Lecture Notes in Artificial Intelligence   990

Subseries of Lecture Notes in Computer Science
Edited by J. G. Carbonell and J. Siekmann

Lecture Notes in Computer Science

Edited by G. Goos, J. Hartmanis and J. van Leeuwen

Springer
Berlin
Heidelberg
New York
Barcelona
Budapest
Hong Kong
London
Milan
Paris
Santa Clara
Singapore
Tokyo

Carlos Pinto-Ferreira
Nuno J. Mamede (Eds.)

Progress in
Artificial Intelligence

7th Portuguese Conference
on Artificial Intelligence, EPIA '95
Funchal, Madeira Island, Portugal
October 3-6, 1995
Proceedings

 Springer

Series Editors

Jaime G. Carbonell, Carnegie Mellon University, USA
Jörg Siekmann, University of Saarland, DFKI, Germany

Volume Editors

Carlos Pinto-Ferreira
ISR/IST, Torre Norte
Av. Rovisco Pais, P-1000 Lisboa, Portugal

Nuno J. Mamede
INESC/IST
Av. Alves Redol, 9, P-1000 Lisboa, Portugal

Cataloging-in-Publication Data applied for

Die Deutsche Bibliothek - CIP-Einheitsaufnahme

Progress in artificial intelligence : proceedings / 7th
Portuguese Conference on Artificial Intelligence, EPIA '95,
Funchal, Madeira Island, Portugal, October 3 - 6, 1995. Carlos
Pinto-Ferreira ; Nuno J. Mamede (ed.). - Berlin ; Heidelberg ;
New York ; Barcelona ; Budapest ; Hong Kong ; London ;
Milan ; Paris ; Tokyo : Springer, 1995
  (Lecture notes in computer science ; Vol. 990 : Lecture notes in
  artificial intelligence)
  ISBN 3-540-60428-6
NE: Pinto-Ferreira, Carlos [Hrsg.]; EPIA <7, 1995, Funchal>; GT

CR Subject Classification (1991): I.2

ISBN 3-540-60428-6 Springer-Verlag Berlin Heidelberg New York

© Springer-Verlag Berlin Heidelberg 1995
Printed in Germany

Typesetting: Camera ready by author
SPIN 10485765   06/3142 – 5 4 3 2 1 0   Printed on acid-free paper

Preface

EPIA'95 is the seventh conference organized under the auspices of the Portuguese Association for Artificial Intelligence (APPIA). Since its first conference, in 1985, the EPIA has grown steadily in quality, particularly since its first international conference (1989), when English was adopted as the official language, allowing the exchange of information between Portuguese and foreign researchers.

When we proposed the organization of the EPIA'95 conference, we committed ourselves to the following strategic objectives: the achievement of high standards of quality, the broadening of its audience, and, last but not least, the motivation of young researchers for the most exciting area of research humankind has ever approached: Artificial Intelligence. As a matter of fact, what unites researchers working in such different fields as non-monotonic logics, vision, planning, connectionism, and the lambda calculus, to name but a few, is the sharing of the very same objective: *the dream of building an intelligent agent.*

In regard to standards of quality, few words need to be said when outstanding invited lecturers such as Marvin Minsky, Manuela Veloso, Luís B. Almeida, and Rodney Brooks participate in the event, or when very distinguished members of the AI community accepted to participate in the EPIA'95 Program Committee — to make it the first with a strong international component. We dared to invite these researchers to be present at our conference, and we are honored and glad for their acceptance: To all of them we address our thanks.

The EPIA'95 paper revision process was very tough: We received 167 submissions (from Russia to Canada, from the USA to China, from Portugal to Singapore). From that initial set, we rejected 17 for being received after the deadline, and out of the remaining 150, 30 papers were selected as full papers and 15 for poster presentation. Twenty-one Program Committee members and almost 200 reviewers worked very hard to ensure a very strict paper revision process (triple, blind, AAAI-94 style). However, it is impossible to manage such a process, taking place in a very limited amount of time, without making mistakes and being unfair (at least, unconsciously). The responsibility for these mistakes rests completely with the Program Co-chairs. We would like to take this opportunity to thank the authors and reviewers for their co-operation and patience! The remarkable quality of the papers collected here result from their work and enthusiasm.

At the time we started organizing EPIA'95, we decided that this year's conference should serve as a forum for a debate on the foundations of Artificial Intelligence. Although being logicists and theoreticians, we share the point of view that there are neither "good" nor "bad" approaches to Artificial Intelligence: The problem the AI community has is certainly too difficult to have a single, canonical, and orthodox answer. Therefore, we have committed ourselves to motivating researchers from the various sub-fields of AI, hence broadening the scope of the conference.

Our third concern was about the responsibility of transmitting our enthusiasm to young students and researchers in AI. This was the reason we contacted sponsors in order to finance about 150 scholarships to help graduate, master's, and Ph.D. students to participate in the conference. Without the support of BNU (Banco Nacional Ultramarino) and ACM Sigart, this critical aspect would not have been possible.

Some comments should also be made about the venue we have chosen for this year's conference. The Madeira Island offers ideal conditions for conferences: the warmth of their people, the mildness of the climate, and very good logistic conditions. We would like to take this opportunity to thank the Governo Regional da Madeira, particularly the Secretaria Regional de Educação, the Secretaria Regional de Turismo e Cultura, and CITMA for their support and enthusiasm from the very beginning of this process.

Finally, we would like to thank all the EPIA'95 supporters, namely,

BNU - Banco Nacional Ultramarino
Governo Regional da Madeira
CITMA - Centro de C&T da Madeira
IST - Instituto Superior Técnico
INESC - Instituto de Engenharia de Sistemas e Computadores
COMPULOG-NET
FLAD - Fundação Luso-Americana para o Desenvolvimento
JNICT - Junta Nacional de Investigação Científica e Tecnológica
Fundação para a Divulgação das Tecnologias de Informação
Fundação Calouste Gulbenkian
ACM - Sigart
SISCOG - Sistemas Cognitivos
IBM Portuguesa
EDP - Electricidade de Portugal, S.A.
TAPair Portugal

Without their support, neither the conference nor these proceedings would have been possible.

Lisbon, June 1995

Carlos Pinto-Ferreira
Nuno João Mamede

Programme & Conference Co-Chairs

Carlos Pinto-Ferreira
Technical Univ. of Lisbon - IST
ISR, Av. Rovisco Pais
1000 Lisboa, Portugal
Voice: +351 (1) 8418270
Fax: +351 (1) 8418291
E-mail: cpf@isr.isr.ist.utl.pt

Nuno João Mamede
Technical Univ. of Lisbon - IST
INESC, Apartado 13069
1000 Lisboa, Portugal
Voice: +351 (1) 3100234
Fax: +351 (1) 525843
E-mail: Nuno.Mamede@inesc.pt

Program Committee

António Porto *(Universidade Nova de Lisboa, Portugal)*

Benjamin Kuipers *(University of Texas at Austin, USA)*

Bernhard Nebel *(University Ulm / DFKI Saarbruecken, Germany)*

Carlos Pinto-Ferreira *(Technical Univ. of Lisbon - IST / ISR, Portugal)*

David Makinson *(UNESCO, France)*

Erik Sandewall *(Linköping University, Sweden)*

Ernesto Costa *(Universidade de Coimbra, Portugal)*

Helder Coelho *(Technical University of Lisbon - ISEG / INESC, Portugal)*

João Pavão Martins *(Technical University of Lisbon - IST, Portugal)*

John Self *(Lancaster University, UK)*

José Carmo *(Tech. Univ. of Lisbon - IST / Univ. da Madeira, Portugal)*

Lauri Carlson *(University of Helsinki, Finland)*

Luc Steels *(VUB AI Lab, Belgium)*

Luigia Carlucci Aiello *(Universitá di Roma La Sapienza, Italy)*

Luís B. Almeida *(Technical University of Lisbon - IST / INESC, Portugal)*

Luís Moniz Pereira *(Centro de Informática e Int. Art., DI/UNL, Portugal)*

Luís Monteiro *(Universidade Nova de Lisboa, Portugal)*

Manuela Veloso *(Carnegie Mellon University, USA)*

Maria Cravo *(Technical University of Lisbon - IST, Portugal)*

Miguel Filgueiras *(University of Porto, Portugal)*

Nuno Mamede *(Technical University of Lisbon - IST / INESC, Portugal)*

Yoav Shoham *(Stanford University, USA)*

Yves Kodratoff *(CNRS, France)*

Reviewers

A. Brunie-Taton
Aaron Sloman
Abhaya Nayak
Alvaro del Val
Ana Fred
Ana P. Tomás
Antónia Lopes
António Leitão
Arlindo M. Oliveira
Aurélien Slodzian
Bernadete Ribeiro
Carlos Bento
Carsten Kindermann
Daniel Borrajo
David Makinson
Elissa Feit
Ernesto Costa
Fernando A. Silva
Francesco M. Donini
Francisco M. Dionísio
Geoff Gordon
Gilles Bisson
Graça Gaspar
H. Mignot
Harald Ruess
Hélder Araujo
Henry Soldano
Hudson Turner
Isabel Ribeiro
Jim Blythe
João Lemos
João P. Martins
Joaquim N. Aparício
John Zelle
José J. Alferes
José L. Fiadeiro
Jürgen Dix
Kimmo Koskenniemi
Laurent Miclet
Luís B. Almeida
Luís Correia
Luís Monteiro
Marco Cadoli
Maria R. Cravo
Maurice Pagnucco
Michele Sebag
Nicolas Graner
Nuno Mamede
Paulo C. Reis
Pedro Aguiar
Pedro Lima
Peter Stuer
Raman Rajagopalan
Rich Caruana
Ronald Schrooten
Sabine Broda
Salvador P. Abreu
Syed S Ali
Timo Honkela
Vitor S. Costa
Yury Smirnov

A. Cornuejols
Artur M. Dias
Alberto Tomé
Amílcar Cardoso
Ana M. Moreira
Andrea Hemprich
António Branco
António M. Florido
Armando Matos
Austin Tate
Bernard Manderick
Carlos V. Damásio
Christer Bäckström
Daniele Nardi
Deepak Kumar
Erica Melis
Eva Ejerhed
Fernando M. Silva
Francisco A. Veiga
Gabriel David
Gerd Brewka
Giovanni Rumolo
Greg Restall
Hans Chalupsky
Harri Arnola
Helder Coelho
Herbert Jaeger
Ilkka Niemelä
Jana Koehler
João Balsa
João P. Costeira
Joaquim Baptista
Joel Quinqueton
José Santos-Victor
José P. Leal
José V. Oliveira
Karen Ehrlich
Kris Van Marcke
Luis M. Custódio
Luís Caires
Luis Moniz
Luc Goossens
Marco Schaerf
Mark Ryan
Micheal Hewett
Miguel Filgueiras
Norman McCain
Paolo Liberatore
Paulo J. Oliveira
Pedro A. Matos
Pedro Resende
Philip Goetz
Renwei Li
Richard Wyatt
Ronen Brafman
Sabine Geldof
Stefan Wrobel
Thibault Langlois
Ulf Hermjakob
William J. Rapaport
Yvonne Waern

Aarno Lehtola
Abdelhamid Mellouk
Alistair E. Campbell
Ana Cardoso
Ana Paiva
Andrea Schaerf
Anthony Cohn
António Porto
Astro Teller
Bart De Boer
Bernhard Hollunder
Carlos Pinto-Ferreira
Claire Nedellec
David Hogg
Dietmar Dengler
Erik Sandewall
Fabio Massacci
Fernando M. Pires
Francisco Menezes
Gabriel P. Lopes
Gerd Wagner
Gordon Novak
Grigorios Antoniou
Hans-Jürgen Bürckert
Hans-Jürgen Profitlich
Helena Sofia Pinto
Herbert Kay
Irene P. Rodrigues
Jeff Rickel
João Cachopo
João P. Neto
Joaquim Filipe
John Self
José Carmo
José L. Ferreira
Juergen Paulokat
Karen Haigh
Lars Ahrenberg
Luis Antunes
Luís Camarinha-Matos
Luís Moniz Pereira
Luigia Carlucci Aiello
Margarida Mamede
Mary-Anne Williams
Michel Wermelinger
Nelma Moreira
Nuno Guimarães
Paulo B. Menezes
Pavlos Peppas
Pedro Barahona
Peter Clark
Pierre Brezellec
Riccardo Poli
Rita Ribeiro
S. Augier
Siddarth Subramanian
Stuart C. Shapiro
Thierry Van de Merckt
Vasco Vasconcelos
Witold Lukaszewicz
Zaron Wirth

Table of Contents

Distributed Artificial Intelligence

Genetic Algorithms

Machine Learning

Neural Networks

Non-Monotonic Reasoning

Planning and Case-Based Reasoning

Table of Contents — Posters

Terminological Meta-Reasoning by Reification and Multiple Contexts

Klemens Schnattinger, Udo Hahn & Manfred Klenner*

Freiburg University
Computational Linguistics Group (CLIF)
Werthmannplatz
D-79085 Freiburg, Germany
e-mail: {schnattinger,hahn,klenner}@coling.uni-freiburg.de
phone: +49 - 761 - 203 - {3356,3255,3252}
fax: +49 - 761 - 203 - 4929

Abstract. We introduce a model and a system architecture for second-order reasoning about statements expressed in a (first-order) terminological representation language. This meta-reasoning approach is based on the reification of first-order propositions and the mediation between second- and first-order expressions via translation rules operating on multiple contexts. An application to a concept learning task in a text understanding environment shows how different degrees of credibility can be assigned to alternative concept hypotheses on the basis of such a schema for terminological meta-reasoning.

1   Introduction

We introduce a model and a system architecture for second-order reasoning about statements expressed in a (first-order) terminological representation language. This meta-reasoning approach is motivated by various requirements which emerged from our work in the overlapping fields of natural language parsing and concept learning and the common need to evaluate alternative representation structures. For instance, global ambiguities determined by a natural language parser can be associated with different degrees of plausibility in order to provide a reason-based ranking among alternative readings which takes, e.g., preference criteria or discourse context factors into account. Similarly, in the course of concept learning from natural language texts various and often conflicting concept hypotheses for a single item are formed, as the learning environment usually provides only inconclusive evidence for exactly determining the properties of the concept to be learned. This underspecification is often due to incomplete knowledge provided for that concept in the data, but it may also be due to imperfect parsing results (originating from lacking lexical, grammatical, conceptual specifications, or ungrammatical input). Again, we face the problem of choosing from among several alternatives to which different degrees of *credibility* can be assigned depending on the *reasons* which led to their formation.

* This work was supported by a grant from DFG under the account Ha2097/2-1.

Both, the parser (Hahn et al., 1994) and the learner (Hahn et al., 1995), in our system environment operate on terminological knowledge representation structures. We thus consider it appropriate to uniformly design and execute the evaluation procedures involved in both types of reasoning processes within the same terminological reasoning environment. As we will be dealing with second-order terminological statements about basic (first-order) terminological statements in order to properly select the most credible hypotheses, we have to provide a formal mapping between both language layers. This is achieved by a reification procedure (see Section 4) yielding different contexts and by various lifting/translation rules mediating between those contexts (see Section 5). Given such a homogeneous framework, we inherit the full-blown classification mechanism from standard (first-order) terminological systems (MacGregor, 1994) for processing reified second-order expressions in order to aggregate preference descriptions.

2   Architecture for Meta-Reasoning

The main requirements for the architecture we propose can be phrased as:

- Expressing *qualitative assertions* about propositions in a terminological language; these meta statements capture the ascription and strength of belief to these propositions, the reasons why they came into existence, the support/weakening they may have received from other propositions, etc.
- *Meta-reasoning* in a terminological knowledge base about properties and relations that certain propositions and conceptual relations may have; the corresponding *second-order expressions* are not only directed at ABox relations (propositions, factual knowledge), but also incorporate TBox relations (like ISA relations or concept-name relations). Thus, we place our approach to meta-reasoning under the heading of increased expressive power of the underlying knowledge representation language (Aiello and Levi (1988) provide a survey of the different meanings associated with that ubiquitous term).

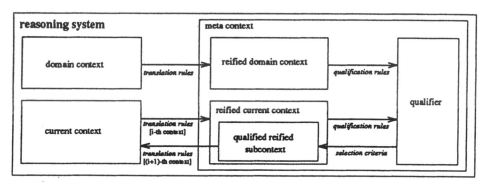

Figure 1: Architecture for Meta-Reasoning Based on Multiple Contexts

The notion of context (informally, a knowledge base partition) on which we build as a formal device for meta-knowledge and meta-reasoning goes back to Weyhrauch's seminal work on the FOL system (Weyhrauch, 1980), the introspective aspects of which are considered in depth by Nardi (1988). While reflection and meta-reasoning <u>within</u> a single context are properly dealt with in FOL-style systems, translations <u>between</u> different contexts are not as well treated in a formally satisfactory way. This gap is closed by McCarthy's context model (McCarthy, 1993; Buvač and McCarthy, 1994), which provides a formally grounded, i.e., truth-preserving notion of translatability between multiple contexts (cf. also Subsection 5.2). We here distinguish several types of contexts, viz. the domain context, the current context, and the meta context (as depicted in Fig. 1). The *domain context* contains the protected part of the original terminological knowledge base (so-called domain knowledge base), which cannot be changed in the course of the text analysis, whereas the *current context* incorporates the incrementally assembled knowledge of the underlying text (so-called text knowledge base) as created by the text parser. In order to map descriptions from the domain context and the current context to the meta context various *translation* (or *lifting*) *rules* are supplied which carry out reification. The *meta context* then holds the reified knowledge of the domain context and of the current context, yielding two parallel data repositories, viz. the *reified domain context* and the *reified current context*, resp. By *reification*, we mean a common reflective mechanism (Friedman and Wand, 1984), which splits up terminological expressions into their constituent parts and, in particular, introduces a unique anchor term, the *reificator*, on which *reasoning about* this expression, e.g., the annotation of qualifying assertions, can be based (cf. also MacGregor (1993)). Among the reified structures in the reified current context there is a subcontext embedded the elements of which carry several qualifications, e.g., reasons to believe a proposition, indications of consistency, certainty, support, etc. In Section 6 we will treat the annotation of reified knowledge representation structures with qualification labels by a set of (second-order) qualification rules. These are the basis for the selection of those representation structures which are assigned the highest degree of plausibility/credibility. Only those will be remapped to the current context by way of (inverse) translation rules and, thus, the circle becomes closed. In particular, at the end of each cycle the original i-th current context is replaced by the $(i+1)$-th current context, the one which reflects the most recent qualifications computed by the *qualifier* in the meta context. The $(i+1)$-th current context then is the input of the next qualification round. This architecture meets the above requirements:

- Qualitative knowledge can be described by a relation between each reified relation of the domain context and the current context and a particular qualitative 'data structure' (concepts that describe several qualifications) interpreted by a specialized inference engine which computes various quality labels in the meta context, viz. the qualifier.
- Second-order queries addressed to the domain and current context can be evaluated as first-order expressions in the meta context. Accordingly, we pro-

vide a particular 'data structure' to operate on reified ABox/TBox relations using ordinary first-order expressions.

These are the technical prerequisites for quality-based meta-reasoning about various degrees of plausibility of parsing ambiguities or credibility of learning hypotheses within a coherent terminological framework. Meta-reasoning heavily relies upon the classifier's capability to assess the plausibility or credibility for each required relation in the meta context. Morik (1986) also stresses the need for meta-reasoning in the machine learning domain and, at the same time, criticizes ordinary terminological systems for their incapability to support this type of reasoning. We claim that our reification mechanism remedies this flaw. Furthermore, given the ordinary truth-maintenance system (TMS) of the LOOM system (it is based on the principles described by Doyle (1979)), we are able to trace and manage possibly occurring revisions of 'quality assertions' and their consequences in the qualifier. This results from the fact that in the meta context only ordinary first-order terminological logic statements are held which are revisable using the common TMS machinery.

3   Terminological Logic

The fairly standard concept language, $\mathcal{TL}$, on which our considerations are based has constructors to define the terminology of a domain (for a subset, see Table 1). We start from *atomic* concepts, roles and individuals. *Concepts* are unary predicates and *roles* are binary predicates over a domain Δ, with *individuals* being the elements of Δ. Correspondingly, an interpretation $\mathcal{I}$ of the language is a function that assigns to each concept symbol (taken from the set $\mathbf{A}$) a subset of the domain Δ, $\mathcal{I} : \mathbf{A} \to 2^{\Delta}$, to each role symbol (taken from the set $\mathbf{P}$) a binary relation of Δ, $\mathcal{I} : \mathbf{P} \to 2^{\Delta \times \Delta}$, and to each individual symbol (taken from the set $\mathbf{I}$) an element of Δ, $\mathcal{I} : \mathbf{I} \to \Delta$. Therefore, $\mathcal{I}$ constitutes a partial function.

Syntax	Semantics
C_{atom}	$\{d \in \Delta^{\mathcal{I}} \mid C_{atom} \text{ atomic}, \mathcal{I}(C_{atom}) = d\}$
$C \sqcap D$	$C^{\mathcal{I}} \cap D^{\mathcal{I}}$
$C \sqcup D$	$C^{\mathcal{I}} \cup D^{\mathcal{I}}$
$\neg C$	$\Delta^{\mathcal{I}} \setminus C^{\mathcal{I}}$
$\exists R.C$	$\{d \in \Delta^{\mathcal{I}} \mid R^{\mathcal{I}}(d) \cap C^{\mathcal{I}} \neq \emptyset\}$
$\forall R.C$	$\{d \in \Delta^{\mathcal{I}} \mid R^{\mathcal{I}}(d) \subseteq C^{\mathcal{I}}\}$
$\exists_{\geq n} R$	$\{d \in \Delta^{\mathcal{I}} \mid \|R^{\mathcal{I}}(d)\| \geq n\}$
$\exists_{\leq n} R$	$\{d \in \Delta^{\mathcal{I}} \mid \|R^{\mathcal{I}}(d)\| \leq n\}$
R_{atom}	$\{(d, e) \in \Delta^{\mathcal{I}} \times \Delta^{\mathcal{I}} \mid R_{atom} \text{ atomic}, \mathcal{I}(R_{atom}) = (d, e)\}$
$R \sqcap S$	$R^{\mathcal{I}} \cap S^{\mathcal{I}}$
R^{-1}	$\{(d, d') \in \Delta^{\mathcal{I}} \times \Delta^{\mathcal{I}} \mid (d', d) \in R^{\mathcal{I}}\}$

Table 1: Syntax and Semantics for a subset of $\mathcal{TL}$

Terminol. Axioms

Axiom	Semantics
$A \doteq C$	$A^{\mathcal{I}} = C^{\mathcal{I}}$
$A \sqsubseteq C$	$A^{\mathcal{I}} \subseteq C^{\mathcal{I}}$
$Q \doteq R$	$Q^{\mathcal{I}} = R^{\mathcal{I}}$
$Q \sqsubseteq R$	$Q^{\mathcal{I}} \subseteq R^{\mathcal{I}}$

Assertional Axioms

Axiom	Semantics
$a : C$	$a^{\mathcal{I}} \in C^{\mathcal{I}}$
$a \, R \, b$	$(a^{\mathcal{I}}, b^{\mathcal{I}}) \in R^{\mathcal{I}}$

Table 2: $\mathcal{TL}$ Axioms

5

Concept terms and *role terms* are defined inductively. Table 1 contains some useful constructors, together with their corresponding semantics. Each constructor defines a concept term. C and D denote concept terms, R and S denote roles and n stands for a natural number. $R^{\mathcal{I}}(d)$ represents the set of role fillers of the individual d, i.e., the set of individuals e with $(d,e) \in R^{\mathcal{I}}$. $\|R^{\mathcal{I}}(d)\|$ denotes the number of role fillers.

By means of *terminological axioms* (see Table 2) a symbolic name is definable for each concept and role. It is possible to define sufficient and necessary constraints for a concept and a role (using $\doteq$) or only necessary constraints (using $\sqsubseteq$). A finite set of such axioms is called the *terminology* (*TBox*). Each symbolic name must be defined only once.

The formulation of assertions associates concepts and roles with concrete individuals. Formally, this can be expressed by *assertional axioms* (see Table 2; a, b denote individuals). A finite set of such axioms is called the *world description* (*ABox*). An interpretation $\mathcal{I}$ is a model of an ABox with regard to a TBox, iff $\mathcal{I}$ satisfies the assertional and terminological axioms.

4 Reification

We here restrict ourselves to the reification of the assertional and terminological axioms and the constructors $C \sqcap D$ and $\forall R.C$. The remaining constructors can be reified in a straightforward way based on the scheme outlined below.

In our running example symbolic names such as COMPANY, PRODUCER, PRODUCT and ACCU (an abbreviation for accumulator) represent concepts, while symbolic names such as DEVELOPS stand for roles. Consider the following terminological theory:

(P1) IBM DEVELOPS $PS/2$
(P2) $Compaq$: PRODUCER
(P3) PRODUCER $\doteq$ COMPANY $\sqcap$ $\forall$DEVELOPS.PRODUCT

We equate the proposition labelled by P1 with the reification of the tuple $\langle IBM, PS/2\rangle$ which belongs to the DEVELOPS relation, the proposition labelled by P2 with the reification of the tuple $\langle Compaq, $PRODUCER$\rangle$ which belongs to the INST-OF relation (see below) and the proposition labelled by P3 with the reification of the tuple $\langle$PRODUCER,COMPANY$\rangle$ which belongs to the ISA relation (see below) as well as the reification of the tuple $\langle$PRODUCER,PRODUCT$\rangle$ which belongs to the DEVELOPS relation. Additionally, our reification mechanism is sensitive to hypothesis spaces, i.e., each reified proposition must be true in at least one hypothesis space H. A hypothesis space is here considered a formal device for grouping non-alternative propositions about the underlying domain (cf. also Section 7). Qualifying assertions about a tuple (e.g., "IBM DEVELOPS $PS/2$" is multiply deduced) are represented by making assertions about its reified form (e.g., P1 QUALIFIED q $\sqcap$ q : MULTIPLY-DEDUCED). Unlike many other formal reasoning systems, we have chosen a particular 'data structure', itself expressed

$$\text{REIF} \doteq \forall\text{BINARY-REL}.\mathbf{P}^{ext} \sqcap \forall\text{DOMAIN}.\mathbf{A} \sqcap \forall\text{RANGE}.\mathbf{A} \sqcap \forall\text{HYPO}.\mathbf{H}$$

Table 3: General Data Structure for Reification

in ordinary terminological logic, to make the reification process explicit. It is defined by the terminological term in Table 3 and provides the common ground for making qualifying assertions and also serves as the foundation for the evaluation of second-order expressions in order to determine various degrees of plausibility or credibility (see Sections 6 and 7). We only use a single data structure, as the assertional axiom $a : C$ can be considered a role (called INST-OF), like a INST-OF C. Similarly, in all terminological axioms the relation between two concepts (the defined concept and the defining concept(s)) can be considered a role (called ISA), like A ISA C. This extended role set is called $\mathbf{P}^{ext}$ (supplementing the one given in Section 3, $\mathbf{P} \cup \{\text{INST-OF},\text{ISA}\}$). Additionally, $\mathbf{H}$ is the set of all hypothesis spaces.

The symbol REIF denotes a concept and BINARY-REL, DOMAIN, RANGE and HYPO denote roles, resp. With these conventions, we are able to define the (bijective) reification function $\Re : t.term_H \to r.term$, where $t.term_H$ is a terminological term known to be true in hypothesis space H and $r.term$ is the corresponding reified term (see Table 4).

$\Re(a : C)$	$r : \text{REIF} \sqcap r$ BINARY-REL INST-OF $\sqcap r$ DOMAIN $a \sqcap$ r RANGE $C \sqcap r$ HYPO H
$\Re(a\ R\ b)$	$r : \text{REIF} \sqcap r$ BINARY-REL $R \sqcap r$ DOMAIN $a \sqcap$ r RANGE $b \sqcap r$ HYPO H
$\Re(A \doteq C)$	$\Re^*(A, C)$
$\Re^*(A, C_{atom})$	$r : \text{REIF} \sqcap r$ BINARY-REL ISA $\sqcap r$ DOMAIN $A \sqcap$ r RANGE $C_{atom} \sqcap r$ HYPO H
$\Re^*(A, \forall R.C_{atom})$	$r : \text{REIF} \sqcap r$ BINARY-REL $R \sqcap r$ DOMAIN $A \sqcap$ r RANGE $C_{atom} \sqcap r$ HYPO H
$\Re^*(A, \forall R.(C \sqcap D))$	$\Re^*(A, \forall R.C) \sqcap \Re^*(A, \forall R.D)$
$\Re^*(A, C \sqcap D)$	$\Re^*(A, C) \sqcap \Re^*(A, D)$

Table 4: Reification Functions $\Re$ and $\Re^*$

Note that $\Re$ is a purely syntactic transformation. By analogy, we may also define the inverse function $\Re^{-1}$ of $\Re$ with the corresponding inverse mapping. In Subsection 5.2 we will then define so-called *translation* (or *lifting*) *rules* using $\Re$ and $\Re^{-1}$. Furthermore, the function $\Re^*$ is introduced which covers those basic expression types considered in this paper (see Table 4); supplementing this list for the remaining expression types from Tables 1 and 2 is obvious. The semantics of the reified expressions is the standard one for terminological logics.

Given the reification schemata from Table 4, the following expressions contain the terminological terms and their corresponding reified forms in terminological logic for the above examples, P(1) to P(3). We assume that the terminological terms hold in a particular hypothesis space H:

$\Re(IBM \text{ DEVELOPS } PS/2) = p_1 : \text{REIF} \sqcap p_1 \text{ BINARY-REL DEVELOPS} \sqcap$
$p_1 \text{ DOMAIN } IBM \sqcap p_1 \text{ RANGE } PS/2 \sqcap p_1 \text{ HYPO } H$

$\Re(Compaq : \text{PRODUCER}) = p_2 : \text{REIF} \sqcap p_2 \text{ BINARY-REL INST-OF} \sqcap$
$p_2 \text{ DOMAIN } Compaq \sqcap p_2 \text{ RANGE PRODUCER} \sqcap p_2 \text{ HYPO } H$

$\Re(\text{PRODUCER} \doteq \text{COMPANY} \sqcap \forall \text{DEVELOPS.PRODUCT}) = p_{3_1} : \text{REIF} \sqcap$
$p_{3_1} \text{ BINARY-REL ISA} \sqcap p_{3_1} \text{ DOMAIN PRODUCER} \sqcap p_{3_1} \text{ RANGE COMPANY} \sqcap$
$p_{3_1} \text{ HYPO } H \sqcap p_{3_2} : \text{REIF} \sqcap p_{3_2} \text{ BINARY-REL DEVELOPS} \sqcap$
$p_{3_2} \text{ DOMAIN PRODUCER} \sqcap p_{3_2} \text{ RANGE PRODUCT} \sqcap p_{3_2} \text{ HYPO } H$

5 Multiple Contexts

In this section we describe the use of contexts and the corresponding translation rules in our architecture (see Section 2). We here primarily build on previous work by McCarthy (1993), Buvač and McCarthy (1994) and Buvač *et al.* (1994); some technical results (see Subsection 5.2) are due to Buvač *et al.* (1995).

5.1 The Nature of Contexts

We will now concentrate on two major types of contexts already introduced in Section 2 (cf. Fig. 1). The current context contains those alternatives (ambiguities or hypotheses) which are created by the parsing or the learning component. The meta context contains the reification of each terminological and assertional term from the current context. In addition, some of these terms may also be augmented by qualifying assertions. *Quality-based reasoning* then can be considered as a cycle of transformations. Translation rules map expressions from the current context to the reified current context (in the meta context), while qualification rules map some reified expressions to the qualifier in the meta context and, after evaluation, some of these (those with a salient degree of plausibility or credibility) are remapped to the qualified reified subcontext from which they are recast, at last, to a newly instantiated successor version of the current context (this type of evaluation can be considered the reflection part of our meta-reasoning scheme; cf. Nardi (1988)). By definition, the meta context contains more information than the domain and current context, viz. qualitative statements about basic terminological assertions. Note also that the *reified current context* of the meta context keeps the same information as the current context before the evaluation of the qualification rules, while the *qualified reified subcontext* of the meta context keeps the same information as the current context after the evaluation of the qualification rules.

At first glance, one might be tempted to require that any theory in one context should be translatable into another one. However, translations must be sensitive to substantial differences of the knowledge structures among the contexts to be mapped. Therefore, we have to restrict the notion of translatability such that only moves from less informative contexts (e.g., the current context) to more informative ones (e.g., the meta context) are generally allowed, but not *vice versa*. Only some properties may be translated from more informative contexts (e.g., the qualifier of the meta context) into less informative ones (e.g., the qualified reified subcontext of the meta context). This explains the nested structure of the contexts in our architecture and the corresponding domain/range restrictions on mapping rules indicated by the arrows in Fig. 1.

Consider, e.g., some current context for which the learner has produced two alternative propositions, viz. (P1) $NiMH$: ACCU and (P2) $NiMH$: HARDDISK. Both propositions are translatable from the current context into the reified current context of the meta context using $\Re$. In the reified current context the original propositions (P1) and (P2) occur as instances p_1 and p_2; the two reified propositions may have additional properties, e.g., p_1 is alternative to p_2 (cf. the ALTER-TO role in the expression below) and p_1 is (cross-)supported by p_3 via its associated quality proposition q_1 and a relation CROSS-SUPPORTED-BY (cf. Section 6, Rule II). These quality propositions are generated immediately after reification and are related via the role QUALIFIED to their corresponding reified propositions (see Section 5.2, axiom $\mathcal{TR}$). Additionally, the classifier is able to conclude that the quality q_1 has the quality label CROSS-SUPPORTED. These additional propositions come into existence as the result of applying qualification rules, i.e., mapping reified statements to the qualifier of the meta context:

p_1 : REIF $\sqcap$ p_1 BINARY-REL INST-OF $\sqcap$ p_1 DOMAIN $NiMH$ $\sqcap$ p_1 RANGE ACCU $\sqcap$
p_1 HYPO H $\sqcap$ p_1 QUALIFIED q_1 $\sqcap$ q_1 CROSS-SUPPORTED-BY p_3 $\sqcap$
q_1 : CROSS-SUPPORTED $\sqcap$ p_1 ALTER-TO p_2

The transformation from the qualified reified subcontext to the new version of the current context only affects some properties. The reified propositions themselves are translated by $\Re^{-1}$, while the qualitative assertions (e.g., p_1 QUALIFIED q_1 $\sqcap$ q_1 : CROSS-SUPPORTED) remain hidden to the new current context. This is motivated by the intention to reduce the number of hypotheses. Therefore, only those reified propositions are translated which have a sufficient degree of credibility (e.g., p_1 should be translated, but p_2 should not, because p_1 is supported, while p_2 is not; therefore, p_1 has more credibility than p_2).

5.2   Formal Aspects of Translatability

In this section we sketch a formalism for translatability between multiple contexts in terms of a first-order language. We assume a context formalism in the sense of McCarthy (1993). Accordingly, a context is an object in a first-order language which has an associated vocabulary (we use that of the terminological logic $\mathcal{TL}$, see Section 3) and therefore denotes a set of models. Formulas from the vocabulary of a context are referred to as *meaningful* in that context. $\mathrm{ist}(\kappa, \phi)$ *holds* iff formula ϕ is true in all the models denoted by context κ (formally, $\models_\kappa \phi$; similarly, the relation $\vdash_\kappa \phi$ is defined in the usual way, see Buvač *et al.* (1995), chapter 2). For finitely axiomatizable theories T and the theorems Th derived from a finite set of axioms A we require $T = Th(A)$. We then stipulate that $\mathrm{ist}(\kappa, T)$ holds iff $\mathrm{ist}(\kappa, \sqcap A)$ holds, i.e., the conjunction of the axioms is true in context κ.

Translation rules are syntactic transformations which derive sentences in the meta context that are equivalent to sentences in the domain and current context. A translation rule from context κ to context κ' is any axiom of the form $\mathbf{ist}(\kappa, \phi) \leftrightarrow \mathbf{ist}(\kappa', \phi')$. These translation rules are *lifting rules* in the sense of McCarthy (1993) as they also relate the truth in one context to the truth in another one.

Given the set $\mathcal{R}$ which denotes all $\Re(x \ R \ y)$ and the set $\mathcal{P}$ of all instances p of the class REIF (i.e., p : REIF), the function $\pi : \mathcal{R} \mapsto \mathcal{P}$ maps each reified term to the corresponding instance of REIF, i.e., the reificator:

$$\pi\,(\Re(x \ R \ y)) \equiv \pi\,(p : \text{REIF} \ \sqcap \ p \ \text{BINARY-REL} \ R \ \sqcap$$
$$p \ \text{DOMAIN} \ x \ \sqcap \ p \ \text{RANGE} \ y \ \sqcap \ p \ \text{HYPO} \ H\,) = \ p$$

Now we can formulate translations rules like the following one, mapping expressions from the current context to the reified current context (briefly referred to as *current* and *meta*, resp.):

$$\forall q, p : \mathbf{ist}\,(current, NiMH : \text{ACCU}) \leftrightarrow$$
$$\mathbf{ist}\,(meta, \pi(\Re\,(NiMH : \text{ACCU})) \ \text{QUALIFIED} \ q)$$

A set of translation rules Tr from context κ to context κ' translates a theory T into another theory T' iff $Tr \vdash \mathbf{ist}(\kappa, T) \leftrightarrow \mathbf{ist}(\kappa', T')$. If the main purpose is the translation of theories, we only need to translate the theory defined by a set of sentences, rather than translate the sentences themselves.

Definition (equivalence preservation): A translation with a set of translation rules Tr from context κ into κ' is *equivalence preserving* iff for any ϕ and ψ for which there exist ϕ' and ψ' with $Tr \vdash \mathbf{ist}\,(\kappa, \phi) \ \leftrightarrow \ \mathbf{ist}\,(\kappa', \phi')$ and $Tr \vdash \mathbf{ist}\,(\kappa, \psi) \leftrightarrow \mathbf{ist}\,(\kappa', \psi')$ it is the case that $\phi \vdash_\kappa \psi$ iff $\phi' \vdash_{\kappa'} \psi'$.

Intuitively speaking, this formalism can be thought of as "blocking" any translation which is not equivalence preserving. A standard FOL theorem prover can be used to show that any theory in one given context is (or is not) translatable to another context via a given set of translation rules.

Proposition (compositionality of translation): A context κ is translatable to another context κ' via translation rules Tr iff all the theories axiomatized by atomic formulas are translatable from κ to κ' via translation rules Tr. (For a proof using induction on the formula length, cf. Buvač *et al.* (1995)).

According to these conventions, we have to supply a translation rule for each role in our domain (i.e., $p \in \mathbf{P}^{ext}$), e.g.,

$$\forall d, r : \mathbf{ist}\,(current, d \ \text{DEVELOPS} \ r) \leftrightarrow$$
$$\exists q : \mathbf{ist}\,(meta, \pi\,(\Re\,(d \ \text{DEVELOPS} \ r)) \ \text{QUALIFIED} \ q)$$
$$\forall d, r : \mathbf{ist}\,(current, d \ \text{INST-OF} \ r) \leftrightarrow$$
$$\exists q : \mathbf{ist}\,(meta, \pi\,(\Re\,(d \ \text{INST-OF} \ r)) \ \text{QUALIFIED} \ q)$$

With these translation rules the current context is translatable to the meta context. For brevity, we may state a single second-order axiom called $\mathcal{TR}$:

$$\forall R : R \in \mathbf{P}^{ext} \rightarrow$$
$$(\forall d, r : \mathbf{ist}\,(current, d \ R \ r) \leftrightarrow \exists q : \mathbf{ist}\,(meta, \pi\,(\Re\,(d \ R \ r)) \ \text{QUALIFIED} \ q))$$

In a similar way, we may construct a translation rule according to which the qualified reified subcontext of the meta context is translatable to (a new version of) the current context. This rule incorporates the quality of some reified element p, which must exceed a specific quality THRESHOLD. But the inverse translation restricts itself to the data only available in the qualified reified subcontext (denoted by *subcontext*) of the meta context. Since the translation rule uses only the roles from the set $\mathbf{P}^{ext}$, this translation is equivalence preserving:

$$\forall R : R \in \mathbf{P}^{ext} \rightarrow (\forall p, d, r, H \ \exists q :$$
$$ist(subcontext, p : \text{REIF} \ \sqcap \ p \ \text{BINARY-REL} \ R \ \sqcap \ p \ \text{DOMAIN} \ d \ \sqcap$$
$$p \ \text{RANGE} \ r \ \sqcap \ p \ \text{HYPO} \ H \ \sqcap \ p \ \text{QUALIFIED} \ q \ \sqcap \ q : \text{THRESHOLD}) \leftrightarrow$$
$$ist(current, \Re^{-1}(p : \text{REIF} \ \sqcap \ p \ \text{BINARY-REL} \ R \ \sqcap \ p \ \text{DOMAIN} \ d \ \sqcap$$
$$p \ \text{RANGE} \ r \ \sqcap \ p \ \text{HYPO} \ H)))$$

The notion of contexts we have sketched (following the exposition of McCarthy (1993) and Buvač *et al.* (1995)) allows us to reason about contexts in a formal sense which is superior to alternative proposals. In particular, it contrasts with related ideas from the field of modal and hierarchical logics:

- *Modal logics* is a standard vehicle to represent beliefs (e.g., Hintikka (1962), Halpern and Moses (1992)). The results of this research indicate that first-order languages are entirely sufficient to state a consistent theory of beliefs (everything that is believed to be true is captured this way). However, truth in a context (assuming a Kripke-style semantics) in our model is not sufficient, because we want contexts to be reified as first-order objects. This allows us to state relations between contexts (e.g., conceptual specialization) and to specify how sentences can be lifted from one context into another.
- Giunchiglia and Serafini (1994) specify a hierarchy of first-order languages (called ML systems or *hierarchical logics*) as an alternative to modal logics. Included in ML systems are further propositions which do not hold in modal logics, while the concept of modality is entirely abandoned. So-called *bridge rules* (special inference rules which allow to deduce formulas in one context based on facts derived in another one) have a procedural semantics only and thus are formally inferior to lifting rules for contexts.

6 Quality-Based Reasoning

Within second-order logic we may quantify over relations of first-order terms, e.g., $\forall R : R(a, b)$ quantifies over all roles R which relate a and b. Our intention is to use second-order expressions in order to reason about the properties of conceptual descriptions and thus to determine degrees of plausibility or credibility. Such expressions can be integrated into the condition-part of production rules in order to deduce quality labels for concept hypotheses. In our architecture, quality labels are modelled as concept classes, too. They have unique roles and, thus, can be attached to a hypothesis by instantiating the role filler through the application of the action-part of the production rules (but see rule I for an exception). Then the classifier is able to assert the INST-OF relation to the corresponding quality class. Those reified elements that have reached a certain credibility threshold after each quality assessment cycle are transferred back from the meta context to the initial context (cf. Fig.1).

Next, we will describe some of our production rules for quality-based reasoning (the symbol $\Longrightarrow$ separates the condition part from the action part). Note that these rules are tested in the meta context immediately after the reification function $\Re$ has been applied to some proposition in the initial context. In addition, the operator **TELL** is used to initiate the assertion of terminological terms. The procedural semantics of the operator **EXISTS** should be intuitively clear. We also need a function $\hbar$ that retrieves the role filler of the role HYPO, which refers to the relevant hypothesis space, for a given instance that belongs to the class REIF, i.e. $\hbar : \mathcal{P} \rightarrow \mathbf{H}$:

$$\hbar(p) \equiv \hbar \left(\pi(p : \text{REIF} \; \sqcap \; p \; \text{BINARY-REL} \; R \; \sqcap \; p \; \text{DOMAIN} \; x \; \sqcap \right.$$
$$\left. p \; \text{RANGE} \; y \; \sqcap \; p \; \text{HYPO} \; H) \right) = H$$

We start with the formal description of three qualification rules and then turn to a more informal style for the remaining ones. Each hypothesis is related by the role QUALIFIED to its qualifying instance q. An illustration of the working of these rules will be provided in Section 7.

Rule I: Inconsistent-Hypo. Any hypothesis in a hypothesis space which is related to an inconsistent hypothesis receives the negative quality label INCONSISTENT-HYPO. A hypothesis space consists of non-alternative hypotheses.

> **EXISTS** o_1, p, q :
> $\quad \hbar(\pi(\Re(o_1 : \text{INCONSISTENT}))) = \hbar(p) \; \sqcap \; p \; \text{QUALIFIED} \; q \; \Longrightarrow$
> **TELL** q : INCONSISTENT-HYPO

Rule II: Cross-Supported. The second rule covers the case, where a relation between two instances can independently be confirmed from another (structurally admitted, though not yet instantiated) relation incorporating the same but "inverted" filler instances. This causes the role CROSS-SUPPORTED-BY of the qualifying instance q to be filled with the reificator of the non-inverted relations's domain. The classifier then deduces the positive quality label CROSS-SUPPORTED. This rule captures the inherent symmetry between concepts related via quasi-inverse relations.

> **EXISTS** $o_1, o_2, q, R_1, R_2, C_1, C_2$:
> $\quad \Re(o_1 \; R_1 \; o_2) \; \sqcap \; \Re(o_1 : C_1) \; \sqcap \; \Re(o_2 : C_2) \; \sqcap \; \Re(C_2 \doteq \ldots \forall R_2.C_1) \; \sqcap$
> $\quad \hbar(\pi(\Re(o_1 \; R_1 \; o_2))) = \hbar(\pi(\Re(o_1 : C_1))) = \hbar(\pi(\Re(o_2 : C_2))) \; \sqcap$
> $\quad \pi(\Re(o_1 \; R_1 \; o_2)) \; \text{QUALIFIED} \; q \; \Longrightarrow$
> **TELL** q CROSS-SUPPORTED-BY $\pi(\Re(o_2 : C_2))$

Rule III: Supported. We here consider the case, where an INST-OF relation between o_1 and C can independently be confirmed from another INST-OF relation between o_2 and C iff an instance o_3 exists which is itself related to o_1 and o_2 via a role R. This causes the role SUPPORTED-BY of the qualifying instance q

to be filled with the reificator of the INST-OF relation between o_2 and C. The classifier then deduces the positive quality label SUPPORTED. This rule reflects the conceptual proximity a relation induces on its component fillers provided they share a common concept class.

EXISTS o_1, o_2, o_3, q, R, C :
$$\Re(o_1 : C) \ \sqcap \ \Re(o_2 : C) \ \sqcap \ \Re(o_3 \ R \ o_1) \ \sqcap$$
$$\Re(o_3 \ R \ o_2) \ \sqcap \ \pi(\Re(o_1 : C)) \ \text{QUALIFIED} \ q \ \sqcap$$
$$\hbar(\pi(\Re(o_1 : C))) = \hbar(\pi(\Re(o_2 : C))) = \hbar(\pi(\Re(o_3 \ R \ o_1))) = \hbar(\pi(\Re(o_3 \ R \ o_2))) \ \implies$$
TELL q SUPPORTED-BY $\pi(\Re(o_2 : C))$

Rule IV: Additional-Role-Filler. This rule accounts for the case, where an already filled conceptual relation receives an additional, yet different role filler. This causes the role ADDITIONALLY-FILLED-BY of the qualifying instance q to be filled with the already available proposition(s). The classifier then deduces the negative quality label ADDITIONAL-ROLE-FILLER. This is a special-purpose application rule, particularly suited to our natural language understanding task. Actually, this heuristics can be traced down to the distinction between mandatory and optional case role fillers.

Rule V: Multiply-Deduced. This rule covers the multiple assignment of the same role filler to one specific conceptual relation. Any such repetitive assignment causes the role MULTIPLY-DEDUCED-BY of the qualifying instance q to be filled with the same role filler, but one which is associated with a different reified element. The classifier then deduces the (very) positive quality label MULTIPLY-DEDUCED. This rule captures the assumption that a role filler which has been multiply derived at different occasions must be granted more strength than one which has been derived at a single occasion only.

Taking the direction (positive/negative) and the individual 'strength' of each label into account, we might, e.g., prefer labels such as MULTIPLY-DEDUCED over others such as ADDITIONAL-ROLE-FILLER. We are currently investigating reasonable combinations and the associated ordering among various labels in terms of a *qualification calculus*, work that is admittedly in an early phase.

7 A Simple Concept Learning Example

We now demonstrate the effects of quality-based reasoning by considering a concept learning task in the domain of information technology. As a result of applying the qualification rules from Section 6 different degrees of credibility are assigned to alternative concept hypotheses and, finally, one of them is selected as the most credible one.

Assume the following alternative INST-OF hypotheses about a new object denoted by $NiMH$, as they might have been delivered by the parser or learner component:

(H1) $NiMH$: ACCU
(H2) $NiMH$: HARDDISK
(H3) $NiMH$: PRODUCER

The following computations are based on the terminological theory P(1)-P(6):

(P1) PRODUCER $\doteq$ COMPANY $\sqcap$ $\forall$DEVELOPS.PRODUCT
(P2) ACCU-PRODUCER $\doteq$ PRODUCER $\sqcap$ $\forall$DEVELOPS.ACCU
(P3) $Compaq$: ACCU-PRODUCER
(P4) PRODUCT $\doteq$ $\forall$DELIVERED-BY.PRODUCER $\sqcap$ $\neg$PRODUCER
(P5) HARDDISK $\doteq$ PRODUCT
(P6) ACCU $\doteq$ PRODUCT

We will now describe the qualification processes that result from integrating an additional hypothesis (H4),

(H4) $NiMH$ DELIVERED-BY $Compaq$

which comes in as text understanding proceeds, into the set of hypotheses H1, H2, H3. A (single) hypothesis is extended by adding a new conjunct to it. We call such an augmented structure a *hypothesis space*:

(H1$_{ext}$) $NiMH$: ACCU $\sqcap$ $NiMH$ DELIVERED-BY $Compaq$
(H2$_{ext}$) $NiMH$: HARDDISK $\sqcap$ $NiMH$ DELIVERED-BY $Compaq$
(H3$_{ext}$) $NiMH$: PRODUCER $\sqcap$ $NiMH$ DELIVERED-BY $Compaq$

Note that qualitative reasoning processes are triggered <u>after</u> the integration of a new hypothesis into the existing ones, i.e., (H4) is not evaluated prior to its integration into (H1), (H2), and (H3). Two rules are applied after the integration of (H4). Rule I is triggered, since an inconsistency is detected by the classifier in (H3$_{ext}$). (H3) postulates that $NiMH$ is an instance of PRODUCER. However, given (H4), $NiMH$ is also the domain object of the role DELIVERED-BY which is restricted to PRODUCT (but not PRODUCER). Since PRODUCT and PRODUCER are exclusive classes (cf. P4), an inconsistency is detected by the classifier mechanism: $NiMH$ is asserted to be a PRODUCER and a PRODUCT, simultaneously. After the inconsistency has been detected and that proposition been translated, rule I fires (in the reified current context) and a negative support label (here: INCONSISTENT-HYPO) is assigned to each (reified) element of the hypothesis space (H3$_{ext*}$):

(H3$_{ext*}$) $NiMH$: PRODUCER $\sqcap$ $NiMH$ DELIVERED-BY $Compaq$ $\sqcap$
$NiMH$: INCONSISTENT

The qualified reified structures of (H3$_{ext*}$) are given below:

$\pi(\Re(NiMH : $ PRODUCER$))$ QUALIFIED q_1 $\sqcap$ q_1 : INCONSISTENT-HYPO $\sqcap$
$\pi(\Re(NiMH $ DELIVERED-BY $Compaq))$ QUALIFIED q_2 $\sqcap$ q_2 : INCONSISTENT-HYPO $\sqcap$
$\pi(\Re(NiMH : $ INCONSISTENT$))$ QUALIFIED q_3 $\sqcap$ q_3 : INCONSISTENT-HYPO

Note that (H4), the inconsistency-provoking proposition, itself is a hypothesis, i.e., it might be subject to later revisions. In such a case, (H3$_{ext*}$) needs to recover from its negative status, i.e., the negative support label possibly needs to be retracted from it (using the ordinary TMS facilities in the qualifier).

There is a second qualification assignment that results from the integration of (H4), namely that rule II fires and the reified equivalent of ($H1_{ext}$) receives the positive quality label CROSS-SUPPORTED. Given the reified equivalents of ($H1_{ext}$), (P2) and (P3), rule II is instantiated as follows:

$$\Re(NiHM \text{ DELIVERED-BY } Compaq) \ \sqcap \ \Re(NiMH : \text{ACCU}) \ \sqcap$$
$$\Re(Compaq : \text{ACCU-PRODUCER}) \ \sqcap \ \Re(\text{ACCU-PRODUCER} \doteq \forall \text{DEVELOPS.ACCU}) \ \sqcap$$
$$\hbar(\pi(\Re(NiHM \text{ DELIVERED-BY } Compaq))) = \hbar(\pi(\Re(NiMH : \text{ACCU})))$$
$$= \hbar(\pi(\Re(Compaq : \text{ACCU-PRODUCER}))) \ \sqcap$$
$$\pi(\Re(NiMH \text{ DELIVERED-BY } Compaq)) \text{ QUALIFIED } q \ \Longrightarrow$$
$$\textbf{TELL } q \text{ CROSS-SUPPORTED-BY } \pi(\Re(Compaq : \text{ACCU-PRODUCER}))$$

Under the hypothesis that $NiMH$ is an accumulator, $Compaq$ (a designated developer of accumulators) is assumed to be the developer of $NiMH$ (accus), which clearly fits well. Hypotheses space ($H2_{ext}$) receives no further support. Hence, we end up with a hypothesis ranking that qualifies ($H1_{ext}$) as the most credible hypothesis space and (H1) being the currently most preferred concept hypothesis.

8 Related Work

Concept learning which is deeply rooted in the framework of terminological logics is just beginning to attract the machine learning community. For instance, KLUSTER (Kietz and Morik, 1994) is a system that builds a TBox from a given ABox by way of constructive induction. To keep the learning task tractable several restrictions on the expressiveness of the language are introduced (disjunctions and transitive relations are not allowed). The authors also discuss numeric measures for the evaluation of concept hypotheses, which lead to discrimination processes on the induced concepts (e.g., the constructive induction of new relations). These measures score the classification accuracy of the induced concepts w.r.t. the given ABox. Similarly, Cohen and Hirsh (1994) compare several subsets of a given terminological logic to identify a PAC-learnable subset of it. As in KLUSTER, the learning task consists of the induction of a TBox from a given ABox, but no constructive induction is realized.

The main difference to our work lies in the overall learning task: We start with an already specified TBox and plenty of hypotheses concerning a new concept. The immediate goal is to build up concept hypotheses for that concept and to evaluate and rank these alternative concept descriptions in qualitative terms according to credibility. This *quality-based* approach reflects our conviction that quantitative accounts dealing with uncertainty (for a survey, cf. Sombe (1990)) are not appropriate for dealing with the *reasons* which favor one alternative hypothesis over another one. As far as our quality-based assessment model is concerned (cf. Section 6), the primitives of the underlying decision logic resemble those considered by Cohen's model of endorsements (Cohen, 1985). Such a quality-based evaluation of competing hypotheses in a learning system has also been suggested by Clark (1988). However, the resolution strategy he proposes is not flexible enough as it crucially depends on a *stronger-than* relation between sets of hypotheses that must be pre-specified (some flexibility comes in through adaptive processes performed by a case-based reasoner). In our scenario, however, we encounter unrestricted combinations of quality assessments which cannot be specified in advance.

9 Conclusion

We have introduced a model and a system architecture for second-order reasoning about statements expressed in a (first-order) terminological representation language. Meta-reasoning, as we conceive it, is based on the reification of first-order terminological expressions, the assignment of qualifications to these reified structures, and reasoning about the degrees of plausibility and credibility of different qualifications based on the evaluation of second-order qualification rules. A major result of our work is that this kind of meta-reasoning is completely embedded in the homogeneous framework of first-order terminological logic using multiple contexts. Thus, we may profit from the full-blown classification mechanism of standard (first-order) knowledge representation systems for quality-based meta-reasoning.

Given this formal framework, we intend to complete the specification of second-order qualification rules in order to capture more significant configurations occurring in the course of parsing and learning processes. Part of this task, and a particular challenging one, will be the further refinement of the qualification criteria in terms of a *qualification calculus* on which terminological meta-reasoning should be based, at last.

References

Aiello, L. and Levi, G. (1988). The uses of metaknowledge in AI systems. In P.Maes and D.Nardi, editors, *Meta-Level Architectures and Reflection*, pages 243–254. Amsterdam: North-Holland.

Buvač, S., Buvač, V., and Mason, I. (1995). Metamathematics of contexts. *Fundamenta Informaticae*, 23(3). Also distributed via <http://sail.stanford.edu/buvac/metamathematics-of-context.ps>.

Buvač, S. and McCarthy, J. (1994). More notes on formalizing context. Distributed via <http://sail.stanford.edu/buvac/more-notes-on-formalizing-context.ps>.

Buvač, S.; Buvač, V. and Mason, I. (1994). The semantics of propositional contexts. In *Proc. 8th Intl. Symposium on Methodologies for Intelligent Systems*. Springer. Also distributed via <http://sail.stanford.edu/buvac/semantics-of-propositional-contexts.ps>.

Clark, P. (1988). Representing arguments as background knowledge for constraining generalisation. In *EWSL'88 - Proc. 3rd European Working Session on Learning*, pages 37–44.

Cohen, P. (1985). *Heuristic Reasoning about Uncertainty: An Artificial Intelligence Approach.* Los Altos/CA: Morgan Kaufmann.

Cohen, W. and Hirsh, H. (1994). The learnability of description logics with equality constraints. *Machine Learning,* 17:169–199.

Doyle, J. (1979). A truth maintenance system. *Artificial Intelligence,* 12:231–272.

Friedman, D. and Wand, M. (1984). Reification: reflection without metaphysics. In *Proc. 1984 ACM Symposium on Lisp and Functional Programming,* pages 348–355, Austin, Texas.

Giunchiglia, F. and Serafini, L. (1994). Multilanguage hierarchical logics, or: how can we do without modal logics? *Artificial Intelligence,* 65:29–70.

Hahn, U., Klenner, M., and Schnattinger, K. (1995). Learning from texts – A terminological meta-reasoning perspective. In *Proc. IJCAI'95 Workshop on New Approaches to Learning for Natural Language Processing.* Also distributed via <http://www.coling.uni-freiburg.de/public/papers/ijcai95.ps>.

Hahn, U., Schacht, S., and Bröker, N. (1994). Concurrent, object-oriented dependency parsing - the PARSETALK model. *International Journal of Human-Computer Studies,* 41(1/2):179–222.

Halpern, J. and Moses, Y. (1992). A guide to completeness and complexity for modal logics of knowledge and belief. *Artificial Intelligence,* 54:319–379.

Hintikka, J. (1962). *Knowledge and Belief. An Introduction to the Logic of the Two Notions.* Ithaca, N.Y.: Cornell University Press.

Kietz, J.-U. and Morik, K. (1994). A polynomial approach to the constructive induction of structural knowledge. *Machine Learning,* 14:193–217.

MacGregor, R. (1993). Representing reified relations in LOOM. *Journal of Experimental and Theoretical Artificial Intelligence,* 5:179–183.

MacGregor, R. (1994). A description classifier for the predicate calculus. In *AAAI'94 - Proc. 12th National Conf. on Artificial Intelligence,* pages 213–220.

McCarthy, J. (1993). Notes on formalizing context. In *IJCAI'93 - Proc. 13th Intl. Joint Conf. on Artificial Intelligence,* pages 555–560, Chambery, France.

Morik, K. (1986). Anything you can do I can do meta. Technical Report KIT-Report 40, TU Berlin, FB Informatik, Projektgruppe KIT.

Nardi, D. (1988). Evaluation and reflection in FOL. In P.Maes and D.Nardi, editors, *Meta-Level Architectures and Reflection,* pages 61–74. Amsterdam: North-Holland.

Sombe, L. (1990). *Reasoning Under Incomplete Information in Artificial Intelligence: A Comparison of Formalisms Using a Single Example.* New York: John Wiley.

Weyhrauch, R. W. (1980). Prolegomena to a theory of mechanized formal reasoning. *Artificial Intelligence,* 13(1):133–170.

A New Continuous Propositional Logic

Riccardo Poli, Mark Ryan and Aaron Sloman

School of Computer Science, The University of Birmingham,
Edgbaston, Birmingham B15 2TT, UK

Abstract. In this paper we present Minimal Polynomial Logic (MPL), a generalisation of classical propositional logic which allows truth values in the continuous interval $[0, 1]$ and in which propositions are represented by multi-variate polynomials with integer coefficients.

The truth values in MPL are suited to represent the probability of an assertion being true, as in Nilsson's Probabilistic Logic, but can also be interpreted as the degree of truth of that assertion, as in Fuzzy Logic. However, unlike fuzzy logic MPL respects all logical equivalences, and unlike probabilistic logic it does not require explicit manipulation of possible worlds.

In the paper we describe the derivation and the properties of this new form of logic and we apply it to solve and better understand several practical problems in classical logic, such as satisfiability.

1 Introduction

There are many proposals in the literature for extending logic beyond the simple truth values {false, true} or {0, 1} to truth values in the interval $[0, 1]$. Two well-known such extensions are *fuzzy logic* and *probabilistic logic*.

Fuzzy logic [1] is motivated by the wish to express degrees of truth/falsity of propositions. For example, as the property of being tall admits of degrees, fuzzy logic allows the truth value of the sentence 'John is tall' to be some number in the interval $[0, 1]$ depending on how tall John is relative to the ambient population. Although fuzzy logic has several important applications, one of its weaknesses is that it does not respect some logical equivalences such as $\neg(x_1 \wedge \neg x_2) \equiv x_2 \vee (\neg x_1 \wedge \neg x_2)$ in the presence of non-binary variables [3].

Nilsson's probabilistic logic [8, 9], on the other hand, is not concerned with inherent degrees of truth, but with the fact that we may have only partial knowledge about the truth or falsity of sentences. In probabilistic logic, a 'truth value' in $[0, 1]$ is taken to be the probability that the sentence is true. From the perspective of probabilistic logic, 'John is tall' is either true or it is false, but we may have only partial information about his size and on that basis we may assign to the sentence a number in $[0, 1]$ representing the probability that it is true. Despite its clear and precise definition, Nilsson's probabilistic logic requires the explicit computation of the truth or falsity of a proposition in all possible worlds (see section 4 for more details).

In this paper we present a generalisation of classical propositional logic, called *Minimal Polynomial Logic* (MPL), initially developed to facilitate incremental searching for solutions to logical problems, which allows handling continuous truth values in the range $[0, 1]$. The properties of MPL which we will describe suggest that the most suitable interpretation of such truth values is the probability of the assertion being true, as in Nilsson's probabilistic logic. However, unlike probabilistic logic MPL does not require explicit manipulation of all possible worlds.

Despite this probabilistic orientation, for specific applications in which a logic which respects all logical equivalences is required, the truth values of MPL could also represent the degree of truth of the assertion, as in fuzzy logic or fuzzy control. Unfortunately, when this interpretation is adopted, some identities that are universally considered fundamental in fuzzy logic (but not in fuzzy control) do not hold.

The paper is organised as follows. In Section 2 we introduce Polynomial Logics (PLs), which are simple generalisations of classical predicate logic in which propositions are represented by multi-variate polynomials. The simplest form of polynomial logic, which we will denote as PL_0, is the precursor of MPL which is described (Section 3). Some applications of these two types of logic as well as their relations with fuzzy logic and probabilistic logic are discussed in Section 4. We make some final remarks in Section 5.

2 Polynomial Logics

In classic logic the variables x_i which are present in a proposition e can only take two values, 0 and 1. Given the standard definitions of the connectives $\wedge$, $\vee$ and $\neg$ (e.g. $x_1 \wedge x_2 = 1$ iff $x_1 = x_2 = 1$), the same is true of the values taken by e. One way of generalising this kind of binary (or Boolean) logic would be to consider expressions with variables that can take continuous values between 0 (false) and 1 (true) and to generalise the ordinary logic connectives.

A natural way of generalising such connectives is to consider functions that can fit the datapoints represented by the truth tables of the ordinary connectives. For example, if we want to generalise the $\vee$ function, $x_1 \vee x_2$, we have to select a function $o(x_1, x_2)$ such that $o(0, 0) = 0$, $o(0, 1) = 1$, $o(1, 0) = 1$ and $o(1, 1) = 1$.

A simple form of such functions is obtained by using polynomials that can fit the truth tables of the ordinary logic connectives. For example, the polynomials $a(x_1, x_2) = \frac{1}{4} x_1 x_2 (1 + x_1)(1 + x_2)$, $o(x_1, x_2) = 1 - a(1 - x_1, 1 - x_2) = 1 - \frac{1}{4}(1 - x_1)(1 - x_2)(2 - x_1)(2 - x_2)$ and $n(x_1) = (1 - x_1)(1 + x_1)$ generalise the logical connectives $\wedge$, $\vee$ and $\neg$, respectively.[1] There are infinitely many such generalisations.

Having defined a set of generalised connectives any ordinary logic expression e can be generalised by simply replacing the ordinary connectives with the generalised ones. With polynomial connectives an entire class of polynomial propositional logics, PL, can thus be defined.

---

[1] Other connectives such as $\rightarrow$ and $\leftrightarrow$ can be obtained likewise using standard equivalences.

The *lowest degree* polynomials that can fit the truth-table entries of the ordinary logic connectives,

$$
\begin{aligned}
o(x_1, x_2) &= x_1 \vee x_2 = 1 - (1 - x_1)(1 - x_2), \\
a(x_1, x_2) &= x_1 \wedge x_2 = x_1 x_2, \\
n(x_1) &= \neg x_1 = 1 - x_1,
\end{aligned}
\tag{1}
$$

define the most parsimonious (lowest-degree) polynomial logic which we will denote with the symbol PL_0. More formally:

Definition 1. Given a propositional formula e, its PL_0 version e_p is the polynomial obtained by replacing the ordinary connectives with those given in Eq. 1.

Example 1. Consider the expression $e = (x_1 \vee (x_2 \wedge \neg x_3)) \wedge (x_1 \rightarrow x_2)$. The PL_0 version of it is:

$$
\begin{aligned}
e_p &= (1 - (1 - x_1)(1 - (x_2(1 - x_3))))(1 - x_1(1 - x_2)) \\
&= 2x_1 x_2 x_3 - x_1{}^2 x_2 x_3 + x_1{}^2 x_2{}^2 x_3 - 2x_1 x_2 + 2x_1{}^2 x_2 - \\
&\quad - x_1{}^2 x_2{}^2 - x_2 x_3 - x_2{}^2 x_3 x_1 + x_1 - x_1{}^2 + x_2 + x_1 x_2{}^2.
\end{aligned}
$$

PL_0 and classical logic give the same truth values when the propositional variables take the values 0 and 1.

Theorem 2. $\forall x_i \in \{0, 1\}$, $e = e_p$.

Proof. Since the polynomials $o(x_1, x_2)$, $a(x_1, x_2)$ and $n(x)$, when evaluated with $x_i \in \{0, 1\}$, take the same values of their discrete (binary/Boolean) counterparts, this is also true for the expression e_p. $\square$

Example 2. If the original expression e is in conjunctive normal form (CNF), i.e. a conjunction ($\wedge$) of disjunctions ($\vee$) of literals (variables or negated variables) of the form

$$
e = \bigwedge_{i=1}^{M} \left(\bigvee_{j=1}^{K_i} l_{ij} \right),
\tag{2}
$$

where $l_{ij} \in \{x_1, \cdots, x_N, \neg x_1, \cdots, \neg x_N\}$, then its PL_0 version is given by:

$$
e_p = \prod_{i=1}^{M} \left(1 - \prod_{j=1}^{K_i} (1 - l_{c,ij}) \right),
\tag{3}
$$

where $l_{c,ij} \in \{x_1, \cdots, x_N, (1 - x_1), \cdots, (1 - x_N)\}$. The fact that $e_p = 1$ iff $\forall i \, \exists j : l_{c,ij} = 1$ clarifies the equivalence between e and e_p in the case of binary variables.

3 Minimal Polynomial Logic

In the previous section we have introduced the notion of polynomial logics in general and described PL_0 in particular. In this section we will obtain from PL_0 a new form of continuous logic that we call Minimal Polynomial Logic (MPL).

Definition 3. Given a propositional formula e, its MPL version e_m is obtained from the PL_0 version e_p by distributing $+$ over $\times$ throughout and then substituting subexpressions of the form x_i^k (with $k > 1$) with x_i. This substitution will be sometimes be denoted with $(\cdot)_m$.

Example 3. Let us consider the exclusive or function: $e = (x_1 \wedge \neg x_2) \vee (\neg x_1 \wedge x_2)$. Its PL_0 and MPL versions are $e_p = x_1 + x_2 - 3x_1x_2 + x_1^2 x_2 + x_1 x_2^2 - x_1^2 x_2^2$ and $e_m = x_1 + x_2 - 2x_1x_2$, respectively.

This simple substitution is one of the main ideas in this paper. As will be seen, it has significant consequences (e.g. Thm. 5).

As before this logic agrees with classical logic on the Boolean truth values:

Theorem 4. $\forall x_i \in \{0,1\}$, $e_p = e_m = e$.

Proof. If $x_i \in \{0,1\}$ then $x_i^k = x_i$ $(k > 1)$, therefore the substitution given in Def. 3 does not change the value of e_p. $e_m = e$ follows from Thm. 2. $\quad\square$

However, MPL has an important property which distinguishes it from other PLs:

Theorem 5. *Two propositions e and e' are logically equivalent iff their MPL versions e_m and e'_m are the same polynomial.*

Proof. $\Leftarrow$ If $e_m \equiv e'_m$ then, in particular, $\forall x_i \in \{0,1\}$ $e_m = e'_m$. Thus, by Thm. 4 $e \equiv e'$.
$\Rightarrow$ Suppose $e_m \not\equiv e'_m$, then there exist some coefficients $c_i \neq 0$ such that

$$e_m - e'_m = c_1 x_{k_1^1} \cdots x_{k_{L_1}^1} + \cdots + c_D x_{k_1^D} \cdots x_{k_{L_D}^D}.$$

Let c_m be the coefficient of any term of minimal degree. Set the variables which occur in that term to 1 and all the other variables occurring either in e_m or e'_m to 0. Then $e_m - e'_m = c_m \neq 0$, so by Thm. 4 $e \neq e'$ for that assignment. $\quad\square$

Corollary 6. 1. *e is satisfiable iff $e_m \not\equiv 0$. Moreover, the second part of the proof of Thm 5 gives an assignment making e true.*

2. *e is a tautology iff $e_m \equiv 1$. Moreover, if $e_m \not\equiv 1$ then the second part of the proof of Thm 5 gives an assignment making e false.*

Example 4. Let us consider again the expression $e = (x_1 \vee (x_2 \wedge \neg x_3)) \wedge (x_1 \to x_2)$. The MPL version of it is:

$$e_m = x_1 x_2 x_3 - x_2 x_3 + x_2.$$

The lowest degree term of e_m is x_2, therefore, according to the procedure outlined in the proof of Theorem 5, the assignment $x_1 = 0$, $x_2 = 1$, $x_3 = 0$ satisfies e. This is correct, as

$$e = (0 \vee (1 \wedge \neg 0)) \wedge (0 \to 1) = (0 \vee (1 \wedge 1)) \wedge 1 = (0 \vee 1) \wedge 1 = 1 \wedge 1 = 1.$$

Example 5. Let us now consider the expression $e = x_1 \wedge x_2 \wedge (\neg x_1 \vee \neg x_2)$. The PL$_0$ version of it is:

$$e_p = x_1 x_2 (1 - x_1 x_2) = x_1 x_2 - x_1^2 x_2^2,$$

while its MPL version is

$$e_m = x_1 x_2 - x_1 x_2 \equiv 0$$

which shows that e is unsatisfiable. This is correct as can be readily seen by rewriting $e = e' \wedge \neg e'$ with $e' = x_1 \wedge x_2$.

This result gives a new and interesting way of checking entailment between propositional formulas:

Corollary 7. $e \models e'$ *iff* $e_m \equiv (e_m e_m')_m$.

Proof. $e \models e'$ iff $e \to e' \equiv \top$ iff $(1 - e_m(1 - e_m'))_m \equiv 1$ iff $e_m \equiv (e_m e_m')_m$. □

Example 6. Let us consider the expressions $e = (x_1 \vee x_2) \wedge (\neg x_2 \vee x_3)$ and $e' = x_1 \vee x_3$. We want to check if e entails e'. As $e_m = x_2 x_3 + x_1 - x_1 x_2$ and $e_m' = x_1 + x_3 - x_1 x_3$, simple calculations can show that $e_m \equiv (e_m e_m')_m$.

The next two lemmas are used for the following decomposition theorem 10 and Thm. 17.

Lemma 8. *Let P_1, P_2 be polynomials.*

1. *$(P_1 + P_2)_m \equiv (P_1)_m + (P_2)_m$.*
2. *$(P_1 P_2)_m \equiv (P_1)_m (P_2)_m$ if P_1 and P_2 have no variables in common.*

Proof. 1. Suppose x_i^k is a subexpression in $P_1 + P_2$, then it is a subexpression in P_1 or P_2 or both, and so will be reduced to x_i in $(P_1)_m + (P_2)_m$. 2. Suppose P_1 and P_2 have no variables in common and x_i^k is a subexpression in $P_1 P_2$, then it is a subexpression in P_1 or P_2, and so will be reduced to x_i in $(P_1)_m (P_2)_m$. □

Lemma 9. $e_m \equiv x_1 (e[\top/x_1])_m + (1 - x_1)(e[\bot/x_1])_m$.

Proof. First note that $e \equiv (x_1 \wedge e[\top/x_1]) \vee (\neg x_1 \wedge e[\bot/x_1])$ therefore:

$$
\begin{aligned}
e_m &\equiv ((x_1 \wedge e[\top/x_1]) \vee (\neg x_1 \wedge e[\bot/x_1]))_m && \text{Thm. 5}\\
&\equiv (1 - (1 - x_1 e[\top/x_1]_p)(1 - (1 - x_1)e[\bot/x_1]_p))_m \\
&\equiv (x_1 e[\top/x_1]_p + (1 - x_1)e[\bot/x_1]_p \\
&\quad + x_1(1 - x_1)e[\top/x_1]_p e[\bot/x_1]_p)_m \\
&\equiv (x_1 e[\top/x_1]_p)_m + ((1 - x_1)e[\bot/x_1]_p)_m \\
&\quad + (x_1(1 - x_1)e[\top/x_1]_p e[\bot/x_1]_p)_m && \text{Lemma 8}\\
&\equiv x_1(e[\top/x_1]_p)_m + (1 - x_1)(e[\bot/x_1]_p)_m && \text{Lemma 8}\\
& && x_1 \text{ does not occur in } e[\cdot/x_1]\\
& && (x_1(1 - x_1))_m \equiv 0 \\[1.2em]
&\equiv x_1 e[\top/x_1]_m + (1 - x_1)e[\bot/x_1]_m
\end{aligned}
$$

$\square$

The following theorem shows how an MPL expression can be decomposed as a linear combination of orthogonal basis of MPL expressions.

Theorem 10. $e_m = \sum_{i=1}^{2^N} y_i(e_i)_m$, *where*

$$
\begin{aligned}
y_1 &= x_1 x_2 \cdots x_N, \\
y_2 &= (1 - x_1)x_2 \cdots x_N, \\
y_3 &= x_1(1 - x_2) \cdots x_N, \\
&\cdots \\
y_{2^N} &= (1 - x_1)(1 - x_2) \cdots (1 - x_N),
\end{aligned}
$$

are an orthogonal basis for MPL with the scalar product $\langle y_i, y_j \rangle = (y_i y_j)_m$ *and*

$$
\begin{aligned}
e_1 &= e[\top/x_1, \top/x_2, \ldots, \top/x_N], \\
e_2 &= e[\bot/x_1, \top/x_2, \ldots, \top/x_N], \\
e_3 &= e[\top/x_1, \bot/x_2, \ldots, \top/x_N], \\
&\cdots \\
e_{2^N} &= e[\bot/x_1, \bot/x_2, \ldots, \bot/x_N].
\end{aligned}
$$

Proof. Apply Lemma 9 recursively to all the variables in e. $\square$

Using the results just introduced, we are now able to give an alternative characterisation of entailment:

Theorem 11. $e \models e'$ *iff* $e_m \le e'_m$, $\forall x_i \in [0, 1]$.

Proof. $\Leftarrow$ immediate.
$\Rightarrow e_m - e'_m = \sum_i y_i((e_i)_m - (e'_i)_m) \le 0$ as $(e_i)_m \le (e'_i)_m$. $\square$

4 Applications and Relations with Other Logics

4.1 Use and Interpretations of PL_0

In addition of being the precursor of MPL, PL_0 can have practical applications on its own.

Algebraic Logical Calculus. As a first application, PL_0 can be used to study or to teach classical logic by using only (or mostly) familiar algebraic techniques. The two theorems and the corollary given in this section are an example of this.[2]

The following definition and lemma are required for the next two theorems.

Definition 12. The dual $\hat{e}$ of e is the expression obtained by exchanging $\wedge$ with $\vee$ and $\perp$ with $\top$ in e.

Lemma 13. *e is unsatisfiable iff its dual $\hat{e}$ is a tautology*

Proof. The duality theorem [11, p.26] states that any two expressions e and e' are logically equivalent iff their duals $\hat{e}$ and $\hat{e'}$ are logically equivalent. Therefore, e is unsatisfiable iff $e \equiv \perp$ iff $\hat{e} \equiv \top$. $\qquad\square$

Theorem 14. *Let e be a proposition in CNF such as Equation 2. e is unsatisfiable iff $\forall (x_1, \ldots, x_N) \in \{0,1\}^N, \exists i \, \forall j \, l_{ij} = 1$.*

Proof. If $\hat{e}$ is the dual of e, i.e. $\hat{e} = \bigvee_{i=1}^{M} \left(\bigwedge_{j=1}^{K_i} l_{ij} \right)$, then

$$\hat{e}_p = 1 - \prod_{i=1}^{M} \left(1 - \prod_{j=1}^{K_i} l_{c,ij} \right).$$

By Lemma and Thm. 2, e is unsatisfiable iff $\forall (x_1, \ldots, x_N) \in \{0,1\}^N \, \hat{e}_p = 1$ iff $\forall (x_1, \ldots, x_N) \in \{0,1\}^N, \exists i \prod_{j=1}^{K_i} l_{c,ij} = 1$ iff $\forall (x_1, \ldots, x_N) \in \{0,1\}^N, \exists i \, \forall j \, l_{ij} = 1$. $\qquad\square$

Corollary 15. *Let e be a proposition in CNF.*

1. *If $\forall i \, \exists j$ such that $l_{ij} \in \{\neg x_1, \cdots, \neg x_n\}$ then e is satisfiable.*
2. *If $\forall i \, \exists j$ such that $l_{ij} \in \{x_1, \cdots, x_n\}$ then e is satisfiable.*

Proof. For 1. $(x_1, \ldots, x_N) = (0, \ldots, 0)$ and for 2. $(x_1, \ldots, x_N) = (1, \ldots, 1)$. $\qquad\square$

Theorem 16. *Let e be a proposition in Disjunctive Normal Form (DNF), i.e. $e = \bigvee_{i=1}^{M} \left(\bigwedge_{j=1}^{K_i} l_{ij} \right)$. e is unsatisfiable iff $\forall (x_1, \ldots, x_N) \in \{0,1\}^N, \forall i \, \exists j \, l_{ij} = 1$.*

Proof. The PL_0 version of the dual $\hat{e}$ of e is $\hat{e}_p = \prod_{i=1}^{M} \left(1 - \prod_{j=1}^{K_i} (1 - l_{c,ij}) \right)$. $\forall (x_1, \ldots, x_N) \in \{0,1\}^N \, \hat{e}_p = 1$ iff $\forall (x_1, \ldots, x_N) \in \{0,1\}^N, \forall i \, \exists j \, l_{ij} = 1$. $\qquad\square$

---

[2] Of course, there are direct proofs based on classical logic only for the results obtained with PL_0.

Relations with Probability. If we interpret the variables occurring in the polynomial e_p as probabilities of being true of the corresponding atomic propositions in e, then the value taken by e_p can be interpreted as the probability that e is true.

To illustrate this, let us consider the expression $e = x_1 \vee x_2$ and imagine that x_1, x_2 and consequently e are stochastic binary variables. If we denote with $\mathcal{P}(x_1)$, $\mathcal{P}(x_2)$ and $\mathcal{P}(e)$ the probability of the events $\{x_1 = 1\}$, $\{x_2 = 1\}$ and $\{e = 1\}$, then on the hypothesis that x_1 and x_2 are independent variables we can write:

$$
\begin{aligned}
\mathcal{P}(e) &= \Pr\{e = 1\} \\
&= \Pr\{x_1 \vee x_2 = 1\} \\
&= \Pr\{x_1 = 1\} + \Pr\{x_2 = 1\} - \Pr\{x_1 = 1\}\Pr\{x_2 = 1\} \\
&= \mathcal{P}(x_1) + \mathcal{P}(x_2) - \mathcal{P}(x_1)\mathcal{P}(x_2) \\
&= 1 - (1 - \mathcal{P}(x_1))(1 - \mathcal{P}(x_2))
\end{aligned}
$$

This expression is formally identical to the PL_0 form of e, namely $e_p = 1 - (1 - x_1)(1 - x_2)$, provided that e_p, x_1 and x_2 are interpreted as the probability of being true of the related binary counterparts. The same observation is valid for the $\neg$ and $\wedge$ polynomial functions.

However, as already mentioned in this example, the probabilistic interpretation of the polynomial connectives is correct only on the hypothesis of independent arguments. As a result, the probabilistic interpretation of e_p is correct if no variable occurs more than once in e. Nonetheless, in many cases e_p can be considered as a reasonable approximation of the exact probability and therefore used for many practical purposes. An example of this is given is in the following subsection.

Towards an explanation for GSAT. The problem of deciding if a proposition is satisfiable is a well known NP-complete problem for which time required for exact solutions is an exponential function of the number of variables [2]. This imposes a serious limit to the number of variables of the expression to be checked. For example, it is reported in the literature that one of the best known exact algorithms for satisfiability checking, the Davis-Putnam procedure [2], cannot practically handle expressions with more than a few hundred of variables [10].

Recently a new, very promising approach to the solution of hard satisfiability problems has been proposed which is based on greedy local search procedures (GSAT) [10, 5]. Given an expression e in CNF such as Eq. 2, GSAT works as follows:

1. Randomly initialise the variables in e.
2. If $e = \top$ then return($\top$).
3. Select a variable such that a change in its truth assignment gives the largest increase in the total number of clauses of e that are satisfied and reverse its assignment.
4. Iterate steps 2–3 for N_{flips} times.
5. Iterate steps 1–4 for N_{tries} times.

This procedure allows finding solutions for satisfiability problems including several hundred (or even thousands) of variables. Although a theoretical analysis of the the algorithm has been undertaken [5], the reason why the simple optimisation of the number of true clauses in an expression leads so frequently to finding an assignment that satisfies such an expression is actually not completely understood. PL_0 provides a possible explanation for this.

If e_p is the PL_0 version of an expression e in CNF such as Eq. 2, then

$$\log(e_p) = \sum_{i=1}^{M} \log \left(\bigvee_{j=1}^{K_i} l_{ij} \right)_p$$

Note that $\log \left(\bigvee_{j=1}^{K_i} l_{ij} \right)_p \in [0, -\infty]$. However, to understand GSAT we imagine that $\log(0) = -K$, for some suitably large number K. On this hypothesis, given any (binary) assignment of the variables,

$$\log(e_p) = -K \times M_\perp = K \times (M_\top - M),$$

$M_\top$ and $M_\perp$ being the number of true and false clauses in e, respectively. Being the logarithm a monotonic increasing function, the probabilistic interpretation of this equation is: *maximising the number of true clauses in e (e.g. using the GSAT algorithm) is equivalent to maximising an approximation (e_p) of the probability of being true of e in the corners of the hypercube $[0, 1]^N$*. Searching for the maxima of e_p moving only on the corners of the hypercube is overconstraining, and GSAT can therefore be generalised and improved by using any optimisation procedure (e.g. gradient ascent or a genetic algorithm) working in $[0, 1]^N$.

Relations with Fuzzy Logic. If we interpret the variables occurring in the polynomial e_p as the degree of truth of the corresponding atomic propositions in e, then the value taken by e_p can be interpreted as the degree of truth of e. In this sense, PL_0 is actually equivalent to a well-known form of fuzzy logic which is often used in fuzzy control [6]. The disadvantages of PL_0 are: a) unlike min/max-based fuzzy logic, it does not respect idempotency properties ($x_1 \wedge x_1 \equiv x_1$ and $x_1 \vee x_1 \equiv x1$), b) like fuzzy logic, it fails to respect some other logical equivalences such as

$$(\neg(x_1 \wedge \neg x_2))_p \equiv 1 - x_1(1 - x_2)$$
$$\not\equiv 1 - x_1 - x_2 + 2x_1x_2 + x_2^2 - x_1x_2^2$$
$$\equiv (x_2 \vee (\neg x_1 \wedge \neg x_2))_p.$$

An advantage of PL_0 as a fuzzy logic is that it is minimally sensitive to errors in the estimation of the degrees of truth of atomic sentences [7].

4.2 Use and Interpretations of MPL

The examples given in Section 3 show how MPL can be used to effectively and naturally answer questions about satisfiability and entailment in classical logic by using algebraic manipulations.

As in the case of MPL, the variables in e_m can be interpreted either as probabilities or fuzzy truth values. In the following we will show how in the first case MPL overcomes all the independency requirements of PL_0, while in the second case it further departs from the usual features of min/max fuzzy logic.

Relations with Probability. The probabilistic interpretation of MPL requires additional work carried out in the following theorem.

Theorem 17. $\mathcal{P}(e) = e_m[\mathcal{P}(x_i)/x_i]$.

Proof. Induction on the number of variables in e.
Base case: 0 variables. Trivial.
Inductive case: Suppose there are k variables in e and the theorem holds for all expressions with $k-1$ variables. Let x_1 be any variable.

$$
\begin{aligned}
\mathcal{P}(e) &= \Pr\{x_1 = 1\}\Pr\{e = 1 \mid x_1 = 1\} \\
&\quad + \Pr\{x_1 = 0\}\Pr\{e = 1 \mid x_1 = 0\} \\
&= \mathcal{P}(x_1)\mathcal{P}(e[\top/x_1]) + (1 - \mathcal{P}(x_1))\mathcal{P}(e[\bot/x_1]) \\
&= \mathcal{P}(x_1)(e[\top/x_1])_m[\mathcal{P}(x_i)/x_i] \\
&\quad + (1 - \mathcal{P}(x_1))(e[\bot/x_1])_m[\mathcal{P}(x_i)/x_i] \qquad \text{Ind. Hyp.} \\
&= (x_1 e[\top/x_1]_m + (1 - x_1)e[\bot/x_1]_m)[\mathcal{P}(x_i)/x_i] \\
&= e_m[\mathcal{P}(x_i)/x_i] \qquad\qquad\qquad\qquad\qquad \text{Lemma 9}
\end{aligned}
$$

$\square$

Example 7. If $e = (x_1 \vee (x_2 \wedge \neg x_3)) \wedge (x_1 \rightarrow x_2)$, then the probability of e being true is $\mathcal{P}(e) = e_m[\mathcal{P}(x_i)/x_i] = (x_1 x_2 x_3 - x_2 x_3 + x_2)[\mathcal{P}(x_i)/x_i] = \mathcal{P}(x_1)\mathcal{P}(x_2)\mathcal{P}(x_3) - \mathcal{P}(x_2)\mathcal{P}(x_3) + \mathcal{P}(x_2)$.

As clarified by the previous results, MPL yields the correct probability of an expression being true, even in the case of dependent subexpressions (i.e. reused variables).

Relations with Nilsson's Probabilistic Logic. In probabilistic logic, each world w_i is an assignment for the variables present in a proposition e to which a probability p_i of being the case is associated. The probability of e being true is then represented by

$$
\Pr\{e = 1\} = \sum_i p_i w_i(e), \tag{4}
$$

where $w_i(e)$ is the result of evaluating e in w_i. This expression shows that Nilsson's probabilistic logic requires the explicit computation of the truth or falsity of a proposition in all possible worlds.

The relation between probabilistic logic and (the probabilistic interpretation of) MPL is clarified by the following

Corollary 18. $\mathcal{P}(e) = \sum_{i=1}^{2^N} y_i [\mathcal{P}(x_i)/x_i](e_i)_m$ *where y_i and e_i are defined as in Thm. 10.*

Proof. Apply Thm. 17 to e_m expressed as in Thm. 10. □

By considering for example that $y_1[\mathcal{P}(x_i)/x_i] = \mathcal{P}(x_1 \wedge x_2 \wedge \ldots \wedge x_N) = \mathrm{Pr}\{x_1 = \top, x_2 = \top, \ldots, x_N = \top\}$, it can be easily understood that $y_i[\mathcal{P}(x_i)/x_i] = \mathrm{Pr}\{w_i\} = p_i$. On the other hand $(e_i)_m = w_i(e)$, and therefore the last corollary can be reformulated as

$$\mathcal{P}(e) = \sum_{i=1}^{2^N} p_i w_i(e),$$

which is exactly the same expressions as in Eq. 4.

This clarifies how (the probabilistic interpretation of) MPL generalises probabilistic logic as the atoms it adopts are are not entire worlds but the sentences composing such worlds.

Relations with Fuzzy Logic. Let us now reconsider the interpretation of MPL as fuzzy logic. Thm. 5 guarantees that MPL respects logical equivalence. For example, $(x_1 \wedge x_1)_m \equiv x_1 \equiv (x_1)_m$, $(x_1 \vee x_1)_m \equiv x_1 \equiv (x_1)_m$,

$$(\neg(x_1 \wedge \neg x_2))_m \equiv 1 - x_1 + x_1 x_2$$
$$\equiv (x_2 \vee (\neg x_1 \wedge \neg x_2))_m,$$

$(x_1 \wedge \neg x_1)_m \equiv 0 \equiv (\bot)_m$ and $(x_1 \vee \neg x_1)_m \equiv 1 \equiv (\top)_m$. Note that the last three equivalences are not valid in the various forms of fuzzy logic.

However, while on the one hand the fuzzy interpretation of MPL seems to have better properties than fuzzy logic, on the other hand it departs even more than PL_0 from the behaviour of the standard min/max fuzzy logic. An example of this is the expression $x_1 \wedge \neg x_1$ which evaluates to something in $[0.5, 1]$ in fuzzy logic, to something in $[0, 0.5]$ in PL_0, and to 0 in MPL. This would certainly be considered an anomalous result if the expression represents the degree of truth of the fact that some property is partly present and partly not present at the same time.

5 Conclusions

In this paper we have presented minimal polynomial logic, a generalisation of classical propositional logic which allows continuous truth values.

In its non-minimal form PL_0, our logic can be used either as a fuzzy logic or as an approximate probabilistic logic. We have used this form of logic to prove some results about classical logic, which are transparent in MPL. The proofs of such results are based on a natural integration of calculus and standard logical techniques. In addition, with a simple logarithm transformation PL_0 provides a long-sought explanation for the enigmatic GSAT algorithm [4].

MPL has all these properties but it also respects logical equivalence (Theorem 5). This means that whatever we can prove to be true for MPL, for example using calculus, is true in classical logic and vice versa. An application of this theorem, Corollary 6, provides a new way of checking the satisfiability of a proposition based only on algebraic manipulations. Thanks to Cor. 7 and Thm. 11, the same is also true for checking entailment.

Finally, the probabilistic interpretation of MPL, supported by Thm. 17, gives the probability of a proposition being true even in the case in which there are repeated variables. This does not require the explicit evaluation of the expression in all possible worlds needed by Nilsson's probabilistic logic. However, Thm.10 guarantees that the probabilities computed with MPL and probabilistic logic are the same.

Acknowledgements

The authors thank Alan P. Sexton of the School of Computer Science, The University of Birmingham, for useful discussions and suggestions. The second author acknowledges partial support from Esprit WG ModelAge (8319).

References

1. J. C. Bezdek. Fuzzy models – what are they and why? *IEEE Transactions on Fuzzy Systems*, 1(1):1–6, 1993.
2. M. D. Davis and E. J. Weyuker. *Computability, Complexity and Languages*. Academic Press, London, 1983.
3. C. Elkan. The paradoxical success of Fuzzy Logic. *IEEE Expert*, 9(4):3–8, August 1994.
4. I. Gent and T. Walsh. The enigma of SAT hill-climbing procedures. Technical Report 605, Department of Artificial Intelligence, University of Edinbrugh, 1992.
5. I. P. Gent and T. Walsh. An empirical analysis of search in GSAT. *Journal of Artificial Intelligence Research*, 1:47–59, 1993.
6. V. Kreinovich, C. Quintana, R. Lea, O. Fuentes, A. Lokshin, S. Kumar, L. Boricheva, and L. Reznik. What non-linearity to choose? A mathematical foundation of fuzzy control. In *Proceedings International Conference on Fuzzy Systems and Intelligent Control*, pages 349–412, Louisville, KY, 1992.
7. H. T. Nguyen, V. Kreinovich, and D. Tolbert. A measure of average sensitivity for fuzzy logics. *International Journal of Uncertainty, Fuzziness, and Knowledge-Based Systems*, 2(4):361–375, 1994.
8. N. J. Nilsson. Probabilistic logic. *Artificial Intelligence*, 28:71–87, 1986.
9. N. J. Nilsson. Probabilistic logic revisited. *Artificial Intelligence*, 59(1–2):39–42, 1993.
10. B. Selman, H. Levesque, and D. Mitchel. A new method for solving hard satisfiability problems. In *Proc. 10-th National Conference of Artificial Intelligence AAAI'92*, pages 440–446, San Jose, CA, July 1992.
11. D. van Dalen. *Logic and Structure*. Universitext. Springer Verlag, third edition, 1994.

Super-Polynomial Speed-Ups in Proof Length by New Tautologies

Uwe Egly

FG Intellektik, TH Darmstadt
Alexanderstraße 10, D–64283 Darmstadt
e-mail: uwe@intellektik.informatik.th-darmstadt.de

Abstract. In this paper, we propose different new techniques for introducing additional clauses in a rather restricted way. Most of the new techniques are based on the introduction of a formula $C \to C$ and a simple decomposition technique. In order to restrict the introduction of such formulae, we choose C from redundant clauses like clauses $C \vee L$ with a pure literal L which are derived in the deduction. We prove the correctness of these techniques and introduce a class of propositional formulae for which any resolution refutation has length super-polynomially related to the length of the input formula. We demonstrate how a super-polynomial decrease of proof length can be achieved for these formulae by applying our new techniques in combination with resolution.

1 Introduction

In the last three decades, many calculi have been developed which are well suited for implementing automated deduction on a computer. Among these calculi, there are different resolution calculi [14], different calculi based on the connection method [1], and different forms of the propositional proof procedure DP of Davis and Putnam [7]. It has been emphasized from the beginning that removing irrelevant parts from a proof yields less alternatives in the search for a proof and, therefore, smarter search spaces. Many reductions, most of them are included as rules in DP, have been proposed to eliminate redundant parts from a given input formula or during a derivation. For instance, the deletion of tautological clauses[1], i.e., clauses containing an atom and its negation, is such a reduction. There are, however, cases, where the deletion of redundant information causes severe problems in finding a proof. The reason is the removal of lemmata, which are necessary to get a short proof. If these lemmata disappear, the shortest proof may be super-polynomially longer than a shortest proof with these lemmata.

In this paper, we propose different new techniques for introducing additional clauses in a rather restricted way. We restrict our attention to propositional resolution. Most of the new techniques are based on the introduction of a formula $C \to C$ and a simple decomposition technique. For instance, let $C \vee P$ be a

---

[1] There are, however, rather restricted variants of resolution like lock resolution [3], where such clauses are necessary for preserving completeness.

clause[2], $\mathcal{D} = \{C \vee P\} \cup \mathcal{C}$ be a clause set, and let P be a pure atom in $\mathcal{C}$, i.e., $\neg P$ does not occur in any clause of $\mathcal{C}$. Let C be a clause of the form $L_1 \vee \ldots \vee L_m$, where L_i $(1 \leq i \leq m)$ is a literal. $\neg C$ denotes a set of unit clauses of the form $\{\neg L_1, \ldots, \neg L_m\}$. An application of PURE would remove $C \vee P$ from $\mathcal{D}$. In our case, the clause $C \vee P$ is not only removed from $\mathcal{D}$, but a formula of the form $C \to C$ is introduced, where C is the maximal subclause not containing the pure literal. Note that this introduction preserves satisfiability and unsatisfiability. Hence, we have an intermediate formula of the form $(C \to C) \wedge \mathsf{F}(\mathcal{C})$, where $\mathsf{F}(\mathcal{C})$ denotes a formula in conjunctive normal form corresponding to $\mathcal{C}$. Two clause sets $\mathcal{D}_1 = \{C\} \cup \mathcal{C}$ and $\mathcal{D}_2 = \neg C \cup \mathcal{C}$ are derived from this intermediate formula by a simple decomposition technique, where $\mathcal{D}$ is unsatisfiable iff $\mathcal{D}_1$ and $\mathcal{D}_2$ are unsatisfiable. The procedure illustrated so far is called NPURE which is called a reduction because the number of pure literals in any of the resulting clause set is less than the number of pure literals in $\mathcal{D}$. The new variants of other well-known reductions can be described in a similar way.

Common subsets of the clause sets introduced by the decomposition can be handled by structure-sharing techniques, thereby minimizing the overhead introduced by the copy of $\mathcal{C}$. Alternatively, the resulting clause sets can be worked with in parallel. This decomposition technique can be considered as a generalization of the well-known splitting rule of Davis and Putnam [7, 6]. In order to simulate this splitting rule, $A \to A$ is introduced (for an atom A occurring in the clause set). The decomposition of $\mathcal{C}$ into $\{A\} \cup \mathcal{C}$ and $\{\neg A\} \cup \mathcal{C}$ has the same effect as giving A the alternative values true and false.

Although such a problem reduction of one clause set into two clause sets might look strange, there are often shorter refutations for $\mathcal{D}_1$ and $\mathcal{D}_2$ compared with the length of refutations of $\mathcal{D}$. The reason is that C as well as $\neg C$ may act as a lemma enabling shorter refutations as in the case of $\mathcal{D}$. The introduction of C and $\neg C$ may have similar effects as the application of the cut rule in the calculus LK. If C is an arbitrary formula instead of a clause, then introducing $C \to C$ simulates the cut rule if a suitable translation of the formula into clause form is assumed. What we propose in this paper is a restricted version of the cut rule, where the possible cut formulae are obtained from redundant information.

There is a second possibility to handle clauses with pure literals. Let P be a pure atom occurring in two clauses $C_1 = D_1 \vee P$ and $C_2 = D_2 \vee P$ of $\mathcal{D}$. An intermediate formula of the form $P \vee (D_1 \wedge D_2)$ is generated and all clauses containing P are deleted from the clause set. Let $\mathcal{C}$ be the resulting clause set. The intermediate formula may be regarded as one half of a definition, namely $(\neg P) \to (D_1 \wedge D_2)$. The introduction of a definition $(\neg P) \equiv (D_1 \wedge D_2)$ can be performed without sacrificing correctness, because P is now a new predicate symbol with respect to $\mathcal{C}$.[3] Let $\mathcal{E}$ be the clause set obtained by the translation

---

[2] Since we are interested in the length of a deduction, we use $A \vee B$ and a contraction operation instead of the usual set-oriented notation $\{A, B\}$, because the latter notation covers deduction steps.

[3] This is a variant of Tseitin's extension [15]. Therefore, the introduction of this definition preserves satisfiability and unsatisfiability.

of this definition to clause form. Then $\mathcal{C} \cup \mathcal{E}$ is the result of the new reduction EXTPURE. The extension of $\mathcal{C}$ by clauses obtained from definitions may yield super-polynomially shorter refutations of $\mathcal{C} \cup \mathcal{E}$ compared with the length of a shortest refutation of $\mathcal{C}$. Again, the new reduction can simulate a restricted version of the cut rule.

The paper is structured as follows. In Section 2, definitions and notations are introduced. Section 3 is devoted to a description of the new reductions. Moreover, the correctness of these reductions is proved. In Section 4, a class of formulae is presented for which any resolution refutation has length super-polynomial in the length n of the input formula, but there exist refutations of length polynomial in n if the new reductions are applied in combination with resolution. Section 5 concludes with a brief discussion of an extension to first order clause logic.

2 Definitions and Notations

In this section, we define some concepts which are needed later. We restrict our attention to propositional logic.

A *clause* is a disjunction of literals. The *empty clause* is denoted by $\square$. For all clauses A and B, $A \vee \square \vee B = A \vee B$. Observe that the order of the literals in a clause is irrelevant. A clause containing an atom and the negation of the atom is called a *tautological clause*. Tautological clauses can be deleted from a clause set by the reduction TAUT. A clause C *subsumes* a clause D if $C \subset D$ and C and D are considered as sets of literals. Clauses which are subsumed by other clauses can be deleted from a clause set by the reduction SUBS.

The complementary literal of L, denoted by $\overline{L}$, is $\neg L$ if L is positive and A if $L = \neg A$. We introduce the following notation. Let C be a clause of the form $L_1 \vee \ldots \vee L_n$. Then $\neg C$ is an abbreviation for the set of n unit clauses $\{\overline{L_1}, \ldots, \overline{L_n}\}$. Let $\mathcal{C}$ be a clause set and let $D = P \vee D$, where P is a literal, $D \in \mathcal{C}$, and $\overline{P}$ does not occur in any clause of $\mathcal{C}$. Then P is called a *pure* literal. Clauses with pure literals can be deleted from a clause set by the reduction PURE.

Two formulae F and G are *satisfiability-equivalent* (sat-equivalent), denoted by $F \equiv_{\text{sat}} G$, if F has a model iff G has a model. It is well-known (cf [1]) that the usual reductions like TAUT, PURE, and SUBS are sat-preserving.

The formula represented by a clause set $\mathcal{C}$ is denoted by $\mathsf{F}(\mathcal{C})$. We often do not distinguish between a clause or a clause set and the corresponding formula which is represented by the clause or by the clause set.

We need the translation of a formula into clause form denoted by $\mathsf{TCF_S}$. This is the translation technique recommended in almost all textbooks [4, 1]. $\mathsf{TCF_S}$ is based on the application of distributivity laws and translates a propositional formula into an equivalent conjunctive normal form (clause form).

A propositional *factor* of a clause is obtained by omitting multiple literals. For instance, $A \vee B$ is a factor of $A \vee B \vee A$. Let $C = C_1 \vee L \vee C_2$, $D = D_1 \vee \overline{L} \vee D_2$ be two clauses where the different C_i, D_i may be $\square$. Then $(C_1 \vee C_2 \vee D_1 \vee D_2)$ is called a propositional *resolvent* of C and D.

Let $\mathcal{C}$ be a set of clauses. The elements of this clause set are called input clauses. A sequence $C_1, \ldots, C_n$ is called propositional *resolution deduction* of a clause C from $\mathcal{C}$ if the following conditions hold.

1. $C_n = C$
2. for all $i = 1, \ldots, n$
   a. C_i is an input clause, or
   b. C_i is a propositional factor of a C_j for $j < i$, or
   c. C_i is a propositional resolvent of a C_j, C_k for $j, k < i$.

A *resolution refutation* of $\mathcal{C}$ is a resolution deduction of $\square$ from $\mathcal{C}$. In the following, we omit the adjective propositional.

The following rule, called *extension* rule, allows for the introduction of abbreviations (or definitions) for formulae. Let $\mathcal{C}$ be a set of clauses and let Q be a predicate symbol not occurring in $\mathcal{C}$. Let A and B be any literals. Then, $\mathsf{TCF_S}(Q \equiv (A \wedge B)) \cup \mathcal{C}$ is the result of an extension. It is well-known that $\mathcal{C} \equiv_{\mathsf{sat}} (\mathsf{TCF_S}(Q \equiv (A \wedge B)) \cup \mathcal{C})$ [15]. *Extended resolution* is the resolution calculus with the possibility to introduce three clauses of the form

$$C_1 = \neg Q \vee A$$
$$C_2 = \neg Q \vee B$$
$$C_3 = Q \vee \neg A \vee \neg B$$

at any point of the deduction, where Q is new with respect to the set of clauses derived so far (including all input clauses).

Let Γ be a resolution deduction of a clause C from $\mathcal{C}$. Then the *length* of Γ, denoted by $|\Gamma|$ is the number of clauses occurring in Γ. If we use the term *short refutation*, we mean a resolution refutation with length polynomial in the length of the input formula.

3   New Reductions

In this section, we introduce different new reductions. Most of them are based on a simple decomposition technique. For instance, let $C \vee P$ be a clause, $\mathcal{D} = \{C \vee P\} \cup \mathcal{C}$ be a clause set, and let P be a pure literal in $\mathcal{C}$. An application of **PURE** would remove $C \vee P$ from $\mathcal{D}$. Instead of simply deleting this clause, two clause sets $\mathcal{D}_1 = \{C\} \cup \mathcal{C}$ and $\mathcal{D}_2 = \neg C \cup \mathcal{C}$ are derived from $\mathcal{D}$ by a simple decomposition technique, where $\mathcal{D}$ is unsatisfiable iff $\mathcal{D}_1$ and $\mathcal{D}_2$ are unsatisfiable. This new reduction is called **NPURE**. It is called a reduction because the number of pure literals in any of the resulting clause set is less than the number of pure literals in $\mathcal{D}$. There are often shorter refutations for $\mathcal{D}_1$ and $\mathcal{D}_2$ compared with the length of refutations of $\mathcal{D}$ because the introduction of C and $\neg C$ can have similar effects like the application of the cut rule in the calculus **LK**.

First recall that the introduction of a clause form of $C \rightarrow C$ (for a clause C) does not destroy unsatisfiability.

Lemma 1. *Let $\mathcal{C}$ be a clause set and let C be an arbitrary clause. Then $\mathcal{C}$ is unsatisfiable iff* $\mathsf{TCF_S}(C \to C) \cup \mathcal{C}$ *is unsatisfiable.*

Since C is restricted to a clause, the cardinality of the resulting clause set $\mathsf{TCF_S}(C \to C)$ equals the number of literals in the clause provided that there are no two identical literals in C.

There are two different mechanisms for handling pure literals. The two reductions are introduced and proved correct. In the following, completeness is not a problem, because we use resolution, and TAUT, PURE, and SUBS are completeness-preserving for unrestricted resolution as well as for many resolution refinements.

Definition 2. Let $\{C \vee P\} \cup \mathcal{C}$ be a clause set, where P is a pure literal. An application of NPURE yields two clause sets $\mathcal{D}_1 = \{C\} \cup \mathcal{C}$ and $\mathcal{D}_2 = \neg C \cup \mathcal{C}$.

Lemma 3. *Let $\mathcal{D}$ be a clause set. Let $C \vee P$ be a clause in $\mathcal{D}$ with a pure literal P and let $\mathcal{D}_1$ and $\mathcal{D}_2$ be the two clause sets obtained by an application of NPURE. Then $\mathcal{D}$ is unsatisfiable iff $\mathcal{D}_1$ and $\mathcal{D}_2$ are unsatisfiable.*

Proof. Remove the clause $C \vee P$ from $\mathcal{D}$ by PURE. Let $\mathcal{C}_1$ be the resulting clause set. Introduce a tautology $C \to C$ and obtain the formula $F_1 = (C \to C) \wedge \mathsf{F}(\mathcal{C}_1)$. Clearly, $F_1 \equiv_{\mathrm{sat}} \mathsf{F}(\mathcal{D})$ and $F_1 \equiv ((\neg C \wedge \mathsf{F}(\mathcal{C}_1)) \vee (C \wedge \mathsf{F}(\mathcal{C}_1)))$. Hence, $\mathsf{F}(\mathcal{D})$ is unsatisfiable iff $(\neg C \wedge \mathsf{F}(\mathcal{C}_1)) \vee (C \wedge \mathsf{F}(\mathcal{C}_1)))$ is unsatisfiable. But then both constituents of the disjunction must be unsatisfiable. Therefore, $\mathcal{D}$ is unsatisfiable iff $\mathcal{D}_1$ and $\mathcal{D}_2$ are unsatisfiable. ∎

There is another possibility to handle pure literals. Assume there are several clauses $Q \vee C_i$ $(1 \le i \le n)$ with the same pure literal Q in a clause set $\mathcal{C}$. Let $\mathcal{C}' = \mathcal{C} \setminus \{Q \vee C_i \mid 1 \le i \le n\}$ and Q does not occur in $\mathcal{C}'$. Then there is an equivalent formula $(\overline{Q} \to \bigwedge_{i=1}^{n} C_i) \wedge \mathsf{F}(\mathcal{C}')$. The implication can be considered as one half of an equivalence introduced by an extension step. Hence, $\mathcal{C}'$ can be extended by the clauses in $\mathsf{TCF_S}((\bigwedge_{i=1}^{n} C_i) \to \overline{Q})$.

Definition 4. Let $\{Q \vee C_i \mid C_i \ne \square, 1 \le i \le n\} \cup \mathcal{C}$ be a clause set, where Q is a pure literal and Q does not occur in $\mathcal{C}$. An application of EXTPURE yields the clause set $\mathcal{D}_1 = \mathsf{TCF_S}((\bigwedge_{i=1}^{n} C_i) \equiv \overline{Q}) \cup \mathcal{C}$.

The requirement that Q does not occur in $\mathcal{C}$ is necessary, since otherwise, EXTPURE would not be correct. The following example illustrates this.

Example 1. Let $\mathcal{D} = \{Q \vee A \vee \neg A\} \cup \mathcal{C}$ be a clause set with $\mathcal{C} = \{Q\}$. Obviously, $\mathcal{D}$ is satisfiable. If we would allow $\mathcal{C}_1$ being of the form $\mathsf{TCF_S}((A \vee \neg A) \equiv \neg Q) \cup \mathcal{C}$, then $\mathcal{D}_1$ would be unsatisfiable. $\mathsf{TCF_S}((A \vee \neg A) \equiv \neg Q)$ results in the clause set $\{Q \vee A \vee \neg A, \neg Q \vee \neg A, \neg Q \vee A\}$ and two resolutions with clause Q yield A and $\neg A$. One further resolution yields $\square$. Therefore, without the restriction mentioned above, EXTPURE would transform a satisfiable clause set into an unsatisfiable one.

Since $\mathsf{TCF_S}$ uses distributivity laws to convert a formula into conjunctive normal form, the resulting clause set may have cardinality exponential in the length of the input clause set. The next example illustrates this problem and its solution.

Example 2. Let $C_1 = L_1 \lor L_2 \lor Q$ and $C_2 = K_1 \lor K_2 \lor Q$ occur in a clause set S derived so far. Then the formula $C_1 \land C_2$ is equivalent to

$$\neg Q \rightarrow ((L_1 \lor L_2) \land (K_1 \lor K_2)).$$

EXTPURE yields the introduction of clauses obtained from the formula $I = ((L_1 \lor L_2) \land (K_1 \lor K_2)) \rightarrow \neg Q$ by $\mathsf{TCF_S}$. The resulting clause set is as follows.

$$A_1 = \neg L_1 \lor \neg K_1 \lor \neg Q$$
$$A_2 = \neg L_1 \lor \neg K_2 \lor \neg Q$$
$$A_3 = \neg L_2 \lor \neg K_1 \lor \neg Q$$
$$A_4 = \neg L_2 \lor \neg K_2 \lor \neg Q$$

In general, the cardinality of such a resulting clause set can, in the worst case, be exponential in the length of the input clause set, because a formula which is essentially in disjunctive normal form has to be transformed into conjunctive normal form. There are well-known translations which completely avoid the exponential explosion of the cardinality of the resulting clause set. The basic idea is to replace $\mathsf{TCF_S}$ by a translation introducing labels for subformulae. Such translations are called definitional or structure-preserving translations in the literature [8, 15, 13].

Instead of introducing $A_1, \ldots, A_4$, the following clauses are introduced instead.

$$D_1 = \neg R \lor \neg L_1$$
$$D_2 = \neg R \lor \neg L_2$$
$$D_3 = \neg R \lor \neg K_1$$
$$D_4 = \neg R \lor \neg K_2$$
$$D_5 = \neg Q \lor R \lor S$$

Observe that both clause sets are sat-equivalent to the original implication I. Although the cardinality of the clause set introduced in such a way for our example implication I is greater than the cardinality of the clause set introduced above, this is not true in general. The cardinality of the latter clause set is only polynomial in the number of literal occurrences.

For our purposes here, it is sufficient to consider the translation $\mathsf{TCF_S}$.

Lemma 5. *Let $\mathcal{D}$ be a clause set. Let $\mathcal{D}_1$ be the result of an application of* EXTPURE, *where Q is the pure literal. Then $\mathcal{D}$ is unsatisfiable iff $\mathcal{D}_1$ is unsatisfiable.*

Proof. Let $\mathcal{D} = \{Q \vee C_i \mid C_i \neq \Box, 1 \leq i \leq n\} \cup \mathcal{D}'$, where Q is a pure literal not occurring in $\mathcal{D}'$. $\mathcal{D} \equiv_{\text{sat}} \mathcal{D}'$ because $\{Q \vee C_i \mid C_i \neq \Box, 1 \leq i \leq n\}$ can be removed from $\mathcal{D}$ by PURE resulting $\mathcal{D}'$. Let $\mathcal{D}_1 = (\text{TCF}_\text{S}((\bigwedge_{i=1}^{n} C_i) \equiv \overline{Q}) \cup \mathcal{D}')$ by Definition 4. Then $\mathcal{D}_1 \equiv_{\text{sat}} \mathcal{D}'$ because Q and $\overline{Q}$ are new literals w.r.t. $\mathcal{D}'$. Hence, $\mathcal{D}_1 \equiv_{\text{sat}} \mathcal{D}$. $\blacksquare$

Definition 6. Let $\{C \vee B, B\} \cup \mathcal{C}$ be a clause set. An application of NSUBS yields two clause sets $\mathcal{D}_1 = \{C, B\} \cup \mathcal{C}$ and $\mathcal{D}_2 = \neg C \cup \{B\} \cup \mathcal{C}$.

Lemma 7. *Let $\mathcal{D}$ be a clause set. Let $C \vee B$ be a clause in $\mathcal{D}$ which is subsumed by another clause B in $\mathcal{D}$, and let $\mathcal{D}_1$ and $\mathcal{D}_2$ be the two clause sets obtained by an application of NSUBS. Then $\mathcal{D}$ is unsatisfiable iff $\mathcal{D}_1$ and $\mathcal{D}_2$ are unsatisfiable.*

Proof. Remove the clause $C \vee B$ from $\mathcal{D}$ by SUBS. Let $\mathcal{C}_1$ be the resulting clause set. Introduce a tautology $C \rightarrow C$ and obtain the formula $F_1 = (C \rightarrow C) \wedge F(\mathcal{C}_1)$. The remaining part of the proof is similar to the proof of Lemma 3. $\blacksquare$

Definition 8. Let $\{C \vee P \vee \neg P\} \cup \mathcal{C}$ be a clause set. An application of NTAUT yields two clause sets $\mathcal{C}_1 = \{C\} \cup \mathcal{C}$ and $\mathcal{C}_2 = \neg C \cup \mathcal{C}$.

By a similar proof as in the case of Lemma 7, we get the following.

Lemma 9. *Let $\mathcal{D}$ be a clause set. Let $C \vee P \vee \neg P$ be a clause in $\mathcal{D}$ and let $\mathcal{D}_1$ and $\mathcal{D}_2$ be the clause sets obtained by an application of NTAUT. Then $\mathcal{D}$ is unsatisfiable iff $\mathcal{D}_1$ and $\mathcal{D}_2$ are unsatisfiable.*

4 Short Proofs of Extended Pigeon Hole Formulae

In this section, we show that an extended version of the pigeon hole formulae [5] can be refuted by a short refutation if the new reductions are applied in combination with resolution. For plain resolution or for resolution extended by the traditional forms of reductions, the length of any refutation is super-polynomial in the length of the input formula. We start with the definition of the pigeon hole formulae.

Definition 10. Let $P_{i,j}^n$ $(i, j > 1)$ be a propositional variable with the intuitive meaning that i gets mapped to j. The following propositional formula PHF_n $(n > 1)$ is the pigeon hole formula for n pigeons and $n - 1$ holes.

$$\text{PHF}_n = \bigwedge_{i=1}^{n} \bigvee_{j=1}^{n-1} P_{i,j}^n \wedge \bigwedge_{1 \leq i < j \leq n, 1 \leq k \leq n-1} \neg P_{i,k}^n \vee \neg P_{j,k}^n$$

A one-to-one map from $\{1, \ldots, n\}$ to $\{1, \ldots, n-1\}$ is asserted by PHF_n. Clearly, PHF_n is inconsistent what can be shown by an automated theorem prover. Although there are intuitive (informal) proofs which are quite short, this class of formulae is intractable for nearly all calculi used in the field of automated deduction. Let

$$m_n = \min\{|\Gamma| \mid \Gamma \text{ is a resolution refutation of } \mathsf{PHF}_n\}.$$

Haken [10] proved a super-polynomial (w.r.t. n) lower bound for the length of any resolution refutation of PHF_n, i.e., m_n cannot be bounded by a polynomial function. Cook [5] showed that there are short refutations of PHF_n if extended resolution is applied. In [11, 12, 2, 9] short proofs of PHF_n are presented using renamings of propositional variables.

The problems of the unrestricted extension rule is a potentially infinite branching degree of the search space because we have to enumerate all possible formulae. In contrast, the possibility of the renaming of propositional variables does not yield infinite branching degrees but the computation of such renamings are variants of the graph isomorphism or subgraph isomorphism problems known to be in $\mathcal{NP}$.

We define a sequence of formulae with ePHF_n being its nth element.

Definition 11. Let n be a positive, odd integer, $n > 2$, $1 \leq i \leq n-1$, $1 \leq j \leq n-2$, $l = 3, 5, \ldots, n-2, n$, and let $\mathcal{A}_n$ be a clause set consisting of the clauses

$$A^l_{i,j,1} = P^{l-1}_{i,j} \vee \neg P^l_{i,j}$$
$$A^l_{i,j,2} = P^{l-1}_{i,j} \vee \neg P^l_{i,n-1} \vee \neg P^l_{n,j}$$
$$A^{l-1}_{i,j,3} = \neg P^{l-2}_{i,j} \vee P^{l-1}_{i,j} \vee P^{l-1}_{i,n-1}$$
$$A^{l-1}_{i,j,4} = \neg P^{l-2}_{i,j} \vee P^{l-1}_{i,j} \vee P^{l-1}_{n,j}$$

Then, ePHF_n is defined as follows, where PHF_n is the pigeon hole formula from Definition 10.

$$\mathsf{ePHF}_n = \mathsf{PHF}_n \wedge \bigwedge_{\substack{1 \leq i \leq n-1 \\ 1 \leq j \leq n-2 \\ l=3,5,\ldots,n-2,n}} (A^l_{i,j,1} \wedge A^l_{i,j,2} \wedge A^{l-1}_{i,j,3} \wedge A^{l-1}_{i,j,4})$$
$$= \mathsf{PHF}_n \wedge E_n$$

Theorem 12. *Let Γ be any resolution refutation of $\mathsf{TCF_S}(\mathsf{ePHF}_n)$. Then $|\Gamma| \geq m_n$.*

Proof. In any clause $A^l_{i,j,k} \in \mathcal{A}_n$, there is a pure literal $P^{l-1}_{i,j}$. A clause with a pure literal cannot occur in a shortest resolution refutation because there is no resolution partner for it. Therefore, clauses with pure literals can be removed from a clause set without increasing the length of a shortest resolution refutation. $\mathsf{TCF_S}(\mathsf{ePHF}_n)$ degenerates to PHF_n for which there are only resolution refutations with length super-polynomial in n. ∎

Cook's proof of PHF_n in extended resolution is adapted for our purpose. Let $n > 2$, $1 \leq i \leq n-1$, $1 \leq j \leq n-2$, and $1 < l \leq n$. Each of the following clauses can be generated by extension steps and short resolution deductions consisting of 9 clauses.

$$A_{i,j,1}^l = P_{i,j}^{l-1} \vee \neg P_{i,j}^l$$
$$A_{i,j,2}^l = P_{i,j}^{l-1} \vee \neg P_{i,n-1}^l \vee \neg P_{n,j}^l$$
$$A_{i,j,3}^l = \neg P_{i,j}^{l-1} \vee P_{i,j}^l \vee P_{i,n-1}^l$$
$$A_{i,j,4}^l = \neg P_{i,j}^{l-1} \vee P_{i,j}^l \vee P_{n,j}^l$$

These clauses can be obtained by transforming

$$(\neg P_{i,j}^{l-1}) \equiv (\neg P_{i,j}^l \wedge (\neg P_{i,n-1}^l \vee \neg P_{n,j}^l))$$

to clause form. Cook uses the resulting clauses and PHF_n to generate PHF_{n-1} by a short (cubic) resolution deduction. PHF_{n-1} uses predicate symbols $P_{i,j,k}^{n-1}$ ($k = 1, 2, 3, 4$). Iterating this construction eventually yields a short extended resolution refutation.

In the definition of ePHF_n, $A_{i,j,3}^k$ and $A_{i,j,4}^k$ are omitted for $k = 3, 5, \ldots n$ and $A_{i,j,1}^k$ and $A_{i,j,2}^k$ are omitted for $k = 2, 4, \ldots n - 1$. It will be demonstrated below that the omission of these clauses is responsible for a super-polynomial lower bound of refutation length.

In the following, we show that ePHF_n has a refutation of polynomial length if the new reduction operations are applied in combination with resolution. We neither introduce new propositional variables as in the case of extended resolution nor do we compute and apply renamings of propositional variables. Since our proof is adapted from Cook's extended resolution refutation, which is based on a short reduction of PHF_n to PHF_{n-1}, we present a reduction of PHF_4 to PHF_3 for illustration.

Example 3. Let $n = 4$. We use $P_{i,j}$ ($1 \leq i \leq 4, 1 \leq j \leq 3$) in order to denote $P_{i,j}^4$ and $Q_{i,j}$ in order to denote $P_{i,j}^3$. Let $D_i = P_{i,1} \vee P_{i,2} \vee P_{i,3}$ be the positive clauses occurring in PHF_4. Each of the following clauses can be generated by extension steps and short resolution deductions consisting of 9 clauses.

$$A_{2,2,1} = Q_{2,2} \vee \neg P_{2,2}$$
$$A_{2,2,2} = Q_{2,2} \vee \neg P_{2,3} \vee \neg P_{4,2}$$
$$A_{2,2,3} = \neg Q_{2,2} \vee P_{2,2} \vee P_{2,3}$$
$$A_{2,2,4} = \neg Q_{2,2} \vee P_{2,2} \vee P_{4,2}$$
$$A_{3,1,1} = Q_{3,1} \vee \neg P_{3,1}$$
$$A_{3,1,2} = Q_{3,1} \vee \neg P_{3,3} \vee \neg P_{4,1}$$
$$A_{3,1,3} = \neg Q_{3,1} \vee P_{3,1} \vee P_{3,3}$$
$$A_{3,1,4} = \neg Q_{3,1} \vee P_{3,1} \vee P_{4,1}$$
$$A_{3,2,1} = Q_{3,2} \vee \neg P_{3,2}$$
$$A_{3,2,2} = Q_{3,2} \vee \neg P_{3,3} \vee \neg P_{4,2}$$
$$A_{3,2,3} = \neg Q_{3,2} \vee P_{3,2} \vee P_{3,3}$$
$$A_{3,2,4} = \neg Q_{3,2} \vee P_{3,2} \vee P_{4,2}$$

In the following resolution deduction, $Q_{3,1} \vee Q_{3,2}$ is derived.

$A_{3,2,2}$, D_3, $Q_{3,2} \vee P_{3,1} \vee P_{3,2} \vee \neg P_{4,2}$, D_4, $Q_{3,2} \vee P_{3,1} \vee P_{3,2} \vee P_{4,1} \vee P_{4,3}$,
$\neg P_{3,3} \vee \neg P_{4,3}$, $Q_{3,2} \vee P_{3,1} \vee P_{3,2} \vee P_{4,1} \vee \neg P_{3,3}$,
$Q_{3,2} \vee P_{3,1} \vee P_{3,2} \vee P_{4,1} \vee P_{3,1} \vee P_{3,2}$, $Q_{3,2} \vee P_{3,1} \vee P_{3,2} \vee P_{4,1}$, $A_{3,1,2}$,
$Q_{3,1} \vee Q_{3,2} \vee P_{3,1} \vee P_{3,2} \vee \neg P_{3,3}$, $Q_{3,1} \vee Q_{3,2} \vee P_{3,1} \vee P_{3,2} \vee P_{3,1} \vee P_{3,2}$,
$Q_{3,1} \vee Q_{3,2} \vee P_{3,1} \vee P_{3,2}$, $A_{3,1,1}$, $Q_{3,1} \vee Q_{3,2} \vee Q_{3,1} \vee P_{3,2}$, $A_{3,2,1}$,
$Q_{3,1} \vee Q_{3,2} \vee Q_{3,1} \vee Q_{3,2}$, $Q_{3,1} \vee Q_{3,2}$

The other positive clauses $Q_{1,1} \vee Q_{1,2}$ and $Q_{2,1} \vee Q_{2,2}$ are derived similarly. Next, $\neg Q_{2,2} \vee \neg Q_{3,2}$ is derived.

$A_{3,2,4}$, $\neg P_{2,2} \vee \neg P_{4,2}$, $\neg Q_{3,2} \vee P_{3,2} \vee \neg P_{2,2}$, $\neg P_{2,2} \vee \neg P_{3,2}$,
$\neg Q_{3,2} \vee \neg P_{2,2} \vee \neg P_{2,2}$, $\neg Q_{3,2} \vee \neg P_{2,2}$, $A_{2,2,4}$, $\neg Q_{2,2} \vee \neg Q_{3,2} \vee P_{4,2}$,
$\neg P_{2,3} \vee \neg P_{3,3}$, $A_{3,2,3}$, $\neg Q_{3,2} \vee P_{3,2} \vee \neg P_{2,3}$, $A_{2,2,3}$,
$\neg Q_{3,2} \vee P_{3,2} \vee \neg Q_{2,2} \vee P_{2,2}$, $\neg Q_{3,2} \vee P_{3,2} \vee \neg Q_{2,2} \vee \neg Q_{3,2}$,
$\neg Q_{3,2} \vee P_{3,2} \vee \neg Q_{2,2} \vee P_{2,2}$, $\neg P_{3,2} \vee \neg P_{4,2}$, $\neg Q_{3,2} \vee \neg P_{4,2} \vee \neg Q_{2,2}$,
$\neg Q_{3,2} \vee \neg Q_{2,2} \vee \neg Q_{3,2} \vee \neg Q_{2,2}$, $\neg Q_{2,2} \vee \neg Q_{3,2}$

The other negative clauses are derived similarly. As a result, PHF$_3$ is obtained.

Theorem 13. *There exists a resolution refutation of* ePHF$_n$ *of length polynomial in n if* EXTPURE *is applied in combination with resolution.*

Proof. Recall the definition of ePHF$_n$ where $n > 2$ is an odd integer. We use the clauses from A_n and PHF$_n$ to generate PHF$_{n-2}$ by a short (cubic) resolution deduction. The resolution derivation is similar to Cook's derivations of PHF$_{n-1}$ from PHF$_n$ and PHF$_{n-2}$ from PHF$_{n-1}$. Iterating this construction eventually yields a short extended resolution refutation of ePHF$_n$.

Apply EXTPURE $(n-1) \cdot (n-2)$ times and obtain the clauses $A_{i,j,3}^n$ and $A_{i,j,4}^n$. Another $(n-1) \cdot (n-2)$ applications of EXTPURE yield the clauses $A_{i,j,1}^{n-1}$ and $A_{i,j,2}^{n-1}$. As a result, all clauses are obtained by EXTPURE which occur in Cook's extended resolution derivation of PHF$_{n-2}$ from PHF$_n$. Hence, resolution in combination with EXTPURE can simulate the extended resolution refutation of ePHF$_n$ with only a quadratic increase of refutation length. Therefore, there is a short refutation of ePHF$_n$ if resolution is applied in combination with EXTPURE.

∎

Theorem 12 and Theorem 13 yield the following

Theorem 14. *For an infinite sequence* (ePHF$_n$)$_{n \in \mathbb{N}}$ *of clause sets, any resolution refutation of* ePHF$_n$ *has length exponential in n, but there exists a short resolution refutation of* ePHF$_n$ *of length polynomial in n if* EXTPURE *is applied in combination with resolution.*

5 Conclusion

We introduced new mechanisms for the generation of clauses from redundant information in a restricted way. A special case of this new technique is the splitting rule of Davis and Putnam. If more than one clause set is obtained by the decomposition, then these clause sets can be worked with in parallel without any communication. We demonstrated that the application of our new reductions enables super-polynomially shorter proofs for a class of formulae which are hard for resolution. We restricted our attention to propositional logic. In the following, we briefly discuss the extension of these reductions to first order clause logic.

A clause C represents a formula $\forall x_1 \ldots \forall x_m C$, where $x_1, \ldots, x_m$ are the variables of C. The existential quantifiers are removed by Skolemization during the transformation of a formula into its clause form, and, therefore, disappear in the clause. For example, let $\mathcal{D} = \{Q(x, g(x)) \vee P\} \cup \mathcal{C}$, whereby P is a pure literal and g is a Skolem function symbol. If $(\forall x Q(x, g(x))) \rightarrow \forall x Q(x, g(x))$ is introduced, then the resulting clause sets are $\{\neg Q(m, g(m))\} \cup \mathcal{C}$ and $\{Q(x, g(x))\} \cup \mathcal{C}$, where m is a new Skolem constant symbol not occurring elsewhere in $\mathcal{C}$.

Alternatively, a formula of the form $(\forall x \exists y Q(x, y)) \rightarrow \forall x \exists y Q(x, y)$ can be introduced yielding two clause sets $\{\neg Q(m, y)\} \cup \mathcal{C}$ and $\{Q(x, h(x))\} \cup \mathcal{C}$, whereby m, h are new function symbols. In this case, a new Skolem term is introduced at the second argument position of the positive Q literal. From a proof-theoretic point of view, the latter formula seems to have advantages because implication of formulae with alternative quantifiers may enable short refutations. A detailed analysis is subject to further research.

Acknowledgment: The author would like to thank Wolfgang Bibel, Stefan Brüning, Stephan Schmitt, and the three referees for their constructive criticism and for their useful comments on an earlier draft of this paper.

References

1. W. Bibel. *Automated Theorem Proving*. Vieweg, Braunschweig, second edition, 1987.
2. W. Bibel. Short Proofs of the Pigeonhole Formulas Based on the Connection Method. *Journal of Automated Reasoning*, 6:287–297, 1990.
3. R. Boyer. *Locking: A Restriction of Resolution*. PhD thesis, The University of Texas at Austin, 1971.
4. C. L. Chang and R. C. Lee. *Symbolic Logic and Mechanical Theorem Proving*. Academic Press, New York, 1973.
5. S. A. Cook. A Short Proof of the Pigeon Hole Principle Using Extended Resolution. *SIGACT News*, 1976.
6. M. Davis. Elimating the Irrelevant from Mechanical Proofs. *Proc. Symp. Appl. Math.*, 15:15–30, 1963.
7. M. Davis and H. Putnam. A Computing Procedure for Quantification Theory. *Journal of the ACM*, 7(3):201–215, 1960.

8. E. Eder. An Implementation of a Theorem Prover Based on the Connection Method. In W. Bibel and B. Petkoff, editors, *AIMSA 84, Artificial Intelligence - Methodology, Systems, Applications, Varna, Bulgaria*, Amsterdam, September 1984. North-Holland.

9. U. Egly. A Simple Proof for the Pigeonhole Formulae. In B. Neumann, editor, *Proceedings of the European Conference on Artificial Intelligence*, pages 70–71. John Wiley & Sons, 1992.

10. A. Haken. The Intractability of Resolution. *Journal of Theoretical Computer Science*, 39:297–308, 1985.

11. B. Krishnamurthy. Short Proofs for Tricky Formulas. *Acta Informatica*, 22(3):253–275, Aug. 1985.

12. N. V. Murray and E. Rosenthal. Short Proofs of the Pigeonhole Formulas Using Path Dissolution. Technical report, Dept. of Computer Science, State Univ. of N.Y. at Albany, Albany N.Y. 12222, 1988.

13. D. A. Plaisted and S. Greenbaum. A Structure-Preserving Clause Form Translation. *Journal of Symbolic Computation*, 2:293–304, 1986.

14. J.A. Robinson. A Machine-Oriented Logic Based on the Resolution Principle. *Journal of the ACM*, 12(1):23–41, Jan. 1965.

15. G. S. Tseitin. On the Complexity of Derivation in Propositional Calculus. In A. O. Slisenko, editor, *Studies in Constructive Mathematics and Mathematical Logic, Part II*, pages 234–259. Seminars in Mathematics, V.A. Steklov Mathematical Institute, vol. 8, Leningrad, 1968. English translation: Consultants Bureau, New York, 1970, pp. 115–125.

Belief Revision in Non-Monotonic Reasoning

José Alferes[*]
DM, U. Évora and CRIA Uninova
2825 Monte da Caparica, Portugal
(jja@fct.unl.pt)

Luís Moniz Pereira[*]
DCS, U.Nova de Lisboa and CRIA Uninova
2825 Monte da Caparica, Portugal
(lmp@fct.unl.pt)

Teodor C. Przymusinski[**]
Department of Computer Science
University of California
Riverside, CA 92521, USA
(teodor@cs.ucr.edu)

1 Introduction

Moore's autoepistemic logic, AEL [Moo85], was obtained by augmenting classical propositional logic with a modal operator $\mathcal{L}$. The intended meaning of the modal atom $\mathcal{L}F$ in the stable autoepistemic expansion T is "F is known" in T, or, more precisely, "F is logically derivable" from T. Indeed, a formula $\mathcal{L}F$ belongs to the expansion T if and only if F is derivable from T. Thus Moore's modal operator $\mathcal{L}$ can be viewed as a "knowledge operator" which allows us to reason about formulae *known* to be true in the expansion[3]. However, often times we need to reason about formulae that are only *believed* (rather than known) to be true, where what is believed or not believed is determined by some specific *non-monotonic formalism*. In particular, we may want to express beliefs based on *minimal entailment*, or, more generally, on some form of *circumscription*, and thus we may need a modal "belief operator" $\mathcal{B}$ with the intended meaning of $\mathcal{B}F$ given by "F is true in all minimal models" or "F is minimally entailed" (in the expansion).

In order to be able to explicitly reason about beliefs, in [Prz94b, Prz94a] the third author introduced a new non-monotonic formalism, called the *Autoepistemic Logic of Beliefs*, AEB, obtained by augmenting classical propositional logic with a *belief operator*, $\mathcal{B}$. The resulting non-monotonic knowledge representation framework turned out to be rather simple and yet quite powerful. It was proved that propositional circumscription and several major semantics for

---

[*] Partially supported by JNICT-Portugal and ESPRIT project Compulog 2 (no. 6810).
[**] Partially supported by the National Science Foundation grant #IRI-9313061.
[3] This view of Moore's modal operator $\mathcal{L}$ as a knowledge operator is not shared by all researchers. Moore himself considered $\mathcal{L}$ to be a belief operator.

logic programs are *isomorphically embeddable* into AEB. In particular, this is true for the stable, well-founded, stationary and static semantics for normal, disjunctive and extended logic programs [GL88, VGRS90, Prz91b, GL90, Prz94c].

At the same time the Autoepistemic Logic of Beliefs, AEB, has some very natural properties which sharply contrast with those of Moore's AEL. In particular, *every* belief theory T in AEB has the *least* (in the sense of inclusion) static expansion T° which has an *iterative* definition as the *least fixed point* of a monotonic belief closure operator. Moreover, least static expansions are always consistent in the broad class of *affirmative* belief theories defined below.

While static expansions seem to provide a natural and intuitive semantics for many belief theories, and, in particular, for all normal and disjunctive logic programs, they often lead to inconsistent static expansions for theories in which (subjective) beliefs clash with the known (objective) information or with some other beliefs. In particular, this applies to extended logic programs with strong or explicit negation.

Consider the following sentence of AEB:

$$\mathcal{B}\neg FlatTire \wedge \mathcal{B}\neg BadBattery \supset \neg Broken$$

which is intended to say that in the absence of any indication that something is wrong with the tires or with the battery we can conclude that the car is not broken[4]. Assuming this is all we know about the car, we are likely to conclude that it is not broken because we have no indication that would make us believe that there is any problem with either battery or tires. In other words, both *FlatTire* and *BadBattery* are false in all minimal models of our knowledge base and thus both $\mathcal{B}\neg FlatTire$ and $\mathcal{B}\neg BadBattery$ hold true.

Suppose, however, that upon inspection we learn that our car is in fact broken, i.e., suppose that we add *Broken* to our knowledge base. Somewhat surprisingly, the resulting theory turns out to be inconsistent because we still have no indication of any problem with either battery or tires and thus $\mathcal{B}\neg FlatTire$ and $\mathcal{B}\neg BadBattery$ continue to hold true.

A common-sense approach suggests that in order to avoid such inconsistencies we should refrain from adopting beliefs that contradict the existing factual information or are mutually contradictory. In this particular case, we could conclude that at least one of our initial beliefs (assumptions) that the car does not have a flat tire and does not have a bad battery must have been incorrect and thus has to be *revised* and *rejected*.

Accordingly, in this paper we first introduce the notion of a *careful static expansion*, a simple and yet powerful extension of the notion of a static expansion of belief theories, which enables us to incorporate *belief revision* into the framework of AEB. When applied to the above theory our approach results in two consistent careful static expansions. In one of them we believe that the battery is fine but possibly the tires are not, and, in the other we believe that the tires are fine but possibly the battery is dead. When taken together,

---

[4] In other words, if we hypothetically assume $\neg FlatTire$ and $\neg BadBattery$ the conclusion follows.

the two expansions imply that most likely either the tires or the battery, but not both, are to blame for the car's trouble. They represent therefore an intuitively appealing approach of rejecting those beliefs that contradict factual information, while keeping all the remaining ones intact. We prove that every consistent belief theory has a consistent careful static expansion. This result demonstrates that we can always assign a reasonable set of revised beliefs to any belief theory and underscores the important role played by belief revision in commonsense reasoning. We also show that every consistent static expansion of a belief theory T is also a careful static expansion of T and therefore the class of careful static expansions extends the class of consistent static expansions. Moreover, for a broad class of affirmative belief theories, defined below, careful static expansions coincide with static expansions.

Belief revision based on the notion of a careful static expansion can be applied to various reasoning domains. In this paper we illustrate its natural application to the domain of *diagnosis*. Here the fact that all consistent theories have consistent careful expansions plays a crucial role because it is imperative that we should be able to derive a reasonable set of conclusions (diagnoses) from any given knowledge base T even though the observable facts may appear to contradict beliefs resulting from default assumptions contained in T.

Careful static expansions represent a form of belief revision in which the rational epistemic agent abstains from believing formulae which, when believed, would lead to a contradiction. However, simply refraining from believing in certain formulae does not fully take into account all the consequences of the withholding such beliefs. For example, faced with the fact that the car does not run we may decide to revise our belief that the car is not broken (cf. Example 7). However, that should also compel us to refrain from believing that the car does not need to be fixed, i.e. that the car is broken should be admitted as a possibility as well. We propose a natural solution to this problem using the previously introduced notion of careful static expansion. The proposed approach is based on the appropriate *revision* of the *original theory* itself instead of just the revision of our beliefs about it. Specifically, we change the theory by adding to it new information that justifies withholding of contradictory beliefs. In other words, we compile into the theory the knowledge that prevents the same belief inconsistencies from occurring again, by allowing that the car may be broken.

Finally, we observe that in some application domains beliefs can logically depend on other beliefs, which may be viewed as more basic and sometimes considered to be non-revisable. For example, this is true when diagnosing faults in a device: causally deeper component faults are sometimes preferred over surface faults, that are simply consequences of the former. In such cases, one would like to control the level at which diagnosis is performed, by eliminating diagnoses which do not focus on the causally deeper faults. More generally, any revision of beliefs should comply with the logical dependency of beliefs. We illustrate how one can express such dependencies in AEL by means of the so called *Belief Completion Clauses*. These clauses essentially state that a revision of some beliefs requires a revision of beliefs on which they logically depend.

Because of its generality, this method of specifying the logical level of revision in belief theories can be employed to explain and justify, via the embedding of logic programs into AEB, the meta-linguistic devices used for controlling abduction, view updates and contradiction removal in logic programs. However, the lack of space precludes us from presenting these results in here. They will be presented, together with other results relating our work to other approaches to belief revision, in the forthcoming paper [APP95]. In particular, we show in there that the contradiction removal semantics for non-disjunctive extended logic programs, introduced in [PAA91, PA94], can be isomorphically embedded into the more general framework of the Autoepistemic Logic of Beliefs.

2 Autoepistemic Logic of Beliefs

We first briefly recall the definition and basic properties of the *Autoepistemic Logic of Beliefs*, AEB. The language of AEB, is a propositional modal language, $\mathcal{K}_{\mathcal{B}}$, with standard connectives ($\vee, \wedge, \supset, \neg$), the propositional letter $\perp$ (denoting *false*) and a modal operator $\mathcal{B}$, called the *belief* operator. The atomic formulae of the form $\mathcal{B}F$, where F is an arbitrary formula of $\mathcal{K}_{\mathcal{B}}$, are called *belief atoms*. The formulae of $\mathcal{K}_{\mathcal{B}}$ in which $\mathcal{B}$ does not occur are called *objective* and the set of all such formulae is denoted by $\mathcal{K}$. Any theory T in the language $\mathcal{K}_{\mathcal{B}}$ is called an *autoepistemic theory of beliefs*, or, briefly, a *belief theory*.

Definition 1 (Belief Theory). By an *autoepistemic theory of beliefs*, or just a *belief theory*, we mean an arbitrary theory in the language $\mathcal{K}_{\mathcal{B}}$, i.e., a (possibly infinite) set of arbitrary clauses of the form:

$$B_1 \wedge ... \wedge B_k \wedge \mathcal{B}G_1 \wedge ... \wedge \mathcal{B}G_l \wedge \neg \mathcal{B}F_1 \wedge ... \wedge \neg \mathcal{B}F_n \supset A_1 \vee ... \vee A_m$$

where $k, l, m, n \geq 0$, A_is and B_is are objective atoms and F_is and G_is are arbitrary formulae of $\mathcal{K}_{\mathcal{B}}$. Such a clause says that if the B_is are true, the G_is are believed, and the F_is are not believed then one of the A_is is true.

By an *affirmative belief theory* we mean any belief theory all of whose clauses satisfy the condition that $m > 0$. □

Observe that arbitrarily deep level of *nested beliefs* is allowed in belief theories. We assume the following two simple axiom schemata and one inference rule describing the arguably obvious properties of belief atoms:

(D) Consistency Axiom:

$$\neg \mathcal{B} \perp \tag{1}$$

(K) Normality Axiom: For any formulae F and G:

$$\mathcal{B}(F \supset G) \supset (\mathcal{B}F \supset \mathcal{B}G) \tag{2}$$

(N) Necessitation Rule: For any formula F:

$$\frac{F}{\mathcal{B}F} \tag{3}$$

The first axiom states that tautologically false formulae are *not* believed. The second axiom states that if we believe that a formula F implies a formula G and if we believe that F is true then we believe that G is true as well. The necessitation inference rule states that if a formula F has been proven to be true then F is believed to be true.

Definition 2 (Formulae Derivable from a Belief Theory). For any belief theory T, we denote by $Cn_*(T)$ the smallest set of formulae of the language $\mathcal{K}_\mathcal{B}$ which contains the theory T, all the (substitution instances of) the axioms (K) and (D) and is closed under standard propositional consequence and under the necessitation rule (N).

We say that a formula F is *derivable* from theory T in the logic AEB if F belongs to $Cn_*(T)$. We denote this fact by $T \vdash_* F$. We call a belief theory T *consistent* if the theory $Cn_*(T)$ is consistent. Consequently, $Cn_*(T) = \{F : T \vdash_* F\}$. Moreover, T is consistent if and only if $T \not\vdash_* \bot$. □

Remark. It is easy to see that, in the presence of the axiom (K), the axiom (D) is equivalent to the axiom:

$$\mathcal{B}F \supset \neg\mathcal{B}\neg F. \tag{4}$$

stating that if we believe in a formula F then we do *not* believe in $\neg F$.

For readers familiar with modal logics it should be clear by now that we are, in effect, considering here a *normal* modal logic with one modality $\mathcal{B}$ which satisfies the consistency axiom (D) [MT94]. The axiom (K) is called "normal" because all normal modal logics satisfy it [MT94]. □

2.1 Intended Meaning of Belief Atoms

In general, belief atoms $\mathcal{B}F$ can be given different intended meanings. In this paper, the intended meaning of belief atoms $\mathcal{B}F$ is based on Minker's *GCWA* (see [Min82, GPP89]) or McCarthy's *Predicate Circumscription* [McC80], and is described by the principle of *predicate minimization*:

$\mathcal{B}F \equiv F$ is minimally entailed $\equiv F$ is true in all minimal models.

Accordingly, beliefs considered in this paper can be called *minimal beliefs*.

We now give a precise definition of minimal models and minimal entailment. Throughout the paper we represent *models* as (consistent) *sets of literals*. An atom A is *true* in a model M if and only if A belongs to M. An atom A is *false* in a model M if and only if $\neg A$ belongs to M. A model M is *total* if for every atom A either A or $\neg A$ belongs to M. Otherwise, the model is called *partial*. Unless stated otherwise all models are assumed to be total. A (total) model M is *smaller* than a (total) model N if it contains fewer positive literals (atoms). For convenience, when describing models we usually list *only* those of their members that are *relevant* to our considerations, typically those whose predicate symbols appear in the theory that we are currently discussing.

Definition 3 (Minimal Models). [Prz94b, Prz94a] By a *minimal model* of a belief theory T we mean a model M of T with the property that there is *no* smaller model N of T which coincides with M on belief atoms $\mathcal{BF}$. If a formula F is true in all minimal models of T then we write: $T \models_{\min} F$ and say that F is *minimally entailed* by T. □

For readers familiar with *circumscription*, this means that we are considering predicate circumscription $CIRC(T;\mathcal{K})$ of the theory T in which atoms from the objective language $\mathcal{K}$ are minimized while the belief atoms $\mathcal{BF}$ are fixed:

$$T \models_{\min} F \equiv CIRC(T;\mathcal{K}) \models F.$$

In other words, minimal models are obtained by first assigning *arbitrary* truth values to the belief atoms and then *minimizing* objective atoms.

2.2 Static Autoepistemic Expansions

Like in Moore's Autoepistemic Logic, also in the Autoepistemic Logic of Beliefs we introduce sets of beliefs that an ideally rational and introspective agent may hold, given a set of premises T. We do so by defining *static autoepistemic expansions* T° of T, which constitute plausible sets of such rational beliefs.

Definition 4 (Static Autoepistemic Expansion). [Prz94b, Prz94a] A belief theory T° is called a *static autoepistemic expansion* of a belief theory T if it satisfies the following fixed-point equation:

$$T^\circ = Cn_*(T \cup \{\mathcal{BF} : T^\circ \models_{\min} F\}),$$

where F ranges over all formulae of $\mathcal{K_B}$. □

The definition of static autoepistemic expansions is based on the idea of building an expansion T° of a belief theory T by closing it with respect to: (i) the derivability in the logic AEB, and, (ii) the addition of belief atoms $\mathcal{BF}$ satisfying the condition that the formula F is minimally entailed by T°. Consequently, the definition of static expansions *enforces* the intended meaning of belief atoms described above. Note that negations $\neg\mathcal{BF}$ of the remaining belief atoms are not *explicitly* added to the expansion although some of them will be forced in by the Normality and Consistency Axioms (2) and (1).

It turns out that every belief theory T in AEB has the *least* (in the sense of set-theoretic inclusion) static expansion T° which has an *iterative* definition as the *least fixed point* of the monotonic belief closure operator Ψ_T:

$$\Psi_T(S) = Cn_*(T \cup \{\mathcal{BF} : S \models_{\min} F\}),$$

where S is an arbitrary belief theory and the Fs range over all formulae of $\mathcal{K_B}$.

Theorem 5 (Least Static Expansion). *[Prz94b, Prz94a] Every belief theory T in AEB has the least static expansion, namely, the least fixed point T° of the monotonic belief closure operator Ψ_T.*

Moreover, the least static expansion T° of a belief theory T can be constructed as follows. Let $T^0 = Cn_*(T)$ and suppose that T^α has already been defined for any ordinal number $\alpha < \beta$. If $\beta = \alpha + 1$ is a successor ordinal then define:

$$T^{\alpha+1} = \Psi_T(T^\alpha) = Cn_*(\, T \cup \{\mathcal{B}F : T^\alpha \models_{\min} F\}\,),$$

where F ranges over all formulae in $\mathcal{K}_\mathcal{B}$. Else, if β is a limit ordinal then define $T^\beta = \bigcup_{\alpha < \beta} T^\alpha$.

The sequence $\{T^\alpha\}$ is monotonically increasing and has a unique fixed point $T^\circ = T^\lambda = \Psi_T(T^\lambda)$, for some ordinal λ. For finite theories T the fixed point T° is reached after finitely many steps. $\square$

Observe that the *least* static autoepistemic expansion T° of T contains therefore those and only those formulae which are true in *all* static autoepistemic expansions of T. It defines the so called *static semantics* of a belief theory T. It is easy to verify that a belief theory T either has a *consistent* least static expansion T° or it does *not* have any consistent static expansions at all. Moreover, least static expansions of *affirmative* belief theories are always consistent [Prz94b, Prz94a].

Example 1. Consider the following belief theory T:

$$Car$$
$$Car \wedge \mathcal{B}\neg Broken \supset Runs$$

For simplicity, when describing static expansions of this and other examples we list only those elements of the expansion that are "relevant" to our discussion. In particular, we usually omit nested beliefs. In order to iteratively compute the least static expansion T° of T we first let $T^0 = Cn_*(T)$. Let us observe that $T^0 \models Car$ and $T^0 \models_{\min} \neg Broken$. Indeed, in order to find minimal models of T^0 we need to assign an *arbitrary* truth value to the only belief atom $\mathcal{B}\neg Broken$, and then *minimize* the objective atoms $Broken$, Car and $Runs$. We easily see that T^0 has the following two minimal models (truth values of the remaining belief atoms are irrelevant and are therefore omitted):

$$M_1 = \{\mathcal{B}\neg Broken, Car, \ Runs, \ \neg Broken\};$$
$$M_2 = \{\neg\mathcal{B}\neg Broken, Car, \ \neg Runs, \ \neg Broken\}.$$

Since in both of them Car is true, and $Broken$ is false, we deduce that $T^0 \models_{\min} Car$ and $T^0 \models_{\min} \neg Broken$. Consequently, since $T^1 = \Psi_T(T^0) = Cn_*(T \cup \{\mathcal{B}F : T^0 \models_{\min} F\})$, we obtain:

$$T^1 = Cn_*(T \cup \{\mathcal{B}Car, \mathcal{B}\neg Broken\}).$$

Since $T^1 \models Runs$ and $T^2 = \Psi_T(T^1) = Cn_*(T \cup \{\mathcal{B}F : T^1 \models_{\min} F\})$, we obtain:

$$T^2 = Cn_*(T \cup \{\mathcal{B}Car, \mathcal{B}\neg Broken, \mathcal{B}Runs\}).$$

It is easy to check that $T^2 = \Psi_T(T^2)$ is a fixed point of Ψ_T and therefore $T^\diamond = T^2 = Cn_*(T \cup \{\mathcal{B}Car, \mathcal{B}\neg Broken, \mathcal{B}Runs\})$ is the least static expansion of T. The static semantics of T asserts our belief that the car is not broken and thus runs fine. One easily verifies that T does not have any other (consistent) static expansions. □

3 Belief Revision

While static expansions seem to provide a natural and intuitive semantics for many (consistent) belief theories (in particular, for all affirmative belief theories) they often lead to inconsistent expansions for theories in which (subjective) beliefs clash with the observable (objective) facts or with some other beliefs.

Example 2. Consider again the simple belief theory introduced in Example 1. As we have seen, its static semantics implies that we believe that the car is not broken and thus runs fine. Suppose, however, that upon inspection we found out that the car actually *does not* run:

$$\neg Runs.$$

It is clear that the resulting new belief theory does not have any consistent static expansions. Indeed, since there is no evidence that the car is broken, $Broken$ is false in all minimal models and thus $\mathcal{B}\neg Broken$ is derivable. This implies $Runs$ and thus results in a contradiction. In other words, our belief that the car is not broken and thus runs, based on the fact that there is no evidence to the contrary, apparently contradicts the objective fact that the car does not run.

In view of the contradictory factual information that the car does not run, we could very well conclude that our initial belief (assumption) that the car is not broken must have been incorrect and thus has to be *revised* and *rejected*. □

Example 3. Consider now the belief theory discussed in the introduction:

$$\mathcal{B}\neg FlatTire \wedge \mathcal{B}\neg BadBattery \supset \neg Broken$$
$$Broken,$$

which says that, in the absence of any indication that something is wrong with the tires or with the battery, we can safely conclude that the car is not broken, and yet the fact is that it is broken. This theory, again, does not have any consistent static expansions because both $\neg FlatTire$ and $\neg BadBattery$ are minimally entailed and thus the premise $\mathcal{B}\neg FlatTire \wedge \mathcal{B}\neg BadBattery$ is derivable. This implies $\neg Broken$ and results in a contradiction.

Again too, a natural way to remedy this problem is to conclude that, in view of the contradictory objective information that the car is broken, at least one of our initial beliefs (assumptions) that the car does not have a flat tire and does not have a bad battery must have been incorrect and thus has to be *revised* and *rejected*. □

3.1 Careful Static Autoepistemic Expansions

The approach illustrated in the previous two examples is based on the idea of *rejecting* or *revising* beliefs that contradict the existing factual information or are mutually contradictory. It leads to a simple modification of the definition of static expansions which results in a natural and potent framework for belief revision in *AEL*.

Definition 6 (Careful Static Autoepistemic Expansion). A belief theory T° is called a *careful static autoepistemic expansion* of a belief theory T if it satisfies the following fixed-point equation:

$$T^\circ = Cn_*(T \cup \{\mathcal{B}F : T^\circ \models_{\min} F \text{ and } T^\circ \cup \{\mathcal{B}F\} \text{ is consistent}\}),$$

where F ranges over all formulae of $\mathcal{K_B}$. □

The only difference between the definition of static expansions and careful static expansions is the requirement that only those belief atoms $\mathcal{B}F$ should be added to the expansion whose addition does not lead to a contradiction. Recall that, by definition, $T^\circ \cup \{\mathcal{B}F\}$ is consistent if and only if $Cn_*(T^\circ \cup \{\mathcal{B}F\})$ is consistent.

Example 4. It is easy to see that the theory considered in Example 2 has precisely one careful static expansion, namely $T^\circ = Cn_*(T \cup \{\mathcal{B}Car, \mathcal{B}\neg Runs\})$, which does not include any beliefs about the car being broken and corresponds therefore to the intuitive approach of rejecting beliefs that contradict existing factual information. □

Example 5. On the other hand, the theory considered in Example 3 has precisely two careful static expansions namely:

$$T_1^\circ = Cn_*(T \cup \{\mathcal{B}Broken, \mathcal{B}\neg FlatTire\}),$$
$$T_2^\circ = Cn_*(T \cup \{\mathcal{B}Broken, \mathcal{B}\neg BadBattery\}),$$

which reflect the fact that one of the assumptions about not having a bad battery or not having a flat tire has to be rejected while the other can be kept without causing any inconsistency. The resulting careful static semantics implies therefore $\mathcal{B}\neg FlatTire \lor \mathcal{B}\neg BadBattery$ and thus suggests that most likely the car does not have both a bad battery and a flat tire. It represents the intuitively appealing approach of rejecting only those beliefs that contradict factual information, while keeping all the remaining ones intact. □

As the previous examples demonstrate, careful static expansions no longer lead to inconsistencies when we add to our knowledge facts that seem to contradict our (default) beliefs. More generally, it turns out that every consistent belief theory has a consistent careful static expansion.

Theorem 7 (Fundamental Theorem of Belief Revision).
Every consistent belief theory has a consistent careful static expansion. □

This result demonstrates that we can always assign a reasonable set of revised beliefs to any belief theory and thus underscores the important role played by *belief revision* in commonsense reasoning. It is also of crucial importance in applications of belief revision, such as the application to *diagnosis* illustrated below, where it is imperative that we should be able to derive a reasonable set of conclusions (diagnoses) from any given knowledge base T even though the observable facts may appear to contradict beliefs resulting from default assumptions contained in T.

The class of careful static expansions extends the class of consistent static expansions.

Theorem 8. *Every consistent static expansion of a belief theory T is also a careful static expansion of T. Moreover, for affirmative belief theories, the notions of a consistent static expansion and a careful static expansion coincide.* □

3.2 Application to Diagnosis

Belief revision based on the notion of a careful static expansion can be applied to various reasoning domains. Below we illustrate its application to the domain of diagnosis.

For any careful static expansion T° of a belief theory T the set $\mathcal{R}(T^\circ) = \{F : T^\circ \models_{min} F$ and yet $\mathcal{B}F \notin T^\circ\}$, namely, the set of those formulae F which should be believed in (because F is minimally entailed) in the expansion T°, and yet are not believed in T° (because of the resulting inconsistency), plays an important diagnostic role by constituting the set of *possibly false assumptions*.

Definition 9 (Revision Set of a Careful Expansion). The revision set $\mathcal{R}(T^\circ)$ of the careful static autoepistemic expansion T° of a belief theory T is defined by:

$$\mathcal{R}(T^\circ) = \{F : T^\circ \models_{min} F \text{ and } \mathcal{B}F \notin T^\circ\}. \quad \square$$

Clearly, a careful static expansion is a (regular) static expansion if and only if its revision set is empty.

Example 6. Consider the careful static expansions of the theory discussed in Example 3:

$$T_1^\circ = Cn_*(T \cup \{\mathcal{B}Broken, \mathcal{B}\neg FlatTire\})$$
$$T_2^\circ = Cn_*(T \cup \{\mathcal{B}Broken, \mathcal{B}\neg BadBattery\})$$

Their revision sets are:

$$\mathcal{R}(T_1^\circ) = \{\neg BadBattery\}$$
$$\mathcal{R}(T_2^\circ) = \{\neg FlatTire\}$$

i.e. in T_1° we refrain from believing $\neg BadBattery$, while in T_2° we refrain from believing $\neg FlatTire$. As a result, the first revision set suggests that our assumption that the car does not have a bad battery may have been wrong and the second revision set suggests that our assumption that the car does not have a flat tire may have been incorrect. Both of them together provide us with a useful diagnosis of possible reasons why the car does not work. □

4 Belief Revision by Theory Change

In this section we study the issue of belief revision by theory revision, as opposed to belief revision by rejection of contradictory beliefs which was discussed in the previous section.

As remarked earlier, careful static expansions represent a form of belief revision where the rational epistemic agent abstains from believing formulae which, if believed, would lead to contradiction. However, simply refraining from believing in certain formulae is often not enough, as it does not fully take into account all the consequences of withholding such beliefs. In order to produce such consequences we must *revise* the theory by adding to it some statements that justify not holding the contradictory beliefs. In other words, we must compile into the theory *additional* knowledge that will prevent the detected belief inconsistency from occurring. This knowledge is gathered by analyzing the causes of inconsistencies.

Example 7. Suppose that to the theory of Example 2 we add:

$$Car \wedge Broken \supset FixIt$$

It is easy to check that the resulting theory T has a single careful expansion:

$$T^\circ = Cn_*\left(T \cup \{\mathcal{B}Car, \mathcal{B}\neg Runs, \mathcal{B}\neg FixIt\}\right)$$

Even though $\neg Broken$ is true in all minimal models of the expansion, $\mathcal{B}\neg Broken$ is not added since it leads to inconsistency. Since $Broken$ is no longer believed to be false, one would intuitively expect $\neg FixIt$ not to be believed either. However, this is not the case in the careful static expansion above. Indeed, the expansion reflects only the fact that the agent must refrain from believing formulae that lead to contradiction. It does not invalidate the reasons that have led to such beliefs. In our example, we believed in the car not being broken because of the lack of evidence showing otherwise. This lack of evidence must therefore be invalidated by admitting the possibility that the car might in fact be broken.

This is the stance taken by most belief revision systems, where the outcome of revision is a modified theory, in which contradiction is avoided by eliminating the reasons for contradictory beliefs. It is clear that the only way of inhibiting $\neg Broken$ from being believed in static expansions is by introducing some evidence for $Broken$ to be true. This evidence could, for example, be stated in the form that $Broken$ is in fact true. However, this appears too strong in view of the fact that we do not know for sure that the car is indeed broken: absence of belief in $\neg Broken$ does not warrant jumping to such a conclusion. An alternative is to simply state that $Broken$ is *possible*, in which case, $\neg Broken$ would no longer be minimally entailed, and we would no longer believe it. Moreover, $\neg FixIt$ would no longer be minimally entailed, and thus would no longer be believed.   □

Careful expansions already identify and inhibit the addition of beliefs that lead to contradiction. It is thus an easy matter to determine which sets of formulae do lead to contradiction: they are the revision sets $\mathcal{R}(T^\circ)$ of careful expansions T°.

4.1 Revised Static Expansions

Given a careful expansion $T^\diamond$ of a belief theory T one can revise T by adding to it the "possibility of F being false" for every F in the revision set $\mathcal{R}(T^\diamond)$. How can this be done?

Most belief revision systems take the position that if the belief in a given formula F leads to contradiction then its complement $\neg F$ should be assumed to be true. In our opinion this is, in general, unwarranted. First of all, it is not necessary to do so in order to inhibit the belief. Moreover, it is unwarranted to jump to a conclusion that some formula is true simply because belief in its falsity would lead to contradiction. That would be tantamount to adopting on our beliefs the law of the excluded middle, i.e. imposing $\mathcal{B}F \vee \mathcal{B}\neg F$.

In Example 7, we simply would like to prevent $\neg Broken$ from being believed. Given the meaning of beliefs, this can be arranged by changing the theory just enough so that "$Broken$ is no longer false in all minimal models" or, equivalently, by "guaranteeing the existence of a minimal model in which $Broken$ is true". Technically, this is achievable by adding to the theory the clause $Broken \vee Maybe\_Not(Broken)$, where $Maybe\_Not(Broken)$ is an atom not occurring elsewhere in the theory, and thus not constrained in value. This clause can be read as "$Broken$ is possible". Intuitively, this constitutes the "minimal" change of the theory ensuring that contradiction is removed. Indeed, believing $\neg Broken$ leads to contradiction and therefore $Broken$ should be possible, which effectively and declaratively prevents believing in $\neg Broken$.

For the sake of modularity, instead of adding the clauses of the form $F \vee Maybe\_Not(F)$ (where $Maybe\_Not(F)$ is an atom not occurring elsewhere in the theory), we prefer the addition of $Possible(F)$, where $Possible(F)$ is defined by[5]:

$$Possible(F) \equiv F \vee Maybe\_Not(F) \tag{5}$$

Definition 10 (Revision of a Belief Theory). A belief theory T_r is a *revision of a consistent belief theory* T if and only if

$$T_r = T \cup \{Possible(\neg F) : F \in \mathcal{R}(T^\diamond)\}$$

for some careful static expansion $T^\diamond$ of T. □

Theorem 11 (Revised Static Autoepistemic Expansion). *Let T_r be a revision of a consistent belief theory T. Then T_r is consistent and has consistent static autoepistemic expansions. We call the least static expansion of T_r, whose existence is guaranteed by Theorem 5, a revised static autoepistemic expansion of T.* □

Theorem 12 (Relation to Careful Expansions). *Let $T_r^\diamond$ be a revised static expansion of a consistent belief theory T. There exists a careful expansion $T^\diamond$ of T such that $T_r^\diamond \subseteq T^\diamond$.* □

---

[5] This will allow us later on [APP95] to use different, simpler, and more specific definitions of $Possible(F)$ in less general classes of theories (such as logic programs) in which there are other methods of ensuring that F is possible.

Example 8. The only revision of the theory T from Example 7 is given by $T_r = T \cup \{Possible(Broken)\}$. Accordingly, the only revised static expansion of T is:

$$T_r^\circ = Cn_*(T \cup \{Possible(Broken)\} \cup \{\mathcal{B}Car, \mathcal{B}\neg Runs\})$$

It is easy to see that there are minimal models of the theory in which $Broken$ is true, and therefore, since Car is true in all models, those models include $FixIt$ too. Thus, neither $\mathcal{B}\neg Broken$ nor $\mathcal{B}\neg FixIt$ are added to the expansion. □

Example 9. The revisions of theory T from Example 3 are $T_{r_1} = T \cup \{Possible(BadBattery)\}$, and $T_{r_2} = T \cup \{Possible(FlatTire)\}$. Thus, the revised static expansions are:

$$T_{r_1}^\circ = Cn_*(T \cup \{Possible(BadBattery), \mathcal{B}Broken, \mathcal{B}\neg FlatTire\})$$
$$T_{r_2}^\circ = Cn_*(T \cup \{Possible(FlatTire), \mathcal{B}Broken, \mathcal{B}\neg BadBattery\})$$

Each of them constitutes a diagnosis of a possible problem with the car. □

4.2 Controlling the Level of Diagnosis

The belief in a formula may be conditional upon the belief in another formula. This is particularly true when diagnosing faults in a device: causally deeper component faults are sometimes preferred over less deep faults, that are simply consequences of the former. In such cases, one would like to control the level over which diagnosis is performed, by preventing diagnoses which do not focus on the causally deeper faults. We now demonstrate that revised static expansion have sufficient expressive power to control the level of diagnosis.

Example 10. The theory T:

$\neg Runs$	$FlatTire \supset Broken$
$\mathcal{B}\neg Broken \supset Runs$	$BadBattery \supset Broken$

has a single revision: $T \cup \{Possible(Broken)\}$. The revised static expansion contains both $\mathcal{B}\neg FlatTire$ and $\mathcal{B}\neg BadBattery$. This revision can be seen as a diagnosis of the car that just states the car might be broken.

However, in this case, one would like the diagnosis to delve deeper into the car problems, and obtain one diagnosis suggesting a possible problem with a flat tire and another suggesting a possible problem with a bad battery. This is justified by the fact that our belief in the car being broken seems to depend entirely on our belief that it either has a flat tire or a bad battery. □

To obtain this more desirable result one has to somehow ensure that instead of just withholding our belief in the car not being broken we in fact also withhold our belief that the car neither has a flat tire nor a bad battery. In other words, a revision of this theory should not be initiated by revising $Broken$ but instead it should be initiated by revising $FlatTire$ or $BadBattery$ by adding either $Possible(FlatTire)$ or $Possible(BadBattery)$.

Note that, by the rule (N) and the axiom (K), the closure of T already contains:

$$\mathcal{B}FlatTire \vee \mathcal{B}BadBattery \supset \mathcal{B}Broken.$$

Thus, belief in the truth of *Broken* is already determined by the belief in *FlatTire* or in *BadBattery*. But we intend to express the stronger fact that belief in the falsity of *Broken* must also be determined by the beliefs held about the latter literals. This is ensured by stating that if both *FlatTire* and *BadBattery* are believed false then *Broken* must be also believed false:

$$\mathcal{B}\neg FlatTire \wedge \mathcal{B}\neg BadBattery \supset \mathcal{B}\neg Broken \qquad (6)$$

Example 11. The theory T from Example 10, augmented with clause (6) now has two revised expansions:

$$T^{\diamond}_{r_1} = Cn_*(T \cup \{Possible(BadBattery), \mathcal{B}\neg Runs, \mathcal{B}\neg FlatTire\})$$
$$T^{\diamond}_{r_2} = Cn_*(T \cup \{Possible(FlatTire), \quad \mathcal{B}\neg Runs, \mathcal{B}\neg BadBattery\})$$

each corresponding to one of the desired deeper diagnoses.
$T\cup\{Possible(Broken)\}$ is no longer a revision because it still derives $\mathcal{B}\neg Broken$, via clause (6), and thus is inconsistent. ☐

Note the similarities between clause (6) and Clark's completion [Cla78] of *Broken*. Clark's completion states that if both *FlatTire* and *BadBattery* are false then *Broken* is false, whilst (6) refers instead to the corresponding beliefs in their falsity. For this reason we call (6) the *belief completion clause* for *Broken*. More generally:

Definition 13 (Belief Completion Clauses). Let T be an AEB theory, and let:

$$B_{1,1} \wedge \ldots \wedge B_{1,m} \wedge \mathcal{B}\neg B_{1,m+1} \wedge \ldots \wedge \mathcal{B}\neg B_{1,n} \supset A$$
$$\ldots$$
$$B_{k,1} \wedge \ldots \wedge B_{k,m} \wedge \mathcal{B}\neg B_{k,m+1} \wedge \ldots \wedge \mathcal{B}\neg B_{k,n} \supset A$$

be the clauses[6] for A in T, where A is an atom, each Bi,j is a literal, and $k > 0$. The *belief completion clauses for A in T*, $BelComp(A)$, are:

$$(\mathcal{B}\neg B_{1,1} \vee \ldots \vee \mathcal{B}\neg B_{1,m} \vee \mathcal{B}B_{1,m+1} \vee \ldots \vee \mathcal{B}B_{1,n})$$
$$\wedge \ldots \wedge (\mathcal{B}\neg B_{k,1} \vee \ldots \vee \mathcal{B}\neg B_{k,m} \vee \mathcal{B}B_{k,m+1} \vee \ldots \vee \mathcal{B}B_{k,n}) \supset \mathcal{B}\neg A$$

If there are no clauses for A in T then its belief completion is $\mathcal{B}\neg A$. ☐

By adding the completion rules for an atom A, we can therefore prevent revision to be initiated in $\mathcal{B}\neg A$, i.e., in order to revise the belief in $\neg A$, beliefs in other literals on which A depends must also be revised. In diagnosis, the hierarchical component structure of artifacts naturally induces dependency levels into theories modeling them. In other words, we can impose, via belief completion clauses, the desired levels of diagnosis in artifacts.

---

[6] By a clause for an atom A we mean one in which A occurs positively.

References

[ADP94] J. J. Alferes, C. V. Damásio, and L. M. Pereira. SLX – a top-down derivation procedure for programs with explicit negation. In M. Bruynooghe, editor, *Int. Logic Programming Symposium*. MIT Press, 1994.

[ADP95] J. J. Alferes, C. V. Damásio, and L. M. Pereira. A logic programming system for non-monotonic reasoning. *Journal of Automated Reasoning*, Special Issue on Implementation of NonMonotonic Reasoning(14):93–147, 1995.

[Alf93] J. J. Alferes. *Semantics of Logic Programs with Explicit Negation*. PhD thesis, Universidade Nova de Lisboa, 1993.

[AP92] J. J. Alferes and L. M. Pereira. On logic program semantics with two kinds of negation. In K. Apt, editor, *International Joint Conference and Symposium on Logic Programming*, pages 574–588. MIT Press, 1992.

[AP94] J. J. Alferes and L. M. Pereira. Belief, provability and logic programs. In C. MacNish et al., editors, *Logics in AI*, pages 106–121. Springer-Verlag LNAI 838, 1994. Extended version in *Journal of Applied Nonclassical Logics*, 5(1):31–50, 1995.

[APP95] J. J. Alferes, L. M. Pereira, and T. Przymusinski. Strong and explicit negation in non-monotonic reasoning and logic programming. (in preparation), 1995.

[Cla78] K. Clark. Negation as failure. In H. Gallaire and J. Minker, editors, *Logic and Data Bases*, pages 293–322. Plenum Press, 1978.

[GL88] M. Gelfond and V. Lifschitz. The stable model semantics for logic programming. In R. Kowalski and K. Bowen, editors, *Proceedings of the Fifth Logic Programming Symposium*, pages 1070–1080, Cambridge, Mass., 1988. Association for Logic Programming, MIT Press.

[GL90] M. Gelfond and V. Lifschitz. Logic programs with classical negation. In *Proceedings of the Seventh International Logic Programming Conference, Jerusalem, Israel*, pages 579–597, Cambridge, Mass., 1990. Association for Logic Programming, MIT Press.

[GPP89] M. Gelfond, H. Przymusinska, and T. Przymusinski. On the relationship between circumscription and negation as failure. *Journal of Artificial Intelligence*, 38:75–94, 1989.

[Lif92] V. Lifschitz. Minimal belief and negation as failure. Research report, University of Texas at Austin, 1992.

[McC80] J. McCarthy. Circumscription – a form of non-monotonic reasoning. *Journal of Artificial Intelligence*, 13:27–39, 1980.

[Min82] J. Minker. On indefinite data bases and the closed world assumption. In *Proc. 6-th Conference on Automated Deduction*, pages 292–308, New York, 1982. Springer Verlag.

[Moo85] R.C. Moore. Semantic considerations on non-monotonic logic. *Journal of Artificial Intelligence*, 25:75–94, 1985.

[MT94] W. Marek and M. Truszczynski. *Non-Monotonic Logic*. Springer Verlag, 1994.

[PA92] L. M. Pereira and J. J. Alferes. Well founded semantics for logic programs with explicit negation. In B. Neumann, editor, *European Conference on Artificial Intelligence*, pages 102–106. John Wiley & Sons, 1992.

[PA94] L. M. Pereira and J. J. Alferes. Contradiction: when avoidance equal removal. Part II. In R. Dyckhoff, editor, *Extensions of Logic Programming*, number 798 in LNAI, pages 268–281. Springer-Verlag, 1994.

[PAA91] L. M. Pereira, J. J. Alferes, and J. N. Aparício. Contradiction Removal within Well Founded Semantics. In A. Nerode, W. Marek, and V. S. Subrahmanian, editors, *Logic Programming and NonMonotonic Reasoning*, pages 105–119. MIT Press, 1991.

[PAA93] L. M. Pereira, J. N. Aparício, and J. J. Alferes. Non–monotonic reasoning with logic programming. *Journal of Logic Programming. Special issue on Nonmonotonic reasoning*, 17(2, 3 & 4):227–263, 1993.

[PDA93] L. M. Pereira, C. Damásio, and J. J. Alferes. Diagnosis and debugging as contradiction removal. In L. M. Pereira and A. Nerode, editors, *2nd International Workshop on Logic Programming and NonMonotonic Reasoning*, pages 316–330. MIT Press, 1993.

[Prz90] T. C. Przymusinski. The well-founded semantics coincides with the three-valued stable semantics. *Fundamenta Informaticae*, 13(4):445–464, 1990.

[Prz91a] T. C. Przymusinski. Autoepistemic logics of closed beliefs and logic programming. In A. Nerode, W. Marek, and V.S. Subrahmanian, editors, *Proceedings of the First International Workshop on Logic Programming and Non-monotonic Reasoning, Washington, D.C., July 1991*, pages 3–20, Cambridge, Mass., 1991. MIT Press.

[Prz91b] T. C. Przymusinski. Stable semantics for disjunctive programs. *New Generation Computing Journal*, 9:401–424, 1991. (Extended abstract appeared in: Extended stable semantics for normal and disjunctive logic programs. *Proceedings of the 7-th International Logic Programming Conference, Jerusalem*, pages 459–477, 1990. MIT Press.).

[Prz94a] T. C. Przymusinski. Autoepistemic logic of knowledge and beliefs. (in preparation), University of California at Riverside, 1994.

[Prz94b] T. C. Przymusinski. A knowledge representation framework based on autoepistemic logic of minimal beliefs. In *Proceedings of the Twelfth National Conference on Artificial Intelligence, AAAI-94, Seattle, Washington, August 1994*, page (in print), Los Altos, CA, 1994. American Association for Artificial Intelligence, Morgan Kaufmann.

[Prz94c] T. C. Przymusinski. Static semantics for normal and disjunctive logic programs. *Annals of Mathematics and Artificial Intelligence*, 1994. (in print).

[Rei78] R. Reiter. On closed-world data bases. In H. Gallaire and J. Minker, editors, *Logic and Data Bases*, pages 55–76. Plenum Press, New York, 1978.

[Rei87] R. Reiter. A theory of diagnosis from first principles. *Artificial Intelligence*, 32:57–96, 1987.

[RLM89] A. Rajasekar, J. Lobo, and J. Minker. Weak generalized closed world assumption. *Journal of Automated Reasoning*, 5:293–307, 1989.

[RT88] K. Ross and R. Topor. Inferring negative information from disjunctive databases. *Journal of Automated Reasoning*, 4:397–424, 1988.

[VGRS90] A. Van Gelder, K. A. Ross, and J. S. Schlipf. The well-founded semantics for general logic programs. *Journal of the ACM*, 1990. Preliminary abstract appeared in Seventh ACM Symposium on Principles of Database Systems, March 1988, pp. 221–230.

A New Representation of JTMS

Truong Quoc Dung

IRIDIA
Université Libre De Bruxelles
50 Av. F. Roosevelt, CP 194/6
1050 Brussels, Belgium

Abstract.

A Justification -based Truth Maintenance System (JTMS) is classically represented by a network of nodes together with a set of links (justifications) that represent dependencies between nodes. In this representation, the relations between the justifications are not explicit. We propose a dual representation of a JTMS based on the dependencies between justifications. This representation allows us to separate the monotonic and non-monotonic parts of the network of dependencies. Based on this representation, we develop an incremental backtracking algorithm to compute an admissible labeling of a JTMS. This algorithm allows us to go from an admissible labeling to another, and so it always finds an admissible labeling when one exists, and dependency-directed backtracking must be called uniquely when all the admissible labelings are inconsistent.

1 Introduction

A reasoning system often consists of a problem solver and a Reason Maintenance System (RMS). The problem solver passes the inferences it makes to the RMS, and the RMS may be used to record inferences, to support efficient search, to manage inconsistencies and to do non-monotonic reasoning. The problem solver receives information back about the currently supported beliefs by interrogating the RMS.

A JTMS is one of two most common types of RMS. It is commonly regarded as the best tool for non-monotonic reasoning. By using non-monotonic justifications, a JTMS allows to present non-monotonic inferences more naturally and more directly.

An essential component of a JTMS is the labeling algorithm. Unfortunately, most labeling algorithms are incomplete in the sense that they can not find an existing admissible labeling if a so called *unsatisfiable non-monotonic odd loop* arises. Junker and Konolige [Junker and Konolige 90] have proposed a labeling algorithm to find *all* admissible labelings. Unfortunately, this labeling algorithm is not incremental. Moreover, if the admissible labeling so found is inconsistent, a Dependency-Directed Backtracking (DDB) procedure is immediately called to remove this inconsistency without examination of the other admissible labelings. A consequence of this is that these algorithms sometimes produce spurious admissible labelings.

In this paper, we propose to represent a JTMS as a network of dependencies between justifications. This dual representation leads naturally to a chronological backtracking algorithm for efficient and incremental computation of an admissible labeling of a JTMS. A distinctive advantage of this algorithm is the ability to go from an admissible labeling to another. Consequently, our algorithm provides always an admissible labeling whenever one exists, and DDB must be called uniquely in the cases where *all* admissible labelings are inconsistent. In our algorithm, the validity of the so-called terminal justifications, i.e. those belonging to the set of assumption justifications, can be considered as a parameter to determine the validity of the other justifications. Therefore, we can use some preference order on the assumption justifications as a control mechanism for the labeling process. This control mechanism is absent in the Doyle's and Goodwin's algorithms. Our algorithm is NP-complete.

2 Representation of JTMS

2.1 Classical Representation of JTMS

We first recall some basic definitions for JTMS.

A *classical representation* of a JTMS is a pair (N,J) where N is a set of nodes and J is a set of justifications. A *justification* j has the form : $j \equiv (\langle \text{In}(I), \text{Out}(O) \rangle : c)$ where I is a subset of N called the set of *IN-justifiers* of j, O is a subset of N called the set of *OUT-justifiers* of j, c is an element of N called the *consequent* of j. The node representing the contradiction is noted by $\perp$. A *labeling* for a JTMS is a function from N to the set {IN, OUT}. A justification is *valid* iff all of its IN-justifiers are IN and all of its OUT-justifiers are OUT. A labeling is *closed* iff a node is labeled IN iff there is at least one valid justification for it. A labeling is said to be *well-founded* iff for every node labeled IN, there exists a chaining of valid justifications going back to premises, or to nodes labeled OUT. A labeling is *admissible* iff it is both closed and well-founded. An admissible labeling is *consistent* iff $\perp$ is labeled OUT by this labeling. For each admissible labeling, the set of nodes labeled IN by this admissible labeling is called an *extension* of JTMS. A justification having a non-empty set of OUT-justifiers is called an *assumption justification*.

We use a graphical representation for classical JTMSs, where a justification $j \equiv \left(\left\langle \text{In}\left(\{i_1,...,i_k\}\right), \text{Out}\left(\{o_1,...,o_m\}\right)\right\rangle : c \right)$ is depicted as follows :

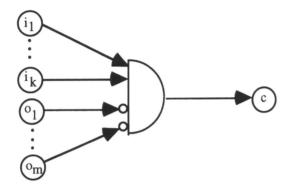

Consider a graphical classical representation of a JTMS. If the number of non-monotonic links (i.e. links with a small circle at the gate) in a path from a node to another is zero (respectively, not zero) then this path is called a *monotonic* (respectively *non-monotonic*) classical path. If this number is greater than zero and even (respectively odd) then this path is called a non-monotonic *even* (respectively non-monotonic *odd*) classical path. A classical path from a node to itself is called a classical *loop*.

The following definitions will be instrumental to the definition of our dual representation.

Definition 2.1.1 Let (N,J) be a classical representation of a JTMS. For every node $c \in N$, we let Jus(J,c) denote the set of justifications belonging to J and having the consequent c:

$$\text{Jus}(J,c) = \left\{ j \in J \mid j \equiv (< \text{In}(I), \text{Out}(O) > : c) \right\}$$

Definition 2.1.2 Let (N,J) be a classical representation of a JTMS. Its *completed classical representation* is $\left(N \cup NOUT \cup \{\Psi\}, J \cup JOUT \cup \{j_\perp\}\right)$ where

1. For every node $c \in N : Jus(J,c) = \varnothing$:
   a new node t_c and a new justification $j_c \equiv \left(\langle\{t_c\},\{\ \}\rangle : c\right)$ are added. Then $JOUT = \bigcup\{j_c\}$ and $NOUT = \bigcup\{t_c\}$.

2. For the contradiction node $\perp$, a new node Ψ and a new justification $j_\perp \equiv \left(\langle\{\perp\},\{\ \}\rangle : \Psi\right)$ are added.

Completing a JTMS according to definition 2.1.2 gives us a representation that is equivalent to the original one in the following sense[1] .

Lemma 2.1.1

Let (N,J) be a classical representation of a JTMS and $\left(N \cup NOUT \cup \{\Psi\}, J \cup JOUT \cup \{j_\perp\}\right)$ its completed classical representation. A subset M of N is an extension of (N,J) iff $M \cup Q$ is an extension of $\left(N \cup NOUT \cup \{\Psi\}, J \cup JOUT \cup \{j_\perp\}\right)$ where

$$Q = \begin{cases} \varnothing & \text{if } \perp \notin M \\ \Psi & \text{otherwise} \end{cases}$$

A fundamental task of a JTMS is to efficiently find an admissible labeling. Generally, a JTMS may have zero, one or more admissible labelings. Doyle [Doyle 79] originally proposed an incremental algorithm for the computation of an admissible and consistent labeling of a JTMS, and Goodwin [Goodwin 87] describes an incremental algorithm that computes an admissible labeling of JTMS. Unfortunately, these algorithms can not find an existing admissible labeling if an unsatisfiable non-monotonic odd loop arises. In this case, Doyle's algorithm does not terminate, whereas Goodwin's algorithm terminates without giving any admissible labeling.

---

[1] The proofs of all the lemmas and theorems can be found in the long version of this paper.

If the found admissible labeling is inconsistent, Doyle's algorithm calls immediatly DDB to remove the inconsistency without examination of the other admissible labelings. This may sometimes produce spurious admissible labelings.

Junker and Konolige [Junker and Konolige 90] and Elkan [Elkan 90] define an operator Apply for a JTMS. Based on this operator, Junker and Konolige propose an algorithm to compute *all extensions* of a JTMS. Unfortunately, it is not an incremental algorithm.

2.2 Dual Representation of a JTMS

In the classical representation of a JTMS, the relations between the justifications are not explicit. Yet, the validity of justifications ultimately decides of the in/out status of the nodes — intuitively, justifications bring more information than nodes. So, we propose a new representation of a JTMS, called dual representation, which is a network consisting of justifications and dependencies that explicitly represent the relations between justifications. Interestingly, we can show that each admissible and consistent dual labeling corresponds exactly to one admissible and consistent labeling of classical representation of a JTMS and vice-versa.

Definition 2.2.1 Let (N,J) be a classical representation of a JTMS and $\left(N \cup NOUT \cup \{\Psi\}, J \cup JOUT \cup \{j_\perp\} \right)$ its completed classical representation. A *monotonic dependency* d has the form : $d \equiv \left(In^*(IJ) : j \right)$, where IJ is a set of subsets of $J \cup JOUT$ called the *IN-components* of d, and j is an element of $J \cup \{j_\perp\}$ called the *consequent* of d. A *non-monotonic dependency* has the form $d \equiv (Out^*(OJ) : j)$, where OJ is a subset of J»JOUT called The *OUT-components* of d, and j is an element of J called the *consequent* of d.

Definition 2.2.2 Let (N, J) be a classical representation of a JTMS and $\left(N \cup NOUT \cup \{\Psi\}, J \cup JOUT \cup \{j_\perp\} \right)$ its completed classical representation.

For every $j \equiv \left(\langle In(I), Out(O) \rangle : c \right) \in J \cup \{j_\perp\}$:

The *monotonic dependency* MD(j) is determined as follows :

$$MD(j) \equiv \left(In^*(IJ) : j \right), \text{ where } IJ = \begin{cases} \{ \} & \text{if } I = \varnothing \\ \{Jus(J \cup JOUT, i_1), ..., Jus(J \cup JOUT, i_k)\} \\ & \text{if } I = \{i_1, ..., i_k\} \end{cases}$$

The *non-monotonic dependency* NMD(j) is determined as follows :

$$NMD(j) \equiv \left(Out^*(OJ) : j\right), \text{ where } OJ = \begin{cases} \{\ \} & \text{if} \quad O = \varnothing \\ Jus(J \cup JOUT, o_1) \cup ... \cup Jus(J \cup JOUT, o_m) \\ & \text{if} \quad O = \{o_1, ..., o_m\} \end{cases}$$

Then, $\left(J \cup JOUT \cup \{j_\perp\}, D\right)$ is called the **dual representation** of this JTMS

$$\text{where } D = \bigcup_{j \in J \cup \{j_\perp\}} \left(MD(j) \cup NMD(j)\right)$$

Definition 2.2.3 A *dual labeling* is a function from $J \cup JOUT \cup \{j_\perp\}$ to the set $\{IN, OUT\}$. A monotonic dependency is *valid* iff every its IN-component contains at least a justification labeled IN and a non-monotonic dependency is *valid* iff all of its OUT-components are labeled OUT. A dual labeling is *closed* iff for each justification j, j is labeled IN if (MD(j) is valid) AND (NMD(j) is valid) and j is labeled OUT otherwise. A dual labeling is said to be *well-founded* iff for every justification labeled IN, there exists a chaining of valid dependencies going back to premise justifications, or to the justifications labeled OUT. A dual labeling is *admissible* iff it is both closed and well-founded. A admissible dual labeling is *consistent* iff $j_\perp$ is labeled OUT by this dual labeling. Finally, for each admissible dual labeling, the set of justifications labeled IN by this admissible dual labeling is called a *dual extension* of JTMS.

We draw a dual representation of a JTMS in a graphical form as follows.

A monotonic dependency $MD(j) \equiv \left(In^*(\{T_1, ..., T_k\}) : j\right)$ and a non-monotonic dependency $NMD(j) \equiv \left(Out^*(\{j_1, ..., j_m\}) : j\right)$ are represented by

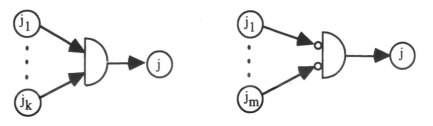

for all $\{j_1, ..., j_k\}$ where $j_q \in T_q$, $q \in \{1, ..., k\}$.

We can define *monotonic, non-monotonic, even and odd dual paths* in a dual representation exactly as we did for the classical representation. A dual path from a justification to itself is called a *dual loop*.

Example 2.2.1

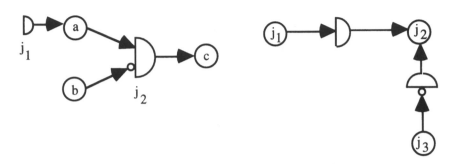

| Classical representation | Dual representation |

where $j_3 \equiv \left(\left\langle \{t_b\}, \{\ \} \right\rangle : b \right)$.

Given a JTMS, its classical representation and its dual representation are equivalent, meaning that both representations admit the same extensions. The following theprem makes this equivalence precise.

Theorem 2.2.1

Let (N,J) be a classical representation of a JTMS, $\left(N \cup NOUT \cup \{\Psi\}, J \cup JOUT \cup \{j_\perp\} \right)$ its completed classical representation and $\left(J \cup JOUT \cup \{j_\perp\}, D \right)$ its dual representation. Then each admissible labeling of $\left(N \cup NOUT \cup \{\Psi\}, J \cup JOUT \cup \{j_\perp\} \right)$ corresponds exactly to an admissible dual labeling of $\left(J \cup JOUT \cup \{j_\perp\}, D \right)$ and vice-versa.

3 Algorithm for Finding of an Admissible and Consistent Dual Labeling

We describe a dual labeling algorithm based on a decomposition of the network in dual representation. This algorithm allows us to go from one admissible dual labeling to another, and thus it always finds an admissible and consistent dual labeling whenever one exists. DDB must still be called to remove inconsistencies, but this will only be done if *all* the admissible dual labelings are inconsistent.

3.1 The Monotonic Connected Components of Dual Representation

The monotonic connected components of the network of dual representation can be obtained by disregarding the non-monotonic dependencies. In the dual representation, the set of non-monotonic dependencies of each justification contains at most one non-monotonic dependency. Using this property, we can build a set of justifications called the *terminals* for every monotonic connected component. The validity of terminals can be considered as *parameters* to determine the validity of the other justifications. The precise definitions of these notations are given below.

Definition 3.1.1 Let (N,J) be a classical representation of a JTMS and $\left(J \cup JOUT \cup \{j_\perp\}, D\right)$ its dual representation, for $\forall\, j \in J \cup JOUT \cup \{j_\perp\}$:

* The set of *monotonic antecedents* of j, noted by $MANT(j)$, is determined as follows :

$$MANT(j) = \bigcup_{T_k \in IJ} T_k \qquad \text{where } MD(j) \equiv \left(In^*(IJ) : j\right)$$

* The set of *monotonic consequences* of j, noted by $MCONS(j)$, is determined as follows :

$$MCONS(j) = \left\{ j' \;\middle|\; \exists MD(j') \equiv (In^*(IJ) : j') : j \in \bigcup_{T_k \in IJ} T_k \right\}$$

* The set of *monotonic connections* of j, noted by $MJOIN(j)$, is determined as follows :

$$MJOIN(j) = MANT(j) \cup \{j\} \cup MCONS(j)$$

* The *transitive closure of the monotonic connections* of j, noted by $MJOIN^*(j)$, is the monotonic connections of j, their monotonic connections, and so on.

Lemma 3.1.1

For every $j, j' \in J \cup JOUT \cup \{j_\perp\}$ and $j \neq j'$:

i) $MJOIN^*(j) \neq \emptyset$

ii) if $MJOIN^*(j) \cap MJOIN^*(j') \neq \emptyset$ then $MJOIN^*(j) \equiv MJOIN^*(j')$

iii) $\bigcup_{j \in J \cup JOUT \cup \{j_\perp\}} MJOIN^*(j) \equiv J \cup JOUT \cup \{j_\perp\}$

Definition 3.1.2 The subsets non-empty and completely separate of $J \cup JOUT \cup \{j_\perp\}$ determined by $MJOIN^*$ are called the *monotonic connected components* of the dual representation.

Definition 3.1.3 A justification j is called a *terminal* of a monotonic connected component iff :

1. $MD(j)$ is valid

2. $NMD(j) \equiv (Out^*(OJ) : j)$ is unknown i.e. :

$$\left(\neg \exists \, j' \in OJ : Label(j') = IN\right) \ AND \ \left(\exists \, j'' \in OJ : Label(j'') = UN\right)$$

Note that a terminal j is an assumption justification because its OUT-justifier set is non-empty. Moreover, its monotonic dependency MD(j) is valid, then its validity depends only on the validity of its non-monotonic dependency NMD(j).

3.2 Description of the Algorithm

Our algorithm maintains permanently an admissible and consistent dual labeling of a JTMS and updates it when a new justification is passed to the JTMS by the problem solver. The algorithm has the following steps :

1°/ Update the monotonic connected components.

2°/ Mark the justifications influenced by introduction of the new justification — i.e. the new justification and all justifications influenced by introduction of the new justification will be labeled UN.

3°/ Update the labeling.

The two first steps are relatively simple. We concentrate on the description of 3rd step. The detailed description of the algorithm can be found in the long version of this paper.

First, the algorithm propagates the label of justifications in accordance with definition 2.2.3. But if there are loops in the dual representation, the propagation process can be blocked. To unlock this situation, we use the following rules to determine an IN-label or an OUT-label of the justifications.

R1 : If there is a monotonic connected component whose set of terminals is empty, then all justifications in this component labeled UN *must be labeled* OUT. (Note : this guarantees the well-foundedness of dual labeling).

R2 : If all sets of terminals are not empty *and* any justification can be labeled IN or OUT in accordance with definition 2.2.3 (i.e., the propagation process is blocked), then the algorithm first *forces an IN-label* for a some terminal j to unlock this situation. The validity of the terminal j depends *only* on the validity of *unique* non-monotonic dependency of NMD(j) having the status unknown now. However, these *forced labels* of terminal j may be not coherent later. Therefore, we introduced a coherence test in our algorithm. These selected terminals are saved in a *stack* for the later uses.

R3 : If there exists a terminal saved in the stack whose validity is not coherent with the validity of its unique non-monotonic dependency, then a *backtracking* process will be invoked: the algorithm removes the terminals from the stack until obtain a terminal whose forced label is IN and, after that, *forces an OUT-label* for this terminal to try to eliminate the non-coherence.

R4 : If all of terminals saved in the stack are coherent, but the validity of $j_\perp$ is IN then the backtracking process will also be invoked to try to resolve the inconsistency.

This algorithm is essentially a chronological backtracking algorithm for the incremental computation of an admissible and consistent dual labeling of a JTMS. Calling Dual_Labeling(new justification) results in an admissible and consistent dual labeling of JTMS whenever one exists. The algorithm always terminates with a finite set of justifications.

Moreover, it is easy to see that this algorithm is incremental. In fact, the old monotonic connected components are used to construct the new ones; and only the justifications affected by the new justification or by the change of terminal validity are recalculated.

Each justification has only one non-monotonic dependency in the dual representation. This facilitates treating the non-monotonic cases — for example, this allows to find efficiently the selected terminal. Moreover, treatment of monotonic dual loop is not explicit in our algorithm. This is replaced by a simple test of terminal sets (cf. rule R1 above).

Using backtracking process, our algorithm always tries to find an admissible and consistent dual labeling for a JTMS. DDB is needed only in the cases where all admissible dual labelings are inconsistent. So no admissible and consistent dual labeling should be excluded unnecessarily. The procedure DDB deals with the cases where an admissible and consistent dual labeling can not be found, either because of an inconsistency or because there is a odd dual loop that can not be ignored. A revised DDB will be presented in a sequence of this paper.

It is interesting to note that our algorithm has provisions for including a preference order between assumption justification, possibly provided by the problem solver — recall that the assumption justifications are the justification whose OUT-justifiers set is non-empty. Because a terminal is also an assumption justification, we can use this ordering to select the terminal. This gives the problem solver some control over the dual labeling process. An equivalent control mecanism is absent in Doyle's and Goodwin's algorithms. Moreover, thanks to its ability to go from one admissible to the other, our algorithm can find different admissible dual labelings if the problem solver so asks.

3.3 Complexity Issues

For a JTMS, the transformation of the classical representation into its dual representation can be performed in $O(|J|*|N|)$ time, and vice-versa. Elkan [Elkan 90] has shown that the problem of finding an admissible labeling of a JTMS is a NP-complete problem. Using these results, we can show that the problem of finding an admissible dual labeling has the same complexity.

4 Conclusion

We have presented a dual representation of a JTMS centered on the relations between justifications. This representation has an advantage over the classical one in that it allows us to split the JTMS (dual) network into separate monotonic components, linked by the non-monotonic dependencies. We have shown how this splitting can be exploited to define an NP-complete algorithm that finds an admissible and consistent dual labeling using a backtracking procedure. Contrary to Doyle's and Goodwin's algorithms, our algorithm always finds an admissible and consistent dual labeling if such a labeling exists, and DDB is only called if all admissible dual labelings are inconsistent. This avoids the generations of spurious dual labelings. A DDB for dual representation of JTMS will be the topic of a forthcoming paper.

An additional advantage of our dual representation is its ability to integrate a preference ordering over the assumption justifications; this order gives the problem solver some control over the labeling process. Moreover, the assumption justifications in a JTMS can be considered as the defaults of a default logic. We plan to integrate the results for prioritized default logic [Besnard 89] to construct this preference order.

References

[Besnard 89] Besnard, P., An Introduction to Default Logic, Springer-Verlag 1989.

[Doyle 79] Doyle, J., A Truth Maintenance System, Artificial Intelligence 12, 1979.

[Elkan 90] Elkan, C., A rational reconstruction of nonmonotonic Truth Maintenance Systems. Artificial Intelligence V.43, Number 2, 1990.

[Goodwin 87] Goodwin, J. W., A Theory and System for Non-monotonic Reasoning. Dissertation 1987.

[Junker and Konolige 90] Junker, U., Konolige, K., Computing the extensions of Autoepistemic and Default Logics with a Truth Maintenance System, Proc. AAAI 90.

[Junker 90] Junker, U., Variations of backtracking for TMS, Proc. Workshop, ECAI 90.

The Retrieval Problem in a Concept Language with Number Restrictions

Aida Vitória, Margarida Mamede and Luís Monteiro

Departamento de Informática
Universidade Nova de Lisboa
2825 Monte da Caparica, Portugal
{av,mm,lm}@fct.unl.pt

Abstract. In this paper, we study the retrieval problem in $\mathcal{ALN}$, which is a tractable concept language with number restrictions. Following the approach proposed in [12], this work differs from the classical framework in two respects. First, the definition of answer has been extended in order to refer to elements whose existence may be deduced but have no explicit representation in the knowledge base. Therefore, our answers are also more informative than the classical ones. Second, the query-answering algorithm is syntax-directed rather than of the generate-and-test sort. Due to number restrictions, answers are possibly infinite sets but, since they are regular languages, they are described by regular expressions. The query-answering algorithm relies on a finite automaton, which can be seen as a preprocessing of the knowledge base, because it is built from its completion and does not depend on the query. Both a declarative and an operational semantics are described, and proved to be equivalent.

1 Introduction

In recent years, much attention has been given to concept-based knowledge bases and several systems have been proposed: KRIS [1, 2], KRIPTON [3], CLASSIC [6, 18], LOOM [11], BACK [15, 19], and NIKL [17]. Much of the research done in this field aims at characterizing concept languages with respect to either their expressive power (see, for example, [5, 13]) or the computational complexity of the following two problems ([4, 7, 8, 9, 15, 16, 20, 21]): knowledge base satisfiability and concept subsumption. In this paper, we study the retrieval problem in $\mathcal{ALN}$, which is a tractable concept language with number restrictions.

According to the classical definition ([1, 2, 9, 10]), the retrieval problem consists of computing the set of individuals that belong to a given concept in all models of the knowledge base. This problem may be reduced to the problem of checking whether a knowledge base is satisfiable, because of the following two facts. On the one hand, given a knowledge base Σ, a concept C, and an individual i, i belongs to C (in all models of Σ) if and only if the knowledge base $\Sigma \cup \{i : \neg C\}$ is unsatisfiable. On the other hand, the number of individuals is always finite. Therefore, the returned set may be computed by generate-and-test.

This approach has been followed both in languages that allow negation of arbitrary concepts (e.g., KRIS [1, 2] or $\mathcal{ALC}$ [9]) and in languages in which negation may only be applied to primitive concepts (like $\mathcal{PL}_1$ [8] and $\mathcal{AL}$ [10]). In this second case, the satisfiability algorithm has been slightly modified in order to handle the kind of assertions the retrieval algorithm generates.

In [9], Donini, Lenzerini, Nardi and Schaerf also reduce the retrieval problem to a finite number of calls to the instance checking problem (the problem of checking if an individual belongs to a concept in all models of a knowledge base), but they solve instance checking by concept subsumption in $\mathcal{AL}$, and, depending on the syntax of the query, by (the common) knowledge base satisfiability or by concept subsumption in the language $\mathcal{ALN}$.

Mamede and Monteiro also studied the retrieval problem in $\mathcal{AL}$ ([12]) and their work differs from the previous approaches in two respects. First, the query-answering algorithm is syntax-directed rather than of the generate-and-test sort. Second, they extended the definition of answer in order to refer to elements whose existence may be deduced but have no explicit representation in the knowledge base. To this end, they introduced the notion of term, which extends that of individual, and defined answer as the set of all terms whose nonempty denotation is contained in the denotation of the query, in all models of the knowledge base. Their query-answering algorithm is sound and complete.

The research described in [14] extends the previous work, studying the same problem in the language $\mathcal{ALC}$ [21] with conjunction of relations and generic terminological axioms. In this case, answers are possibly infinite sets of terms, but since they are regular languages, they are described by regular expressions. The operational semantics relies on a finite automaton, which is built from some completions of the knowledge base. Although sound, this system is not complete in the general case.

Our paper follows the same approach, studying a language that allows number restrictions. As in the above case, an answer is a regular expression that denotes the language accepted by a finite automaton, which is (basically) obtained by first preprocessing the knowledge base. Nevertheless, the construction of these automata is completely different. In [14], most of the problems come from disjunction, existential quantification and terminological axioms, whereas, in our case, difficulties stem from the number restrictions. Moreover, our algorithm is sound and complete.

The rest of the paper is organized as follows. Section 2 is devoted to studying knowledge bases. In Sect. 2.1, the language $\mathcal{ALN}$ is defined and some basic notions are introduced, and Sect. 2.2 presents tractable algorithms for computing the completion of the knowledge base and for testing its satisfiability. The declarative semantics is defined in Sect. 3, while the operational semantics is described in Sect. 4. First, in Sect. 4.1, we show how to build a deterministic finite automaton associated with a knowledge base. Then, in Sect. 4.2, we present the abstract query-answering algorithm. Finally, Sect. 5 includes some comments on the research done in the paper and some directions of future work.

Several examples are included to explain the motivation of some notions or to illustrate some definitions. Due to space limitations, all proofs are omitted. However, they can all be found in [22].

2 Knowledge Bases

2.1 Basic Definitions

The language studied in this work is $\mathcal{ALN}$ ([7, 9]). Given a tuple (Ind, Prim, Rel) of pairwise disjoint sets of *individuals* $i \in$ Ind, *primitive concepts* $P \in$ Prim, and *binary relations* $r \in$ Rel, an $\mathcal{ALN}$-concept C and an $\mathcal{ALN}$-assertion σ are defined by the following grammar, where n is a non negative integer:

$$C \longrightarrow \top \mid \bot \mid P \mid \neg P \mid C_1 \sqcap C_2 \mid \forall r.C \mid (\leq n\, r) \mid (\geq n\, r)$$
$$\sigma \longrightarrow i : C \mid r(i_1, i_2) \ .$$

An $\mathcal{ALN}$-*knowledge base* is a finite set of $\mathcal{ALN}$-assertions. Sometimes we omit the prefix $\mathcal{ALN}$, writing only the words *concept*, *assertion*, and *knowledge base*.

Intuitively, a concept denotes: the domain of discourse ($\top$); the empty set ($\bot$); the set of elements that belong to a primitive concept (P) or to its complement ($\neg P$); the intersection of two concepts ($C_1 \sqcap C_2$); or the set of those elements whose image by the relation r is contained in concept C ($\forall r.C$), has at most n elements (($\leq n\, r$)), or has at least n elements (($\geq n\, r$)). Assertions allow to state that an individual belongs to a concept ($i : C$) and that two individuals are related by some relation ($r(i_1, i_2)$).

Let us give the intuitive meaning of the following knowledge base, Σ_{fam}, assuming that child is a primitive concept, son, play, hate and belong are relation names, and Joe, Peter, Fred, Amy and RedBall are individuals.

(1)	Joe : $(\geq 2\,\text{son})$ Joe : $(\leq 2\,\text{son})$	Joe has exactlty two sons.
(2)	son(Joe, Fred) son(Joe, Peter)	Joe's sons are Fred and Peter.
(3)	Fred : $(\leq 1\,\text{play})$	Fred plays with at most one thing.
(4)	play(Fred, RedBall)	Fred plays with the RedBall.
(5)	Amy : $(\leq 1\,\text{hate})$	Amy hates at most one thing.
(6)	hate(Amy, RedBall)	Amy hates the RedBall.
(7)	RedBall : $(\leq 1\,\text{belong})$	The RedBall has at most one owner.
(8)	belong(RedBall, Amy)	The RedBall belongs to Amy.
(9)	Amy : child	Amy is a child.
(10)	Joe : $\forall\text{son}.(\geq 1\,\text{play})$	Joe's sons play with something.
(11)	Peter : $\forall\text{play}.\forall\text{belong}.\text{child}$	Anything Peter plays with belongs only to children.

An *interpretation* of $\mathcal{ALN}$ over (Ind, Prim, Rel) is a pair $I = (\Delta^I, \cdot^I)$, where Δ^I is a nonempty set, called the *interpretation domain*, and $\cdot^I$ is the *interpretation function* which associates:

- $i^I \in \Delta^I$ with every $i \in$ Ind, in such a way that $(\forall i, j \in \text{Ind})\ i \neq j \Rightarrow i^I \neq j^I$;
- $P^I \subseteq \Delta^I$ with every $P \in$ Prim; and
- $r^I \subseteq \Delta^I \times \Delta^I$ with every $r \in$ Rel.

The interpretation function is extended to arbitrary concepts in the following way, where $r^I(a) = \{b \mid (a,b) \in r^I\}$, for every $a \in \Delta^I$ and every $r \in \text{Rel}$:

$$\top^I = \Delta^I$$
$$\bot^I = \emptyset$$
$$(\neg P)^I = \Delta^I \setminus P^I$$
$$(C_1 \sqcap C_2)^I = C_1^I \cap C_2^I$$
$$(\forall r.C)^I = \{a \in \Delta^I \mid r^I(a) \subseteq C^I\}$$
$$(\geq n\, r)^I = \{a \in \Delta^I \mid \#r^I(a) \geq n\}$$
$$(\leq n\, r)^I = \{a \in \Delta^I \mid \#r^I(a) \leq n\} \ .$$

To simplify the notation, the functions r^I are extended in the usual way to arbitrary subsets X of the interpretation domain, i.e., $r^I(X) = \bigcup_{a \in X} r^I(a)$. Furthermore, we define

$$r^{-I}(a) = \{b \mid (b,a) \in r^I\} \text{ and } r^{-I}(X) = \bigcup_{a \in X} r^{-I}(a) \ .$$

An interpretation I *satisfies* $i : C$ or $r(i_1, i_2)$ if $i^I \in C^I$ or $(i_1^I, i_2^I) \in r^I$, respectively. A knowledge base Σ is *satisfiable* if there is an interpretation I that satisfies all of its assertions. In this case, I is said to be a *model* of Σ. When Σ is not satisfiable, we say it is *unsatisfiable*. An assertion σ is a *logical consequence* of the knowledge base Σ, and we write $\Sigma \models \sigma$, if every model of Σ satisfies σ.

2.2 Completion of the Knowledge Base

It is possible to check if a knowledge base Σ is satisfiable by generation of "propositions" that are logical consequences of Σ. For example, any model of Σ_{fam} satisfies $\text{Peter} : (\geq 1\,\text{play})$, because Peter is a son of Joe (line (2)) and Joe's sons play with something (line (10)). This assertion states that, in every model M of Σ_{fam}, there is an element[1] $a \in \Delta^M$ such that $(\text{Peter}^M, a) \in \text{play}^M$. In order to represent this kind of elements, whose existence is guaranteed by number restrictions of the form $(\geq n\, r)$, for some $n \geq 1$, we define another language of assertions, $\mathcal{ALN}_T$, which accepts "terms" in any place individuals may occur in $\mathcal{ALN}$-assertions.

More formally, a *term* t is an expression of the form $i r_1 \cdots r_k$, with $i \in \text{Ind}$, $r_1, \ldots, r_k \in \text{Rel}$ and $k \geq 0$. We denote by Term the set of all terms (built over the alphabet $\text{Ind} \cup \text{Rel}$). $\mathcal{ALN}_T$-*assertions* are either of the form $t : C$ or $r(t_1, t_2)$, and an $\mathcal{ALN}_T$-*knowledge base* is a finite set of $\mathcal{ALN}_T$-assertions.

The *denotation* of a term t in an interpretation I, written $[t]^I$, is defined as follows:

$$[i]^I = \{i^I\};$$

$$[t'r]^I = \begin{cases} \emptyset & \text{if there is some } a \in [t']^I \text{ such that } r^I(a) = \emptyset, \\ r^I([t']^I) & \text{otherwise.} \end{cases}$$

---

[1] This element will be denoted later by the "term" **Peter play**.

Let us exemplify this notion with an arbitrary model M of Σ_{fam}. Intuitively, the denotation of Joe son play in M is nonempty, because Joe has sons and every son of Joe plays with something. Actually, we know that:

$[\text{Joe}]^M = \{\text{Joe}^M\}$ (by definition);

$[\text{Joe son}]^M = \text{son}^M(\{\text{Joe}^M\}) = \{\text{Fred}^M, \text{Peter}^M\}$ (lines (1) and (2));

$[\text{Joe son play}]^M = \text{play}^M(\{\text{Fred}^M, \text{Peter}^M\}) \neq \emptyset$

   because $\text{play}^M(\text{Fred}^M) = \{\text{RedBall}^M\} \neq \emptyset$ (lines (3) and (4))

     and $\text{play}^M(\text{Peter}^M) \neq \emptyset$ (lines (2) and (10)).

Notice that if the assertion Joe : $\forall\text{son}.(\geq 1\,\text{play})$ did not belong to Σ_{fam}, there would be models M' in which Peter would not play with anything, i.e., $\text{play}^{M'}(\text{Peter}^{M'}) = \emptyset$. As a consequence, the denotation of Joe son play in those models would be the empty set.

An interpretation I *satisfies* an $\mathcal{ALN}_T$-assertion $t : C$ if $\emptyset \neq [t]^I \subseteq C^I$ and I satisfies $r(t_1, t_2)$ if $\emptyset \neq [t_2]^I \subseteq r^I([t_1]^I)$ and $\emptyset \neq [t_1]^I \subseteq r^{-I}([t_2]^I)$.

Note that an $\mathcal{ALN}$-assertion is an $\mathcal{ALN}_T$-assertion and that the two definitions of satisfiability coincide. When the distinction is not important or when it is clear from the context, we use only the word *assertion*. Similarly, a *knowledge base* is either a finite set of $\mathcal{ALN}$-assertions or a finite set of $\mathcal{ALN}_T$-assertions.

The definitions of model, (un)satisfiability and logical consequence of an $\mathcal{ALN}_T$-knowledge base are equal to the ones given for $\mathcal{ALN}$-knowledge bases.

To simplify the remainder of the paper, we now introduce some notation. First, a generic expression of the form $t : \forall r_j. \cdots .\forall r_k.C$ denotes the assertion $t : C$, when $j > k$. Second, given a knowledge base Σ, an individual i, and a relation r, $r(i)$ denotes the following set of individuals $\{i' \in \text{Ind} \mid r(i, i') \in \Sigma\}$. Finally, we say that concepts C_1 and C_2 are *contradictory* when:

1. either one of these concepts has the form P and the other has the form $\neg P$, for some $P \in \text{Prim}$;
2. or one of these concepts has the form $(\leq n_1\, r)$ and the other has the form $(\geq n_2\, r)$, for some $r \in \text{Rel}$ and some integers n_1 and n_2 verifying $n_1 < n_2$.

The algorithm that tests the satisfiability of a knowledge base Σ starts with the set Σ to which it adds new $\mathcal{ALN}_T$-assertions, by applying the following six rules, until no new information can be generated. The final set is called the *completion* of Σ and is denoted by $\overline{\Sigma}$.

More precisely, $\overline{\Sigma}$ is the least set containing Σ that verifies:

     (⊓-r)   If $t : \forall r_1. \cdots .\forall r_n.(C_1 \sqcap C_2) \in \overline{\Sigma}$, with $n \geq 0$,
               then $\{t : \forall r_1. \cdots .\forall r_n.C_1, t : \forall r_1. \cdots .\forall r_n.C_2\} \subseteq \overline{\Sigma}$.

     (#-r)   If $\#r(i) = n$, for some $n > 0$,
               then $i : (\geq n\, r) \in \overline{\Sigma}$.

     (≥-r)   If $t : (\geq n\, r) \in \overline{\Sigma}$, for some $n > 0$,
               then $r(t, tr) \in \overline{\Sigma}$.

     (∀-r)   If $t : \forall r.C \in \overline{\Sigma}$ and $r(t, t') \in \overline{\Sigma}$
               then $t' : C \in \overline{\Sigma}$.

($\forall\perp$-r)   If $t : \forall r_1. \cdots . \forall r_n.\perp \in \overline{\Sigma}$, with $n \geq 1$,
         then $t : \forall r_1. \cdots . \forall r_{n-1}.(\leq 0\, r_n) \in \overline{\Sigma}$.

($\forall C$-r)   If $t : \forall r_1. \cdots . \forall r_n.C_1 \in \overline{\Sigma}$ and $t : \forall r_1. \cdots . \forall r_n.C_2 \in \overline{\Sigma}$,
         for some $n \geq 1$ and some contradictory concepts C_1 and C_2,
         then $t : \forall r_1. \cdots . \forall r_{n-1}.(\leq 0\, r_n) \in \overline{\Sigma}$.

For example, the completion of Σ_{fam} comprises all the following assertions, besides those that belong to Σ_{fam}:

(#-r)   Fred : $(\geq 1\,\text{play})$,   Amy : $(\geq 1\,\text{hate})$,
        RedBall : $(\geq 1\,\text{belong})$;

($\geq$-r)   son(Joe, Joe son),   play(Fred, Fred play),
       hate(Amy, Amy hate),   belong(RedBall, RedBall belong);

($\forall$-r)   Peter : $(\geq 1\,\text{play})$,   Joe son : $(\geq 1\,\text{play})$;

($\geq$-r)   play(Peter, Peter play),   play(Joe son, Joe son play);

($\forall$-r)   Peter play : $\forall$belong.child.

We conclude this section with two propositions. The first one shows that if the completion does not contain an obvious contradiction (formalized by the notion of "clash", below), the knowledge base is satisfiable, and the second one states that the completion process is always tractable. Actually, to prove these propositions, rules ($\forall\perp$-r) and ($\forall C$-r) are not needed and their inclusion gives rise to useless assertions, from the point of view of the satisfiability test. Nevertheless, since the query-answering algorithm (presented in Sect. 4) relies on this definition of completion and these rules do not affect the tractability result, we have already included them to prevent future repetitions.

A knowledge base Σ has a *clash* if it contains: an assertion of the form $t : \perp$, for some term t; or two assertions $t : C_1$ and $t : C_2$, for some $t \in$ Term and some contradictory concepts C_1 and C_2. Otherwise, we say that Σ is *clash-free*.

It is easy to verify that $\overline{\Sigma_{fam}}$ has no clash.

Proposition 1. *An $\mathcal{ALN}$-knowledge base Σ is satisfiable if and only if its completion is clash-free.*

The *length* of an assertion $r(t_1, t_2)$ is one and the length of $t : C$ is equal to the number of subconcepts of C. The *size* of a knowledge base Σ is a pair (N, D), where N is the cardinal of Σ and D is the maximum length of the assertions in Σ.

Back to our example, the size of Σ_{fam} is $(13, 3)$. Notice that the "biggest" assertion, which is Peter : $\forall$play.$\forall$belong.child, has length three[2].

Proposition 2. *The completion of an $\mathcal{ALN}$-knowledge base can be computed in polynomial time with respect to the size of the knowledge base.*

---

[2] The subconcepts are $\forall$play.$\forall$belong.child, $\forall$belong.child and child.

3 Queries and Answers

According to the classical definition ([1, 2, 9, 10]), the retrieval problem consists of computing the set of individuals that belong to a given concept in all models of the knowledge base. Our idea is to extend this definition to the set of all terms.

Let Σ be an $\mathcal{ALN}$-knowledge base. A *query* to Σ is an $\mathcal{ALN}$-concept Q, the *classical answer* to Q is

$$\text{ClassicalAnswer}(\Sigma, Q) = \{i \in \text{Ind} \mid \Sigma \models i : Q\},$$

and the *answer* to Q is

$$\text{Answer}(\Sigma, Q) = \{t \in \text{Term} \mid \Sigma \models t : Q\}.$$

Let us see an example, based on the knowledge base Σ_{fam}. Suppose the query is $Q_1 = \forall \text{belong.child}$. The classical answer is $\{\text{RedBall}\}$, because RedBall is the only individual that belongs only to children, in all models of Σ_{fam}. On the other hand, according to our definition, the answer contains, among others, the term **Peter play**, which can be read as "everything Peter plays with". Notice that, in every model M of Σ_{fam}:

1. there is an element $a \in \Delta^M$ that satisfies $(\text{Peter}^M, a) \in \text{play}^M$
   (due to the second assertion of line (2) and that in line (10)),
   so, $[\![\text{Peter play}]\!]^M \neq \emptyset$; and
2. for every $b \in \Delta^M$, $(\text{Peter}^M, b) \in \text{play}^M \Rightarrow b \in (\forall \text{belong.child})^M$
   (by line (11)), which implies $[\![\text{Peter play}]\!]^M \subseteq (\forall \text{belong.child})^M$.

4 Operational Semantics

This section describes the abstract query-answering algorithm, which relies on the completion of the knowledge base. In order to gain in efficiency, some of the information contained in this set is first preprocessed, resulting in a deterministic finite automaton. We start, in Sect. 4.1, by defining this automaton and then, in Sect. 4.2, we present the query-answering algorithm.

When the knowledge base is unsatisfiable, the answer to any query is the set of all terms. Since, in this case, answers are trivially computed, in the sequel, we shall assume that Σ is a satisfiable $\mathcal{ALN}$-knowledge base.

4.1 Automaton for a Knowledge Base

The main idea is that the language accepted by the automaton for Σ is the set of terms whose denotation, in every model of Σ, is nonempty. First of all, since individuals always have a nonempty denotation, for every $i \in \text{Ind}$, there will be a state $\{i\}$ and a transition from the initial state, by i, into $\{i\}$. Notice that, for every model M of Σ, the denotation of this word i, "accepted" by state $\{i\}$, is the union of the denotations of the terms that are in $\{i\}$, i.e., $[\![i]\!]^M = \bigcup_{t \in \{i\}} [\![t]\!]^M$.

Now suppose that the "image" of i by some relation r is always the set of individuals $\{i_1, \ldots, i_n\}$ — because assertions $r(i, i_1), \ldots, r(i, i_n)$ and $i : (\leq n\, r)$ belong to $\overline{\Sigma}$. In this case, there will be a state $\{i_1, \ldots, i_n\}$ and a transition from $\{i\}$ into $\{i_1, \ldots, i_n\}$ by r. Once more, for every model M of Σ, the denotation of ir, which is a word "accepted" by state $\{i_1, \ldots, i_n\}$, satisfies

$$[ir]^M = \bigcup_{t \in \{i_1, \ldots, i_n\}} [t]^M \ .$$

If term ir occurs in the completion of the knowledge base, which intuitively means that the "image" of i by r is also always nonempty, but we cannot know exactly to which elements i is related, state $\{ir\}$ is created and there is a transition from $\{i\}$ into $\{ir\}$ by r. The next definitions formalize these intuitions.

We denote by Term_Σ, the set of all terms that occur in some assertion of $\overline{\Sigma}$. Recall that Term is the set of all terms built over the alphabet $\mathrm{Ind} \cup \mathrm{Rel}$, so although $\mathrm{Term}_\Sigma \subseteq \mathrm{Term}$, the inverse relation may not hold.

Let $t \in \mathrm{Term}_\Sigma$ and $r \in \mathrm{Rel}$. The *image* of t by r, $\mathrm{Im}(t, r)$, is defined by:

$$\mathrm{Im}(t, r) = \begin{cases} r(t) & \text{if } t \in \mathrm{Ind} \text{ and } (\exists n > 0)\ t : (\leq n\, r) \in \overline{\Sigma} \ \wedge\ \#r(t) = n, \\ \{tr\} & \text{if the above condition does not hold and } r(t, tr) \in \overline{\Sigma}, \\ \emptyset & \text{otherwise.} \end{cases}$$

When $H \subseteq \mathrm{Term}_\Sigma$, the *image* of H by the relation r, $\mathrm{Im}(H, r)$, is:

$$\mathrm{Im}(H, r) = \begin{cases} \emptyset & \text{if there is some } t \in H \text{ such that } \mathrm{Im}(t, r) = \emptyset, \\ \bigcup_{t \in H} \mathrm{Im}(t, r) & \text{otherwise.} \end{cases}$$

The *automaton* for a satisfiable $\mathcal{ALN}$-knowledge base Σ is the deterministic finite automaton $\mathcal{A}_\Sigma = (V, \Omega, \omega, \delta, F)$, where:

- $V = \mathrm{Ind} \cup \mathrm{Rel}$; % Input alphabet.
- $\Omega = \wp(\mathrm{Term}_\Sigma) \cup \{\omega\}$; % Set of states.
- $\omega \notin \mathrm{Ind} \cup \mathrm{Rel} \cup \mathrm{Term}_\Sigma$; % Initial state.
- $F = \Omega \setminus \{\omega, \emptyset\}$; and % Set of final states.
- $\delta : \Omega \times V \longrightarrow \Omega$ is the function: % Transition function.
  - $\delta(\omega, i) = \{i\}$, for every $i \in \mathrm{Ind}$;
  - $\delta(\omega, r) = \emptyset$, for every $r \in \mathrm{Rel}$;
  - $\delta(H, i) = \emptyset$, for every $H \subseteq \mathrm{Term}_\Sigma$ and every $i \in \mathrm{Ind}$;
  - $\delta(H, r) = \mathrm{Im}(H, r)$, for every $H \subseteq \mathrm{Term}_\Sigma$ and every $r \in \mathrm{Rel}$.

Note that the above construction may produce automata in which some states are inaccessible (from the initial state). To simplify, in the sequel we shall assume that any automaton for a satisfiable $\mathcal{ALN}$-knowledge base Σ is obtained from the previous definition by removing the inaccessible states.

Figure 1 shows the automaton for Σ_{fam}. Also to simplify, state $\emptyset$, which somehow plays the role of an "error state", has not been drawn.

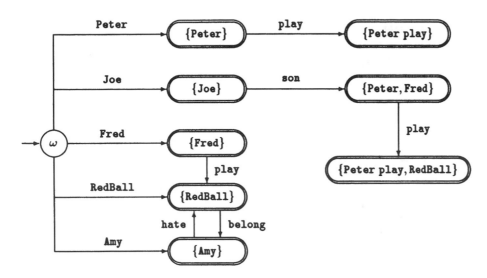

Fig. 1. $\mathcal{A}_{fam}$: the automaton for Σ_{fam}.

Let $\mathcal{A}_{\Sigma} = (V, \Omega, \omega, \delta, F)$ be the automaton for Σ, and $Z \subseteq \Omega$ be a set of states of $\mathcal{A}_{\Sigma}$. We denote by $\mathcal{A}_{\Sigma}(Z)$ the deterministic finite automaton $(V, \Omega, \omega, \delta, Z)$. In addition, given any deterministic finite automaton $\mathcal{A}$, RegExp$(\mathcal{A})$ is a regular expression that denotes the language accepted by $\mathcal{A}$.

For instance, $\mathcal{A}_{fam}(\{\{\mathtt{Amy}\}\})$ is an automaton similar to the one represented in Fig. 1, whose set of final states has just the element $\{\mathtt{Amy}\}$. So, a regular expression denoting the language accepted by $\mathcal{A}_{fam}(\{\{\mathtt{Amy}\}\})$ could be

$$(\mathtt{Amy} + \mathtt{RedBall}\ \mathtt{belong} + \mathtt{Fred}\ \mathtt{play}\ \mathtt{belong})(\mathtt{hate}\ \mathtt{belong})^* \ . \qquad (1)$$

4.2 Query-Answering Algorithm

The query-answering algorithm, presented in Fig. 2, performs three steps. First, the function KbAns(Σ, Q) returns a set X of terms $t \in \text{Term}_{\Sigma}$ that verify $\Sigma \models t : Q$ ((1.1)). Since there may be other terms satisfying the latter condition, the second step looks into the automaton and selects every nonempty state S that is contained in X ((1.2)). Lastly, a regular expression that denotes the language "accepted" by those states is computed and returned ((1.3)).

Let us see an example with the query $Q_2 = \mathtt{child}$, which asks for the children. The function ComputedAnswer$(\Sigma_{fam}, \mathtt{child})$ calls KbAns$(\Sigma_{fam}, \mathtt{child})$ and, since child is a primitive concept, the set $\{t \mid t : \mathtt{child} \in \overline{\Sigma_{fam}}\} = \{\mathtt{Amy}\}$ is returned. Then, we collect all nonempty states S of $\mathcal{A}_{fam}$ contained in $\{\mathtt{Amy}\}$ (see Fig. 1), and the result is $\{\{\mathtt{Amy}\}\}$. So, the returned answer is, for instance, the regular expression (1).

When the query begins with a universal quantifier, the function KbAns starts by calling the procedure Decompose$(Q, Q_1 \sqcap Q_2 \sqcap \cdots \sqcap Q_k)$, which transforms

% $\overline{\Sigma}$ is the completion of Σ, Term$_\Sigma$ is the set of terms occuring in $\overline{\Sigma}$,
% $\mathcal{A}_\Sigma = (V, \Omega, \omega, \delta, F)$ is the automaton for Σ.

ComputedAnswer$(\Sigma, Q) = \{$
(1.1) $X \leftarrow \text{KbAns}(\Sigma, Q);$
(1.2) $Z \leftarrow \{S \in \Omega \mid \emptyset \neq S \subseteq X\};$
(1.3)   **return** $\text{RegExp}(\mathcal{A}_\Sigma(Z))$ $\}.$

KbAns$(\Sigma, Q) = \{$
(2)   **case** Q **of:**

$\top$: **return** Term$_\Sigma$;
$\bot$: **return** $\emptyset$;
$P, \neg P$: **return** $\{t \mid t : Q \in \overline{\Sigma}\};$
$(\leq n\, r)$: **return** $\{t \mid (\exists m \leq n)\ t : (\leq m\, r) \in \overline{\Sigma}\};$
$(\geq n\, r)$: **if** $n = 0$ **then return** Term$_\Sigma$
            else return $\{t \mid (\exists m \geq n)\ t : (\geq m\, r) \in \overline{\Sigma}\};$
$Q_1 \sqcap Q_2$: **return** $\text{KbAns}(\Sigma, Q_1) \cap \text{KbAns}(\Sigma, Q_2);$
$\forall r.Q'$: $\text{Decompose}(Q, Q_1 \sqcap \cdots \sqcap Q_k);$
            return $\bigcap_{i=1}^{k} \text{KbAnsUniv}(\Sigma, Q_i)$

      end case $\}.$

KbAnsUniv$(\Sigma, \forall r_1. \cdots . \forall r_n.C) = \{$
% $n \geq 1$ and C is of the form $\top$, $\bot$, P, $\neg P$, $(\leq m\, r)$ or $(\geq m\, r)$, with $m \geq 0$.
      case C **of:**

$\top$: **return** Term$_\Sigma$;
$\bot$: **return** $\text{KbAns}(\Sigma, \forall r_1. \cdots . \forall r_{n-1}.(\leq 0\, r_n));$
$(\geq 0\, r)$: **return** Term$_\Sigma$;
otherwise :

for $i \leftarrow 0$ **to** n **do**
(3.1) $\Phi_i \leftarrow \{t \mid t : \forall r_{i+1}. \cdots . \forall r_n.C \in \overline{\Sigma}\}$[a]
(3.2) $\cup\ \{t \mid (\exists k = i+1, \ldots, n)\ t : \forall r_{i+1}. \cdots . \forall r_{k-1}.(\leq 0\, r_k) \in \overline{\Sigma}\}$[b]
end for;
for $i \leftarrow n - 1$ **downto** 0 **do**
(3.3) $\Phi_i \leftarrow \Phi_i \cup \{t \mid (\exists S \in \Omega)\ \emptyset \neq \delta(S, r_{i+1}) \subseteq \Phi_{i+1}, t \in S\}$
end for;
return Φ_0
      end case $\}.$

---

[a] When $i = n$, this set is $\{t \mid t : C \in \overline{\Sigma}\}$.
[b] This set is empty when $i = n$, and is $\{t \mid t : (\leq 0\, r_{i+1}) \in \overline{\Sigma}\}$ if $k = i + 1$.

Fig. 2. The abstract query-answering algorithm.

the query Q into a conjunction of $k = j + 1$ queries Q_i where the symbol "$\sqcap$" does not occur (if j is the number of these symbols in Q) by applying the rule

$$\forall r.(C_1 \sqcap C_2) \equiv (\forall r.C_1) \sqcap (\forall r.C_2) \ .$$

For example, if $Q = \forall r.(P \sqcap \forall r'.(\neg P' \sqcap (\geq 3\, r'')))$, the returned query is

$$(\forall r.P) \sqcap (\forall r.\forall r'.\neg P') \sqcap (\forall r.\forall r'.(\geq 3\, r'')) \ .$$

Then, the function KbAnsUniv computes the answer to each

$$Q_i = \forall r_1.\cdots.\forall r_n.C,$$

where $n \geq 1$ and C is of the form $\top$, $\bot$, P, $\neg P$, $(\leq m\, r)$ or $(\geq m\, r)$, with $m \geq 0$. Finally, the answer to Q comprises the terms that are in the answer to all Q_i.

Let us now briefly explain how KbAnsUniv works. In the general case, the algorithm builds $n+1$ sets of terms, Φ_0, Φ_1, ..., Φ_n, which satisfy the following property (with $0 \leq i \leq n$):

$$t \in \Phi_i \Rightarrow [t]^M \subseteq (\forall r_{i+1}.\cdots.\forall r_n.C)^M, \text{ for every model } M \text{ of } \Sigma. \qquad (2)$$

For a term t to belong to Φ_i, at least one of the following conditions must hold:

(3.1) $t : \forall r_{i+1}.\cdots.\forall r_n.C \in \overline{\Sigma}$;
(3.2) $i < n$ and $t : \forall r_{i+1}.\cdots.\forall r_{k-1}.(\leq 0\, r_k) \in \overline{\Sigma}$, for some $k = i+1, \ldots, n$;
(3.3) $i < n$ and there is a state S such that $\emptyset \neq \delta(S, r_{i+1}) \subseteq \Phi_{i+1}$ and $t \in S$.

Condition (3.1) implies (2) because completion rules are sound, i.e., any model of Σ satisfies every assertion generated during the completion process. With respect to (3.2), by hypothesis, $[t]^M \subseteq (\forall r_{i+1}.\cdots.\forall r_{k-1}.(\leq 0\, r_k))^M$, for every model M of Σ, which implies $[t]^M \subseteq (\forall r_{i+1}.\cdots.\forall r_{k-1}.\forall r_k.C')^M$, for every concept C'. Finally, (3.3) follows from the fact that if $t \in S$ and $\delta(S, r_{i+1}) = \{t_1, \ldots, t_k\}$, for some $k \geq 1$, then $r_{i+1}^M([t]^M) \subseteq \bigcup_{j=1}^{k} [t_j]^M$. Since, for every $j = 1, \ldots, k$, $[t_j]^M \subseteq (\forall r_{i+2}.\cdots.\forall r_n.C)^M$, $[t]^M \subseteq (\forall r_{i+1}.\forall r_{i+2}.\cdots.\forall r_n.C)^M$.

Let us see an example, with Σ_{fam} and $Q_3 = \forall play.\forall belong.child$. Since there are no conjunctions in Q_3, procedure Decompose returns Q_3 and function KbAnsUniv(Σ_{fam}, Q_3) is called. Firstly, sets Φ_0, Φ_1 and Φ_2 are initialized with those terms that satisfy either condition (3.1) or (3.2).

$\Phi_0 \leftarrow \emptyset$
$$\emptyset = \{t \mid t : \forall play.\forall belong.child \in \overline{\Sigma_{fam}}\} \qquad (3.1)$$
$$\emptyset = \{t \mid t : (\leq 0\, play) \in \overline{\Sigma_{fam}}\}$$
$$\cup \ \{t \mid t : \forall play.(\leq 0\, belong) \in \overline{\Sigma_{fam}}\} \qquad (3.2)$$

$\Phi_1 \leftarrow \{\text{Peter play}\}$
$$\{\text{Peter play}\} = \{t \mid t : \forall belong.child \in \overline{\Sigma_{fam}}\} \ (3.1)$$
$$\emptyset = \{t \mid t : (\leq 0\, belong) \in \overline{\Sigma_{fam}}\} \qquad (3.2)$$

$\Phi_2 \leftarrow \{\text{Amy}\}$
$$\{\text{Amy}\} = \{t \mid t : child \in \overline{\Sigma_{fam}}\} \qquad (3.1)$$

Secondly, step (3.3) is performed, and some more terms are added to Φ_1 and Φ_0. Note that, in this step, queries are analysed from right to left.

$$\Phi_1 \leftarrow \Phi_1 \cup \{\text{RedBall}\} = \{\text{Peter play}, \text{RedBall}\}$$
$$\text{because} \quad \delta(\{\text{RedBall}\}, \text{belong}) = \{\text{Amy}\} \subseteq \Phi_2 \ .$$

$$\Phi_0 \leftarrow \Phi_0 \cup \{\text{Peter}, \text{Fred}\} = \{\text{Peter}, \text{Fred}\}$$
$$\text{because} \quad \delta(\{\text{Peter}, \text{Fred}\}, \text{play}) = \{\text{Peter play}, \text{RedBall}\} \subseteq \Phi_1$$
$$(\quad \text{or} \quad \delta(\{\text{Peter}\}, \text{play}) = \{\text{Peter play}\} \subseteq \Phi_1$$
$$\text{and} \quad \delta(\{\text{Fred}\}, \text{play}) = \{\text{RedBall}\} \subseteq \Phi_1 \ ) \ .$$

Therefore, the set $\Phi_0 = \{\text{Peter}, \text{Fred}\}$ is returned by $\text{KbAnsUniv}(\Sigma_{fam}, Q_3)$ (and by $\text{KbAns}(\Sigma_{fam}, Q_3)$), which ends phase (1.1). The next step ((1.2)) is to find every nonempty state $S \subseteq \Phi_0$, which led us to the set

$$Z = \{\{\text{Peter}\}, \{\text{Fred}\}, \{\text{Peter}, \text{Fred}\}\} \ .$$

By performing step ((1.3)), the answer Peter + Fred + Joe son is finally computed. Intuitively, it can be read as "Peter, Fred and Joe's sons".

We conclude with the main proposition of this paper.

Proposition 3 (Soudness and Completeness). *Let Σ be a satisfiable $\mathcal{ALN}$-knowledge base and Q be a query. Then, $\text{Answer}(\Sigma, Q)$ is the language denoted by the regular expression $\text{ComputedAnswer}(\Sigma, Q)$.*

5 Conclusion

This work shows that the retrieval problem in a concept language that allows number restrictions can be tackled according to the framework first proposed by Mamede and Monteiro in [12], and later extended in [14]. As in those works, we relied on the notion of term, which extends that of individual, and defined answer as the set of all terms whose nonempty denotation is contained in the denotation of the query, in all models of the knowledge base. We claim that our answers are more informative to the user than the classical ones.

Besides, we proved that concepts of the form $(\leq n\,r)$ and $(\geq n\,r)$, which had not been considered before, are responsible for a possibly infinite number of terms in answers. Due to the fact that answers are regular languages, they may be defined by regular expressions, and we showed how to associate a deterministic finite automaton with the knowledge base, so that answers could be efficiently computed. It turns out that our method is sound and complete.

Concerning future work, and apart from keeping investigating the retrieval problem in other concept languages, we would like to address two points. First of all, we want to study the complexity of this query-answering algorithm. It is easy to verify that if the number of states of the automaton is polynomially bounded by the size of the completion of the knowledge base, we may conclude that our method is tractable. This question is important because Donini, Lenzerini,

Nardi, and Schaerf have already proved that the (classical) retrieval problem in $\mathcal{ALN}$ may be solved in polynomial time (see [9]).

Secondly, we are interested in exploring definitions of answer that eliminate "redundant" terms. For instance, the answer to the last query contains three elements: **Peter**, **Fred**, and **Joe son**. If we took into account that, for every model M of Σ_{fam}, the denotation of **Joe son** in M is the union of the denotations of the first two terms in M (because $[\text{Joe son}]^M = \{\text{Peter}^M, \text{Fred}^M\}$), a more concise answer could contain only the terms **Peter** and **Fred**, or even just the element **Joe son**, in which case the answer would be more intensional[3]. Furthermore, since this redundancy is the source of infinite answers, with these new definitions, answers would become finite sets.

Acknowledgements

This work has been partially supported by ESPRIT BRA 6810 Compulog 2. We would like to thank the referees for their comments and suggestions.

References

1. F. Baader, B. Hollunder. KRIS: Knowledge Representation and Inference System. *SIGART Bulletin*, 2(3):8–14, 1991.
2. F. Baader, B. Hollunder. A Terminological Knowledge Representation System with Complete Inference Algorithms. In *Proc. International Workshop on Processing Declarative Knowledge (PDK'91)*, Kaiserslautern, H. Boley and M. M. Richter (eds.), LNAI 567, Springer-Verlag, 1991.
3. R. Brachman, R. Fikes, H. Levesque. KRYPTON: A Functional Approach to Knowledge Representation. In *Readings in Knowledge Representation*, R. Brachman and H. Levesque (eds.), Morgan Kaufmann, 1985.
4. R. Brachman, H. Levesque. The Tractability of Subsumption in Frame-Based Description Languages. In *Proc. 4th National Conference on Artificial Intelligence (AAAI'84)*, Austin, Texas, 1984.
5. M. Buchheit, F. Donini, A. Schaerf. Decidable Reasoning in Terminological Knowledge Representation Systems. In *Proc. 13th International Joint Conference on Artificial Intelligence (IJCAI'93)*, Chambéry, R. Bajcsy (ed.), Morgan Kaufmann, 1993.
6. W. Cohen, H. Hirsh. Learning the CLASSIC Description Logic: Theoretical and Experimental Results. In *Proc. of the 4th International Conference on Principles of Knowledge Representation and Reasoning (KR'94)*, Bonn, J. Doyle, E. Sandewall and P. Torasso (eds.), Morgan Kaufmann, 1994.
7. F. Donini, M. Lenzerini, D. Nardi, W. Nutt. The Complexity of Concept Languages. In *Proc. of the 2nd International Conference on Principles of Knowledge Representation and Reasoning (KR'91)*, Cambridge, MA, J. A. Allen, R. Fikes and E. Sandewall (eds.), Morgan Kaufmann, 1991.

---

[3] Notice that if we choose the first alternative, answers will still have terms besides individuals. In our knowledge base example, the term **Peter play** cannot be replaced by any set of individuals.

8. F. Donini, M. Lenzerini, D. Nardi, W. Nutt. Tractable Concept Languages. In *Proc. 12th International Joint Conference on Artificial Intelligence (IJCAI'91)*, Sidney, J. Mylopoulos and R. Reiter (eds.), Morgan Kaufmann, 1991.

9. F. Donini, M. Lenzerini, D. Nardi, A. Schaerf. Deduction in Concept Languages: from Subsumption to Instance Checking. *Journal of Logic and Computation*, 4(4):423–452, 1994.

10. M. Lenzerini, A. Schaerf. Querying Concept-based Knowledge Bases. In *Proc. International Workshop on Processing Declarative Knowledge (PDK'91)*, Kaiserslautern, H. Boley and M. M. Richter (eds.), LNAI 567, Springer-Verlag, 1991.

11. R. MacGregor. Inside the LOOM Description Classifier. *SIGART Bulletin*, 2(3):88–92, 1991.

12. M. Mamede, L. Monteiro. Towards Complete Answers in Concept Languages. In *Proc. 6th Portuguese Conference on Artificial Intelligence (EPIA'93)*, Porto, M. Filgueiras and L. Damas (eds.), LNAI 727, Springer-Verlag, 1993.

13. M. Mamede, L. Monteiro. $\mathcal{ALC}$rn: A Decidable Terminological Language with Role Negation. In *Proc. 6th Australian Joint Conference on Artificial Intelligence (AI'93)*, Melbourne, C. Rowles, H. Liu and N. Foo (eds.), World Scientific Publishing, 1993.

14. M. Mamede, L. Monteiro. *Towards More Informative Answers in Terminological Logics*. To appear in *Proc. International KRUSE Symposium — Knowledge Retrieval, Use, and Storage for Efficiency*, Santa Cruz, California, August 1995.

15. B. Nebel. Computational Complexity of Terminological Reasoning in BACK. *Artificial Intelligence*, 34(3):371–383, 1988.

16. B. Nebel. Terminological Reasoning is Inherently Intractable. *Artificial Intelligence*, 43(2):235–249, 1990.

17. P. F. Patel-Schneider. Undecidability of Subsumption in NIKL. *Artificial Intelligence*, 39(2):263–272, 1989.

18. P. Patel-Schneider, D. McGuinness, R. Brachman, L. Resnick, A. Borgida. The CLASSIC Knowledge Representation System: Guiding Principles and Implementation Rationale. *SIGART Bulletin*, 2(3):108–113, 1991.

19. C. Peltason. The BACK System — An Overview. *SIGART Bulletin*, 2(3):114–119, 1991.

20. A. Schaerf. On the Complexity of the Instance Checking Problem in Concept Languages with Existential Quantification. In *Proc. 7th International Symposium on Methodologies for Intelligence Systems (ISMIS'93)*, Trondheim, Norway, J. Komorowski and Z. W. Raś (eds.) LNAI 689, Springer-Verlag, 1993.

21. M. Schmidt-Schauß, G. Smolka. Attributive Concept Descriptions with Complements. *Artificial Intelligence*, 48(1):1–26, 1991.

22. A. Vitória. *Geração de Respostas em Bases de Conhecimento Baseadas em Conceitos*. M.Sc. Thesis, Universidade Nova de Lisboa, 1995 (in portuguese).

Formalizing Local Propagation in Constraint Maintenance Systems

Gilles Trombettoni

INRIA-CERMICS, B.P.93, 06902 Sophia-Antipolis Cedex, France

Abstract. Local propagation is one of the most simple and general ways to maintain the consistency of constraint problems. When some variable's values are changed or when new constraints are added, it allows to incrementally resatisfy a set of constraints by calling local solving methods. This is particularly useful for interactive applications in computer graphics including geometric design and user interface construction.

However, the great weakness of local propagation comes from cycles in the constraint graph so that local propagation is generally viewed as a weak paradigm that should be assisted by more powerful solvers. We claim that local propagation is powerful enough to tackle complex constraint maintenance problems, provided that the solving methods are expressed in a sufficiently general formalism which allows the user to express any solving method in a natural way. Thus, local propagation should be considered the main constraint maintenance engine that can pilot numeric solvers *within* this general formalism. This paper presents this formalism and a local propagation algorithm in two steps that can handle it.

1 Introduction

Local propagation reinstates the constraints initially violated by calling local solving methods. These methods are short procedures that change some variable's values in order to satisfy some constraints, so that the other constraints connected to these variables may become unsatisfied: the application of other methods are necessary and so on by propagation until all the constraints are satisfied. Thus, local propagation mainly deals with *functional* constraints, although this paper extends this notion. For example, the linear and functional constraint $x = y + 1$ has two associated methods calculating a new value for variable x or y: $x \leftarrow y + 1$ and $y \leftarrow x - 1$.

Numerous local propagation algorithms have been embedded in previous systems [2, 11, 1] as a general solving process. Indeed, local propagation allows taking into account heterogeneous types of constraints, in particular non numeric ones. Many development systems of computer graphics applications including *SemDraw* [4], *Thinglab II* [7], *Magritte* [6] and *MultiGarnet* [10] also use local propagation. *MultiGarnet* is based on a powerful propagation algorithm called *SkyBlue* [8, 9].

The basic local propagation mechanism cannot tackle correctly cycles in the constraint graph. Indeed, the application of some methods may lead to a previously encountered state where the same constraints are violated for the second time. And since the variables cannot generally be changed more than once, a failure may occur. Therefore, some existing systems improve the solving process before local propagation by simplifying the constraint graph with rewriting rules [6]. Some systems call external solvers to use iterative methods [2] when a failure caused by a cycle occurs during a stage of local propagation. Finally, others simplify the constraint problem by managing *constraint hierarchies* where sets of required and preferential constraints are maintained [3]. So, most of the improvements take place *outside* local propagation.

This article does deal with the inside of the local propagation process. Using a general formalism to express solving methods, we are able to include any solving knowledge for constraint maintenance within methods. So the algorithm can be viewed as an engine that schedules methods among which some are evaluated by specialized solvers.

First of all, we will present our formalism. Then a small computer graphics example will show the significance of the formalism. Finally, a more theoretical part will present two local propagation algorithms of increasing complexity that deal with the formalism, and the properties they hold.

2 A General Method Formalism

Different levels of method expression derive from existing systems based on local propagation. The most simple systems only authorize *one way* constraints, i.e. methods that only allow constraints to be satisfied in one direction. One way constraints cancel the declarative and multi-directional aspect of constraints which is so important in interactive applications. More powerful systems handle what we will call *simple methods*. This formalism allows *several* methods to satisfy the same constraint in multiple directions (*multi-way* constraints). However these methods only determine *one* variable in order to satisfy only *one* constraint, which prevents the user from describing complex numeric or symbolic solving methods. SkyBlue [8, 9] allows *multi-output* methods that output to several variables. Moreover one SkyBlue constraint may be a conjunction of several more simple ones[1].

The formalism we are going to present is even more general and subsumes the previous ones. We work with a constraint problem (V, C, M) where V and C are the usual sets of variables and constraints. M is the set of methods $m_i = (V_i^{out}, V_i^{in}, C_i, rm_i)$. Every method m_i is a procedure that binds new values to the *output variables* V_i^{out} in order to satisfy the set of *constraints* C_i. During the evaluation of m_i, these new values are calculated by function rm_i that replaces the *input variables* V_i^{in} by their current values in C_i.

We will assume that function rm_i cannot fail. This non fail condition prevents the formalism from dealing with variable's domains: no failure can occur when checking the adequacy of a computed value with its corresponding variable

---

[1] SkyBlue is even more complex since it is conceived to manage constraint hierarchies. Its behavior is described when all the constraints are required.

domain. This hypothesis over methods is far from reality (Take numerical methods depending on input conditions about a matrix or a divide-by-zero error.), but it simplifies the presentation of the paper.

The following terminology will be used in this paper. A *constraint graph* is an undirected bipartite graph formed by constraints and variables, respectively represented by rectangles and circles. It includes edges between each constraint and its variables. This is a syntactic view of a constraint problem and a helpful support to understand local propagation. In order to represent a m_i method, we will use an hyper-arc connecting output variables V_i^{out} and constraints C_i together. A method that satisfies more than one constraint will be called *global* (in opposition to simple methods that satisfy exactly one constraint). We will speak about *more* (or *less*) *global* (or *local*) *methods* according to the number of constraints they can satisfy.

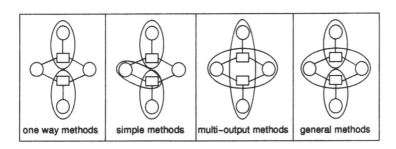

Fig. 1. Four method formalisms of increasing complexity

At first glance, our method formalism seems equivalent to the SkyBlue one. Certainly, this is not far from it but there is a significant difference: plunged in our formalism, the SkyBlue methods M form a partition of the set of constraints. A SkyBlue method m_i that belongs to one element S of the partition is $(V_i^{out}, V_i^{in}, C_S, rm_i)$[2] Even if the SkyBlue constraint C_S is in fact a conjunction of constraints, this means that all the methods in S satisfy the *same set of constraints*. Figure 1 shows a trivial constraint graph where the four types of methods are expressed. Note that we can always express methods of a given formalism by using a more general one.

3 Segments Scared by Walls

This section shows a small example of local propagation for which the general method formalism is necessary. Constraints hold between two horizontal segments I_1 and I_2 whose horizontal position and length may be changed. Figure 2 shows the initial state in plain lines: I_1 and I_2 are vertically centered (constraint

---

[2] In the rest of the article, a maintenance problem where all methods are expressed with this formalism will be named Skyblue problem.

c_2) and must not go beyond their corresponding walls in the right (constraints c_1 and c_3). When the user moves segment I_2, the only solution (according to the methods yielded) is represented in dashed lines.

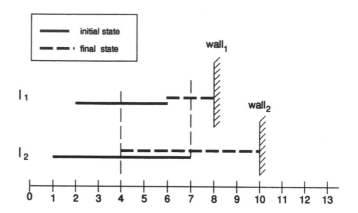

Fig. 2. A global method changes the offset and the length of I_1

We can handle this problem with local propagation as follows. A segment is described by two variables: the horizontal offset of its lower bound (x) and its length (l). The system of simultaneous (in)equations is:

$$\begin{cases} c_1 : x_1 + l_1 \leq wall_1 \\ c_2 : 2x_1 + l_1 = 2x_2 + l_2 \\ c_3 : x_2 + l_2 \leq wall_2 \end{cases}$$

All the simple methods are available. For example, the following method changes l_1 to satisfy c_2: $(\{l_1\}, \{x_1, x_2, l_2\}, \{c_2\}, return\,(2x_2 + l_2 - 2x_1))$. Method m_1 changes variable l_2 to satisfy c_3:

$$m_1 = (\{l_2\}, \{x_2\}, \{c_3\}, when\,(x_2 + l_2 > wall_2)\,then\,return\,(wall_2 - x_2))$$

$wall_1$ and $wall_2$ are constant and m_1 does not change l_2 unless it is necessary. Two more global methods are necessary to maintain the consistency of this system when any variable may be changed. They are symmetric and are represented in figure 3 by hyper-arcs that include their two output variables and their two constraints. One of them, method m_2, deduces values for x_2 and l_2 from the system of simultaneous equations formed with c_2 and the equation corresponding to c_1:

$$m_2 = (\{x_1, l_1\}, \{x_2, l_2\}, \{c_1, c_2\}, return\,(2x_2 + l_2 - wall_1, 2wall_1 - 2x_2 - l_2))$$

Thus, when segment I_2 is moved, local propagation behaves as follows. x_2 is changed so both c_2 and c_3 may be violated. First m_1 is applied to satisfy c_3: in

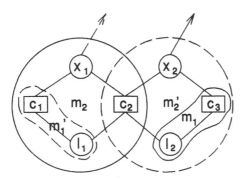

Fig. 3. Constraint graph and methods of the segment problem

our example, c_3 remains satisfied, so method m_1 does not change l_2 (the *when* condition is false). Second, m_2 is applied to satisfy c_2 (and c_1).

Note that the evaluation of the global method m_2 is necessary. Indeed, we could rather evaluate the simple method that changes x_1 to satisfy c_2 (i.e. that makes back the two segments vertically centered by moving segment I_1). However, this may violate c_1 so a simple method that satisfies c_1 must be applied, which violates c_2 for the second time: this cycle cannot be solved with simple methods.

Since the problem is symmetric, the alteration of x_1 implies the application of the sequence of methods m_1', m_2'. The principle is the same when the length of one of these segments is changed. Thus, both m_2 and m_2' must be expressed to handle constraint maintenance when any variable may be changed: a local propagation algorithm that only allows simple methods cannot tackle this problem. Moreover, even SkyBlue cannot tackle this problem: within the Skyblue formalism, m_2 and m_2' cannot be expressed together. Indeed, they both satisfy c_2 while m_2 satisfies c_1 and m_2' satisfies c_3. In fact, the only way to handle this problem with Skyblue is to express all the constraints of the problem with *one* Skyblue constraint. Four methods must then be defined, one for each variable alteration. Each of them is equivalent to two of our methods. This means that the user has to think about all the possible behaviors of his problem. First, local propagation should precisely avoid considering the problem globally and should rather add incrementally the maintenance knowledge split in declarative methods. Second, when the problem grows, this quickly becomes out of question since the number of behaviors may increase in an exponential manner.

4   First Algorithm

Our algorithm is an extension of the Prose one [1] which only handles simple methods. Its mechanism is very close to the SkyBlue one. It works in two steps. The first step builds an *acyclic* directed graph giving a partial order between the methods to apply. The methods are the nodes of the directed graph and the arcs come from the propagation mechanism: an arc from m_i to m_j indicates that at least one output variable v of m_i may violate at least one constraint c of m_j (because c is connected to v). This acyclic directed graph of methods will be named DAGM hereafter. The second step is a topological sort of the partial order computed during the first step. The methods of the obtained sequence are evaluated one by one. Figure 4 describes the first step of the algorithm in details. Function $BuildDagm1$ manages a set L of pairs (m_f, c) where m_f is a method that belongs to the current DAGM and c is a constraint to satisfy. At each step, $BuildDagm1$ handles a pair: a method m_c that satisfies c is added to the current DAGM if necessary and an arc is added from m_f to m_c if a path does not already exist. If a method is added to DAGM, then L is updated with the constraints connected to the output variables of m_c. This process goes on by propagation until L becomes empty (in this case the algorithm succeeds) or until a pair cannot be correctly handled.

```
function BuildDagm1 (DAGM , L)
if L is empty then return DAGM and exit /* first solution found */
else let (m_f, c) be a pair in L:
      if there is already a node m_c in the DAGM that satisfies c then
          if there is a path from m_c to m_f then /* this branch of
             the combinatorial search fails to avoid a cycle */
          else add an arc from m_f to m_c (if necessary)
                  return BuildDagm1 (DAGM , L - (m_f, c))
          e-if
      else /* we must add a method m_c and an arc from m_f to m_c */
          calculate the set S_m of methods that satisfies at least c without
          altering an output variable nor satisfying a constraint
          already enclosed in the DAGM
          if S_m is empty then /* failure: no method to satisfy c */
          else for all method m_c in S_m do /* choice points */
                  – add m_c to the DAGM and an arc from m_f to m_c
                  – let S_new be the set of pairs (m_c, c_i) such that:
                      c_i is connected to an output variable of m_c,
                      c_i is not already satisfied by m_c
                  – return BuildDagm1 (DAGM , L ∪ S_new - (m_f, c))
          e-if
      e-if
e-if
```

Fig. 4. First algorithm

Propagation algorithms are generally called for incremental modifications.

Therefore, this algorithm is able to reuse the previous DAGM when the user incrementally adds new constraints. Thus, parts of the DAGM may remain unchanged.

Compared to existing algorithms, *BuildDagm*1 has several advantages. First, *BuildDagm*1 can handle the general method formalism described above. Second, some existing systems only work over acyclic constraint graphs, which does not allow tackling complex interactive applications. Prose and SkyBlue are more powerful but they may build, during the first step, a *cyclic* directed graph that may be rejected or handled at the second step. The problem is that the first step may yield a cyclic directed graph that will be rejected later, whereas an acyclic one does exist. Although *BuildDagm*1 only builds acyclic directed graphs, the method formalism we propose allows dealing with cyclic problems, as we will see in section 6. *BuildDagm*1 holds the following completeness proposition:

Proposition 1 *BuildDagm*1 *can find every* DAGM *where the output variables are changed at most once and the constraints are satisfied at most once.*

The proof is made by induction over the set of all possible DAGM and is based on the fact that a DAGM necessary increases in a monotone way: *BuildDagm*1 only adds methods or arcs to the current DAGM. Note that any pair in L can be chosen at each step of *BuildDagm*1. Thus, we must carefully check whether no solution is lost when a given pair is handled before another one. In order to ensure this completeness result, each time a pair (m_f, c) is handled, *BuildDagm*1 may make several choice points for every method that can satisfy constraint c. Indeed, the problem of finding a DAGM is NP-complete: reference [7] proved that finding a directed graph for a constraint problem with multi-output methods is already NP-Complete. Page 43 of [9] shows a case where the time complexity is the theoretical worst case, i.e. $O(m^n)$ (n constraints that have m methods each). However, we hope that *BuildDagm*1 has an acceptable average time complexity[3]. This combinatorial search generally works depth first until the first suitable directed graph is found: *BuildDagm*1 may backtrack to reconsider the last choice of method.

Proposition 2 *Consider a SkyBlue problem.*
If a DAGM *(built by any algorithm) satisfies several times some constraints, there is also another* DAGM *that satisfies these constraints at most once. The second* DAGM *uses a subset of the methods used in the first one.*

Note that the algorithm is necessary able to find the second DAGM because of proposition 1. That is why *BuildDagm*1 always prevents from evaluating several methods that all satisfy the same constraints, which limits the choice points. These two propositions emphasize that we do not need a more powerful algorithm to handle any type of solution maintenance problem expressed in

---

[3] According to experimental results in the field of user interface, SkyBlue, which is close to this algorithm, is linear in the number of constraints: the average time is about the double of DeltaBlue [5] (which is $O(mn)$ in the theoretical worst case).

a SkyBlue formalism. This good result also holds for SkyBlue since the two algorithms behave nearly identically over SkyBlue problems.

5 Second Algorithm

Unfortunately, a proposition comparable to proposition 2 does not hold for a general problem.

Proposition 3 *Consider the general method formalism.*
Problems can be found for which the only DAGMs enclose some methods that satisfy the same constraint several times.

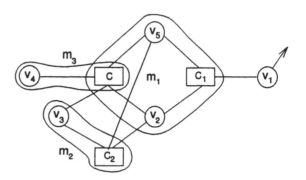

Fig. 5. An example where the only solution satisfies constraint c twice

A proof is given in figure 5. We assume that the only global method is m_1 and that all the simple methods are available except the two ones that satisfy c_1 by changing v_5 or v_2. The only sequence of methods that can lead to a solution is then m_1, m_2, m_3. This sequence is necessarily obtained after a topological sort of a DAGM where both m_1 and m_3 satisfy the same constraint c. This example corresponds to the smallest constraint graph we have found, but does not correspond to a linear constraint problem since, in this case, every simple method could be given. However, even in the field of user interfaces, all constraints are not linear and global methods may include more than two constraints. Moreover, the user may omit an existing method by mistake or on purpose. Indeed, for an obvious runtime complexity preoccupation, local propagation is rarely used to find out all the solutions but only the first one. Thus, faced to an underconstrained problem, the user may be more interested in a solution than in another one: without additional features, including (but not limited to) constraint hierarchies, the main way to force such or such behavior of the system is to forbid some solutions by omitting some of the local methods. Moreover, methods cannot always be deduced automatically by a computer algebra system when constraints of heterogeneous types (especially non numeric constraints) describe the application, which is a cause of user mistakes. For these two main reasons, we do not believe that the expression of methods can be entirely automatized. That is why we have decided to build a new algorithm that can take into account the fact that expressing a method is not always easy and may be a cause of user mistakes. The frame of the algorithm is close to the first one. Figure 6 shows a detailed description of it.

```
function BuildDagm2 (DAGM , L)
if L is empty then return DAGM and exit /* first solution found */
else let (m_f, c) be a pair in L:
    let S_mc be the set of the methods that satisfy c
    let S_mc^{InDag} be the subset of S_mc such that:
        m_c belongs to DAGM,
        m_c has no descendant that satisfies c, (co_1)
        m_c is not an ancestor of m_f
    let S_mc^{OutDag} be the subset of S_mc such that:
        m_c does not belong to DAGM, m_c does not have an output variable
        that is already an output variable of a method in DAGM and
        no set of constraints of a method in S_mc and in DAGM that is
        an ancestor of m_c, is a subset of the constraint's set of m_c (co_2)
    for all method m_i in S_mc^{InDag} ⋃ S_mc^{OutDag} do
        if m_i ⊂ S_mc^{InDag} then
            when there is no path from m_i to m_f then
                add an arc from m_f to m_i in DAGM
            return BuildDagm2 (DAGM , L - (m_f, c))
        else
            add m_i to the DAGM and an arc from m_f to m_i
            let S_new be the set of pairs (m_c, c_i) such that:
                c_i is a constraint connected to an output variable of m_c,
                c_i is not satisfied by m_c
            return BuildDagm2 (DAGM , L ⋃ S_new - (m_f, c))
        e-if
e-if
```

Fig. 6. Second algorithm

Note that if both S_{mc}^{InDag} and S_{mc}^{OutDag} are empty then nothing is done, i.e. the corresponding branch of the combinatorial search fails.

Proposition 4 *If there are DAGMs that prevent methods from changing an output variable several times, then BuildDagm2 can find one of them.*

This is a semi-completeness result (An algorithm is called semi-complete if it can always find at least one possible DAGM, but not all of them.). The algorithm does not find all the DAGMs on purpose: co_1 and co_2 (see figure 6) reject some DAGMs that are not interesting and make useless work. More precisely:

Proposition 5 *If a DAGM (built by any algorithm) does not hold conditions co_1 and co_2, there is also another DAGM that holds these conditions. The second DAGM uses a subset of the methods used in the first one.*

Compared to *BuildDagm1*, the number of choice points is greater. Indeed, an arc is added from m_f to *every* method in S_{mc}^{InDag}, whereas at most one such choice could be made by *BuildDagm1*. Fortunately, the following property holds:

Proposition 6 *Consider a SkyBlue problem and BuildDagm1, BuildDagm2, the two algorithms presented above.*
Both algorithms make the same choice points and thus behave identically.

This proposition comes from condition co_2 that always avoids choosing several methods that satisfy the same constraint when tackling a SkyBlue problem. The additional choice points only occur in the local parts of the constraint graph where the problem cannot be described in a weaker formalism.

6   Handling Cycles

Given the method formalism and the corresponding propagation algorithms, a natural question is how the user can deal with an engine based on them.

In *Constraints* [12], where only simple methods can be expressed, a method is declared in the same location as its corresponding output variable. In SkyBlue, the meaning of a constraint is specified entirely by its methods. Our formalism leads to clearly separate methods from constraints and variables. Compared to existing systems, this should not make less easy to predict the behavior of propagation. First, although the method formalism is useful, we think that an overriding majority of methods can be expressed in a SkyBlue formalism. Second, we have only proposed algorithms but not a complete system. So, additional syntactic features would allow putting in one location all the simple methods concerned by the same constraint, just like in SkyBlue: only rare global methods would then make more complex the approach of a system behavior.

Moreover, all the constraint maintenance knowledge can be described within the method formalism. In fact, we should compare the first step of our propagation algorithms with a compiler. The returned DAGM can then be viewed as the result of the compilation. This "runtime program" is executed during the second step and behaves according to the variable's values and the way in which the methods are evaluated. The compiler is able to schedule precisely when such or such external program (i.e. solver) will be called. Thus, our local propagation algorithms are able to be the main engine that schedules methods among which some may be evaluated by external solvers including symbolic (computer algebra) and numeric systems. And since our algorithms hold completeness properties that ensure that any solution will be found if it does exist, then these properties will hold over classical methods as well as over external ones.

The main issue is a way to deal with cycles in the constraint graph, because the compiler is able to know whether a powerful method can or cannot break a cycle by only considering its inputs and outputs. Therefore a cyclic directed graph can be rejected as soon as it appears *during* the first step (every node in a DAGM contains the set of its ancestors).

We encourage to express the solving methods as follows. We should first add local methods. If cycles prevent from finding a solution, we should then add more global ones to break them and so on until a solution is obtained: the methods should be global enough to avoid such failures, but local enough to prevent solutions from changing too many variables.

7   Conclusion and Future Works

We have proposed a new formalism to express local methods. This formalism makes the methods independent of the constraint graph. The user should express methods local enough to allow an incremental constraint maintenance when perturbations are added. However, more global methods are sometimes necessary to avoid failures due to cycles in the constraint graph.

Two new algorithms have been developed to take into account this formalism. The first one is powerful enough to tackle SkyBlue problems. The second one is semi-complete over general problems, provided that all the variables cannot be determined more than once. It is useful when some methods are missing. Indeed, we have considered that all the methods are not generally given and that they may be given by hand, which is a cause of mistakes.

The two algorithms make a combinatorial search with an increasing complexity. The second one makes some additional choice points since it returns DAGMs in which several methods may satisfy several times the same constraint. However, it is carefully built to forestall a combinatorial explosion and it behaves just like the first one when tackling SkyBlue problems. Although the general method formalism is useful, we think that an overriding majority of methods can be expressed in a SkyBlue formalism. Thus, we trust that the algorithms presented are nearly as efficient as SkyBlue.

We intend to implement the algorithms with efficient data structures and to apply them to a real world software in the field of computer graphics. This would also get a better idea of the average time complexity of the algorithms. A small language for expressing the methods should also be developed in order to allow the user to manage our method formalism. Furthermore, we will see how far the expression of methods can be automatized with symbolic or numeric systems. If the time complexity makes the algorithms usable for an interactive behavior, we will think about four main improvements.

First, we will maybe remove the hypothesis of *BuildDagm2* stating that a variable can be altered at most once. Are there cases for which this hypothesis can avoid finding a solution? Second, the algorithms should be changed (especially the second step) in order to allow a method to return *several* possible values for the ouput variables. Third, up to now, the user can modify the behavior of the algorithms by only giving some of the methods. This is contrary to declarativity. Maybe, the formalism should be extended by additional features that dynamically allow choosing first such method rather another one. Finally, when the algorithm will be stable, we will improve it in order to take into account priorities between constraints.

Acknowledgements

Thanks to B. Neveu for many useful discussions. Thanks to P. Berlandier, N. Chleq and B. Vigot for comments on the paper.

References

1. P. Berlandier. *A Study of Constraint Interpretation Mechanisms and of their Integration in a Knowledge Representation Language*. PhD thesis, University of Nice, 1992. (in french).
2. A. Borning. THINGLAB: *A Constraint-Oriented Simulation Laboratory*. PhD thesis, Stanford University, 1979.
3. A. Borning, B. Freeman-Benson, and Molly Wilson. Constraint hierarchies. *Lisp and Symbolic Computation*, 5(3):223–270, September 1992.
4. B. Chabrier. *Interfaces par contraintes graphiques*. PhD thesis, Université de Nice Sophia–Antipolis, 1993.
5. B. Freeman-Benson, J. Maloney, and A. Borning. An incremental constraint solver. *Communications of the ACM*, 33(1), 1990.
6. J. Gosling. *Algebraic Constraints*. PhD thesis, Carnegie–Mellon University, 1983.
7. J. Maloney. *Using Constraints for User Interface Construction*. PhD thesis, University of Washington, August 1991. PhD Thesis, published as Departement of Computer Science and Engineering Technical Report 91-08-12.
8. M. Sannella. The skyblue constraint solver and its applications. In *Proc. workshop PPCP*, Rhode Island, USA, 1993.
9. M. Sannella. The skyblue constraint solver. Technical Report 92–07–02, Department of Computer Science and Engineering, University of Washington, February 1993.
10. M. Sannella and A. Borning. Multi-garnet: Integrating multi-way constraints with garnet. Technical Report 92–07–01, Department of Computer Science and Engineering, University of Washington, September 1992.
11. G. Steele. *The Definition and Implementation of a Computer Programming Language Based on Constraints*. PhD thesis, Massachusetts Institute of Technology, 1980.
12. G. Sussman and G. Steele. CONSTRAINTS: A language for expressing almost-hierarchical descriptions. *Artificial Intelligence*, 14:1–39, 1980.

A Dependency Parser of Korean Based on Connectionist/Symbolic Techniques*

Jong-Hyeok Lee and Geunbae Lee

Department of Computer Science,
Pohang University of Science and Technology,
San 31 Hyoja-dong Nam-ku, Pohang 790-784, Korea

Abstract. This paper suggests a hybrid method for dependency parser of Korean which integrates both connectionist and symbolic techniques. First, the dependency parser tries to identify syntactic dependencies between individual words, specifying the grammatical role of dependency in each case. In most normal cases, a symbolic approach can work well, but a connectionist approach is also used for handling the cases where case-markers are omitted in a sentence. All the plausible dependencies are kept in a Syntactic Dependency Graph (SDG). Then, structural disambiguation is carried out by a constraint satisfaction process, in which various constraints on dependency structure are propagated through SDG to filter out inconsistent dependencies. For an efficient control mechanism, a forward checking algorithm is used together with both variable-ordering and value-ordering heuristics. Finally, the experiment showed very promising results with parsing accuracy of above 90% for sentences of less than 10 Korean words.

1 Introduction

Traditionally most syntactic parsers of a rigid word-order language like English or French have been developed on the basis of a phrase-structure grammar (PSG). However, it has been argued that PSG is not adequate for a relatively free word-order language like Korean, Japanese, Turkish, or Finnish. In such languages, there is no syntactic constraint on the ordering of the nominal arguments of a verb, as long as the verb remains in final position. Furthermore, the variable word order often results in discontinuous constituents. A phrase-structure tree for such a scrambled sentence would have crossing branches, which PSG disallows. Unlike PSG, a dependency grammar (DG) does not divide a sentence up into constituents; instead, it identifies the grammatical relations that connect one word to another. This is known to be advantageous for dealing with discontinuity [1]. Almost all known parsing algorithms are based on PSG, while efficient parsing strategies for DG are still unavailable.

---

* This research was supported by KOSEF(Korea Science and Engineering Foundation), Korea-China cooperative project (93.5-95.5)

In this paper, we propose a two-phase parsing method for DG: the first phase is to identify the syntactic dependencies that connect one word to another, specifying the type of dependencies in each case, and then to build a Syntactic Dependency Graph (SDG), and the second is to remove all the inconsistent dependencies from the SDG. For these, both connectionist and symbolic techniques are used, because they show mutually complementary properties so that a hybrid symbolic/connectionist system may be more powerful than a system operating only within one paradigm [2]. In this paper, Yale Romanization is used for representing Korean words and sentences.

2 Characteristics of Korean Compared with English

Korean, as an agglutinative language, has a rich and complex morphology as opposed to English with simple word structures. ¿From the viewpoint of word order typology, Korean is a relatively free word-order SOV language, while English is a rigid word-order SVO language. And also, according to the typology based on the grammatical relations, Korean is topic-prominent as well as subject-prominent. English is, however, only subject-prominent, which means that English has almost no topic notion. Because of these typological differences, Korean shows the following characteristics as opposed to English, some of which are very hard to model only within a symbolic rule-based paradigm:

Word Order Variations Korean allows considerably more variation of word order than does English. In fact, Korean has almost no constraints on word order, except for the very rigid constraint that the verb must appear in final position of a sentence. The variable word order may often results in discontinuous constituents. A phrase-structure grammar (PSG) has been argued to be inadequate for dealing with discontinuity even though many linguists have tried to augment PSG [1]. Unlike PSG, a dependency grammar (DG) analyzes a sentence by establishing dependency relationships between individual words, specifying the type of dependency in each case. This is advantageous in languages where the word order is variable and many of the constituents are discontinuous.

Postpositioning of Governor Even a variable word-order language has some constraints on word order. In verb-final languages such as Korean and Japanese, a governor (head) appears after its dependent (modifier) in a sentence, while in English there is no consistent rule of word order between a governor and its dependent [3]. The governor's postpositioning constraint must be strictly obeyed in normal sentences.

Complex Word Structures A Korean word called *eojeol* usually consists of one lexical morpheme accompanied by one or more grammatical morphemes. In other words, a lexical stem may be combined with several inflectional suffixes to form a word. In dependency analysis, the governing attribute of an *eojeol* is determined by part-of-speech of its lexical stem, while the dependent attribute by its inflectional suffixes such as case-marking particles, auxiliary particles, and verb endings.

Auxiliary Particles Instead of Case-markers Korean, as a topic-prominent
language, has a morphological topic-marker *(n)un* as well as a subject-marker
ka/i. The topic-marker can be used in place of some case-markers such as
subject and *object* to represent which constituent is the topic in a sentence.
In that case, it becomes difficult to distinguish the type of case marking.
Besides the topic-marker, there are also lots of auxiliary particles that can
take place of case-markers.

Frequently-Occurred Ellipses In a Korean sentence, many constituents may
be omitted more frequently than in English. In general, although the missing
parts need not be recovered completely, types of their grammatical relations
should be inferred to correctly interpret the other relations.

3   Overview of Two-Phase Dependency Parser

In this section, we'll give an overall introduction of the two-phase dependency
parser that has been developed under a hybrid connectionist/symbolic approach.

3.1   Syntactic Dependency Relationship

There are two diametrically opposed methods of describing the syntactic structure of natural sentences: phrase-structure (PS-) trees and dependency (D-)
trees. Since the PS-tree is based on grouping of words into larger constituents,
non-terminal nodes stand for groupings, and terminal nodes for words. And also
some linear order of nodes is unavoidable. On the contrary, D-tree is based on relationships between words, so that a D-tree should contain only terminal nodes,
and moreover the nodes need not be in linear order at all. As mentioned above,
this is advantageous in languages with word order variability. And further, the
D-tree is known to be an ideal bridge between a semantic structure and a morpheme chain. However, there have been also a number of unjustified criticisms
of D-tree that claim its insufficiency or inadequacy. These can be divided into
three major groups: double dependency, mutual dependency, and no dependency.
But all of these are mostly due to the failure to distinguish a purely syntactic
dependency from semantic and morphological dependencies as discussed by [4].
As a result, all dependencies that we try to establish between words are purely
syntactic.

Consider, for instance, a simple sentence of three words '*na-nun say-lul po-
nta*' which means that I see a bird. The first word *na-nun* (I-TOP) can be
syntactically connected to the third word *pon-ta* (see), and the syntactic dependency between them should be labeled with the grammatical role *subject*. In
general the grammatical role labeling is not so simple, especially when a case-
marker is omitted or replaced with other auxiliary particles like topic-marker
-nun. Since the second word *say-lul* (bird-OBJ) has an *object* case-marker, it can
be easily connected to the predicate *pon-ta* (see), but it cannot have any connection with the first one *na-nun* (I-TOP). Unlike English, the double-subject and
double-object constructions are common in Korean. So we define 11 grammatical

roles for labeling the interword dependencies: *subject, subject2, object, object2, indirect object, complement, adverbial, adjectival, subordinate, coordinate,* and *connective.*

3.2 Two-Phase Parsing Strategy

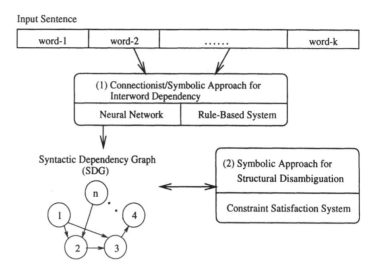

Fig. 1. Overall Architecture of Two-Phase Dependency Parser

The proposed parser consists of two phases as shown in Fig. 1. The first phase is to identify the syntactic dependencies between individual words, specifying the grammatical role of dependency in each case. Here, we do not have to check all possible pairs of words in a sentence, because, as mentioned above, Korean obeys the so-called *governor's postpositioning* constraint. So we can reduce a large amount of checking time. All the plausible syntactic dependencies between words are collectively represented in a Syntactic Dependency Graph (SDG).

Since the initial SDG is built only from the viewpoint of interword level, it is natural that lots of structural ambiguities appear in it. The second phase is to resolve such structural ambiguities, that is, to remove all inconsistent (i.e. ungrammatical) dependencies from the initial SDG. The structural disambiguation can be viewed as a constraint satisfaction problem, in which various sentence-level constraints on dependency are propagated through SDG to effectively eliminate inconsistent dependencies.

4 Identifying Syntactic Dependencies between Words

Among the inflectional suffixes of words, the case-marking particles are essential for the identification of syntactic dependency between a predicate and its nominal arguments. So, in most normal cases, a symbolic rule-based system works well only relying on case-markers. But, if a case-marker is omitted or replaced with an auxiliary particle like topic-marker, to make matters worse, if two or more nominal arguments of a predicate lose their case-markers, it is almost impossible to identify the type of dependency between them without semantic information.

4.1 Learning Dependencies in Backpropagation Network

Since, in a symbolic rule-based system, it is very hard to find regularities of *syntactic* dependencies between *semantic* categories, a connectionist approach is used to learn the underlying regularities from a training set.

For this, two backpropagation nets are used: one for checking whether the dependency is possible or not, and the other for determining the type of grammatical roles of dependency. Each net consists of three layers of units as shown in Fig. 2. The input layer, which is shared by the two nets, consists of 35 binary units (value 0 or 1). Among them, 15 binary units are for directly representing 15 syntactic features, and 20 units for encoding 2,000 semantic features of two words. SYN stands for the local representation of syntactic features, and SEM for the distributed coding of semantic features. For output layers, the first net has a single binary unit indicating Yes/No of dependency, while the second net has eleven real-valued units each of which produces the plausibility value of its corresponding grammatical role. Seven real-valued hidden units encode the mapping from the input units to output units from a training set, and the hidden layers are fully connected between the input and output layers.

First, we randomly extracted 463 sentences from our corpus, and then built one training set for each net based on them. Each training example of training sets consists of two feature vectors for two input words together with a feature vector for the dependency between these words. The training set for the first net consists of 933 positive and 2,809 negative examples. However, the second net uses only the positive exampes. After the training phase was completed, the trained nets were tested with both the training and test sets, which showed error rates of 9% and 17%, respectively.

4.2 Syntactic Dependency Graph

A Syntactic Dependency Graph (SDG), which keeps all the plausible syntactic dependencies between words, is a labeled weighted digraph. As shown in Fig. 3, a node stands for a single category of word, so a multi-category word should be represented as several nodes, one for each syntactic/semantic category. An arc stands for a syntactic dependency between two nodes with an arrow directed from *governor* to *dependent*, and also is labeled with a grammatical role. An arc weight, a plausibility value, is computed by the neural network on the basis of

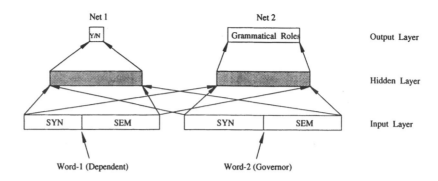

Fig. 2. Two Backpropagation Nets for Learning Dependency Relationships

semantic features as well as syntactic ones. This means that semantic knowledge must be reflected in arc weights to some extent. So, in the structural disambiguation, the plausibility values can be used to eliminate inconsistent arcs from the semantic viewpoint. All words are numbered to indicate their linear order in a sentence. Because of the principle of *postpositioning of governor*, an SDG can be internally represented by a triangular table rather than a whole one.

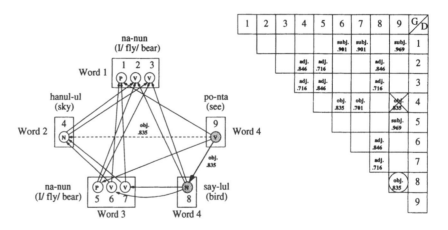

	1	2	3	4	5	6	7	8	9	G/D
						subj. .901	subj. .901		subj. .969	1
				adj. .846	adj. .716			adj. .846		2
				adj. .716	adj. .846			adj. .716		3
						obj. .835	obj. .701	obj. .835		4
								subj. .969		5
								adj. .846		6
								adj. .716		7
									obj. .835	8
										9

Fig. 3. Initial SDG for sentence *na-nun hanul-ul na-nun say-lul po-nta* (I see a bird flying in the sky)

5 Structural Disambiguation

5.1 Formulation of Disambiguation as CSP

In an initial SDG, any word with two or more incoming arcs indicates that its syntactic role is not determined yet. Such dependent word has to be assigned a single incoming arc (that is, grammatical role) toward its unique governor. This constraint is so universal that any dependency structure should obey it regardless of languages. Since our goal is to find all such assignments to words such that the assignments satisfy all dependency constraints including the principle of *uniqueness of governor*, the structural disambiguation can be viewed as a constraint satisfaction problem (CSP) over a finite domain as discussed in [5]:

1. A set of variables V_i : *dependent* words
2. A set of domain D_i : arcs (grammatical roles)
3. A set of constraints C_i : dependency constraints

5.2 Dependency Constraints

Since all the so-far-identified dependencies are only based on knowledge of inter-word level, it is no wonder that an initial SDG should contain lots of structural ambiguities, which have to be solved with dependency constraint knowledge of sentence level. In our system, several kinds of dependency constraints are used for structural disambiguation:

Uniqueness of Governor No word may simultaneously depend on two or more other words. That is, every word, except the root word, has just one syntactic governor. So, the *double dependency* is not allowed [4] [6].

Postpositioning of Governor A governor (head) appears after its dependent (modifier) in a sentence. This holds true in most of OV languages such as Korean and [3].

Uniqueness of Category A multi-category word is represented by more than one node at the same word position. But, even in such case one and only one node, except the root, must participate in every meaning interpretation [7].

Non-Crossing of Arcs In a dependency structure, any arc cannot cross another. This constraint is sometimes called *adjacency condition* or *projectivity*. In general, the variable word order may often result in discontinuous constituents, that are represented by crossing arcs. However, unlike Russian, the discontinuity is not so common in Korean, so we impose the constraint as did many linguists [1].

Uniqueness of Grammatical Role No word can govern more than one word with the same grammatical role.

5.3 Forward Checking Algorithm and Heuristics

There are two major schemes for solving constraint satisfaction problems (CSP): backtracking and constraint propagation [8]. The first scheme tries to test different possible combinations of variable assignments until a complete solution is found. It is essentially a depth-first search process, and its time complexity for most nontrivial problems is exponential. The second scheme propagates constraints between different variables to derive a simpler problem. This approach is usually more expensive than simple backtracking.

As a third possible scheme, a number of hybrid algorithms have been investigated by various researchers. And the forward checking (FC) by [9] is one of the well-known hybrid algorithms: Whenever a new variable instantiation is made, the domains of all as-yet-uninstantiated variables are filtered to contain only those values that are consistent with this instantiation. If the domains of any of these uninstantiated variables become null, then failure is recognized, and backtracking occurs [8].

In the FC algorithm, the order in which variables are chosen for instantiation is very important to the efficiency of backtrack search. One powerful variable-ordering heuristic by [10] is to select the variable with the fewest possible remaining alternatives. Once a variable is selected for instantiation, it can have several values available. Since the order in which these values are considered can have substantial impact on the time to find the first solution, we also need a good value-ordering heuristic.

5.4 Control Flow of Disambiguation

The structural disambiguation as CSP is based on the FC algorithm with both variable-ordering and value-ordering heuristics. The control flow of disambiguation is illustrated in Fig. 4.

As mentioned above, the variable-ordering heuristic is very important to the efficiency of backtracking search. To realize the powerful heuristic developed by [10] that is often used with the FC algorithm, we select variables (i.e. words) for instantiation as follows:

1. First, select the word that has the fewest total sum of incoming arcs.
2. If there exists more than one satisfying the above, then select the word with the fewest categories.

The value-ordering heuristic can also have substantial impact on the time to find the first solution. We prefer the incoming arc (i.e. grammatical role) with the largest plausibility value at the selected word position.

6 Example: Disambiguation Process

In this section, we will give a step-by-step example of structural disambiguation based on FC algorithm. Consider an example sentence '*na-nun hanul-ul na-nun*

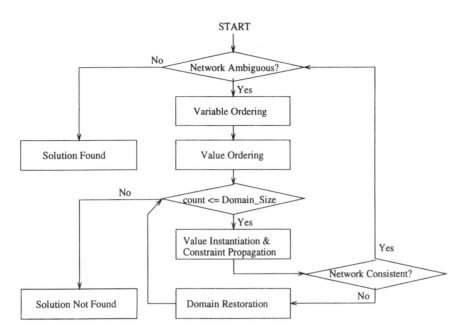

Fig. 4. Control Flow of Disambiguation

say-lul po-nta' which means that I see a bird flying in the sky. Figure 3 shows its initial SDG together with its internal triangular representation, where some information is omitted to simplify the following explanation. Note that the word *na-nun* has multiple categories, and appears twice in a sentence, at the word 1 and 3 positions. But, the former is used as a personal pronoun (I) while the latter as a verb (fly).

First, according to the variable-ordering heuristic, the word 4 *say-lul* (bird) is selected for variable instantiation, because it has the fewest incoming arcs except the word 5 that is a root node. The selected word 4 (i.e. node 8) has only one incoming arc (9,8), the value ordering is unnecessary. Here, as a notation, let (i,j) represent a directionality from node i to node j. Once the word 4 is assigned the incoming arc (9,8) labeled *object*, the domains of all as-yet-uninstantiated nodes are filtered by constraint propagation to contain only those values that are consistent with this instantiation. For example, the arc (9,4) labeled *object* can be removed from the domain of node 4, because it violates the constraint of *uniqueness of grammatical role*. Figure 5 illustrates the result of SDG after filtering, where with a circle, and the deleted value with a cross in the triangular table.

Second, for the next instantiation, the variable-ordering heuristic selects the word 2 because it has the fewest two incoming arcs like (6,4) and (7,4) The arc (6,4) has larger plausibility value than the arc (7,4), so the arc (6,4) is assigned to the word 2 (i.e. node 4). After instantiation of word 2, the constraint propagation

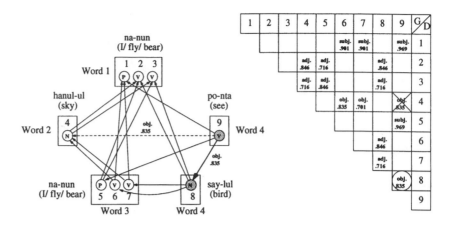

Fig. 5. Constraint Propagation Process (I)

can remove six inconsistent arcs such as (9,5), (8,7), (7,1), (7,4), (5,2), and (5,3), as shown in Fig. 6. This is because they violate the constraint of *uniqueness of category*.

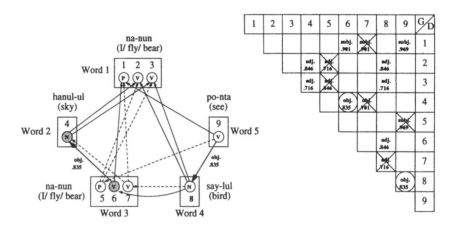

Fig. 6. Constraint Propagation Process (II)

In a similar way, we can assign the arc *modifier* to node 2, and then a value *subject* to node 0. Consequently, we obtain the most preferable dependency structure for the given sentence as shown in Fig. 7. In case of an ambiguous sentence, other dependency structures can be also selected by backtracking.

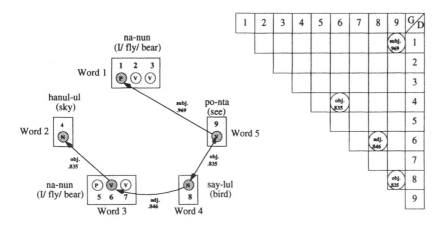

Fig. 7. Final SDG

7 Experiment

The proposed two-phase parser has been implemented on a Sun 10 workstation in C language. In the experiment, two hundred and more sentences of various constructions were parsed. These sentences were mostly from the book by [11], because it is the first book on Korean grammar written from the viewpoint of computational linguistics, giving a lot of examples of various sentence types. And further, we added somewhat long sentences from elementary text books. The length of sentences ranged from 2 to 24.

The experimental results are summarized in Table 1. For the sentences of less than 10 *eojeols* (Korean words), the two-phase dependency parser shows the high accuracy of above 90%. Especially, all sentences of 7 *eojeols* and below were all parsed correctly. This is a surprising result. As mentioned previously, the first phase of our parser for identifying dependencies relies on semantic features as well as syntactic ones. So, the high accuracy may be due to the shallow processing of semantics. On the other hand, for the long sentences, the parsing accuracy dropped radically to about 70%. The longer a sentence is, the more rapidly the number of candidate dependencies increases. What is worse, such a long sentence usually has a complex conjunctive structure that the parser still cannot handle it. As a result, although the proposed parser still has some problems that have to be solved, it shows a very promising accuracy for dependency parsing.

8 Conclusion

We have proposed a hybrid connectionist/symbolic method for two-phase dependency parsing of Korean. The first phase uses both symbolic rules and neural nets for establishing all plausible syntactic dependencies between words. The second one is a symbolic system for structural disambiguation that can be formulated

Table 1. Results of Dependency Parsing

Sentence size (eojeols)	Number of sentences	Average number of dependencies	Number of correctly parsed sentences	Parsing accuracy
below 3	37	5.96	37	100%
4-5	94	10.74	94	100%
6-7	25	18.19	25	100%
8-9	20	24.62	18	90%
10-11	11	29.67	9	81.8%
12-13	14	37.42	10	71.4%
above 14	11	58.92	7	63.6%
Total	212	17.40	200	94.3%

as a constraint satisfaction problem. The experiment showed very promising results with parsing accuracy of above 90% for sentences of less than 10 *eojeols* (Korean words). We plan to use the two-phase dependency parser for a Korean-to-Chinese machine translation system that has been under development as a joint project with Northeastern University of China.

References

1. Covington, M. A.: *A Dependency Parser for Variable-Word-Order Languages.* Research Report AI-1990-01, Artificial Intelligence Programs, Univ. of Georgia, (1990)
2. Wermter, S., Lehnert, W. G.: *A Hybrid Symbolic/Connectionist Model for Noun Phrase Understanding.* In N. Sharkey(ed) it Connectionist Natural Language Processing: Readings from Connection science. London: Kluwer Academic Publishers (1992) 101–118
3. Kodama, T.: *Studies in Dependency Grammar.* Tokyo: Kenkyusha (1987) (written in Japanese).
4. Mel'čuk, I. A.: *Dependency Syntax: Theory and Practice.* New York: State University of New York Press (1988)
5. Maruyama, H.: *Structural Disambiguation with Constraint Propagation.* Proceedings of the 28th Annual Meeting of the ACL (1990) 31–38
6. Robinson, J. J.: *Dependency Structures and Transformation Rules.* Languages **46** (1970) 259–285
7. Seo, J., Simmons, R.: *Syntactic Graphs: a Representation for the Union of All Ambiguous Parse Trees.* Computational Linguistics **15(7)** (1988) 19–32
8. Kumar, V.: *Algorithms for Constraint-Satisfaction Problems: A Survey.* AI Magazine **Spring** (1992) 32–44
9. Haralick, R., Elliot, G.: *Increasing Tree Search Efficiency for Constraint-Satisfaction Problems.* Artificial Intelligence **14(3)** (1980) 263–313
10. Bitner, J., Reingold, E. M.: *Backtrack Programming Techniques* **18** (1975) 651–655
11. Chang, S.: *Information-Based Korean Grammar.* Seoul: Language & Information Research Assn. (1993) (written in Korean)

A Symbiotic Approach
to Arc and Path Consistency Checking

Pierre Berlandier

SECOIA Project, INRIA-CERMICS,
2004, Route des Lucioles, B.P. 93, 06902 Sophia-Antipolis Cedex

Abstract. The resolution of constraint satisfaction problems heavily relies on the use of local consistency enforcement procedures which are used to filter the problems before or during their resolution. While procedures based on arc-consistency are almost a standard, path-consistency checking is often neglected because it is costly and it filters out pairs of assignments instead of single assignments. This paper presents a domain filtering procedure that tightly combines the use of arc and path-consistency, each one helping the other to achieve further or faster work. We show, on an experimental evaluation, that the proposed procedure offers a considerable filtering power at relatively low cost.

1 Introduction

Constraint satisfaction problems (CSP) have proved useful in the encoding of various instances of practical combinatorial problems (e.g. planning, scheduling, resource allocation). A great part of the success of the CSP approach is due to the simplicity of the formalism: a CSP is simply defined by a set of variables, each having a finite domain, and a set of constraints, each connected to a subset of the variables. Constraints are partial informations that restrict the values that can be assigned simultaneously to their variables.

Still, enforcing the *global consistency* of a CSP (i.e. finding a solution) is an NP-complete problem. It is usually attacked with now sophisticated [1] but still exponential search procedures. Therefore, it is crucial to narrow the search space as much as possible by enforcing some level of *local consistency* with a polynomial time filtering procedure.

Currently, the best known levels of local consistency are arc and path consistency (resp. AC and PC). The first one is used almost universally because it can be computed at low cost and its enforcement simply comes down to the elimination of some value assignments (which is quite valuable since value elimination represents a maximal simplification operation with regard to the problem combinatorics).

Now, except for some temporal reasoning applications, path-consistency (PC) does not have the same good press. We can give at least two reasons for this. A first one is that the ratio between the complexity of computing PC and the simplification factor it brings is far less interesting than the one brought by AC. A second reason is that enforcing PC entails the deletion of *couples* of value assignments, by opposition to single value assignments with AC [2]. To rule out a given couple between two variables, it is necessary either to tighten the constraint between the two variables or to create this constraint if it does not exist. These two possible actions are illustrated respectively on figure 1 and 2.

- *Couples deletion.* Figure 1.1 shows a very simple constraint problem between three variables i, j and k such that $i \neq j$, $i = k$ and $j = k$. As it is displayed, the problem is arc-consistent. Now, if we check the path-consistency of variables i and j, we realize that there is no path from the assignment $\langle i, a \rangle$ (resp. $\langle i, b \rangle$) to $\langle j, b \rangle$ (resp. $\langle j, a \rangle$) through k. The two couples (a, b) and (b, a) can thus be ruled-out from the relation R_{ij} as shown on figure 1.2 and the problem is left trivially unsatisfiable.

  Here, tightening the constraint was an easy operation since it was linked to a set of tuples. However, it would not be so straightforward if the constraint was linked to an intensive representation as it is the case for most real-world CSP-encoded problems.

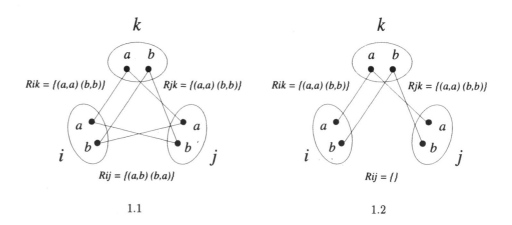

1.1   1.2

Fig. 1. enforcing path-consistency deletes some tuples

- *Constraint addition.* Figure 2.1 shows a problem which has only two constraints: $i = k$ and $j = k$. Figure 2.2 shows the resulting problem after path-consistency filtering has been applied: the constraint C_{ij} has been created to represent the fact that the couples of assignments $(\langle i, a \rangle, \langle j, b \rangle)$ and $(\langle i, b \rangle, \langle j, a \rangle)$ are inconsistent. Such a dynamic change (increase) of the connectivity of the constraint graph is often not desirable and sometimes not even feasible.

So, with the above two drawbacks in mind, we decided to implement an algorithm that restrict the scope of problem filtering with path-consistency to

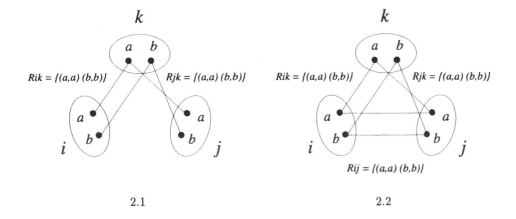

Fig. 2. enforcing path-consistency adds a new constraint

the case where the deletion of some couples of value assignments implies the deletion of one of the two assignments.

Such a situation occurs when all the couples that are representing the supports of an assignment are deleted by path-consistency. For example, in figure 1, after we had determined by PC that the couple $(\langle i,a\rangle,\langle j,b\rangle)$ is inconsistent, $\langle i,a\rangle$ was left without any support on j. Then, instead of going on with some costly path-consistency filtering, we could immediately ask to check again the arc-consistency, an operation that would quickly determine that the problem is inconsistent.

Our principle of cooperation between arc and path-consistency is thus the following: when AC is enforced and cannot filter any additional values, PC is used with the goal of finding an unsupported assignment. As soon as one such assignment is found, AC is called back to work. The rest of the paper details the implementation of this symbiosis: in section 2, after recalling some definitions about CSP, arc and path-consistency, we present our filtering algorithm and in section 3, we evaluate experimentally its merits on some randomly generated constraint problems.

2 Algorithm

For the sake of clarity, we will restrict ourselves in this paper to binary CSPs. A binary constraint satisfaction problem P can be formally defined by a quadruple $\langle \mathcal{V}, \mathcal{D}, \mathcal{C}, \mathcal{R} \rangle$ in which:

- $\mathcal{V}$ is a set of n variables $\{1, \ldots, n\}$;
- $\mathcal{D}$ is the set of domains $\{D_1, \ldots, D_n\}$ corresponding to each variable. A value assignment $\langle i,a\rangle$ is possible iff $a \in D_i$. We note d the maximum size of the domains.

- $\mathcal{C}$ is the set of constraints. Each constraint is a pair of distinct variables $\{i, j\}$ noted C_{ij} for convenience. We note e the size of $\mathcal{C}$.
- $\mathcal{R}$ is the set of relations associated to the constraints. The relation R_{ij} defines the set of legal pairs of values for i and j.

Reaching global consistency for a CSP means finding a value assignment for each variable in $\mathcal{V}$ so that all the constraints in $\mathcal{C}$ are satisfied. Local consistency imposes some weaker conditions about the possible value assignments of the problem. For arc and path-consistency, the conditions are the followings:

- a variable i is arc-consistent iff:

  for all $a \in D_i$,
  for all $j \in \mathcal{V}$ such that $C_{ij} \in \mathcal{C}$,
  there exists $b \in D_j$ such that $(a, b) \in R_{ij}$.

- a pair of variables $\{i, j\}$ is path-consistent iff:

  both i and j are arc-consistent,
  for all $(a, b) \in D_i \times D_j$,
  for all $k \in \mathcal{V}$ such that C_{ik} and $C_{kj} \in \mathcal{C}$,
  there exists $c \in D_k$ such that $(a, c) \in R_{ik}$ and
  $\qquad (c, b) \in R_{kj}$.

A CSP is said arc-consistent iff all of its variables are arc-consistent and none of them have an empty domain. Similarly, a CSP is said path-consistent iff all of the possible pairs of variables are path-consistent.

Filtering procedures that are based on local consistency properties are generally complete, i.e. they only stop when the considered property is fully established in the constraint problem. Ensuring this completeness usually requires a big workload that is of little profit from a domain filtering point of view. That is why we have decided to implement a *partial* but fast filtering procedure which is going to check only once each value assignment after arc-consistency has been enforced. The corresponding algorithm is presented on figure 3. It works as follows. We suppose that before calling the procedure *check-paths*, arc-consistency was enforced in the current CSP. For each possible assignment $\langle i, a \rangle$ and for each variable j linked to i, we are going to compute the set of supporting value of $\langle i, a \rangle$ on j, i.e. the values x in D_j such that $(a, x) \in R_{ij}$. These values are counted. Then, for each supporting value and each variables k connected by a constraint to both i and j, we are going to check the existence of a path from $\langle i, a \rangle$ to $\langle j, x \rangle$ passing through k. If no such path is found, the number of supporting values is decremented. If this number becomes zero, we can rule out the value a from the domain of i and restart arc-consistency checking from variable i.

The worst-case time complexity of the algorithm depends on the arc-consistency procedure it is used with. If we rely on an AC3 scheme [3], the computation of the sets of supports (line 2 of *check-assignment* is done in $O(d)$ and checking the existence of a path (line 1 and 2 of *check-couple*) is achieved in $O(nd)$. This

```
procedure check-paths;
1 for each i ∈ V do
2       for each a ∈ D_i do
3             check-assignment(⟨i, a⟩).

procedure check-assignment(⟨i, a⟩);
1 for each j ∈ V such that C_{ij} ∈ C do
2       let S = supports(⟨i, a⟩, j) and N = |S|;
3             for each x ∈ S do
4                   check-couple(⟨i, a⟩, ⟨j, x⟩, N);
5             if N = 0 then
6                   D_i ← D_i \ {a};
7                   arc-consistency({⟨i, a⟩});
8                   return.

procedure check-couple(⟨i, a⟩, ⟨j, x⟩, var N);
1 for each k ∈ V such that C_{ik} et C_{kj} ∈ C do
2       if supports(⟨i, a⟩, k) ∩ supports(⟨j, x⟩, k) = ∅ then
3             N ← N − 1;
4             return.
```

Fig. 3. the arc and path-consistency mix

latter computation is done at most ed^2 times to cover all possible couples. The complexity is thus in $O(ned^3)$.

Now, if we use an AC$_4$ scheme [4], checking the existence of a path can be achieved in $O(n)$ if the sets $supports(⟨i, a⟩, j)$ are explicitly represented by bit-vectors. The worst-case complexity with AC$_4$ is thus in $O(ned^2)$.

Note that the complexities of *check-paths* with AC$_3$ and AC$_4$ are not really comparable since the basic operations that are counted in each case are different. For AC$_3$, we speak in terms of constraint evaluations; for AC$_4$, basic operations are access to arrays and intersections on bit-vectors. The complexities that are given here are to be compared with the ones of the corresponding arc-consistency algorithms (i.e. $O(ed^3)$ for AC$_3$ and $O(ed^2)$ for AC$_4$).

3 Experimental Evaluation

In order to study the performances of the *check-paths* procedure, we have experimented it on a range of randomly generated constraint problems. As usual, the generation of random problems is based on four parameters: the number n of variables, the size d of the variables domain, the constraint density cd in the graph and the constraint tightness ct. The constraint density corresponds to the fraction of the difference in the number of edges between a n-vertices clique and a n-vertices tree. A problem with density 0 will show $n − 1$ constraints; a problem with density 1 will show $n(n − 1)/2$ constraints. The constraint tightness ct

corresponds to the fraction of the number of tuples in the cross-product of the domain of two variables that will not be allowed by the constraint between these two variables. Tightness 0 stands for the universal constraint and tightness 1, the unsatisfiable constraint.

In the results we are displaying here, we have fixed $n = 16$ and $d = 8$. For four values of the constraint tightness (0.3, 0.4, 0.5 and 0.6), we had the density varying from 0 to 1 by 0.1 steps and for each step, we have repeated the executions of the following procedures on 100 different instances (and reported the average of the results).

- An arc-consistency filtering procedure, noted AC, which will serve as a lower-bound for both the execution time and the filtering power.
- A conventional and complete path-consistency filtering procedure, noted cPC, which will serve as the upper-bound for the execution time and the filtering power.
- Our partial filtering procedure, noted pPC.

Figure 4 shows the execution time ratios. We can clearly see that pPC is much less sensible to the evolution of the problem structure than cPC which shows neatly marked peaks. This regularity is a consequence of our choice to only check once each possible variable assignment which prevent the excessive iteration of the path-checking process.

But let us seen now what is the extent of the simplifications brought by pPC. The curves on figure 5 report the percentage of the initial search space that has been ruled out after the application of a filtering procedure i.e. the quantity:

$$1 - \frac{\prod_{i \in \mathcal{V}} \Delta_i}{\prod_{i \in \mathcal{V}} D_i}$$

where Δ_i represents the domain of variable i after it has been filtered. This quantity measures the impact of the filtering work on the problem simplification.

As it can be seen on the first graphic of figure 5, the gain in search-space pruning begins early, for problems with high satisfiability (note that AC alone is not able to filter anything for $ct = 0.3$). Then, this gain increases considerably in the transition zone between satisfiable and unsatisfiable problems.

For $ct = 0.5$, AC is still too weak to detect a unsatisfiable problem whereas pPC finds out that all the problems are unsatisfiable from a constraint density of 0.4.

We should also note that the gap between cPC and pPC that was sensible for $ct = 0.3$ is filling quickly as ct increases. Now, for $ct = 0.6$, the gap between AC and pPC is also filling since the problems are now becoming trivially unsatisfiable.

As a conclusion to these tests, we are inclined to think that our filtering procedure offers a good tradeoff between the additional cost it requires over arc-consistency checking and the benefits that are obtained from the domain filtering point of view.

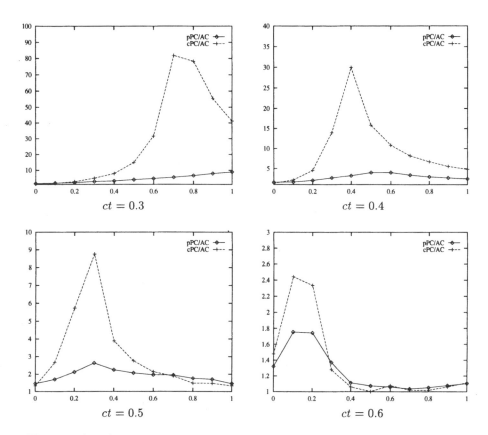

Fig. 4. ratios of execution time

4 Conclusion

Very seldom has path-consistency been considered as a useful filtering procedure in the constraint satisfaction problem literature (one exception can be found in [6]). Also, we think that the resolution of CSPs needs the implementation of pragmatic processes to improve its efficiency. In this paper, we have proposed such a process that uses the path consistency property.

Guided by efficiency goals, we chose to implement a partial filtering procedure which is not interested in establishing a local consistency property in the constraint problem but more in exploiting this property at the best possible cost. As a consequence of this partial filtering, the link between local consistency and satisfiability should still be based on consistency level that is completely enforced which in our case is arc-consistency.

Further work involve the generalization of the filtering procedure to n-ary constraints and its integration in the solution search process following the MAC model [7].

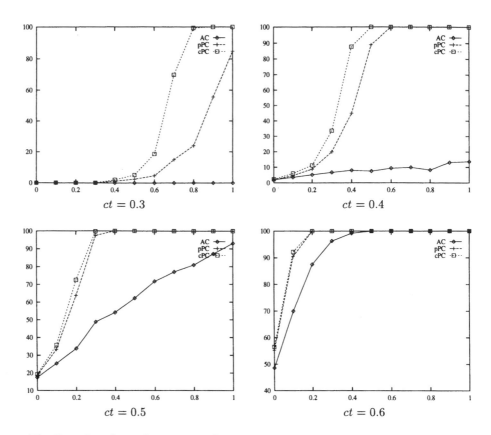

Fig. 5. ratios of search-space pruning

References

1. E. Tsang. *Foundations of Constraint Satisfaction.* Academic Press, 1993.
2. C. Han and C. Lee. Comments on Mohr and Henderson's path consistency algorithm. *Artificial Intelligence*, 36:125–130, 1988.
3. A. Mackworth. Consistency in networks of relations. *Artificial Intelligence*, 8:99–118, 1977.
4. R. Mohr and T. Henderson. Arc and path consistency revisited. *Artificial Intelligence*, 28:225–233, 1986.
5. H. Bennaceur. Partial consistency for constraint satisfaction problems. In *Proc. ECAI*, Amsterdam, Netherlands, 1994.
6. Ph. Codognet and G. Nardiello. *Path Consistency in* CLP*(FD)*, volume 845 of *Lecture Notes in Computer Science.* Springer–Verlag, 1994.
7. D. Sabin and E. Freuder. Contradicting conventional wisdom in constraint satisfaction. In *Proc. ECAI*, Amsterdam, Netherlands, 1994.

Where Do Intentions Come from ?:
A Framework for Goals and Intentions Adoption, Derivation and Evolution

Graça Gaspar and Helder Coelho

Departamento de Informática
Faculdade de Ciências de Lisboa
Bloco C5, Piso 1 - Campo Grande, 1700 Lisboa, Portugal
gg@di.fc.ul.pt, hcoelho@inesc.pt

Abstract. Current agent models usually address the definition of agents' intentions and their relationship to other components of the mental state of an agent. However, the genesis of goals and intentions, and the question of why the agent decides to commit itself or to abandon a particular goal, are questions that have not yet been clearly answered. Moreover, when we look for foundations on which to base implementations of agencies, we get in real trouble because the existence of such a gap in formal models of agents do not allow them to guide crucial aspects of agents' programming. Also, a formal model of agents should take into account their limited reasoning capability in order to lead up to realistic agents. In this paper, we defend a model of goals and intentions, based on deductive structures, and an integrated framework for revising them, that can and has been adopted as a specification for designing and building up artificial agents. The model of goals and intentions is part of the formalization of a complete multi-agent model whose development has guided the parallel development of a workbench, which in turn provided guidance for the refinement and extension of the conceptual model. We argue that research for theoretical foundations of multiagent systems should provide such a guidance.

1 Introduction

Defining intentions, as well as relating intentions to other components of an agent's mental state, has been the topic of much research lately [Cohen and Levesque 90], [Rao and Georgeff 91], [Werner 91], [Shoham 93], [Cawsey et al 93], [Konolige and Pollack 93]. Nevertheless, when one looks for foundations on which to base implementations of societies of agents [Coelho et al 94], all the models of intention that have been presented so far have serious drawbacks:

- They employ modal logics and adopt idealistic assumptions, like for instance, that agents believe all logic consequences of their beliefs. Even if a theorem prover for the particular modal logic proposed by one of those authors was available, the unrealistic assumptions about the agents' reasoning capability that would follow would not be adequate for most applications.

- The models do not give a clue on where do goals or intentions come from, that is to say, they do not address the circumstances under which a goal should be formed or, when the goal has been proposed by another agent, the circumstances under which it should be adopted. For instance, Cohen and Levesque's model of intentions conceals this problem behind the choice of possible worlds representing goals, that they postulate to be a subset of the possible worlds for beliefs. They define intentions as goals to which the agent is committed, but do not address the question of why it decided to commit itself to those particular goals.

- The models do not address the problem of revising intentions or goals during a communication process. In any realistic application in a multiagent environment, the goals and intentions of an agent, as well as its beliefs, will have to be revised in the face of new incoming information.

In this paper, we present a model of the goals and intentions of an agent and an integrated framework for revising them, that can and has been used as a specification for implementing agents. This model builds on and extends a model of the belief component of the mental state of an agent that has been previously presented [Gaspar 91]. Both the belief and the goal models are deductive models, incorporating sets of inference rules used by the agent to derive beliefs or goals. Also they make explicit the preferences that an agent may use to choose a preferred subset of beliefs or goals among a set of possibly inconsistent possibilities.

The adoption of new goals depends on the plans the agent is able to formulate to try to achieve one of its intentions, on the solicitation for the adoption of goals by other agents, and on the inferencing capability of the agent in order to derive subgoals and related goals according to its beliefs. The revision of goals depends on the reasoning capability of the agent, on the achievement of the expected results of planned actions, but it also depends on the opinions the agent has formed regarding the other agents' authority and credibility and also on the agent's personal characteristics, for instance, its will to assist others.

In the next section, we will briefly review the definition of belief model of an agent that was the starting point for this research. In section 3 we will proceed to define the model of goals and intentions. In sections 4 and 5 we will discuss the evolution of the agent as a result of the execution of plans and as a result of communication acts with other agents.

2   Background: Preferred Subtheories and the Belief Model

We will present the basic notions that underlie the belief model of an agent and that will also be used to define the goal model. For further details and examples, the reader should refer to [Gaspar 91], [Costa et al 94], [Gaspar 94].

The belief state of an agent is characterised by several deductive structures: one deductive structure that determines the beliefs of the agent itself and several others that determine its beliefs about the other agents it is aware of.

The idea of basing the definition of the belief model of an agent in deductive structures was motivated by the work of Konolige [Konolige 86]. Nevertheless, our definition of deductive structure departs from Konolige's definition in several aspects, namely in considering sets of possibly inconsistent formulas and preference relations as the basis for the definition of belief sets, as will be clarified in the following.

Agents must be able to reason with inconsistent information, as human beings do. In order to do so, they will maintain sets of possibly inconsistent formulas, viewed as belief hypotheses or assumptions, from which they will try to select the most preferred ones. Therefore, deductive structures include a set of formulas from a so called internal language of belief, IL^B, and a partial preference order relation on that set of formulas.

We will assume that IL^B is identical for all agents and that it is a first order language extended with some operators to speak about the effects believed to result from the execution of actions. Briefly, if α is an action expression and f and g are first order formulas in IL^B, then ($\overset{\alpha}{\to}$ g) and (f $\overset{\alpha}{\to}$ g) are formulas in IL^B. The intended meaning of the formula (f $\overset{\alpha}{\to}$ g) is the following: if f is believed in a mental state s, then immediately after executing α starting from s, the agent will be in a new mental state where it believes g.

Action expressions may be atomic expressions, built up from an action symbol with arity n applied to n terms, or composed action expressions, considering the usual forms of action composition, for instance (α, β) denoting the sequential composition of α and β, and (f? α, β) denoting 'if f then α else β'.

We want to model agents with a limited reasoning ability, and even to model agents that sometimes perform incorrect inferences, in order to approach realistic societies. Therefore, deductive structures will also include a set of inference rules that are used by the agent in question.

Definition 1. A belief deductive structure D^B_a, where a is an agent identifier, is a triple $(H^B_a, <^B_a, R^B_a)$ where

   H^B_a is a set of belief hypotheses, that is, formulas of IL^B ;

   $<^B_a$ is a partial order relation on H^B_a;

   R^B_a is a set of inference rules.

Δ

From a belief deductive structure, we will define the set of basic beliefs of the agent, denoted by $BBase(D^B_a)$, as well as its closure relative to the set of inference rules considered, the set of beliefs denoted by $B(D^B_a)$.

Ideally, the set of basic beliefs of an agent would be a maximal preferred consistent subset of H^B_a, but since the set of inference rules R^B_a may be incomplete or even unsound, the agent may be incapable of determining the inconsistency of a set of belief hypotheses. Therefore, when defining the notion of maximal preferred subset of formulas, we replace the semantic notion of inconsistency with the syntactic notion of a contradictory set of formulas defined in the following way:

Definition 2. Given a set of inference rules R, a set of formulas H is contradictory if it is possible to derive false from H using the rules in R, that is if $H \vdash_R$ false.

Δ

The definition of maximal preferred subset that we present in the following is closely related to the one presented in [Brewka 89] [Brewka 91] but it has the advantage of taking into account the limited reasoning capability of the agents, and also of capturing the progressive construction of a preferred subtheory from a nucleus set corresponding to a previously determined preferred subtheory, which will be of great help in defining the set of goals of an agent from its set of beliefs.

Definition 3. T is a preferred subtheory of a deductive structure $D = (H, <, R)$, starting from a given non-contradictory set of formulas T_0, if there exists a total descending ordering $(f_1, f_2, ..., f_n)$ of the formulas in H, respecting $<$, such that $T = T_n$ and such that, for $0 \leq i < n$,

$T_{i+1} :=$ if f_{i+1} is contradictory with T_i, considering the rules in R,

then T_i

else $T_i \cup \{f_{i+1}\}$.

Δ

Since the preference relation in a deductive structure is only a partial order, in principle there may be several alternative preferred subtheories. In practice, we would like the set of basic beliefs of an agent to be uniquely defined, given its deductive structure. That could be enforced by defining it to be the intersection of all the preferred subtheories, which would be expensive to compute. Alternatively, we may guarantee that there is only one preferred subtheory by imposing restrictions on the preference order, namely that for each minimal set of contradictory belief hypotheses the preference order determines the least preferred one.

Example 1. Consider an agent x and the following deductive structure D^B_y, that agent x maintains relative to agent y with which it communicates:

$H^B_y = \{$ quaker(nixon), $\qquad\qquad\qquad\qquad\qquad\qquad$ (f.a)

republican(nixon), $\qquad\qquad\qquad\qquad\qquad\qquad$ (f.b)

quaker(X) $\rightarrow$ pacifist(X), $\qquad\qquad\qquad\qquad$ (f.c)

republican(X) $\rightarrow$ ~pacifist(X) $\}$ $\qquad\qquad$ (f.d)

$<^B_y = \{$ (f.c, f.d), (f.c, f.a), (f.c, f.b) $\}$

$R^B_y = \{$ modus-ponens, instantiation, direct_contradiction $\}$

The direct_contradiction rule of inference is by default considered to be included in all deductive structures, and it corresponds to

$$\{ L, \sim L \} \vdash \text{false}$$

where L is a positive literal.

Notice that, using the given inference rules and starting from the formulas f.a, f.b, f.c and f.d, it is possible to derive false and, according to the relation $<^C_y$, formula f.c is the least preferred formula of that contradictory set.

Considering then a possible descending total ordering respecting $<^C_y$, for instance (f.a, f.b, f.d, f.c), and constructing the sequence of T_i sets, we would obtain:

$T_0 = \{ \}$

$T_1 = \{$ quaker(nixon) $\}$

$T_2 = \{$ quaker(nixon), republican(nixon) $\}$

$T_3 = \{$ quaker(nixon), republican(nixon), republican(X) $\rightarrow \sim$pacifist(X) $\}$

$T = T_4 = T_3$

T represents a preferred subtheory, according to this ordering. Another ordering, also compatible with $<^C_y$ would be for instance (f.d, f.b, f.a, f.c). This ordering would result in the same T, also excluding formula f.c. In fact, for this example, there is a single preferred subtheory T, whatever the ordering we consider as long as it is compatible with $<^C_y$. This subtheory corresponds to the set of basic beliefs of x about the beliefs of agent y.

$\triangle$

3 Goal Model

The goals of an agent are chosen from among a set of formulas that represent desires of the agent, or goal hypotheses, that may be contradictory. The agent will choose a subset of preferred non-contradictory desires, that must also be non-contradictory with its beliefs. An agent may also use special inference rules, besides the rules it uses for beliefs, to derive desires. So, we will define goal deductive structures in the same way we used to define belief deductive structures.

Definition 4. A goal deductive structure D^G_a, where a is an agent identifier, is a triple $(H^G_a, <^G_a, R^G_a)$ where

> H^G_a is a set of formulas of the internal language of goals IL^G, representing
> desires of the agent;

$<^G_a$ is a partial order relation on H^G_a, representing preferences between desires;

R^G_a is a set of goal inference rules.

Δ

The syntax and intuitive meaning of the formulas of IL^G are the following:

- If b is an agent and α is an action expression then do(b, α) is a formula of IL^G. Informally do(b, α) represents the goal of agent b doing action α in the present or future.

- If b is an agent and f is a formula in IL^B, then s(b, f) is a formula in IL^G. Informally s(b, f) represents the goal of agent b satisfying f, in the present or future, that is to say, of b coming to believe f.

- If g1 and g2 are formulas in IL^G, then before(g1, g2) is a formula in IL^G. Informally before(g1, g2) represents a relation between two goals indicating that while goal g2 exists then the goal of satisfying g1 before satisfying g2 will also exist. That is, g1 is a goal conditioned to the existence of g2 and g1 must be satisfied in a state no later than the state where g2 is satisfied.

- IL^G includes all the formulas in IL^B. The formulas of IL^B are included in IL^G for technical reasons, namely so that goal inference rules may have belief formulas as antecedents. If f is a formula in IL^B then f may be interpreted as equivalent to s(a, f).

Note that, in our approach, goals are not maintenance goals, that is to say that an agent tries to satisfy them, in a present or future state, but it will not try to keep satisfying them thereafter. Therefore, the execution of a sequence of actions satisfies a goal s(a,f) if it makes agent a pass through a state that satisfies f.

A set of goal formulas is said to be contradictory if it is possible to derive false from that set, using the goal inference rules, which corresponds intuitively to proving that no possible sequence of future states of the agent can satisfy all the goals in the set. As goal inference rules we can consider all the belief inference rules, plus specific goal rules as the ones that we illustrate in the following.

Example 2. The first rule allows the derivation of the goal of satisfying simultaneously f1 and f2, that is to say in the same belief state, from the goal of satisfying f1 and the restrictions that f1 must be satisfied before f2 and that f2 must be satisfied before f1.

{ s(a, f1), before(s(a, f1), s(a, f2)), before(s(a, f2), s(a, f1)) } $\vdash$ s(a, f1 & f2)

The second rule allows the derivation of false from the goal of satisfying f and the belief that f implies false.

$\{ s(a, f), \ f \rightarrow false \ \} \quad \vdash \ false$

The third rule allows the derivation of goal o1 from goal o2 and the restriction that o1 must be satisfied before o2.

$\{ o2, \ before(o1,o2) \ \} \ \vdash \ o1$

The fourth rule allows the derivation of goal s(a, f) from goal do(a, α) when a believes that doing α will result in a state where it believes f.

$\{ do(a, \alpha), \ (\overset{\alpha}{\rightarrow} f) \ \} \ \vdash \ s(a, f)$

Δ

Notice that such inference rules allow the agent both to detect contradictory goals and to derive goals based on goal dependence relations ("before" formulas) and beliefs about actions, but do not allow it to derive as a subgoal one of several possible actions that it believes will lead to the satisfaction of one of its goals. The choice and commitment to such actions or subgoals will be the subject of the planning activity of the agent.

We can now define the set of basic goals of an agent, in an similar way as we did for the set of basic beliefs.

Definition 5. Given a belief deductive structure D^B_a and a goal deductive structure $D^G_a=(H^G_a, <^G_a, R^G_a)$, a set of basic goals $GBase(D^B_a, D^G_a)$ is a preferred subtheory of $(H^G_a, <^G_a, R^B_a \cup R^G_a)$ starting from the set $BBase(D^B_a)$.

Δ

The set of basic goals of an agent includes therefore the set of basic beliefs and is non-contradictory with it. The set $G(D^B_a, D^G_a)$ of all the goals of the agent, derived or not, is defined as the deductive closure of $GBase(D^B_a, D^G_a)$, considering the inference rules in $R^B_a \cup R^G_a$.

Let us now proceed to define the intentions of an agent as a concept derived from the concept of a goal. The considerations that led us to this definition of intention were based on the arguments of Bratman [Bratman 90] over the functionality of intentions and their relation with the goals and beliefs of the agent, but were also based on the assumption that agents have limited reasoning capabilities and should therefore avoid planning in detail before committing themselves to a goal.

Our intentions must be basic goals. Therefore, intentions are non-contradictory (not necessarily consistent with the agent beliefs, but only believed to be compatible with its beliefs and believed to be possible to satisfy). The consequences of an intention are not considered as intentions, unless they are themselves intentional, that is, unless they are themselves basic goals.

We also impose that an intention be a goal that is not already satisfied, since an already satisfied goal does not have the fundamental characteristic of intentions of forcing the agent to do something to satisfy them.

Informally, a goal g is considered to be satisfied in a belief and goal state of an agent in the following cases:

- If g is of the form s(a, f) then g is satisfied if f is a belief of a;

- If g is of the form do(a, α) then g is satisfied if done(a, α) is a belief of a;

- If g is of the form before(o1, o2) then g is satisfied if o2 is not a goal of a or if o1 is satisfied.

The agent must also be able to establish ways to satisfy intentions. Therefore we impose a restriction on intentions that, on one side, forces the agent to sketch a plan to satisfy an intention, and on the other side, does not force it to detail that plan nor commits it to follow that plan in the future under all conditions. With that aim, we will define satisfiable goals and restrict intentions to being satisfiable goals.

A goal g is considered satisfiable by an agent in two different situations:

- g is satisfiable if the agent has beliefs that allow it to decompose g into a set of goals {g$_1$, ..., g$_n$}, that will constitute a plan for g.

- g is satisfiable if the agent is able to determine an action expression such that it believes that its execution will satisfy g. That is, for instance assuming g is of the form s(a,f), if ($\overset{\alpha}{\rightarrow}$ f) is one of a's beliefs.

To represent the beliefs of an agent about the possibility of decomposing a goal into a set of subgoals, we will extend the internal language of beliefs with formulas of the form

$$\text{in\_order\_to}(g, \{g_1, ..., g_n\})$$

Agents may include such formulas in their set of belief hypotheses directly, or they may come to believe them as a result of applying inference rules to beliefs about actions. That is to say, "in_order_to" formulas may also be used to record and operationalize ways to achieve goals, previously derived from a long chain of inferences about actions.

Example 3. An agent a having the goal of another agent b doing α, may try to use the following decomposition formula to determine a plan to achieve that goal:

$$\text{in\_order\_to}(\text{do}(b, \alpha),$$
$$\{ \text{before}(\text{do}(a, \text{send\_msg}(sol, b, \text{do}(b, \alpha))),$$
$$\text{do}(a, \text{receive\_msg}(rep, b, \text{done}(b, \alpha)))),$$
$$\text{do}(a, \text{receive\_msg}(rep, b, \text{done}(b, \alpha))) \})$$

According to this decomposition formula, a possible plan for a to achieve do(b, α) would be to send a solicitation message to agent b, asking him to adopt the goal of doing α and to wait until it receives a reply from b saying that α has been done.
Agents may also use inference rules that allow them to infer such formulas from belief formulas about actions. For instance,

$$\{ g \overset{\alpha}{\rightarrow} h, h \overset{\beta}{\rightarrow} f \} \vdash \text{in\_order\_to}(s(a, f),$$
$$\{ \text{before}(s(a, g), do(a, (\alpha,\beta))), \ do(a, (\alpha,\beta)) \})$$
$$\Delta$$

In short, an intention is defined as a basic goal that is not already satisfied and that is considered satisfiable.

This definition of intention is obviously discussible and was chosen mainly because it does not impose much on the agent reasoning capabilities. Notice that it does not guarantee that all the intentions of the agent are considered to be jointly satisfiable, nor that the plans that the agent is able to consider for each individual intention are themselves satisfiable. More restrictive definitions of intentions can be replaced for the one presented here, if need be for a particular application.

As for the degree of commitment to an intention, it will depend on the revision of the belief and goal deductive structures resulting either from the execution of plans or actions, or from the reception of messages from other agents, as will be presented in the following sections.

4   Evolution by Execution of Plans

A plan for a goal g is either an action α or a set of goals $\{g_1, ..., g_n\}$. The execution of a plan is specified in our agent's model by a function called plan_execution that, given an agent a, its current model M, an intention g and a plan p for g, produces a new model M' for a. We will describe only informally the changes in the belief and deductive structures of an agent that correspond to the result of plan_execution.

If plan p is a set of goals $\{g_1, ..., g_n\}$, then plan_execution will introduce n new goal hypotheses of the form before(g_i, g) and it will introduce new tuples (before(g_i,g) < g) in the preference order relation between goal hypotheses. In this way, the execution of a plan results in the adoption of the subgoals g_i if they are not contradictory with the previous goals of the agent. Subgoal g_i will not be an intention in itself, because it is only a derived goal, but before(g_i,g) will, if it is not satisfied yet and if it is satisfiable. Therefore, the execution of a plan results in the adoption of the components of that plan as intentions, conditioned to the existence of the original intention g. Agent a will continue to have g as an intention, but it will try to satisfy each g_i before trying to satisfy g, so it will stick to that plan as long as possible, before trying alternative ones.

If plan p is an action α, then its execution will correspond to a sequence of changes that will start with the execution of action α itself.

Execution of an action is specified by a function action_execution whose results we will describe only briefly. The execution of an atomic action α by a may be successful, in which case a will have as new preferred belief hypotheses (and therefore as new beliefs, if non-contradictory) all the formulas g such that $(f \overset{\alpha}{\to} g)$ is a basic belief and f is a belief. After successfully executing α, agent a will also have the belief done(a, α). The execution of atomic action α may also be unsuccessful[1], in which case the agent model will be unchanged. The execution of composed actions is defined in such a way that it reflects the usual semantics of the composition and that it guarantees the adoption of a belief done(a, β) for all the subactions β successfully executed.

After the execution of action α, the execution of α as a plan for g will proceed by eliminating, from the set of goal hypotheses of a, all the goals considered to be satisfied. In this way, if the plan for g was successful, g will no longer be an intention. Finally, all the belief hypotheses of the form done(a, α) will be eliminated, so that new goals of the form do(a, α) later adopted will not be considered automatically satisfied.

5   Evolution by Communication

The goals and intentions of an agent may change as a consequence of communication with other agents. Such a change is specified in our model by a function called assimilation that, given an agent a, its current model M and a message m received by a from another agent b, produces a new model M' for a. Function assimilation defines the revision of beliefs and goals of the agent, in terms of changes in the corresponding deductive structures, as a result of the reception of a message. It is not defined directly in an explicit form, in an agent model, but it is indirectly defined through the specification of general revision principles, that all the agents in a society must conform to, and through the indication of an ordered list of heuristic criteria, that may be different for different agents and that determine the attitude of an agent toward the others. The list of adopted heuristic criteria can be considered as defining the agent's "personality". The principles and heuristic criteria that together define the assimilation function depend on the type of message received. For lack of space we will present only an example regarding the reception of a solicitation message, that is, a message that requests that an agent adopt a goal. Nevertheless, is should be stressed that the intentions of an agent can also change as a result of the assimilation of other types of messages, for instance information messages.

Most of the general revision principles that we adopt, to control evolution by communication, are not justifiable by purely logical arguments. Instead, they result

---

[1] The unsuccessful execution of an action depends on a component of the agent model called the action model, that we do not detail here for lack of space [Gaspar, 94]. Briefly, the action model lists the basic actions an agent knows how to execute, and may impose restrictions that must be satisfied before such an action is executed. An attempt to execute an action in a state where the action restrictions are not met, will result in an unsuccessful execution.

from a consideration of what might be "reasonable" communication principles, taking into account the type of applications that we intend to model. Considering that the societies of agents that we intend to model correspond typically to groups of knowledge based agents that interact to update and correct the information they have and to request the execution of subtasks, we may consider it "reasonable" to model such agents as being honest and disposed to help others whenever that does not interfere with their own activity. Therefore, we may consider agents as being cooperative as long as they have no specific reasons not to cooperate. That leads us to considering the following revision principle:

Principle of Cooperation of the Receiving Agent. If an agent a, in a mental state characterised by a model M with belief and goal deductive structures D^B_a and D^G_a, receives a solicitation message m from another agent b with content $f \in IL^G$, and if

$$GBase(D^B_a, D^G_a) \cup \{f\} \not\vdash false \quad \text{and} \quad f \text{ is satisfiable by a in M}$$

then in the new model M' resulting from the assimilation of m in M, f must be a goal of a.

$$\Delta$$

This principle does not stipulate what should happen if, for instance, the request f is contradictory with previous goals of a. In such a case, f would always be introduced as a new goal hypothesis but whether it would or would not become a new goal of a depends on the preference order relation between goal hypotheses adopted as a result of the assimilation. It should also be noted that the "conditioned benevolence" of the agents that this principle asserts is not an intrinsic characteristic of our model but instead characterises a certain type of society of agents. For different societies, different principles might be adopted without changing the formal model of agents' beliefs and goals.

The heuristic criteria that we mentioned above, given a current model M of agent a and a set H of contradictory hypotheses, aim precisely at defining new preferences between those hypotheses. Therefore, such criteria correspond basically to criteria for revising preferences. One such criterion might be for instance the following:

Criterion of Preference to Help Agent c. For each goal g1 in H, if agent a believes that agent c has the goal that a should satisfy g1, that is if

$$GBase(D^B_c, D^G_c) \vdash g1$$

where D^B_c and D^G_c are the belief and goal deductive structures relative to agent c included in agent's a current model M, then

$$g2 \leq g1, \text{ for all } g2 \text{ in } H.$$

$$\Delta$$

A sequence of such heuristic criteria may be applied, resulting in the determination of a least preferred element in H. The previous preference order between goal hypotheses is changed accordingly, resulting in new deductive structures for a, and leading eventually to the dropping of some intentions and the adoption of others. For lack of space, we cannot present here a detailed example of goals and intentions revision.

6   Conclusions

We presented a deductive approach to the modeling of agents' beliefs, goals and intentions, as well as to the change of agents' goals resulting from the execution of plans and actions and from the communication between agents.

Such a model of the mental state of an agent presents the advantages that it can directly be used as a specification for implementations and that it incorporates the aspects relating to goal adoption and revision that must be considered before real agents can be put to work.

The model, partially presented herein, has been the base for the specification of a workbench and of an agent programming language, that are being used for implementing experiments with small societies of agents. The workbench, described in [Gaspar 94], runs on a DECstation and has been implemented in Prolog. The implementation experiments began very early with an initial and very limited version of the workbench [Monteiro 89] and since then they have accompanied and partially guided the refinement and extension of the model.

References

[Bratman 90] M. E. Bratman, What is intention, In P. R. Cohen, J. Morgan and M. E. Pollack (Eds.), *Intentions in Communication*, pp.15-32, MIT Press, 1990.

[Brewka 89] G. Brewka, Preferred subtheories: an extended logical framework for default reasoning, in *Proceedings of IJCAI'89*, pp. 1043-1048, 1989.

[Brewka 91] G. Brewka, Belief revision in a framework for default reasoning, in A. Fuhrmann and M. Morreau (Eds.),*The Logic of Theory Change*, Lecture Notes in AI, 465, Springer Verlag, 1991.

[Cawsey et al 93] A. Cawsey, J. R. Galliers, B. Logan, S. Reece and K. S. Jones, Revising beliefs and intentions: a unified framework for agent interaction, in A. Sloman et al (Eds.), *Prospects for Artificial Intelligence*, IOS Press, 1993.

[Coelho et al 94] H. Coelho, L. Antunes and L. Moniz, On agent design rationale, in T. Pequeno and F. Carvalho (eds.), *Proceedings of the 11th Brazilian Symposium on Artificial Intelligence*, SBC, 1994.

[Cohen and Levesque 90a] P. R. Cohen and H. J. Levesque, Persistence, intention and commitment, in P. R. Cohen, J. Morgan and M. E. Pollack (Eds.), *Intentions in Communication*, pp.34-69, MIT Press, 1990.

[Cohen and Levesque 90b] P. R. Cohen and H. J. Levesque, Intention is choice with commitment, *Artificial Intelligence*, 42, pp.213-261, 1990.

[Costa et al 94] E. Costa, G. Gaspar and H. Coelho, A formal approach to intelligent learning environments, in J. E. Greer and G. McCalla (Eds.), *Student Modelling: the Key to Individualized Knowledge-based Instruction*, (Proceedings of the NATO ARW on Student Modelling, Quebec, Canada, May 1991), Springer-Verlag, NATO ASI Series F 125, pp. 281-294, 1994.

[Gaspar 91] G. Gaspar, Communication and belief changes in a society of agents: towards a formal model of an autonomous agent, in Y. Demazeau and J.-P. Müller (Eds.), *Decentralized AI 2*, North Holland, 1991.

[Gaspar 94] G. Gaspar, *Modeling of autonomous intelligent agents inserted in agent societies*, Ph.D. Thesis (in Portuguese), University of Lisbon, 1994.

[Konolige 86] K. Konolige, *A deduction model of belief*, Pitman, 1986.

[Konolige and Pollack 93] K. Konolige and M. E. Pollack, A Representationalist theory of intention, in *Proceedings of IJCAI'93*, pp.390-395, 1993.

[Monteiro 89] J. C. Monteiro, *A Model for a Society of Intelligent Agents* (in Portuguese), LNEC and FCUL, December 1989.

[Rao and Georgeff 91] A. S. Rao and M. P. Georgeff, Modeling rational agents within a BDI-architecture, in *Proceedings of the 2nd International Conference on Principles of Knowledge Representation and Reasoning*, pp.473-484, Morgan Kaufmann, 1991.

[Shoham 93] Y. Shoham, Agent-Oriented Programming, *Artificial Intelligence*, 60, pp.51-92, 1993.

[Werner 91] E. Werner, A Unified View of Information, Intention and Ability, in Y. Demazeau and J.-P. Müller (Eds.), *Decentralized AI 2*, North Holland, 1991.

Acknowledgements

This work was partially supported by CEC under ESPRIT-III MODELAGE project.

A Closer Look to Artificial Learning Environments

Helder Coelho[1], Augusto Eusébio[1] and Ernesto Costa[2]

[1] Departamento de Informática
Faculdade de Ciências de Lisboa
Bloco C5 Piso1, Campo Grande
1700 Lisboa (Portugal)
hcoelho@inesc.pt

[2] Departamento de Engenharia Informática
Universidade de Coimbra
Polo II, Vila Franca-Pinhal de Marrocos
3030 Coimbra (Portugal)
ernesto@moebius.uc.pt

Abstract. The so-called Intelligent Tutoring Systems evolved in the past five years to Intelligent Learning Environments. This shift was supported by the stronger role of software agents and the possible ways they can be used to promote human learning. The aim of this paper is to explore further on one possible style of formalization taking now a point of view from DAI in stead of AI and Education: a classroom is a small society of agents that can be simulated according to some specific goal defined by the user (say, the teacher). It will be based on a modification of the idea of deductive structures (DS), first proposed by Konolige. These DS will be accompanied by heuristic principles and criteria that define different types of societies and agents. The technical apparatus can be adopted in distinct educational scenarios from history to mathematics, and we will show, with an example, recent work in high school linear algebra.

1 Introduction

When we accept the paradigm of Computational Mathetics, advocated by [Self 92], we must shift our research focus in the direction of formal theories for Intelligent Learning Environments (ILE's). As a consequence, our research can be easily considered also within the field of Distributed Artificial Intelligence (DAI), and from now on we stand by this wide open perspective.

One possible way of formalization in DAI [Wooldridge and Jennings 95], which we will explore here, is based on the two following hypothesis: 1) learning and teaching are particular cases of interaction between autonomous rational agents (RAs); and, 2) RAs can be modelled in terms of belief states and of how they change as a consequence of interactions with other RAs and the environment.

From the two hypothesis above it is clear that one important research direction is, on one hand, the construction of a formal theory about the dynamics of belief systems [Konolige and Pollack 93] and, on the other hand, its evaluation in a learning context. The main aim of the present paper is to look again to that sort of artificial learning environment, following previous research [Costa et alli 91], and by setting up experiments in a classroom society in order to enhance and improve the agent model.

Running educational processes in some sort of a workbench is helpful for a teacher not only for demonstrating and evaluating reasoning mechanisms in particular situations, but also for simulating the student doings and debugging his errors in working sessions and future tests. Such teaching apparatus can be viewed as a tool where we may model specific student´s understanding and abilities to explore learnable pieces of knowledge.

Our approach to model an agent is presented briefly in section 2 [Costa et alli 91]. It is based on a first modification, done by [Gaspar 90], of the idea of deductive structures (DS) that was proposed earlier by [Konolige 86]. In section 3, we discuss how these DS accompanied by heuristic principles and criteria define different types of societies and agents. In section 4, we show how this apparatus is used to construct distinct educational scenarios. In section 5, we present a new agent architecture behind that agent model, that evolved from a first attempt and through experimentation. In section 6, we give an example of a computational classroom session with three participants. Finally, we summarize the main aspects of the paper.

2 The Agent Model

The agent model is defined by looking into its statics (structure) and its dynamics (communication). First, let us see the structural side. An autonomous rational agent's (hereafter called simply agent) belief state can be characterized by several structures, one that determines his own beliefs about the world and one for each one of the others agents whose existence he is aware of (agent's beliefs about the beliefs of the other agents). So each agent will have, at a particular moment, a base set of beliefs which is in fact an indexed set of sets of beliefs, B_A, where A is a set of agent identifiers. The set A includes the special identifier *own* denoting the agent itself. Each element of a set B_a, where a is the name of an agent, is a sentence in the internal language of that agent. We will assume that the internal language, L, is the same for all agents and that it is a first order language [Gaspar 90].

An agent must have some inferential capability in order to reason. This will be expressed by a set of deduction rules. As with the base set of beliefs what we have in fact, for each agent, is an indexed set of sets of deduction rules denoted by R_A, where A is a set of identifier names of agents.

We will assume also that our agents are imperfect reasoners [Konolige 86]. This means that the set of deduction rules an agent has is not necessarily complete or sound. Moreover the whole set of beliefs explicitly held by the agent may be inconsistent. This situation leads us to introduce a partial order relation on the base set of formulas (candidate beliefs) of an agent, $<_a$, allowing us to define at each moment the preferred subtheories T of that agent.

<u>Definition</u>. T is a preferred subtheory of B_a if there is a total ordering of formulas (f1, f2, ..., fn) respecting $<_a$ such that T is the deductive closure of Tn where:

- T0 = { } and, for $0 \leq i < n$
- Ti+1 = Ti   <u>if</u> f_{i+1} is contradictory with Ti else $Ti \cup \{f_{i+1}\}$

that is, T is a maximal non-contradictory subtheory of B_a relative to $<_a$.

<u>Definition.</u> A deductive structure of an agent a, D_a, is a triple formed by a set of formulas (candidate beliefs), B_a, a partial order on that set, $<_a$, and a set of deduction rules, R_a. It is denoted by $<B_a, <_a, R_a>$.

If $<_a$ is a partial order, several total orders may exist that respect $<_a$, leading therefore to several possible preferred subtheories. From those the agent will choose one non-contradictory, T, according to heuristic criteria presented below or arbitrarily.

<u>Example 1</u>

Let us consider the deductive structure $<B_a, <_a, R_a>$ of a general agent called a able to deal with the commutative property of a general operation in linear algebra $\otimes$. He knows the definition of the set e and the non-commutativity of + in e. He has an example, a piece of knowledge about the fact: "the addition operation + is commutative in the set of real numbers $\Re$".

B_a= {
    commutative($\otimes$,V) $\Leftrightarrow$ (X$\otimes$Y=Y$\otimes$X, $\forall$X, Y$\in$ V)),
    e = { (X,Y,0) : X, Y$\in\Re$},
    (X1,X2,0) + (Y1,Y2,0) = (X1+Y1,X2+Y2,0), $\forall$ (X1,X2,0), (Y1,Y2,0) $\in$ e,
    not commutative(+,e),
    example(commutative(+,$\Re$),because($\forall$x, y$\in\Re$ x+y=y+x))
    }
$<_a$= { commutative($\otimes$,V) $\Leftrightarrow$ (X$\otimes$Y=Y$\otimes$X, $\forall$X, Y$\in$ V) $<_a$ not commutative(_,_) }
R_a= {modus-ponens}

To obtain a preferred subtheory of a (his beliefs) we start by building the sequence Ti:

T0={};
T1={commutative($\otimes$,V) $\Leftrightarrow$ (X$\otimes$Y=Y$\otimes$X, $\forall$X, Y$\in$ V) };
T2={commutative($\otimes$,V) $\Leftrightarrow$ (X$\otimes$Y=Y$\otimes$X, $\forall$X, Y$\in$ V), e = { (X,Y,0) : X, Y$\in\Re$ }};
T3={commutative($\otimes$,V) $\Leftrightarrow$ (X$\otimes$Y=Y$\otimes$X, $\forall$X, Y$\in$ V), e = { (X,Y,0) : X, Y$\in\Re$}, (X1,X2,0) + (Y1,Y2,0) = (X1+Y1,X2+Y2,0), $\forall$ (X1,X2,0), (Y1,Y2,0) $\in$ e };
T4=T3;
T5={commutative($\otimes$,V) $\Leftrightarrow$ (X$\otimes$Y=Y$\otimes$X, $\forall$X, Y$\in$ V), e = { (X,Y,0) : X, Y$\in\Re$}, (X1,X2,0) + (Y1,Y2,0) = (X1+Y1,X2+Y2,0), $\forall$(X1,X2,0), (Y1,Y2,0) $\in$ e, example (commutative (+,$\Re$), because($\forall$x, y$\in\Re$ x+y=y+x))} }.

Now T, a maximal non-contradictory subset of B_a relative to $<_a$ and R_a , is:

T={ commutative($\otimes$,V) $\Leftrightarrow$ (X$\otimes$Y=Y$\otimes$X, $\forall$X, Y$\in$ V)), e = { (X,Y,0) : X, Y$\in\Re$}, (X1,X2,0) + (Y1,Y2,0) = (X1+Y1,X2+Y2,0),$\forall$ (X1,X2,0),(Y1,Y2,0)$\in$ e,example(commutative(+,$\Re$), because($\forall$x, y$\in\Re$ x+y=y+x)), commutative(+,e) }.

End of Example 1.

It is reasonable to assume that the set of beliefs held by an agent is structured. This means that an agent has tendency to group together beliefs that are related in some way, and this guides and speeds up his reasoning because reduces the amount of available information. So the whole set of beliefs may be viewed as divided in several (possibly intersecting) spaces each one defining a context or a viewpoint [Costa et alli 88, Martins and Shapiro 88]. To define this we introduce a relation rel between belief formulas and contexts, rel $\subseteq$ F x C, where F is the set of wff of L and C is the set of names of contexts (topic domains). In practice there is more than one way to define rel. We can define it intentionally: instead of formulas we use the names of the predicates and define the criteria, for instance syntactic criteria, that establish when a formula belongs to a context. We can also define rel extensionally: when the formulas themselves are linked to a context. In each context the beliefs are organized in groups, sub-contexts, allowing their fast identification, and a belief may belong to several contexts. The precise instant of time an agent acquires a new belief is recorded in his memory to be explored later on.

Moreover agents have a tendency to ascribe some credibility for the fact that another agent is knowledgeable in a certain context, and therefore able to explain their doubts. This aspect can be formally defined by introducing the function, cred: A x C $\rightarrow$ I, where A is the set of agent names (identifiers) and I is the interval [0,1]. For example, a credibility of 0.2 assigned to an agent means that he knows only a small fraction in some particular context, and a credibility of 1 means that the agent is an expert in that context. The initial credibility ascribed by an agent a to an agent b, in the context C, is N1/N, where N is the number of beliefs of c (the agent with the greatest number of beliefs in the society) and N1 is the number of beliefs of b.

If we assemble all these pieces we arrive to the notion of model of the belief state of an agent.

<u>Definition.</u> The belief state of an agent a is the five-tuple: $m_a = < A, C, cred, rel, D_A>$.

Note that contexts may intersect each other, and therefore we can have contradictory beliefs in different contexts and even inconsistent information inside the same context.

3 Agent Communication Power

The agent belief system is based upon deductive structures and it has four components: a model of belief states, a valuation function that allows the interpretation of sentences about the beliefs held by an agent in some state, a classification of the messages that may be received by the agents, and a belief change function capable to fix a new belief state for each belief state and the received message. Let us see now the communication side of the agent model.

3.1 Structure of Messages

Agents communicate among each other by a mechanism of message passing. It is thus important to see how this communicative process can affect their epistemic state

[Galliers 90]. In particular we have to introduce a function called Assimilation, that given a model of an agent and a message shows how its belief state is modified:

Assimilation: M x Mess → M.

Lets look more closely to the structure of messages. First of all messages can have a different nature and a distinct type. Concerning the nature they can be public or (exclusively) private. Public messages are those addressed to a particular agent or agents but that can be accessed by other agents. Private are those that, in contrast, can only be "used" by the recipients of the message.

Concerning the types of possible messages (speech acts) agents can exchange we may have: presentation messages, sent by an agent to introduce himself to other agents; request messages, that essentially state questions about the receiving agent's belief state (whether a given formula is believed or not) or ask the agent to perform some action; reply messages, that send back answers to previous request messages; information messages, that communicate some information about the belief state of the sending agent. Special cases are considered such as: forbidden to talk, forbidden peculiar dialogues, no conversation, and out of context.

A message itself has six components: the nature of the message, the type of the message, the sending agent, the receiving agent (or agents), the content of the message and the time of occurrence. The way the content of a message is interpreted depends on the nature and type of the message. For instance, the content of a private reply message can be the sequence (A, A → B, B). In that case the content has the role of an explanation.

3.2 Situations and Assimilation

In order to see how communication affects the belief state of an agent we must introduce some basic principles that define possible attitudes of agents in particular situations. These principles cannot be justified in purely logical grounds being only "reasonable" principles [Gaspar 90, Costa et alli 91]. For instance, if we want to model a classroom society based on the idea of honesty we can introduce the two following principles:

Principle 1 (Sincerity of the sending agent): If an agent a at a given belief state m_a sends a message of type presentation, request or information with content f then a believes in f, ie. $f \in bel(D_a)$.

Principle 2 (Confidence of the receiving agent): If an agent a, at a given belief state m_a, receives a message, from agent b, of type presentation, reply or information with content f then he/she believes that the sender believes in f, ie. $f \in bel(D_b)$. Again using the learning metaphor this means that the student believes in the information message sent to him by the teacher.

Principle 3 (Credulity of the receiving agent): If an agent a, at a given belief state m_a, receives a message from an agent b of type presentation, reply or information with content f and if he/she does not believe f to be false he/she enters a new believe state where he/she believes in f, ie. in the new model m'_a $f \in bel(D_a)$.

It is clear that these principles (and other, alternative or complementary) define the behavior of agents in particular situations, ie. they define different types of societies and they support simple mechanisms for implementing the assimilation function. For instance, with principle 2, after receiving an information message with content f from an agent a the agent b will introduce in its B_a the formula f. Using Principle 3 he will include f in D_b.

3.3 Types of Agents and Assimilation

Until now we have not discussed the possibility that incoming messages may contradict the beliefs that an agent has himself or those that he/she has about the other agents. This problem will again be treated at an heuristic level. The heuristics reflect the existence in the society of distinct types of agents or, in other words, the existence of agents with different personalities: arrogant and shy [Costa et alli 91]. We assume that we are only concerned with messages of type information and with their effects in D_{own}. We can easily generalize to other types of messages and to the possible modifications in the deductive structure of the sending agent included in the model of the receiving agent.

Let us suppose that Cont is the set of formulas belonging to D_{own} that participate in the proof of the contradiction: when there are two contradictory beliefs in some context only one of them is included in the preferred subtheory of the agent. For example, an arrogant agent is the one which uses the:

Criteria 1 - Highest support given by $<_{own}$
That is he will order the formulas in Cont according with $<_{own}$ and will choose accordingly.

And, a shy agent will look to the support that the other agents give to the contradictory formulas in Cont and will decide using the:

Criteria 2 - Highest support given by context
We consider that all agents, other than own, that believe in a formula f of Cont are the sources of knowledge represented in that formula. Each one will support f with a strength corresponding to their credibility in the formula topics. For each of the formulas in Cont we calculate its maximal support and we order Cont according to that measure. The maximal support is defined as:

$$max\_support(f) = max\{support(f,b) : \models_m[b] f\} \qquad support(f,b) = max\{cred(b,c) : rel(f,c)\}$$

One can think of many other types of agents that may use other criteria (for instance: a "simpler" formula will be preferred over a more "complex" one): lazzy, innattentive, obstinate, and theoretical. In a learning environment, each agent reacts is a specific way when receives several messages. A lazy agent does not put questions, ie. he does not send request messages. The shy agent sends a particular request message to all agents that he does not know having or not the eliminated contradictory message, and in order to have access to the total credibility for that belief. All the other agents send a request message of explaining sort to the teacher agent whenever a belief is rejected. The theoretical agent uses an inductive method to discover new rules, checking whether that rule is known by the teacher. The obstinate agent sends a request message to the teacher in order to confirm the validity of the generated beliefs.

4 Different Learning Scenarios

The previous model plus the assimilation function is the kernel of the simplest image of the agents in the communicative society of a classroom. Using this framework we shall model different educational situations (one-to-one, one-to-many, and many-to-many), enhance that agent model and later on simulate the computational classroom on a workbench in order to achieve common aims of a teacher, such as prepare the plan of a future class, evaluate the difficulty of a test, structure problems according to expected student reasoning types (the profile of a class about the most common reasoning types of the students was obtained through a survey), and even generate automatic teaching.

Let us concentrate only on the one-to-many tutoring scenario. This is the typical classroom situation, where the artificial agents are the teacher, the students and a particular agent called public. The teacher has a model of each student. The students in turn have a teacher's model plus a model of each one of their colleagues. This society works as follows: in a particular moment the teacher may address the whole classroom with public informative messages. Students send request and receive reply messages from the agent public. Request messages are addressed to a particular student concerning the subject matter being thought but, being public, can be answered by another student. The assimilation process proceeds in the same way as before.

A class is set up by the teacher who defines his aims, say a general topic or particular goals that each student may achieve, such as knowing facts and solving exercises (from some data X conclude Y). Afterwards, the teacher prepares a class plan by collecting all the beliefs, organized into contexts and subcontexts, related with those goals already introduced. All the different scenarios are tuned according to the leading role played by the agent teacher. In this type of learning environment the teacher has control of the dialogue among all the students. He has not access to the private messages exchanged by the agents, but he may interfere to interrupt the dialogues or other manifestations of the sudents, by issuing special information messages. Four scenarios may be devised: one-sided communication (vertical teaching, strong gap between teacher and students, authoritarian teacher), two-sided communication (semi-strong gap between teacher and students, semi-authoritarian teacher), coordinated many-sided communication (weak gap between teacher and students, dialoguing teacher), and many-sided communication (no gap between teacher and students, permissible teacher).

5 A New Agent Architecture

The agent model defined in section 2 was firstly defended by [Gaspar 90]. Several architectures were experimented later on based on it, in particular one by [Caldas and Coelho 92] in Arity-Prolog for modelling economic markets and another by [Trancas and Godinho 93] in Smalltalk for a learning environment in history for the high school. The research reported here is a further enhancement directed to the learning of college mathematics (linear algebra) and written in Arity-Prolog. A different agent architecture approach, with more mental states, was also taken by [Corrêa and Coelho 93] for modeling conversations among robots moving in a building, and the discussion about the design methodology behind experiments was presented in [Coelho et alli 94, 95].

The two features, time and intention, that were point out earlier in [Costa et alli 91] to be further investigated were explored along the development of the present new agent architecture. The first novel aspect consisted of using effectively the time dimension present in the messages. In point of fact each formula in the deductive structure of an agent has attached information concerning the instant of time when it was believed (or not believed) plus the corresponding justification. With that information it is possible to build histories for each formula because it is recorded the precise instant (date) when a belief is accepted or rejected, and we have also the origin (justification) of each belief. So, the agent can select the beliefs that are adequated to be kept for further reasoning.

The second novel aspect consisted of adding motivation to the agent, by moving him to a course of action. With this new element we are able to define more clearly the intentions of an agent and how they can be achieved. In educational terms this means having the goals of the teacher and of the students together with the strategies they prefer to attain these goals, ie. observing the way how students evolve along their learning, modifying their attitudes in the classroom, and also the sort of questions raised by the students. The increased importance of the agent mentality is necessary to approach the classroom as a society.

The introduction of these new elements obliged a revision of the previous agents' model (see 2). The belief state of an agent is now a 8-tuple:

$$ma = < A, CxSc, rel, cred, D_A, mem, Tl, mot>$$

The elements A, cred and D_A have the same meanings as in the old model. The relation rel associates now to each belief of an agent a pair (Context, Sub-context). The relation mem represents the state of a belief in terms of memory, and it can have six values, such as permanent, transitory, instantaneous, gray, dark, and irrecoverable. The first three states are used during reasoning and communication, and correspond to the positive side of memory. The other three states correspond to the negative side, the ones that are eliminated, following the shape of forgetting of Hermann Ebbinghaus: "the key to a good memory is the ability to retain important details, while letting go of unimportant ones". The element Tl records the amount of time the agent needs to reason, to communicate, and to organize its knowledge The motivation of the agent depends on the relationship between the pair (Context,Sub-context) and the base beliefs, and it is built upon a relation motivation degree, mot, given by the maximal non-contradictory set, receiving one of the following values, non_motivated, little_motivated, motivated and very_motivated, according to the proportion of interests, within that pair of contexts, is below or above some threshold. The overall motivation structure, in charge of generating mot, is a 4-tuple $<M_a, I_a, <_a, R_a>$, where M_a denotes the set of motives of the agent a, I_a is the set of his interests, in teaching and learning, organized in a pyramid shape, and $<_a$ and R_a were already defined before. The notion of interest has an intuitive flavour and presents some similarities to the notion of intention adopted by [Gaspar 95].

6 A Computational Classroom Workbench

The computational classroom workbench consists of three main parts: a user interface, a general knowledge base about mathematics domain, and the computational agents (teacher and students). The teacher agent has a structure similar to the student agent plus a module with teaching methods [Eusébio 95].

Each computational agent is organised into three modules, the belief base plus the working memory (universe), the reasoning machinery (based upon a preferred subtheory), and the communication base. The belief base is structured into three parts: the first one covering the agent intial knowledge, where each belief (facts, definitions, theorems, examples and partial order) is set in some frame defined by a context, a sub-context, and a date; the second one for its self knowledge, where each belief is set in another frame defined by a context, a sub-context, a date, a state, and a justification; and, finally, the third part is responsible for the motivation of the agent. The working memory is a space necessary to cover four activities: 1) store the self knowledge of the agent, the agent knowledge about the agents in touch to a specific society; 2) organize a set of features (the agent name, the initial belief base, the list of known agents, the list of the agent reasoning types, the list of contexts, the assimilation type associated to those contexts, and the credibility ascribed to the agent in some context); 3) have a mail box with all the received messages; and, 4) take notes about the doubts the agent has in particular contexts. The reasoning machinery has two capabilities: one for the type of assimilation and the other for the type of reasoning (four types are available: modus ponens, abduction, inheritance, and analogy), selected for a specific agent. Finally, the communication base is where the mechanism for understanding and sending messages is located.

Example 2

In the one-to-many-tutoring situation (see 4) let us illustrate now an example of interaction among three agents, a, b and c. Agent a (the same that was presented in Example 1) is the teacher, and agents b and c are the students.

The agent teacher a is semi-authoritarian. He has the following belief state in the context alga (linear algebra and analytic geometry) and in the subcontext ev (vectorial spaces):

A = { self,b,c }
$CxSc$ = { (alga,ev) }
cred(b,alga) = 0, cred(c,alga) = 0
B_{own} = {definition($operation addition, usual in e$, operand(triple(X1,X2,0), triple(Y1,Y2,0),addition,triple(R1,R2,0),e),def(#simpl_exp(X1+Y1,R1),#simpl_exp(X2+Y2,R2),));definition($commutative property$,commutative(Op,V),def(operation(Op,V),set(V), any (X,V),any(Y,V),operand(X,Y,Op,R1,V),operand(Y,X,Op,R2,V),#equal_exp(R1,R2)));set(e); operation(addition,e);not_commutative(addition,e);definition($any element of e$,§ any(triple(X,Y,o),e),def(# aux_name(X),# aux_name(Y)));example($example1 $ex(data(set(r), element(x,r),element(y,r),operation(addition,r)),conclude if(commutative(addition,r))), just(operand(x,y,addition,res1,r),operand((y,x,addition,res2,r),#equal_exp(res1,res2)));oper ation(addition,r);element(triple(x1,x2,0),e) }
B_b = {}, B_c = {}
$<_a$ = { partial_order($ord 1$,not_commutative(_,_) '«' $commutative property$) }
R_a = {modus_ponens}
mem(Belief) = permanent
Tl = 0:0:0
mot(alg,ev) = very_motivated
M_a = {goal(alga,ev,discipline(alga))}

I_a = {}

The agent *b* is shy (see 3.3) and he has the following features:

A = { own }
CxSc = {}
B_b={}
$<_{own}$ = {}
R_b={by_analogy}
mem(_) = unspecified
Tl = 0:0:0
mot(_,_) = unspecified
M_{own} ={ theorem($electrical circuits$, if,head(agent(X), electrotechnical_engineer(X)), body(electrical_circuits(X)));theorem($electricity$,if,head(agent(X),electrotechnical_engin eer(X)),body(electricity(X)));theorem($electrical machines$, if, head(agent(X), electrotechnical_engineer(X)),body(electrical_machines(X)));theorem($electrotechnical engineer1$,if,head(agent(X),course(electrotechnical_engineering,X)),body(electrotechnical _engineer(X))); theorem($electrotechnical engineer 2$, if, head(agent(X), discipline(alga, X), discipline(electricity,X)),body(course(electrotechnical_engineering,X))) }
I_b={electrical_circuits; electricity; electrical_machines}

The agent *b* builds up his pyramid of interests by inserting the belief agent(self) in the set of his motives. In the top of this pyramid we may find the base interests, fixed by the user, and in the lower layers we find the interests generated by the motivation structure. So, the interest electrical_circuits can be satisfied when the interest electrotechnical_engineer is attained, this one when the interest course(electrotechnical_engineering) is attained, and this one when the interests discipline(alga) and discipline(electricity) are satisfied.

The agent *c* is theoretical (see 3.3) in the base context of soccer, and he has the following features:

A = { own }
CxSc = { (soccer,teams) }
B_{own} = { team(benfica, team(oporto), team(sporting)}
$<_{own}$ = {}
R_{own} = { modus_ponens }
mem(Belief in (soccer,teams)) = permanent
Tl = 0.0.0
mot(soccer, teams)=very_motivated
M_{own} ={ theorem($informatics engineer 2$, if, head(agent(X), technician_course(computers, X)), body(programming(X)));theorem($informatics engineer 2$, if, head(agent(X),informatics_engineer(X)),body(programming(X)));theorem($informatics engineer 2$, if,head(agent(X), course(informatics_engineering,X)),body(informatics_engineer(X))); theorem($informatics engineer 3$, if, head(agent(X), discipline(alga,X), discipline(computers, X),body(course(informatics_engineering,X)));theorem($soccer 1$, if, head(agent(X), read(sports_papers,X)),body(soccer(X))) }
I_{own} = { soccer; programming }

Again, in the top of the agent *c* pyramid of interests we may find the base interests, fixed by the user (soccer, programming), and in the lower layers we find the interests generated by the motivation structure (discipline(alga) and discipline(computers)).

The following scenario was built up: two-sided communication (semi-strong gap between teacher and students, and semi-authoritarian teacher). The goal of this classroom lesson consists of both students learn the concept of commutativity, say 'know(commutativity(_,_))' in the language of the agent. The plan of the lesson is structured by the agent teacher with the set of those beliefs, related indirectly or undirectly with that goal. In the present case, the plan consists of the beliefs that are in the preferred subtheory of agent a. The teaching method consists of two steps: 1) the selection of the set of beliefs to be taught (the class plan) and 2) the presentation of the knowledge content, in a sorted manner for each pair (Context, Sub-context).

The overall communication has four phases: 1) motivated introduction, 2) presentation of contents (related to the pair Context and Sub-context), the so-called base beliefs, 3) confirmation of goals in that pair, and 4) presentation of the generated beliefs, when unknown for the student agents, and repetition when necessary of other beliefs not assimilated by the student agents. The interaction among the above three agents (31 steps) is presented below in a reduced version:

(1) a --> soc (public)
    inform: presents(a)
...
(5) a --> soc (public)
    inform: goal(alga,ev,discipline(alga))
...
(14) c --> a (private)
    request: request(question_1,p(alga,ev, theorem(_7DFC,if, head(set(_7E18)), mbody(operation(addition, _7E18)))))
(15) a --> c (private)
    answer: answer(question_1,empty)
(16) b --> c (public)
    request: request(question_2,p(alga,ev,definition(operation addition in e,operand(triple(_1088, _108C,0), tripple(_1098,_109C,0), addition, tripple(_10A8,_10AC,0),e), def(# simplify(_1088 + _1098, _10A8), # simplify(_108C + _109C, _10AC)))))
(17) c --> b (public)
    answer: answer(question_2,r(alga,ev, definition(operation addition in e, operand(triple(_1C8C,   _1C9C,0),   tripple(_1C9C,_1CA0,0),   addition, tripple(_1CAC,_1CB0,0),e), def(# simplify(_1C8C + _1C9C, _1CAC), # simplify(_1C90 + _1CA0, _1CB0)))))
(18) a --> b (private)
    inform: no_conversation
(22) b --> a (public)
    request: request(question_5,p(alga,ev,example(_7E1C,_7E20,_7E24)))
(23) a --> b (private)
    answer: answer(question_5, r(alga, ev, example(example1, ex(data(set(r), element(x, r), element(y, r), operation(addition, r)), conclude_if(commutative(addition, r))), just(operand(x, y, addition, res1, r), operand(y, x, addition, res2, r), # equal_exp(res1,res2)))))
(24) b --> a (public)
    request: request(question_6, p(alga, _7E68, operand(triple(x1, x2, 0), triple(x1, x2, 0), addition, _7E80, e)))
(25) a --> b (private)
    answer: request(question_6,r(alga,ev,operand(triple(x1,x2,0), triple(x1,x2,0), addition, triple(2*x1, 2*x2,0), e)))
(26) b --> a (public)

request: request(question_7, p(alga, _7E68, operand(triple(x1,x2,0), triple(x1,x2,0), addition, _7E80, r)))
(27) a --> b (private)
   answer: answer(question_7, r(alga,ev,operand(triple(x1,x2,0), triple(x1,x2,0), addition, triple(2*x1, 2*x2,0), e)))
(28) a --> b (private)
   request: request(question_8,p(commutativity(addition,e)))
(29) b --> a (private)
   answer: answer(question_8,r(commutativity(addition,e)))
(30) a --> c (private)
   request: request(question_8,p(commutativity(addition,e)))
(31) c --> a (private)
   answer: answer(question_8,r(commutativity(addition,e)))

End of Example 2.

Interaction is the visible part of any teaching session. But with classical intelligent tutors there was only a transfer of knowledge to the student mind. Along ILE's, and with a DAI approach, we can simulate the natural environment of a classroom by introducing more flexible agent architectures, allowing the processing of action and reaction (belief revision). For example, the request of agent c in (14) is generated by his inductive reasoning and constrained by his theoretical role. Again in (21), agent b discovers that he has no sufficient data to proceed, reasoning by analogy, and he is forced to ask the teacher for help. At the end, the two students, b and c, arrived to the conclusion about commutativity, and, therefore, the goal of the classroom is achieved.

The key feature in our new proposal is the motivation capability that allows the agent student to accomplish a successful learning process. Note that the 3-tuple $<M_A, <_a, R_a>$ serves as a kind of deductive structure for motives, like D_A for beliefs, giving to the agent the preferred subtheory of motives. The all set of motives is viewed as a set of general beliefs (meta-level), upon any context, and always present along all interactions.

7 Conclusions

We have presented a new attempt in looking closer to the Intelligent Learning Environments, taking now a point of view from DAI and discussing agent architectures and multi-agent interactions. We hope it is clear from the discussion above that our approach is general enough to deal with different educational scenarios. Moreover, being based on a formal model helps in clarifying some concepts used in the field of Artificial Intelligence and Education like, for instance, what a student (agent) model really is. Such a decision helps also to view these environments as teaching and learning workbenches where we can evaluate how to build a student relationship by tuning key features, such as reasoning and motivation, and with the explicit goal of educating the individual. Advisory, tutoring or assistance styles can be simulated for the sole benefit of the teacher in charge of some class with "difficult" students and a forecast of bad results.

Acknowledgements

The background ideas of this follow-up paper were advanced for the first time in 1990 by Graça Gaspar, with whom we had fruitful discussions along years. The authors are also grateful to the three anonymous referees for critical and helpful comments. This work was partially supported by CEC under ESPRIT-III MODELAGE project.

References

[Caldas and Coelho 92] J. C. Caldas and H. Coelho, Strategic interaction in oligopolistic markets: experimenting with real and artificial agents, in the Proceedings of the Fourth European Workshop on Modeling Autonomous Agents in a Multi-Agent World (MAAMAW´92), Rome (Italy), 29-31 August, 1992 and in Artificial Social Systems, C. Castelfranchi and E. Werner (eds.), Springer-Verlag, pp. 147-163, 1994.

[Coelho et alli 94] H. Coelho, L. Antunes and L. Moniz, On agent design rationale, in the Proceedings of the XI Brazilian Symposium on Artificial Intelligence (SBIA-94), Fortaleza (Brazil), 17-20 October, 1994, T. Pequeno and F Carvalho (eds.), BSC, 1994.

[Coelho et alli 95] H. Coelho, L. Antunes and L. Moniz, Building multi-agent societies from descriptions to systems: inter-layer translation, Proceedings of the Seventh Portuguese Conference on Artificial Intelligence (EPIA´95), Funchal (Portugal), 3-6 October, 1995.

[Corrêa and Coelho 93] M. Corrêa and H. Coelho, Around the architectural agent approach to model conversations, in the Proceedings of the Fifth European Workshop on Modeling Autonomous Agents in a Multi-Agent World (MAAMAW´93), Neuchâtel (Switzerland), 24-27 August, 1993.

(Costa et alli, 1988) E. Costa, S. Duchénoy and Y. Kodratoff, A resolution-based method for discovering student's misconceptions, in J. Self (Ed.) Artificial Intelligence and Human Learning, Chapman and Hall, 1988.

(Costa et alli 91] E. Costa, G. Gaspar and H. Coelho, A formal approach to Intelligent Learning Environment (ILE)´s: a first tentative, in the Proceedings of the NATO Advanced Research Workshop on Student Modelling, Montréal (Canada), May, 1991 and also in Student Modelling: the key to individualized knowledge based instruction, Jim Greer and Gordon McCalla (eds.), Springer-Verlag, pp. 281-294, 1994.

[Eusébio 95] A. Eusébio, Learning environment for mathematics supported upon autonomous intelligent agents (in Portuguese), M. Sc. Thesis (submitted to UTL), 1995.

[Galliers 90] J. Galliers, Belief revision and a theory of communication, Technical Report 193, Computer Laboratory, University of Cambridge, UK, 1990.

[Gaspar 90] G. Gaspar, Communication and belief changes in a society of agents: towards a formal model of an autonomous agent, in the Proceedings of the 5th Rocky Mountains Conference on AI, Pragmatics in AI, Las Cruces, 28-30, 1990. Revised version published in "Decentralized Artificial Intelligence 2", Elsevier Science Publishers, 1991.

[Gaspar and Coelho 95] G. Gaspar and H. Coelho, Where do intentions come from? A framework for goals and intentions adoption, derivation and evolution, Proceedings of the Seventh Portuguese Conference on Artificial Intelligence (EPIA´95), Funchal (Portugal), 3-6 October, 1995.

[Konolige 86] K. Konolidge, A deduction model of belief, Pitman, London, 1986.

[Konolige and Pollack 93] K. Konolige and M. E. Pollack, A representationalist theory of intention, in the Proceedings of the Thirteenth International Joint Conference on Artificial Intelligence (IJCAI-93), Chambéry (France), pp. 390-395, 1993.

[Martins and Shapiro 88] J. P. Martins and S. C. Shapiro, A model for belief revision, in Artificial Intelligence, 35, pp. 25-79, 1988.

[Self 92] J. Self, Computational Mathetics: the missing link in Intelligent Tutoring Systems research?, in New Directions for Intelligent Tutoring Systems, E. Costa (ed.), Springer-Verlag, pp. 38-56, 1992.

[Trancas and Godinho 93] J. Trancas and P. Godinho, Multi-agent interaction (in Portuguese), FCT Research report, Coimbra University, 1993.

[Wooldridge and Jennings 95] M. Wooldridge and N.R. Jennings, Intelligent agents: theory and practice, in Knowledge Engineering Review, 1995 (to appear).

Building Multi-Agent Societies from Descriptions to Systems: Inter-Layer Translations

Helder Coelho, Luis Antunes and Luis Moniz
Departamento de Informática
Faculdade de Ciências de Lisboa
Bloco C5 - Piso 1, Campo Grande, 1700 Lisboa, Portugal
E-mail: {hcoelho, xarax, hal}@di.fc.ul.pt

Abstract. When we focus on (Distributed) Artificial Intelligence as an experimental science, it is not always clear which are the best experiments to try and how they should be conducted. It is up to the designer of the experiment the choice from a wide range of languages, models and architectures for his agents, and even from a numerous set of computational environments (namely, workbenches and testbeds).

In the follow-up of some methodological remarks recently made, concerning the journey from the first idealization of a problem until a final system is completed and running, with this paper we aim to enlighten the importance of maintaining consistent and coherent links between levels of description. Only in this way, we can debug experiments at the higher levels of abstraction, and hope the implementation results we get are sound, in order to make the journey backwards and be re-interpreted in a high-level context.

1 Introduction

It is possible to look at a discipline such as Artificial Intelligence (AI) as a branch of engineering, whose aim is to build artifacts considered interesting by the application of some criterion. On the other hand, it is more challenging and potentially more rewarding to see AI as a science, its aim being now to understand the structure and mechanisms of certain phenomena, then to try to produce models of those phenomena, and ultimately to contribute not only to the construction of artificial replicates, but also to the understanding of the natural events observed.

But for this goal to be correctly accomplished, it doesn't suffice to say AI is a science. It is necessary to do AI in a scientific manner. And nowadays more and more people defend that AI is an experimental science [Hanks et al 93, Simon 93]. Nevertheless, the "Look Ma, no hands!" phase hasn't passed yet. There should be some concern about methodologies to correctly develop AI experiments.

In a recent paper, [Coelho et al 94] have debated the designer's activity, when picking up problems to be approached by Distributed AI, describing them in an informal manner, and then making a journey from those descriptions to completed systems, passing through (possibly) several stages of increasingly formal descriptions. They provided some reasons for also making that journey in the opposite direction, so that the designer can better (and rightfully) evaluate the results of his experiment, or even redesign the whole experiment. And, by doing that, they gave a first critical answer to the [Shoham 93] challenge.

In this paper, we re-address the issue of designing experiments as a journey from the idealization of a problem to a running system (possibly in a simulated environment), and passing through several stages, such as the informal description, and one or more formalizations, that are closer and closer to a concrete system. Our main focus here is to observe what happens between two levels of these successive descriptions, what is gained and what is lost when we travel along that line. Instead of blindly jumping from a specification to a running system, we propose a sequence of smaller steps, that will bring us to a more continuous approach of this voyage. Moreover, we intend to make backwards journeys (cf. [Coelho et al 94]), which reiterates the necessity of correctness and completeness between levels. In section 2, we further present this methodological view and discuss some of its related issues. In section 3, we present a small and simple example, adopt a formalism to represent it and translate this formalization into a SSAE ADL architecture [Moniz 93]. In section 4, we provide a generalization of the translation rules we used in section 3. And, in the last section, we present our conclusions and some ideas of work to be done in the future.

2 Designing Experiments

In a not yet published paper, [Jones 93] commented an earlier version of Shoham's paper on Agent-Oriented Programming [Shoham 93], and he extended his strong criticism to the research carried out in DAI on describing the behaviour of computer systems (so-called agents) in terms of logics of human agency and deliberation. The points put forward are quite relevant to be further studied and thought about, and in our present paper we present another contribution to clarify the whole space of discussion suggested firstly by [Sloman 93].

In general, we observe two main perspectives taken over autonomous agents: (1) an AI programming and engineering perspective, following the old ideas of Hewitt's Actor formalism [Hewitt 77, 85] around objects, and (2) an applied modal logic perspective, inspired in Philosophy, around some class of modalities to characterize their mental states and attitudes [Pörn 77].

The main criticism presented by Jones was that Shoham, when trying to combine these two perspectives, failed to provide the necessary links between the modal logic formalization and the actual implementation of the systems we wanted to conceive. There is no mapping between the formal descriptors and the real features of the computational environment he provided. So, the intuitive (first) and formal (afterwards) motivations for developing the system (in the way it was done) fall down.

In this case (like in many other) evaluation criteria are missing, with common sense intuitions about intentional terms not clearly separated (or related) from formal demands or computational needs. However, an effort has been done by [Cohen et al 89] in order to set up some order in AI, and the ecology (or MAD: Modelling, Analysis and Design) methodology is a good example to view the agent architecture in function of its behaviour and environment.

As benchmarks, testbeds and controlled experimentation are becoming more common in AI [Hanks et al 93], the need for an appropriate methodology for agent design is well recognized in order to evaluate not only theories as interpretations of results of experimental studies, but also to evaluate designs as the correct translations of formal descriptions. [Coelho et al 94] have made a contribution to clarify these issues, and to open new alleys of research around the most appropriate languages for formal and system engineering work (how can we relate their primitives?).

It is common to conceive the whole journey as composed of only three steps: providing a description, formalizing, and building the system (e.g. MAD: modelling, analysis, and design). It could be argued that it suffices to provide a correct algorithm to translate the specification into a system. The only remaining problem would be to provide adequate formalisms to think about and to represent the informal descriptions.

But this view is oversimplified, and several points have to be made. There is a need to make the translation back to previous languages (and abstraction levels). This is necessary both to debug and to evaluate the descriptions (and ultimately the working system). It isn't evident that an absolutely correct algorithm can be built, one that avoids the need to debugging. Even Shoham admits he doesn't want to addres theorem proving in modal logic. Think, for instance, of a first system that simulates a robot's arm functioning and a second system composed by a real arm and the software that operates it. The kind of control required by the second system is so different from the first one that one should expect some problems to arise when developing the systems [Sloman 92]. How to debug the system, or to account for unexpected features in the system behaviour, if we cannot relate our observations to the specification we have made?

On the other hand, we can have final systems that do not differ that much from the formal specifications. They could be symbol manipulating programs. In this case, where is the relation between the symbols in our system and the objects in the world? Why is this relation more present in the working system than it would be in the specification? The answer to these questions is: it depends on what happens in the designer's mind. But it is easy for him to draw those relations, because he has the global picture of the whole path from the initial description to the desired system. There is no less need for the journeys back and forth, since in these conditions it is easy to wrongly introduce features in a level that weren't in a previous one, for instance, solutions to unspecified problems.

3 The Journey of a Simple Experiment

In this section we will present our experimental environment and describe a small and simple exercise, in a step-by-step manner. First, we present the SSAE workbench and its Agent Definition Language (ADL), and afterwards we state an example and formalize it by using Temporal Linear Logic [Wolper 89]. Finally, we discuss the translation from this formal description to ADL.

3.1 The SSAE workbench and its Agent Definition Language (ADL)

The structure of the SSAE workbench is described in [Moniz 93b] and is composed of four sections: the agents, the libraries, the interpreter, and the implementation of parallelism. The architecture of the agents is depicted in figure 1, where the arrows represent the access channels. For instance, units are connected to modules and internal states. This means that units can use both of them in their definition, but they can't use methods or other units. It is a general architecture, intended to support the definition and test of different agent models. The different activities an agent can carry out are associated with the notion of unit. The control part of the agent is in charge of enabling or desabling the units. The modules can be said to implement atomic actions. These actions can either consist of a change in the agent's internal states or have consequences in the world. The methods are procedures or plan schemes to perform calculations, or verify internal situations.

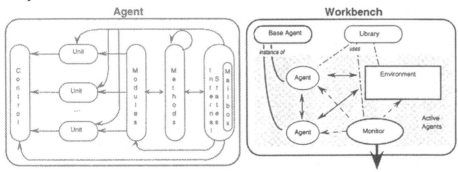

Figure 1: General structure of an agent in SSAE.   Figure 2: The context structure of an experiment.

In figure 2 we present the context organization of a possible experiment with our workbench. The dotted area contains all entities that can change their behaviour within the simulation time. The Base Agent and the Library are shared by several agents but do not participate actively in the simulation. The full lines represent visible communication channels between agents, the dotted lines represent invisible channels for the active agent, and the arrows represent active access to an object, during the simulation. The Monitor is the agent that allows the user to watch the other agent's states, without interacting with them. So its channels to and from the other agents are for its exclusive use.

3.2 Informal children story

Jack, the mole, lives in a garden near the big river. In this environment, Jack has lots of friends, Joe the toad, Mr. Rufus the badger and Andrew the water rat. One day, waking up in a foggy and cloudy morning Jack, our hero, noticed that all his friends had disappeared. Now, the quest begins...

Let us specify the narrative description in order to observe the agent skills and behaviour. Jack can walk around his world (the garden), look for his friends, become hungry, search for food, and eat seeds. Jack's main goal is to find his friends, but to acomplish that he will spend energy, so he must eat first. He will only look for his friends when he's not hungry.

3.3 Logical formalization of the narrative

Let us start to formalize the narrative by taking Jack's point of view: Jack can perform several actions and be engaged in simple behaviours. A possible formal language is Temporal Linear Logic [Wolper 89], with two operators, X and F.

- **Xa** means: **a** will be true the following instant.
- **Fa** means: **a** will be true sometime in the future.

Our first aim is to isolate the five actions that Jack can perform and his mental attributes (knowledge that will dynamically change value).

Actions:	Mental Attributes:
Eat food (**eat**)	he is hungry (**hungry?**)
Walk (**walk**)	he has found food (**found?**)
Search for food (**search**)	he has reached food (**reached?**)
Become hungry (**bc_hungry**)	he has found friends (**friends?**)
Look for friends (**lk_friends**)	

Jack's mental attributes are directly connected to his actions. They will be used to define in what circumstances the agent should finish an action and start another. To keep this experiment simple we will consider that the values that can be asserted to Jack's mental attributes are only TRUE or FALSE.

We must also define the various interactions between mental attributes and actions. For instance, which are the attributes that change by the execution of an action. There are four sets of rules for governing these interactions: security rules, that indicate the conditions to perform an action; liveness rules, that indicate when an action should be initiated; transition rules, that describe the change of values on the attributes caused by the execution of an action; and initial values, that indicate the starting values of the attributes.

Which are the initial values of the agent's mental attributes? When the agent's execution begins, its mental attributes have values. The following rule states which is the value of each attribute.

BEG –> (hungry?=false) and (found?=false) and (reached?=false) and (friends?=false)

When must Jack start an action? This can be represented by rules, that state what are the necessary conditions to initiate an action. These liveness rules have the generic structure: *Condition* → M*Action*, meaning that the *Action* will start as soon as (according to the modal operator M) the *Condition* is true. The following rules state the liveness rules for the actions of our agent.

¬hungry? –> Fbc_hungry
hungry? –> Xsearch
found? –> Xwalk
reached? –> Xeat
¬hungry? –> Xlk_friends

When can Jack perform an action? Each action is regulated by a set of conditions that define when it can be performed. The generic structure of these security rules is: *Action → Conditions*, where the *Conditions* define the state in which the *Action* can be performed. In our example:

```
eat -> (reached?)
walk -> (found?) and (¬reached?)
search -> (hungry?) and (¬found?)
lk_friends -> (¬hungry?)
```

Which are the consequences of each action on his mental attributes ? When an action is performed the agent's mental attributes changes. These transition rules state what happens to each one of the attributes when the action is completed.

```
bc_hungry -> (Xhungry?=true) and (Xfound?=found?) and (Xreached?=reached?) and (Xfriends?=friends?)
eat -> (Xhungry?=false) and (Xreached?=false) and (Xfound?=found?) and (Xfriends?=friends?)
walk -> (Xreached?=true) and (Xfound?=false) and (Xhungry?=hungry?) and (Xfriends?=friends?)
search -> (Xfound?=true) and (Xhungry?=hungry?) and (Xreached?=reached?) and (Xfriends?=friends?)
lk_friends -> (Ffriends?=true) and (Xfound?=found?) and (Xreached?=reached?) and (Xhungry?=hungry?)
```

3.4 Agent representation in ADL

The formal narrative description we have just presented is not complete, but neither was the informal description from which we started. It does not specify what is meant by walking or searching, how much time does Jack take for walking one meter, etc. We will ignore these difficulties, and consider by now that the way the agent performs those actions is *hardwired*, and will be defined later as modules (atomic actions) in the SSAE workbench. For instance, we consider walk to be an instantaneous action, that takes no time to perform, and define it in the corresponding module.

Jack can perform all five previous actions, four of which are strongly interdependent: search, walk, eat and look for friends. He cannot start one of these actions without finishing the previous one. These four actions can be grouped together and define an independent behaviour, which may be broken into related behaviours: eat food and look for friends. The last action defines a completely independent behaviour: become hungry, which doesn't depend of the completion or initialization of any other action, because it can be activated any time. In figure 3 we illustrate the two independent behaviours of Jack: eat and find friends, and become hungry.

Figure 3: Two behaviours of Jack

We can have several alternatives for representing agent Jack in our SSAE workbench [Moniz93]. At least, these following three ways are a consequence of how actions are connected to compose behaviours, and how we want to represent these connections.

1) We can associate each one of these two behaviours (illustrated in figure 3) to an ADL unit:

Control level

```
execute(unit(eat_find_friends)),
execute(unit(become_hungry))
```

Unit *become_hungry*

```
bc_hungry
```

Unit *eat_find_friends*

```
if(hungry?,
    if(¬found?,
        search,
        if(¬reached?, walk, eat)),
    lk_friends)
```

2) The second alternative is to assign a unit to each action the agent may perform. In each unit we include the triggers to that action (corresponding to the liveness and security rules defined earlier). The control level only defines which are the agent's units. Each unit consists of a selection command that activates an action if its security rule becomes true.

Control level	Each unit can be defined as:
execute(unit(do_walk)), execute(unit(do_search)), execute(unit(do_lk_friends)), execute(unit(do_eat)), execute(unit(become_hungry))	do_search: if(hungry? & ¬found?, search,nothing) do_walk: if(found? & ¬reached?, walk,nothing) do_eat: if(reached?, eat,nothing) do_lk_friends: if(¬hungry?, lk_friends,nothing) become_hungry: bc_hungry

3) The triggers we defined can also be represented in the control level. This option defines, in the control level, the conditions in which a unit is activated.

The control level is composed of a sequence of selection commands, which use the security rule as selection condition.

```
if(hungry? & ¬found?,execute(unit(do_search)),nothing)
if(found? & ¬reached?,execute(unit(do_walk)),nothing)
if(reached?,execute(unit(do_eat)),nothing)
if(¬hungry?,execute(unit(do_lk_friends)),nothing)
```

The units are defined only as a module execution.

```
do_search: search
do_walk: walk
do_eat: eat,
do_lk_friends: lk_friends
become_hungry: bc_hungry
```

The alternatives proposed above correspond to different architectures for our final agent, thus its behaviour remains the same in each proposal. For instance the alternative 1, represents an agent with two independent behaviours and almost no higher level control, the control is performed locally and the high level control only indicates which are the active units. This can be useful to study agents with a strong reactive architecture, although each component may have some global view of the agent knowledge in order to avoid conflicts. On the opposite side we have the option 3, where the high level control takes charge of the resolution of all potential conflicts. The control has all the information regarding the agent structure and when each action should be performed. This approach emphasizes the traditional mentalistic view of an agent, with a strong centralized control and almost no global knowledge in the agent components. The second option represents an agent where his behaviour is fragmented in independent simple behaviours. Each simple behaviour has the triggers to enable or disable the actions. The main difference between this and option 1 is the fragmentation of the behaviour, which in this case is reduced to simple actions. In this case, the responsability for the execution of the action is represented explicitly in each component. This could be an advantage if we want to build agents in a bottom-up fashion.

4 The Issue of Translation

It was suggested, in [Shoham 93], that there should be desirable to design an automatic process to bridge the gap between the formal description (high abstraction level, in his case in mental terms) and the low level machine programs. Shoham calls this process an 'agent interpreter.' But unfortunately, Shoham does not say anything about the way that agent is built. Nor does he provide a table of conversions linking the mental (intentional) high-level specifications to the low-level primitives of his language: Is he assured that the two 'agents' (the abstract one and the computational one) are the same? How and by what means?

In our present paper, we chose not to use mental terms to describe our agents, in order to make easier the discussion of the translation process. In this section we pick up the formalism we have chosen, and propose some rules of translation to the workbench language we have taken. We define explicitely the rules of translation that must be obeyed, in order to transform the logical representation into a system description. We try to observe what is gained and what is lost in this translation, and look at some possibilities for retroversion, in order to re-engineer the experiment if necessary, as is illustrated in figure 4. We infer the rules we present from the example in section 3, showing how the translation can be made in a detached way. These rules should be applied to the logical definition of an agent in order to obtain its ADL definition.

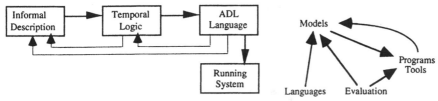

Figure 4: From reality to systems.   Figure 5: Evolution along research.

This voyage is not made only in one direction, as depicted in figure 5. Sometimes in the last steps we find out that something is missing, then we must go back and complete the previous stages in order to get what we need in the end level. This evaluation of results allows the tuning up of our informal descrition of the initial situation. It also may allow for the detection of deficiencies in the adopted frameworks, and suggest ways of reformulating them.

4.1 Converting a formal language to a system language

In order to achieve the automatic bridge pointed earlier, we draw now the outline of an automatic translator, the so-called agent interpreter. This meta-agent performs the translation between the description language and the agent architecture (see figure 6).

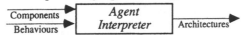

Figure 6: The agent interpreter.

We define the structure of the agent interpreter as a table. This table maps the components and the description of the behaviours of our agent to the workbench generic architecture (see the table in figure 7). The map provides us a set of alternatives to define an agent, and it is a direct consequence of the experiments made in agent representation with ADL. From the map, we can't draw a unique algorithm for the translation. As we have seen in the previous section, there are several alternatives for the ADL programming of an agent, given its TLL description. What the table gives us is a family of designs for the formal specification confirming [Sloman 94] thesis.

	Control	Units	Modules	Procedures	Internal States
Actions		•	•		
Behaviours		•			
Attributes					•
Initial Conditions					•
Security Rules	•	•	•		
Transition Rules			•	•	
Liveness Rules	•	•			

Figure 7: The internal structure of an agent interpreter.

The problem of translation can be viewed from two distinct standpoints. On one hand, is the question of how to translate the formal rules in our architecture, converting those rules in agent components. The other standpoint is how can a agent component arise from those conversions, integrating all the translations of rules. For instance, if we choose to represent a liveness rule in a unit, it make no sense to put the corresponding security rule in the control. Next we present a detailed view of the rows of the table in figure 7.

1) Initial Values/Attributes ⟶ Internal States

The translation between attributes and internal states is straightforward. It is only an association of each attribute to a variable in the agent internal states. The initial values of the attributes are translated by assigning to the corresponding variable its initial value.

Initial Values	Internal States
BEG –> (Attribute1? = Value1) and (Attribute2 ?= Value2)	eq(Variable1, Value1), eq(Variable2, Value2)

Figure 8: Translation from Initial Values to Internal States.

2) Liveness Rules ⟶ Units/Control

These properties define the agent triggers, and the conditions for a unit or module to be activated. In figure 9, we show how this translation can be achieved.

Liveness Rule	Unit	Control
Condition –> Action	if(Condition, mod_Action, nothing)	if(Condition,execute(unit(do_Action)),nothing)

where *mod_Action* is the name of the module and *do_Action* is the name of the unit, both connected to the action *Action* defined in the liveness rule.

Figure 9: Translation from Liveness Rules to Units and Control.

3) Security Rules ⟶ Control/Units/Modules

Security Rules are tools to inibit actions. These rules can be represented anywhere in the units, in the control or modules according to the user needs. The representation of this rule in a module is similar to the representation of a liveness rule (as in 2). In the next table we present the translation of security rules in units and modules.

Security Rule	Unit	Module
Action –> CondA and CondB	if(CondA & CondB, mod_Action, nothing)	execute(action) <– CondA & CondB

where action is a sequence of commands to achieve Action defined in the security rule.

Figure 10: Translation from Security Rules to Units and Modules.

4) Transition Rules ⟶ Modules/Procedures

These rules define what happens to the attributes when an action is executed. These rules must be represented in the modules as part of the action definition.

Transition Rule	Module/Procedure Action
Action –> (Attrib1? = Val1) and (Attrib2? = Val2)	remember(eq(Var1, Val1)) & remeber(eq(Var2, Val2)).

Note that the *Module/Procedure* is associated to the *Action* of the transition rule. The translation is similar if made in module or procedure.

Figure 11: Translation from Transition Rules to Modules and Procedures.

5) Behaviour/Action ⟶ Control/Unit

In our formal model the behavior of the agent is represented by rules. The Liveness rules and Security rules are the ones that control the execution of the action. As we saw in 2) and 3) these rules are represented, in our architecture, into units and control.

There are several alternatives of building the control and units. Let U be the set of agent's units, *SecurityCondition* the right member of the security rule, *LivenessCondition* the left member of the liveness rule, and *action* a module name associated to the action.

	Alternative 1	Alternative 2	Alternative 3
Control	$\forall i \in U$: execute((unit(i))	$\forall i \in U$: if(LivenessCondition & SecurityCondition , execute((unit(i)), nothing)	$\forall i \in U$: if(LivenessCondition, execute(unit(i)), nothing)
Units	if(LivenessCondition& SecurityConditio, action, nothing)	action	if(SecurityCondition , action, nothing)

Figure 12: Composition of control and units.

We must note that in our previous example the security condition overlaps the liveness condition, then the conjunction of both could be reduced to the security condition.

6) Actions ─────► Modules/Procedures

Each atomic action should be defined as a module. This action could be a decomposed in a set of actions. For instance, we have defined walk as an atomic action, but in a real simulation we must specify what their components are: check and make a step or stop. After, we must define what is check, step and stop. This decomposition is not in our formal definition of the problem, we chose to keep it out to make a clearer description. This specification should be made in a module or in a procedure. For an example, look at figure 13, where the module language is similar to Prolog. If the module is activated the interpreter will test (by definition order) the right-hand side of each instruction. If all clauses are true, it will execute the left-hand side.

Module Walk	Procedure Step
execute(remember(reached),forget(found)) <– check?, execute(step) <– true	step <– lift_paw & put_down_paw

Figure 13: Action representation in modules and procedures.

We can begin to address the issue of correctness by looking at what is gained and what is lost between translation levels. We can outline some criteria to measure this. It seems clear that in ADL we have a smaller representation space than we had in TLL (which in turn is smaller than the informal description). We can have less designs than we have specifications, since the SSAE architecture imposes further constraints. On the other hand, in ADL we have more grounding. To execute real experiments we must have concrete objetcs, and the objects that inhabit our simulated environment are closer to reality than the formal objects specified in TLL, even though it may be a simulated reality. It is fundamental to further explore this question, so that the advantages of the backwards journey (as proposed in [Coelho et al 94]) can be fully expoited, to achieve benefits in agent and experiment re-engineering, and so generate developments both in abstract description techniques and in the formalisms that support them. For instance, suppose we were to add new features, such as mental states, to our agent idealization. We would represent those features and their dynamics in TLL, apply the conversion table and get a new design. This process teminates successfully if this new agent behaves in the way it was supposed to. In any other case (either the conversion wasn't possible, or it produced a wrongly-behaving agent), we should re-address the translation process, using the discovered limitations as guidelines.

5 Conclusions and Future Work

It is nowadays commonly acknowledged by the AI community, the need to conduct the research in a principled way. The management of experiments and proper evaluation of results can provide a way of reducing to tractable complexity the design space [Sloman 94] where we are searching. Only by really conducting the experiments can we check whether our idealizations are correct and feasible.

In this paper we argue for more principled experiment design, in particular addressing the issue of translation between levels of description. We took a toy example, formalized it in Temporal Linear Logic and then looked into the problem of translating this formal description into a system language and a (simulated) experimental setting. With this simple example, we were able to produce a simple conversion table from TLL to ADL. This table will not generate a unique design for an agent, given its TLL description. The table only gives the designer some guidelines for the construction of the agent. Nevertheless, these guidelines can be used to define a policy for agent design. Taking into account fundamental design options (something like a third dimension in the table) this policy can address a broad spectrum of agent architectures, from purely reactive to completely cognitive and deliberative.

There are several unanswered questions we leave for further research. One main issue we couldn't address here was the maintenance of correctness during the travel along the design-line, allowing the designer to claim that in each performed step he has all the properties (and not more) he had in the previous step. This is closely related with another problem, the choice of the formal language to use, and the set of its primitives. Another issue is the evaluation of results. It is possible that we cannot be less formal when evaluating the behaviours we observe than we are when designing the agents. This would mean that even for the observation of behaviours we can't have an ad hoc approach, we rather ought to postulate clearly what are the properties we expect to see, and then compare that with the collected results. One further link can be explored, between real experiments (with real societies and real agents), and simulated experiments.

Acknowledgments

We would like to thank Igmar Pörn, Andrew Jones, and Cristiano Castelfranchi, with whom we have had fruitful discussions about the ideas in this paper. The present work was partially carried out within the ESPRIT III project MODELAGE.

References

[Coelho et al 94] H. Coelho, L. Antunes and L. Moniz, On agent design rationale, Proceedings of the XI Brazilian Symposium on Artificial Intelligence, Fortaleza, Brazil, October 1994.

[Cohen et al 89] P. R. Cohen, M. L. Greenberg, D. M. Hart and A. E. Howe, Trial by fire: understanding the design requirements for agents in complex environments, AI Magazine, Fall 1989.

[Hanks et al 93] S. Hanks, M. E. Pollack and P. R. Cohen, Benchmarks, testbeds, controlled experimentation and the design of agent architectures, AI Magazine, volume 14, no. 4, Winter, 1993.

[Hewitt 77] C. Hewitt, Viewing control as patterns of passing messages, Artificial Intelligence, volume 8, 1977.

[Hewitt 85] C. Hewitt, The challenge of open systems, Byte, April, 1985.

[Jones 93] A. J. I. Jones, Practical reasoning, California-style: some remarks on Shoham's agent-oriented programming (AOP), Working Report, Dept. of Philosophy, University of Oslo, 1993.

[Moniz 93] L. Moniz, SSAE: system for simulation of agents and environments, MSc. Thesis, IST/UTL, Lisboa, June 1993 (in portuguese).

[Moniz 93b] L. Moniz, SSAE: A workbench for the simulation of heterogeneous environments and agents, Proceedings of the X Brazilian Symposium on Artificial Intelligence, Porto Alegre, Brazil, October 1993 (in portuguese).

[Pörn 77] I. Pörn, Action theory and social science, vol. 120, Synthese Library, D. Reidel Publishing Company, Dordrecht, Holland, 1977.

[Shoham 93] Y. Shoham, Agent-oriented programming, Artificial Intelligence Journal, volume 60, Number 1, March, 1993.

[Simon 93] Invited lecture in AAAI'93.

[Sloman 92] A. Sloman, The emperor's real mind: review of Roger Penrose's The Emperor's New Mind: concerning computers, minds and the laws of physics, Artificial Intelligence, vol. 56, numbers 2-3, August 1992, Elsevier, pp. 355-396.

[Sloman 93] A. Sloman, Prospects for AI as the general science of intelligence, in Prospects for Artificial Intelligence - Proceedings of AISB'93, Birmingham, IOS Press, 1993.

[Sloman 94] A. Sloman et al., Explorations in design space, Proceedings of the European Conference Artificial Intelligence, Amsterdam (Holland), August 8-12, 1994.

[Wolper 89] P. Wolper, On the relation of programs and computations to models of temporal logic, in B. Banieqbal, H. Barringer, and A. Pnueli (eds.), Temporal Logic in Specification, LNCS 398, Springer-Verlag, 1989, pp. 75-123.

GA/TS : A Hybrid Approach for Job Shop Scheduling in a Production System

José Ramón Zubizarreta Aizpuru and Javier Arrieta Usunáriz

Universidad del País Vasco, Facultad de Informática,
Plaza de Manuel de Lardizabal, 20009 San Sebastián, Spain

Abstract. This paper outlines a new efficient approach to solve combinatorial optimization problems making use of a hybrid search method. The approach integrates genetic algorithms (GA) and tabu search (TS) techniques to be incorporated into a generic architecture for a knowledge-based manufacturing system.

In this paper, a new method, called GA/TS, has been developed. The proposed method pursues a hybrid schedule generation strategy wherein it effectively combines knowledge acquired via genetics-based induction with tabu search methodology. We have used this hybrid approach to explore new strategies that may result in more powerful solution methods. Experiments on randomly generated problems of practical complexity, the notorious 10x10 instance of Muth&Thompson's benchmark and several instances of Lawrence [22] show that the hybrid scheduler strategy produces good results, better than previous efforts using genetics algorithms, and comparable to existing search-based methods [2, 4, 21].

Keywords : Genetic algorithms, production scheduling, tabu search.

1 Introduction

The task of production scheduling [14, 26] is temporal planning of the processing of a given set of orders. The scheduling problems have important characteristics: they are very difficult, and good quality solutions bring highly tangible benefits. In general, scheduling problems are NP-hard, consequently there are no known algorithms guaranteed to give an optimal solution and run in polynomial time. The processing of an order corresponds to the production of a particular product. It is accomplished by the execution of a set of operations in a sequence on certain resources, under consideration of several additional constraints, e.g. limited capacities or earliest start times. The result of scheduling is a (production) schedule showing the temporal assignment of operations of orders to the resources to be used, i.e. which resources should be used when for the manufacturing of a particular product.

The job shop scheduling problem is formally defined as follows. Given are a set O of l operations, a set M of m machines, and a set J of n jobs. For each operation $v \in O$ there is a processing time $p(v) \in \mathbb{N}$, a unique machine $M(v) \in M$ on which it requires processing, and a unique job $J(v) \in J$ such that $v \in J(v)$. On O a binary relation A is defined, which represents precedences between operations : if $(v, w) \in A$, then v has to be performed before w. A is such that all operations v with the same value $J(v)$ are totally ordered.

A schedule is a function $S : O \to \mathbb{N} \cup \{\emptyset\}$ that for each operation v defines a start time $S(v)$. A schedule S is feasible if

$$
\begin{aligned}
&\forall v \in O : && S(v) \geq 0 \\
&\forall v, w \in O, (v, w) \in A : && S(v) + p(v) \leq S(w) \\
&\forall v, w \in O, v \neq w, M(v) = M(w) : && S(v) + p(v) \leq S(w) \text{ or } S(w) + p(w) \leq S(v)
\end{aligned}
$$

The quality of a schedule is measured by means of an evaluation function, which assigns a numerical value to a schedule. Several different evaluation criteria can be relevant for a particular application, e.g. project duration (makespan), mean flow time, maximum lateness ...

The scheduling problems in an industrial environment often have a more complex problem structure, some additional parameters that are relevant to many real problem situations have to be considered as well, e.g. alternative process plans for the production of a product, alternative machines for the execution of an operation, cleaning times, special production structures, and so forth.

Heuristic tree search methods [4, 9] for locating good answers in scheduling include breadth-first search, depth-first search, hill climbing, best-first search, beam search and filtered beam search. Of course, each method has particular strengths and weaknesses. The drawbacks of relying wholly on tree search methods when examining the total space of legal schedules illustrate the desirability of exploring other alternatives. Genetic algorithms [10, 24] and Tabu search [17, 18] are efficient tools for searching and optimizing scheduling problems. Search remains tractable in terms of computing time and resources, even for considerable large problems.

The application scenario investigated was the production scheduling in a manufacturing plant. All experiments were run with real-world sample problem instances supplied by our industrial partners. The factory is organized as a series of specialized production units and manufactures 'to order'. The factory has planning and scheduling needs that are well matched by the tools provided by manufacturing information systems, as its activities require both detailed operational plans and frequent revisions of purchase orders and shop-floor activity.

2 The Knowledge-Based Architecture

The scheduling process, described above, uses a knowledge-based system to detect and react to conflicts between a predictive schedule and the actual events on the shop floor. The knowledge-based architecture is structured as a blackboard system. This system can be thought of as a framework in which the knowledge can be arranged so that it can be distributed and yet shared among a number of cooperating processes. The process by which the system construct solutions is incremental and opportunistic and is based on the progressive application of a variety of knowledge sources to solution space at varying levels of abstraction. The problem-solving schema has no predefined priority schedule determining how and when the individual knowledge sources are allowed access to the blackboard. Each source responds to changes in the state of the blackboard by altering its contents. The solution is therefore built incrementally, based on the cooperative behavior of these knowledge sources. A control component makes control decisions on the basis of the state of the blackboard. This component coordinates the knowledge sources recommend actions that they can take and performs these actions to make changes to the description of the problem and its solution.

The system was implemented as a BB1-like blackboard architecture. As in [8] the basic unit of control is the KSAR (Knowledge-Source Activation Record). KSAR's are created whenever a knowledge source is triggered by a blackboard event. The basic control loop consists in a three-step problem-solving cycle. First update the To-Do-Set (Update-To-Do-Set knowledge source) according to both domain and control blackboard modifications that satisfies Choose-KSAR's Conditions. Then select a pending KSAR using the control knowledge source Choose-KSAR and at last execute the selected KSAR that satisfies Interpret-KSAR's Condition producing a blackboard modification. In addition, two high-level control knowledge sources are employed to update heuristics used by scheduling process and to control the propagation of the consequences of scheduling decisions. Fig. 1 shows an overview of the system.

Basically, the system uses three different types of knowledge sources. The analysis knowledge source determines which of the available predictive and reactive components should be applied for schedule generation. The resource analyzer detects bottleneck and under-loaded resources and the conflict analyzer chooses those available reactive components which are most efficient in terms of conflict resolution. The planification knowledge source is responsible for generating a predictive scheduling and to resolve conflicts between the predictive schedule and the current situation on the shop floor. The interface knowledge source provides a flexible way to maintain a natural language dialogue between the user and the scheduling system.

The following sections describe in detail the planification knowledge source. Two search techniques will be investigated in a hybridization context with the main purpose to produce a good and efficient scheduler system.

3 Genetic Algorithms Approaches to Scheduling

Genetic Algorithms are adaptive procedures [10, 24] that find solutions to problems by an evolutionary process based on natural selection. The basic idea is to maintain a population of solutions for a given problem. The population evolves over time through competition (survival of the fittest) and controlled variation (crossover and mutation).

GA have been applied to a wide range of different problem domains. Diverse areas such as routing and scheduling, machine learning, gas pipeline control systems, VLSI design and strategy planning have profited from this method. One important domain of research and application of GA is the operations management problem of scheduling. In this arena, GA-based schedulers have

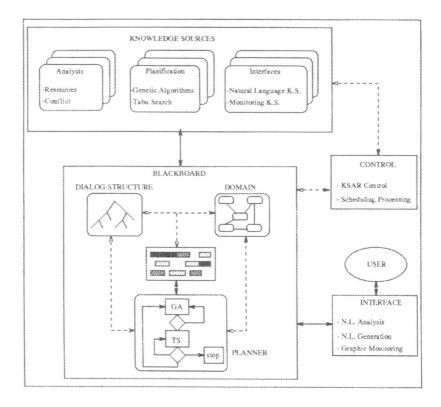

Fig. 1. Knowledge-Based Architecture.

been examined in the context of single-machine job shop scheduling, the time-constrained scheduling of limited resources, open shop sheduling and so forth.

Like other approaches [6, 25, 28, 30] we think that all information that pertains to the scheduling problem should be represented in the chromosome. For this reason, we use a direct problem representation in the GA by using the schedule itself as a chromosome. With this approach neither a transformation procedure nor a schedule builder are necessary anymore. The GA searches the space of all job order permutations and assigns process plan using advanced crossover and mutation operations. In our approach each individual represents an active schedule based on the classic Giffler and Thompson's algorithm [16] for generating active schedules. Individuals (parents) which are active schedules results in new active schedules (offsprings) which inherit the parents characteristics. A new solution is created selecting among the possible operations at every step the most advanced one in mother or father (crossover operator). Mutation randomly selects one of the possible operations introducing variability into the population. After the creation of offsprings some individuals are removed from the population in order to reduce it to its initial size.

4 Tabu Search Techniques in Production Scheduling

Tabu Search is an iterative descendent optimization method. The search presupposes a neighborhood structure. When the search arrives at a local optimum, it moves beyond the local optimum by choosing the best possible neighbor. However, such a procedure may introduce cycling. To avoid this one introduces so-called tabu list as a data structure storing in a queue all the solutions visited in the last i iterations. The moves which are classified as forbidden (tabu) are recorded on the list, where they reside for a specified number of iterations and then are removed. However, it may happen that an interesting move is tabu. In order to perform such moves an 'aspiration level' is defined. In this case, the tabu status of a move from solution i to solution j may be ignored allowing a move to be selected regardless of its tabu status.

We represent the job shop problem in disjunctive graph theoretical terms. The technological precedence ordering of the job operations is represented by directed paths of conjunctive arcs in the graph. The machining sequence that have to be processed by a machine is detailed by a selection of the direction of the disjunctive edges. The selection is consistent and the sequence is feasible if and only if the directed graph is acyclic, i.e., if and only if there is no path in the graph that begins and ends on the same vertex. In this formulation, the fundamental difficulty is to find the directed graph with the minimum critical path.

Like other approaches [11, 27, 29] the neighborhood function used in our TS approach is based on structural properties [5] of such graphs. To improve a schedule, a directed disjunctive arc on the critical maximum length path must be reversed. Each step of TS consists of examining the neighborhood and then of choosing the best allowed neighbor. The length of a neighbor equals the length of the new schedule when both operations involved are still on a longest path, and otherwise it is a lower bound.

5 The GA/TS Hybrid Algorithm

The proposed approach uses a direct problem representation where the production schedule itself is used as a chromosome. The used crossover operator is based on the classic Giffler and Thompson's algorithm for generating active schedules.

We have observed that the two search methods separately working offer relatively good solutions in production sequencing. However, the initial solution in TS and local minima in both cases can be hard obstacles in the search. One way of coping with this problems is to profit from the advantages of both GA and TS. The combination of these methods can be as simple as a successive application of them or cooperate in a more complex way. We have actually tried three different approaches :

- H1 : a successive application of GA, TS on the best solution and TS on a randomly selected solution.

- H2 : the user selects successively one of the methods and is allowed to change the parameters in order to favour the detected improvement.
- H3 : similar to H2, but TS is also embedded as a local optimizer in the GA.

The genetic-tabu(GA/TS) algorithm

```
Initialize ( GA, TS);
Generate P; Sort P;                    – P: Population
repeat selection
    → P := Genetic Algorithms ( P);
    → i_ts := Tabu Search ( i ∈ P); P := Select Population ( P, i_ts);
    → Display improvement; Change parameters;
until stop criterion;
end;
```

Tabu Search (i_{start})

```
Initialize ( L);                       – L: tabu list
i_best := i_start; i := i_start; k := 0;
limit := itemin + itemore;
repeat
    Find a longest path in i;
    Generate N;                        – N: Neighborhood
        – j ∈ N such that j is not tabu or γ(j) < γ(i)
    Choose j* minimizing γ over N;     – γ: objective function
    Update L;
    if γ(j*) < γ(i_best) then
        i_best := j*;
        if k > itemin then limit := limit + itemore;
        end;
    i := j*;
    k := k + 1;
until k > limit;
return i_best;
end;
```

Genetic Algorithms (P)

```
k := 0;
repeat
    Select i_father and i_mother from P;
    Select operator;                   – crossover operator
    i_child := Create Schedule ( i_father, i_mother, operator);
    P := Select Population ( P, i_child);
    k := k + 1;
until k > genmax;                      – genmax: # of generations
return P;
end;
```

Select Population (P, i_{new})
        if $\gamma(i_{new}) > \gamma(i_{worst})$ then return P;
        if $\gamma(i_{new}) = \gamma(i \in P)$ then
                – prevents a solution from being repeated in P
           if $local < random[0, 1)$ then
               begin
               $i_{ts} :=$ **Tabu Search** (i_{new});
               $P :=$ **Select Population** (P, i_{ts});
               end;
           return P;
           end;
        Eliminate i_{worst} from P;
        $P := P + i_{new}$;
    return P;
    end;

Create Schedule ($i_{father}, i_{mother}, operator$)
    Initialize ($SO = \emptyset, PO$);   – SO: scheduled operations
                                    – PO: possible operations

    repeat
        Choose φ^* minimizing φ over PO;   –φ_j: earliest completion time
        $m^* :=$ machine assigned to φ^*;
        Generate CO^{m^*};   – CO^{m^*}: candidate oper. for m^*
           – $j \in CO^{m^*}$ such that $j \in PO$, assigned to m^* and $\sigma_j < \varphi^*$
           – σ_j: earliest starting time for operation j
        if $mutation < random[0, 1)$ then
           $j^* :=$ at random over CO^{m^*};
        else
           Choose i from i_{father} or i_{mother} using $operator$;
           $j^* :=$ most advanced from i over CO^{m^*};
           end;
        $SO := SO + j^*$;
        $PO := PO - j^* +$ (next to j^*);
        until $PO = \emptyset$;
    return $i_{child} := SO$;
    end;

6   Experimental Results

This section summarizes the results of experimentation with the GA/TS hybrid scheduler. The experiments have been developed on randomly generated problems of practical complexity, the notorious 10x10 instance of Muth and Thompson's benchmark and several instances of Lawrence [22]. For that purpose, the three versions (H1, H2 and H3) of the scheduler were tested.

Tables 1 and 2 present the computational results obtained by our scheduler comparing with another good algorithms [1, 2, 7, 21]. In Table 1 for each method[1] we show the mean relative error (MRE) and the standard deviation of the relative error (SRE). Table 2 gives the CPU-times for the corresponding results of Table 1. Each of these instances from the classical benchmark has exactly one operation for each job-machine pair, and the problem is to minimize the total elapsed time between the beginning of the first operation and the completion of the last one (makespan). But in the industrial world each product has its own type of process plan, usually including different parts or by-products, other objectives are searched (as minimize tardiness for due dates), there are job priorities, etc. Thus, we have considered 3 more instances:

- SP10: similar to FT10 but with due dates,
  Objective function= Σ (tardiness[job] +50$\times$ out_of_date[job]).
- SP2 and SP3: same product catalogue, including by-products. There are 10 machines; 49 jobs and 241 operations for SP2; 31 jobs and 184 operations for SP3, which also has job priorities. Due dates and objective functions are different.

Table 3 presents the best and mean results over 10 runs for the three last instances and FT10 and LA38 from the classical benchmark. In this experiment we have separately applied TS and GA, and the three hybrid versions of our scheduler (with similar CPU times). Fig. 2 shows the comparison of the mean results. The two extreme values are the mean obtained by random generation, 100%, and by the most efficient method, 0%. We see that TS gives poor results for the three SP instances. In fact, on these instances, TS usually improves the solution in the first 20 - 30 iterations, which means that the tabu list (the short-term memory) does not start working and it just act as a local optimizer. Other neighborhood definition could enlarge the applicability of TS. In another way, GA results are not very strong, but they show that it is a robust method.The hybrid methods produce the best results, specially when there is an interaction with the user. H2 and H3 results are similar, but H3 is faster and demands less control from the user.

In Fig. 3 we present the performance of H3 on two different instances. There is not interaction with the user in these sample runs. On FT10 instance improvement is usually obtained up to 100% by TS, but on SP3 each method shares the improvement of the search. Thus, TS as local optimizer embedded in GA may contribute more than half to the optimization on these non classical instances, while acting separately as TS hardly improves the best solution randomly obtained.

---

[1] method^x: best result after x runs; method^{mx}: mean over x runs.

Table 1. Performance comparison of various algorithms: Results

Lower bound *optimal		*930	1040	1235	1184	*1222		
Author	method	FT10	LA21	LA27	LA38	LA40	MRE	SRE
Adams	SB1[1]	1015	1172	1325	1280	1326	9.15	2.09
Balas	SB4[1]	940	1071	1272	1294	1262	3.92	3.13
Adams	SB11[1]	930	1084	1291	1255	1269	3.72	2.23
Applegate	Bottle-6[1]	938	1084	1286	1268	1255	3.80	2.29
Applegate	Shuffle2[1]	938	1046	1269	1267	1238	2.50	2.66
Aarts	TA1[m5]	1003	1104	1289	1323	1295	7.22	2.81
V.Laarhoven	SA[5]	951	1063	1269	1215	1234	2.16	0.70
Aarts	SA1[5]	969	1083	1282	1235	1256	3.84	0.62
Matsuo	CSSA[1]	946	1071	1274	1231	1235	2.58	1.17
Taillard	TS1[5]	930	1047	1240	1202	-	0.65	0.64
Barnes	TS2[1]	935	1053	1256	1211	1239	1.43	0.64
Dell'Amico	TS3[5]	935	1048	1242	1203	1233	0.88	0.43
Nowicki	TSAB[3]	930	1047	1236	1196	1229	0.47	0.42
Aarts	GLS1[m5]	978	1084	1303	1285	1273	5.52	1.78
Dorndorf	P-GA[1]	960	1139	1378	1296	1321	8.38	3.14
Dorndorf	SB-GA(40)[m2]	938	1074	1272	1251	1274	3.41	1.77
Nuijten	RCS[5]	930	1069	1285	1278	1247	3.36	2.95
Hybrid Scheduler	GA/TS[1]	930	1056	1255	1210	1239	1.35	0.81

Table 2. Performance comparison of various algorithms: CPU times

Author	computer	FT10	LA21	LA27	LA38	LA40	MRE
Adams	VAX 780/11	10	2	46	58	77	9.15
Balas	Sparc 330	11	20	38	30	52	3.92
Adams	VAX 780/11	851	362	837	1079	899	3.72
Applegate	Sparc st ELC	8	301	667	182	154	3.80
Applegate	Sparc st ELC	25	87478	604	17799	150	2.50
Aarts	VAX 8650	99	243	492	636	597	7.22
V.Laarhoven	VAX785	779	1991	4535	5480	5373	2.16
Aarts	VAX 8650	99	243	492	636	597	3.84
Matsuo	VAX 780/11	987	205	286	672	603	2.58
Taillard	-	-	-	-	-	-	0.65
Barnes	IBM RS 600	16	174	248	181	90	1.43
Dell'Amico	PC 386	156	199	254	242	237	0.88
Nowicki	AT 386DX	-	-	-	-	-	0.47
Aarts	VAX 8650	99	243	492	636	597	5.52
Dorndorf	DEC st 3100	933	352	565	525	526	8.38
Dorndorf	DEC st 3100	107	135	242	336	348	3.41
Nuijten	Sparc st ELC	256	863	1156	1149	842	3.36
Hybrid Scheduler	Sparc st 10	218	147	255	371	351	1.35

Table 3. Best and mean results after 10 runs

method	FT10	LA38	SP2	SP3	SP10
random	1361	1773	981	8278	1794
TS	937 / 959	1214 / 1248	399 / 547	1177 / 2348	587 / 792
GA	938 / 988	1288 / 1324	28 / 91	-2542 / -1237	386 / 536
H1	937 / 956	1216 / 1248	31 / 116	-2918 / -1305	386 / 470
H2	930 / 951	1210 / 1245	27 / 80	-3410 / -1697	288 / 390
H3	930 / 951	1236 / 1250	34 / 80	-2551 / -1481	360 / 450

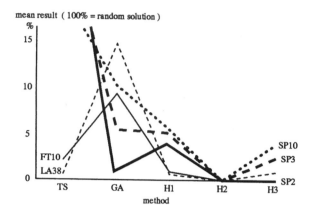

Fig. 2. Comparison of the mean results.

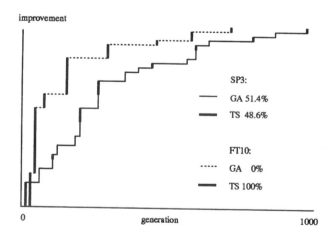

Fig. 3. Performance of H3 on some instances.

7 Conclusion and Further Work

In this paper, a genetic-tabu (GA/TS) hybrid approach for the solution of real-world production scheduling problems has been presented. Since the weakness of GA for local search is well acknowledged, we improve the quality and stability of the solution using a local search method. Specifically, we have combined GA with TS techniques. Experiments have demonstrated that the hybrid approach produces good results, better than previous efforts using GA alone.

Future work will include investigation of this approach in more complex domains. We want to improve the utility of the algorithm in rescheduling and reactive scheduling contexts incoming orders onto an existing schedule and revising predictive schedules when conflicts and problems in real time force changes.

References

1. Aarts, E., Laarhoven, P. van, Lenstra, J., Ulder, N.: A Computational Study of Local Search Algorithms for Job Shop Scheduling. ORSA Journal of Computing **6** (1994) 118-125
2. Adams, J., Balas, E., Zawack, D.: The Shifting Bottleneck Procedure for Job Shop Scheduling. Management Science **34** (1988) 391-401
3. Applegate, D.,Cook, W.: A Computational Study of the Job-Shop Scheduling Problem. ORSA Journal of Computing **3** (1991) 149-156
4. Atabakhsh, H.: A Survey of Constraint Based Scheduling Systems Using an Artificial Intelligence Approach. Art. Int. in Engineering **6** (1991) 58-73
5. Balas, E.: Machine Sequencing via Disjunctive Graphs: An Implicit Enumeration Algorithm. Operational Research **17** (1969) 941-957
6. Bruns, R.: Direct Chromosome Representation and Advanced Genetic Operators for Production Scheduling. Proc. of the fifth Int. Conf. on Gen. Alg. (1993) 352-359
7. Carlier, J.,Pinson, E.: An Algorithm for Solving the Job Shop Problem. Management Science **35** (1989) 164-176
8. Collinot, A., Le Pape, C.: Adapting the Behavior of a Job Shop Scheduling System. Decision Sup. Sys. **7** (1991) 341-353
9. Charalambous, O., Hindi. K.: A Review of Artificial Intelligence Based Job Shop Scheduling Systems. Information and Decision Technologies **17** (1991) 189-202
10. Davis, L.: Handbook of Genetic Algorithms. Van Nostrand Reinhold (1991)
11. Dell'Amico, M., Trubian, M.: Applying Tabu Search to the Job Shop Scheduling Problem. Ann. of Op. Res. **41** (1993) 231-252
12. Dubois, D., Koning, J.: A Decision Engine Based on Rational Aggregation of Heuristic Knowledge. Decision Sup. Sys. **11** (1994) 337-361
13. Fang, H., Ross, P., Corne, D.: A Promising Genetic Algorithm Approach to Job Shop Scheduling, Rescheduling and Open Shop Scheduling Problems. Proc. of the fifth Int. Conf. on Gen. Alg. (1993) 375-382
14. Fox, M.: Constraint Directed Search: A Core Study of Job-Shop Scheduling. Pitman Publ. (1987)
15. Fox, B., McMahon, M.: Genetic Operators for Sequencing problems in Foundations of Genetic Algorithms. G. Rawlins Eds. (1991) 284-300
16. Giffler, J., Thompson, G.L.: Algorithms for Solving Production Scheduling Problems. Operational Research **8** (1969) 487-503

17. Glover, F.: Tabu search-Part I. ORSA Journal of Computing **1** (1989) 1909-206
18. Glover, F.: Tabu search-Part II. ORSA Journal of Computing **2** (1990) 4-32
19. Holsapple, C., Jacob, V., Pakath, R., Zaveri, J.: A Genetics Based Hybrid Scheduler for Generating Static Schedules in Flexible Manufacturing Contexts. IEEE Tran. on systems, man and cybernetic **23** (1993) 953-972
20. Husbands, P.: An Ecosystems Model for Integrated Production Planning. Int. J. CIM **6** (1993) 74-86
21. Laarhoven, P. van, Aarts, E., Lenstra, J.: Job Shop Scheduling by Simulated Annealing. Operations Research **40** (1992) 113-126
22. Lawrence, S.: Resource Constrained Project Scheduling : an Experimental Investigation of Heuristic Scheduling Techniques. Graduate School of Ind. Adm., Carnegie Mellon Un. (1984)
23. Lin, F., Kao, C., Hsu, C.: Applying the Genetic Approach to Simulated Annealing in Solving some NP-hard Problems. IEEE Tran. on systems, man and cybernetic **23** (1993) 1752-1767
24. Michalewicz, Z.: Genetic Algorithms and Data Structures = Evolution Programs. Springer-Verlag (1992)
25. Nakano, R.: Conventional Genetic Algorithm for Job-Shop Problems. Proc. of the forth Int. Conf. on Gen. Alg. (1991) 474-479
26. Rodammer, F.: A Recent Survey of Production Scheduling. IEEE Trans. on systems, man and cybernetic **18** (1988) 841- 851
27. Taillard, E.: Parallel Taboo Search Techniques for the Job Shop Scheduling Problem. ORSA J. of Comp. **6** (1994) 108-117
28. Uckun, S., Bagchi, S., Kawamara, K.: Managing Genetic Search in Job Shop Scheduling. IEEE Expert **8** (1993) 15-24
29. Wesley, J., Laguna, M.: A Tabu Search Experience in Production Scheduling. Ann. Oper. Res. **41** (1993) 141-156
30. Yamada, T., Nakano, R.: A Genetic Algorithm Applicable to Large-scale Job Shop Problems. Parallel Problem Solving from Nat., 2. Elsevier Sc. Pub. (1992) 281-290

A Controlled Experiment: Evolution for Learning Difficult Image Classification

Astro Teller and Manuela Veloso

Carnegie Mellon University, Pittsburgh PA 15213, USA

Abstract. The signal-to-symbol problem is the task of converting raw sensor data into a set of symbols that Artificial Intelligence systems can reason about. We have developed a method for directly learning and combining algorithms that map signals into symbols. This new method is based on evolutionary computation and imposes little burden on or bias from the humans involved. Previous papers of ours have focused on PADO, our learning architecture. We showed how it applies to the general signal-to-symbol task and in particular the impressive results it brings to natural image object recognition. The most exciting challenge this work has received is the idea that PADO's success in natural image object recognition may be due to the underlying simplicity of the problems we posed it. This challenge implicitly assumes that our approach suffers from many of the same afflictions that traditional computer vision approaches suffer in natural image object recognition. This paper responds to this challenge by designing and executing a controlled experiment specifically designed to solidify PADO's claim to success.

1 Introduction

The goal of the PADO (Parallel Algorithm Discovery and Orchestration) project is the supervised autonomous learning of signal understanding for arbitrary signal types. PADO accomplishes this goal through a new evolutionary computation architecture. In previous work, we have argued and demonstrated that PADO is already able to learn to accomplish difficult signal understanding tasks [10, 12]. In recent talks given on PADO, and through correspondence with other researchers, the idea has been expressed that because the end result of the PADO architecture is so opaque, it may be that PADO is accomplishing little and that the problems we have posed it may instead actually be quite simple [3].

This worry is analogous to the worry that, while the mechanism of Neural Networks (NNs) is easy to understand, typical NNs generated are very hard to understand, *and therefore* NNs may not really be doing anything of interest. 15 years ago this was a concern for the NN community, but it has been overcome. One of the main reasons why this worry about the opacity of learned NNs has been alleviated is that controlled experiments like *auto-encoders* effectively convinced the research community that the hidden units of the NN were in fact finding useful, compressed versions of their inputs [1, 2, 6].

While we are confident that the PADO learning architecture, through evolutionary computation, does learn non-trivial algorithms and can be applied to real world signals, it seems that a tangent is in order. This paper is that tangent. We will show, through a controlled experiment, using manufactured images, that PADO can indeed learn abstract, "high-level" features of a signal in order to accomplish signal classification. These experiments, detailed in Sect. 4 of this paper, were specifically designed to dispel potential scepticism about PADO's power.

This paper will first give a brief description of PADO and the process involved in the creation of a PADO system: the discovery of algorithms that can be parallelly executed and the orchestration of these algorithms into a useful system. Then, two past experiments [10] will be summarized to situate this paper's controlled experiments. The heart of the paper follows, in which two controlled experiments remove doubt about "secretly simple features" available for signal classification.

The concept of this paper is simple and should be appealing. PADO has performed well in seemingly difficult object recognition tasks and this performance has excited many of our colleagues. A few of our colleagues, because the end result of the PADO architecture is so difficult to decipher, have wondered whether these tasks were in fact difficult, and therefore, whether PADO is capable of automatically learning algorithms that achieve reasonable recognition rates in truly difficult signal domains. Our response, this paper, is "Well, let's make a domain that we can all agree is not trivial to learn and see how PADO does."

2   The PADO Architecture

While we believe PADO does have merit as an original system, that is not the claim we are trying to substantiate in this paper. For the same reason that a paper on auto-encoding for NNs need explain the NN process, but need not justify the existence of NNs as a research tool, the purpose of this section is not to convince, but to explain. We will first sketch the PADO architecture and its extension of genetic programming (GP) [4]. Then, the section will detail exactly what kind of programs PADO is evolving and what access these programs have to the experimental signals in Sects. 3 and 4.

The goal of the PADO architecture is to learn to take signals as input and output correct class labels. *When there are C classes to choose from, PADO starts by learning C different "systems"*. System$_I$ is responsible for taking a signal as input and returning a confidence that class I is the correct label. System$_I$ is built out of several programs learned by PADO. Each of these programs does exactly what the system as a whole does: it takes a signal as input and returns a confidence value that label I is the correct label. The reason for this seeming redundancy can be found in [10]. PADO performs object recognition by orchestrating the responses of the C systems. Here is a description of a simple orchestration scheme that was used in the experiments described in this paper. System$_I$ is built from the S programs that best (based on the training results) learned to recognize the instances of class I. The S responses that the S programs return on seeing a particular image are all weighted and their weighted average of responses is interpreted as the confidence that System$_\mathcal{I}$ has that the signal in question contains an object from class $\mathcal{I}$. The responses of the C systems are weighted and combined in a similar way. Figure 1 summarizes the main functionality of PADO's evolutionary learning of signal understanding algorithms.

```
function PADO(population, signals, C, S) returns C groups of S algorithms
   inputs: population, a set of P randomly generated algorithms
           signals, a set of training signals
           C, the number of classes
           S, the number of algorithms from each class to return
   Repeat
      Loop over signals
              EvaluateFitness(population,signal_i)
      Split population into C distinct subpools of size P/C based on fitness
      Loop i from 1 to C
              MatingPool_i ← Reproduction(SubPool_i)
              NewSubPop_i ← Recombination(MatingPool_i)
           population ← ΣNewSubPop_i
   Until return requested
   return the most fit S algorithms in each of the C subpools
```

Fig. 1. A top level of view of PADO's algorithm evolution learning process.

PADO evolves programs in a PADO-specific graph structured language. At the beginning of a learning session, the main population is filled with $\mathcal{P}$ programs that have been randomly generated using a grammar for the legal syntax of the language. All programs in this language are constrained by the syntax to return a number that is interpreted as a confidence value between some minimum confidence and some maximum confidence. Crossover and mutation in PADO are more complicated than their standard forms in genetic algorithms or GP. Both the crossover and mutation operators are "SMART" operators that are co-evolved with the main population, as we describe in [9, 10].

2.1 PADO Program Representation

Figure 2 sketches the structure of a PADO program. Each program is constructed as an arbitrary directed graph of nodes. As an arbitrary directed graph of N nodes, each node can have as many as N *arcs* outgoing. These arcs indicate possible flows of control in the program. In a PADO program each node has two parts: an *action* and a *branch-decision*. Each program has a private stack and an indexed memory. All *actions* pop their inputs from this stack and push their result back onto the stack. These actions are the equivalent of GP's terminals and non-terminals. The indexed memory is effected in the usual way via READ and WRITE actions [8].

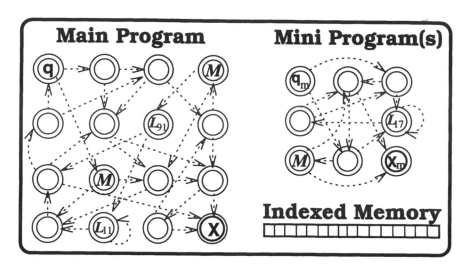

Fig. 2. This is the basic structure of a PADO program. There can be one or more Mini programs for each PADO program. Each Mini program may be referenced from the Main program, another local Mini program, or a *Library* program.

After the action at node i is executed, an arc transfers control to a new node. The branch-decision function at the current node makes this decision. Each node has its own branch-decision function that may use the top of the stack, the previous state number, the memory, and constants to pick an arc. There is a separate (i.e., individually evolved) branch-decision function for each node.

There are several special nodes as illustrated in Fig. 2. Node q is the start node. It is special in no other way than that it is always the first node to be executed when a program begins. Node X is the stop node. When this node is reached, its action is executed and then the program halts. When a program halts, its response is considered to be the current value residing in some particular memory location (e.g., response = Memory[0]). If a program halts sooner than a pre-set time threshold, it is started again at its start node (without erasing its memory or stack) to give it a chance to revise its confidence value.

Node M executes the private *Mini* program as its action. The *Mini* program associated with each *Main* program bears similarity to the concept of ADF's [5]. It may be called at any point in the *Main* program and it evolves along with the *Main* program. The *Mini* programs may recursively call themselves or the globally available *Library* programs, just like a *Main* program may. The *Library* programs (e.g., L_{91} in Fig. 2) are globally available programs that can be executed at any time and from anywhere just like the Mini programs. But unlike the Mini programs, where each Mini may be run only during the execution of the MAIN program to which it belongs, the *Library* programs are available to the entire population. The method by which these *Library* programs change can be seen in [10]. For an example of a learned PADO program, see [10, 12].

We hope that these two subsections have been detailed enough to give a flavor, if not complete details, about the PADO learning architecture. In particular, it should be clear that PADO is *not* simply a genetic algorithm (GA).

2.2 PADO Program Primitives

Here is a brief summary of the language *actions* and their effects:

Algebraic Primitives: {ADD SUB MULT DIV NOT MAX MIN}

These functions allow basic manipulation of the integers. All values are constrained to be in the range 0 to 255. For example, DIV(X,0) results in 255 and NOT(X) maps the set {1..255} to 0 and {0} to 1.

Memory Primitives: {READ WRITE}

These two functions access the memory of the program. Each program has a memory which is organized as an array of 256 integers that can take on values between 0 and 255. READ(X) returns the integer stored in position X of the memory array. WRITE(X,Y) takes the value X and writes it into position Y of the indexed memory. WRITE returns the OLD value of position Y (i.e. a WRITE is a READ with a side-effect). The memory is cleared (all positions set to zero) at the beginning of a program execution.

Branching Primitives: {IF-THEN-ELSE EITHER}

Calling these "Branching" primitives may be misleading. In both cases the primitive pops X,Y, and Z off the stack and then replaces either Y or Z (not both) depending on the value of X. For IF-THEN-ELSE the test is (X less than 0). For EITHER the test is (X less than RandomNumber) where RandomNumber varies between 0 and 255. These primitives can be used as an action or a branch-decision functions. In the former case, they have no effect on the flow of control.

Signal Primitives: {PIXEL LEAST MOST AVERAGE VARIANCE DIFFERENCE}

These are the language functions that can access the signals. In order to demonstrate PADO's power and flexibility, these same primitives were used for both image and sound data [12]. PIXEL returns the intensity value at that point in the image (or sound). The other five "signal functions" each pop the top four values off the stack. These four numbers are interpreted as (X1,Y1) and (X2,Y2) specifying a rectangle in the image. If the points specify a negative area then the opposite interpretation was taken and the function was applied to the positive area rectangle. LEAST, MOST, AVERAGE, VARIANCE, and DIFFERENCE return the respective functions applied to that region in the image. DIFFERENCE is the difference between the average values along the first and second half of the line (X1,Y1,X2,Y2).

Routine Primitives: {MINI LIBRARY[i]}

These are programs that can be called from the Main program. In addition, they may be called from each other. Because they are programs, and not simple functions, the effect they will have on the stack before completion is unknown.

3 Previous Experiments

Several publications already exist about the application of the PADO learning architecture to image understanding [9, 11, 10]. These papers address signal understanding issues such as object recognition in real video images of everyday objects and classification of high-quality sound samples. To illustrate and summarize two of those experiments, Fig. 3 shows some examples from the training and testing sets of two separate image databases. Each of these two databases contain 7 classes of images (only 2 classes from each database are shown in Fig. 3). Each 256x256 image is in 256 shades of grey.

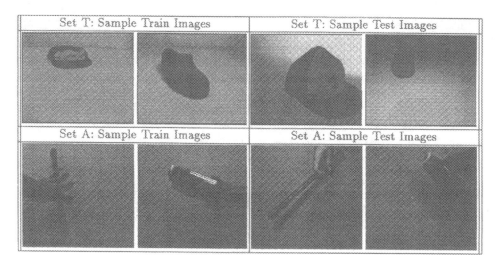

Fig. 3. 8 randomly chosen images from the experimental image database.

Figure 4 shows the ability of PADO to perform object recognition on these two sets of image data. The crux of previous papers has been "Does PADO succeed at the task of object recognition?" It is important to point out that if we constructed a system that simply guessed at the class of the image by choosing one of the seven classes at random, it would be right about 14% of the time (shown as a dotted line in Fig. 4). At generation 80, the percent of the time that PADO correctly identifies the image class is about 4 to 5 times random performance. On images as unconstrained as these images are, of objects as unfriendly as these objects are, this is a real difference.

There is little to which these results can appropriately be compared. The only other learning architecture for which there are vision results with such an unbiased, "low-level" starting point are NNs (e.g., [7]). NN cannot currently be trained on images as rich as these (65536 eight bit inputs). Even if NNs could be trained on inputs of this size, they are notoriously bad at finding "features" that are local, non-stationary, and can not be directly "observed" through the inputs.

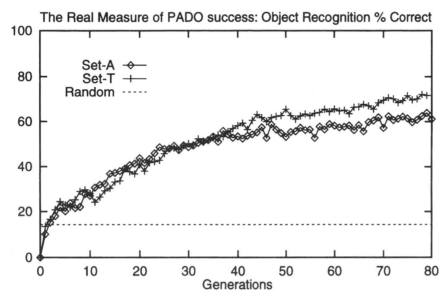

Fig. 4. PADO object recognition percentage correct on Sets A and T test images.

There are, of course, a large number of computer vision techniques that don't involve machine learning. Comparison was not made against any of these for two reasons. The first is that the type of images shown in Fig. 3 are less constrained (translation, rotation, foreshortening, lighting, etc.) than most of the computer vision object recognition domains of today. The second reason is that when learning is not involved, the choice of any particular set of computer vision techniques to solve a particular object recognition problem (like the discrimination of the images in Fig. 3) is effective only for that specific domain. In other words, while traditional computer vision techniques can outperform PADO in almost any specific domain, they do so at the repeated cost of a researcher's time and energy. As computer cycles become increasingly cheap relative to human effort, the attractiveness of machine learning in computer vision rises.

Because there is substantial difference between "guessing" and PADO's actual performance, a few researchers have suggested that these classification problems may be secretly "easy." In other words, how can PADO, a learning architecture with so little initial world knowledge, create a system that so reliably predicts the contents of novel images from the same classes? PADO's performance on images like those shown in Fig. 3 is very good. The question is, "Where does credit belong? With PADO (a successful learning algorithm), or with the images that have subtle but simple distinguishing characteristics?" The following section will *not* explain *how* PADO performs so well. What the following section will provide is conclusive evidence *that* PADO does succeed in difficult (from a learning perspective) image understanding domains.

4 Doing the Controlled Experiment

In order to create a convincing experiment to satisfy the doubting Thomases in the audience, we should first know what criteria we (and they) are looking for in such an experiment. It must be a "good" control to the experiments summarized in the previous section, and it must be a "hard" experiment in order to qualify as a convincing one. The criteria for such an experiment could be summarized as follows:

1. A controlled experiment should be similar to the original one in most details.
2. The classes that we require PADO to "understand" the difference between should be completely separable. That is, the task should be possible.
3. The distinction between the classes should be readily apparent to human observers to make the issues clear.
4. The distinction between the image classes should only exist in abstract (high-level) local features of the imaged objects. By abstract or high-level, we mean a feature that can not be directly measured using a signal primitive.
5. Most importantly, we should be able to *prove* the criteria above true.

4.1 Constructing a Simple Controlled Experiment

In order to satisfy criterion 1, our new experiment will be an object recognition/signal classification problem with a few classes. Let's pick 5 as the number of classes. In order to satisfy criterion 5, we will manufacture the images in the different classes. By manufacturing the images we can *guarantee* certain properties of the images. This image fabrication is *not* an attempt to create a "toy problem", but an attempt to eliminate ambiguity in the image feature space. The classification of these constructed images *is* a simple problem for hand-coded vision systems; it is *not* simple for a learning system (like PADO) that is given no information specific to the task at hand. However, the real need and goal of PADO is to attack and conquer problems that frustrate hand-coded solutions (See Sect. 3).

We chose as the 5 signal classes to manufacture: SQUARE, CIRCLE, GRID, CROSS, and TRIANGLE. To create an image instance for one of these classes:

- The object occupies between 6% and 24% (chosen randomly) of the image.
- The location of the object center in the image is chosen randomly.
- The foreground color is chosen randomly from grey levels {191...255}
- The background color is chosen randomly from grey levels {0...63}

If we take care (which we did) to adjust the relative thicknesses of these object patterns, then no "global" application of the signal primitives (LEAST, MOST, AVERAGE, VARIANCE, DIFFERENCE) to an image can help in distinguishing between classes. This is so because the images were manufactured with that criteria in mind. These images, by the construction just described, satisfy criterion 4. Figure 5 shows two examples from each class. As we can see, these objects are trivial for people to discriminate, satisfying criteria 2 and 3.

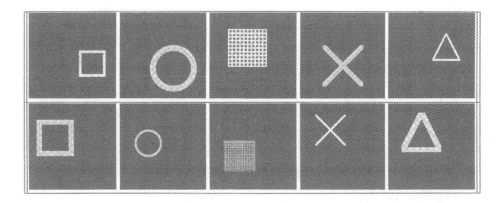

Fig. 5. 2 randomly chosen images from each of the 5 manufactured classes.

To see how difficult these images are for a *learning system* to discriminate among, let's take a look at a few pairs of classes. The only reliable distinction between the SQUARE and CIRCLE images is the *shape* of the brighter area. Both are continuous borders with background in their centers; their curvature sets them apart. Exactly the opposite is true of the SQUARE and GRID. An examination of their external borders shows them to be identical. Internal to their borders is where their distinction lies. For other examples of the difficulty of the space, notice that the bottom leg of the triangle is identical to the bottom of the square, and the top two legs of the triangle are similar to the bottom half of the Cross. Mid-level features like "dark-in-the-middle" or "straight-lines-at-right-angles" can be of some use, but still do not fully disambiguate the image classes (e.g., SQUARE vs. CIRCLE and SQUARE vs. CROSS respectively). In short, the distinctions between these classes are not only abstract, they are conjunctions of abstract features.

The curve labeled "Without Noise" in Fig. 6 shows how PADO learns to classify images its has never seen into their correct classes at a much higher rate (about 60% by generation 100) than random guessing would yield (shown as the dotted line in Fig. 6). This experiment and the experiment in the following section were performed using the same methodology as the experiments whose results on natural images are summarized in Sect. 3. 70 images were used for training during each generation, 100 images were used for orchestration, and each testing phase used 100 images. All images were chosen randomly from the distribution of images described above. Since there are over 2 billion different pictures in each class, the test images, with very high probability, had never been seen during the training phase. The lower curve ("With Noise") will be discussed in the next section.

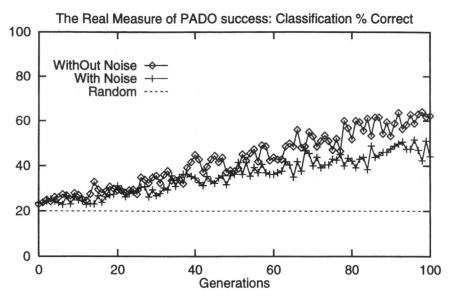

Fig. 6. PADO classification percentage correct on manufactured **test** images.

4.2 Increased Difficulty in the Controlled Experiment

The results in the previous subsection convincingly portray PADO as being able to construct a system that learns non-trivial, abstract features and uses them to successfully perform its signal classification task.

There were many possible ways to increase the difficulty of these images. Among the most traditional (from a computer vision "noise" standpoint) are: Gaussian noise, rotation, and obstruction. Gaussian noise and obstruction were chosen as our images complicators simply because they are both trivial to add to the image construction process. The noise added varies each pixel with a standard deviation of 16 shades of grey. The obstruction was added in the form of two grey bars of constant thickness in random orientations. The color of these bars varies around the central 64 shades of grey. Example images using this new image manufacturing process are shown in Fig. 7.

The curve labeled "With Noise" in Fig. 6 shows that PADO still manages to perform significantly better than random even on this harder set of 5 image classes. Given more time PADO's ability continues to increase. In order to complete a sufficient number of experiments to provide statistically significant data, generation 100 was chosen as a cut-off for the experiments. Each run took about 2.5 days of CPU time on a DECStation5000/20. Both curves in Fig. 6 are averaged over 5 runs. Each program, is given about 30 milliseconds to examine the picture and return a confidence. Because an entire PADO system orchestrates many programs in order utilize a wide variety of learned information, each classification answer was produced in about 1 second.

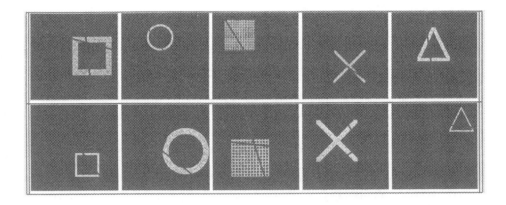

Fig. 7. 2 randomly chosen images from each of the 5 manufactured classes.

5 Discussion and Conclusions

The purpose of this paper has been to convince the reader that PADO can find and utilize local, abstract features of a signal in order to perform its signal classification task. PADO does this by evolving a set of algorithms that can be orchestrated and run in parallel to "analyze" signals. This discovery and utilization of "high-level" features of a signal was accomplished using no domain knowledge.

The goal of the PADO project is the supervised autonomous learning of signal understanding for arbitrary signal types. In previous work, we have argued and demonstrated that PADO is already able to learn to accomplish difficult signal understanding tasks. Because the PADO programs and orchestration do not evolve to be understandable by people, a few researchers have wondered whether PADO is or would be able to achieve the kind of complex understanding necessary to distinguish between everyday objects in natural images. The experiments detailed in Sect. 5 of this paper were designed to dispel this scepticism.

This paper gave a brief description of PADO and the process involved in the creation of a PADO system: the discovery of algorithms that can be parallelly executed and the orchestration of these algorithms into a useful system. Past experiments were then summarized to situate the following controlled experiments. Because the presentation of PADO as a learning model was not the focus of the paper, little direct evidence was given for evaluating of the originality of the PADO architecture.

The first controlled experiment detailed in this paper asked PADO to distinguish between 5 classes of manufactured images. The features of these images that set them apart were purposefully constrained to be high-level features such as "square" or "circle." Mid-level features like "dark-in-the-middle" or "straight-lines-at-right-angles" can be of some use, but still do not fully disambiguate the classes. On this task, where guessing a class would yield a 20% result, PADO manages a 60% classification rate by Generation 100.

The second controlled experiment increased the difficult of the task by adding confusing elements to the images. This confusion was added both through Gaussian noise at every point and through the inclusion of two grey "occluding" bars that obscure the background and foreground they cross. Even under these circumstances, PADO's ability to correctly identify images it has never seen reaches almost 2.5 times the rate that random guessing would provide.

The number of applications in need of increased autonomous signal understanding is innumerable. Most of these applications don't know in advance what form all the signals will take or what aspects of the signals will be of greatest interest. The creation of a system that can meet the needs of these applications is one of the most exciting current demands of the information age.

References

1. H. Bourlard and Y. Kamp. Autoassociation by multilayer perceptrons and singular value decomposistion. In *Biological Cybernetics.*, 1988.
2. G. Cottrell. Extracting features from faces using compression networks. In *Proceedings of the 1990 Connectionist Models Summer School.*, 1990.
3. The Symbolic Visual Learning Group. In *personal correspondence*, 1995.
4. John Koza. *Genetic Programming.* MIT Press, 1992.
5. John Koza. *Genetic Programming II.* MIT Press, 1994.
6. Mark Kramer. Nonlinear principal components analysis using autoassociative neural networks. In *AIChe Journal.*, volume 37:2, 1991.
7. Dean Pomerleau. *Neural Network Perception for Mobile Robot Guidance.* PhD thesis, Carnegie Mellon University School of Computer Science, 1992.
8. Astro Teller. The evolution of mental models. In Jr. Kenneth E. Kinnear, editor, *Advances In Genetic Programming*, pages 199–220. MIT Press, 1994.
9. Astro Teller. Evolving programmers: The co-evolution of intelligent recombination operators. In K. Kinnear and P. Angeline, editors, *Advances in Genetic Programming II*, 1995. Submitted for review.
10. Astro Teller and Manuela Veloso. PADO: A new learning architecture for object recognition. In Katsushi Ikeuchi and Manuela Veloso, editors, *Symbolic Visual Learning.* Oxford University Press, 1995.
11. Astro Teller and Manuela Veloso. PADO: Learning tree structured algorithms for orchestration into an object recognition system. Technical Report CMU-CS-95-101, Department of Computer Science, Carnegie Mellon Unversity, 1995.
12. Astro Teller and Manuela Veloso. Program evolution for data mining. In Sushil Louis, editor, *The International Journal of Expert Systems. Third Quarter. Special Issue on Genetic Algorithms and Knowledge Bases.* JAI Press, 1995.

Minimal Model Complexity Search

Chris McConnell, ccm@cs.cmu.edu

Carnegie Mellon University, School of Computer Science, Pittsburgh PA 15213-3891, USA

Abstract. SURFER is an empirical discovery system that given a set of input data and a modelling vocabulary returns the model that best describes that data. The best model is considered to be the one that minimizes the description length of that model plus the data encoded using that model. The search for models is controlled by the *a priori* estimate of model likelihoods as encoded in the modelling vocabulary. SURFER includes domain independent mechanisms for identifying redundant models and for finding free parameters. The system is described together with the results of running the system on several different types of problems.

Keywords: Bayesian Learning, discovery, explanation-based learning, minimum description length.

1 Introduction

This paper describes the empirical discovery system SURFER (SURface FittER). In empirical discovery, the goal is to find a model to describe a set of observations. AI approaches to this problem are typically data-driven and use the recursive application of heuristics to generate possible models.[3] Another AI approach that has been used with some success generates models using genetic algorithms.[2] Statistical or neural network approaches use algorithmic procedures to find the parameters for a particular class of models. SURFER's design is independent of any particular modelling vocabulary and has model generation heuristics that can plausibly be learned. It is a model-driven approach based on the ideas of Minimum Description Length (MDL).[6]

What is it that makes one model better than another? One answer is a model that fits the data exactly. Unfortunately for a limited set of data there are an infinite number of models with that property. Furthermore, real world data often includes noise. The principle of *Occam's Razor* indicates that the simplest model should be preferred, but model complexity also needs to be traded off against accuracy. A model that fits noisy data exactly or that is simple but doesn't match the data very well will be unlikely to be predictive.

MDL formalizes the tradeoff between model complexity and accuracy.[6] MDL views model selection as a coding problem. Given a coding system for describing models, the best model is the one where the string describing the model plus the string describing the data in terms of the model has the shortest length. This formulation is equivalent to a Bayesian one since the coding cost of a string in bits C can be interpreted as the probability 2^{-C} of that string.[4]

Under this interpretation, the complexity of a model is equivalent to its prior probability and the length of a model plus the data is the posterior probability that the model fits the data.

A model coding system for a particular problem can be considered a *domain theory* for that problem. The coding system defines a partial order based on complexity for all possible models. Furthermore, MDL rules out some models as a possiblility since the complexity of the data places a limit on the most complex model that should be considered. SURFER exploits this partial order to generate models and then evaluates them by the MDL criterion.

There have been other model-driven approaches to empirical discovery such as COPER[1] and the system built by Solomonoff.[9] COPER's domain theory made use of knowledge about units to identify likely theoretical terms and then fit a parameterized model to those terms. Solomonoff's approach is much closer to that of SURFER. Its search process is based on the ideas of Kolmogorov complexity.[8] A model is a program for generating candidate solution strings. The probability P_i of model i being the solution is defined as the product of the probabilities of the concepts making it up. All possible models are generated at once with no attempt at identifying equivalent models. The search procedure selects a time T and then spends time TP_i executing model i. If no model has found a solution, T is doubled and the search continues. Solomonoff's search procedure is theoretically elegant but presents numerous practical difficulties. No results on this system have been published.

The SURFER system described in this paper successfully implements an empirical discovery system that generates models based on a probabilistic domain theory. The models are evaluated in terms of the MDL criterion. The system incorporates domain independent mechanisms for identifying equivalent models and for optimizing free parameters. Despite being a version of generate and test, the system is able to solve moderately difficult problems.

2 SURFER

Given a dataset and a modelling vocabulary, SURFER returns the model that minimizes the description length of the model and the data encoded using that model. Models are generated in order of increasing complexity up to the complexity justified by the dataset.

A *dataset* consists of a dataset signature and k n-tuples of data. The *dataset signature* describes the names, types, ranges and directions associated with each element in an n-tuple. Types can be *integer, boolean* or *real.* Direction is *in* for elements to be used as model arguments and *out* for elements to be predicted by models. Each *n-tuple* has a set of n values with characteristics as described by the signature.

A vocabulary for SURFER consists of a set of terms. Each term can either be a terminal or an operator for combining other terms. Each term has a name, type, relative cost and class. The *type* of a term indicates the type of value the term represents in an expression: boolean, integer or real. *Relative cost* reflects the relative cost of coding a term in a model. The *class* of a term is either constant, parameter, variable or operator.

Constant, parameter and variable terms are all terminals. A *constant term* represents a constant value such as one, π or zero. A *parameter term* represents a free parameter in the model that can be optimized to fit a model to a particular dataset. A *variable term* represents one of the *in* elements in a dataset n-tuple.

Operator terms combine one or more component terms of specified types. If the order of component terms does not matter, an operator is marked as commutative. Operator terms require a fixed number of component terms, but arbitrary arity operators can be simulated by marking an operator as associative. Recursive operator terms are also marked so that the operator can refer to the entire model. Operator terms also include their identity constant and inverse operator if applicable.

Throughout this paper, models will be described in prefix notation. Constants will be represented by c, parameters by p, variables by x, and operators by their name. For example, the addition of a constant and a variable would be shown as: (+ c x).

Name	Args	Identity	Inverse	Commut.	R_t	P_t	C_t
X	Variable				1.0	0.22	2.2
Float	Parameter				1.0	0.22	2.2
*	Float X Float	1.0	/	Y	1.0	0.22	2.2
/	Float X Float	1.0	*	N	1.0	0.22	2.2
LOG	Float		EXP	Y	2.0	0.05	4.3
EXP	Float		LOG	Y	2.0	0.05	4.3

Fig. 1. Depth Complexity Terms

2.1 Models

Models are built out of the terms found in the vocabulary. The *model complexity* of a model is the number of bits required to encode that model. It is the sum of the costs of the terms making up that model. Once a vocabulary V is selected, the cost C_t and probability P_t of each term t can be calculated from its relative cost R_t. To do this, the base coding cost b is calculated as the solution of: $\sum_{t \in V} 2^{-R_t b} = 1.0$. The base coding cost can then be used to calculate $C_t = R_t b$ and $P_t = 2^{-C_t}$. Figure 1 shows a typical vocabulary of terms with the relative cost of unary operators doubled. With these values, models will be generated in terms of increasing model depth. The model (* X (LOG X)) will have the same model length as the model (* (LOG X) (EXP X)) even though the second model has one more term than the first.

The *description length* of a model is the model complexity plus the number of bits required to encode the dataset using that model. Given an n-tuple as input, a model predicts a value m. The n-tuple is encoded using a Gaussian probability distribution $G(m, fm)$ with a standard deviation of $\pm fm$ where f is the desired fractional tolerance. Given $G(m, fm)$ for an n-tuple, the number of bits required to send that n-tuple with the model is $-\log_2 G(m, fm)$.

A model can include free parameters that need to be optimized to the data. To assign free parameters, SURFER uses numerical optimization procedures to minimize the model description length. Functions with one free parameter are optimized using Brent's method. Functions with multiple parameters are optimized using Powell's method with line minimization done by Brent's method. [5] As in most numerical optimization procedures, these are prone to false minima, but they work well for the class of models currently tested with SURFER.

Model vocabularies are usually highly redundant. There are syntactic rearrangements, and parameterized equivalences. For example, Figure 2 shows some of the equivalences present in a vocabulary with some typical mathematical functions. There are several different techniques used in SURFER to handle these equivalences. Pattern 1 is handled by generating only argument combinations for commutative functions. If a term is not commutative then all argument permutations are generated. Term inverse information is used to reject inverse patterns like pattern 2. Since SURFER allows parameterized functions, patterns like 3 and 4 can arise where the parameters are redundant. These are identified by propagating parameters upward through terms that are the same as the top level term or its inverse. If there end up being more than one constant at the top level, the model is rejected. Models with more than doubly recursive functions are also rejected to keep the evaluation of signatures within reasonable bounds.

SURFER uses the domain independent, probablitistic technique of signatures to identify model equivalences. A *model signature* is the evaluation of a model on a random set of probes. Each probe binds the input variables and free parameters to random values. Functions with singularities like division, generate special values at the singularities that contaminate all other operations so that the signature value for the probe causing the singularity is marked as undefined. If the top level term is recursive, no signature is generated since the component's value will depend on the model it is embedded in. If all of the elements in a signature are constant as in pattern 5, the model is rejected. Otherwise it is compared to previously generated models. If there is a match, then the model with the greatest complexity is rejected as in patterns 6 and 7.

Once a model's parameters have been fixed, each model component with a free parameter is checked to see if its parameter is close to the identity constant for that component. If that is the case, the model is kept because the identity constant would cause that model component to have no effect whereas a different parameter value would have an effect. Pattern 8 shows an example with an identity constant. If no components have identity constants, the same random probes used for signatures are used to generate an *instance signature*. The instance signature is then used to find other models with free parameters that converged to the same function. Pattern 9 shows an equivalence caught by instance signatures.

Signatures for integer and boolean valued models must match exactly and are checked using hash tables. Floating point models require special care due to the imprecise nature of floating point calculations. Two signatures are considered the same if each element of the signature is within a fractional tolerance of the value or within an absolute value of zero. *KD-trees* [7] are used to implement this matching efficiently.

The probability of a false match by a signature with b bits per signature and k probes in the signature is 2^{-bk}. In SURFER, models with float outputs usually have $b = 22$ and $k = 5$, so the likelihood of a false match is approximately 1 in 10^{34}. Models with integer outputs have $b = 8$ and $k = 10$ so they have an error of 1 in 10^{24}. Models with boolean outputs have $b = 1$ and $k = 20$, so they have an error of 1 in 10^{20}. The error rate is actually higher than these values would indicate since most functions are relatively smooth. With smooth functions, being close at one point increases the likelihood that the functions will be close at nearby points. To help prevent this effect the random probes are constructed to insure the presence of very small and large positive and negative values for each parameter and variable.

The matching procedure used for floating signatures and instance signatures can have both false positives and false negatives. False positives are bad because they permanently remove a unique model. False negatives are not as bad, but they do cause more models than are necessary to be generated. The incidence of false positives is decreased by verifying matches with an additional probe. If the models do not match on the additional probe, then the match is rejected. In practice, false positive signature matches happen very rarely. False positives happen much more frequently for instance signatures because of the inherent numerical problems involved in optimization. Tightening the tolerances used for matching instance signatures decreases the false positive rate, but increases the false negative rate.

Despite these problems, the signature matching works well in practice. The only problem that has false positives is the *Newton* problem as described in Figure 3. In the 8,361 models generated there were no false positives for signatures, but there were 23 for instance signatures, all of them with more complicated models and frequently involving two free parameters.

```
1. (+ X1 X2) == (+ X2 X1)
2. (LOG (EXP X)) == X
3. (+ P1 (+ X P2)) == (+ X P3)
4. (+ P1 (- X P2)) == (+ x p3)
5. (/ X X) == 1
6. (+ X (- X X)) == X
7. (* X (+ C1 X)) == (+ (* C1 X) (* X X))
8. (+ (* X 1.0) X) == (+ X X), (+ (* X 1.5) X) != (+ X X)
9. (* X P1) == (/ X P2)
```

Fig. 2. Redundant Patterns

2.2 Generation

SURFER generates models in order of increasing complexity. At any given time there are usually many possible models with the same complexity. All of these models are generated before any more complex models are considered. A *model complexity level* consists of all the models with the same complexity that are kept after being generated. All higher model complexity levels are constructed out of components from lower levels. At a given complexity level, the arguments for unary terms all come from the same lower level. For higher arity functions the picture is more complicated. A binary term might have the same complexity models with a level zero component and a level three component as with two level two components.

Each time the system completes a model complexity level, all of the possible model complexity level combinations for each possible term arity are generated. These combinations are then inserted into a list for each arity ordered by complexity total and when the complexity totals are equal, ordered by the smallest maximum complexity level involved. Once a term has generated all possible combinations (or permutations for non-commutative functions) of the models in a given combination of model complexity levels, it moves onto the next combination in the list for its arity.

The first model generated is always a terminal (constant, variable or parameter) since any non-terminal model must include one or more terminals. On each cycle, a term has associated with it pointers to the previously kept models it would like to use as components, the complexity of the candidate model and an accumulated probability. At each stage only terms of the problem output type and with minimal complexity are considered. Within those terms the first term with an accumulated probability greater than one is generated and has its probability decremented by one. If there are no terms with an accumulated probability greater than one, every vocabulary term is incremented by its associated probability P_t. This procedure has the effect of insuring that models are generated in order of increasing complexity while causing terms to appear as often as the top level operation in a model as their probability P_t.

Operators can overlap. For example, both (* x x) and (* x1 x2) can coexist as terms in the same vocabulary even though the first is just a special case of the second. Presumably (* x x) is used enough that using some of the coding space for the special case results in shorter model solutions. Since models are searched in order of complexity, such terms change the model generation order.

Figure 4 shows the model generation process for a simple problem. The problem is defined by the *Example* entry in Figure 3. * has a relative cost R_t twice that of the other terms, so the complexity C_t of * is 3.44 and C_t of the other terms is 1.72. *(Cy)cle* is incremented each time a model is generated. *(K)ept* is incremented each time a model is kept. *(R)ejects* keeps track of the number of models that were rejected during model generation as were models 4, 7 and 11. *(S)ignatures* is the number of models rejected because their signature matched a previously generated model. Model 10 was rejected because its signature was the same as model 9. *(I)signatures* is the number of models that were rejected after their free parameters were optimized to the data. Model 13 was rejected because its instance signature was the same as that for model 6. *(Ev)aluations* is the number of evaluations of the model the optimization procedures took to optimize the free parameters in the model. *(Co)mplexity* is the model complexity in bits. As can be seen in the figure five complexity levels were generated in order of increasing model complexity. *(Len)gth* is the total description length of the model. The end of each line shows the model just generated. If the model is the best so far it is marked with an @ sign. If the model is rejected, an = is printed and its equivalent model is shown. In this example, the original model is found on model 14 of 20 possible models.

Name	Inputs	Output	Constants	Unary	Binary
	Expression				
Example	X	Float			+ *
	(+ 3.0 (* X X))				
Boolean	A B C D	Boolean		NOT	AND OR
	(AND (OR A B) (OR C D))				
Regression	X	Float		- COS SIN EXP LOG	+ * /
	(+ (* 2.718 (* X X)) (* 3.1416 X))				
Fibonacci	J	Integer	0 1 2	SELF	+ -
	(+ (SELF (- J 2)) (SELF (- J 1)))				
Newton	M1 M2 R	Float			+ * /
	(/ (* 6.67 M1 M2) (* R R))				

Fig. 3. Problem Definitions

3 Results

Figure 3 shows some of the problems that SURFER has solved. *Boolean* looks for a simple boolean function of four variables. The problems *Regression* and *Fibonacci* come from work on genetic programming.[2] The *Regression* problem requires finding both the symbolic form of a model and the parameters required to make the model fit the data. The *Fibonacci* problem requires finding a recursive program to generate element J of the Fibonacci sequence. The SELF function returns one for any value less than two and zero if the function would recurse infinitely. *Newton* is just a more complex instance of the regression problem where the goal is to discover Newton's universal law of gravitation including the constant. To prevent numerical problems, the constant used is not of the right magnitude.

Each of these problems was run with two different sets of relative term complexities except *Newton*. In the first run, all terms have the same relative complexity $R(t)$. In the second run, unary functions have a relative complexity R_t

```
Cy    K R S I Ev Co Len Model
00:   0 0 0 0  0  2  98 @X
01:   1 0 0 0 28  2  52 @FLOAT1
02:   2 0 0 0  0  5  98 (+ X X)
03:   3 0 0 0 12  5  54 (+ X FLOAT1)
04:   3 1 0 0  0  5     (+ FLOAT1 FLOAT1) =
05:   4 1 0 0  0  7  54 (* X X)
06:   5 1 0 0 13  7  92 (* X FLOAT1)
07:   5 2 0 0  0  9     (* FLOAT1 FLOAT1) =
08:   6 2 0 0  0  9  97 (+ X (+ X X))
09:   7 2 0 0 12  9  64 (+ X (+ X FLOAT1))
10:   7 2 1 0  0  9     (+ FLOAT1 (+ X X)) = (+ X (+ X 3.00))
11:   7 3 1 0  0  9     (+ FLOAT1 (+ X FLOAT1)) =
12:   8 3 1 0  0 10  58 (+ X (* X X))
13:   8 3 1 1 12 10  95 (+ X (* X 3.00)) = (* X 4.00)
14:   9 3 1 1 11 10  10 @(+ FLOAT1 (* X X))
(+ 3.0143678 (* X X))
```

Fig. 4. Example Problem

twice the complexity of the other terms. Since *Newton* has no unary terms only one run is provided because the results would be the same in both cases.

In the first run, the complexity level of a model is just the number of terms in that model minus one. In the second run, the complexity level of a model is one less than the number of terms in that model minus the number of binary terms. The model (SIN X) would be found at model complexity level one in both runs. Model (+ X (+ X C)) would be found at model complexity level four in the first run and two in the second run. Unless relative complexities are integer multiples of the lowest complexity terminal, determining a model's complexity level is usually not this simple.

Figure 5 shows the best and second best model for each problem run and their respective model complexities and description length. On each run, SURFER ran until it found a model that matched the data exactly. This was just an expedient way to get each run to terminate quickly. In the presence of noise, each run would have to continue to either a preset effort limit or until models get complex enough that they cannot improve on the best description length. As can be seen by the large difference between the best and second best model in each case, there would have to be a lot of noise or very few n-tuples to cause the system to prefer the second best model. As can be seen in the *Regression* problem solutions, the two runs do not always end up generating the same syntactic model although they do generate models that describe the same function.

Figure 6 shows information on the search process for each problem. *Kept* is the number of models that were kept of all of the models *Tried*. *Max* is the maximum number of models that would have to be tried to guarantee finding the eventual solution. It is the number of models that were left in the same complex-

Problem	Best Second Best	Complex (Bits)	Len (Bits)
Regression	(* (+ x 1.15) (/ X 0.37))	23.3	23.3
	(* (+ X X) (+ X 1.21))	23.3	44.5
Regression2	(* (* X 2.7) (+ X 1.2))	18.0	18.0
	(* (+ X X) (+ x 0.8))	18.0	37.0
Boolean	(AND (OR D C) (OR A B))	19.7	19.7
	(OR D C)	8.4	27.2
Boolean2	(AND (OR D C) (OR A B))	18.4	18.4
	(OR D C)	7.9	26.6
Fibonacci	(+ (SELF (- J 1)) (SELF (- J 2)))	25.3	25.3
	(+ (- J 1) (SELF (- J 1)))	22.5	55.8
Fibonacci2	(+ (SELF (- J 1)) (SELF (- J 2)))	28.9	28.9
	(+ (- J 1) (SELF (- J 1)))	23.6	124.0
Newton	(* (/S 6.7 R) (/S (* M1 M2) R))	25.3	25.3
	(* (/S 0.09068619 R) (* M1 M2))	19.7	35.9

Fig. 5. Problem Solutions

ity level as the solution. *Generation* is the number of models that were rejected without being evaluated. *Signature* is the number of models that were rejected as being identical to a previously kept model through the use of signatures. *Instance* is the number of models that were rejected as being equivalent to another once their free parameters were optimized to fit the data. *Evals* is the number of model evaluations that were required including the optimization procedures. Since *regression* and *Fibonacci* came from work on Genetic Programming, *GP Evals* has the number of evaluations Genetic Programming requires.[2]

Problem	Models			Rejects			Evals	GP Evals
	Kept	Tried	Max	Gen	Sign	Inst		
Regression	4519	6121	33224	378	854	370	36184	306,000
Regression2	141	194	1584	20	17	16	1851	306,000
Boolean	332	926	1520		594		926	
Boolean2	332	926	1520		594		926	
Fibonacci	5626	6997	21974	1070	301		6997	484,500
Fibonacci2	5169	6421	73328	316	914		6421	484,500
Newton	4095	8631	62661	323	3166	1047	133106	

Fig. 6. Problem Summary

As can be seen in Figure 6, the solution to *Regression* was found much sooner in the second run than in the first. This is because the solution only involved binary functions and the change in relative complexities caused binary functions to appear at earlier complexity levels. However even if the order of models within the same complexity level had been different, the worst case for the first run was 33,224 models while that for the second run was only 1,584.

Boolean looks like the two runs had exactly the same effect, but the path taken to the results are actually very different. The number of complexity levels explored for the first run was four and for the second was seven. The reason that the size of the final complexity levels are so similar is because of the high redundancy found in the boolean terms.

While problem *Fibonacci* looks similar to *Regression* in that the second run finds a model sooner than the first, that is actually deceptive. The maximum number of models that would have to be generated in the first run is only 21,974 whereas in the second run it is 73,328. It was chance that made it look like run two found a solution more quickly than the first run. The reason that the effect of the two runs is different from their effects in *Regression* is that the solution to *Fibonacci* involves unary functions. The second run causes the size of the model complexity levels to increase because unary functions must be generated for all of the binary functions at the previous model complexity level. Since the final solution must await the generation of all the models at the level of the unary components, the size of the final model complexity level is much larger.

While *Fibonacci* has the runs with the largest final model complexity level and the most number of model complexity levels, *Newton* is the problem that takes the longest to solve. This is because of the large size of the complexity levels and the effort spent finding optimal settings for parameterized models.

How do *Regression* and *Fibonacci* compare to Genetic Programming (GP)? As can be seen in Figure 6, GP requires substantially more evaluations on both of these problems. This is because GP works best when successful building blocks can be found and then combined. In these examples, there are not small successful building blocks and GP does not do very well when compared to SURFER.

4   Conclusion

SURFER as it stands is a able to solve some empirical discovery problems. It is a framework with a single unifying idea–that of generating models in increasing complexity order. It provides domain independent mechanisms for model generation, optimization and testing. If a problem has the additive property that partial models can be identified and then combined, data-driven systems would be better. In systems without this property, but with a good *a priori* idea of likely model components, SURFER would be a good choice. The main advantages of this architecture are its complete coverage of the model space and that the domain theory is amenable to automatic generation. I plan to extend the system to automatically refine the domain theory after solving several similar problems by adjusting the vocabulary to incorporate new terms or to adjust the prior probablilities of the terms. This addition will allow the system over time to more quickly find optimal models in a particular domain.

References

1. M. M. Kokar. Determining arguments of invariant functional descriptions. *Machine Learning*, 1:403–422, 1986.

2. John R. Koza. Genetic programming: A paradigm for genetically breeding populations of computer programs to solve problems. Technical Report STAN-CS-90-1314, Stanford University, 1990.

3. Pat Langley and Jan M. Zytkow. Data-driven approaches to empirical discovery. *Artificial Intelligence*, 40(1):283–312, 1989.

4. John R. Pierce. *An Introduction to Information Theory*. Dover Publications, Inc, New York, NY, 1980.

5. William H. Press, Brian P. Flannery, Saul A. Teukolsky, and William T. Vetterling. *Numerical Recipes in C*. Cambridge University Press, Cambridge, England, 1988.

6. J. Rissanen. Modeling by shortest data description. *Automatica*, 14:465–471, 1978.

7. Hanan Samet. *The Design and Analysis of Spatial Data Structures*. Addison-Wesley, New York, 1990.

8. R. J. Solomonoff. A formal theory of inductive inference. parts i and ii. *Information and Control*, 7:1–22, 224–254, 1964.

9. R. J. Solomonoff. A system for incremental learning based on algorithmic probability. In *AAAI Symposium on the Theory and Application of Minimal-Length Encoding*, pages 140–146, March 1990.

Characterization of Classification Algorithms

J.Gama and P.Brazdil

LIACC, University of Porto
Rua Campo Alegre 823
4150 Porto, Portugal
email: {jgama, pbrazdil}@ncc.up.pt

Abstract

This paper is concerned with the problem of characterization of classification algorithms. The aim is to determine under what circumstances a particular classification algorithm is applicable. The method used involves generation of different kinds of models. These include regression and rule models, piecewise linear models (model trees) and instance based models. These are generated automatically on the basis of dataset characteristics and given test results. The lack of data is compensated for by various types of preprocessing. The models obtained are characterized by quantifying their predictive capability and the best models are identified.

1 Introduction

Previous studies have shown that it is difficult to identify a classification algorithm that would perform well on all tasks [7]. Although some classification algorithms may perform quite well in general, they may be easily surpassed by others. It is then desirable to take the characteristics of the task into account when attempting to identify a suitable algorithm. We are interested to find models that permit us to make reasonably reliable predictions concerning applicability. If we use Shaffer's [11] terminology our aim is to characterize the space in which the individual classification algorithms achieve positive generalization performance.

Shaffer [10] described a method which involves testing competing models using cross-validation. It was demonstrated that the truly best model is selected with high probability. The disadvantage of this approach is that we have to do quite a lot of testing before a decision can be made. As Brodley [4] has shown the decision as to which is the 'best' model can be guided by rules and can thus be potentially quicker. The rules used in [4] incorporate the knowledge of domain experts and hence are not easy to update when new algorithms, or test results, become available.

Various attempts have been made to automate the generation of such rules ([2], [3]). The method in [3] incorporated the process of learning, using decision tree/rule learning system C4.5 [8]. The advantage of this approach is that the rules characterizing the applicability can not only be generated with relative ease, but also updated whenever new results become available.

algorithms are expressed in terms of this error margin (i.e. how many EM's it is above the default error rate).

Normalization Method 3: This method consist of first assembling the test results of all classification algorithms on one particular dataset. These are used to calculate the mean and the standard deviation. All error rates are normalized by subtracting the mean value and by dividing the result by the standard deviation. For the Segment dataset, for instance, the mean error rate of the classification algorithms considered is 8.9%. The standard deviation in this case is 9.8%. If we use these figures to normalize the error rate of, say, ALLOC80, we will get the normalized error rate ERN_3 of -0.605.

The advantage of this method is that the values have rather clear interpretation. Higher negative values (i.e. < -0.5) indicate that the error rate is rather low. Values around 0 show that the error rate is not far from the average. Positive values may be interpreted as worse than average performance. High positive values (such as 10) suggest that the algorithm may have failed to run and hence was attributed maximum error rate.

2.2 Normalization of Dataset Characteristics

Datasets are characterized using certain number of measures which are similar to those in [3] or in [7]. These include simple measures, statistical measures and information based measures. The simple measures include:
- number of examples (N),
- number of attributes (p),
- number of classes (k),
- proportion of binary attributes (Bin_att),
- errors quantified by costs (Cost).

The statistical measures include:
- standard deviation ratio (SDratio),
- mean value of correlation (Correl),
- canonical correlation for the best single combination of attributes (Cancor1),
- the first normalized eigenvalues of canonical discriminant matrix (Fract1),
- skewness,
- kurtosis.

The information based measures include:
- entropy of class (Hc),
- entropy of attributes (Ha),
- mean mutual information of class and attributes (Mca),
- noise-signal ratio (NSratio) equal to (Ha-Mca)/Mca.

In the experiments with regression models the dataset measures were also normalized. The process is similar to normalization 3 of error rates. For each measure mean and standard deviation is calculated across all datasets. Each measure is normalized by subtracting the mean and by dividing the result by the standard deviation. Here all measures normalized in this way are marked by '. For instance, *Kurtosis'* represents the normalized version of *Kurtosis* measure.

The method referred to above had, however, one disadvantage. This is related to the fact C4.5 works with categorical classes. If we want to predict numeric values, the data has to be discretized beforehand. This may introduce certain information loss. It would thus seem that a method that does not require prior discretization should be better suited to this task. We have decided to verify this hypothesis and evaluated the capability of linear regression models, piecewise linear models (model trees [9]) and instance based models [1] to capture the information concerning applicability. This paper describes the results.

The rest of the paper is organized as follows. Section 2 describes the metadata considered in our study and some preprocessing steps carried out. Section 3 describes several models considered here. Section 3.1 describes the method of generating and characterizing regression models. Section 3.2 discusses the rule models. The following two subsections describe the use of model trees and instance based models. Section 4 is dedicated to comparisons between different types of models. Section 5 discusses how we can select, or combine, the outcomes of different models in order to improve the overall prediction. Section 6 concludes the paper.

2   Normalizing Meta-Datasets

The results of the StatLog project represent a valuable source of information [7]. In this project 22 different classification algorithms were tested on more than 20 different datasets. The results can be used to develop models indicating when each algorithm is applicable [7] [3]. In this paper we continue to use this data to carry out further analysis. Before describing this in more detail, we describe how the data available has been normalized.

2.1   Normalization of Test Results

Error rates (and success rates) are not too meaningful in themselves. The error rate of, say 90%, may be excellent for some datasets, but not so good in other cases. In order to achieve minimally meaningful results, the test results need to be normalized. The test results need to be converted to other units comparable across different datasets.

Normalization Method 1: One possible method of normalizing error rates consists of first examining the results of all classification algorithms on a particular dataset and identifying the best performing algorithm. So for example, if we consider the *Segment* dataset, the best performing algorithm is *ALLOC*80 (it achieved 3% error rate). Next, an estimate of the error margin EM is calculated on the basis of the best error rate (ER) and number of examples in the test set (NT) as follows: $EM = sqrt(ER * (1 - ER)/NT)$. In the case of the *Segment* dataset, for instance, the error margin is $EM = 0.35$. The error rates of all other classification algorithms are expressed in terms of this error margin (i.e. how many EM's it is below the best error rate). Although low error rates are comparable across datasets (they are near 0), high error rates are not. The following alternative methods overcome this problem.

Normalization Method 2: This method consists of first calculating the error rate ER of the default rule which simply predicts the most frequent class. Next the error margin EM is calculated in a similar way as above. The error rates of all classification

3 Generating Different Models of Applicability

3.1 Generation of Regression Models

Generation of regression models proceeds as follows. First, the normalized results relative to one particular classification algorithm are separated from the rest. The data consists of pairs of values of the form $< Dataset, ERN_i >$ where $Dataset$ represents the dataset name and ERN_i the error rate, normalized using method "i". Next the dataset name is substituted the corresponding normalized dataset measures described in the previous section. This data is used in the construction of regression models. These are generated in the usual way, following the method described, for instance, in [5] or [7]. Some regression equation generated, for instance, on the basis of given metadata normalized using method 1 were:

$$ERN_1(Bayes) = 60.9 + 115.6* (-1.15 * Skew' + 1.79 * Kurtosis' + 0.53 * Hc')$$
$$ERN_1(Discrim) = 40.6 + 121.9* (1.06 * Kurtosis' + 0.89 * N' - 0.44 * Skew')$$

For simplicity only the most significant terms are shown, and these follow the order of importance. Regression equations enable us to predict the normalized error rate in terms of the error margins (EM's) discussed earlier.

If we consider the equation for the *linear discriminant method (Discrim)*, for instance, we note that the error rate is affected by the measures $Kurtosis'$, $Skew'$ which are considered to be relevant in this case. The term $0.89 * N'$ suggests that number of examples also affects errors. In other words $Discrim$ will not work well, if the number of examples is large. This empirically derived fact appears to be in agreement with other evidence in [7] in the form of learning curves.

The regression equation shown can be used to predict the normalized error rate for a particular dataset. So for instance, if we apply it to the *Segment* dataset, we obtain a prediction of $ERN = 23.4EM's$. In other words, the predicted error rate of $Discrim$ is $23.4EM's$ below the best performance. As it happens the actual value is $24.2EM's$ which is not far from the predicted value.

The pairs of predicted and actual values can be compared. The errors can be quantified using, for instance, *normalized mean squared error* discussed later. However, such comparisons are not very meaningful, as they express how well the regression model fits the data. It represents a *biased estimate* which may not be too reliable when attempting to make predictions. This is why we have decided to characterize the *predictive power* of each model. The method is discussed in the following section.

Characterization of Regression Models

Each model is characterized using the leave-one-out cross-validation method. In each step one case is set aside for an evaluation. The remaining data is normalized and the regression model generated is used to obtain a prediction. The prediction is denormalized and stored together with the actual (observed) value. After the leave-one-out cycles have terminated, the measures characterizing the quality of prediction are calculated. So, essentially we measure the capability of the system to generate reliable models. We assume that the characterization obtained on the basis of N-1 cases is similar to the one we would obtain on N cases.

In literature many different measures have been suggested for the quality of predictions. Here we use a normalized mean squared error ($NMSE$), which has for instance been used in [12] in the context of time series prediction tasks. It is calculated as follows:

$$NMSE = (\textstyle\sum_{i=1}^{N}(Prediction_i - Actual_i)^2)/(\sum_{i=1}^{N}(Actual_i - Mean)^2)$$

where $i = 1..N$ identifies the items in the test set, while $Prediction_i$ and $Actual_i$ represent the predicted and actual values. The $NMSE$ has the following interpretation. Values equal to 1 indicate that the predictor gives similar predictions as the mean. Lower values suggest that the predictions are better than those achieved by the mean. If the value of $NMSE$ is higher than 1, the predictor is worthless.

Model	Regression			Rules			Model Trees			IBL		
Normal.	1	2	3	1	2	3	1	2	3	1	2	3
AC2				.74	.72			.39*			.51	
ALLOC80					.59			.33*			.61	
Backprop						.57*						.77
Bayes	.17*										.55	.58
BayesTree				.79				.51*			.55	.57
C4.5				.84		.48*				.84		.48*
Cal5				.47*		.74		.47*	.74		.57	.67
CART												
Cascade									.82			.67*
CASTLE								.48*			.69	
CN2						.67		.43*			.57	
Dipol92								.39*			.58	
Discrim	.39*							.49			.62	
IndCART								.41*			.56	
ITrule				.88	.44*			.77		.57	.52	
k-NN					.75*						.84	
Kohonen												
LogDisc						.83		.60*			.60	
LVQ					.74			.41*			.56	
NewID								.53*			.54	
QuaDisc								.45*			.62	
RBF						.33*			.89		.57	
SMART				.86				.51*			.60	

Table 1. Predictive capability of regression models, rule models, piecewise linear models (model trees) and instance based models, expressed in terms of $NMSE$.

The table above shows the predictive capability of various models which are characterized using $NMSE$. The first three columns show the results of different regression models. As it happens only normalization method 1 lead to relatively reliable models in this case. All other columns represent other types of models which are discussed later.

We note that the normalized mean square errors of some of the models are quite low indicating that these enable us to generate relatively reliable predictions. All models that appear to be better than others (i.e. have the lowest $NMSE$ compared with other types) are identified by "*". Empty spaces represent useless models whose $NMSE$ is larger than 1.

3.2 Generation of Rule Models

In [3] we have explored the possibility of using a decision tree/rule learning algorithm C4.5 [8] to generate models of applicability of different classification algorithms. The method proceeds as follows. First, the data relative to one particular algorithm (e.g. *Discrim* etc.) is separated out (this is similar to the corresponding step in the regression method). As the decision tree/rule learning algorithm chosen does not accept numeric classes, the normalized error rates need to be converted into categorical values. For normalization 1, all classification algorithms whose error rates are between 0 and 8 error margins, are considered to belong to the class "applicable". The others are considered "non-applicable". For normalization 3 the frontier between the two classes is set to $-.3$ (.3 standard deviations above the mean).

Rules are generated using C4.5rules. The method adopted here is essentially similar to [3] with the exception of how rules are calibrated and characterized. The objective of rule calibration is to determine the numeric value that should be attached to each rule. The value represents the prediction associated with each rule if it fires. It is calculated as follows. First we determine all cases to which the rule applies. The value in question is calculated as the mean of the corresponding numeric classes.

If we follow this method on the StatLog metadata normalized using method 3 relative to the classification algorithm $C4.5$, we obtain a set of rules which include:

$$ERN_3(C4.5) = -0.71 \leftarrow Cost \leq 0, Ha \leq 4.25$$
$$ERN_3(C4.5) = -0.51 \leftarrow N > 18000$$

The first rule states that if the dataset does not include costs ($Cost \leq 0$) and if the entropy of attributes (Ha) is below a certain level, the normalized error rate of $C4.5$ algorithm will be 0.71 standard deviations above average. The other rule can be interpreted in a similar manner. The rules for *Backprop* generated include:

$$ERN_3(Backprop) = -0.58 \leftarrow Cost \leq 0, k \leq 10$$

which also indicates that this algorithm does not work well with datasets with costs. In addition, the number of classes (k) seems to be relevant.

Characterization of Rule Models

Rules are characterized in a similar way as regression equations. First, all cases to which the rule applies are identified, and the predicted and the actual values are stored. These pairs of values are used to calculate the $NMSE$. Table 1 shows the $NMSE$ coefficients associated with various rule models. If we consider normalization method 3, for instance, the best values have been obtained for $C4.5$, *Backprop* and *RBF*.

The method of characterizing models of applicability differs from that used in [3] where predictions were characterized by information scores. These determine the degree to which the class concept is satisfied, and in effect, enable to turn a categorical concept into a fuzzy one.

3.3 Generation of Piecewise Linear Models

We have decided to investigate the applicability of a particular class of piecewise linear models represented by model trees [9]. These can be seen as generalization of both linear regression models and decision trees. Whereas a leaf of a decision tree contains just a class name, the leaf of a model tree can contain a linear model relating a class value to corresponding attribute values.

We have used Quinlan's M5.1 to generate models of applicability. The given meta-data was normalized using all three methods described ealier. The models were generated and evaluated in a similar way as the other types of models discussed earlier. The $NMSE's$ obtained are shown in Table 1.

3.4 Generation of Instance Based Models

We have decided to examine also the ability of *instance based models* to generate predictions concerning applicability. Instance based learning represents one of the simplest forms of learning, in which the solution of previous cases is simply stored for future use. The solution of a new case is found by searching for the most similar cases to the given one ([1]). Here we use the vector of dataset measures discussed earlier and calculate *Euclidian distance* which is used to measure similarity. The three most similar cases are used to estimate the value of ERN. The resulting value is obtained by calculating the mean of normalized errors of the three most similar cases. The instance based models can be evaluated in a similar way as other models which were discussed earlier.

4 Analysis of Results

We have examined three normalization methods in conjunction with four different kinds of models which include regression, rule, model trees and instance based models. Overall this represents 12 different types of models. The results obtained (see Table 1) indicate that it is difficult to determine which set of models is clearly the best one.

Regression models seem to produce good predictions in two cases (*Bayes* and *Discrim*). Both of these models are based on normalization 1. In other cases regression models do not appear to be so good.

Some rule models seem compete very well with other types. If we consider all three normalization methods, about 17 good rule models were obtained in total. About one third of these appear to be overall winners.

Model trees turned out to be quite good in about 18 cases. Most of these are based on normalization 2. Relatively large proportion of these (13) appear to be better than other types.

Instance based learning method lead to about 25 reliable models. However, only two seem better than the models of other types. Most of these good models are associated with normalization 2.

Instance models have, however, one disadvantage. They are much more difficult to comprehend than the other types of models considered here. Lists of cases do not represent a very comprehensible theory. Although this problem could be mitigated by considering only prototypical cases, other simpler types of models still seem preferable, particularly if they are equally reliable.

5 Selecting the Best Models

As the results do not seem to be in favour of one particular set of models, it is reasonable to consider that we should have a method of selecting, or combining, predictions of different models. In this section we describe how this is done. First all complex models that appear to be worse than a simple average (i.e. whose $NMSE$ is greater than 1) are excluded. Then the method of selecting / combining models proceeds in two phases.

Method of Selection

All models related to one normalization method and a particular classification algorithm are identified. The objective is to select the model that appears to be the best one. The quality of models is judged by $NMSE's$. This is repeated for all three normalization methods.

So, for instance, if we consider normalization 1, the *rule model* is selected for $AC2$ ($NMSE = .74$), *default average* for $ALLOC80$ and *Backprop* ($NMSE = 1$), *regression model* for *Discrim* ($NMSE = .39$) etc. The process of selecting models is repeated for normalization 2 and 3. With normalization 2, for instance, *model tree* is selected for $AC2$. because its $NMSE$ is lower (.39) than the corresponding values of other models.

The models selected in this manner can be used to generate predictions concerning applicability. These can be compared with the actual values (see Fig.1).

Combining Outcomes of Different Model Types

The procedure just described reduces the initial number of model types for each classification algorithm from 12 to just to 3. Each type is related to a particular normalization method considered. Let us consider the models for *Discrim*, for instance. Model of type 1 (obtained on the basis of normalization 1) represents the regression model, while type 2 represents a model tree and type 3 the default average.

Combining the predictions of several models has usually positive effects on the overall quality of predictions. Our aim is to do just that. As different model types use somewhat different units, the predictions need to be re-scaled (by subtracting the mean and dividing all values by the standard deviation). This preserves the relative ordering of classification algorithms.

The scaled predictions are combined by taking into account their quality, expressed in terms of $NMSE's$. If this was not done, even a perfect-prediction could be adversely affected by other less reliable ones. The value of combined prediction ERN_c is calculated as a weighted average of $(w_1 * ERN_1(A) + w_2 * ERN_2(A) + w_3 * ERN_3(A))$ $/(w_1 + w_2 + w_3)$ where A represents the classification algorithm and $w_1..w_3$ are weights. Here we follow the standard method and equate each weight w_i to $1/NMSE_i^2$. The larger the error, the lesser is its weight in the combined outcome.

Fig.1 shows the individual predictions as well as the combined predictions for the *Segment* dataset. The combined predictions (lower right figure) correlate reasonably well with the actual values. We have verified that, in general. the combined predictions are usually better than the individual predictions.

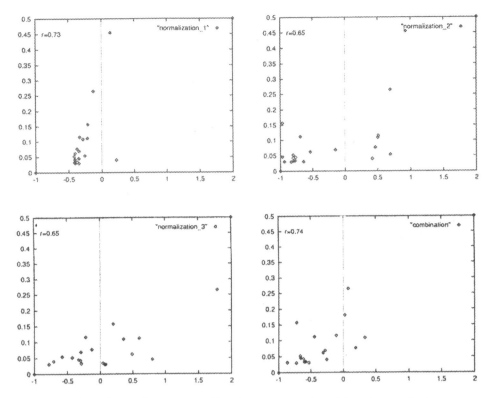

Figure 1: Correlation between predicted error rates (x-axis) and actual error rates (y-axis) for the Segment dataset. The figure shows predictions of models based on normalization 1-3 as well as the combined prediction. The correlation coefficients are shown in the upper left corner. Some outliers are not included in the figures.

Although the method of combining predictions seems to improve the overall outcome, other methods could have been adopted. Ho and Hull [6], for instance, described a method according to which the combination of N different classifiers (Bayes, kNN etc.) is determined using a regression method. The coefficients associated with each classifier determine its weight in the overall outcome. This method could potentially achieve somewhat better results than the one described here.

6 Conclusion

This paper is concerned with the problem of characterization of classification algorithms. The aim is to predict the error rate of a particular classification algorithm in relative terms. The prediction should estimate the performance of the algorithm in relation to other competing algorithms.

In our previous work we have explored the use rule models for this aim. In this paper we have considered other types of models, including regression, piecewise linear model (model trees) and instance based models. As the objective is to predict a numeric value it is natural that we should consider these in our study. In addition we have considered different types of data preprocessing (normalization).

The results indicate that no single method can be considered overwhelmingly better than the others. In some cases a particular combination of preprocessing and model type lead to most reliable predictions. In other cases a different method of preprocessing, or different type of model, works better.

It appears that if the induction task is difficult, then it is worth trying to *search for* a reliable outcome. The method described here attempts not just to apply a single method, but rather, try several of them. The $NMSE$ measure is used to provide a kind of feedback in this process. This way it is possible to spot regularities in the data and capture them in a useful form.

Some of the models generated which are shown in the Appendix provide a very useful source of information. They show, in a condensed form, when a particular classification algorithm seems to work or fail. All of this information could potentially be of interest to the algorithm designers. It could help to determine how the classification algorithms could be improved and thus stimulate further development in this area.

References

[1] Aha D., Kibler D. and Albert M. (1991): "Instance-based learning algorithms". em Machine Learning, Vol.6, No.1, 37-66.

[2] Aha D.(1992): "Generalizing from Case Studies: A Case Study", in *ML92, Machine Learning, Proceedings of the 9th International Workshop*, D.Sleeman and P.Edwards (eds.), Morgan Kaufmann.

[3] Brazdil P., Gama J. and Henery R.(1994): "Characterizing the Applicability of Classification Algorithms using Meta Level Learning", in *Machine Learning - ECML-94*, F.Bergadano and L. de Raedt (eds.), Springer Verlag.

[4] Brodley C. (1993): "Addressing the Selective Superiority Problem: Automatic Algorithm / Model Class Selection Problem", in *ML93, Machine Learning, Proceedings of the 10th International Conference*, P. Utgoff (ed.), Morgan Kaufmann.

[5] Dillon W. and Goldstein M.(1984): *Multivariate Analysis, Methods and Applications*, J. Wiley and Sons, Inc.

[6] T. K. Ho and Hull J.J. (1994): "Decision combination in multiple classifier systems", in *IEEE Transactions on pattern Analysis and Machine Intelligence*, Vol. 16, No. 1.

[7] Michie D., Spiegelhalter D.J. and Taylor C. (1994): *Machine Learning, Neural and Statistical Classification*, Ellis Horwood.

[8] Quinlan R. (1992): *C4.5: Programs for Machine Learning*, Morgan Kaufmann.

[9] Quinlan R. (1993): "Combining Instance-Based and Model-Based Learning", in *ML93, Machine Learning, Proceedings of the 10th International Conference*, P.Utgoff (ed.), Morgan Kaufmann.

[10] Shaffer C. (1993): "Selecting a Classification Method by Cross- Validation", in *Machine Learning*, Vol. 13, No. 1, Kluwer Academic Publishers.

[11] Shaffer C. (1994): "A Conservation Law for Generalization Performace", in *Machine Learning, Proc. of 11th International Conference*, ed. W.Cohen and H.Hirsh, Morgan Kaufmann Publishers.

[12] Weigend A.S. and Gershenfeld N.A.(1993): *Time Series Prediction, Forecasting the Future and Understanding the Past*, Addison Wesley.

Annex

Models Relative to Normalization 1: The errors are expressed in terms of error margins (EM's) which are related to the best error rate. The error rate of the best classification algorithm is 0. Large positive numbers represent high error rates.

$ERN_1(AC2) = 6.3 \leftarrow k \leq 2$

$ERN_1(AC2) = 9.5 \leftarrow p > 9, Fract1 > 0.203$

$ERN_1(AC2) = 33.1 \leftarrow p \leq 9, k > 2$

$ERN_1(AC2) = 76.4 \leftarrow Fract1 \leq 0.2$

$ERN_1(Bayes) = 60.9 + 115.6 * (-1.15 * Skew' + 1.79 * Kurtosis' + 0.53 * Hc')$

$ERN_1(BayesTree) = 6.1 \leftarrow Ha \leq 5.6$

$ERN_1(BayesTree) = 59.8 \leftarrow Ha > 5.6$

$ERN_1(C4.5) = 7.8 \leftarrow Fract1 > 0.2, Cost \leq 0$

(The error rate of C4.5 is 7.8 error margins (EM's) below the best performance if the value of Fract1 is greater than 0.2 and if errors are not characterized by costs.)

$ERN_1(C4.5) = 22.5 \leftarrow Fract1 > 0.2, Cost > 0$

$ERN_1(C4.5) = 58.2 \leftarrow Fract1 \leq 0.2$

$ERN_1(Cal5) = 8.9 \leftarrow Ha \leq 5.6$

$ERN_1(Cal5) = 109.5 \leftarrow Ha > 5.6$

$ERN_1(CN2) = 8.5 \leftarrow Ha \leq 5.6$

$ERN_1(CN2) = 60.4 \leftarrow Ha > 5.6$

$ERN_1(Discrim) = 40.6 + 121.9 * (1.06 * Kurtosis' + 0.89 * N' - 0.44 * Skew')$

$ERN_1(IndCART) = 28.8 + Fract1 * 26.3$

$ERN_1(SMART) = 2.6 \leftarrow Cancor1 \leq 0.8$

$ERN_1(SMART) = 5.5 \leftarrow Cancor1 > 0.8, N \leq 2500$

$ERN_1(SMART) = 35.7 \leftarrow Cancor1 > 0.8, N > 2500$

Models Relative to Normalization 2: The errors are expressed in terms of error margins (EM's) which are related to the default error rate which is considered to be 0. Values near 0 represent thus high error rates. Large negative numbers represent low error rates.

$ERN_2(Ac2) = -277.7 \leftarrow Fract1 \leq 0.31$

$ERN_2(Ac2) = (73.5 - 128.5 * Cancor1) \leftarrow Fract1 > 0.31$

$ERN_2(Alloc80) = -302.6 \leftarrow Fract1 \leq 0.31$

$ERN_2(Alloc80) = (-8.07 - 62.1 * Mca) \leftarrow Fract1 > 0.31$

$ERN_2(BackProp) = -102 \leftarrow Mca > 0.19$

$ERN_2(BackProp) = -7.4 \leftarrow Mca \leq 0.19$

$ERN_2(BayesTree) = -297.7 \leftarrow Fract1 \leq 0.31$

$ERN_2(BayesTree) = (40.3 - 51.3 * SDratio) \leftarrow Fract > 0.31$

$ERN_2(Cal5) = -264.1 \leftarrow Fract1 \leq 0.31$

$ERN_2(Cal5) = (38.5 - 49.8 * SDratio) \leftarrow Fract1 > 0.31$

$ERN_2(CASTLE) = -284.3 \leftarrow Fract1 \leq 0.31$

$ERN_2(CASTLE) = -16.3 \leftarrow Fract1 > 0.31$

$ERN_2(CN2) = -299.3 \leftarrow Fract1 \leq 0.31$

$ERN_2(CN2) = (68.5 - 121.6 * Cancor1) \leftarrow Fract1 > 0.31$

$ERN_2(Dipol92) = -316.7 \leftarrow Fract1 \leq 0.31$

$ERN_2(Dipol92) = (-13 - 69.1 * Cancor1 + 45.2 * Fract1) \leftarrow Fract1 > 0.31$

(The error rate of Dipol92 is 316.7 error margins above the default error rate if $Fract1 \leq .31$. If $Fract1 > .31$, the error rate decreases with Cancor1 and increases with Fract1.)

$ERN_2(IndCART) = -294.2 \leftarrow Fract1 \leq 0.31$

$ERN_2(IndCART) = (46.6 - 56.6 * SDratio) \leftarrow Fract1 > 0.31$

$ERN_2(LVQ) = -320.3 \leftarrow Fract1 \leq 0.31$

$ERN_2(LVQ) = (-0.286 - 80 * Mca) \leftarrow Fract1 > 0.31$

$ERN_2(NewID) = -295.1 \leftarrow Fract1 \leq 0.31$

$ERN_2(NewID) = (70.6 - 125 * Cancor1) \leftarrow Fract1 > 0.31$

$ERN_2(QuaDisc) = -320.2 \leftarrow Fract1 \leq 0.31$

$ERN_2(QuaDisc) = 55 - 100 * Cancor1 \leftarrow Fract1 > 0.31$

$ERN_2(RBF) = -212.5 \leftarrow Fract1 \leq 0.31$

$ERN_2(RBF) = -13.5 \leftarrow Fract1 > 0.31$

$ERN_2(SMART) = -298.9 \leftarrow Fract1 \leq 0.31$

$ERN_2(SMART) = (-11 - 60.9 * Mca) \leftarrow Fract1 > 0.31$

Models Relative to Normalization 3: The errors are expressed in terms of the number of standard deviations from the mean. Value near 0 represents mean error rates. Values below $-.5$ represent low error rates, and values above .5 high error rates.

$ERN_3(BackProp) = -0.6 \leftarrow k \leq 10, Cost \leq 0$

$ERN_3(BackProp) = 4.2 \leftarrow k > 10$

$ERN_3(BackProp) = -0.16 \leftarrow Cost > 0$

$ERN_3(C4.5) = -0.71 \leftarrow Ha \leq 4.25, Cost \leq 0$

(The error rate of C4.5 is .71 standard deviations above average if the entropy of attributes is less than 4.25 and if the errors are not quantified by costs.)

$ERN_3(C4.5) = -0.51 \leftarrow N > 18000$

$ERN_3(C4.5) = 0.276 \leftarrow Ha > 4.25, N \leq 18000$

$ERN_3(C4.5) = 1.9 \leftarrow Cost > 0$

$ERN_3(Cal5) = 1.04 - 1.79 * Fract1$

$ERN_3(CN2) = -0.3 \leftarrow N > 1000$

$ERN_3(CN2) = 0.99 \leftarrow N \leq 1000$

$ERN_3(ITRule) = 0.94 \leftarrow NSratio > 1000$

$ERN_3(ITRule) = 7.33 \leftarrow NSratio \leq 4.9$

$ERN_3(LogDisc) = -1.05 \leftarrow N \leq 1250$

$ERN_3(LogDisc) = -0.6 \leftarrow Ha > 5.6$

$ERN_3(LogDisc) = 0.36 \leftarrow N > 1250, Hx \leq 5.6$

$ERN_3(LVQ) = 0.8$

$ERN_3(RBF) = -0.3 \leftarrow Cost \leq 0$

$ERN_3(RBF) = 1.5 \leftarrow Cost > 0$

Neurons, Glia and the Borderline Between Subsymbolic and Symbolic Processing

J. G. Wallace[1] and K. Bluff[2]

[1] Swinburne University of Technology,
Melbourne, Australia
[2] Department of Computer Science,
Swinburne University of Technology,
Melbourne, Australia

Abstract. Our goal is the exploration of the nature and development of the functional borderline between non or subsymbolic processing and symbolic processing. Newell attributes the existence of a physical symbol system to the fundamental restriction imposed on the amount of information represented and processed in a local neural area by the limited energy available. Symbol tokens overcome the restriction by providing distal access to another local area and further energy while maintaining the linkage necessary for integrated information processing. Critical to further specification of this account of the origins of symbolic processing is clarification of the nature and capabilities of subsymbolic processing proceeding within a local neural area. Contributing to this clarification is our current objective.

We focus on the local cortical neural mechanisms at the millimetric level underlying the acquisition and operation of specific cognitive performance. Our account of the nature of local neural processing significantly deviates from the current norm in assigning a critical information processing role to glia, another type of brain cell, and their interaction with neurons.

Glia appear to possess a type of intracellular and intercellular calcium dynamics which provide a basis of excitability for signaling between them. This raises the possibility that glial networks engage in information processing with very different temporal and spatial characteristics from neuronal signaling. The potential performance capabilities of subsymbolic processing in local neural areas are clarified in a description of mechanisms involved in glia-neuron interaction drawing upon a wide range of neurochemical research. A computational version of the glia-neuron (GN) model has been implemented to permit assessment of local performance capabilities. The results are discussed in terms of their potential significance for cognitive science and artificial intelligence. The complexity of neural-glial interaction in local areas suggests that much specific cognitive processing can occur without the need for symbol tokens to provide distal access to other local areas. The principle that the units in the physical symbol system refer to relatively elaborate local subsymbolic processing areas may assist in explaining the effectiveness of symbolic processing in spite of the constraints of slowness, seriality and limited memory size imposed by its dependence on neural networks. Clarification of the nature of local glial-neural processing and its implications for the relationship between subsymbolic and symbolic processing will assist in the construction of hybrid systems. Our work, also, has the potential to contribute to extension of the biological metaphor underlying ANN.

Introduction

Among the many stimulating and controversial aspects of Newell's (1990) model are the temporal and spatial frameworks adopted in his account of the relationship between neural functioning and cognitive processing. The basic temporal restriction adopted is that a minimal cognitive event requires about a second due to the time required for the generation of a neural action potential and the conduction time within local neural circuits. This constraint has been questioned by, for example, Purves (1993) who cites the brain's ability, in accurately localizing sound in space, to execute precise calculation in resolving differences on the order of tens of microseconds. Our work addresses both time and space since its motivation is the exploration of the nature and development of the functional borderline between non or subsymbolic processing and symbolic processing.

Newell attributes the existence of a physical symbol system to the fundamental restriction imposed on the amount of information represented and processed in a local neural area by the limited energy available. Symbol tokens overcome the restriction by providing distal access to another local area and further energy while maintaining the linkage necessary for integrated information processing. Critical to further specification of this account of the origins of symbolic processing is clarification of the nature and capabilities of subsymbolic processing proceeding within a local neural area. Contributing to this clarification is our current objective.

The Nature of Local Neural Processing

Brain and, more specifically, cortical rhythmic activity provides a means of defining local neural processing. Local resonances are relatively high frequency rhythmic processes in the 30-80 Hz range with a spatial dimension in the millimetric range. A major distinction between local and lower frequency global/regional resonant modes is that the local resonant modes are not coherent over distances of more than a few millimeters. Human regional and global resonant modes, in contrast, are always coherent over a distance of centimeters. It is suggested that cognitive behavioral or perceptual states requiring a high degree of spatio-temporal specificity in neocortical activation are only consistent with local states, (Silberstein, 1994). We will focus on the local cortical neural mechanisms at the millimetric level underlying the acquisition and operation of specific cognitive performance. Although local acquisition or learning depends on the functioning of distant areas such as the hippocampus and the striatum their role is relatively global and complements the spatio-temporal specifics that emerge in local areas, (Wickens, 1993).

Our account of the nature of local neural processing significantly deviates from the current norm in assigning a critical information processing role to glia, another type of brain cell, and their interaction with neurons. This approach is supported by a rapidly expanding range of experimental evidence. Glia, such as the astrocytes of cortical gray matter, have elaborate dendritic morphologies superficially similar to those of neurons. As Dani et al. (1992) point out, their fine processes mingle intimately with those of neurons throughout the synaptic neuropil and astrocyte membranes juxtapose or ensheathe most synapses in the mammalian CNS. Astrocytes actually outnumber neurons in many brain regions and are interconnected by gap junctions into vast networks. While these structural features hint at signaling or even information processing functions, astrocytes have traditionally been assigned relatively passive, background roles in structural, metabolic and trophic support of neurons. This view arose and persisted due to the absence in astrocytes of evidence of the electrical excitability which provides the basis of signaling between neurons. Recent studies of astrocytes, however, suggest that they possess a type of intracellular calcium dynamics which provides an alternative basis of excitability for signaling between them. This raises the possibility that astrocytic networks engage in information processing but with very different temporal and spatial characteristics from neuronal signaling. We will now describe the mechanisms involved in glia-neuron interaction. The account draws upon a wide range of neurochemical research. This excursion proves worthwhile, however, in the clarification which it offers of the potential performance capabilities of subsymbolic processing in local neural areas.

Learning and Synaptic Facilitation

Intracellular calcium levels play a prominent part in the neural mechanism underlying the long term potentiation (LTP) produced by Hebbian learning as a result of conjunction of presynaptic and postsynaptic activity. The mechanism for detecting a conjunction of presynaptic and postsynaptic activity appears to have a postsynaptic locus of control and to be based on postsynaptic depolarization. As Figure 1 indicates, the emergence of LTP is accompanied by a postsynaptic increase in intracellular calcium ion concentration. The neurotransmitter glutamate promotes calcium influx via NMDA-receptor linked channels. Calcium also enters via voltage sensitive calcium channels (VSCC).

Maintenance of LTP is mediated by presynaptic mechanisms. Williams et al. (1989) postulate the existence of a retrograde messenger to carry information from the postsynaptic side of the synapse to recently active presynaptic terminals. Arachidonic acid (AA) is suggested as a candidate retrograde messenger. Activation of NMDA receptors by neurotransmitter glutamate stimulates release of AA. This maintains LTP by increasing the amount of glutamate available for synaptic facilitation. The mechanism underlying this result introduces glia to

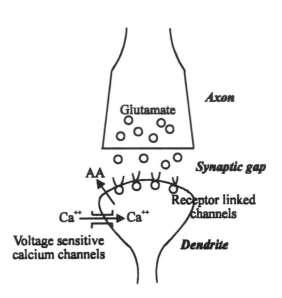

Fig. 1. Long Term Potentiation (LTP)

the scene. Figure 2 presents a process enabling glial cells to absorb glutamate from a synaptic gap and convert it to glutamine which can be transferred to neurons and reconverted to glutamate. This recycling process enables glia to function as a reservoir for glutamate and has been long known to be a feature of the supportive structure supplied to neurons by glia (McGeer et al., 1978). This function offers a ready explanation of the synaptic facilitation produced by AA. Barbour et al. (1989) have discovered that AA inhibits the uptake of glutamate by glial cells and, thus, produces an increase in the amount of glutamate available for synaptic facilitation. We will revisit this mechanism later.

Several comments on temporal and operational aspects of LTP will set the scene for our consideration of the role of glia, in general, and astrocytes, in particular, in synaptic facilitation. LTP begins to develop within 10 seconds of the application of stimulation and its effects are fully present within 20 - 30 seconds, (Gustafsson and Wigstrom, 1990). The potentiation can persist without detectable change for weeks, (Staubli and Lynch, 1987). The linking of long-term synaptic facilitation with the results of experience of very short duration must be achieved by means of processes that avoid the obvious dangers of such 'jumping to conclusions' to the survival of a system. Current versions of the neural mechanisms underlying LTP do not take account of this objective.

It is, also, difficult using current LTP mechanisms to account for experimental data such as the results of Martin et al., (1992). Recording from local groups of discriminated hippocampal neurons revealed that while stimulation produced LTP at the level of population evoked field potentials the local, single neuron response was highly variable. The same stimulation produced different LTP outcomes within a local group of simultaneously recorded neurons. Once again, this

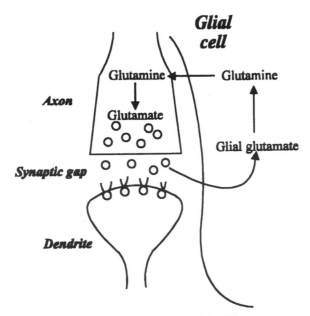

Fig. 2. Glutamate Takeup by Glial Cells

suggests the need for enhancement of our accounts of synaptic facilitation.

In addition to arguments for the inclusion of additional processes based on the shortcomings of current mechanisms there is direct experimental evidence that supports the involvement of two interacting processes in synaptic facilitation. Williams et al., (1989), in addition to producing LTP in hippocampal tissue, explored the effects of a combination of weak stimulation and added AA. This produced an increase in potentiation comparable with maximal LTP but, in contrast to the rapid onset of LTP, the time course of potentiation revealed a slow onset and a gradual climb to a plateau during a 60 - 120 minute period. As with LTP the enhancement of neural transmission was accompanied by an increase in the release of glutamate.

Astrocytes and Synaptic Facilitation

In this section we will present a necessarily brief description of processes capable of producing temporal and operational characteristics which complement those of LTP and carry us towards a more comprehensive account of synaptic facilitation. The account brings together a wide range of experimental evidence derived from independent lines of investigation of the role and functioning of glial cells.

Figure 3 presents a cycle of sequential and concurrent processes begun by registration on astrocytes of glutamate generated by neural synaptic activity. Evidence from calcium-imaging experiments in hippocampal and cortical astrocytes indicates that glutamate receptor activation in these cells leads to an increase in internal calcium, (Cornell-Bell and Finkbeiner, 1991). Rising intracellular calcium (Ca^{2+}) results in two highly interesting chains of events. The first provides a mechanism for the appearance of learned associations between astrocytes; the second enables the extended experience of astrocytes to influence synaptic facilitation in the neural system.

Continued raised levels of intracellular Ca^{2+} frequently propagate as waves, first within the cytoplasm of individual astrocytes and then between adjacent astrocytes, (Dani et al., 1992). Waves have been recorded involving as many as 59 cells before moving beyond the field of view, (Cornell-Bell et al., 1990). The emerging strength of Ca^{2+} based associations between sequences of astrocytes is continuously tested by a chemical reaction chain which reduces conductance across the gap junctions between astrocytes. Decrease in conductance results from a rise in intracellular cyclic GMP (De Vries and Schwartz, 1989). This is produced by the presence of astrocyte derived relaxing factor (ADRF) itself a consequence of raised Ca^{2+} levels in astrocytes.

ADRF provides a link between the processes producing associations between astrocytes and the sequence of events enabling astrocytes to influence synaptic facilitation. Astrocytes are, via specialized end-feet, intimately associated with cerebral blood vessels and have long been regarded as possessing the ability to produce vasodilation for trophic purposes in areas where neural activity is high. Two possible triggers for vasodilation are the vasorelaxant effect of ADRF (Murphy et al., 1990) or of the potassium (K^+) expelled by astrocytes as they absorb Ca^{2+}, (Clarke and Mobbs, 1992). The connection between vasodilation and long term synaptic facilitation hinges on blood borne fatty acids which are converted to AA by a two step process involving endothelial cells, lying between blood vessels and astrocytes, and, finally, astrocytes themselves, (Moore et al., 1991). Extracellular AA produced promotes synaptic facilitation by inhibiting glutamate uptake by glia through the recycling mechanism previously described.

Evaluation of the Glia - Neuron Model

The astrocyte based processes outlined in the previous section are a promising source of a broadened perspective in tackling the shortcomings of current LTP mechanisms. The extended temporal base due to the relative slowness of calcium excitability enables state change in astrocytes to reflect the results of neural activity over more extended periods than the brief duration underlying LTP. This offers the possibility of a modified mechanism involving astrocyte - neuron interaction that preserves the advantages of rapid reaction in LTP while avoiding the dangers of long term synaptic facilitation based on short duration experience. It, also, provides a source of variation in the operational context of single synaptic connections that offers an explanation of the different LTP outcomes at the single neuron level produced by the same stimulation.

With a view to assessing the local performance capabilities of the glia-neuron (GN) model we are progressively implementing a computational version. Only the briefest of outlines can be provided. The basic unit is an element representing

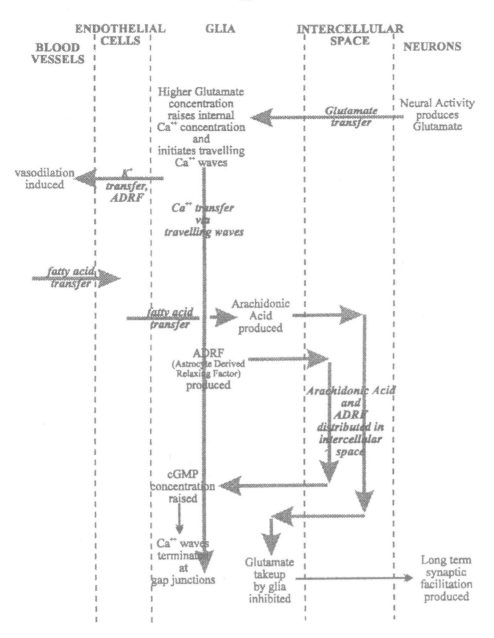

Fig. 3. Glial Influence on Synaptic Facilitation

a small set of spatially adjacent and functionally interactive neurons and astrocytes. As Figure 4 indicates, each element is represented by a hexagonal area.
The six segments of the area provide a simplified representation of dendritic receptors. Variations in the profile of stimulation of the segments by axonal sources
give rise on each cycle to a competition between them for access to glutamate.
The settlement of this process is represented in the values of six synaptic facilitation factors (SFFs) governing the transmission of glutamate from axons to
dendrites. Each hexagon represents a single glial state reflecting the relationship
between glutamate and calcium levels in the area. This state makes an equal
contribution to each of the six SFFs.

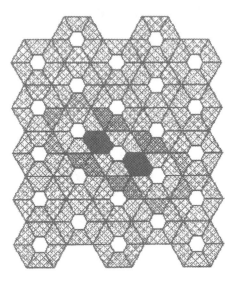

Fig. 4. A simplified illustration of the result of interaction between glial and neural
states. Each larger hexagon represents a single glial state which makes a contribution to
the individual synaptic facilitation factors of the dendritic receptors (the six segments
of each hexagon). Darker shading indicates greater SFF.

The proportion of spatially adjacent and distal axonal sources in the pattern
of neural connectivity varies between segments. This architecture, the current
glutamate level and the appropriate SFFs determine the onward transmission
on the axonal or output sides of dendritic segments. The influence of the glial
state of each hexagon on its six neighbours is determined by its calcium level.
If this is too low or too high no calcium travel across gap junction boundaries
occurs. Within the prescribed bandwidth a smoothing process revises calcium
values on both sides of the boundary.

The computational version of the GN model enables investigation of the effects of variations in neural connectivity between elements, concurrent and sequential axonal stimulation of adjacent elements and the interactive effects of differences in the duration of the neuronal and glial cycles. In the spirit of Newell's approach the results will be viewed from both a cognitive science and artificial intelligence perspective.

Implications for Cognitive Science

The most striking observation to date is the potential complexity of the specific cognitive performance that could be supported by a local neural area when augmented by the interaction with glia exemplified in the GN model. The difference in cycle duration between glia and neurons (10:1, for example) enables the development of a complex range of dendritic profiles before the sequence of activity in an element produces a glia generated calcium level which stabilizes the SFF values at a high LTP level. The stabilization process is assisted by the exclusion of calcium travelling across gap junction boundaries from neighbouring elements. Until this exclusion occurs, the developmental associations between elements formed by travelling calcium can produce an enlargement of a local neural area integrating a specific cognitive performance.

Recent research by Kim et al., (1994) supports a more elaborate and differentiated role for glia than in the current implementation of the GN model. Astrocytes exhibit a large heterogeneity of calcium responses even among neighbouring cells, suggesting that they may differentiate to fulfil different signalling roles. Information can be coded in patterns of behaviour which may provide bases for organization of large groups of astrocytes. In addition to spreading intercellular calcium waves, other potential information encoders are oscillations versus sustained elevations, oscillation frequencies and peak amplitudes. These possibilities further enhance the potential complexity of processing conducted via neural-glial interaction in a local area.

In general, our results support the view of Norman (1991) on the nature of the borderline between non or subsymbolic processing and symbolic processing. The complexity of neural-glial interaction in local areas suggests that much specific cognitive processing can occur without the need for symbol tokens to provide distal access to other local areas. The principle that the units in the physical symbol system refer to relatively elaborate local subsymbolic processing areas may assist in explaining the effectiveness of symbolic processing in spite of the constraints of slowness, seriality and limited memory size imposed by its dependence on neural networks.

Implications for Artificial Intelligence

Even at the current early stage in the development of the GN model it appears likely to produce results of interest in AI research. Clarification of the nature of local glial-neural processing and its implications for the relationship between subsymbolic and symbolic processing will assist in the construction of hybrid systems. As Minsky (1991) argues, the degree of versatility required in machine intelligence can only be achieved via architectures that permit capitalizing on specific strengths of symbolic and non symbolic modes of representation, and enable each to be used to offset the deficiencies of the other. It is not enough to maintain separate symbolic and non symbolic boxes inside separate agencies; we need additional mechanisms to enable each to support the activities of the others.

Our work has the potential to contribute to extension of the biological metaphor underlying artificial neural networks (ANN). This is particularly true in coping with time, an aspect of ANN performance still requiring considerable development. Rogers (1994) supports the need for an expansion of the range and temporal basis of associative memory, describing the neural multiprocess memory model (NMMM), "a new artificial synaptic multistage memory system that replaces the single associative long-term memory that normally modulates the efficacy of ANN element inputs. The NMMM enhances learning in an ANN element by supporting multiple time scales in the acquisition, retention and recall of encoded associative memory traces."

The GN model offers an interesting example of two interactive recurrent networks operating on different time bases. At a more detailed level, the interaction between glial and neural processes determining SFFs between elements is closely related to Hinton's (1990) proposed implementation of working memory using temporary modifications of the connection strengths in a network. Each internal connection in the network is given two different weights: a long-term weight which changes relatively slowly and a short-term weight which is limited in magnitude, changes rapidly and spontaneously decays towards zero. The effective connection strength at any time is the sum of the short-term and long-term weights. Further study of astrocyte mechanisms offers a potential source of new ideas on the achievement of temporal flexibility in ANN.

References

1. Barbour, B., Szatkowski, M., Ingledew, N., and Attwell, D., (1989). Arachidonic acid induces a prolonged inhibition of glutamate uptake into glial cells. *Nature* **342**, 918-920.
2. Clark, A., (1993). *Associative Engines: Connectionism, Concepts and Representational Change*. MIT Press, Cambridge, Mass.
3. Clarke, B. and Mobbs, P., (1992). Transmitter-operated channels in rabbit retinal astrocytes studied in situ by whole-cell patch clamping. *Neuroscience* **12(2)**, 664-673.
4. Cornell-Bell, A.H., Finkbeiner, S.M., Cooper, M.S., Smith, S.J. (1990). Glutamate induces calcium waves in cultured astrocytes: long-range glial signaling. *Science*, **247**, 470-473.
5. Cornell-Bell and Finkbeiner (1991). Ca^{2+} waves in astrocytes. *Cell Calcium*, **12**, 185-204.
6. Dani, J.W., Chernjavsky, A., and Smith, S.J. (1992). Neuronal activity triggers calcium waves in hippocampal astrocyte networks. *Neuron*, **8**, 429-440.

7. De Vries, S.H., and Schwartz, E.A., (1989). Modulation of an electrical synapse between solitary pairs of catfish horizontal cells by dopamine and second messengers. *Journal of Physiology*, **414**, 351-375.

8. Gustafsson, B., and Wigstrom, H., (1990). Long-term potentiation in the CA1 region: its induction and early temporal development. *Progress in Brain Research*, **83**, 223-232.

9. Hinton, G.E., (1990). Mapping part-whole hierarchies into connectionist networks. *Artificial Intelligence*, **46**, 47-75.

10. Lynch, G. and Granger, R., (1994). Variations in synaptic plasticity and types of memory in corticohippocampal networks. In D.L. Schacter, and E. Tulving, (Eds.) *Memory Systems 1994*, MIT Press, Cambridge, Mass., 65-86.

11. Kim, W.T., Rioult, M.G. and Cornell-Bell, A.H. (1994), Glutamate-induced calcium signaling in astrocytes. *Glia*, **11**, 173-184.

12. McGeer, P.L., Eccles, Sir J.C. and McGeer, E.G., (1978). *Molecular Neurobiology of the Mammalian Brain*, Plenum Press, New York.

13. Martin, P.D., Lake, N., and Shapiro, M.L. (1992). Effects of burst stimulation on neighboring single CA1 neurons in rat hippocampus. *Society for Neuroscience*, 22nd Annual Meeting, Anaheim, CA,.

14. Minsky, M. (1991) Logical versus analogical or symbolic versus connectionist or neat versus scruffy. *AI Magazine* Summer 1991, 35-51.

15. Moore, S.A., Yoder, E., Murphy, S., Dutton, G.R., and Spector, A.A. (1991). Astrocytes, not neurons, produce docosahexaenoic acid (22:6w-3) and arachidonic acid (20:4w-6). *Journal of Neurochemistry*, **56**, 518-524.

16. Murphy, S., Minor, R.L., Welk, Jr., G., and Harrison, D.G., (1990). Evidence for an astrocyte-derived vasorelaxing factor with properties similar to nitric oxide. *Journal of Neurochemistry*, **55**, 349-351.

17. Norman, D.A., (1991). Approaches to the study of intelligence. *Artificial Intelligence*, **47**, 327-346.

18. Newell, A., (1990). *Unified Theories of Cognition*, Harvard University Press, Cambridge, Mass.

19. Purves, D., (1993). Brain or mind? A review of Allen Newell's "Unified Theories of Cognition". *Artificial Intelligence*, **59**, 371-373.

20. Rogers, B.L., (1994). New neural multiprocess memory model for adaptively regulating associative learning. *Neural Networks*, **7**, 1351-1378.

21. Silberstein, R.B., (1994). Neuromodulation of Neocortical Dynamics. In P.L. Nunez (Ed.), *Neocortical Dynamics and Human EEG Rhythms*. Oxford University Press, (in press).

22. Staubli, U., and Lynch, G. (1987). Stable hippocampallong-term potentiation elicited by "theta" pattern stimulation. *Brain Research* **435**, 227-234.

23. Wickens, J., (1993). *A Theory of the Striatum*; Pergamon Press, Oxford.

24. Williams, J.H., Errington, M.L., Lynch, M.A., and Bliss, T.V.P. (1989). Arachidonic acid induces a long-term activity-dependent enhancement of synaptic transmission in the hippocampus, *Nature*, **341**, 739-742.

Arguments and Defeat
in Argument-Based Nonmonotonic Reasoning

Bart Verheij

University of Limburg, Department of Metajuridica
P.O. Box 616, 6200 MD Maastricht, The Netherlands
bart.verheij@metajur.rulimburg.nl, http://www.cs.rulimburg.nl/~verheij/

Abstract. Argument-based formalisms are gaining popularity as models of non-monotonic reasoning. Central in such formalisms is a notion of argument. Arguments are formal reconstructions of how a conclusion is supported. Generally, an argument is defeasible. This means that an argument supporting a conclusion does not always justify its conclusion: the argument can be defeated. Whether a conclusion supported by an argument is justified depends on the structure of the argument and on the other arguments available.

In this paper, we argue for four points that are refinements of how arguments and defeat have been used in argument-based nonmonotonic reasoning. First we argue that an argument can be defeated because it contains a weak sequence of steps; second that arguments accrue, which means that arguments for a conclusion reinforce each other; third that defeat can be compound, which means that groups of arguments can defeat other groups of arguments; fourth that defeated arguments must be distinguished from not yet considered arguments. In related work these points are overlooked, or even denied. We describe a formalism that incorporates them.

1 Introduction

Recently, several formalisms for nonmonotonic reasoning have been proposed that are argument-based. In this paper, we argue for the following points that have been overlooked, or even denied.

1. An argument can be defeated because it contains a weak *sequence* of steps.
2. Arguments *accrue*, i.e., arguments for a conclusion reinforce each other.
3. Defeat can be *compound*, i.e., groups of arguments can defeat other groups of arguments.
4. *Defeated* arguments must be distinguished from *not yet considered* arguments.

In the next section, we discuss what distinguishes argument-based formalisms from other formalisms for nonmonotonic reasoning. Section 3 contains the main points of the paper. In section 4, a formalism is described that incorporates them. In the last section, we summarize the conclusions of the paper.

2 Why argument-based?

Argument-based formalisms can be distinguished from nonmonotonic logics in general by a notion of 'argument'. An argument is a reconstruction of how a conclusion is supported. Arguments can consist of several steps from their premises to their conclusion. In this sense, arguments are similar to proofs. Unlike proofs, however, arguments are not strict, but defeasible. Arguments can be defeated by other arguments. If an argument is defeated, it does not justify its conclusion.

So, there is a close relation between the defeat of arguments and the justification of conclusions. This results in two main reasons to take the arguments into account to find out which conclusions are justified. First, the *structure* of the argument determines whether it is defeated or not. Second, whether an argument is defeated is determined by *other* available arguments.

The structure of an argument. An argument can be defeated if it is not sufficiently cogent to support its conclusion. The cogency of an argument is influenced by its structure. For instance, an argument is more cogent if it contains less weak steps, and if it contains more information to support its conclusion. When one only considers conclusions and single argument steps, the influence of the structure of arguments is overlooked.

Other arguments. An argument can be defeated by other arguments. For instance, there can be an exception to the conclusion of an argument or to a step in an argument. Arguments can attack other arguments, resulting in the defeat of the attacked arguments. Arguments can also reinforce each other, so that they remain undefeated. As a result, it is not sufficient to consider arguments in isolation.

Examples of argument-based formalisms are those described by Loui (1987), Pollock (1987-1994), Nute (1988), Lin (1993), Vreeswijk (1991, 1993), Dung (1993), Prakken (1993), and Verheij (1995).

3 The defeat of arguments

In this section, we discuss four points concerning the defeat of arguments that form the crux of this paper.

3.1 Defeat by sequential weakening

In most argument-based formalisms, an argument can be defeated in two ways: at the conclusion (or an intermediate conclusion) and at a step. Let's for instance consider the argument that it will be a sunny day since the weather forecast says so. If we look out the window and see that it is raining, the conclusion simply is false. In this case we say that the argument is defeated *at the conclusion*. If we learn that we mistakenly read the weather forecast in yesterday's paper, the argument step breaks down: yesterday's forecast does not say much about the weather today. In this case we say that the argument is defeated *at the step*.

We think that there is a third way in which an argument can be defeated: *at a sequence of steps*. The reason for this is that an argument gets weaker at each step. If the chain of steps gets too long, it breaks down.

An extreme example of this is the Sorites paradox. The basis of the paradox is the argument step that taking a grain of sand from a heap leaves you with a heap. In principle, this argument step can be repeated many times. This leads to a long argument that supports the conclusion that you are left with a heap of sand. But some reflection shows that in the end the argument becomes unacceptable: after taking away the last grain of sand we are certainly not anymore left with a heap. An explanation of this paradox is that the more steps the argument contains the weaker it becomes, until it does not anymore justify the conclusion, and is defeated.

We call this the *sequential weakening* of arguments. Only Vreeswijk's (1991) formalism allows for defeat by sequential weakening. This is however hidden in his conclusive force relation, and left implicit.

3.2 Accrual of arguments

The following example is taken from Verheij (1994, 1995). Assume that John has robbed someone, so that he should be punished (α_1). Nevertheless, a judge decides that he should not be punished, because he is a first offender (β). Or, assume that John has injured someone, and should therefore be punished (α_2). Again, the judge decides he should not be punished, being a first offender (β). Now assume John has robbed and injured someone at the same time, so that there are two arguments for punishing him (α_1, α_2). In this case, the judge might decide that John should be punished, even though he is a first offender (β).

This is an example of what Pollock (1991) has called the *accrual* of arguments. The arguments α_1 and α_2 together give better support to the conclusion that John must be punished than on their own. As a result, they can on their own be defeated by the argument β, but together remain undefeated. We have the following situation:

- The argument β defeats the argument α_1, if α_1 and β are the arguments available.
- The argument β defeats the argument α_2, if α_2 and β are the arguments available.
- The arguments α_1 and α_2 defeat the argument β, if α_1, α_2 and β are the arguments available.

Even though Pollock (1991) finds it a natural supposition that arguments reinforce each other in such a way, he surprisingly rejects it. We do not agree, and think that arguments can accrue. Pollock's main point against the accrual of arguments is the following thought experiment. He asks to imagine a linguistic community in which speakers tend to confirm each other's statements, only when they are fabrications. So, in this community it is not true that arguments, based on speakers' testimonies, accrue. Indeed, two equal testimonies reduce their value to zero.

In our opinion, this is not an argument against the accrual of arguments in general, but only an example that shows that defeat information can be overruled by more specific defeat information. *Normally*, different arguments for a conclusion make the conclusion more plausible. *In exceptional situations*, however, such as in Pollock's thought experiment, this is not the case.

The idea to incorporate accrual of arguments in a formalism for defeasible reasoning is inspired by the research on Reason-Based Logic (Hage, 1993; Hage and Verheij, 1994; Verheij, 1994).

3.3 Compound defeat

In other formalisms, only single arguments defeat single arguments. We think however that defeat can be *compound*, which means that groups of arguments defeat other groups of arguments. We give two situations that involve compound defeat. First, defeat by accruing arguments is compound. Second, skeptical defeat is compound.

Defeat by accruing arguments. We have already seen an example of defeat by accruing arguments in the previous subsection. In the example two arguments were on their own defeated by another, but could together defeat the latter. In this case, a group of arguments defeats another argument, and the defeat is compound.

Skeptical defeat. The second reason why we think that defeat can be compound involves our view on the distinction between skeptical and credulous reasoning. In nonmonotonic reasoning it can be the case that incompatible conclusions are supported. Now, a skeptical reasoner withholds from drawing a conclusion, while a credulous reasoner considers both conclusions as separate possibilities.

Both options are reasonable, and all reasoning formalisms we know make a choice: they are either skeptical or credulous. We propose a formalism in which no choice is made and both skeptical and credulous reasoning can be modeled. We can do this because we think that skeptical reasoning involves compound defeat: the arguments with incompatible conclusions are together defeated. In this case, a group of arguments is defeated at once, and the defeat is compound.

Vreeswijk's (1991) formalism suggests a restricted form of compound defeat. Among a group of arguments that leads to a contradiction one argument is defeated, if it is not better (with respect to a given conclusive force relation) than the other arguments in the conflict. So, the group of undefeated arguments can be considered to defeat the defeated argument. This is however left implicit.

Our notion of compound defeat should not be confused with Pollock's (1994) notion of *collective* defeat, that is only a variant of the choice for skeptical reasoning.

3.4 Defeated vs. not yet considered arguments

Argumentation is a process. Not all information, in the form of arguments, is available at once. At each stage of argumentation new arguments are taken into account. If arguments are defeasible, this results in the possible change of the status of arguments, depending on which arguments have been considered.

An overlooked aspect of argumentation is the influence of the defeated arguments that have been considered. A good example can be given in case of accrual of arguments (section 3.2). Suppose we have again the situation that there are three arguments, denoted α_1, α_2 and β, available to a reasoner, and that the arguments α_1 and α_2 are both on their own defeated by β, but together remain undefeated, and even defeat β.

There are several orders in which the arguments can be taken into account by a reasoner, such as first α_1, then α_2, and finally β or first α_2, then β, and finally α_1. In figure 1, these orders are shown in a diagram. Each node in the diagram represents an argumentation stage and has a label representing which arguments are undefeated at that stage. The 0 represents that no argument has been considered yet. Each arrow denotes that a new argument is taken into account. For instance, if at stage α_2 the argument β is taken into account, α_2 is defeated, and only β is not. If at stage α_2 the argument α_1 is taken into account, both α_2 and α_1 are undefeated.

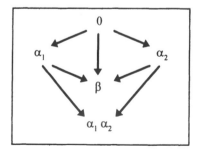

Fig. 1. A first attempt

Figure 1 is wrong, for two reasons:

1. *It does not properly represent all different stages of the argumentation process.*
   For instance, the stage that only β has been taken into account is represented by the same node as the stage that both α_2 and β have been taken into account.
2. *Orders of argumentation have disappeared.*
   For instance, there is no arrow from β to $\alpha_1 \alpha_2$, because it has become unclear what it means to go from stage β to stage $\alpha_1 \alpha_2$ by taking one extra argument into account.

The picture is wrong because defeated arguments are not distinguished from not yet considered arguments. Figure 2 is the right picture. Each corner of the 'block' in the picture again represents a stage in the argumentation process, and has a label representing which arguments have been considered at that stage. The arguments in brackets are defeated. Again, each arrow denotes that a new argument is taken into account. For instance, the arrow from α_2 to β (α_2) means that the argument α_2 becomes defeated after β has been taken into account.

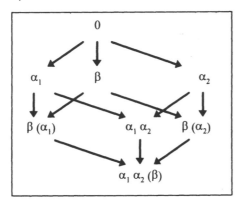

Fig. 2. The right picture

In this picture all different stages of the argumentation process can be distinguished and no orders of argumentation have disappeared. The intermediate stages β (α_1), β (α_2), and $\alpha_1 \alpha_2$ (β) dissolve the problems.

In our formalism, argumentation stages are represented as in figure 2; they contain not only the undefeated, but also the defeated arguments at the stage. Other formalisms either do not treat argumentation as a sequence of stages, or neglect the influence of the defeated arguments.

4 An appropriate formalism

In this section, we describe a formalism that incorporates the main points of this paper. We start with the formal definition of *arguments* that represent how conclusions are supported. Then we formally define *defeaters* that represent when arguments defeat other arguments. In the last subsection, we formally define *argumentation stages*. They represent which arguments have been considered at a stage of the argumentation process, and which of them are defeated at that stage.

4.1 Arguments

Our notion of an argument is related to that of Lin (1993) and Vreeswijk (1991, 1993), and is basically a tree of sentences in some language. Our approach to argumentation is independent of the choice of a language. Therefore, we treat a language as a set without any structure. A language does not even contain an element to denote negation or contradiction.

Definition 1. A *language* is a set, whose elements are the *sentences* of the language.

Lin (1993), Vreeswijk (1991, 1993) and Dung (1993) do more or less the same. Lin and Shoham use a language with negation, and Vreeswijk one with contradiction. Dung even goes a step further, and uses completely unstructured arguments.

The structure of an argument is like a proof. An argument supports its conclusion (relative to its premises), but unlike a proof, an argument is defeasible. Any argument can be defeated by other arguments. Each argument has a *conclusion* and *premises*. An argument can contain arguments for its conclusion. Arguments contain *sentences*, and have *initial* and *final* parts. A special kind of argument is a *rule*.

Definition 2. Let L be a language. An *argument* in the language L is recursively defined as follows:

1. Any element s of L is an argument in L. In this case we define

    $Conc(s) = s$

    $Prems(s) = Sents(s) = Initials(s) = Finals(s) = \{s\}$

2. If A is a set of arguments in L, s an element of L, and $s \notin Sents[A]$,[1] then $A \to s$ is an argument in L. In this case we define

    $Conc(A \to s) = s$

    $Prems(A \to s) = Prems[A]$

    $Sents(A \to s) = \{s\} \cup Sents[A]$

    $Initials(A \to s) = \{A \to s\} \cup Initials[A]$

    $Finals(A \to s) = \{s\} \cup \{B \to s \mid \exists f: f \text{ is a surjective function from A}$
    $\text{onto B, such that } \forall \alpha: f(\alpha) \in Finals(\alpha)\}$

$Conc(\alpha)$ is the *conclusion* of α. An element of $Prems(\alpha)$, $Sents(\alpha)$, $Initials(\alpha)$, and $Finals(\alpha)$ is a *premise*, a *sentence*, an *initial argument*, and a *final argument* of α, respectively. The conclusion of an initial argument of α, other than the argument α itself, is an *intermediate conclusion* of α. An argument in L is a *rule*, if it has the form $S \to s$, where $S \subseteq L$ and $s \in L$. For each argument α we define the set of arguments $Subs(\alpha)$, whose elements are the *subarguments* of α:

$$Subs(\alpha) = Initials[Finals(\alpha)]$$

A *proper subargument* of an argument α is a subargument other than α. If α is a subargument of β, then β is a *superargument* of α. A subargument of an argument α that is a rule is a *subrule* of α.

Notation. If A is finite, i.e. $A = \{\alpha_1, \alpha_2, ..., \alpha_n\}$, we write $\alpha_1, \alpha_2, ..., \alpha_n \to s$ for an argument $A \to s = \{\alpha_1, \alpha_2, ..., \alpha_n\} \to s$, if no confusion can arise.

Intuitively, if $A \to s$ is an argument (in some language L), the elements of A are the arguments supporting the conclusion s. It may seem strange that also sentences are considered to be arguments. An argument of the form s, where s is a sentence in the language L, represents the degenerate (but in practice most common) kind of argument that a sentence is put forward without any arguments supporting it.

Some examples of arguments in the language $L = \{a, b, c, d\}$ are $\{\{a\} \to b\} \to c$ and $\{\{a\} \to c, \{b\} \to c\} \to d$. They are graphically represented in figure 3.

---

[1] If f: $V \to W$ is a function and $U \subseteq V$, then f[U] denotes the image of U under f.

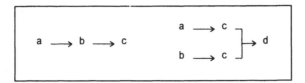

Fig. 3. Examples of arguments

The *premise*s of the argument {{a} → c, {b} → c} → d are a and b. It has d as its conclusion. Some of its initial arguments are b, {a} → c and the argument itself. Some of its final arguments are d, {c} → d, and {c, {b} → c} → d. Among its subarguments are c and {b} → c.

The structure of our arguments differs from those of Lin (1993) and Vreeswijk (1991, 1993). In these formalisms, the conclusion of an argument (or an intermediate conclusion) can only be supported by a single argument. Because we think that arguments accrue, in our formalism the same conclusion can be supported by several arguments. As a result, we can make *parallel strengthening* (and *weakening*) of an argument explicit. Intuitively, an argument becomes stronger if more arguments support its conclusion and intermediate conclusions. For instance, the argument {{a} → c, {b} → c} → d is a *strengthening* of the argument {{b} → c} → d. The former contains {a} → c and {b} → c to support the intermediate conclusion c, while the latter only contains {b} → c.

Definition 3. Let L be a language. For any argument α in the language L we recursively define a set of arguments Weaks(α):

1. For α = s, s ∈ L,

   Weaks(s) = {s}.

2. For α = A → s, A ⊆ Args(L), s ∈ L,

   Weaks(A → s) = {B → s | B ⊆ Weaks[A] and Conc[B] = Conc[A]}

An element of Weaks(α) is a *weakening* of α. A weakening of α, other than α, is a *proper* weakening of α. If α is a weakening of β, then β is a *strengthening* of α.

Weakenings are in general not subarguments. For instance, {{a} → c} → d is not a subargument of {{a} → c, {b} → c} → d.

4.2 Defeaters

Arguments are defeasible. In our formalism, *all* arguments can be defeated. Except for Dung (1993), other authors have separate classes of strict and defeasible arguments. In our formalism, arguments remain undefeated, if there is no information that makes them defeated. So, if one wants a class of strict arguments, for instance, to model deductive argumentation, it can be defined, by not allowing information that leads to the defeat of the arguments in that class. In our formalism this is straightforward, because the defeat of arguments is the result of defeat information that is *explicit* and *direct*.

Explicit defeat information. Pollock's (1987-1994) defeaters, Prakken's (1993) kinds of defeat, Vreeswijk's (1991, 1993) conclusive force, and Dung's (1993) attacks are examples of explicit defeat information. Instead of hiding the information in a general procedure, for instance based on specificity, explicit information determines which arguments become defeated and which remain undefeated. Explicit defeat information is required because no general procedure can be flexible enough to be universally valid.

Direct defeat information. By direct defeat information, we mean explicit defeat information directly specifying when arguments are defeated. Pollock's defeaters and Dung's attacks are examples of direct defeat information. Explicit defeat information is not always direct. Examples of indirect defeat information are Prakken's kinds of defeat and Vreeswijk's conclusive force. In their formalisms defeat of arguments is triggered by a conflict of arguments. If there is a conflict, one of the arguments involved is selected using the defeat information. The selected argument becomes defeated, and the conflict is resolved. We think that indirect defeat information is not sufficient. An important kind of defeat requiring direct defeat information is defeat by an undercutting argument (Pollock, 1987). An undercutting argument only defeats another argument, without contradicting the conclusion.

In our formalism the defeat information is specified by explicit and direct *defeaters*. A defeater consists of two sets of arguments: The arguments in one set become defeated if the arguments in the other set are undefeated.

Definition 4. Let L be a language. A *defeater* of L has the form A (B), where A and B are sets of arguments of L, such that no argument in A has a subargument or weakening that is an element of B. The arguments in A are the *activating* arguments of the defeater. The arguments in B are its *defeated* arguments. A $\cup$ B is the *range* of the defeater.

Notation. A defeater A (B) with finite range, i.e. A = $\{\alpha_1, \alpha_2, ..., \alpha_n\}$ and B = $\{\beta_1, \beta_2, ..., \beta_m\}$, is written $\alpha_1 \alpha_2 ... \alpha_n (\beta_1 \beta_2 ... \beta_m)$, if no confusion can arise.

The meaning of a defeater A (B) is that if the arguments in A are undefeated, the arguments in B must be defeated. For instance, the defeater a (b $\rightarrow$ c) defeats the rule b $\rightarrow$ c, if the argument a is undefeated. By the requirement in the definition a defeater cannot defeat a subargument or strengthening of one of its own activating arguments. For instance, if the argument a $\rightarrow$ b $\rightarrow$ c is activating a defeater, it cannot defeat the argument b $\rightarrow$ c. If the argument a $\rightarrow$ c $\rightarrow$ d is activating a defeater, it cannot defeat the argument $\{$a $\rightarrow$ c, b $\rightarrow$ c$\} \rightarrow$ d.

In contrast with Pollock's (1987-1994) defeaters, and Dung's (1993) attacks, our defeaters can represent compound defeat which occurs in case of defeat by accruing arguments and in case of skeptical defeat (section 3.3). The example of accruing arguments in section 3.2 requires not only the regular defeaters $\beta (\alpha_1)$ and $\beta (\alpha_2)$, but also a defeater that represents compound defeat, namely $\alpha_1 \alpha_2 (\beta)$. If α and β are incompatible arguments, a credulous reasoner can use the regular defeaters $\alpha (\beta)$ and $\beta (\alpha)$, while a skeptical reasoner can use the defeater $(\alpha \beta)$ that represents compound defeat. Defeaters of the form (α_1, α_2), where α_1 and α_2 represent different testimonies, can be used to model Pollock's (in our view mistaken) counterexample for the accrual of arguments (section 3.2).

Our defeaters can also represent defeat by sequential weakening (section 3.1). If for instance the sequence of steps a $\rightarrow$ b $\rightarrow$ c makes an argument so weak that it must be defeated, this can be represented by the defeater (a $\rightarrow$ b $\rightarrow$ c).

4.3 Argumentation stages

We are about to define an *argumentation theory*. It formally represents which arguments are available to a reasoner, and when arguments can become defeated. Our notion of an argumentation theory is related to that of an argument system (Vreeswijk, 1991, 1993) and of an argumentation framework (Dung, 1993). A theory consists of a language, arguments, and defeaters. The language of a theory specifies the sentences that can be used in arguments. The arguments of a theory are the arguments that are available. The defeaters of a theory represent the situations in which arguments defeat other arguments.

Definition 5. An *argumentation theory* is a triple (L, Args, Defs), where
1. L is a language,
2. Args is a set of arguments in L, closed under initial arguments, and
3. Defs is a set of defeaters of L, with their ranges in Args.

For instance, a theory that represents the example of accruing arguments in section 3.2 is defined as follows:

$L = \{a_1, a_2, a, b\}$,
$Args = \{a_1, a_1 \rightarrow a, a_2, a_2 \rightarrow a, b\}$,
$Defs = \{\beta\,(\alpha_1), \beta\,(\alpha_2), \alpha_1\,\alpha_2\,(\beta)\}$, where $\alpha_1 = a_1 \rightarrow a$, $\alpha_2 = a_2 \rightarrow a$, $\beta = b$.

So we have two separate arguments α_1 and α_2 that support the conclusion a, and an argument β that supports b. The defeaters say that α_1 and α_2 are on their own defeated by β, but together defeat β. We use this theory as an illustration of the coming definitions. It is chosen, because it is a key example of accrual of arguments, and therefore suitable to show some important aspects of our formalism. It is however too simple to illustrate all aspects of the definitions.

The next definition is that of an *argumentation stage*. It can represent the arguments that at a certain stage in the process of argumentation have been taken into account, and which of them are then defeated. (Later we define argumentation stages that are *acceptable* with respect to a theory. These are the actual stages of argumentation that are made possible by an argumentation theory.) Each of the requirements in our definition corresponds to a simple intuition on stages in argumentation. For instance, one requirement is that an argument can only be taken into account if all its initial arguments already have been. The *range* of an argumentation stage consists of the arguments taken into account at that stage.

Definition 6. Let (L, Args, Defs) be an argumentation theory. An *argumentation stage* of (L, Args, Defs) has the form Σ (T), where Σ and T are subsets of Args, such that:
1. Σ is closed under initial arguments.
2. No argument can be an element of both Σ and T.
3. No proper subargument of an element of Σ can be an element of T.
4. Not all proper weakenings of an element of T that has proper weakenings can be elements of Σ.

The arguments in Σ are *undefeated*, and those in T *defeated*. The set $\Sigma \cup T$ is the *range* of Σ (T).

Remark: defeaters and argumentation stages are the same in form.

Some argumentation stages of the example theory are $a_1\,\alpha_1\,(\beta)$, $a_2\,\beta\,(a_1\,\alpha_2)$, and $a_1\,\alpha_1\,a_2\,\alpha_2\,(\beta)$.

Our definition of an argumentation stage is related to the argumentation structures of Lin and Vreeswijk. They require however that it is a set without contradicting arguments and do not include defeated arguments. Definition 6 is crucial for the point made in section 3.4: the arguments that are defeated at a stage are distinguished from the arguments not yet considered.

Which arguments of a theory become defeated and which don't is determined by its defeaters. Arguments are normally undefeated, but can at some stage of argumentation be defeated because of *relevant* defeaters. A defeater is relevant at some argumentation stage if all its arguments have been taken into account at that stage, or are parts of such arguments. Formally, this means that its range is a subset of the final parts of the arguments taken into account.

Definition 7. Let (L, Args, Defs) be an argumentation theory, A (B) a defeater in Defs, and Σ (T) an argumentation stage of (Args, Defs). A (B) is *relevant* for Σ (T), if $A \cup B \subseteq \text{Finals}[\Sigma \cup T]$.

So, in the example theory, β (α_2) is relevant for a_2 β (a_1 α_2), and all three defeaters of the theory are relevant for a_1 α_1 a_2 α_2 (β).

This notion of relevance of defeaters has no analogue in other formalisms. Normally, *all* defeaters are considered relevant. We can do better, because our argumentation stages explicitly represent which arguments are taken into account, including the defeated arguments.

A defeater only justifies the defeat of its defeated arguments, if its activating arguments are parts of the undefeated arguments, i.e., if they are subarguments of the undefeated arguments. The defeater is then *activated*.

Definition 8. Let (L, Args, Defs) be an argumentation theory, A (B) a defeater in Defs, and Σ (T) an argumentation stage of (Args, Defs). A (B) is *activated* in Σ (T), if it is relevant and $A \subseteq \text{Finals}[\Sigma]$.

In the argumentation stage a_2 β (a_1 α_2) the defeater β (α_2) is activated. In the stage a_1 α_1 a_2 α_2 (β) all three defeaters are activated.

Argumentation stages only represent actual stages of the process of argumentation, if they are *acceptable* with respect to an argumentation theory. An argumentation stage is acceptable, if

1. *The defeat of each of its defeated arguments is forced by an activated defeater.*
2. *If the defeat of an argument is forced by an activated defeater, it must actually be defeated in the stage.*
3. *No relevant defeater is unjustly ignored.*

The latter requirement requires yet another definition. Relevant defeaters must be *deactivated*, for instance, because one of its activating arguments is defeated. A defeater is deactivated, if two conditions hold. First, there must be another defeater that forces the defeat of one of its activating arguments. (It is even sufficient that the defeat of a subargument or a strengthening of one of the activating arguments is forced.) However, α_1 α_2 (β) and β (α_1) do not deactivate each other. Only the former can deactivate the latter. The reason for this is the accrual of the arguments α_1 and α_2. The defeater α_1 α_2 (β) overrules β (α_1), and therefore cannot be deactivated by it. This leads to the second condition: a defeater can only be deactivated by a defeater it does not overrule. Formally, this is captured in the following definition.

Definition 9. Let (L, Args, Defs) be an argumentation theory, A (B) and Γ (Δ) defeaters in Defs, and Σ (T) an argumentation stage of (Args, Defs). A (B) *deactivates* Γ (Δ), if both are relevant for Σ (T), and the following hold:

1. There is an element of B that is a subargument or a strengthening of an element of Γ.
2. If B is a proper subset of Γ, then A is not a subset of Δ.

We can finally define when an argumentation stage is *acceptable* with respect to an argumentation theory. The requirements in our definition have already been briefly explained just after definition 8.

Definition 10. Let (L, Args, Defs) be an argumentation theory, and Σ (T) an argumentation stage of (L, Args, Defs). Σ (T) is *acceptable* with respect to (Args, Defs), if the following hold:

1. If $\tau \in$ T, there is an activated A (B) $\in$ Defs, such that $\tau \in$ B.
2. If A (B) $\in$ Defs is activated, then B $\subseteq$ T.
3. If A (B) $\in$ Defs is relevant, but not activated, then there is an activated Γ (Δ) $\in$ Defs that deactivates A (B).

An acceptable argumentation stage of our example theory is β (a_1 α_1). The stage a_1 a_2 α_2 (β) is not acceptable, because the defeat of β is not justified, and because β (α_2) is not deactivated. It can be checked that the acceptable argumentation stages of our example theory correspond exactly to the stages represented in figure 2.

The way we define acceptable defeasible argumentation stages is related to the way Dung (1993) defines his admissible sets of arguments, and Pollock (1994) his partial status assignments. However, these do not represent *stages* in the process of argumentation, but are merely convenient formal structures on the way to the definition of extensions.

An *extension* of an argumentation theory is an acceptable stage of argumentation that has no succeeding argumentation stage, i.e. there is no argumentation stage with larger range. It must therefore be maximal with respect to set inclusion. Dung's (1993) preferred extensions and Pollock's (1994, p. 393) status assignments are defined similarly.

Definition 11. Let (L, Args, Defs) be an argumentation theory, and Σ (T) an argumentation stage of (L, Args, Defs). Σ (T) is an *extension* of (L, Args, Defs), if the following hold:

1. Σ (T) is acceptable with respect to (L, Args, Defs), and
2. There is no argumentation stage Σ' (T'), acceptable with respect to (L, Args, Defs), such that $\Sigma \cup$ T is a proper subset of $\Sigma' \cup$ T'.

As usual, a theory can have any number of extensions: zero, one, or several. The unique extension of our example theory is a_1 α_1 a_2 α_2 (β). The example is a real case of the accrual of the arguments α_1 and α_2, as can be seen by looking at other acceptable argumentation stages: β a_1 (α_1) and β a_2 (α_2). Here α_1 and α_2 are on their own defeated by β. The arguments α_1 and α_2 only remain undefeated if they reinforce each other.

5 Conclusions

This paper is an example of the argument-based approach to nonmonotonic reasoning. We have indicated why this is a valuable approach: First, because defeat is determined by the structure of arguments, and second, because defeat is determined by other available arguments.

The main points of this paper were the following. First, arguments can be defeated by sequential weakening. Second, arguments accrue. Third, defeat can be compound. Fourth, defeated arguments must be distinguished from not yet considered arguments.

We have provided a formalism that captures these ideas. To this end, we used a definition of arguments that makes parallel strengthening explicit, a definition of defeaters that can represent defeat by sequential weakening and compound defeat, and a definition of argumentation stages that explicitly represent the defeated arguments that have been considered.

Acknowledgments

This research was partly financed by the Foundation for Knowledge-based Systems (SKBS) as part of the B3.A project. SKBS is a foundation with the goal to improve the level of expertise in the Netherlands in the field of knowledge-based systems and to promote the transfer of knowledge in this field between universities and business companies. I thank Jaap Hage, Arno Lodder and Gerard Vreeswijk for our stimulating and lively arguments about argumentation.

References

1. Bondarenko, A., Toni, F. and Kowalski, R. A. (1993). An assumption-based framework for non-monotonic reasoning. *Logic programming and non-monotonic reasoning. Proceedings of the second international workshop* (eds. L. M. Pereira and A. Nerode), pp. 171-189. The MIT Press, Cambridge (Massachusetts).

2. Dung, P. M. (1993). On the acceptability of arguments and its fundamental role in nonmonotonic reasoning, logic programming, and human's social and economical affairs.

3. Hage, J. and Verheij, B. (1994). Reason-Based Logic: a logic for reasoning with rules and reasons. To appear in *Law, Computers and Artificial Intelligence*.

4. Lin, F. (1993). An argument-based approach to nonmonotonic reasoning. *Computational Intelligence*, Vol. 9, No. 3, pp. 254-267.

5. Loui, R. P. (1987). Defeat among arguments: a system of defeasible inference. *Computational Intelligence*, Vol. 3, No. 2, pp. 100-106.

6. Nute, D. (1988). Defeasible reasoning: a philosophical analysis in Prolog. *Aspects of Artificial Intelligence* (ed. James H. Fetzer), pp. 251-288. Kluwer Academic Publishers, Dordrecht.

7. Pollock, J. L. (1987). Defeasible reasoning. *Cognitive Science* 11, pp. 481-518.

8. Pollock, J. L. (1991). Self-defeating arguments. *Minds and Machines* 1, pp. 367-392.

9. Pollock, J. L. (1994). Justification and defeat. *Artificial Intelligence* 67, pp. 377-407.

10. Poole, D. (1988). A logical framework for default reasoning. *Artificial Intelligence* 36, pp. 27-47.

11. Prakken, H. (1993). A logical framework for modelling legal argument. *The Fourth International Conference on Artificial Intelligence and Law. Proceedings of the Conference*, pp. 1-9. ACM, New York.

12. Simari, G. R. and Loui, R. P. (1992). A mathematical treatment of defeasible reasoning and its applications. *Artificial Intelligence* 53, pp. 125-157.

13. Touretzky, D. S., Horty, J. F., and Thomason, R. H. (1987). A clash of intuitions: the current state of nonmonotonic multiple inheritance systems. *IJCAI 87; Proceedings of the Tenth International Joint Conference on Artificial Intelligence* (ed. J. McDermott), pp. 476-482. Morgan Kaufmann Publishers, Los Altos (California).

14. Verheij, H. B. (1994). Reason Based Logic and legal knowledge representation. *Proceedings of the Fourth National Conference on Law, Computers and Artificial Intelligence* (eds. I. Carr and A. Narayanan), pp. 154-165. University of Exeter.

15. Verheij, B. (1995). The influence of defeated arguments in defeasible argumentation. Accepted for the *Second World Conference on the Fundamentals of Artificial Intelligence (WOCFAI 95)*.

16. Vreeswijk, G. (1991). Abstract argumentation systems: preliminary report. *Proceedings of the First World Conference on the Fundamentals of Artificial Intelligence* (eds. D. M. Gabbay and M. De Glas), pp. 501-510. Angkor, Paris.

17. Vreeswijk, G. (1993). *Studies in defeasible argumentation*. G. A. W. Vreeswijk, Amsterdam.

A Preference Semantics
for Ground Nonmonotonic Modal Logics

Daniele Nardi and Riccardo Rosati

Dipartimento di Informatica e Sistemistica,
Università di Roma "La Sapienza",
Via Salaria 113, I-00198 Roma, Italy
email: {nardi,rosati}@dis.uniroma1.it

Abstract. In this paper we provide a semantic characterization of ground logics, a family of nonmonotonic modal logics obtained by means of a variant of the well known Mc Dermott and Doyle fixed point equation. The term ground logics carries the idea of restricting the negative introspection capabilities of the reasoning agent to the objective (i.e. non modal) part of the theory. This intuition was nicely formalized for modal logic $S5$ by a semantic definition based on a preference relation on Kripke models, which was obtained as the semantic counterpart to the notion of minimal knowledge initially defined by Halpern and Moses. We have then found a preference relation on Kripke models that both generalizes this notion of minimal knowledge and provides a semantic characterization for a significant subset of ground logics.

1 Introduction

The interplay of nonmonotonic reasoning and reasoning about knowledge and belief has been recognized from the beginning of the research on commonsense reasoning. Since then modal epistemic logics have been studied with the aim of characterizing the reasoning of an agent who is capable to perform introspective reasoning by making assumptions on its own knowledge. The first formalizations of nonmonotonic reasoning based on the use of a modal operator have been proposed in [13, 15]. The knowledge of an agent is characterized in terms of a fixed-point equation that expresses its introspective capabilities.

A different approach for defining nonmonotonic modal logics was taken in [3, 22, 7], where the knowledge of the agent is characterized on a semantic ground, following the idea of selecting those models in which knowledge is minimal.

Recently, there have been a number of attempts to reconcile the fixed-point and semantic characterizations of modal nonmonotonic logics. In order to introduce the issue, let us recall McDermott and Doyle equation which applies to the consequence operator of a monotonic modal logic. The equation is a general scheme for defining expansions, namely possible sets of sentences representing the knowledge of an agent reasoning introspectively from an initial body of knowledge. We use $\mathcal{L}$ to denote a fixed propositional language, $\mathcal{L}_K$ to denote its modal extension with the only modality K; the set of formulae $I \subseteq \mathcal{L}_K$ stands for the initial knowledge of the agent.

Given a modal logic $\mathcal{S}$, a consistent set of formulae T is an $\mathcal{S}_{MDD}$-*expansion* for a set of initial knowledge $I \subseteq \mathcal{L}_K$ if

$$T = Cn_{\mathcal{S}}(I \cup \{\neg K\varphi \mid \varphi \notin T\}), \tag{1}$$

where $Cn_{\mathcal{S}}$ is the consequence operator in (classical) modal logic $\mathcal{S}$.

The resulting consequence operator is defined as the intersection of all $\mathcal{S}_{MDD}$-expansions for I. Such operator is in general nonmonotonic: thus for every modal logic $\mathcal{S}$, the (nonmonotonic) modal logic $\mathcal{S}_{MDD}$ is obtained by means of equation (1).

The McDermott and Doyle's family of nonmonotonic modal logics has been extensively studied [15, 11, 10, 12]: McDermott [13] analyzed the case of $\mathcal{S} =$ S5 and found out that the resulting logic S5$_{MDD}$ is monotonic, in the sense that the intersection of all S5$_{MDD}$-expansions of a theory I is exactly the set of consequences of I in monotonic S5. Schwarz [17] proved the equivalence of Moore's autoepistemic logic [15] with logic KD45$_{MDD}$. He also defined in [18] a preference semantics for McDermott and Doyle's family, thus giving a true possible-world semantic characterization of this class of modal nonmonotonic formalisms.

This result allows us to study properties of logics $\mathcal{S}_{MDD}$ by reasoning on Kripke structures, which is often easier than analyzing sets of modal formulae. From this semantic viewpoint it is easy to show that S5$_{MDD}$ is not the only degenerate (i.e. monotonic) case for logics $\mathcal{S}_{MDD}$. More specifically, it can be shown that for every normal modal logic $\mathcal{S}$, characterized by a class of Kripke models whose accessibility relation is symmetric, its nonmonotonic variant $\mathcal{S}_{MDD}$ is equivalent to monotonic logic S5. Therefore there is a whole class of logics in the McDermott and Doyle's family degenerating to the case of monotonic S5, precisely the logics characterized by a class of Kripke models whose accessibility relation is symmetric, i.e. all logics in which every instance of the modal axiom schema B, that is $\neg K \neg K \varphi \supset \varphi$, is valid.

Let us now turn the attention to the nonmonotonic modal logics that have been proposed on the basis of semantic considerations and, more precisely, on the intuition that in the models the knowledge attributed to the agent should be minimal. This principle was introduced in [3] and it was enforced by minimizing the set of objective facts known by the agent. In its most general version, this notion of minimal knowledge can be stated as follows:

Definition 1. A model $\mathcal{M}$ is a model of minimal knowledge for $I \subseteq \mathcal{L}_K$ in the logic $\mathcal{S}$, if $\mathcal{M}$ is a model for I in $\mathcal{S}$ and for every model $\mathcal{M}'$ of I in $\mathcal{S}$, $Th(\mathcal{M}') \cap \mathcal{L} \not\subseteq Th(\mathcal{M}) \cap \mathcal{L}$, where $Th(\mathcal{M}) = \{\varphi \in \mathcal{L}_K \mid \mathcal{M} \models \varphi\}$.

We say that a logic $\mathcal{S}$ is a logic of minimal knowledge if for every theory $I \subseteq \mathcal{L}_K$, every model for I in $\mathcal{S}$ is a model of minimal knowledge for I in $\mathcal{S}$.

In [3] the notion of minimal knowledge is applied to modal logic S5 and in [7] a possible-world semantics for this logic is given as follows. A model $\mathcal{M}$ is constituted by a set of interpretations: a sentence $K\varphi$ is true in a world w belonging to $\mathcal{M}$ if φ is true in all worlds w' belonging to $\mathcal{M}$. This amounts to considering the so-called universal S5 models, i.e. connected structures whose accessibility relation is reflexive, symmetric and transitive. However, not every such structure that satisfies the initial assumptions I of the agent is taken into consideration: the interesting models are the minimal ones, namely those which do not have any proper superset satisfying I. In other words, an S5-model is minimal if it satisfies I and cannot be extended by adding a new possible world. Therefore, minimization of knowledge is obtained by maximizing the set of possible worlds, sometimes explained as maximizing ignorance. The nonmonotonic character of this construction becomes evident when looking at the case in which I is the empty set. In this case one can conclude $\neg Kp$ for every atomic sentence p.

This idea has been further developed in [7][1] and in [9] where it is embedded in a bimodal logic that combines minimization of knowledge with justified assumptions.

In [21] the minimization of knowledge is formulated in terms of a preference criterion on Kripke models which differs from the one shown in [7]: in particular, a different class of models is taken into consideration, that is the class of models characterizing modal logic S4F. However, this way of minimizing knowledge does not correspond to the minimization of objective facts, so this logic is not a logic of minimal knowledge in the sense of the definition above.

The idea of minimal knowledge can be easily captured by a fixed point equation in the McDermott and Doyle style, by bounding introspection in the right-hand side of Equation (1) to modal-free formulae only. Given a normal modal logic $\mathcal{S}$, a consistent set of formulae T is a *ground $\mathcal{S}$-expansion* for a set $I \subseteq \mathcal{L}_K$ if

$$T = Cn_{\mathcal{S}}(I \cup \{\neg K\varphi \mid \varphi \in \mathcal{L} \setminus T\}). \qquad (2)$$

This equation defines a family of logics $\mathcal{S}_G$ called *ground* nonmonotonic modal logics (see [19, 23, 4]). These logics are logics of minimal knowledge in the sense of Definition (1), as stated by the following proposition, which directly follows from a property of minimality of ground $\mathcal{S}_G$-expansions proved in [12].

Proposition 2. *If a theory $T \subseteq \mathcal{L}$ is a ground $\mathcal{S}$-expansion for $I \subseteq \mathcal{L}_K$, then T is a model of minimal knowledge for I. Hence every ground logic $\mathcal{S}_G$ is a logic of minimal knowledge.*

The goal of our work is to study the generalization of the idea of minimal knowledge intended as the minimization of objective facts, or, in other terms, to study the family of ground logics, for which we find an appropriate semantic characterization, that has been advocated in [21]. In particular, the characterization we present is an instance of the preference semantics introduced by Shoham [22], where the preference criterion is given by a partial ordering over possible-world models. We show the correspondence between such semantic characterization

---

[1] A more recent version of this work [8] contains a technical difference which makes the resulting logic a logic of "minimal belief", that is no longer captured by our definition.

and the fixpoint definition of ground logics for a subclass of normal modal logics, called cluster-decomposable logics, which includes the most studied cases in nonmonotonic modal logics.

In the next section we present some preliminary definitions. We then introduce the semantic characterization of the family of ground logics. We finally briefly discuss some interesting properties of this family of logics.

2 Preliminaries

In this section we recall some basic definitions and theorems which will be referred to in the rest of the paper (see [12] for further details).

A *Kripke model* $\mathcal{M}$ is defined as usual by a triple $\langle W, R, V \rangle$, where W is a set (whose elements are called worlds), R is a binary relation on W (called the accessibility relation on $\mathcal{M}$), and V is a function assigning a propositional valuation to each world $w \in \mathcal{M}$.

The following is the definition of *concatenation* between Kripke models.

Definition 3. Given Kripke models $\mathcal{M} = \langle W, R, V \rangle$, $\mathcal{M}_1 = \langle W_1, R_1, V_1 \rangle$, $\mathcal{M}_2 = \langle W_2, R_2, V_2 \rangle$, such that $W_1 \cap W_2 = \emptyset$, $\mathcal{M} = \mathcal{M}_1 \odot \mathcal{M}_2$ if $W = W_1 \cup W_2$, $V = V_1 \cup V_2$ and $R = R_1 \cup (W_1 \times W_2) \cup R_2$.

Now we recall the definitions of stable theory and of canonical model for a stable theory, which will be used in the proof of the semantical characterization of ground nonmonotonic modal logics.

Definition 4. A theory $T \subseteq \mathcal{L}_K$ is *stable* if

1. T is closed under propositional consequence;
2. for every $\varphi \in \mathcal{L}_K$, if $\varphi \in T$ then $K\varphi \in T$;
3. for every $\varphi \in \mathcal{L}_K$, if $\varphi \notin T$ then $\neg K\varphi \in T$.

Definition 5. The *canonical model for a stable theory* T is a Kripke model $\mathcal{M}_T = \langle W, R, V \rangle$ such that W consists of all propositional valuations in which all formulas from $T \cap \mathcal{L}$ are true, R is the universal relation on W (hence $\mathcal{M}_T$ is an S5-model) and $V(w) = w$ for every $w \in W$.

$ST(S)$ will be used to indicate the (unique) stable theory T such that $T \cap \mathcal{L} = Cn(S)$, where Cn is the propositional consequence operator.

The following definition is derived from [12], Definition 9.17.

Definition 6. A class $\mathcal{C}$ of Kripke models is *cluster-decomposable* if every model in $\mathcal{C}$ is of the form $\mathcal{M}_1 \odot \mathcal{M}_2$, where $\mathcal{M}_2$ is a universal Kripke model, and for every such model $\mathcal{M}_1 \odot \mathcal{M}_2$ and every universal model $\mathcal{M}'_2$ whose set of worlds is disjoint from that of $\mathcal{M}_1$, the model $\mathcal{M}_1 \odot \mathcal{M}'_2$ is in $\mathcal{C}$.

We remark that most of the modal logics studied in the nonmonotonic setting, in particular the logics $S5$, $KD45$, $S4f$ and $Sw5$, are all characterized by a cluster-decomposable class of Kripke models.

The following definition characterizes a class of modal logics for which Theorem 8 states an important characterization of ground expansions in terms of minimal McDermott and Doyle's expansions.

Definition 7. A logic S characterized by a class $\mathcal{C}$ of models satisfies the *terminal cluster property* if for every $\mathcal{M} = \langle W, R, V \rangle \in \mathcal{C}$ and for every world $w \in W$ there is a terminal cluster for w, i.e. a maximal subset Y of W such that $Y \times Y \subseteq R$ and:

1. for every $w' \in Y, (w, w') \in R$;
2. for every $w' \in Y$ and every $w'' \in W \setminus Y$, $(w', w'') \notin R$.

Theorem 8. *Given a modal logic S such that $K \subseteq S \subseteq S5$, if S satisfies the terminal cluster property then a theory T is a ground S-expansion for a theory $I \subseteq \mathcal{L}_K$ iff T is a minimal S_{MDD}-expansion for I, i.e. for every stable theory T' containing I, $T \cap \mathcal{L} \subseteq T' \cap \mathcal{L}$.*

Notice that modal logics $S4F$, $KD45$ and $SW5$ satisfy the terminal cluster property, hence for such logics the notions of ground S-expansion and of minimal S_{MDD}-expansion coincide.

3 Minimal model semantics for ground nonmonotonic modal logics

We now present the semantic characterization for a relevant subset of ground nonmonotonic modal logics. The path we follow is similar to the one used in [18, 12], to provide a semantic characterization for the McDermott and Doyle's family of logics. Although the steps of the construction are the same, there are significant differences in the proofs, that will be pointed out in the presentation.

The structure is as follows. We first introduce a notion of ground-intended model, that constitutes a first step to the semantic characterization of theories formulated through a fixed point equation. We then focus on the preference relation, starting from the intuition that the syntactic notion of minimization of objective sentences can be formulated in terms of a partial ordering relation on Kripke models. This is achieved by enforcing the preference relation defined in [18], which in turn is obtained by weakening the preconditions for the comparison of Kripke models. The preference relation is then used to characterize ground-minimal models. The final step shows the correspondence between the notions of ground-intended and ground-minimal models.

We start by defining the notion of *ground-intended* model, which follows from the properties a reasoning agent should satisfy. Such properties correspond to those stated in [12], par. 9.1, but for the formulae it is possible for the agent to assume: in particular, we restrict the introspection capability of the agent to modal-free formulae only.

Definition 9. Given a normal modal logic $S \subseteq S5$ characterized by the class $\mathcal{C}$ of Kripke models and a theory $I \subseteq \mathcal{L}_K$, a model $\mathcal{M} \in \mathcal{C}$ is *ground $\mathcal{C}$-intended* for I iff:

1. $\mathcal{M} \models I$;
2. for every model $\mathcal{N} \in \mathcal{C}$, if $\mathcal{N} \models I \cup \{\neg K\varphi \mid \varphi \in \mathcal{L} \setminus Th(\mathcal{M})\}$, then $Th(\mathcal{M}) = Th(\mathcal{N})$.

Then, we show that the notion of ground $\mathcal{C}$-intended model exactly corresponds to that of ground $\mathcal{S}$-expansion, if $\mathcal{C}$ is the class of Kripke models characterizing modal logic $\mathcal{S}$.

Theorem 10. *Given a modal logic $\mathcal{S}$ such that $K \subseteq \mathcal{S} \subseteq S5$, let $\mathcal{C}$ be the class of Kripke models characterizing $\mathcal{S}$. An $S5$-model $\mathcal{M}$ is a ground $\mathcal{C}$-intended model for $I \subseteq \mathcal{L}_K$ iff $Th(\mathcal{M})$ is a ground $\mathcal{S}$-expansion for I.*

Proof. First, assume $\mathcal{M}$ is ground $\mathcal{C}$-intended for I, and define $T = Th(\mathcal{M})$. Since $\mathcal{M}$ is an $S5$-model, T is stable, therefore $T \supseteq \{\neg K\varphi \mid \varphi \in \mathcal{L} \setminus Th(\mathcal{M})\}$. Besides, $I \subseteq T$ and $\mathcal{S} \subseteq S5$, consequently

$$T \supseteq Cn_{\mathcal{S}}(I \cup \{\neg K\varphi \mid \varphi \in \mathcal{L} \setminus Th(\mathcal{M})\})$$

Since $\mathcal{M}$ is ground $\mathcal{C}$-intended, every model of $I \cup \{\neg K\varphi \mid \varphi \in \mathcal{L} \setminus Th(\mathcal{M})\}$ in $\mathcal{C}$ is a model of T, therefore

$$T \subseteq Cn_{\mathcal{S}}(I \cup \{\neg K\varphi \mid \varphi \in \mathcal{L} \setminus Th(\mathcal{M})\})$$

Hence, T is a ground $\mathcal{S}$-expansion for I.

Conversely, assume that T is a ground $\mathcal{S}$-expansion for I. Then, $T = Th(\mathcal{M}) = Cn_{\mathcal{S}}(I \cup \{\neg K\varphi \mid \varphi \in \mathcal{L} \setminus Th(\mathcal{M})\})$. Consider a model $\mathcal{N} \in \mathcal{C}$ such that $\mathcal{N} \models I \cup \{\neg K\varphi \mid \varphi \in \mathcal{L} \setminus Th(\mathcal{M})\}$; it follows that $T \subseteq Th(\mathcal{N})$. And if $\varphi \in \mathcal{L} \setminus T$, then $\mathcal{N} \models \neg K\varphi$, which implies that $\mathcal{N} \not\models \varphi$. Therefore $\mathcal{L} \setminus T \subseteq \{\varphi \in \mathcal{L} \mid \mathcal{N} \not\models \varphi\}$, from which we obtain $Th(\mathcal{N}) \cap \mathcal{L} \subseteq T \cap \mathcal{L}$. But $T = Th(\mathcal{M}) \subseteq Th(\mathcal{N})$, consequently $Th(\mathcal{M}) \cap \mathcal{L} = Th(\mathcal{N}) \cap \mathcal{L}$, and since T is stable, we can conclude $Th(\mathcal{M}) = Th(\mathcal{N})$ (see [12], Theorem 8.16). Therefore $\mathcal{M}$ is a ground $\mathcal{C}$-intended model for I. $\qquad \square$

Now we turn our attention to Kripke models and define a notion of minimality based on a partial ordering relation on models. First, we need to define a relation between Kripke models that differ only with respect to the accessibility relation.

Definition 11. Given the two Kripke models $\mathcal{M}_1 = \langle W_1, R_1, V_1 \rangle$ and $\mathcal{M}_2 = \langle W_2, R_2, V_2 \rangle$, $\mathcal{M}_2 \supset_G \mathcal{M}_1$ if $W_1 = W_2$, $V_1 = V_2$ and $R_2 \supset R_1$.

Using the $\supset_G$ relation, we are now able to define a partial ordering relation on Kripke models.

Definition 12. Given two Kripke models $\mathcal{M}_1, \mathcal{M}_2$, $\mathcal{M}_2 \sqsubset_G \mathcal{M}_1$ if there exists a Kripke model $\mathcal{M}$ such that:

1. $\mathcal{M}_2 \supset_G \mathcal{M} \odot \mathcal{M}_1$;
2. there exists a world $a \in W_2 \setminus W_1$ such that for each world $b \in W_1$, $V_2(b) \neq V_2(a)$.

The above notion of partial ordering among Kripke models can informally be explained as follows: $\mathcal{M}_2$ is "less than" $\mathcal{M}_1$ if $\mathcal{M}_2$ is built on top of $\mathcal{M}_1$, by adding at least one world whose corresponding interpretation is different from those contained in $\mathcal{M}_1$, in such a way that each new world must be connected to all the worlds belonging to $\mathcal{M}_1$. Moreover, connections between worlds belonging to $\mathcal{M}_1$ and the new worlds are allowed.

Finally, minimal models are characterized using the $\sqsubset_G$ ordering, as a special case of Shoham's preference semantics [22].

Definition 13. Given a normal modal logic $\mathcal{S}$ characterized by the class of Kripke models $\mathcal{C}$, a model $\mathcal{M} \in \mathcal{C}$ is a *ground $\mathcal{C}$-minimal model* for I if $\mathcal{M} \models I$ and for every model $\mathcal{M}' \in \mathcal{C}$ such that $\mathcal{M}' \models I$, $\mathcal{M}' \not\sqsubset_G \mathcal{M}$.

The preference criterion obtained through the definition of the relation $\sqsubset_G$ can be seen as a stronger version of the minimality criterion found by Schwarz for Mc Dermott and Doyle's logics [18]. We try to give an intuitive argument to this claim.

Informally, the difference between Schwarz's ordering relation and $\sqsubset_G$ is the following: Schwarz compares the $S5$-model $\mathcal{M}$ with all $\mathcal{S}_{MDD}$-models $\mathcal{N}$ such that $\mathcal{N} = \mathcal{M}' \odot \mathcal{M}$, therefore $\mathcal{N}$ is such that

1. every world of $\mathcal{M}'$ is connected to every world in $\mathcal{M}$;
2. no world in $\mathcal{M}$ is connected to any world in $\mathcal{M}'$.

In the ground case the second condition does not hold, therefore connections between worlds in $\mathcal{M}'$ and worlds in $\mathcal{M}$ are allowed (this is the intuitive meaning of $\mathcal{N} \supset_G \mathcal{M}' \odot \mathcal{M}$).

Therefore, when checking for the minimality of a model $\mathcal{M}$, the ground criterion allows more monotonic models of the theory to be compared with $\mathcal{M}$. Hence, every ground model is also a McDermott-Doyle's model for I, while the converse in general does not hold.

In the rest of this section we show the correspondence between the notion of ground expansion and the semantic notion of ground minimal model, which in turn establishes a preference semantics for ground nonmonotonic modal logics. To prove such a correspondence, we need the following lemmata.

Lemma 14. *Let $\mathcal{N}$ be a Kripke model and $\mathcal{M}$ be an $S5$-model such that:*

1. $\mathcal{N} \models \{\neg K\varphi \mid \varphi \in \mathcal{L} \setminus Th(\mathcal{M})\}$;
2. $Th(\mathcal{N}) \cap \mathcal{L} = Th(\mathcal{M}) \cap \mathcal{L}$.

Then, $Th(\mathcal{N}) = Th(\mathcal{M})$.

Proof. The proof easily follows from the fact that $Th(\mathcal{M})$ is a stable theory and from [12], Theorem 8.16. $\square$

Lemma 15. *Let $\mathcal{M}'$, $\mathcal{M}''$ be $S5$-models. If $Th(\mathcal{M}') \cap \mathcal{L} = Th(\mathcal{M}'') \cap \mathcal{L}$ then $Th(\mathcal{N} \odot \mathcal{M}') = Th(\mathcal{N} \odot \mathcal{M}'')$ for any Kripke model $\mathcal{N}$.*

Proof. Since $\mathcal{M}'$ and $\mathcal{M}''$ are $S5$-models, it follows that $Th(\mathcal{M}')$ and $Th(\mathcal{M}'')$ are stable theories, hence $Th(\mathcal{M}') \cap \mathcal{L} = Th(\mathcal{M}'') \cap \mathcal{L}$ implies $Th(\mathcal{M}') = Th(\mathcal{M}'')$, which in turn implies $Th(\mathcal{N} \odot \mathcal{M}') = Th(\mathcal{N} \odot \mathcal{M}'')$ (see [12], Lemma 9.19). □

Finally, we state the equivalence between the syntactic and semantic characterizations above defined. This equivalence is proved under the restriction of cluster-decomposable classes of Kripke models.

Theorem 16. *Given a normal modal logic S, characterized by a cluster-decomposable class of Kripke models $\mathcal{C}$, a theory $I \subseteq \mathcal{L}_K$ and a stable theory T, let $\mathcal{M}$ be the canonical model for T. Then T is a ground S-expansion for I if and only if $\mathcal{M}$ is a ground $\mathcal{C}$-minimal model for I.*

Proof. The proof makes use of the intermediate semantic notion of intended model above defined. From Theorem 10 it follows that theory T is a ground S-expansion for I if and only if $\mathcal{M}$ is a ground $\mathcal{C}$-intended model for I, hence we only have to show that the model $\mathcal{M}$ is ground $\mathcal{C}$-intended for I if and only if $\mathcal{M}$ is a ground $\mathcal{C}$-minimal model for I.

First, assume $\mathcal{M}$ is ground $\mathcal{C}$-intended. Then $\mathcal{M} \models I$ and for any $\mathcal{M}' \in \mathcal{C}$, if $\mathcal{M}' \models I \cup \{\neg K\varphi \mid \varphi \in \mathcal{L} \setminus Th(\mathcal{M})\}$, then $Th(\mathcal{M}) = Th(\mathcal{M}')$. Now, suppose $\mathcal{M}$ is not ground $\mathcal{C}$-minimal for I. Then, there exists a Kripke model $\mathcal{N} \in \mathcal{C}$ such that $\mathcal{N} \models I$ and $\mathcal{N} \sqsubset_G \mathcal{M}$. Since $\mathcal{M}$ is ground $\mathcal{C}$-intended, it cannot be the case that $\mathcal{N} \models \{\neg K\varphi \mid \varphi \in \mathcal{L} \setminus Th(\mathcal{M})\}$, therefore there exists a formula $\varphi \in \mathcal{L}$ such that $\mathcal{M} \models \neg K\varphi$ and $\mathcal{N} \not\models \neg K\varphi$. This implies that there exists a world b in $\mathcal{M}$ such that $V_M(b) \neq V_N(a)$, for every world $a \in \mathcal{N}$. But this contradicts the hypothesis $\mathcal{N} \subseteq_G \mathcal{M}$, which concludes the proof of the first part of the theorem.

Next, assume $\mathcal{M} = \langle W, R, V \rangle$ is ground $\mathcal{C}$-minimal for I, i.e. $\mathcal{M} \models I$ and for any $\mathcal{M}' \in \mathcal{C}$, if $\mathcal{M}' \models I$, then $\mathcal{M}' \not\sqsubset_G \mathcal{M}$. Then, suppose $\mathcal{M}$ is not ground $\mathcal{C}$-intended for I, i.e. there exists a model $\mathcal{N} = \langle W_N, R_N, V_N \rangle \in \mathcal{C}$ such that $\mathcal{N} \models I \cup \{\neg K\varphi \mid \varphi \in \mathcal{L} \setminus Th(\mathcal{M})\}$ and $Th(\mathcal{M}) \neq Th(\mathcal{N})$. Since $\mathcal{N} \models \{\neg K\varphi \mid \varphi \in \mathcal{L} \setminus Th(\mathcal{M})\}$, it follows that if $\varphi \in Th(\mathcal{N}) \cap \mathcal{L}$, then $\varphi \in Th(\mathcal{M}) \cap \mathcal{L}$ (otherwise $\mathcal{N} \models \neg K\varphi$), hence $Th(\mathcal{N}) \cap \mathcal{L} \subseteq Th(\mathcal{M}) \cap \mathcal{L}$. Now, it cannot be the case that $Th(\mathcal{N}) \cap \mathcal{L} = Th(\mathcal{M}) \cap \mathcal{L}$, otherwise by lemma 14 we would conclude $Th(\mathcal{N}) = Th(\mathcal{M})$, which contradicts the hypothesis. Therefore, $Th(\mathcal{N}) \cap \mathcal{L} \subset Th(\mathcal{M}) \cap \mathcal{L}$, thus there exists a world $a \in W_N$ such that $V_N(a) \neq V(b)$, for each world $b \in W$.

Now, the class $\mathcal{C}$ is cluster-decomposable, therefore there exists a model $\mathcal{N}'$ and an $S5$-model $\mathcal{M}'$ such that $\mathcal{N} = \mathcal{N}' \odot \mathcal{M}'$. Since $\mathcal{N} \models \{\neg K\varphi \mid \varphi \in \mathcal{L} \setminus Th(\mathcal{M})\}$, it follows that $\mathcal{M}' = \langle W', R', V' \rangle$ is such that for each world w belonging to W there exists a world w' belonging to W' such that $V(w) = V'(w')$. In other words, $\mathcal{M}'$ must contain all the interpretations belonging to $\mathcal{M}$. Thus, we only have two possible cases:

1. there exists a world $a \in W'$ such that $V'(a) \neq V(b)$, for each world $b \in W$. In this case we have $\mathcal{M}' \sqsubset_G \mathcal{M}$, and since $\mathcal{N} \models I$ implies $\mathcal{M}' \models I$, it follows that $\mathcal{M}$ is not a ground $\mathcal{C}$-minimal model for I, thus contradicting the hypothesis.

2. the interpretations belonging to $\mathcal{M}'$ are exactly the same belonging to $\mathcal{M}$, i.e. $Th(\mathcal{M}) \cap \mathcal{L} = Th(\mathcal{M}') \cap \mathcal{L}$. So, consider the Kripke model $\mathcal{M}'' = \mathcal{N}' \odot \mathcal{M}$: since $\mathcal{C}$ is cluster-decomposable, it follows that $\mathcal{M}'' \in \mathcal{C}$. Moreover, we have $\mathcal{M}'' \sqsubseteq_G \mathcal{M}$. Finally, by Lemma 15 we have that $\mathcal{M}'' \models I$. Therefore, $\mathcal{M}$ is not a ground $\mathcal{C}$-minimal model for I, which again contradicts the hypothesis. Consequently, $\mathcal{M}$ is a ground $\mathcal{C}$-intended model for I.

□

The last theorem provides a semantic characterization for a subset of the family of ground non-monotonic logics $\mathcal{S}_G$, since it relates the solutions of equation 2 to ground-minimal models. In particular, the correspondence is shown to hold for the ground logics built from modal logics $S5, KD45, S4f, Sw5$.

The semantic characterization above presented can be used to prove some properties of ground logics, that we briefly outline in the following.

– none of the ground logics collapses into a monotonic logic (in particular for $\mathcal{S} = S5$ the logic defined in [3] is obtained, as stated in [19]);
– all cluster-decomposable ground logics $\mathcal{S}_G$ are insensitive to the axiom schema D (i.e. schema $K\varphi \supset \neg K \neg \varphi$), in the sense that, for each ground logic $\mathcal{S}_G$, every istance of schema D is a tautology in $\mathcal{S}_G$;
– $S5_G$ shows monotonicity with respect to objective formulae, in the sense that for each $I, \varphi \in \mathcal{L}_K$ and for each $\psi \in \mathcal{L}$, if $I \models_{S5_G} \psi$ then $I \cup \{\varphi\} \models_{S5_G} \psi$. Therefore, when adding new information in $S5_G$, only modal formulae only can be lost, no longer being derivable in the resulting theory.
– the above property implies that defaults [16] are not expressible in $S5_G$, in the sense that there exists no faithful modular translation (i.e. a translation which translates each default into a modal formula, independently from other defaults and from the theory) from default logic to $S5_G$. Since for no other ground logic the property of monotonicity with respect to objective formulae holds, this behaviour seems to be restricted to the logic $S5_G$ only: for example in the logic $S4F_G$ (and in any normal modal logic contained in $S4F_G$) defaults are expressible with the same translation used in the corresponding Mc Dermott and Doyle's logic (see [2] for a detailed analysis on the embedding of defaults into ground logics).
– given any two cluster-decomposable modal logics $\mathcal{S}, \mathcal{S}'$, each containing the axiom schema D, $\mathcal{S}$ is equivalent to $\mathcal{S}'$ if and only if their ground non-monotonic extensions $\mathcal{S}_G, \mathcal{S}'_G$ are equivalent. Namely, with the exception of schema D, every cluster-decomposable modal logic $\mathcal{S}$ produces a different nonmonotonic logic $\mathcal{S}_G$.

4 Conclusions

In this paper we have presented a semantic characterization of ground logics [19, 23, 4], a family of nonmonotonic modal logics obtained by a modification of the well known Mc Dermott and Doyle fixpoint equation [14]. Ground logics owe their name to the idea that the negative introspection capability of the reasoning agent is bounded to his objective knowledge only. This intuition was nicely formalized for modal logic $S5$ by a semantic definition based on a preference relation on Kripke models, which was obtained as the semantic counterpart to the notion of minimal knowledge initially defined by Halpern and Moses [3, 22, 7]. Therefore our minimal model characterization can be viewed as a generalization of this semantic account of minimal knowledge to a broader class of modal logics. Moreover, the preference relation can be viewed as an enforcing of the one used by Schwarz [18] to provide a minimal model semantics for Mc Dermott and Doyle's logics. We are currently working at a generalization of the semantic characterization above presented, with the aim of identifying the semantic counterpart to the fixpoint definition for every ground modal logic. Moreover, we are addressing the use of ground logics in knowledge representation: our first results in this direction are reported in [1, 2].

Acknowledgements

We would like to thank Francesco Maria Donini for many discussions on the subject of the paper.

References

1. F. M. Donini, D. Nardi and R. Rosati. Ground Nonmonotonic Modal Logics for Knowledge Representation. To appear in *Proceedings of WOCFAI-95*.

2. F. M. Donini, D. Nardi and R. Rosati. Non-first-order features in concept languages. To appear in *Proceedings of AI*IA-95 - Fourth congress of the Italian Association for Artificial Intelligence*.

3. J. Halpern and Y. Moses. Towards a theory of knowledge and ignorance: preliminary report. In K. Apt editor, *Logics and models of concurrent systems*, pages 459–476, Springer-Verlag, 1985.

4. M. Kaminski. Embedding a default system into nonmonotonic logic. *Fundamenta Informaticae*, 14:345–354, 1991.

5. K. Konolige. On the relationship between default and autoepistemic logic. *Artificial Intelligence Journal*, 35:343–382, 1988.

6. H. J. Levesque. All I know: a study in autoepistemic logic. *Artificial Intelligence*, 42:263–310, 1990.

7. V. Lifschitz. Nonmonotonic databases and epistemic queries. In *Proc. of the 12th Int. Joint Conf. on Artificial Intelligence IJCAI-91*, Sydney, 1991.

8. V. Lifschitz. Minimal belief and negation as failure. *Artificial Intelligence Journal*, 70:53–72, 1994.

9. F. Lin and Y. Shoham. Epistemic semantics for fixed-point non-monotonic logics. *Artificial Intelligence Journal*, 57:271–289, 1992.

10. W. Marek, G.F. Shvarts and M. Truszczyński. Modal nonmonotonic logics: ranges, characterization, computation. In *Proceedings of the 2nd international conference on principles of knowledge representation and reasoning (KR-91)*, pages 395–404, Morgan Kaufmann, 1992.

11. W. Marek and M. Truszczyński. Autoepistemic logic. *Journal of the ACM*, 38:588–619, 1991.

12. V.W. Marek and M. Truszczyński. Nonmonotonic logic. Context-dependent reasoning. Springer-Verlag, 1993.

13. D. McDermott. Non-monotonic logic II: Non-monotonic modal theories. *Journal of the ACM*, 29:33–57, 1982.

14. D. McDermott and J. Doyle. Non-monotonic logic I. *Artificial Intelligence Journal*, 13:41–72, 1980.

15. R. C. Moore. Semantical considerations on nonmonotonic logic. *Artificial Intelligence Journal*, 25:75–94, 1985.

16. R. Reiter, A Logic for Default Reasoning. *Artificial Intelligence Journal*, 13:81–132, 1980.

17. G. Schwarz. Autoepistemic logic of knowledge. In A. Nerode, W. Marek and V.S. Subrahmanian editors, *Logic programming and nonmonotonic reasoning*, pages 260–274, MIT press, 1991.

18. G. Schwarz. Minimal model semantics for nonmonotonic modal logics. In *Proceedings of LICS-92*, pages 34–43, IEEE Computer Society Press, 1992.

19. G. Schwarz. Bounding introspection in nonmonotonic logics. In *Proceedings of the 3rd international conference on principles of knowledge representation and reasoning (KR-92)*, pages 581–590, Morgan Kaufmann, 1992.

20. G. Schwarz and M. Truszczyński. Modal logic S4f and the minimal knowledge paradigm. In *Proceedings of the Fourth Conference on Theoretical Aspects of Reasoning about Knowledge (TARK-92)*, pages 184–198, 1992.

21. G. Schwarz and M. Truszczyński. Minimal knowledge problem: a new approach. *Artificial Intelligence Journal*, 67:113–141, 1994.

22. Y. Shoham. Nonmonotonic logics: meaning and utility. In *Proc. of the 10th Int. Joint Conf. on Artificial Intelligence IJCAI-87*, Milan, 1987.

23. M. Tiomkin and M. Kaminski. Nonmonotonic default modal logics. In *Proceedings of the Third Conference on Theoretical Aspects of Reasoning about Knowledge (TARK-90)*, pages 73–84, 1990.

24. M. Truszczyński. Modal interpretations of default logic. In *Proc. of the 12th Int. Joint Conf. on Artificial Intelligence IJCAI-91*, Sydney, 1991.

Logical Omniscience vs. Logical Ignorance on a Dilemma of Epistemic Logic

Ho Ngoc Duc

Institute of Logic and Philosophy of Science, University of Leipzig
P.O. Box 920, D-04009 Leipzig, Germany
phone: +49 (0341) 97 35 775, fax: +49 (0341) 97 35 798
e-mail: duc@informatik.uni-leipzig.de

Abstract. We propose in the paper a new solution to the so-called Logical Omniscience Problem of epistemic logic. Almost all attempts in the literature to solve this problem consist in weakening the standard epistemic systems: weaker sytems are considered where the agents do not possess the full reasoning capacities of an ideal reasoner. We shall argue that this solution is not satisfactory: in this way omniscience can be avoided, but many intuitions about the concepts of knowledge and belief get lost. We shall show that axioms for epistemic logics must have the following form: if the agent knows all premises of a valid inference rule, and if she thinks hard enough, then she will know the conclusion. To formalize such an idea, we propose to "temporalize" epistemic logic, that is, to introduce a temporal component into the language. We develop a logic based on this idea and show that it is suitable for formalizing the notion of explicit belief.

Keywords: Knowledge representation, Logics of knowledge and belief, Logical omniscience, Dynamic epistemic logic, Knowledge and time

1 Introduction and Preliminaries

Epistemic logic, or the logic of the concepts of knowledge and belief, has established as an autonomous branch of logic since the work of Hintikka ([6].) The subject has been studied extensively by philosophers, linguists and, more recently, computer scientists. Most systems of epistemic logic have been developed in analogy to modal logic. Many results and methods of modal logic can be tranferred to epistemic logic, notably the techniques of the possible worlds semantics. There are, however, severe objections against the modal approach in epistemis logic. The most serious problem of this approach is perhaps the so-called "logical omniscience problem (LOP)." It can be described informally

---

* I thank my teachers Peter Steinacker and Heinrich Herre for their invaluable help during the last several years. I have learned much from Werner Stelzner's works on non-modal epistemic logic. I had the chance to discuss preliminary versions of this paper with several people at different occasions. I thank all of them for their comments which have helped me very much to improve the presentation of the paper.

as follows. According to the standard approach, the agent should be an ideal logician and reasoner in the following sense: she knows all logical truths, can (actually) draw all consequences of a certain sentence and can identify all logical equivalences of a given sentence. Such requirements are clearly too strong for a real agent, human or non-human. Thus, the standard systems cannot capture the notion of knowledge and belief adequately. The problem of logical omniscience is a severe obstacle for the applicability of epistemic logic. For that reason, many attempts have been undertaken to solve this problem. The goal of my paper is to assess how successful these attempts can be and then to propose another solution to the LOP.

Before going on, let us state the problem more precisely. For simplicity's sake I consider only the propositional case with only one agent. I use the terms "knowledge" and "belief" as synonyms in the paper. (It is therefore not distinguished between epistemic and doxastic logic.) Knowing p only means "having good reasons to believe that p", but does not imply that p is true. By "modal epistemic logic" I mean, as proposed by Wuttich in [13], those systems of epistemic logic which are developed in the modal tradition. The language of modal epistemic logic is built up from a set At_M of propositional letters using the usual Boolean connectives of negation and implication and the unary operator K. The set of formulae of this language will be denoted by Fml_M. (The index M indicates the modal approach.) Formally, Fml_M is the least set which includes At_M and is closed under the following rules: if p and q are members of Fml_M then so are $\neg p$, $p \supset q$ and Kp. The formula Kp is to be read: "the agent knows p". The other Boolean connectives are defined in the usual way. The minimal normal modal epistemic logic K is the least system which contains all theorems of the propositional calculus (PC) together with all instances of the axiom schema K, i.e., the schema $K(p \supset q) \supset (Kp \supset Kq)$, and is closed under modus ponens and the so-called Gödel rule: if p is a theorem then so is Kp. It is well-known that K is characterized by the class of all Kripke models (cf. [1].)

The logical omniscience problem for this minimal normal logic can be stated as follows. The following inference rules are valid for the system K:

(R1) If p is a theorem then so is Kp

(R2) If $p \supset q$ is a theorem then so is $Kp \supset Kq$

(R3) If $p \leftrightarrow q$ is a theorem then so is $Kp \leftrightarrow Kq$

The three rules (R1), (R2), (R3) are called Gödel rule, monotony rule, and congruence rule, respectively. These rules not only hold for K, but also for all of its normal extensions. An agent who is described by such a logic is said to be logically omniscient, because she knows all logical truths (according to R1), she knows all logical consequences of a sentence that she knows (according to R2), and she can identify all logical equivalent sentences of a given sentence, according to (R3). Such an agent cannot be a real one. The logic K and its normal extensions can only describe ideal agents. For modelling realistic agents we need other logics which do not suffer from the LOP. In the next section we shall discuss some common ways to solve this problem. After showing that the strategy of weakening epistemic logic has many disadvantages I shall propose an alternative approach to the problem. The intuitions of my strategy will be explained in section 3. A formal system which can cope with the problems of the traditional approaches will be developed in section 4 following the new strategy.

2 Strategies to Avoid Logical Omniscience

An obvious strategy to solve the logical omniscience problem is to weaken epistemic logic. One denies the universal validity of the mentioned inference rules (R1)–(R3). In fact, almost all attempts to solve the LOP have in common that they consider systems that are weaker than the standard modal epistemic logics (cf. [3], [4], [7], [8], [9], [10], [11], [12], [13].) But here some care is needed: some systems solve the original version of the LOP, but not other versions. For example, the agent in Levesque's logic ([9]) does not know all truths of classical logic, but she knows all theorems of a relevance logic. In the same way, an agent in Ho Ngoc Duc's system ([8]) does not know all classical theorems, but knows all theorems of a three-valued logic. Thus, such solutions cannot be regarded satisfactory. Modal systems which are not normal can also be used to describe an agent who does not know all logical truths (cf. [11], for example.) However, if the monotony rule and/or the congruence rule are valid for a system, then the agent in this system must still be viewed as ideal: real agents simply never achieve such reasoning capacities which can be described by these rules. Thus, a solution to the LOP must provide us with a logic for which neither of the rules (R1)–(R3) is valid. We shall note that the notion of "theorem" in these rules not only applies to classical logic, but also to other logical systems as well.

A number of systems have been proposed which are not closed under any of the rules (R1)–(R3). To construct such a system we can postulate, for example, that the agent only knows some "obvious" logical truths, but not necessarily the "more complicated" ones. We can assume that the agent can draw all "obvious" consequences, but not any arbitrary consequence, of a certain sentence. We can consider logics which allow only the rules of classical logic (e.g., modus ponens) as inference rule. The properties of the knowledge concept must then be described by a set of axioms. The more axioms are assumed, the more rational is the agent. With the aid of such weak epistemic logics we can classify the agents according to their logical capacities. (cf. [12], [13].) In general those weak epistemic logics lack logical omniscience. Besides this axiomatic approach we can also pursue a more semantical approach. One can show that logical omniscience can be avoided if one allow "impossible possible worlds" in which the valuation of the sentences of the language is arbitrary. In other words, the logical laws do not hold in the "impossible possible worlds" ([11], [10]). Another solution is to introduce a new operator of awareness into the language and to require that belief include awareness ([4].) Because it is possible that the agent is aware of some sentence but she is not aware of its logical consequences or its equivalent sentences, the monotony rule (R2) and the congruence rule (R3) do not hold in general.

Although the approach with impossible possible worlds and the approach with the awareness operator solve the LOP technically, they cannot be regarded satisfactory. New problems arise in these approaches besides the old problems of the possible worlds approach. Here I shall not discuss these problems in details, nor shall I try to improve any of these approaches. I shall rather present a more fundamental criticism of the common strategy of all these approaches, namely the strategy of weakening epistemic logic.

The discussion of the logical omniscience problem in the literature has concentrated mainly on the issue: in which way can logical omniscience be avoided. But the LOP has another aspect which is often overlooked in the discussion: what is left if one restrict the reasoning capacities of the agents, for example by denying the validity of the rules (R1), (R2) and (R3)? Is there still a reasonable way to describe the agent's knowledge if the regularities of the agent's knowledge is too weak to be described by these rules?

An attempt to cope with this challenge is to postulate axioms which describe the regularities of the agent's knowledge. Such axioms shall express the intuitive idea that the agent is somehow rational, or logical. The axioms are generally of the form: the belief set of the agent is closed under a certain valid rule of inference of logic, i.e., if all premises of the rule are known, then the conclusion is known. (This is also the general form of a theorem of a standard epistemic logic.) In this way we can get subsystems of the logic K which do not suffer from the LOP. Let us see how far such a strategy may take us. We consider a simple example of a ultra-weak epistemic logic.

Definition 1. Let L be the logic whose axioms consist of all theorems of the propositional calculus (PC) and all instances of the schema K. The only inference rule of L is modus ponens.

L is thus the system obtained from the smallest normal system K by dropping the Gödel rule (without any substitute!) L is a very weak epistemic logic lying between PC and K. It describes an agent, or more correctly, a class of agents who can only use modus ponens reliably: whenever they know the premises of modus ponens then they can infer the conclusion (i.e., if Kp and $K(p \supset q)$ then Kq.) It is not required that such an agent know any other inference rule or axiom. It is clear that the agent lacks logical omniscience.

It is possible to find an adequate semantics for L using impossible possible worlds. However, we can also provide L with a simple truth-functional semantics.

Definition 2. An L-evaluation is a function V from the set Fml_M of formulae to the set $\{0, 1\}$ of truth-values, which satisfies the following conditions for arbitrary formulae:

- $V(\neg p) = 1$ if and only if $V(p) = 0$
- $V(p \supset q) = 0$ if and only if $V(p) = 1$ and $V(q) = 0$
- If $V(Kp) = 1$ and $V(K(p \supset q)) = 1$ then $V(Kq) = 1$

The first two clauses guarantee that all classical theorems are valid, and the last one ensures the validity of the axiom schema K. It can be seen easily that if a formula is provable in L then it has the value 1 under all L-valuations. It turns out that the converse is also true, that is, the system L is complete with respect to the given semantics.

Theorem 3. *If $V(p) = 1$ for all L-valuations V then p is L-provable.*

Proof. (Sketch) If p is not a theorem of L, then $\neg p$ is L-consistent. Therefore $\neg p$ is contained in a maximal L-consistent set X, by the standard Henkin argument. The valuation V defined by $V(p)=1$ iff $p \in X$ for all $p \in Fml$ satisfies the three conditions above, as we can check easily. Thus, V is an L-valuation and V is a model of $\neg p$. By contraposition we have the desired result. □

As the example of system L shows, the strategy of weakening epistemic logic allows us to consider agents who are very restricted in their reasoning capacities. We can describe and classify them according to their rationality. We would have a hierarchy of agents: some agents are ideal, who are modelled by the logic K or its extensions, others are less ideal and can be described by, e.g., the logic L. The agents described by the intermediate systems between L and K are not as ignorant as those of L, neither are they ideal reasoners as those of K.

The strategy of weakening epistemic logic solves the logical omniscience problem. However, the disadvantages cannot be overlooked. First, this approach is only suited to analyze static knowledge, that is, we can at most describe the knowledge sets at one single time point. This is of course not a deficiency of these logics alone, but of most epistemic logics developed up to now. Second, the categories of agents we describe and classify by our logics are merely imaginary: they do not exist in reality. It is very implausible to assume that there are agents who always think in some fixed patterns which can be captured by one of our logics. Each agent represents rather some mixture of several logics, at some time point they can be described by one, at other time points by another, and still at other by none of our logics at all. Third, we have the feeling that our logics are too weak. Surely, we want to avoid logical omniscience. On the other hand, we are interested in having epistemic logics which are strong enough to allow sufficiently many conclusions from a given set of facts we know about the agent's propositional attitudes. For example, if we know that the agent know the conjunction $p \wedge q$ then we may expect that she knows p and that she knows q. This inference is, however, not sound for L and many related systems. We want to have agents who do know at least a (sufficiently) large class of logical truths, and can draw sufficiently many conclusions from their knowledge. This is the dilemma on logical omniscience on the one side and logical ignorance on the other side. That is why I ask the question before: what is left from belief logic if we deny the validity of the congruence rule and stronger principles? What we need is something between two extremes. Can we have some reasonable thing like that?

My goal is to show that we can solve this dilemma. I shall now propose another strategy to solve the logical omniscience problem which also solves the problem of logical ignorance. My strategy starts with the observation that the laws of (classical) logic are not sentences about the world, they do not tell us anything about what is the case in the world. If we say that the epistemic agent knows the laws of logic, we do not mean that she knows some facts about the world, but rather that she is able to use these laws to draw conclusions from what she already knows. The laws of logic are what the agent knows implicitly; she does not need to possess them permanently. It suffices if she can recall them when she needs them in order to infer new information from her explicit data base. At a given time the set of logical laws that the agent has in her memory is restricted, and so is the set of logical consequences of all what she knows explicitly. In this way we can achieve a good tradeoff between logical omniscience and logical ignorance: the agent is surely not omniscient with respect to her actual or explicit knowledge, but neither is she logically ignorant. Our task is to find a suitable way to express this idea formally.

3   Temporalizing Epistemic Logic

Let us consider an inference rule, say R. It can be a valid inference rule of classical logic, or some other (non-classical) logic, for example, intuitionist logic, conditional logic or relevant logic. Assume that the agent accepts R as valid and she can use R. What does it mean? In the modal approach we formalize this idea by an axiom saying that the knowledge set of the agent is closed under this rule, that is, if all premises of the rule are known then the conclusion of R is also known. However, as we noted above, it is only true of implicit knowledge. In the context of explicit knowledge it must mean something different. It means rather that, if the agent knows all premises of the rule, and if she perform the inference according to the rule R, then she will know the conclusion. The agent does not know the conclusion automatically, but rather as the result of some action, viz. the (mental) action of performing the corresponding inference. If she does not perform this action, then we cannot require her to know (or believe) the conclusion, although this conclusion may seem to be an obvious consequences of the sentences under consideration. Especially, a logical axiom can be viewed as an inference rule without any premises. We cannot require the agent to know all axioms automatically and permanently, but she must also carry out some action before she can acquire knowledge of a certain axiom. It is possible that the agent knows all logical truths, but merely in principle. This knowledge is only implicit. Factually she never knows them all at once explicitly. As the idea of "time shift" ("before / after the reasoning") is implicit in the idea of performing an inference we call our approach the strategy of "temporalizing epistemic logic."

For formalizing the reasoning actions it is natural to use (a form of) dynamic logic (cf. [5].) We can associate each valid inference rule with an atomic action. Thus, we can add a set of basic actions to the language of epistemic logic. The set of formulae now includes formulae like $[R]Kp$ or $\langle R \rangle Kp$ with the intended meaning: "always after using rule R (or sometimes after using R) the agent knows p". The formalization of the idea that the agent accepts and is able to use an inference rule is straightforward. For example, the idea that the agent accepts modus ponens can be formalized by the axiom: $Kp \wedge K(p \supset q) \supset \langle MP \rangle Kq$. This axiom says no more than if the agent knows p and she also knows that p implies q, then after a suitable inference step she will know q.

As the axioms can be viewed as special inference rules we can introduce an action corresponding to each axiom of the basis logic, which describes the ability of the agent to use this axiom in her reasoning. By means of the familiar program connectives for dynamic logic (such as composition or iteration) we can formalize the idea that the agent may know the consequences of some sentence which she already knows explicitly, provided that she performs the right reasoning steps. For example, assume that the agent knows the conjunction of p and $p \supset q$, that is, $K(p \wedge (p \supset q))$. There is no guarantee that she will know $p \wedge q$ automatically, as the logic K suggests. We can only say that if the agent reasons correctly then she will know $p \wedge q$. In our concrete case, let CE, CI, MP be the conjunction elimination rule, the conjunction introduction rule, and modus ponens, respectively, and let the symbol ";" denote the composition of actions. Then our theorem must be: $K(p \wedge (p \supset q)) \supset \langle CE; MP; CI \rangle K(p \wedge q)$, and not $K(p \wedge (p \supset q)) \supset K(p \wedge q)$ as in the standard modal approach.

In gerenal, assume that q follows from p in some basis logic (which is accepted by the agent) and that the agent knows p. For explicit knowledge we cannot assume that the agent automatically knows q. Let a proof of q from p be given, where the axioms and inference rules used in the proof are $R_1,...,R_n$ (in this order, where the same axiom or inference rule may occur at different places in the sequence.) Then, instead of the monotonicity rule in the standard modal approach we have the axiom: $Kp \supset \langle R_1; \ldots ; R_n \rangle Kq$. This axiom says that if the agent perform the sequence of actions from R_1 to R_n then she may know q under the given circumstances. Whether or not the agent can come to this conclusion depends crucially on her logical ability. In this way we see that the logical omniscience problem can be solved easily in a natural way. On the other hand we can still say that the agent thinks rationally, that she is not logically ignorant.

Often we do not need to care about what course of actions the agent just carried out; we are only interested in the result of the actions, so to speak. We only need to know that the agent has carried out some reasoning steps, and after that she gain certain new information. In this case it is convenient to introduce an auxiliary action F with the following intended reading: do any one of the atomic actions (we don't know what action;) repeat the non-deterministic choice finitely many times (we don't know how many!) The action F could be interpreted as a course of thought. (For dynamic logicians: if the set of all atomic actions associated with the basis logic is a finite set $\{r_1, \ldots, r_n\}$, then F can be viewed as $(r_1 \cup r_2 \cup \ldots \cup r_n)^*$, where the symbols $\cup$ and * denote choice and iteration, respectively.) The choice of the symbols F is not accidental at all: in temporal logic its stands for the operator "Future". It turns out that our auxiliary action behaves in the same manner as the mentioned operator of temporal logic. The formal language in which our dynamic epistemic logics are formulated is called DE and will be defined in the following section.

4   A System of Dynamic Epistemic Logic

Definition 4 (The language DE). We assume the propositional calculus (PC) as our basis logic. Atomic formulae of DE are of the form Kp, where p is a formula of PC. The set of DE-formulae is the least set which contains all atomic formulae and is closed under the usual Boolean connectives and the following condition: if A is a DE-formula then so is $\langle F \rangle A$. Let At denote the set of atomic formulae and Fml be the set of all DE-formulae.

The formula Kp is read: p is known. $\langle F \rangle A$ means "A is true after some course of thought"; $[F]A$ means "A is true after any course of thought". (We could think of $\langle F \rangle$ and $[F]$ as the modalities "at some future times" and "at all future times" of temporal logic.) Note that we consider only sentences about the agent's current and future knowledge such as $K(\neg p)$ or $[F]K(p \vee q)$, but no sentences about "the world" (i.e., sentences of PC) or "mixed" sentences such as $Kp \supset p$. Thus, we must be careful to distinguish between the basis language (i.e., the language of PC) and the language DE of our epistemic logic. Moreover, nested knowledge is not allowed. We do it just for simplicity's sake, but the restrictions are not essential. We use the symbols A, B, ... as meta-variables to denote DE-formulae.

Definition 5 (A minimal logic of growing knowledge). Let $TAUT$ be the set of all tautological PC-formulae. The logic BDE (Basic Dynamic-Epistemic Logic) has the following axiom schemata:

A1. All classical tautologies of the language DE.
A2. $[F](A \supset B) \supset ([F]A \supset [F]B)$
A3. $[F]A \supset [F][F]A$
A4. $Kp \wedge K(p \supset q) \supset \langle F \rangle Kq$
A5. $Kp \supset [F]Kp$
A6. $\langle F \rangle Kp$, where $p \in TAUT$

The rules of inference are:

R1. Modus ponens: if A and $A \supset B$ are theorems then B is a theorem.
R2. Necessation: if A is a theorem then so is $[F]A$

The first three axioms together with the rules R1, R2 axiomatize the minimal temporal logic of transitive time. Axiom A4 says that the agent is capable of using modus ponens. Axiom A5 says that the agent does not forget what she knows. Finally, axiom A6 says that the agent is able to use the theorems of classical logic in her reasoning. (Note that the elements of $TAUT$ belong to the basis language and not to the language DE.) The notions of a proof, a theorem, and a consistent formula or set of formulae are defined as usual. Unless otherwise stated these notions are used relatively to the system BDE.

The following list comprises some provable formulae of BDE. They say that if all premises of a valid inference rule are known or will be known, then after some steps of reasoning the agent will know the conclusion. (Compare them with the corresponding theorems of the standard approach.) The proof of them is not difficult and is omitted.

Theorem 6. *The following formulae are theorems of BDE:*

1. $Kp \wedge \langle F \rangle K(p \supset q) \supset \langle F \rangle Kq$
2. $Kq \supset \langle F \rangle K(p \supset q)$
3. $Kp \wedge Kq \supset \langle F \rangle K(p \wedge q)$
4. $Kp \wedge \langle F \rangle Kq \supset \langle F \rangle K(p \wedge q)$
5. $K(p \wedge q) \supset \langle F \rangle Kp \wedge \langle F \rangle Kq$
6. $K(p \wedge q) \supset \langle F \rangle (Kp \wedge Kq)$
7. $Kp \supset \langle F \rangle K(p \vee q)$
8. $Kq \supset \langle F \rangle K(p \vee q)$

Instead of the monotony rule in modal epistemic logic we have now the theorem: if $p \supset q$ is a theorem of classical logic, then $Kp \supset \langle F \rangle Kq$ is a theorem of BDE. This is a simple consequence of the axioms of BDE. (Note that this rule is formulated cross the two languages of PC and BDE.) It is obvious that BDE solves the logical omniscience problem. Now we define a semantics for our basic dynamic epistemic logic. Recall that a temporal frame is a structure $\mathcal{F} = (S, R)$ where S is a non-empty set and R is a binary relation on S. We assume that R is transitive. A valuation on the frame $\mathcal{F}$ is a function V from S to the set of subsets of At. A temporal model is a pair $(\mathcal{F}, V)$ comprising a temporal frame and a valuation. Models of the Basic Dynamic Epistemic are temporal models which satisfy certain conditions.

Definition 7 (Models for BDE). A *BDE*-model M consists of a temporal frame $\mathcal{F}$ and a valuation V which satisfies the following conditions:

1. For all $s \in S$, if $Kp \in V(s)$ and sRt then $Kp \in V(t)$
2. For all $s \in S$, if $Kp, K(p \supset q) \in V(s)$ then $Kq \in V(t)$ for some $t \in S$ with sRt.
3. If $p \in TAUT$ then for all $s \in S$ there is a $t \in S$ such that sRt and $Kp \in V(t)$.

We can interpret $V(s)$ as the agent's explicit knowledge (or her information state) at time s. From the definition we see that if sRt then $V(s) \subseteq V(t)$, that is, the agent's knowledge always grows.

Definition 8. For any temporal model M the relation "the formula A is true at state s in M", in symbol $M, s \models A$, is defined recursively for each $s \in S$ as follows:

1. $M, s \models Kp$ iff $Kp \in V(s)$ for any atomic formula Kp
2. $M, s \models \neg A$ iff $M, s \not\models A$
3. $M, s \models A \supset B$ iff $M, s \models B$ or $M, s \not\models A$
4. $M, s \models \langle F \rangle A$ iff there is some t such that sRt and $M, t \models A$

A formula A is said to be BDE-satisfiable if and only if it is true at some state in some BDE-model. We say that A is true in M just in case A is true at all states in M. A is valid (with respect to BDE-models) iff it is true in all BDE-models.

Theorem 9 (Soundness and Completeness). *A formula A is a theorem of BDE if and only if A is valid.*

Proof. Soundness is straightforward: we have only to show that all BDE-axioms are valid and the application of the inference rules leads from valid premises to valid consequences. Completeness follows immediately from the next lemma. □

Lemma 10. *Every consistent set of formulae is satisfiable.*

Proof. Assume that the set X is consistent. We show that it has a model, i.e., that it is satisfiable. We define a model for X as follows. By the standard Lindenbaum argument, X is contained in a maximal consistent set. Let M be the following structure: $M = ((S, R), V)$ where

- S is the set of maximal consistent sets of BDE-formulae.
- sRt if and only if $\langle F \rangle A \in s$ whenever $A \in t$ (if and only if $A \in t$ whenever $[F]A \in s$).
- $V(s) = \{Kp : Kp \in s\}$ for all atomic formulae Kp.

We show that M is a BDE-model. First, we show that (S, R) is a transitive temporal frame. Assume that sRt and tRu, and let $A \in u$. From tRu we have $\langle F \rangle A \in t$, therefore $\langle F \rangle \langle F \rangle A \in s$, because sRt. By axiom (A3) we can infer $\langle F \rangle A \in s$, hence sRu, i.e., R is transitive.

Next, we prove that for all states s in the temporal model M and all formulae A, $M, s \models A$ if and only if $A \in s$. The base case (A is atomic) is trivial. If A is $\neg B$ then $M, s \models A$ iff $M, s \not\models B$ iff $B \notin s$ (by induction hypothesis) iff $\neg B \in s$ (by maximality of s,) i.e., $A \in s$. If A is another Boolean connection then the argument is similar. Let A be the formula $\langle F \rangle B$. Assume that $M, s \models A$. Then there is some t such that sRt and $M, t \models B$. By induction hypothesis, $B \in t$. By definition of M, $\langle F \rangle B \in s$. Conversely, assume that $A \in s$, i.e., $\langle F \rangle B \in s$. We show that there is some t such that sRt and $M, s \models t$. It suffices to show that the set $Y = \{B\} \cup \{C : [F]C \in s\}$ is consistent. Assume that Y is inconsistent. In this case there must be some $C_1, \ldots, C_n$ such that $[F]C_i \in s$ and $\neg(B \wedge C_1 \wedge \ldots \wedge C_n)$ is provable. It follows that $(C_1 \wedge \ldots \wedge C_n) \supset \neg B$ is provable. By the rule of necessation and the distribution axiom, $([F]C_1 \wedge \ldots \wedge [F]C_n) \supset [F]\neg B$ is provable, so this formula belongs to s. It follows that $[F]\neg B \in s$, contradicting the assumption that $\langle F \rangle B \in s$. Thus, X is consistent. Let t be any maximal consistent extension of X. Then sRt by definition of R, and $B \in t$. By induction hypothesis $M, t \models B$ and so $M, s \models A$.

It remains to show that the temporal model M is a BDE-model. Assume that $Kp \in V(s)$ and sRt. We show that $Kp \in V(t)$. By definition of V we have

$Kp \in s$. As $Kp \supset [F]Kp$ is an axiom it must belong to s, thus $[F]Kp \in s$. It follows that $M, s \models [F]Kp$, hence $M, t \models Kp$, so $Kp \in t$, therefore $Kp \in V(t)$.

Now let $Kp \in V(s)$ and $K(p \supset q) \in V(s)$. We show that $Kq \in V(t)$ for some t such that sRt. By maximality of s all theorems of BDE belong to s, thus $(Kp \wedge K(p \supset q) \supset \langle F \rangle Kq) \in s$. But $V(s) \subseteq s$, so $Kp \in s$ and $K(p \supset q) \in s$. It follows that $\langle F \rangle Kq \in s$, therefore $M, s \models \langle F \rangle Kq$, that is, there must be some t such that sRt and $M, t \models Kq$. From the latter we conclude $Kq \in t$, hence $Kq \in V(t)$.

Finally, we show that if $p \in TAUT$ then for all $s \in S$ there is a $t \in S$ such that sRt and $Kp \in V(t)$. But this is a simple consequence of the fact that $\langle F \rangle Kp \in s$, by axiom A6 and the maximality of s.

Thus, the canonical model is a BDE-model. If X is a consistent set then all formulae of X are satisfied at a state of the canonical model, which is a maximal consistent extension of X, i.e., X has a model. □

5 Conclusions

We have shown how to solve the logical omniscience problem of epistemic logic while preserving the intuition that the agents *are* logical beings. Our strategy consists in taking the dynamic aspect of knowledge into account. We have argued that the correct form of an axiom for epistemic should be: if the agent knows all premisses of a valid inference rule, and if she performs the right reasoning, then she will know the conclusion as well. This intuitive idea has been captured formally within an axiomatic system, and the calculus has been given an adequate semantics. Our strategy can do justice to the intuition that the agent is neither logically omniscient nor logically ignorant. She is non-omniscient, because her actual (or explicit) belief at a single time point need not be closed under any law. It is even possible that she does not believe any logical truth at some of her information states. On the other hand, she is non-ignorant, because she is capable of logical thinking. She can use her reasoning capacities to infer new information from what she already knows. If she performs the correct inferences and if she has enough time, then she might arrive at an ideal information state where all logical consequences of her current beliefs have been drawn. This ideal state can never been achieved if the underlying logic is rich enough, but this is another matter.

On the basis of our basis logic BDE we can develop further epistemic logics which capture other desirable properties of knowledge. It is not hard to write down, for example, axioms saying that the agent is (in principle) capable of introspection and to develop the corresponding model conditions. (In this case we have to extend our language to allow nested belief, of course.) A more interesting problem is to develop dynamic epistemic logics based on non-monotonic logic, where the agent can revise her knowledge when she finds out that her knowledge is inconsistent. We may expect to find interesting connections with two other, very active fields of AI research, viz. to non-monotonic reasoning and to the logic of belief revision. This seems to be a promising field of research and needs further investigations.

References

1. Chellas, B.: Modal Logic: An Introduction. Cambridge 1980
2. Cresswell, M. J.: Logics and Languages. London 1973
3. Eberle, R.: A Logic of Believing, Knowing and Inferring. Synthese **26** (1974) 356–382
4. Fagin, R., Halpern, J.: Belief, Awareness and Limited Reasoning. Artificial Intelligence **34** (1988) 39–76
5. Harel, D.: Dynamic Logic. In: Handbook of Philosophical Logic, ed. D. Gabbay and F. Guenthner, vol. II, 1984, 497–604
6. Hintikka, J.: Knowledge and Belief. New York 1962
7. Hintikka, J.: Impossible Possible Worlds Vindicated. Journal of Philosophical Logic **4** (1975) 475–484
8. Ho Ngoc Duc: Ein System der epistemischen Logik. In: Philosophie und Logik. Frege-Kolloquien Jena 1989/1991, ed. W. Stelzner, Berlin 1993, 205–214
9. Levesque, Hector: A Logic of Implicit and Explicit Belief. Proceedings AAAI-84, 198–202
10. Rantala, V: Impossible Worlds Semantics and Logical Omniscience. Acta Philosophica Fennica **35** (1982) 18–24
11. Steinacker, Peter: Superschwache Modalkalküle und einige epistemische Anwendungen. Dissertation. Leipzig, 1979
12. Stelzner, Werner: Epistemische Logik. Berlin 1984
13. Wuttich, Klaus: Glauben, Zweifel, Wissen. Eine logisch-philosophische Studie. Berlin 1991

On the Role of Splitting and Merging Past Cases for Generation of a New Solution

Carlos Bento Penousal Machado Ernesto Costa

Departamento de Engenharia Informática
Universidade de Coimbra
Vila Franca - Pinhal de Marrocos
3030 Coimbra - PORTUGAL
E-mail: bento@alma.uc.pt   ernesto@moebius.uc.pt

Abstract. This paper introduces RECIDE, an implementation of our approach to case-based reasoning. A qualitative and a quantitative metric are used for case retrieval. RECIDE has a library of successful and failure cases. Generation of new solutions is driven by splitting and merging operations on successful cases. Failure cases represent constraints on the application of splitting and merging operators. RECIDE$_{PSY}$, an application of RECIDE in the domain of psychology, is introduced in this paper. We present the results obtained with RECIDE$_{PSY}$ when splitting and merging operations are considered for generation of a new solution and compare them with the ones produced when solutions are constructed from a single case.

1 Introduction

A Case-Based Reasoning (CBR) System depends strongly on its methods for retrieval and reuse of previous experiences. This distinguishes these systems from those relying on the generalisation of solutions from first principles (abstract knowledge).

The combination of CBR and abstract knowledge-guided techniques led to the development of knowledge-based retrieval systems [5]. These systems use domain knowledge for construction of explanations of why a problem had a specific solution in the past. Explanations are necessary to judge the relevance of the facts describing a past problem [1, 7, 2]

In our work on CBR we are mainly concerned with two aspects. One has to do with the fact that the CBR approach is mostly used when a strong theory is not available and past experience is accessible. Lack of a strong theory means that, in general, case explanations are imperfect. We consider three kinds of imperfections and use them for retrieval [2]. A second aspect relates to the role of failure cases in CBR. Some current CBR systems make use of failure cases to represent and explain past unsuccessful experiences [3]. In our approach, failure cases represent *intra* and/or *inter*-case dependencies which were violated during case reuse.

This paper introduces results obtained with RECIDE$_{PSY}$ (<u>RE</u>asoning with <u>C</u>ases <u>I</u>mperfectly <u>D</u>escribed and <u>E</u>xplained in the domain of <u>PSY</u>chology), an expert system developed from RECIDE which is a CBR shell that implements our CBR approach.

2 Overview of RECIDE

RECIDE functional structure comprises: a case retriever, and a case reuser (Figure 1). The case retriever accesses successful cases in the case library. For case selection we use a qualitative and a quantitative metric.

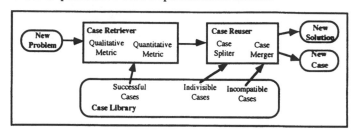

Fig. 1. Functional Structure of RECIDE.

The qualitative metric clusters past cases by the way in which they are potentially useful for creation of a new solution. The quantitative metric ranks cases in each cluster by its similarity with the new problem. The case reuser takes case clusters ordered by decreasing similarity and generates new cases that potentially have the same solution as the new problem. New cases are generated by applying splitting and merging operators, constrained by indivisible and incompatible cases. The need for splitting and merging operations on past cases follows from the fact that in general it does not exist a case in memory that comprises a complete solution for the new problem. In those situations catching the case pieces that have part of the solution for the new problem and merging them hopefully leads to a case comprising the new solution. This method of generating a solution shows to be particularly suitable for design tasks. The drawback of it is that, when a case is split, some *intra*-case constraints may be violated making this operation illegal. Also, in the merging step may be *inter*-case dependencies disable the synthesis of a new case from case pieces.

Within our approach *inter* and *intra*-case dependencies are represented in the form of indivisible and incompatible cases which are two kinds of failure cases. Their syntax is similar to the one for successful cases. Indivisible cases represent case pieces that when occurring in a case cannot be split. Incompatible cases represent case pieces that cannot occur in a new case by means of merging case parts from different cases. The semantic for failure cases is formally introduced in this section.

2.1 Case Library

The case library comprises: successful, indivisible, and incompatible cases. A successful case is represented by a triple $<P, S, R>$ (Figure 2) with P and

S, respectively, a set of facts representing past problem and solution, and R a set of rules given by the expert, representing a set of causal explanations. An explanation is a proof tree that links facts in the problem with a fact in the solution. We consider three kinds of imperfections in explanations: (1) incomplete set of explanations; (2) partial explanations; (3) broken explanations.

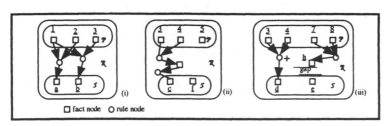

Fig. 2. A case with (i) a complete set of explanations; (ii) an incomplete set of explanations; (iii) a partial and broken explanation.

In a successful case with an incomplete set of explanations some solution facts are not explained and hence are not conclusion for any proof tree (e.g., Cases ii and iii in Figure 2. Facts $\underline{f}$ and $\underline{e}$ in these case solutions are not leaves of a proof tree). A partial explanation is one whose proof tree omits some branches. This means that one or more steps in the proof tree apply a rule for which the conditions are necessary but not sufficient. Rule nodes representing these rules are labelled by '+' (e.g., In Figure 2, case iii, the proof tree at the left). A broken explanation is one in which there is a gap between the proof tree and the case solution (e.g., In Figure 2, case iii, the proof tree at the right).

Failure cases (indivisible and incompatible), are represented by a triple $<Pf,$ $Sf, Rf>$ with Pf and Sf the sets of facts representing, respectively, the problem and solution components, and Rf a set of rules. The semantic for these cases is different from the one defined for successful cases and is related to the splitting and merging operations performed during case reuse. The semantic for indivisible cases is (P, S, and R represent, respectively, the components of the case candidate for splitting):

i) If $Pf \neq \emptyset$, $Sf = \emptyset$, $Rf = \emptyset$ and $Pf \subseteq P$ then the subset Pf in P cannot be split.
ii) If $Pf = \emptyset$, $Sf \neq \emptyset$, $Rf = \emptyset$, and $Sf \subseteq S$ then the subset Sf in S cannot be split.
iii) If $Pf = \emptyset$, $Sf = \emptyset$, $Rf \neq \emptyset$, and $Rf \subseteq R$ then the subset Rf in R cannot be split.
iv) If $Pf \neq \emptyset$, $Sf \neq \emptyset$, $Rf \neq \emptyset$, and $Pf \subseteq P \wedge Sf \subseteq S \wedge Rf \subseteq R$ then subsets Pf, Sf, and Rf in P, S, and R have to remain in the same past case piece after the splitting process.
v) If $Pf \neq \emptyset$, $Sf \neq \emptyset$, $Rf = \emptyset$, and $Pf \subseteq P \wedge Sf \subseteq S$ then the subsets Pf and Sf in P and S have to remain in the same past case piece after the splitting process.
vi) If $Pf = \emptyset$, $Sf \neq \emptyset$, $Rf \neq \emptyset$, and $Sf \subseteq S \wedge Rf \subseteq R$ then the subsets Sf and Rf in S and R have to remain in the same past case piece after the splitting process.

vii) If $Pf \neq \emptyset$, $Sf = \emptyset$, $Rf \neq \emptyset$, and $Pf \subseteq P \wedge Rf \subseteq R$ then the subsets Pf and Rf in P and R have to remain in the same past case piece after the splitting process.

Indivisible cases of types i, ii, and iii constrain the splitting of facts in a problem or solution, or in a set of rules. Indivisible cases of type iv through vii constrain splitting between parts of the problem, solution, or set of rules.

Incompatible cases represent merging constraints on cases in memory. The semantic for incompatible cases is (P, S, and R are the components of the new case created by merging two or more cases or case pieces):

i) If $Pf \neq \emptyset$, $Sf = \emptyset$, and $Rf = \emptyset$ then Pf cannot occur in P as a results of merging.

ii) If $Pf = \emptyset$, $Sf \neq \emptyset$, and $Rf = \emptyset$ then Sf cannot occur in S as a results of merging.

iii) If $Pf = \emptyset$, $Sf = \emptyset$, and $Rf \neq \emptyset$ then Rf cannot occur in R as a results of merging.

iv) If $Pf \neq \emptyset$, $Sf \neq \emptyset$, $Rf \neq \emptyset$ and $Pf \subseteq P \wedge Sf \subseteq S \wedge Rf \subseteq R$ then Pf, Sf, and Rf cannot occur all together in the new case as a result of merging.

v) If $Pf \neq \emptyset$, $Sf \neq \emptyset$, $Rf = \emptyset$ and $Pf \subseteq P \wedge Sf \subseteq S$ then Pf and Sf cannot occur all together in the new case as a result of merging.

vi) If $Pf = \emptyset$, $Sf \neq \emptyset$, $Rf \neq \emptyset$ and $Sf \subseteq S \wedge Rf \subseteq R$ then Sf and Rf cannot occur all together in the new case as a result of merging.

vii) If $Pf \neq \emptyset$, $Sf = \emptyset$, $Rf \neq \emptyset$ and $Pf \subseteq P \wedge Rf \subseteq R$ then Pf and Rf cannot occur all together in the new case as a result of merging.

As with indivisible cases, incompatible ones of type i, ii, and iii relate to merging constraints at the fact level. Remaining case types report to constraints at the case component level.

2.2   Case Retrieval

Case retrieval is performed on a flat memory of successful cases. The retrieval process involves two steps:

i) Clustering of potentially useful past cases (qualitative metric).
ii) Ranking of case clusters (quantitative metric).

In the first step five clusters of past cases are created. Let S be the set of facts representing the solution for a case in memory and S' the set of facts representing the solution for a new problem. Each cluster comprises the following cases (in the examples that follow it is assumed the case library is composed by cases in Figure 2, and represented again in Figure 3):

CLUSTER_1 - Cases with $S = S'$.
  e.g. If the new problem is described by the set of facts $\{\underline{1}, \underline{2}, \underline{3}\}$, CLUSTER_1 will be composed of case i (see Figure 2). Case i is completely explained, that is,

facts $\{\underline{1}, \underline{2}, \underline{3}\}$ describing case problem and the new problem are necessary and sufficient for the solution $S = \{\underline{a}, \underline{b}\}$, therefore the new problem solution is $S' = S = \{\underline{a}, \underline{b}\}$.

CLUSTER_2 - Cases possibly with $S = S'$.

e.g. For a new problem described by the set $\{\underline{3}, \underline{4}, \underline{5}\}$, CLUSTER_2 will be composed of case ii. As the new problem is the same as the one described in case ii it is possible that case and new problem solutions are also similar. The reason why we are not certain about this is that case ii is not completely explained. Therefore we do not know if fact $\underline{5}$ is causally linked with fact $\underline{f}$ in the solution. This means the problem that has the solution $S = \{\underline{c}, \underline{f}\}$ may be different from the one represented in case ii provided it contains facts $\underline{3}$ and $\underline{4}$.

CLUSTER_3 - Cases possibly with $S \supset S'$.

e.g. Considering a new problem $\{\underline{1}, \underline{2}\}$, case i is the one in CLUSTER_3. As $\underline{1}$ and $\underline{2}$ are the causal premises for fact $\underline{a}$ in this case solution, it is possible that the new problem solution is $\{\underline{a}\} = S' \subset S$. The uncertainty about this is due to unknown *intra*-case dependencies which may be violated by splitting case i.

CLUSTER_4 - Cases possibly with $S \subset S'$.

e.g. With a new problem $\{\underline{1}, \underline{2}, \underline{3}, \underline{4}, \underline{5}\}$, cases i and ii are the ones in CLUSTER_4. As case i has the solution $S = \{\underline{a}, \underline{b}\}$ for problem $\{\underline{1}, \underline{2}, \underline{3}\}$ and case ii solution $\{\underline{c}, \underline{f}\}$ is supposed to be the one for problem $\{\underline{3}, \underline{4}, \underline{5}\}$ then it is possible that $\{\underline{a}, \underline{b}\} = S_i \subset S'$ and $\{\underline{c}, \underline{f}\} = S_{ii} \subset S'$, with S_i and S_{ii}, respectively, the solutions for cases i and ii. We are not certain about this as we do not know the *inter* and *intra*-case dependencies between and within cases i and ii.

CLUSTER_5 - Cases possibly with $S \cap S' \neq \emptyset$.

e.g. Assuming the new problem is $\{\underline{1}, \underline{3}, \underline{6}, \underline{9}\}$, CLUSTER_5 is composed by case i. As $\underline{1}$ and $\underline{3}$ are necessary and sufficient for $\underline{b}$ in the context of case i then $S_i \cap S' = \{\underline{b}\}$. The uncertainty on this is related to possibly unknown *intra* and *inter*-case dependencies.

Clusters above are not mutually exclusive. Considering, for instance, a new problem $\{\underline{3}, \underline{4}, \underline{5}\}$ case ii will belong to CLUSTER_2, as explained above, but it will also belong to CLUSTER_5 as it is possible that fact $\underline{5}$ in case ii is not the one responsible for fact $\underline{f}$ in the solution. If this happens then as $\underline{3}$ and $\underline{4}$ are necessary and sufficient for $\underline{c}$ in the context of case ii then $S_i \cap S' = \{\underline{c}\}$, with the constraint that no *intra* and *inter*-case dependencies are violated.

Cases within each cluster are ranked by an explanation-based similarity metric [2]. It assigns a distinct relevance to each fact in a case problem that matches a fact in the new problem, depending on the fact being premise of a complete, partial, broken, or no explanation at all. Clusters are sorted by decreasing similarity values.

Clustering of cases for retrieval embodies two main properties: (1) case clustering organises memory cases accordingly to their kind of potential usefulness for the new problem solution; and (2) it provides information on the most suitable method for creation of a new case. In the next subsection we describe how the reuse unit deals with these clusters.

2.3 Case Reuse

RECIDE reuse unit works with successful cases in terms of case pieces. Four types of pieces are considered (Figure 3): strong, weak, undetermined, and unexplained.

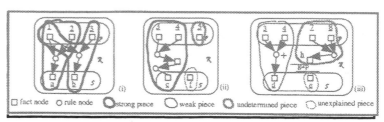

Fig. 3. Types of case pieces.

A strong piece comprises a complete explanation, the facts that are premises of it, and the fact that is its conclusion (e.g. In Figure 3, the pieces in case i). A partial explanation, its premises and its conclusion embody a weak piece (e.g. In Figure 3, case iii, the case piece at its left). A broken explanation and its premises or any single fact that is not premise of an explanation form an undetermined piece (e.g. In Figure 3, case ii, the piece composed by the single fact 5 and the piece in case iii at top right). Any fact in a case solution that is not conclusion of an explanation determines an unexplained piece (e.g. In Figure 3. single facts f and e in cases ii and iii are unexplained pieces). Case splitting is performed at the case piece level.

As described in section 2.2, after giving the system a new problem, successful cases in memory are clustered accordingly to their usefulness for the generation of a new solution. The reuse unit gets those clusters and performs the following steps:

1) generation of new cases;
2) selection of the new case most promising for the solution of the new problem;
3) validation of the solution provided by the selected case.

Each new case is created by splitting and merging operations on cases from a cluster. Two heuristics are applied for selection of the new case most likely to have the same solution as the new problem:

H1: Prefer new cases from clusters with lower index (e.g. CLUSTER_1 over CLUSTER_2).
H2: Prefer new cases with higher similarity values.

Heuristic 1, favours cases from those clusters with lower indexes. The reason to choose CLUSTER_1 is obvious. It is the only cluster that, if not empty, has a case known to have the correct solution. For the other clusters, preferring those with lower index means to choose new cases that required fewer splitting and merging operations for its generation. The more splitting and merging operations are performed, the more likely it is that unknown *intra* and/or *inter*-case dependencies are disregarded.

Heuristic 2 assumes cases with a problem description closer to the new problem description (matching more facts in the new problem, weighted the fact of being premise of a complete, partial, or interrupted explanation) have a higher chance of comprising the same solution as the new problem.

The next step comprises validation of the solution provided by the selected new case. In the validation step, RECIDE searches for a new case for which the splitting and merging operations involved in its construction do not violate the constraints imposed by failure cases in memory. Then it outputs the new case solution and the cases in the origin of it. If the user accepts the solution the validation process is finished.

If the new solution is not accepted, the user is encouraged to give the *intra* and *inter*-case dependencies in the origin of the wrong solution. Those descriptions are recorded as indivisible and/or incompatible cases. With the memory of indivisible and incompatible cases updated in this way the system starts another validation cycle selecting a new case that does not conflict with the updated library of failure cases.

If the user cannot explain why the new solution is wrong in terms of indivisible and incompatible cases then she/he is asked to give the solution for the new problem together with a causal justification. This input is recorded as a new successful case and the process is completed.

3 An Application in the Domain of Psychology

In this section we present an application of RECIDE in the domain of psychology. Results obtained with this application are also described in this section.

3.1 The Domain

$RECIDE_{PSY}$ is an advising system for scholar underachievers. It suggests a new program for improvement of scholar performance supported on previous successful experiences.

A past experience comprises a context (past problem) in which a set of intervention strategies (past solution) was applied successfully. Figure 4 represents a case in the domain as it is output by $RECIDE_{PSY}$[1]. A '->' symbol in the explanations represents a complete explanation and a '->+' a partial explanation. This case describes a male client between twelve and fourteen years old, with two siblings, both younger and with a conflicting relation with relatives. The level of education achieved is six years of basic education and he is unfavourably

---

[1] The taxonomy introduced for context and intervention strategies is only relevant at the user's level. For matching a case with a new problem, $RECIDE_{PSY}$ only considers ground facts organised in a flat structure.

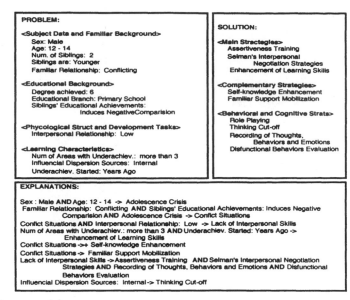

Fig. 4. A successful case.

compared with his siblings due to their scholar achievements. Interpersonal relationship is low. His grades comprise more than three unsuccessful disciplines, shows internal sources of dispersion and has a long history of underachievement.

The main intervention strategies being applied are assertiveness training, Selman's interpersonal negotiation strategies, and enhancement of learning skills. The complementary strategies are self-knowledge enhancement and familiar support mobilisation. The behavioural and cognitive intervention strategies are role playing, thinking cut-off, recording of thoughts, behaviours and emotions, and dysfunctional behaviours evaluation.

The explanations provided by the experts for this intervention program are: (1) being a male client aged between twelve and fourteen are causing an adolescence crisis, (2) a conflicting familiar relationship marked by negative comparison, associated with the adolescence crisis characterise a conflict situation, (3) the conflicting situation, under development and his low level of interpersonal relationship describe his lack of interpersonal skills, (4) the number of underachievement areas being higher than three and the duration of this problem (starting years ago) cause the need for enhancement of learning skills, (5) the conflicting situation is a partial cause (the only partial explanation step in this case) for using self-knowledge enhancement, (6) the conflict situation is the cause for mobilisation of familiar support, (7) the lack of interpersonal skills is the motive for applying assertiveness training, Selmans interpersonal negotiation strategies, recording of thoughts, behaviours and emotions, and evaluation of dysfunctional behaviours, and (8) presence of internal sources of dispersion is the cause for using thinking cut-off.

In this task indivisible cases are of types i and ii (see subsection 2.1.). Incompatible cases are of types ii, iii, and v. The set of cases given by the experts comprises 47 successful cases and 65 failure cases (43 indivisible and 22 incompatible).

3.2 Experimental Results

Two kinds of tests (labelled TEST #1 and #2) were performed. In TEST #1 each iteration comprises input of the problem component of a case not in memory, generation of new cases in the way described in section 2.3, selection of the potentially best new case, output of its solution, and validation by the user. TEST #2 is like #1 with the difference that a new case is not created by splitting and merging operations but by selecting from memory the case most similar to the new situation. Then its solution is given as the solution for the new problem.

The parameters we consider in judging the quality of a proposed solution are: (1) rate of facts belonging to the generated solution appearing in the correct solution per total number of facts in the correct solution; (2) rate of facts in the generated solution that not belong to the correct solution per total number of facts in the correct solution; (3) difference between the first and second ratios.

The set of successful cases used in these tests was randomly ordered and this ordering was maintained along all the experiments.

Results showing the evolution of these parameters along a working session are presented in Figures 5 through 7.

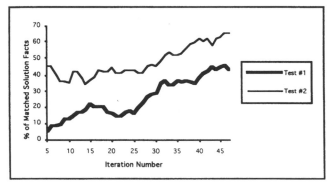

Fig. 5. Percentage of correct facts in the proposed solution relative to the total number of facts in the problem solution.

The number of facts correctly included in the new solution is higher in TEST #2 than in TEST #1 along the 47 iterations (see Figure 5), but it is also TEST #2 that shows the highest rate of facts wrongly included in the new solution (see Figure 6). In particular, till the 12th iteration, solutions produced by TEST #2 involve a high number of facts wrongly included in the generated solution. Figure 7 shows a measure of global quality of solutions as it takes into account the facts correctly and wrongly included in it. It is evident from this figure that till the 25th iteration, generation of a new solution by splitting and merging past

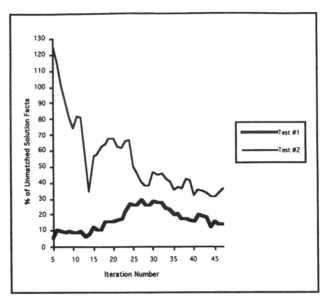

Fig. 6. Percentage of wrong facts in the proposed solution relative to the total number of facts in the problem solution.

cases produces better results than when these operations are disabled. After the 25th iteration using the best case in memory as the solution of a new problem or creating a new case by splitting and merging past cases does not make a difference.

3.3 Analysis of the Experimental Results

Considerations on the experimental results relate, at first to the facts (intervention strategies) correctly proposed by the system for a solution (treatment).

In contrast with previous expectations, the system performs better in terms of this parameter when only the best case in memory is retrieved then when a new one is created from previous cases. Our explanation for this is that when a single case is selected it tends to suggest a huge set of intervention strategies, many of them being correct (see Figure 5), but also with many wrong ones (see Figure 6). When a new case is generated by splitting and merging previous cases, the system leans to be more conservative in the sense that it only chooses case pieces comprising a causal relation between problem and solution pieces. In this way, when splitting and merging takes place for generation of a new solution the rate of facts wrongly included in the solution keeps low along the 47 iterations, never being higher than 30 % of the number of facts in the correct solution. A different result is obtained when a single case is retrieved for generation of a new solution. In this mode the rate of facts wrongly considered is high till the 25th iteration and very high till the 12th iteration.

When the number of correct and wrong facts is weighted for judgement of the solution quality (see Figure 7), it is clear that till the 25th iteration it is

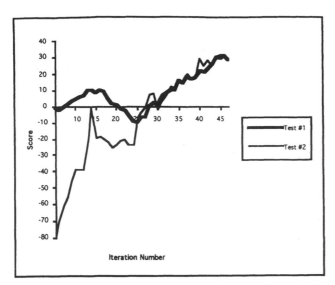

Fig. 7. Difference between percentage of correct and wrong facts in the proposed solution.

worth applying splitting a merging for generation of a new solution. After the 25th iteration no improvement is obtained with this method.

4 Final Remarks

Our last comments concern to the way RECIDE solves and learns and to the role of splitting and merging operations in the generation of new solution.

With respect to problem solving, the retrieval method used by RECIDE takes into consideration two important aspects - usefulness and similarity - assigning a higher importance to usefulness. As pointed out by other authors [4, 6] we believe search driven by usefulness plays a main role in case retrieval. Case clustering. as performed within our approach, relates to the role cases can play in the construction of a new one. Similarity is considered for case ranking within clusters.

Failure cases as they are defined in our framework constrain the generation of new cases by *intra* and *inter*-case dependencies. Many times, the reason why cases created by splitting operations do not have the correct solution roots in *intra*-case dependencies that were not perceived *a priori*. A similar problem takes place when case pieces are merged due to *inter*-case dependencies. Indivisible and incompatible cases are a powerful way to represent those dependencies.

An aspect that needs to be taken into consideration is that if the combination strategies used for case generation are not maintained under control the process leads to combinatory explosion. This is prevented by limiting combination of case pieces to the most promising cases within each cluster.

In RECIDE, the learning process comprises interactive acquisition of failure and successful cases. In general the acquisition *a priori* of *intra* and *inter*-case dependencies is not feasible. The problem-solving process provides a context of failure in which the analysis of the cases in the origin of a wrong solution is a way to detect violated dependencies that were the cause for the wrong solution. Incompatible cases also make possible to represent that a solution proposed by the system is incompatible with the new problem given to the system.

Another remark relates to the role of splitting and merging operators. It is clear that results are improved when this method is applied. Although in this domain the improvements which are obtained are not as important as we would expect. We believe this is related to the way cases are selected for splitting and merging. In this approach we select the most similar cases for splitting and merging. Intuitively, it is better to select cases which are complementar in terms of usefulness for splitting and merging than those which are most similar to the new situation. At the moment we are studding different strategies for selection of cases for splitting and merging.

A last comment has to do with the fact that these results were obtained for a specific domain. It is expected that in different domains a slightly different behaviour is detected.

5 Acknowledgements

We would like to thank Paula Vieira and Eduarda Góis who provided the case library. Fundação Luso-Americana para o Desenvolvimento and Fundação Calouste Gulbenkian financially supported our contacts with other groups working on CBR in the USA.

References

1. Barletta, R., and Mark, W., Explanation-Based Indexing of Cases, in Proceedings of a Case-Based Reasoning Workshop, Morgan-Kaufmann, 1989.
2. Bento, C., and Costa, E., A Similarity Metric for Retrieval of Cases Imperfectly Explained, in Wess, S.; Althoff, K.-D.; and Richter, M. M., eds., Topics in Case-Based Reasoning - Selected Papers from the First European Workshop on Case-Based Reasoning, Springer Verlag, Berlin: Germany, 1994a.
3. Hammond, K., CHEF: A Model of Case-Based Planning, in Proceedings of AAAI-86, Cambridge, MA: AAAI Press / MIT Press, 1986.
4. Kolodner, J., Judging Which is the Best Case for a Case-Based Reasoner, in Proceedings of a Case-Based Reasoning Workshop, Morgan-Kaufmann, 1989.
5. Koton, P., Using Experience in Learning and Problem Solving, Massachusets Institute of Technology, Laboratory of Computer Science (Ph D diss., October 1988). MIT/LCS/TR-441, 1989.
6. Smyth, B., and Keane, M., Retrieving Adaptable Cases: The Role of Adaptation Knowledge in Case Retrieval, in Wess, S.; Althoff, K.-D.; and Richter, M. M.. eds., Topics in Case-Based Reasoning - Selected Papers from the First European Workshop on Case-Based Reasoning. Springer Verlag, Berlin: Germany, 1994.
7. Veloso, M., Learning by Analogical Reasoning in General Problem Solving. Ph D Thesis. School of Computer Science, Carnegie Mellon University, Pittsburgh. PA. 1992.

Theorem Proving by Analogy – A Compelling Example*

Erica Melis

University of Edinburgh**, Department of AI, 80 South Bridge, Edinburgh EH1 1HN,
Scotland

Abstract. This paper shows how a new approach to theorem proving
by analogy is applicable to *real maths* problems. This approach works
at the level of proof-plans and employs reformulation that goes beyond
symbol mapping. The Heine-Borel theorem is a widely known result in
mathematics. It is usually stated in R^1 and similar versions are also true
in R^2, in topology, and metric spaces. Its analogical transfer was proposed
as a challenge example and could not be solved by previous approaches
to theorem proving by analogy. We use a proof-plan of the Heine-Borel
theorem in R^1 as a guide in automatically producing a proof-plan of the
Heine-Borel theorem in R^2 by analogy-driven proof-plan construction.

1 Introduction

Theorem proving by analogy has been clearly recognized as a powerful heuristic
in mathematical problem solving [16, 18]. In automated and interactive theorem
proving, analogy is particularly useful in situations where much search is necessary, e.g., where many proof assumptions or long proof paths are involved.
Analogy in automated theorem proving is, however, still a challenging problem
[1, 20].

Previous approaches to theorem proving by analogy had problems with real,
complex maths examples because they have been dominated by the idea of mapping symbols of the source theorem to symbols of the target theorem and employing an extended symbol map for transferring single calculus level proof steps
of the source proof[3]. Empirical investigations [12], however, have provided evidence that this idea does not appropriately cover the analogies drawn by mathematicians, not even all the analogies in the textbook [5].

In [14] we developed a new approach to theorem proving by analogy and
explained why the *plan* level is an appropriate one for the analogical transfer.
As shown in [11] this method can cope with the analogies in the mentioned textbook. In order to prove this approach to be successful, we now show that, unlike

---

* This work was supported in part by the HC&M grant CHBICT930806 and by a
research grant of the Deutsche Forschungsgemeinschaft.
** On leave from University Saarbrücken, Germany
[3] Though Bledsoe transfers larger steps calling an automated prover but again uses
symbol mapping.

other approaches, it is even able to deal with more complicated maths theorems that are considered challenge. Our method can handle a non-trivial Heine-Borel theorem, proposed in [2] as a challenging example for theorem proving by analogy. This example could not be solved by previous approaches to analogy in theorem proving.

The paper is organized as follows: First the new approach is presented. Then we introduce the challenge example and describe its analogy-driven proof-plan construction step by step.

2 The Approach

Our method transfers proof-plans analogically and incorporates the reformulation of problems and operators that may include abstraction and other reformulations different from symbol mapping. For employing the full range of reformulations, the operator representation has to be mainly declarative. Therefore we describe the operators designed for Ω-MKRP [6]. We briefly review how the specific operators and plans are defined, introduce reformulation, and discuss the analogy procedure.

2.1 Preliminaries

Proof planning operators have been introduced by Bundy [3]. Our planning operators, called *methods*, are frame-like structures defined in [7] with pre- and postconditions just as the common planning operators. More specifically, methods M have the following slots: parameter, preconditions (pre(M)), postcondition (post(M)), constraints, proof schema and procedure. pre(M) is a set of sequents[4] from which the application of the method derives post(M) which is a set of sequents as well. pre(M) and post(M) both are needed for planning.

The constraints are formulated in a meta-language and serve to restrict the search during planning, e.g., restrictions of pre(M), post(M), or of the parameters. The standard program in the slot procedure executes the application of the proof schema. The proof schema is a declarative schematic representation of proofs in the object logic, relying on the Natural Deduction (ND) calculus and on invoking automated theorem provers such as OTTER [10]. The proof schema lines contain a label, a sequent, and a line-justification. The line-justification consists of the name of an ND-rule, the name of a prover, or LEMMA in case, the sequent is in pre(M). Additionally it may include supporting lines. For instance,

3. $\Delta \vdash F$ (IP;2)

describes that $\Delta \vdash F$ is derived from the sequent in line 2 of the proof schema by the ND-rule IP[5]. An example of a method is

---

[4] *Sequents* $\mathsf{P} = (\Delta \vdash F)$, are pairs of a set Δ of formulas and a formula F in an object language that is extended by meta-variables for functions, relations, formulas, sets of formulas, and terms.

[5] The IP rule is a combination of the ND-rules $\neg I$ and $\neg E$ that has been proved to be correct.

method: **Indirect Proof**		
parameter	F: formula, Δ: set of formulas	
preconditions	$(\Delta \cup \{\neg F\} \vdash \bot)$	
postcondition	$(\Delta \vdash F)$	
constraints		
proof schema	1. $\neg F$ $\vdash$ $\neg F$ 2. $\Delta, \neg F$ $\vdash$ $\bot$ 3. Δ $\vdash$ F	(HYP) (LEMMA) (IP;2)
procedure	standard schema-interpreter	

Our methods mainly differ from those in [3] in that the tactic slot is replaced by a declarative proof schema *and* a procedure interpreting this schema[6]. The intention behind this difference is to enable reformulations of methods.

A method is *verifiable* if, given pre(M), then the method yields a correct proof of post(M) in case the constraints are satisfied. For verifying a line with an OTTER-call, a time limit is set for OTTER to prove the sequent.

Since maths proofs are constructed top down and bottom up, we consider backward *and* forward search in proof planning and define plan operators to be an f-method or a b-method respectively. f-methods work with their preconditions as input and postcondition as output; b-methods work vice versa. For instance, the method corresponding to the ND-rule $\wedge$-elimination is a typical f-method, whereas the method $\wedge$-introduction is a typical b-method. f- and b-methods will be treated differently by the analogy procedure.

Goals and assumptions are sequents, and a *proof-plan* is a forest the trees of which consist of sequent nodes and method nodes that satisfy the "link condition": A method node M follows a sequent node **g** and precedes the sequent nodes $\mathbf{g}_1, \ldots, \mathbf{g}_n$ if

$\mathbf{g} \in \sigma(\text{post}(M))$ and $\sigma(\text{pre}(M)) = \{\mathbf{g}_1, \ldots, \mathbf{g}_n\}$ for a substitution σ of parameters.

Proof planning starts with a goal **g** and assumptions $(\emptyset \vdash F_i)$, where F_i are proof-assumptions, axioms, definitions, or lemmata. The proof planning proceeds by inserting methods and sequents: A b-method follows a goal and yields new (sub)goals as its successors. An f-method precedes assumptions and yields a new preceding assumption. Planning aims at reducing the gap between leaf goals and assumptions. Leaf goals that are not equal to an assumption are called *open goals*. As soon as a goal $\mathbf{g}_i$ equals an assumption, the two nodes collapse. Then $\mathbf{g}_i$ is no longer an open goal but *satisfied*. The planning terminates if there are no open goals.

The source proof-plans are trees with the source problem at the root, with no open goals, and with verifiable methods. For the analogy procedure we use *linearized* proof-plans ordered by the sequence in which the nodes have been

---

[6] Besides, the slots are renamed, e.g., our preconditions are named input there.

added to the plan. As in [19] justification structures, used to encode justifications for the decision made, annotate the plan nodes. These *justifications* capture the subgoaling structure of a plan and point to reasons for the choice, such as application conditions of a method, user-given guidance, or pre-programmed control knowledge. The verifiability of a method is one of the justifications.

Reformulations are mappings ρ of a proof-plan to a proof-plan which usually but not necessarily preserve the verifiability of methods in the plan. They encode mathematical heuristics on how a proof-plan changes dependent on certain changes of the problem to be proved. Reformulations may insert subplans or replace methods and may change methods, sequents, and justifications of plan nodes. Reformulations are carried out by meta-methods which are represented by data structures with the slots parameters, application-condition, effect, program. The purpose of the slots application-condition, effect is to meta-plan a sequence of reformulations. program executes the reformulation dependent on parameters.

The reformulation Add-Arguments is applied in the example below. It is applicable if a function f is to be mapped to a function f', where arguments x_i (or tuples of arguments) of f are mapped to k_i arguments (or tuples of arguments) x_{ij} of f'; for instance, if the function $[-,-]$ mapping a pair of real numbers x, y to a real interval $[x, y]$ is mapped to a function $[-,-,-,-]$ with two pairs $(x, y), (z, w)$ of real numbers as arguments that yields an interval $[x, y, z, w]$ in R^2. The program of Add-Arguments replaces the function f by f' with duplicated arguments in goals, assumptions, justifications, and methods. It yields additional related changes in the proof schema of effected methods such as replacing certain subformulas by conjunctions and duplicating certain lines of the proof schema which may also cause the duplication of related preconditions of the method (see [13] for more details). If a method's precondition P became duplicated, then Add-Arguments modifies the structure of the proof-plan by duplicating the subplan that yields the goal/assumption P in the original proof-plan.

For example, for the functions $[-,-]$ and $[-,-,-,-]$ to be mapped and $(x, y), (z, w)$ corresponding to (x, y) a proof-schema line
$\emptyset \vdash a \in R \wedge b \in R \rightarrow clsdint([a, b])$ would be changed to the line
$\emptyset \vdash a \in R \wedge b \in R \wedge c \in R \wedge d \in R \rightarrow clsdint([a, b, c, d])$ and

$\emptyset \vdash \forall x \forall y \forall z \forall w (lf([x, y, z, w]) = x \wedge rt([x, y, z, w]) = y)$ is replaced by
$\emptyset \vdash \forall x \forall y \forall z \forall w (lf([x, y, z, w]) = x \wedge lf'([x, y, z, w]) = z \wedge rt([x, y, z, w]) = y \wedge$
$rt'([x, y, z, w]) = w)$

Even so it might seem that Add-Arguments was designed exactly for the Heine-Borel example or that this particular example was chosen according to the reformulation, this is *not* the case. Add-Arguments proved to be a fairly frequent and general reformulation that has been used in several examples and was documented in [11, 7]. Moreover, the particular Heine-Borel example was chosen independently in [2].

2.2 Analogy-Driven Proof-Plan Construction

The general idea of analogy-driven proof-plan construction is to use the linearized source proof-plan as a guide for constructing an analogous target proof-plan, to reformulate the source plan, and to transfer methods, goals, and assumptions of a reformulated source proof-plan to the target proof-plan. The analogy-driven proof-plan construction is a derivational analogy [4, 19], which has not been used for theorem proving before, extended by reformulation and bidirectional planning.

During the analogical transfer it is checked whether the justifications from the source node hold for the corresponding node in the target, e.g. whether the application conditions hold in the target. Checking the justifications makes it possible to consider information that is not available in the source and target problems, but relevant to the proof. This idea goes back to Carbonell's derivational analogy [4], where a decision in the target is made correspondingly to the decision in the source only if the justifications of the decision hold in the target as well. Thereby the requirement of a semantic justification of analogical reasoning [17] can be met.

Our analogy employs reformulation that aims at matching a source goal with a target goal or as many preconditions of a source f-method with target assumptions respectively and that yield corresponding changes of the proof-plan. Table 1 shows the top-level procedure of the analogy-driven proof-plan construction. Given a linearized source proof-plan, target assumptions, and a target goal (the first open goal), the output of the procedure is a target proof-plan.

Step 4 is relevant for a planner with backward search only whereas step 5 and 6 apply to the treatment of forward planning. The two branches differ mainly in that ρ aims at matching a source goal to one target goal, whereas ρ' aims at matching as many source assumptions as possible to target assumptions. $|missing(\rho'M)| < m$[7] means that less than m preconditions of the currently treated reformulated f-method M do not match a target assumption. The sequents of $missing(\rho'M)$ become new open goals if ρ' is an acceptable reformulation. m is a procedure parameter and indicates the confidence in an analogical transfer despite mising target lemmata.

According to the order of the source plan the first goal, usually the source problem P_S, is chosen. If P_S can be reformulated by a ρ such that it matches the target problem P_T, then ρ will be applied to the (current) source plan and the method M with $post(M) = \rho P_S$ is a candidate for the transfer to the target plan. If the original justifications hold for the M in the target, then M is transferred and the open goals are updated by removing $post(M)$ and introducing all sequents from $pre(M)$ as open goals. The procedure is repeated, first testing termination reasons.

If the justifications do not hold for M in the target, then different actions can be taken dependent on the kind of violated justification. For instance, a

---

[7] For *missing(M)* := set of preconditions of M that do not match a current target assumption.

---

input: linearized source plan, (open) target goal

output: (linearized) target plan

1. **while** there are open target goals **do**
2. **if** source plan is exhausted, **then** base-level plan for the open goals.
3. Get next sequent P from source plan. The sequent is either an assumption or a goal. **if** P is an assumption, **then** go to 5.
4. **if** there is a reformulation ρ, such that ρP matches an open target goal g_T for which the justifications hold, **then**
   - reformulate source plan by ρ and link g_T to source plan.
   - Select from the reformulated source the relevant b-method M.
   - Check M's justifications.
   - **if** justification does not hold, **then** choose suitable action:
     - Advance the source if M is not necessary.
     - Try to establish the justifications by other means.
     - Or base-level plan.
5. Select from the reformulated source the relevant f-method M.
6. **if** there is a reformulation ρ' left such that $|missing(\rho'M)| < m$ and that justifications hold for the matched target assumptions **then**
   - reformulate source plan by (best) ρ' and link the matched target assumptions to source plan.
   - Check M's justifications.
   - **if** justification does not hold, **then** choose suitable action as above.

Table 1. Outline of the analogy-driven proof-plan construction

reformulated method might not be verifiable because reformulations do not necessarily preserve verifiability. If the verifiability-justification does not hold for M, then try to *modify* M to a verifiable method M'. One possible modification technique decomposes M such that a verifiable submethod M' results with post(M)= post(M') and M' replaces M. This technique creates a new open goal as well. If a precondition of M does not hold in the target, then it can be made an open goal that has to be proved by other means (e.g., base-level planning).

Another action is taken if the current goal is satisfied in the target already. Then M is superfluous in the target and can be skipped. The last option is to replace M by another method M', and this requires base-level planning for M'.

When all methods of the source plan have been visited, then the remaining open goals have to be proved (by base-level planning). This situation is similar to human theorem proving by analogy that usually leaves new details to prove.

The argument that every new example would need a new reformulation did not prove to be true during experiments with the analogy procedure. In fact, few normalizing and abstracting reformulations were used and most often **Symbol-Mapping**, **Term-Mapping**, and **Add-Arguments** were used (see [11, 15]). This claim needs, however, further experience and evaluation.

3 The Heine-Borel Example

Theorem 1 Heine-Borel-1 (HB1). *If a closed interval $[a, b]$ of R^1 is covered by a family G of open sets (in R^1), then there is a finite subfamily H of G which covers $[a, b]$.*[8]

Formalized: $\{a \in R \land b \in R \land a \leq b, \forall B(B \in G \rightarrow open(B)), [a, b] \subset \cup G\}$
$\vdash \exists H(H \subseteq G \land finite(H) \land [a, b] \subset \cup H)$

Theorem 2 Heine-Borel-2 (HB2). *If a closed rectangle $[a, b, c, d]$ of R^2 is covered by a family G of open sets (in R^2), then there is a finite subfamily H of G which covers $[a, b, c, d]$.*

Formalized: $\{a \in R \land b \in R \land c \in R \land d \in R \land a \leq b \land c \leq d, \forall B(B \in G \rightarrow open(B)), [a, b, c, d] \subset \cup G\} \vdash \exists H(H \subseteq G \land finite(H) \land [a, b, c, d] \subset \cup H)$.

Figure 1 shows the complex proof-plan for HB1 which, in fact, yields a proof of HB1 when executed.

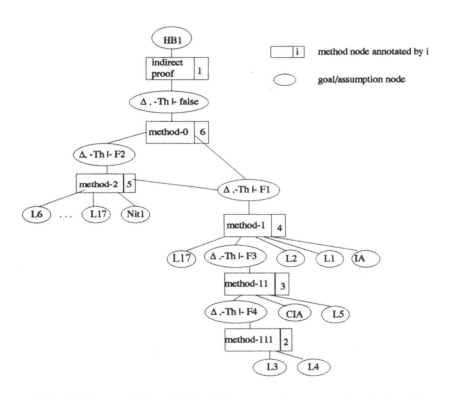

Fig. 1. The proof-plan of HB1 with annotated sequence of method nodes

---

[8] R^1 denotes the set of sets of real numbers and R^2 denotes the set of sets of ordered pairs (x,y) of real numbers x and y.

One of its (verifiable) methods, method-111, is shown below. This example has been proceeded detail in [13]. Here we cannot go into detail and just explain the bottom line.

3.1 Proving HB2 by Analogy

The lemmata of HB1 L1, L2, L6, L8, L10, L12, L13, L14, L17 are potential lemmata for HB2 as well because they contain only symbols not specific for R^1. m is set to a large number because many lemmata are missing for HB2.

The reformulations are assisted by a user-supplied connection-table CT, which contains connections of the kinds, ([-,-] [-,-,-,-]), ($clsdint\ clsdrect$), and ($R^1 R^2$). (Here [-,-] is written for $\lambda x, y.[x, y]$ and [-,-,-,-] for $\lambda x, y \lambda z, w[x, y, z, w]$). In our example the association $[-, -][-, -, -, -]$ also points to an association of the pair (x, y) with the two pairs $(x, y)(z, w)$.

CT restricts the search for reformulations and reduces the number of parameters that have to be instantiated to be able to prove suggested target lemmata after the analogy procedure. CT is a *permanent* connection table, which contains information for an area of mathematics, and can be used for other analogy problems as well. Not surprisingly, CT may carry *semantic* information which often is important for the support of analogical transfer in mathematics. In fact, the association of (x, y) with $(x, y), (z, w)$ is a semantic information.

The source proof-plan is reformulated stepwise along with a step by step transfer of methods

1. The source goal HB1 has to be reformulated such that it matches HB2. The reformulation consists of the **Symbol-Mapping** instantiating the parameters $a, b, G, open, finite$ to the constants $a, b, G, open, finite$ of HB2 and of **Add-Argument** which inter alia replaces the binary function $[-, -]$ by the 4-ary function $[-, -, -, -]$ and introduces the additional parameters lf', rt' and constants c, d. No duplication of subplans occurs in this application of **Add-Argument**. The indirect proof method stays unchanged but all other methods are changed by the reformulation.

2. Next, the source assumption L3 (reformulated in step 1) leads the f-method method-111'. No lemmata corresponding to L3, L4 are given for HB2 but, since m is large, this does not matter. The parameter $clsdint, lf, rt, lf', rt'$ occur in the reformulated L3, L4, thus the **Symbol-Mapping** $clsdint \Rightarrow clsdrec$ is forced by CT while lf, rt, lf', rt' cannot be instantiated and remain parameters. method-111 is reformulated to the verifiable method-111' by the reformulations of step 1 and 2:

method: -111	
parameter	$a, b, G, clsdint, open, rt, lf, [-,-], finite$
preconditions	L3,L4
postcondition	$(\Delta, \neg Th \vdash F4)$
constraints	

proof schema			
	0-1.Δ	$\vdash$ $a \in R \wedge b \in R \wedge a \leq b$	(HYP)
	1. Δ	$\vdash$ $a \in R \wedge b \in R$	($\wedge$E,0-1)
	2. Δ	$\vdash$ $a \in R \wedge b \in R \rightarrow clsdint([a,b])$	($\forall$E;L3)
	3. Δ	$\vdash$ $clsdint([a,b])$	($\rightarrow$E,1,2)
	4. $\{\neg Th\}$	$\vdash$ $\neg \exists H(H \subseteq G \wedge finite(H) \wedge [a,b] \subset \cup H)$	(HYP)
	5. Δ	$\vdash$ $lf([a,b]) \leq rt([a,b])$	(OTTER;L4, 1)
	6. Δ	$\vdash$ $[a,b] \subset \cup G$	(HYP)
	7. $\Delta, \neg Th$	$\vdash$ $F4$	($\wedge$I,3,4,5,6)

procedure	schema-interpreter

method: -111'	
parameter	rt, lf, rt', lf'
preconditions	L3',L4'
postcondition	$(\Delta', \neg Th' \vdash F4')$
constraints	type(rt)=type(rt'), type(lf)=type(lf')

proof schema			
	0-1.Δ'	$\vdash$ $a \in R \wedge b \in R \wedge a \leq b \wedge c \in R \wedge d \in R \wedge c \leq d$	(HYP)
	1. Δ'	$\vdash$ $a \in R \wedge b \in R \wedge c \in R \wedge d \in R$	($\wedge$E,0-1)
	2. Δ'	$\vdash$ $a \in R \wedge b \in R \wedge c \in R \wedge d \in R \rightarrow clsdrec([a,b,c,d])$	($\forall$E;L3')
	3. Δ'	$\vdash$ $clsdrec([a,b,c,d])$	($\rightarrow$E,1,2)
	4. $\{\neg Th'\}$	$\vdash$ $\neg \exists H(H \subseteq G \wedge finite(H) \wedge [a,b,c,d] \subset \cup H)$	(HYP)
	5. Δ'	$\vdash$ $lf([a,b,c,d]) \leq rt([a,b,c,d])$ $\wedge lf'([a,b,c,d]) \leq rt'([a,b,c,d])$	(OTTER;L4', 1)
	6. Δ'	$\vdash$ $[a,b,c,d] \subset \cup G$	(HYP)
	7. $\Delta', \neg Th'$	$\vdash$ $F4'$	($\wedge$I,3,4,5,6)

procedure	schema-interpreter

3. The next (previously reformulated) source sequent is $(\Delta', \neg Th' \vdash F4')$ and the corresponding f-method is method-11'. No lemmata corresponding to L5',CIA' are given in the target which does not matter because of the large m. No reformulations are necessary. method-11' is verifiable.

4. Essentially the same is true for the next assumption and method-1'.

5. Now it is method-2's turn. *center* occurs in the preconditions of method-2' and remains a parameter since no lemma to match L7 or L9 is given in the target. No reformulation takes place.

   - Checking the justifications of method-2' we find that method-2' is not verifiable because line2'-5

$\Delta', \neg Th' \vdash \exists i (i \in \mathbb{N} \wedge (rt([a,b,c,d]) - lf([a,b,c,d]))/2^i \leq (rt([u,v,s,t]) - lf([u,v,s,t]))/2 \wedge (rt'([a,b,c,d]) - lf'([a,b,c,d]))/2^i \leq (rt'([u,v,s,t]) - lf'([u,v,s,t]))/2)(\ldots)$ is not.

In order to establish the justification method-2' is decomposed into a plan consisting of the verifiable method-21' with post(method-2') = post(method-21'), the subgoal g'_{5a} which is in pre(method-2'), and a not verifiable method-22' with post(method-22') = g'_{5a}.

- method-21' can be transferred and g'_{5a} remains an open goal.

6. $(\Delta', \neg Th' \vdash F2)$ is the next source assumption and leads to method-0'. No further reformulation happens in this step and method-0' is verifiable.

3.2 The Resulting HB2 Proof Plan

The analogy procedure yields the copy of the source plan, shown in Figure 2, with reformulated goals, assumptions and methods proved to be verifiable. The target plan for HB2 looks like that for HB1 except that some new lemmata $L3'\ldots$ replace $L3\ldots$ and all methods but method-2 are replaced by the corresponding reformulated methods. method-2 is replaced by its reformulated submethod method-21'.

Actually this proof-plan has been produced by interactively choosing the reformulations but applying it automatically. The analogy procedure suggests as open goals the lemmata L3', L4', L5', L7', L9', L11', L17', Nit2, CIA', IA', and g'_{5a} which are left to be proved in the target.

4 Conclusion and Related Work

The presented analogy method was developed independently from the Heine-Borel example by learning lessons from the analogy examples in the standard textbook [5]. Solving the Heine-Borel analogy shows that substantial progress has been made by the analogy-driven proof-plan construction because it is able to cope with complicated real maths examples.

Our approach advances ideas of previous systems for theorem proving by analogy and of derivational analogy [4, 19]. The power of the analogy procedure partially stems from the supplied source proof-plan which guides the search for target subplans. Besides, the reformulation contributes to the strength of the analogy procedure. The remaining open goals have to be satisfied by base-level proof planning. Hence, in order for the analogy procedure to succeed, it has to be embedded into a problem solver (proof planner) which is a good idea for analogy methods ins general.

More techniques for *automatically* modifying the target methods are required such as abduction or "debugging" [2] which automatically provides additional preconditions in order to verify target methods and which has handled the proof of some difficult mathematical theorems. As also recognized in [8][9] and [9] more frequently needed reformulations have to be found.

---

[9] where a reformulation very similar to **Add-Argument** is used

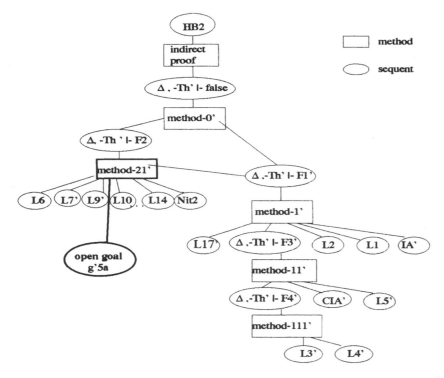

Fig. 2. The proof-plan of HB2

5   Acknowledgement

Special thanks to Woody Bledsoe who proposed a proof-plan and lemma list of HB1 [2]. He implemented a version of **Add-Argument** and also checked the validity of the plans for HB1 and HB2. Because of health problems he decided not to coauthor.

References

1. W.W. Bledsoe. The use of analogy in automatic proof discovery. Tech.Rep. AI-158-86, Microelectronics and Computer Technology Corporation, Austin, TX, 1986.
2. W.W. Bledsoe. Heine-Borel theorem analogy example. Technical Report Memo ATP 124, University of Texas Computer Science Dept, Austin, TX, August 1994.
3. A. Bundy. The use of explicit plans to guide inductive proofs. In E. Lusk and R. Overbeek, editors, *Proc. 9th International Conference on Automated Deduction (CADE)*, volume 310 of *Lecture Notes in Computer Science*, pages 111–120, Argonne, 1988. Springer.
4. J.G. Carbonell. Derivational analogy: A theory of reconstructive problem solving and expertise acquisition. In R.S. Michalsky, J.G. Carbonell, and T.M. Mitchell,

editors, *Machine Learning: An Artificial Intelligence Approach*, pages 371–392. Morgan Kaufmann Publ., Los Altos, 1986.

5. P. Deussen. *Halbgruppen und Automaten*, volume 99 of *Heidelberger Taschenbücher*. Springer, 1971.

6. X. Huang, M. Kerber, M. Kohlhase, E. Melis, D. Nesmith, J. Richts, and J. Siekmann. Omega-MKRP: A Proof Development Environment. In *Proc. 12th International Conference on Automated Deduction (CADE)*, Nancy, 1994.

7. X. Huang, M. Kerber, M. Kohlhase, and J. Richts. Methods - the basic units for planning and verifying proofs. In *Proceedings of Jahrestagung für Künstliche Intelligenz*, Saarbrücken, 1994. Springer.

8. Th. Kolbe and Ch. Walther. Patching proofs for reuse. In N. Lavrac and S. Wrobel, editors, *Proceedings of the 8th European Conference on Machine Learning 1995*, Kreta, 1995.

9. P. Madden. *Automated Program Transformation Through Proof Transformation*. PhD thesis, University of Edinburgh, 1991.

10. W.W. McCune. Otter 2.0 users guide. Technical Report ANL-90/9, Argonne National Laboratory, Maths and CS Division, Argonne, Illinois, 1990.

11. E. Melis. Change of representation in theorem proving by analogy. SEKI-Report SR-93-07, Universität des Saarlandes, Saarbrücken, 1993.

12. E. Melis. How mathematicians prove theorems. In *Proceedings of the Sixteenth Annual Conference of the Cognitive Science Society*, pages 624–628, Atlanta, Georgia U.S.A., 1994.

13. E. Melis. Analogy-driven proof-plan construction. Technical Report DAI Research Paper No 735, University of Edinburgh, AI Dept, Dept. of Artificial Intelligence, Edinburgh, 1995.

14. E. Melis. A model of analogy-driven proof-plan construction. In *Proceedings of the International Conference on Artificial Intelligence*, Toronto, 1995. Morgan Kaufmann.

15. E. Melis and M.M. Veloso. Analogy makes proofs feasible. In D. Aha, editor, *AAAI-94 Workshop on Case Based Reasoning*, pages 13–17, Seattle, 1994.

16. G. Polya. *How to Solve it*. 2nd ed. Doubleday, New York, 1957.

17. S.J. Russell. Analogy by similarity. In D. Helman, editor, *Analogical Reasoning*, pages 251–269. Kluwer Academic Publisher, 1988.

18. B.L. van der Waerden. Wie der Beweis der Vermutung von Baudet gefunden wurde. *Abh.Math.Sem.Univ.Hamburg*, 28, 1964.

19. M.M. Veloso. Flexible strategy learning: Analogical replay of problem solving episodes. In *Proc. of the twelfth National Conference on Artificial Intelligence 1994*, Seattle, WA, 1994.

20. L. Wos. *Automated Reasoning: 33 Basic Research Problems*. Prentice-Hall, Englewood Cliffs, 1988.

Non-Atomic Actions in the Situation Calculus

José Júlio Alferes, Renwei Li, and Luís Moniz Pereira

Centre for Artificial Intelligence, UNINOVA and
Department of Computer Science, U. Nova de Lisboa
2825 Monte da Caparica, Portugal*

Abstract. In this paper we investigate non-atomic actions and changes in the framework of the situation calculus. We classify non-atomic actions into three types: simultaneous actions, inclusive selective actions, and exclusive selective actions. We show that the extended situation calculus with non-atomic actions has the same expressive power as the basic situation calculus. We identify a problem, called composition problem, which relates effects of non-atomic actions to those of their component actions. A defeasible solution to the composition problem is proposed. The believability of some choices of default rules for the composition problem are discussed. We also provide some simple examples to illustrate the usefulness of our default rules.

1   Introduction

The situation calculus [10] is a general framework for reasoning about actions and changes. Actually, it is a many-sorted first-order theory including three basic elements: actions, situations, and fluents. Its expressiveness and limitations had never been systematically studied until Gelfond, et al [5] argued that the attractive syntax of the situation calculus is not tied to the primitive ontology that was usually associated with its use. In line with [5], further efforts for formalizing concurrent actions were proposed in [9, 2, 1].

Inspired by [5, 9, 2, 1], in this paper we investigate three types of non-atomic actions: simultaneous actions, inclusive selective actions, and exclusive selective actions. We will show that the extended situation calculus with non-atomic actions has the same expressive power as the basic situation calculus. We will identify a problem, called composition problem, which relates effects of non-atomic actions to those of their component actions. A defeasible solution to the composition problem is proposed. The believability of some choices of default rules for the composition problem are discussed. We also provide some simple examples to illustrate the usefulness of our defeasible rules.

The rest of the paper is organized as follows. In Section 2 we briefly introduce the basic situation calculus. In Section 3 we extend the basic situation calculus [10] with non-atomic actions, and argue that the extended situation calculus has

---

* This work was partially supported by ESPRIT Project COMPULOG II (No. 6810) and a post-doctoral fellowship from JNICT. We would also like to thank Gerd Wagner and Carlos Damásio for helpful discussions.

the same expressive power as the original situation calculus. In Section 4 we identify a problem, termed composition problem, concerning descriptions of effects of non-atomic actions. The composition problem is as follows: given descriptions of the effects of atomic actions how do we avoid *unnecessary* descriptions of effects of non-atomic actions? It will be indicated that the composition problem also exists in other formalisms for reasoning about non-atomic actions. In Section 5 and 6 we make use of defeasible rules of inference to solve the composition problem about simultaneous actions and selective actions, respectively. In Section 7 we discuss the believability of defaults for reasoning about simultaneous actions. In Section 8 we compare our work with others and make some discussions.

2 Basic situation calculus

In this paper a situation calculus without non-atomic actions is referred to as a basic situation calculus (BSC). In order to make a serious study of the situation calculus, it suffices to give a domain-specific alphabet Σ and then define the basic situation calculus as a first-order formalism on Σ.

The alphabet Σ of the situation calculus is defined to include: (i) A set of sorts including three special sorts: *Act*, *Sit* and *Bool*; (ii) A set A of sorted action symbols; (iii) A set of sorted predicate symbols including a special symbol *holds* of the sort *Bool* $\times$ *Sit*; (iv) A set of sorted function symbols including two special symbols: *do* of the sort *Act* $\times$ *Sit* $\rightarrow$ *Sit*, and S_0 of the sort *Sit*. There is a distinguished subset $\mathcal{F}$ of function symbols, called fluent symbols.

From the alphabet we can define terms and formulas as usual. In particular, we are interested in terms of sorts *Act*, *Sit* and *Bool*. All terms of the sort *Act* are actions. Terms of the sort *Bool* used as first parameter of *holds* are fluents. Situations are either S_0 or terms of form $do(a, s)$. We require that actions and fluents cannot have parameters of sorts *Act* and *Sit*.

Using terms and formulas we can describe domain-specific axioms. In particular, the initial conditions can be specified by formulas of the form $holds(F, S_0)$. The effect of actions can be specified by formulas of the form $holds(\phi, s) \rightarrow holds(\psi, do(a, s))$. In order to formally reason about changes, we may need *unique name axioms for actions* and *unique name axioms for states* [13]:

In order to correctly formalize dynamic world, in addition to which fluents are changed by which actions we need to indicate which fluents are *not* changed by which actions. This is the frame problem identified in [10]. One solution is simply to use the *frame axioms*. In order to avoid explicitly specifying frame axioms, many efforts have been made. One approach is to implicitly represent frame axioms as entailments of some uniform non-monotonic policy, as for example in [8, 7]. Another approach is Reiter [13], using *successor state axioms* and *precondition axioms for actions* in [13], which are from the combination of Pednault [11] and Haas-Schubert's explanation closure axioms [6, 15]. Although the solution of [13] is very elegant and parsimonious, it only applies in a class of domains satisfying the completeness assumption: For any action a and any fluent F, all the conditions under which a can lead to F becoming true or false in the successor state are known and characterized by some first-order formulas. When we admit non-atomic actions in the situation calculus, it is hardly possible to determine all the conditions under which a can lead to F becoming true or false in the successor state. In this paper we prefer to appeal to non-monotonic solutions to the frame problem. For example, we can also follow [4] to introduce four *inertia axioms* to represent the frame axioms. There are some subtleties here. For the purpose of this paper, we leave it open. For simplicity we will simply use Reiter's extension semantics [12] for the default rules proposed in this paper, although there are several other possibilities of choices.

3   Non-atomic actions

We consider two types of non-atomic actions: simultaneous actions and selective actions. Selective actions are further classified into exclusive selective actions and inclusive selective actions. By *simultaneous action* we mean that an agent performs several actions at the same time. For example, *to lift a bowl of soup* and *to open the door* at the same time can be regarded as a simultaneous action. By *selective action* we mean that an agent performs one or more of a set of actions at the same time. For example, *to go to Army* or *to perform an alternative service* can be regarded as an *exclusive* selective action. As another example, *to take an examination* or *to do an experimental work* or both can be regarded as an inclusive selective action.

Let a and b be two actions. We use $a \parallel b$ to represent a simultaneous action for performing a and b at the same time, $a+b$ to represent an (inclusive) selective action, $a\dot{+}b$ to represent an (exclusive) selective action. The situation calculus extended with non-atomic actions is generally called extended situation calculus (ESC). To be more specific, given an alphabet Σ, all actions ACT of the extended situation calculus for Σ is defined as follows: (i) All actions of the basic situation calculus for Σ are in ACT; (ii) If $a, b \in ACT$, then $a \parallel b, a + b, a\dot{+}b \in ACT$; (iii) No other actions are in ACT.

In general, the situation $do(a \parallel b, s)$ is different from $do(a, s)$ and $do(b, s)$, but the situation $do(a + b, s)$ is one of $do(a, s)$, $do(b, s)$, and $do(a \parallel b, s)$, and $do(a\dot{+}b, s)$ is one of $do(a, s)$ and $do(b, s)$. We will admit the commutative law for $\parallel$, $+$ and $\dot{+}$.

It can be seen that the extended situation calculus has *more* actions than the basic situation calculus. The *structure* of actions in the extended situation calculus is much richer than that in the basic situation calculus. In order to apply the extended situation calculus we need to describe effects of all non-atomic actions in the same way as for atomic actions.

Example 1. Let *Switchon* and *Shoot* denote two actions: switching on the light and shooting, respectively. Then *Switchon* $\parallel$ *Shoot* is a simultaneous action to denote *switching on the light and shooting at the same time*. The effects of actions can be described as follows:

$$holds(Lighton, do(Switchon, s))$$
$$holds(Loaded, s) \rightarrow holds(Dead, do(Shoot, s))$$
$$holds(Lighton, do(Switchon \parallel Shoot, s))$$
$$holds(Loaded, s) \rightarrow holds(Dead, do(Switchon \parallel Shoot, s))$$

Note that, however, the situation $do(Switchon \parallel Shoot, s)$ is not the same as $do(Switchon, s)$, nor as $do(Shoot, s)$.

Example 2. Let $Air, Train, Bus$ denote three actions: go to Paris by air, by train, and by bus, respectively. Then $Air \dotplus Train \dotplus Bus$ is a selective action to denote *going to Paris by air or by train or by bus*. We can use the following formulas as its effect descriptions:

$$holds(Paris, do(Air \dotplus Train \dotplus Bus, s))$$

Note that we also have the following three formulas as effect descriptions of the constituent component actions of $Air \dotplus Train \dotplus Bus$:

$$holds(Paris, do(Air, s))$$
$$holds(Paris, do(Train, s))$$
$$holds(Paris, do(Bus, s))$$

The situation $do(Air \dotplus Train \dotplus Bus, s)$ is the same as one of $do(Train, s))$, $do(Air, s)$, and $do(Bus, s))$, but different from the other two, although the fluent $Paris$ is true in all of them.

It can be seen that any basic situation calculus (BSC) of [10] is a subset of an extended situation calculus (ESC). That is to say, ESC is as expressive as BSC. But is BSC as expressive as ESC? Our conclusion is that ESC does not increase the expressive power of BSC. Note that if we ignore the internal structure of the expressions $Switchon \parallel Shoot$ and $Air \dotplus Train \dotplus Bus$ and consider them as atomic ones, say $\overline{Switchon \parallel Shoot}$ and $\overline{Air \dotplus Train \dotplus Bus}$, then the extended situation calculus becomes the same as the non-extended one. This observation can be used to prove the equivalence between ESC and BSC. The following claim is formalized and proved in the extended version of this paper as a proposition.

Claim 1. The extended situation calculus (ESC) has the same expressive power as the basic situation calculus (BSC) in the sense that for any ESC we can construct an equivalent BSC.

4   The composition problem

When the extended situation calculus is applied to a practical universe of discourse, each non-atomic action α should be considered as being uninterrupted and look like an atomic action, and its effect should be given in the form of $holds(\phi, s) \rightarrow holds(\psi, do(\alpha, s))$. It is, however, often difficult or unnecessary to do so, since there are too many non-atomic actions. On the other hand, given the description of effects of atomic actions, we may be able to derive the effects of non-atomic actions.

Example 3. Suppose there is a banking account for donations. Let the atomic action set be { $donate(n) \mid n \in \aleph$ }. The effects of atomic actions may be described as follows:

$$holds(balance(x), s) \rightarrow holds(balance(x + d), do(donate(d), s))$$

Assume two donators donate their money d_1 and d_2 at the same time. Then, we can use $donate(d_1) \parallel donate(d_2)$ to represent the simultaneous donations. The effect of $donate(d_1) \parallel donate(d_2)$ may be described by the following formula:

$$holds(balance(x), s) \rightarrow$$
$$holds(balance(x + d_1 + d_2), do(donate(d_1) \parallel donate(d_2), s))$$

In the above example it seems that the description of effects of the simultaneous action $donate(d_1) \parallel donate(d_2)$ is *unnecessary and redundant*, and thus can be omitted, since it can be derived from effects of atomic actions by using the so-called interleaving model.

Example 4. Consider the *Going To Paris* example. We have the following four formulas to describe the effects of three atomic actions and a selective action.

$$holds(Paris, do(Air, s)) \qquad holds(Paris, do(Train, s))$$
$$holds(Paris, do(Bus, s)) \qquad holds(Paris, do(Air \dotplus Train \dotplus Bus, s))$$

The description of the effect of $Air \dotplus Train \dotplus Bus$ does not seem to be necessary; it is actually redundant, since $Paris$ is true in all the situations $do(Air, s)$, $do(Train, s))$, $do(Bus, s))$, $do(Air \dotplus Train \dotplus Bus, s)$.

We can find many other examples in which effects of non-atomic actions *may* be derived from effects of their component actions. It is certainly favoured to avoid describing unnecessary descriptions of effects of non-atomic actions, if the effects of the non-atomic actions can be derived from the effects of their component actions. Now the problem is: how do we avoid unnecessary descriptions of effects of non-atomic actions, given descriptions of effects of atomic actions? If a description of effects of non-atomic actions has been omitted, how do we derive it later? This problem is referred to as the composition problem for non-atomic actions in this paper.

The composition problem concerns the relationship between effects of non-atomic actions and their component actions. In reality, when some atomic action is performed, it has some certain effect; when it is performed simultaneously with other actions, either it may have the same effect as if it were performed atomically, or it may have additional side-effects, or it may have different effects from those when it is performed atomically. The following example is about side-effects of simultaneous actions.

Example 5. For the sake of business a shop has a special policy: If a client buys toothpaste and toothbrush, then the shop gives a soap to the client free of charge. Let the atomic actions be $\{buy(x) \mid x \in \{paste, brush, soap\}\}$. Then, the effects of atomic actions may be described as follows: $holds(has(x), do(buy(x), s))$. The effects of the simultaneous action $buy(paste) \parallel buy(brush)$ are as follows:

$$holds(has(paste), do(buy(paste) \parallel buy(brush), s)) \tag{1}$$

$$holds(has(brush), do(buy(paste) \parallel buy(brush), s)) \tag{2}$$

$$holds(has(soap), do(buy(paste) \parallel buy(brush), s)) \tag{3}$$

The formula (3) above may be regarded as a side-effect of the simultaneous action $buy(paste) \parallel buy(brush)$. The formulas (1) and (2) can be omitted, but it does not seem to be possible to omit (3), since we don't have general knowledge about how to derive it from effects of atomic actions.

5 Effects of simultaneous actions

Defeasible reasoning allows for "jumping to conclusions" or reaching conclusions which rely in part on the "absence of evidence to the contrary". In this paper we make use of normal default rules of the form $\frac{\phi : \varphi}{\varphi}$, where ϕ and φ are first-order sentences. Recall that there is always an extension for a normal default theory [12].

By using default rules of the above form, now we can solve the composition problem for simultaneous actions. For simultaneous actions composed of two atomic actions we propose to use the following default:

$$\frac{\begin{array}{l} holds(p, do(a; b, s)) \\ holds(p, do(b; a, s)) \end{array} : holds(p, do(a \parallel b, s))}{holds(p, do(a \parallel b, s))} \tag{4}$$

where we use $holds(p, do(x; y, s))$ denote $holds(p, do(y, do(a, s)))$. It can be seen that the above default rule characterizes a class of so-called interleaving traces of the simultaneous actions. Now let's consider some examples to see whether the above default works in practice.

If we apply the above default to the donation example we can achieve the correct answer. For a very large class of domains, the above default really works. We should emphasize that by use of the above rule of inference we can only omit *unnecessary* descriptions of effects of simultaneous actions. Sometimes we still need to give the *necessary* descriptions of effects. In the brush-paste-soap scenario, for example, we still need to give the formula (3) to describe the *side-effect* of the simultaneous action, while formulas (1) and (2) for the simultaneous action $buy(paste) \parallel buy(brush)$ can be omitted.

The default (4) can be extended for simultaneous actions composed of more than two atomic actions. Let $A = \{a_1, \cdots, a_n\}$ for any $n \geq 1$. We use $Per(A)$ to stand for the set of all ordered permutations of A. For example, $Per(\{a, b, c\}) =$

$\{a; b; c, a; c; b, b; a; c, b; c; a, c; a; b, c; b; a\}$. For simultaneous actions $a_1 \parallel \cdots \parallel a_n$, we propose to use the following default:

$$\frac{\Pi(p, A, s) \; : \; holds(p, do(a_1 \parallel \cdots \parallel a_n, s))}{holds(p, do(a_1 \parallel \cdots \parallel a_n, s))} \tag{5}$$

where $\Pi(p, A, s)$ denotes $\bigwedge_{e \in Per(A)} holds(p, do(e, s))$. Thus reasoning about change caused by simultaneous actions amounts to computing extensions for a default theory. Hence we can use properties of default logic to study properties of changes caused by simultaneous actions.

6 Effects of selective actions

Intuitively, the situation $do(a + b, s)$ is one of $do(a, s)$, $do(b, s)$, and $do(a \parallel b, s)$. Thus we immediately have the following non-default rule of inference for effects of selective actions:

$$\frac{holds(p, do(a, s)), holds(p, do(b, s)), holds(p, do(a \parallel b, s))}{holds(p, do(a + b, s))} \tag{6}$$

Combining it with (4), we then have the following default rule:

$$\frac{\begin{array}{l} holds(p, do(a, s)) \\ holds(p, do(b, s)) \\ holds(p, do(a; b, s)) \; : \; holds(p, do(a \parallel b, s)) \\ holds(p, do(b; a, s)) \end{array}}{holds(p, do(a + b, s))} \tag{7}$$

Later we will see that there are also a few other alternatives to (4), thus there are a few other alternatives to (7). On the other hand, the default (7) is not a normal one. In addition, the effect of $a \parallel b$ may be just directly given. Taking all these factors into account, we propose the following default to replace (6) and (7).

$$\frac{\begin{array}{l} holds(p, do(a, s)) \\ holds(p, do(b, s)) \; : \; holds(p, do(a + b, s)) \\ holds(p, do(a \parallel b, s)) \end{array}}{holds(p, do(a + b, s))} \tag{8}$$

Note that although (6) is not a default, conclusions from it may still be defeasible, since reasoning about $a \parallel b$ may involve the default (4), not additionally mentioning that the action a and b may also denote simultaneous actions. There are some subtle discussions and arguments here on (6), (7) and (8). For the space limitation we will not go into deeper discussions.

In practice we often use the exclusive selective action. Intuitively, the situation $do(a \dotplus b, s)$ is one of $do(a, s)$ and $do(b, s)$. In this case, we simply modify (6) into the following rule of inference:

$$\frac{holds(p, do(a, s)), holds(p, do(b, s))}{holds(p, do(a \dotplus b, s))} \tag{9}$$

Note that the action a and b may be also simultaneous actions. Thus, conclusions from (9) may also be defeasible. For conservative reasoning we propose the following default for effects of exclusive selective action:

$$\frac{\begin{array}{l} holds(p, do(a, s)) \\ holds(p, do(b, s)) \end{array} \;:\; holds(p, do(a \dot{+} b, s))}{holds(p, do(a \dot{+} b, s))} \tag{10}$$

The above discussions can be extended for selective actions composed of more than two actions.

7 Believability

Since defaults are used to solve the composition problem, conclusions from default rules should be understood as beliefs, which can be defeated by new facts. On the other hand, we can use other defaults instead of the previous defaults. That is to say, some defaults will lead our reasoning more non-monotonic than others. In this section, we discuss believability of defaults for simultaneous actions.

Note that the prerequisites of the default rule (5) are conjunctions of some formulas of the form $holds(p, do(e, s))$. More credulous people may think that the prerequisites might be too strong, and thus the conclusions would be too conservative. A simple modification of the prerequisites in the default (5) is just to change conjunction into disjunction. That is to say, for simultaneous action $a_1 \parallel \cdots \parallel a_n$, we may use the following default rule:

$$\frac{\Sigma(p, A, s) \;:\; holds(p, do(a_1 \parallel \cdots \parallel a_n, s))}{holds(p, do(a_1 \parallel \cdots \parallel a_n, s))} \tag{11}$$

where $A = \{a_1, \cdots, a_n\}$ and $\Sigma(p, A, s)$ denotes $\bigvee_{e \in Per(A)} holds(p, do(e, s))$. Obviously, the beliefs from (11) are less believable than those from (5), but (11) can also be justified by practical examples. For example, in the donation scenario if we use (11) instead of (5), we still achieve the same result.

In what follows, we will define a partial ordering relation among default theories to indicate some beliefs are more believable than others. We start with the general definition of believability, then present some defaults alternative to (4), and then discuss their believability.

Definition 2. Let $D = \{D_i \mid D_i$ is a set of defaults for any $i \geq 1\}$. We define a partial ordering relation $\preceq$ on D as follows: $D_i \preceq D_j$ iff $M_i \subseteq M_j$, where M_i and M_j are the extensions for $\langle W, D_i \rangle$ and $\langle W, D_j \rangle$, respectively, for any set of first-order sentences W. When $D_i \preceq D_j$, we say that beliefs in M_i for D_i are more believable than those in M_j for D_j. The partial ordering relation $\preceq$ is simply called believability relation.

In particular, $\{\} \preceq D_i$ for any D_i. The extension for $\langle W, \{\}\rangle$ is just $Th(W)$, which cannot be defeated by any new facts. Hence, $\{\}$ is the most believable. Now consider two sets of normal defaults D_1 and D_2. Suppose $D_1 \subseteq D_2$. Then, $D_1 \preceq D_2$. That is to say, the more normal defaults are used, the less believable the conclusions from them. Thus, the empty set of normal defaults are the most believable. The following proposition is particularly useful for the following discussion.

Proposition 3. *Let D_1 and D_2 be two sets of closed normal defaults. Suppose for any normal default $\{\frac{\phi \, : \, \psi}{\psi}\} \in D_1$ there is a normal default $\{\frac{\varphi \, : \, \psi}{\psi}\} \in D_2$ such that $\vdash \phi \rightarrow \varphi$. Then, $D_1 \preceq D_2$.*

For non-atomic actions, by admitting different set of default rules we have different default theories. Some of them are more believable than others. For example, for $a \parallel b$ we can have four possible default rules :

$$(\delta_1) \quad \frac{\begin{array}{c} holds(p, do(a; b, s)) \\ holds(p, do(b; a, s)) \end{array} \, : \, holds(p, do(a \parallel b, s))}{holds(p, do(a \parallel b, s))}$$

$$(\delta_2) \quad \frac{holds(p, do(a; b, s)) \, : \, holds(p, do(a \parallel b, s))}{holds(p, do(a \parallel b, s))}$$

$$(\delta_3) \quad \frac{holds(p, do(b; a, s)) \, : \, holds(p, do(a \parallel b, s))}{holds(p, do(a \parallel b, s))}$$

$$(\delta_4) \quad \frac{\begin{array}{c} holds(p, do(a; b, s)) \\ \vee \\ holds(p, do(b; a, s)) \end{array} \, : \, holds(p, do(a \parallel b, s))}{holds(p, do(a \parallel b, s))}$$

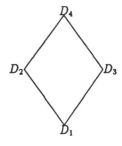

Fig. 1. Lattice of default rules.

Let $D_i = \{\delta_i\}$ for $i = 1, 2, 3, 4$. Then, by use of the above proposition it is easy to verify $D_1 \preceq D_2$, $D_1 \preceq D_3$, $D_2 \preceq D_4$, and $D_3 \preceq D_4$, as shown in figure 1.

The above discussion can be generalized for simultaneous actions of the form $a_1 \parallel \cdots \parallel a_n$. Generally, there are $n! + 2$ particularly interesting defaults for the simultaneous action $a_1 \parallel \cdots \parallel a_n$. For the sake of space limitation we will not delve into deeper discussions.

8 Comparison and discussion

The situation calculus was proposed as a general framework for reasoning about changes [10]. It was long believed that the expressiveness was rather restricted and limited, but no serious study on its expressive power had been made until Gelfond, et al [5] presented a pioneering effort and made a clarification. The main purpose of [5] is to clarify some misbeliefs on the situation calculus. The recent popularity enjoyed by the situation calculus is due to [5]. With respect to concurrent actions, a few interesting examples are given about independence, cancellation, conflict, etc. Although the ideas of [5] are profound, the specific details need to be elaborated. Recent approaches to dealing with concurrent actions in the framework of the situation calculus include [1, 2, 9], all of them are in line with the pioneering work [5]. Although there are some similarities between this paper and [1, 2, 9], some technical differences still exist, summarized as follows.

The focus of [1] is only on the concurrent actions. In particular, it discusses the concurrent actions where a constituent action may be composed of a sequence of actions. In [1] the exact meaning of "concurrent actions" is not clearly defined, and selective actions are totally ignored. In this paper we indicated that simultaneous actions are those composed of some actions which are performed at the same time. Thus we are dealing with common-sense actions in our reality, but not those concurrent actions introduced in software engineering. In addition, in this paper we have proposed some default rules to deal with (exclusive and inclusive) selective actions.

In [2], a language denoted by $\mathcal{A}_C$ and a translation methodology of theories from $\mathcal{A}_C$ to extended logic programs ELPs of [3] are proposed. In the translation, the following axioms, which are among major contributions of [2], play a vital rôle:

$$(a)\ holds(f, do(a, s)) \quad \leftarrow subsetof(b, a), holds(f, do(b, s)),$$
$$not\ noninherit(f, a, b, s)$$

$$(b)\ \neg holds(f, do(a, s)) \quad \leftarrow subsetof(b, a), \neg holds(f, do(b, s)),$$
$$not\ noninherit(\overline{f}, a, b, s)$$

$$(c)\ noninherit(\overline{F}, x, y, s) \leftarrow subsetof(y, x), subsetof(A, x),$$
$$\neg subsetof(A, y), not\ \overline{holds(P_1, s)},$$
$$\cdots, not\ \overline{holds(P_n, s)}$$

where $noninherit(e, a, b, s)$ means "action a does not inherit fluent literal e from subaction b in situation s." According to these axioms, concurrent actions normally inherit their component actions' effects. This is the case when subactions are independent of each other. For example, the effect of $Switchon\|Opendoor$ is the *net aggregation* of effects of *Switchon* and *Opendoor*. When subactions are independent of each other, both [2] and our default rules can achieve the same conclusions. When subactions are dependent on each other, some effect descriptions of concurrent actions can be omitted by use of our default rules and some cannot, as shown before. In the donation example, however, it is not clear whether and how to use the above ELP rules (a), (b) and (c) to derive effects of $donate(d_1)\|donate(d_2)$ from effects of $donate(d)$. It seems that the default rules (5) are more expressive than the above axioms.

The focus of [9] is on the epistemological completeness proposed in [8]. Intuitively, a theory of an action is epistemologically complete if, given a complete description of the initial situation, the theory enables us to predict a complete description of the resulting situation when the action is performed. Lin and Shoham use some circumscriptive minimization techniques to deal with their generalized frame problem, which looks similar to our composition problem (a study of the precise relationship is still needed). Lin and Shoham's formalism enjoys the epistemological completeness. It seems that all of our formalism, and formalisms in [2, 1] do not have precisely this property. Actually it is questionable that epistemological completeness is always required. For example, $Holds(Open, do(Opendoor\|Closedoor, s))$ could be derivable in [9] as indicated in [2], but it cannot be derived in either our formalism or [2, 1]: the effect of $Opendoor\|Closedoor$ is unknown. In this case, we think that the epistemological completeness should not be required.

References

1. Alferes, J.J., R. Li, and Pereira, L.M., Concurrent Actions and Changes in the Situation Calculus, *Proc. of IBERAMIA 94*, Hector Geffner (ed.), McGraw-Hill, 1994, 93–104

2. Baral, C. and Gelfond, M., Representing concurrent actions in extended logic programming, *IJCAI*, 1993, pp. 866–871

3. M. Gelfond and V. Lifschitz, Logic programs with classical negation, In. *Logic Programming: proc. of the 7th Int'l Conf.*, D. Warren and P. Szeredi, eds., 1990, pp. 579–597

4. M. Gelfond and V. Lifschitz, Representing actions in extended logic programs, *Joint International Conference and Symposium on Logic Programming*, K. Apt (ed.), 1992, 559–573

5. Gelfond, M., Lifschitz, V., and Rabinov, A., What are the limitaions of the situation calculus?, Automated Reasoning: Essays in Honor of Woody Bledsoe, R. Moore (ed.), 1991, 167–179

6. Haas, A., The case for domain-specific frame axioms, *Proc. of the Workshop on the Frame Problem in Artificial Intelligence*, Morgan Kaufmann Publishers, Inc., 1987, 343–348

7. V. Lifschitz, Toward a metatheory of action, *Proc. of KR'91*, J. Allen, R. Fikes and E. Sandewall (eds.), Morgan Kaufmann Publishers, Inc., 376–386

8. F. Lin and Y. Shoham, Provably correct theories of actions: preliminary report, *Proc. of AAAI-91*, 1991

9. F. Lin and Y. Shoham, Concurrent actions in the situation calculus, *Proc. of AAAI-92*, 1992, 590–595

10. McCarthy, J. and Hayes, P.J., Some philosophical problems from the standpoint of artificial intelligence, in: B. Meltzer and D. Michie, (eds.), *Machine Intelligence*, 4, Edinburgh, 1969, 463–502

11. Pednault, E. P. D., ADL: Exploring the middle ground between STRIPS and the situation calculus, *Proc. of KR'89*, R. J. Brachman, H. Levesque, R. Reiter (eds.), Morgan Kaufmann Publishers, Inc., 324–332

12. Reiter, R., A logic for Default Reasoning, *Artificial Intelligence*, 13, 1980, 81–132

13. Reiter, R., The frame problem in the situation calculus: A simple solution (sometimes) and a completeness result for goal regression, *Artificial Intelligence and Mathematical Theory of Computation: Papers in Honor of John McCarthy*, V. Lifschitz (ed.), Academic Press, San Diego, CA, 1991, 359–380

14. Reiter, R., Proving properties of states in the situation calculus, *Artificial Intelligence*, 64:2, 1993, 337–351

15. Schubert, L., Monotonic solution of the frame problem in the situation calculus: An efficient method for worlds with fully specified actions, *Knowledge Representation and Defeasible Reasoning*, H. E. Kyberg, R. P. Loui, and G. N. Carlson (eds.), Kluwer Academic Press, Boston, 1990, 23–67

Planning Under Uncertainty: A Qualitative Approach

Nikos I. Karacapilidis

Artificial Intelligence Research Division
Institute for Applied Information Technology
GMD - German National Research Center for Computer Science
Schloss Birlinghoven, 53757 Sankt Augustin, Germany
e-mail: karacapilidis@gmd.de

Abstract. Hierarchical planners create descriptions of abstract states and divide their planning task into subproblems for refining these states. In spite of their success in reducing the search space, they classically assume the existence of certain and complete information. In real world planning instances, one has to select among alternative strategies at each abstract state, observing both incomplete knowledge of the attributes that each strategy may pose, and partial ordering of these attributes. In addition, reasoning is defeasible: further information may cause another alternative to be more preferable than what seems optimal at the moment. This work presents a planning framework based on qualitative value decision making formalisms. Sketching the appropriate strategy operator schemata for hierarchical planning, it focuses on aspects of uncertainty handling by combining abilities of constraint programming languages with the introduced concepts of credulous and skeptical conclusions of an issue. The topics of argumentation among the planning agents and common conflicts in the ordering of defaults are discussed by means of a real planning example.

Keywords: planning, qualitative reasoning, uncertainty.

1 Introduction

Classical planning systems assume the existence of certain and complete information. However, uncertainty is inherent in various instances of a planning problem, due to the incomplete knowledge of the world one has at most times. Planning is usually performed through a lot of debates, negotiations and arguments between various agents. In such a case, planning agents have to confront the existence of partial information regarding the alternative choices. This is due both to incomplete argumentation about the alternative goals or assignments and their attributes, and to weaknesses of totally weighing this set of attributes. Decision making formalisms could provide the desired platform, yet lack some computational advantages of planners. Consequently, planning systems require the specification of a framework with which to express beliefs and goals. Such a framework should provide the basis upon which to build representations of actions, plans and operators. Predominant conditions in real world planning paradigms are:

- Planning agents assert arguments supporting or against alternative solutions. Conflicts are rather unavoidable and a rational planning framework is required;
- Reasoning is defeasible. Further information may cause another alternative to be more preferable than what seems optimal at the moment;
- There may be arguments supporting or against the choice of a certain alternative, but this should not yield to the consideration of the whole system as irrational or inconsistent;
- Factual knowledge is not always sufficient. Usually, value judgements on aspects like weighing of attributes, that alternative solutions possess, appear as the most critical issues. In addition, these judgements should be derivable and subject to debate;
- The planner has to face the existence of both not enough and too much information, as well as of limited resources for finding a solution;
- Assignment of quantitative values to arguments is difficult. Planning agents usually need a framework to express preferences qualitatively.

Hierarchical planning has been rendered a promising approach, at least in that it significantly reduces the search space [15]. Planning first at the abstract levels, the method expands coarse plans into more detailed ones. The above procedure is taking place recursively until all levels of abstraction have been reached. Consequently, it recursively enforces pruning of search space at each level. Hierarchical planning is supported by a scalable description of the existing knowledge at a number of abstraction levels. As it can been concluded from the above, the hierarchical tree is not prespecified, but it should be able to be expanded dynamically by the introduction of new information from various planning agents. A representation scheme of the possible knowledge states (i.e., worlds) revealing at various abstraction levels is illustrated in Figure 1. Each instance of the planning procedure comprises goals and knowledge (i.e., belief[1]). Goals and knowledge are interacting in the following way:

- The status of knowledge enforces the selection of a certain route in the planning tree by triggering the appropriate reduction operators and, consequently, refines the current set of goals. This is achieved with the classical planning operator schemata (see for example [14]);
- The current set of goals may imply consideration of further and more specific knowledge. Knowledge acquisition operators should require from the planning agents attachment of extended argumentation.

The remainder of the paper is organized as follows: The integration of a planning framework, that efficiently handles the adequacies of classical planners

---

[1] The exact relationship between belief and knowledge is still under long philosophical debates. In the context of this paper we simply adopt that knowledge is true belief.

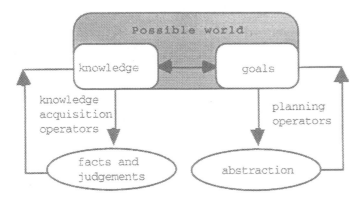

Fig. 1. Possible world representation scheme

discussed above, is presented in Section 2. The qualitative approach introduced eliminates the need of assigning numerical costs to arguments. The corresponding plan-schema is sketched and the issues of operator selection and plan reviewing are discussed. The suggested framework is validated with an extended example in Section 3. Further issues regarding the planning procedure, related work, and future research directions are discussed in Section 4.

2 The planning framework

In spite of the success of the predominant form of hierarchical non-linear planning in search reduction, such systems lack a sufficient basis for choice of action [17] and an adequate representation for consistency and replanning [14, 18]. The rough distinction of states into those satisfying and those not some goals poses problems in real world instances.

2.1 Operator selection: the suggested plan-schema

The decision to apply an operator instance to a goal usually results in a conjunction of new subgoals and assignments. An assignment is something like the cost of a part of a trip in a route planning exercise or the allocation of a resource to a specific role in an allocation task. The assignments are the effects of choosing a decision. Assignments can also be functions which compute specific consequences of the new state, so that constraints can be evaluated.

The primary representation task of an operator is to describe how the world changes after the action it represents has been performed. Consequently, operators contain information about the objects that participate in the actions, the constraints that must be placed on them, the goals that the actions are attempting to achieve, the way actions in this operator relate to more or less abstract descriptions of the same action, and the conditions necessary before the actions can be performed (i.e., admissibility conditions). The structure of the strategy operator used in this approach is as follows:

$$OPERATOR < name > \{ \; instance\_variables$$
$$antecedents : applicable\_goals$$
$$admissibility\_conditions$$
$$consequents : new\_instance$$
$$new\_goal$$
$$assignments \; \}$$

The suggested plan schema makes use of a tactical language similar in syntax to common relational database query languages (like SQL). The language allows such structured queries to be made as part of the admissibility test for each operator prior to final selection of a particular operator, i.e., as antecedent conditions. This is desirable for the tactical variable binding of the operator to be done early, enabling the fulfilment criteria to be supplied with dynamic values from the knowledge base.

Each alternative strategy, caused by the selection of a particular operator, may fulfil each problem instance at a specific level. In addition, the likelihood of each selected strategy depends on the current information available. In other words, each strategy has a different probability of success and a different degree to which it fulfils a specific goal[2].

2.2 Handling uncertainty

In [4] a new logic for defeasible qualitative decision making has been suggested, called Qualitative Value Logic. According to this, decision making is governed by preferences among arguments for and against an alternative choice. Rather than hardwiring into the logic a single principle, such as specificity, for resolving conflicts among arguments, knowledge about preferences is encoded as part of the domain theory. Arguments pro and con each choice are weighed against each other. Combined weak arguments may defeat a strong argument and preferences may be expressed qualitatively.

Constraints provide a qualitative way to argue about preferences and value judgements. In other words, they give to the users the ability of ranking the quality of alternative choices. We assume the existence of an axiomatization of the integer operations $+$ and $-$, and the predicates $=, >$ and $<$ with their standard meanings to express preferences between arguments. Constraints comprise attributes that are linked to the corresponding alternative via supporting and counter arguments.

We define an *issue* as the set of alternative choices. A reserved function symbol, v, is used to represent the value of an attribute (for more precise definitions see [4]). In addition, we assume that any assertion related to an attribute

---

[2] The corresponding concepts of expected fulfilment of an operator and degree of fulfilment of a concequence have been introduced in [12]. However, they rely on precise numerical estimations which is rather an illusion in real world planning instances and, therefore, they are not addressed here.

(represented in the following as $d_1, d_2, ..., d_n$) has a qualitative value out of a predetermined domain, but this value is identical for each alternative it refers to[3]. Asserted constraints on attributes provide the means of weighing among them. Representing real world cases, we allow for not totally ordered attributes. Finally, value judgements are represented with equations and inequations about the values of the different attributes. For instance:

$$v(d_1) < v(d_2)$$
$$v(d_1) + v(d_2) = v(d_3)$$
$$v(d_3) + v(d_4) > v(d_5)$$

The representation of the above is that attribute d_1 is considered less important than d_2, coexistence of attributes d_1 and d_2 is considered equally important with the existence of attribute d_3, and attributes d_3 and d_4 together overweigh d_5. Regarding negations of attributes we assume:

$$v(\neg d_n) = -v(d_n).$$

Jointly regarding the constraints holding and the arguments asserted to alternative choices we define the following inference relations regarding an optimistic or pessimistic, and a credulous or skeptical conclusion of an issue. As it will be made clear later, the corresponding rectangular they provide (that is, skeptical-optimistic, skeptical-pessimistic, credulous-optimistic, and credulous-pessimistic conclusions), is used in order for the planner to decide about the best alternative in cases of incomplete information.

Definition 1. *The conclusion of an issue is credulous (skeptical) iff it is entailed regarding the full (common) set of asserted attributes.*

Definition 2. *The conclusion of an issue is optimistic (pessimistic) iff it is entailed regarding the maximum (minimum) possible values of alternative choices.*

Allowing the planning agents to assert their preferences between attributes, facilities for consistency checking of the set of corresponding constraints is needed. Inconsistencies are common and have to be revealed. In addition, following to the above formalism, a type of constraint optimization problems is rendered. Both the above problem aspects are illustrated with an example in Section 3.

2.3 Belief Revision

It is desirable to review earlier decisions while planning. In addition, in plan monitoring situations, reviewing is desirable after the plan has been constructed. The proposed framework allows and advocates for the review of selected operators as the knowledge state is augmented with more details of the plan. Decisions

---

[3] Note that the proposed formalism allows both for qualitative and numerical representations of the importance of the asserted attributes.

about previous world states can be reviewed at each stage of a plans evolution to enable an agent to check that a decision taken towards a certain planning direction is still recommended.

Regarding the set of conclusions an issue returns, planning agents may assert new arguments for and against the alternative selections, new constraints aiming at a more complete ordering among the corresponding attributes, or even more alternative selections. Acting in this way, belief revision will render a reviewing of the existing plan[4].

3   An example

We apply our framework to a real world instance. The goal at a part of our planning problem is to find a constructor for the BOO–1 part of a car engine. Let the following three, asserted so far, alternatives: to construct it in the home factory, where the fitting of the various parts is being performed (Do–It–Yourself alternative), or to order it from two candidate subcontractor companies, Constructor–1 and Constructor–2. The asserted attributes concern the quality, service, delivery time and cost that each of the alternatives provide. The corresponding operator schema is illustrated in Figure 2. Figure 3 concludes the existing knowledge about the attributes that each alternative possesses (or not). As in this special case, there is not always complete linking between each alternative of an issue and every asserted attribute. For instance, there is no argumentation about the service provided for the Do–It–Yourself and Constructor–1 alternatives.

Let the following constraints asserted so far:

$fair\,cost > good\,quality$,
$meet\,due\,date < fair\,cost$, and
$good\,quality + meet\,due\,date > fair\,cost$.

We observe that with the above set of constraints only a partial ordering among the already asserted attributes is efficient. We exploit abilities of constraint satisfaction programming languages on the revealing constraint (optimization) problem. In particular, we report experiments with ECLiPSe. Such a language guarantees consistency checking for the asserted constraints. We assume the following:

- all attributes take values greater than zero;
- an arbitrary but identical domain for each attribute's qualitative value (we consider here the interval $[1..10]$[5]).

---

[4] The method of antecedents and consequents checking followed in our problem specification language, has the advantage of placing backtracking under user control. The complete presentation of such a method is not in the context of this paper.

[5] Although we have experimented with various intervals (resulting to the same outputs), a more thorough sensitivity analysis needs to be done.

```
operator:           choose_constructor
goal:               (choose_constructor ?constructor ?job_part)
instance variables:
                    ?job_part, cost, quality,
                    service_provided, meet_due_date
admissibility conditions:
                    (in_product_list ?constructor ?job_part)
                    (available ?constructor ?job_part)
consequents:
   new_goal:
        (prepare_interface ?job_part ?constructor_type)
   assignments:
        (makes ?constructor ?job_part)
        (equals ?job_part_cost ?constructor_cost)
        (equals ?job_part_quality ?constructor_quality)
        (equals ?job_part_service ?constructor_service)
        (equals ?job_part_due-date ?constructor_delivery-date)
```

Fig. 2. The operator schema for the planning example

One can see that the alternative Do It Yourself is worst than that of Constructor-1 because it does not provide good quality ($\neg$ *good quality*). Thus, the final selection should be between Constructor-1 and Constructor-2. Note that there is not any information about service provided related to Constructor-1, not even any constraints related to this attribute asserted so far.

Using the definitions of the alternative conclusions of an issue we have:

- considering a skeptical conclusion of the issue, that is ignoring any argument about *service provided* (since we lack such information for one alternative), the value domain of the alternative Constructor-1 is the interval [1..18], while that one of the alternative Constructor-2 is [1..16];
- considering a credulous conclusion of the issue, that is taking the argument about *service provided* into account, the value domain of Constructor-1 is the interval [1..18] and of Constructor-2 is [1..26].

Choices indicated by the above conclusions yield the table illustrated in Figure 4. For instance, considering a skeptical-optimistic conclusion, Constructor-1 appears to be the most promising alternative choice (with value 18), while considering the credulous-pessimistic conclusion, no decision can be made (both alternatives have the same pessimistic value).

4 Discussion

We have presented a planning framework, based on qualitative value decision making formalisms, that allows for handling uncertain and incomplete knowl-

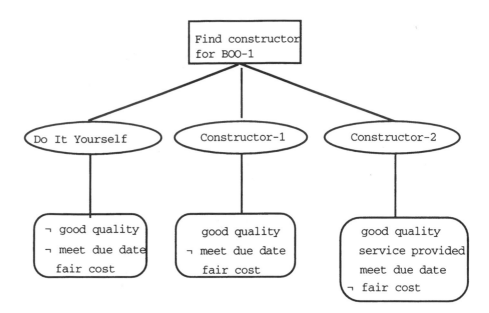

Fig. 3. A part of a planning instance

	optimistic	pessimistic
sceptical	Constructor-1	no decision
credulous	Constructor-2	no decision

Fig. 4. Conclusions for the problem instance

edge at various abstract levels of a hierarchical planning tree. This framework combines aspects of classical planners and reasoning formalisms focusing on the support of a sufficient basis for choice of action. The motivations behind this joint integration are:

- to support and reason about commonly prevailed conditions in dynamic planning environments, such as argumentation, negotiation, and conflict resolution, and
- to facilitate and rationalize the communication among the various agents in the planning process;

Among the most interesting, related to our formalism, works are:

- The BURIDAN planning algorithm [11]: BURIDAN is a fully implemented least-commitment planner whose underlying semantics is probabilistic. A probability distribution over states represents the agents uncertainty. The planner uses a mixed symbolic and probabilistic representation of action. It takes as input a probability distribution over initial states, a set of action descriptions, a goal expression, and a probability threshold which represents the minimum acceptable success probability. The definition of a symbolic action representation and its probabilistic semantics is formal and promising. The algorithm searches a space of partial plans. Each plan consists of a set of actions, a partial *temporal ordering* relation over them, a set of *causal links*, and a set of *subgoals*. BURIDAN starts searching from the *null plan* (it contains only two dummy actions A_0 and A_G which encode the initial probability distribution and the goal), and performs two basic operations: (i) *Plan Assessment*, where it is determined whether the probability that the current plan will achieve the goal exceeds the abovementioned threshold – ending successfully if so, and (ii) *Plan Refinement*, where the algorithm tries to increase the probability of goal satisfaction by refining the current plan; the algorithm signals failure if there are no possible refinements, otherwise deterministically chooses a new current plan and makes a loop. The algorithm has been proved *sound* (i.e., every consistent total order of the actions is a solution to the problem), and *complete* (it always returns a solution plan if such a plan exists).

- The work of Haddawy and Hanks on utility models for planners [8]: It exploits together strengths arising from classical AI *goal–directed* planners (where success is measured in terms of whether a goal is satisfied, and the process is driven by goals), and *decision–theoretic* problem solvers (where there are not explicit goals, and success is measured in terms of preferences and utility functions). The work presents a unification of the above approaches to planning, by providing utility models that support rational decision making while retaining the goal information needed to support algorithms for plan generation. The limitations of a goal–directed behaviour are highlighted and, based on them, utility models addressing issues like *temporally scoped goals* (i.e., propositions that must be true by a deadline or over an interval), *partial goal satisfaction*, and the cost of resource consumption are proposed. Finally, it is described how symbolic AI planning algorithms can exploit these utility models in order to effectively produce rational plans.

The PYRRHUS planning system from Williamson and Hanks [19]: Their work extends the definition of plan quality to take into account the cost of resources used by the plan and partial satisfaction of the goal. The system is based on an effective planning algorithm by exploiting classical planning techniques like *backward chaining* and knowledge–based *search control rules*. The system finds optimal plans for a class of goal–directed utility models suggested by Haddawy and Hanks [8] and briefly described above. More specifically, Haddawy and Hanks characterize deadline goals as having two components: an *atemporal* (describing *what* must be done) and a *temporal* one (describing by *when* it must be done). PYRRHUS system does not allow for partial satisfaction of the atemporal component. The utility model addressed is called PSTC (Partial Satisfaction of the Temporal Component).

As concluded in [19], the algorithm achieves heuristic tractability by taking advantage of the goal component of the PSTC utility model, and by employing the kind of search control knowledge used by classical planners. It is claimed that the information provided through the utility model can sometimes make planning easier. We intend to explore and exploit utility theory concepts on our framework.

— The work of Tan and Pearl [16] on Qualitative Decision Theory: They describe a framework for specifying conditional desires (i.e., "desire α if β"), and evaluating preference queries (i.e., "would you prefer σ_1 over σ_2 given ϕ") under uncertainty. The aim of the work is to equip an agent with decision making capabilities based on two types of inputs: beliefs and preferences. They allow some of the beliefs to be defeasible, and preferences are encoded in conditional sentences such as "if high quality products are needed, then I prefer Constructor-2 than Constructor-1". Their work addresses the unstructured nature of the input information in decision making environments and deploy preference evaluation and rankings in terms of *specificity*. The work refines *ceteris paribum* (i.e., other things being equal) semantics enabling the handling of specificity of conditional desires, generalizing the notion of believability, and extending preferential dominance so that the evaluation of preference queries may be qualified by an integer indicating the strength of the confirmation. All these concepts are very close to the planning–as–negotiation paradigm.

— The TRAINS project [1]: This is a long–term effort to develop a system that can use English conversation to interact with and assist humans in problem solving tasks. Viewing the system as a planning assistant rather than a natural language system some interesting remarks arise: Such a system has the potential to allow humans and machine to best exploit their own strengths. More specifically, humans can use their expertise at making high–level decisions about the best strategy to search for solutions, whereas the system can use its capabilities for detailed evaluation of plans, scheduling large amounts of interrelated events. On the other hand, as claimed by the system developers, it seems clear that a natural language is not always the best medium for communicating all information about plans. The project is still under refinement trying to build future generations of conversational and collaborative planning systems[6].

We intend to further strengthen the concepts of the Qualitative Value Logic, first introduced in [4] extending previous works on reasoning about priorities (see for example [2] and [3]). Currently, we experiment on the combination of the presented approach with asserting by default constraints of the type $p > \neg p$, where p represents an attribute and $\neg p$ its negation (as discussed in [6]). We also intend to explore the concepts of *expected fulfilment* of an operator and *degree of fulfilment* of a goal concequence, introduced in [12], in order to qualitatively

---

[6] We have recently coined the term "Dialectical Planning" in order to describe such issues (see [9]).

handle the notions of utilities and probabilities (these concepts are also discussed in [10] and [13]). According to them, goals are not precise requirements, but can be fulfilled to various degrees by achieving alternative subgoals. In addition, not all subgoals are equally likely to be achieved. The above instances are often addressed in real world planning instances.

Finally, we focus our research on developing efficient mediating systems for supporting and reasoning about rational and effective decision-making, when information is limited and uncertain, and conflicts of interest and opinion are common. Models of rational decision-making in groups are needed, taking these considerations into account (see [7] about computational models of norms of rational discourse). These models should provide such services in the planning paradigm as managing the dependencies between arguments, claims, positions and issues, helping the participant agents to be aware of their rights and obligations in a planning problem, and providing access to procedures for negotiation and conflict resolution. The specified role of such a system should be that one of an assistant and advisor, that is it should recommend its solutions leaving the final enforcement of decisions and actions to the agents. Such a system, called *Zeno*, is currently under development at GMD (see [5] for an introduction to its architecture).

Acknowledgements: The author thanks Jim Blythe, Gerhard Brewka, Tom Gordon, Dionysios Pothos and two anonymous referees for providing useful suggestions and comments on various topics of the paper. This work draws substantially on valuable discussions with John Bigham and Kelvyn Scrupps, when the author was with Queen Mary and Westfield College, University of London.

References

1. Allen, J.F., Schubert, L.K., Ferguson, G., Heeman, P., Hwang, C.H., Kato, Ts., Light, M., Martin, N., Miller, Br., Poesio, M., Traum, D.R.: The TRAINS project: a case study in building a conversational planning agent. Journal of Experimental and Theoretical Artificial Intelligence **7**, (1995) 7–48.
2. Brewka, G.: Preferred Subtheories – An Extended Logical Framework for Default Reasoning. Proceedings of IJCAI-89, Detroit (1989) 1043–1048.
3. Brewka, G.: Reasoning about Priorities in Default Logic. Proceedings of AAAI-94, Seattle (1994) 940–945.
4. Brewka, G., Gordon, Th.: How to Buy a Porsche: An Approach to Defeasible Decision Making. Working Notes of AAAI-94 Workshop on Computational Dialectics, Seattle (1994) 28–38 (available in http://nathan.gmd.de/projects/zeno/zeno2.html).
5. Brewka, G., Gordon, Th., Karacapilidis, N.I.: Mediating Systems for Group Decision Making: the Zeno System. KI-95 (German National AI Conference) Workshop on Computational Dialectics: Models of Argumentation, Negotiation and Decision Making, Bielefeld, Germany (1995); to appear.
6. Doyle, J., Shoham, Y., Wellman, M.P.: A Logic of Relative Desire. in Z.W. Ras and M. Zemankova (eds.) Proceedings of the 6th Int. Symposium on

Methodologies for Intelligent Systems, ISMIS-91 (1991) 16–31 (available in http://medg.lcs.mit.edu/ftp/doyle).

7. Gordon, Th.: Computational Dialectics. Proceedings of Workshop Kooperative Juristische Informationssysteme, Wien, Austria, GMD Studien Nr. 241 (1994) 25–36 (available in http://nathan.gmd.de/projects/zeno/zeno2.html).

8. Haddawy, P., Hanks, St.: Utility Models for Goal–Directed Decision–Theoretic Planners. Technical Report TR 93–06–04, University of Washington, Dept. of CS and Engineering (1993); also under review in JAIR.

9. Karacapilidis, N.I., Gordon, Th.: Dialectical Planning. Proceedings of 14th International Joint Conference on Artificial Intelligence (IJCAI-95) Workshop on Intelligent Manufacturing Systems, Montreal (1995); to appear.

10. Karacapilidis, N.I., Pappis, C.P., Adamopoulos, G.I.: Designation of abstraction levels for handling uncertain and incomplete information in planning problems. 14th European Conference on Operational Research (EURO XIV), Jerusalem, Israel (1995); to appear.

11. Kushmerick, N., Hanks, St., Weld, D.: An Algorithm for Probabilistic Least–Commitment Planning. Proceedings of AAAI-94, Seattle (1994) 1073–1078.

12. Mansell, T.M.: A method for planning given uncertain and incomplete information. Proceedings of the 9th Conference on Uncertainty in Artificial Intelligence, Washington (1993) 350–358.

13. Pearl, J.: Probabilistic reasoning in intelligent systems: Networks of plausible inference. Morgan Kaufmann Publishers, San Mateo, CA (1988).

14. Petrie, C.: Constrained Decision Revision. Proceedings of the Tenth National Conference on Artificial Intelligence, AAAI-92, San Hose (1992) 393–400.

15. Sacerdoti, E.D. : Planning in a Hierarchy of Abstraction Spaces. Artificial Intelligence 5 (1974) 115–135.

16. Tan, S., Pearl, J.: Qualitative Decision Theory. Proceedings of AAAI-94, Seattle (1994) 928–933.

17. Wellman, M.P., Doyle, J.: Preferential Semantics for Goals. Proceedings of AAAI-91 (1991) 698–703 (available in http://medg.lcs.mit.edu/ftp/doyle).

18. Wilkins, D.E., Myers, K.L.: A Common Knowledge Representation for Plan Generation and Reactive Execution. SRI AI Center Technical Note 532R (1994); also to appear in Journal of Logic and Computation (available in http://www.ai.sri.com/people/wilkins/papers.html).

19. Williamson, M., Hanks, St.: Optimal Planning with a Goal–Directed Utility Model. Proceedings of 2nd International Conference on Artificial Intelligence Planning Systems, Chicago (1994) 176–181.

Qualitative Reasoning Under Uncertainty

Pacholczyk Daniel

LERIA

U.F.R. Sciences d'Angers. 2, Boulevard Lavoisier. 49045- ANGERS CEDEX 01
pacho@univ-angers.fr

Abstract

In this paper we propose a Symbolic Probability Theory for the Management of Uncertainty encoded into a Qualitative way. A semantic model of Uncertainty Representation is made with the aid of nonlogical tools built on the substrate of a M-valued Predicate Logic. In order to exploit Uncertain Knowledge, we have constructed deductive processes founded upon Logical or Conditional inferences. We have obtained Generalizations of either classical Deduction Rules, or classical Conditional Probabilities.

Keywords

Artificial Intelligence, Conditional Probabilities, Independence, Knowledge Representation, Many-valued predicate Logic, Qualitative Reasoning, Symbolic Uncertainty Representation.

1 Introduction

Our purpose in this paper is to present a Logico-symbolic Probability Theory for the Management of Uncertainty encoded into a Qualitative way. Qualitative Models have been proposed to deal with Qualitative Reasoning, Natural Language or Decision Processes. Some are based upon Heuristical or Logical Procedures (*Cf.* [CoGr83], [Cohe85], [FPKE93], [PaMa93]) or Qualitative/Comparative Probabilities or Possibilities (*Cf.* [Bobr84], [Will86], [Stru88], [Bell90], [Davi90], [Well90], [HeDr91], [CGSc91], [Gold92], [GoPe92], [Haec92], [DrHe93], [PaDo93], [Pars93], [Bout94]). More recently, a Symbolic Probability Concept, conceived as a Symbolic extension of the classical one, has been defined to represent States of Belief, Probabilistic Knowledge or Uncertain statements of natural language (*Cf.* [Pear88(a), (b)], [Alel88, 90], [XBPo90], [ADGP92], [HaFa92], [DaGi92], [Darw92], [Pacd92(a), (b), 93, 94], [Pool93], [PdjH95]). As noted by Poole (*Cf.* [Pool91]), a propositional representation does not have the modelling power of logic-based models.

The Semantic Model presented here has been conceived in a M-valued Predicate Logic initially defined to deal with Imprecise Predicates. So, our system allows us to deal with Vagueness and Uncertainty.

In section 2, we present our Semantic Model of Uncertainty Representation. Within the algebraic framework presented in § 2.1, we have enriched a M-valued Logic by adjoining a peculiar predicate Prob and by specifying its Axiomatics (§ 2.2). So, we can propose some Generalizations of classical Deduction Rules and Probabilistic results allowing us to deal with Uncertainty (§ 2.3).

The section 3 is devoted to the study of the Conditional Certainty. First of all, we present the Algebraic Structures (§ 3.1) with which one can define this notion. The notions of C-conditional Certainty, Independence and Conditional Independence (§ 3.2) lead to properties which can be presented as Generalizations of the classical numerical Conditional Probabilities (§ 3.3).

2 Uncertainty Representation

In our approach, rather than extending a logic by adding a new operator, we have enriched a M-valued Predicate Logic by adjoining a peculiar predicate, denoted Prob, and by specifying its symbolic Axiomatics [1].

2.1 The Algebraic Context of Uncertainty Representation.

♦ Given an odd integer $M \geq 2$, one calls by $\mathcal{M}$ the interval $[1, M]$ totally ordered by the relation $\leq$ and by n the mapping defined by $n(x)=M+1-x$. Obviously $\{\mathcal{M}, \vee, \wedge, n\}$ is a De Morgan's lattice with : $a \vee b = \max(a, b)$ and $a \wedge b = \min(a, b)$.

Let $\mathcal{L}_M = \{\tau_\alpha, \alpha \in \mathcal{M}\}$ be a set of M elements totally ordered by the following relation : $\tau_\alpha \leq \tau_\beta \Leftrightarrow \alpha \leq \beta$. Thus, $\{\mathcal{L}_M, \leq\}$ is a chain whose least element is τ_1 and greatest element is τ_M. One may then define in $\mathcal{L}_M$, two operators $\vee$ and $\wedge$ and a decreasing involution $\sim$ as follows : $\tau_\alpha \vee \tau_\beta = \tau_{\max(\alpha, \beta)}$, $\tau_\alpha \wedge \tau_\beta = \tau_{\min(\alpha, \beta)}$ and $\sim \tau_\alpha = \tau_{n(\alpha)}$. We have also defined in $\mathcal{L}_M$ the operators $(v_\beta)_{\beta \in \mathcal{M}}$ as follows :

$$\text{if } \alpha = \beta \text{ then } v_\beta \tau_\alpha = \tau_M \text{ else } v_\beta \tau_\alpha = \tau_1.$$

♦ In this paper, *we use the Lukasiewicz's implication* defined as follows [2] :

$$\text{if } \alpha \leq \beta \text{ then } \tau_\alpha \to \tau_\beta = \tau_M \text{ else } \tau_\alpha \to \tau_\beta = \tau_{M-\alpha+\beta}.$$

♦ The T-conorm S (*Cf.* Figure 1 with M=7) associated with Lukasiewicz' implication is defined as follows [3] : if $\alpha + \beta \geq M+1$ then $S(\tau_\alpha, \tau_\beta) = \tau_M$ else $S(\tau_\alpha, \tau_\beta) = \tau_{\alpha+\beta-1}$.

♦ Moreover, the corresponding T-norm T verifies : $T(\tau_\alpha, \tau_\beta) = \sim S(\sim \tau_\alpha, \sim \tau_\beta)$.

2.2. The Semantics of the predicate Prob.

♦ The uncertainty is a notion attached to the reference of a sentence : a truth degree (*true* or *false*) reflects its adequation (or not) to reality and uncertainty appears when the available knowledge cannot enable to do this assignment. In this case, one cannot define a new truth degree, denoted *indeterminate*, since its truth degree is either *true* or *false*. One can only assign a certainty degree to its truthfulness.

---

[1] Our enriched logic can be viewed as a peculiar *M-valued Modal Logic* within which the predicate Prob is a modal operator.

[2] This choice results from the fact that its properties lead to a satisfactory interpretation of natural inference processes.

[3] The peculiar definitions of T-norm and T-conorm can be viewed as restrictions to a finite chain of the classical definitions in the real interval [0, 1]. We can point out that the Symbolic properties of a T-conorm (resp. a T-norm) are similar to the ones of the *numerical operator +* (resp. x) used within Probability Theory.

It is the matter of partial Knowledge of Truth which must be distinguished from partial Truth of Knowledge.

Definition. A statement is said to be uncertain if one can assert that it is true or that it is false but one cannot decide which of the two terms of the alternative holds. Otherwise the statement is said to be certain.

$S(\tau_\alpha, \tau_\beta)$	τ_1	τ_2	τ_3	τ_4	τ_5	τ_6	τ_7
τ_1	τ_1	τ_2	τ_3	τ_4	τ_5	τ_6	τ_7
τ_2	τ_2	τ_3	τ_4	τ_5	τ_6	τ_7	τ_7
τ_3	τ_3	τ_4	τ_5	τ_6	τ_7	τ_7	τ_7
τ_4	τ_4	τ_5	τ_6	τ_7	τ_7	τ_7	τ_7
τ_5	τ_5	τ_6	τ_7	τ_7	τ_7	τ_7	τ_7
τ_6	τ_6	τ_7	τ_7	τ_7	τ_7	τ_7	τ_7
τ_7	τ_7	τ_7	τ_7	τ_7	τ_7	τ_7	τ_7

Fig. 1 : T-conorm S associated with Lukasiewicz' Implication

Example : When we assert that Smith is *very* rich, we estimate to *very* the truth degree of the many-valued proposition "Smith is rich", and when we assert that it is *rather probable* that Smith is *very* rich, we estimate to *rather* the certainty degree of the sentence Smith is *very* rich. More precisely, the wealth of Smith is so that the proposition "Smith is *very* rich" is either *true* or *false*, but we don't know the real wealth statement of Smith. However, the available knowledge is so that we bet that this assertion is *rather probable*.

♦ The human understanding of certainty degrees is generally better when the Scale of Valuation is Discrete and Qualitative rather than continuous and quantitative. So, a user will understand a qualitative valuation using terms as little, moderately, very or totally. It should then be clear that a qualitative valuation of uncertainty leads experts and users to an opinion consensus.

Example : A patient understands the diagnosis "it is very probable that you suffer from hepatitis" of his doctor. In the same way, one discerns the meaning of the following weather forecast "it is rather probable that it will rain tomorrow".

♦ Commonly the two valuation scales that people use to evaluate Truth and Certainty are restricted to 7 symbolic values.

The following choices can lead to an opinion consensus.

- *Truth degrees :* $\mathcal{U}_7 = \{u_1,...,u_7\} = \{$*not-at-all, very-little, little, moderately, rather, very, totally*$\}$.

- *Certainty degrees :* $\mathcal{P}_7 = \{v_1,...,v_7\} = \{$impossible, very-little, little, moderately, rather, very, certain$\}$.

For these reasons, we use only Valuation scales containing 7 Symbolic values.

♦ Let us denote by $\mathcal{A}$ an interpretation of our Predicate logic [4], and by $\mathcal{C}$ the set of formulas ϕ such that, for any valuation x, either x *totally* satisfies ϕ in $\mathcal{A}$ or x *not at all* satisfies ϕ in $\mathcal{A}$.

$$\mathcal{C} = \{\phi \mid \forall x, \mathcal{A} \models_M^x \phi \; or \; \mathcal{A} \models_1^x \phi\}, \text{ where } x \text{ is a valuation of variables.}$$

The predicate Prob is such that : if $\phi \in \mathcal{C}$, then Prob(ϕ) is a M-valued formula.

The assertion Φ is v_α-probable in $\mathcal{A}$ will be denoted $\mathcal{A} \models_\alpha$ Prob(Φ). In other words, we can say that : Prob(Φ) is u_α-*true* in $\mathcal{A}$ [5].

- *Axiomatics. The predicate* Prob *satisfies the following axiomatics* [6] :

[P1] : $\forall \phi \in \mathcal{C}, \forall \Phi \in \mathcal{C}, \models_M \phi \equiv \Phi \Rightarrow \{\mathcal{A} \models_\alpha$ Prob(ϕ) $\Leftrightarrow \mathcal{A} \models_\alpha$ Prob(Φ)$\}$.

[P2] : $\forall \phi \in \mathcal{C}, \mathcal{A} \models_M \phi \Rightarrow \mathcal{A} \models_M$ Prob(ϕ).

[P3] : $\forall \phi \in \mathcal{C}, \mathcal{A} \models_1 \phi \Rightarrow \mathcal{A} \models_1$ Prob(ϕ).

[P4] : $\forall \phi \in \mathcal{C}, \mathcal{A} \models_\alpha$ Prob(ϕ) $\Rightarrow \mathcal{A} \models_{n(\alpha)}$ Prob($\neg \phi$).

[P5] : $\forall \phi \in \mathcal{C}, \forall \Phi \in \mathcal{C}, \{\mathcal{A} \models_1 (\phi \cap \Phi), \mathcal{A} \models_\alpha$ Prob(ϕ), $\mathcal{A} \models \beta$Prob($\Phi$)$\}$

$$\Rightarrow \{\mathcal{A} \models_\gamma \text{Prob}(\phi \cup \Phi) \text{ with } \tau_\gamma = S(\tau_\alpha, \tau_\beta)\}[7]$$

Remark : We can give the intuitive meaning of the previous Certainty Axiomatics. Two semantically equivalent formulas have the same certainty degree ([P1]). A true formula is certain ([P2]). A false formula is impossible ([P3]). If a formula is v_α-probable, its logical negation is v_β-probable with $\tau_\beta = \tau_{n(\alpha)} = \sim\tau_\alpha$. Since $n(\alpha) = M+1-\alpha$, the symbolic value $\sim\tau_\alpha$ takes the place of 1-p(A) within classical Probability Theory ([P4]). The axiom [P5] gives us a symbolic translation of the classical probabilistic one : p(A∪B) = p(A)+p(B), for disjunct events A and B.

---

[4] All the formal definitions as well as the properties expressed in the framework of our M-valued Predicate Logic can be found in [Pacd92(a), 92(b), 94].

[5] Let's recall that, Φ is u_α-*true* in $\mathcal{A}$ is denoted $\mathcal{A} \models_\alpha \Phi$.

[6] One has to remember that the certainty degree v_1-probable (resp. v_M-probable) stands for impossible (resp. certain).

[7] S denotes the T-conorm associated with the Lukasiewicz' implication.

2.3 Fundamental properties.[8]

Proposition 2.1. Let ϕ and Φ be formulas of C. Then :

-a- $\{\mathcal{A}\models_M(\phi\supset\Phi),\ \mathcal{A}\models_\alpha\text{Prob}(\phi),\ \mathcal{A}\models\beta\text{Prob}(\Phi)\}\Rightarrow\tau_\alpha\leq\tau_\beta.$

b- $\{\mathcal{A}\models_\alpha\text{Prob}(\phi),\ \mathcal{A}\models_\lambda\text{Prob}(\phi\cap\Phi)\}\Rightarrow\{\mathcal{A}\models\gamma\,\text{Prob}(\phi\supset\Phi)\ with\ \tau_\gamma=\tau_\alpha\rightarrow\tau_\lambda\}$

Remark : This first result can be viewed as a *Symbolic Generalization of the classical Probabilistic property* : if $A\subset B$ then $p(A)\leq p(B)$. The second result corresponds to the axiom (A3) in the theory of Darwiche & Ginsberg (*Cf.* [DaGi92]).

Remark : In our model, the certainty of a *logical implication* is based upon *the informative part* of the implication, i.e. ϕ *and* $\phi\cap\Phi$. The same motivations have led to the definition of classical *Conditional Probabilities*.

Proposition 2.2. Let ϕ and Φ be formulas of C. Then :

$$\{\mathcal{A}\models_\alpha\text{Prob}(\phi),\ \mathcal{A}\models\beta\text{Prob}(\Phi)\}$$

$$\Rightarrow\{\mathcal{A}\models_\delta\text{Prob}(\phi\cup\Phi),\ \mathcal{A}\models_\gamma\text{Prob}(\phi\cap\Phi)\}$$

$$with\ \tau_\gamma\in[T(\tau_\alpha,\tau_\beta),\ \tau_\alpha\wedge\tau_\beta],\ \tau_\delta\in[\tau_\alpha\vee\tau_\beta,\ S(\tau_\alpha,\tau_\beta)]\ and\ \delta=\alpha+\beta-\gamma.$$

Remark : We obtain a *Symbolic relation similar to the classical Probabilistic one*, i.e.
$$p(A\cup B)=p(A)+p(B)-p(A\cap B).$$

Proposition 2.3. Let ϕ and Φ be formulas of C. Then :

$\{\mathcal{A}\models_\alpha\text{Prob}(\phi),\ \mathcal{A}\models\beta\text{Prob}(\phi\supset\Phi)\}\Rightarrow\mathcal{A}\models_\gamma\text{Prob}(\Phi)\ with\ \tau_\gamma\in[T(\tau_\alpha,\tau_\beta),\ \tau_\beta].$

Remark : Classical Probability Theory leads to a similar result.

Proposition 2.4. The S-additivity Property.
 Let $\phi_i,\ \phi_2,\ ...,\ \phi_n$ be n formulas of C such that
 (i): $\mathcal{A}\models\alpha_i\,\text{Prob}(\phi_i)\ (i=1,...,\ n)$;
 (ii): $\mathcal{A}\models_1(\phi_i\cap\phi_j)$ for $i=1,...,n,\ j=1,...,\ n$ *with* $i\neq j$.
 Put : $\tau_{\gamma_1}=\tau_{\alpha_1}$ *and* $\tau_{\gamma_k}=S(\tau_{\gamma_{k-1}},\ \tau_{\alpha_k})$ *for* $k=2,...,\ n$

 Then, we have : $\mathcal{A}\models\gamma_n\text{Prob}(\phi_1\cup...\cup\phi_n).$

Remark. This additivity property can be presented as a *Symbolic Generalization of the classical Additivity property* :
$$p(A_1\cup A_2...\cup A_n)=p(A_1)+p(A_2)...+p(A_n).$$

---

[8] Proofs of all propositions can be found in [Pacd94].

3 Uncertainty Management Within a Conditional Inference Process

3.1 The Algebraic Context of Conditional Certainty

◆ We have introduced a mapping of $\mathcal{L}_M^2$ into $\mathcal{P}(\mathcal{L}_M)$ which will allows us to propose a Symbolic extension of classical Conditional Probability.

Definition. A Conditioning Criterion is a mapping C *of* $\mathcal{L}_M^2$ *into* $\mathcal{P}(\mathcal{L}_M)$ *which satisfies the following properties:*

[C1] : $C(\tau_\alpha, \tau_\lambda) \subset [\tau_\lambda, \tau_\alpha \to \tau_\lambda]$.

[C2] : $\{\tau_\alpha < \tau_\lambda \Rightarrow C(\tau_\alpha, \tau_\lambda) = \varnothing \}$ *and* $\{\tau_\alpha \geq \tau_\lambda \Rightarrow C(\tau_\alpha, \tau_\lambda) \neq \varnothing\}$.

[C3] : $\cup_\lambda C(\tau_\alpha, \tau_\lambda) = \mathcal{L}_M$.

[C4] : $\forall \tau_{\lambda 1} \leq \tau_\alpha, \forall \tau_{\lambda 2} \leq \tau_\alpha, \{\tau_{\lambda 1} \neq \tau_{\lambda 2} \Rightarrow C(\tau_\alpha, \tau_{\lambda 1}) \cap C(\tau_\alpha, \tau_{\lambda 2}) = \varnothing\}$.

[C5] : $\forall \tau_{\lambda 1} < \tau_{\lambda 2} \leq \tau_\alpha, \{\tau_{\xi 1} \in C(\tau_\alpha, \tau_{\lambda 1}), \tau_{\xi 2} \in C(\tau_\alpha, \tau_{\lambda 2})\} \Rightarrow \tau_{\xi 1} < \tau_{\xi 2}$.

[C6] : $C(\tau_\alpha, \tau_\lambda) = \{\tau_\beta \mid \tau_\alpha \in C(\tau_\beta, \tau_\lambda)\}$.

[C7] : $C(\tau_\alpha, \tau_{\lambda 1}) \cap C(\tau_\beta, \tau_{\lambda 2}) \neq \varnothing \Rightarrow \{\exists \tau_\lambda \in \mathcal{L}_M, \tau_\beta \in C(\tau_{\lambda 1}, \tau_\lambda), \tau_\alpha \in C(\tau_{\lambda 2}, \tau_\lambda)\}$.

[C8] : $\exists \tau_\alpha \in \mathcal{L}_M, \{\tau_1 < \tau_\alpha \leq \tau_a, \tau_\alpha \in C(\tau_\alpha, \tau_\alpha)\}$, where $a = (M+1)/2$.

Remark : It is important to note that generally, for any value of M, there exists several tables C. The following table C (*Cf.* Figure 2) leads to results "consistent" with classical Probability ones.

$\tau_\alpha \backslash \tau_\lambda$	τ_1	τ_2	τ_3	τ_4	τ_5	τ_6	τ_7
τ_1	$[\tau_1, \tau_7]$	$\varnothing$	$\varnothing$	$\varnothing$	$\varnothing$	$\varnothing$	$\varnothing$
τ_2	$\{\tau_1\}$	$[\tau_2, \tau_7]$	$\varnothing$	$\varnothing$	$\varnothing$	$\varnothing$	$\varnothing$
τ_3	$\{\tau_1\}$	$[\tau_2, \tau_6]$	$\{\tau_7\}$	$\varnothing$	$\varnothing$	$\varnothing$	$\varnothing$
τ_4	$\{\tau_1\}$	$[\tau_2, \tau_5]$	$\{\tau_6\}$	$\{\tau_7\}$	$\varnothing$	$\varnothing$	$\varnothing$
τ_5	$\{\tau_1\}$	$[\tau_2, \tau_4]$	$\{\tau_5\}$	$\{\tau_6\}$	$\{\tau_7\}$	$\varnothing$	$\varnothing$
τ_6	$\{\tau_1\}$	$[\tau_2, \tau_3]$	$\{\tau_4\}$	$\{\tau_5\}$	$\{\tau_6\}$	$\{\tau_7\}$	$\varnothing$
τ_7	$\{\tau_1\}$	$\{\tau_2\}$	$\{\tau_3\}$	$\{\tau_4\}$	$\{\tau_5\}$	$\{\tau_6\}$	$\{\tau_7\}$

Fig. 2 : Conditioning Criterion C.

Remark : We can compare our C-conditional Certainty Axiomatics to the ones chosen by Aleluinas (*Cf.* [Alel90]) in order to define Conditional Probability within Propositional Probabilistic Logic. It is explicit that Prob (resp. ~) takes the place of Probability Assignment f (resp. i).

It is obvious to verify that only the axioms 1-6 are satisfied. But, we have not the equalities for axioms 7-8. So, restricted to propositional Logic, our system differs from Aleluinas' Probabilistic Logic.

◆ We have defined a C-independence criterion like in standard Probability Theory.

Definition. A mapping I *of* $\mathcal{L}_M{}^2$ *into* $\mathcal{L}_M$, *is said to be an Independence Criterion for* C, *if* I *possesses the following properties :*

[I1] : $I(\tau_\alpha, \tau_\beta) = I(\tau_\beta, \tau_\alpha)$.

[I2] : $I(\tau_1, \tau_\beta) = \tau_1$.

[I3] : $I(\tau_\alpha, \tau_M) = \tau_\alpha$.

[I4] : *If* $\tau_{\beta1} \leq \tau_{\beta2}$ *then* $I(\tau_\alpha, \tau_{\beta1}) \leq I(\tau_\alpha, \tau_{\beta2})$.

[I5] : $C(\tau_\alpha, \tau_\lambda) = \{\tau_\beta \mid I(\tau_\alpha, \tau_\beta) = \tau_\lambda\}$.

[I6] : $I(I(\tau_\alpha, \tau_\beta), \tau_\gamma) = I(\tau_\alpha, I(\tau_\beta, \tau_\gamma))$.

[I7] : $\exists\ \tau_\alpha \in \mathcal{L}_M, \{\tau_1 < \tau_\alpha \leq \tau_a, I(\tau_\alpha, \tau_\alpha) = \tau_\alpha\}$, *where* $a=(M+1)/2$.

Example (M=7) *:* The mapping C defined in the Figure 2 is a Conditioning criterion. Then, the figure 3 defines the Independence Criterion I for C.

Remark : The axioms [C2] to [C5] have been chosen to obtain, for any value, an "increasing" partition of the chain of possible Certainty degrees. The axiom [C6] (resp. [C7]) is necessary to the commutativity property (resp. the associativity property) of the Independence criterion I. The last axiom [C8] has been introduced to avoid that the T-norm T, can be chosen as Independence Criterion I. Indeed, T being so that : if $(\alpha+\beta \leq M+1)$ then $T(\tau_\alpha, \tau_\beta) = \tau_1$, it cannot give us a satisfactory Independence Criterion.

Remark : We can establish a link with the structure of Probability Algebra (*Cf.* [Alel88], [XBPo90]). In this case, the function I (resp. ~) taking the place of * (resp. i), axioms 1-10 (*Cf.* [XBPo90]) are verified. So, Axiomatics of I lead to a structure of Finite Totally Ordered Probability Algebra.

Remark : We have taken into account the fact that people can define precisely Product Operator I but approximatively Quotient Operator C. This connection between Independence and Conditionalization, resulting from the connection between Product and Quotient Operators, appears in Axiom [I5] :
$$\tau_\lambda = I(\tau_\alpha, \tau_\mu) \Leftrightarrow \tau_\mu \in C(\tau_\alpha, \tau_\lambda).$$

Proposition 3.1. Let C *be a Conditioning Criterion. Then the mapping* I *such that :*
$$\tau_\lambda = I(\tau_\alpha, \tau_\mu) \Leftrightarrow \tau_\mu \in C(\tau_\alpha, \tau_\lambda),$$ *is the only Independence Criterion for* C. *The pair* (C, I) *is said to be a C-independence Criterion.*

NB : (C, I) *resulting from Figures 2 and 3 will be denoted* System CL_7.

$\tau_\alpha \backslash \tau_\mu$	τ_1	τ_2	τ_3	τ_4	τ_5	τ_6	τ_7
τ_1	τ_1	τ_1	τ_1	τ_1	τ_1	τ_1	τ_1
τ_2	τ_1	τ_2	τ_2	τ_2	τ_2	τ_2	τ_2
τ_3	τ_1	τ_2	τ_2	τ_2	τ_2	τ_2	τ_3
τ_4	τ_1	τ_2	τ_2	τ_2	τ_2	τ_3	τ_4
τ_5	τ_1	τ_2	τ_2	τ_2	τ_3	τ_4	τ_5
τ_6	τ_1	τ_2	τ_2	τ_3	τ_4	τ_5	τ_6
τ_7	τ_1	τ_2	τ_3	τ_4	τ_5	τ_6	τ_7

Fig. 3 : Independence Criterion I for C.

3.2 C-conditional Certainty and unconditionally or conditionally C-independence.

In the following, (C, I) being a C-independence Criterion, $U(v_\alpha, v_\lambda)$ denotes the interval of Certainty degrees associated with the set $C(\tau_\alpha, \tau_\lambda)$.

Definitions. Let ϕ and Φ be formulas of C such that $\mathscr{A} \models {}_\alpha Prob(\phi)$ and $\mathscr{A} \models {}_\lambda Prob(\phi \cap \Phi)$. Then :

- *$U(v_\alpha, v_\lambda)$ is the C-conditional Certainty Interval of Φ, given ϕ, and*
- *v_μ the C-conditional Certainty degree of Φ, given ϕ, belongs to $U(v_\alpha, v_\lambda)$.*
- *v_μ the C-conditional certainty of Φ, given ϕ, will be denoted : $\mathscr{A} \models \mu Prob(\Phi|\phi)$.*

Definitions [9]. Let ϕ, Φ and ψ be formulas of C. Then :

- *ϕ and Φ are said to be (unconditionally) C-independent if and only if :*

$$\{\mathscr{A} \models \beta Prob(\Phi) \Leftrightarrow \mathscr{A} \models \beta Prob(\Phi|\phi)\} \text{ and } \{\mathscr{A} \models {}_\alpha Prob(\phi) \Leftrightarrow \mathscr{A} \models {}_\alpha Prob(\phi|\Phi)\}.$$

- *ϕ and Φ are said to be conditionally C-independent given ψ, if and only if:*

$$\{\mathscr{A} \models \mu Prob(\phi|\psi) \Leftrightarrow \mathscr{A} \models \mu Prob(\phi|\Phi \cap \psi)\} \text{ and }$$

$$\{\mathscr{A} \models \mu' Prob(\Phi|\psi) \Leftrightarrow \mathscr{A} \models \mu' Prob(\Phi|\phi \cap \psi)\}.$$

---

[9] The definition of C-independence corresponds to the intuitive meaning that people give to this concept : for both formulas, their conditional certainty degrees do not differ from their certainty degrees. Generally, people are more able to evaluate independence of events A and B given an event C : the happening or not of B does not modify the conditional certainty degree of A given C. So, this natural conditionally independence concept fulfills the chosen definition.

3.3 Uncertainty Management based upon C-conditional Inference Process

The following results allow us to exploit Symbolic Uncertainty by using the notions of C-conditional Certainty and Independence.

Proposition 3.2. Let ϕ, Φ and ψ be formulas of C.

- *Put $\mathcal{A} \models {}_\alpha \mathrm{Prob}(\phi)$, $\mathcal{A} \models \beta \mathrm{Prob}(\Phi)$ and $\mathcal{A} \models {}_\lambda \mathrm{Prob}(\phi \cap \Phi)$.*

(a): *If ϕ and Φ are C-independent, then $\tau_\lambda = I(\tau_\alpha, \tau_\beta)$.*

(b): *If $\tau_\lambda = I(\tau_\alpha, \tau_\beta)$, then ϕ and Φ are C-independent if $\mathrm{Card}(C(\tau_\alpha, \tau_\lambda)) = 1$ and $\mathrm{Card}(C(\tau_\beta, \tau_\lambda)) = 1$.*

- *Put $\mathcal{A} \models \gamma \mathrm{Prob}(\psi)$, $\mathcal{A} \models \mu \mathrm{Prob}(\phi|\psi)$, $\mathcal{A} \models \mu' \mathrm{Prob}(\Phi|\psi)$ and $\mathcal{A} \models {}_\lambda \mathrm{Prob}(\phi \cap \Phi \cap \psi)$*

(a): *If ϕ and Φ are Conditionally C-independent given ψ, then*

$$\tau_\lambda = I(\tau_\gamma, I(\tau_\mu, \tau_{\mu'})).$$

(b): *If $\tau_\lambda = I(\tau_\gamma, I(\tau_\mu, \tau_{\mu'}))$, then ϕ and Φ are Conditionally C-independent given ψ if*

$$\mathrm{Card}(C(I(\tau_\gamma, \tau_\mu), \tau_\lambda)) = \mathrm{Card}(C(I(\tau_\gamma, \tau_{\mu'}), \tau_\lambda)) = 1.$$

Remark : The relation $\tau_\lambda = I(\tau_\alpha, \tau_\beta)$ (resp. $\tau_\lambda = I(\tau_\gamma, I(\tau_\mu, \tau_{\mu'}))$) is not sufficient to assert that ϕ and Φ are C-independent (resp. conditionally C-independent given ψ). The weakening of probabilistic results is due to the fact that people use a finite number of certainty degrees to express their imprecise knowledge.

Proposition 3.3. Let ϕ and Φ be two formulas of C. Then :

$$\{\mathcal{A} \models {}_\alpha \mathrm{Prob}(\phi), \quad \mathcal{A} \models \mu \mathrm{Prob}(\Phi|\phi)\} \Rightarrow \{\mathcal{A} \models {}_\lambda \mathrm{Prob}(\phi \cap \Phi) \ \text{with} \ \tau_\lambda = I(\tau_\alpha, \tau_\mu) \ \text{and}$$
$$\mathcal{A} \models \mu' \mathrm{Prob}(\phi \cap \Phi|\phi) \ \text{with} \ \tau_{\mu'} \in C(\tau_\alpha, \tau_\lambda)\}.$$

Remark : This result can be presented as a *Symbolic Generalization of Compound Probabilities Formula.*

Proposition 3.4. Let ϕ_1, ..., ϕ_n and Φ be formulas of C such that :

(i) : $\mathcal{A} \models {}_M (\phi_1 \cup ... \cup \phi_n)$,

(ii) : $\mathcal{A} \models {}_1 (\phi_i \cap \phi_j)$ *for* $i=1,...,n$, $j=1,...,n$ *with* $i \neq j$,

(iii) : $\mathcal{A} \models {}_{\alpha i} \mathrm{Prob}(\phi_i)$ $(i=1,...,n)$,

(iv) : $\mathcal{A} \models \mu i \mathrm{Prob}(\Phi|\phi_i)$ $(i=1,...,n)$.

Put : $\tau_{\gamma 1} = I(\tau_{\alpha 1}, \tau_{\mu 1})$ *and* $\tau_{\gamma k} = S(\tau_{\gamma(k-1)}, I(\tau_{\alpha k}, \tau_{\mu k}))$ *for* $k=2,...,n$

Then, we have : $\mathcal{A} \models \beta \mathrm{Prob}(\Phi)$ *with* $\tau_\beta = \tau_{\gamma n}$.

Remark : This property gives us a *Symbolic Generalization of the classical Total Probabilities Formula :*

$$p(B) = \sum_{j=1}^{n} p(A_j).p(B| A_j)$$

Example (system CL_7*) : The Cheats Problem.*

An individual is chosen at random among a population including a third of cheats. This person draws a card out of a pack which contains 32 cards. We admit that a cheat is certain to turn up an ace. What is the certainty degree that the chosen individual turns up an ace ? Put Φ="the individual turns up an ace" and ϕ="the individual is a cheat".

In other words, we have : $\tau_\alpha = \tau_3$, $\tau_{\mu 1} = \tau_7$, $\sim \tau_\alpha = \tau_5$, $\tau_{\mu 2} = \tau_2$. Then, we obtain $\tau_\beta = \tau_4$. So, it is moderately-probable that "the individual turns up an ace".

If we suppose now that it is very-probable that a cheat turns up an ace, then we have

$\tau_\alpha = \tau_3$, $\tau_{\mu 1} = \tau_6$, $\sim \tau_\alpha = \tau_5$, $\tau_{\mu 2} = \tau_2$. Since we obtain : $\tau_\beta = \tau_3$, it is little-probable that "the individual turns up an ace".

Proposition 3.5. C-conditional Detachment Rule.

Let ϕ and Φ be two formulas of C such that : $\mathcal{A} \models {}_\alpha Prob(\phi)$ and $\mathcal{A} \models {}_\mu Prob(\Phi|\phi)$. If $\tau_\lambda = I(\tau_\alpha, \tau_\mu)$, then $\mathcal{A} \models \beta Prob(\Phi)$ with $\tau_\beta \in [\tau_\lambda, \tau_\alpha \to \tau_\lambda]$.

Remark : The precise Certainty interval can be viewed as a *Symbolic Generalization of the similar one obtained within classical Probability Theory.*

Proposition 3.6. Generalization of Bayes' Formula.

Let ϕ_1 , ...,ϕ_n and Φ be formulas of C such that :

(i) : $\mathcal{A} \models {}_M (\phi_1 \cup ... \cup \phi_n)$,

(ii) : $\mathcal{A} \models {}_1 (\phi_i \cap \phi_j)$ *for* i=1,...,n, i=1,...,n *with* i≠j,

(iii) : $\mathcal{A} \models {}_{\alpha i} Prob(\phi_i)$ (i=1,...,n),

(iv) : $\mathcal{A} \models {}_{\mu i} Prob(\Phi| \phi_i)$ (i=1,...,n).

Put $\tau_{\gamma 1} = I(\tau_{\alpha 1}, \tau_{\mu 1})$ and $\tau_{\gamma k} = S(\tau_{\gamma(k-1)}, I(\tau_{\alpha k}, \tau_{\mu k}))$ for k=2,...,n.

Then, $\mathcal{A} \models {}_{\eta i} Prob(\phi_i| \Phi)$ with $\tau_{\eta i} \in C(\tau_{\gamma n}, I(\tau_{\alpha i}, \tau_{\mu i}))$ (i=1,...,n).

Remark : This result appears as a *Generalization of classical Bayes' Formula*

$$p(A_i|B) = \frac{p(A_i).p(B|A_i)}{\sum_{j=1}^{n} p(A_j).p(B|A_j)}$$

Example (system CL_7) : *The Cheats Problem again.*

Let us come back to the cheats problem with the first hypothesis. The previous result leads to : $\tau_{\mu 1}=\tau_6$. So, it is very-probable that an individual obtaining an ace is a cheat.

Proposition 3.7. Let ϕ, Φ and Ψ be formulas of C such that :

$$\mathcal{A}\models {}_\alpha Prob(\phi),\ \mathcal{A}\models {}_{\mu 1}Prob(\Phi|\phi)\ and\ \mathcal{A}\models {}_{\mu 2}Prob(\Psi|\phi\cap\Phi).$$

Then $\mathcal{A}\models {}_\mu Prob(\Phi\cap\Psi|\phi)$ *with* $\tau_\mu\in C(\tau_\alpha, I\ (\ I\ (\tau_\alpha, \tau_{\mu_1}),\ \tau_{\mu_2}))$.

Example (system CL_7) : *Young Students.*

Let us suppose that "it is very-little-probable that young students are wage earners" and that "it is very-probable that students are young".

Put $\phi(m)=$student(m), $\Phi(m)=$young people (m) and $\psi(m)=$wage earner(m). We have : $\mathcal{A}\models {}_2 Prob(\psi(m)|\phi(m)\cap\Phi(m))$ and $\mathcal{A}\models {}_6 Prob(\Phi(m)|\phi(m))$. If we examine the students population, we obtain, "it is very-little-probable that students are young wage earners".

Proposition 3.8. Let ϕ and Φ be two formulas of C such that :

(i) : $\mathcal{A}\models {}_\alpha Prob(\phi),$

(ii) : $\mathcal{A}\models {}_\mu Prob(\Phi|\phi),$

(iii) : $\mathcal{A}\models {}_{\mu'}Prob(\neg\,\Phi|\phi).$

Then :

(a) : $\tau_\alpha=S(I(\tau_\alpha, \tau_\mu), I(\tau_\alpha, \tau_{\mu'})),$

(b) : *if* $\tau_\mu\in C(\tau_\alpha, \tau_\lambda)$ *then* $\tau_{\mu'}\in C(\tau_\alpha,\ \tau_{\alpha+1\ -\lambda}),$

(c) : *With the system* CL_7, *we have :* $S(\tau_\mu, \tau_{\mu'})=\tau_M$, *for any* $\tau_\alpha>\tau_1.$

Remark : With the system CL_7, S taking the place of *Summation operator*, we obtain a *Symbolic Generalization of the classical Probabilistic result* :

$$p(\neg\,A|B) + p(A|B) = 1\ (property\ (c)).$$

Remark : We can point out that our model can be applied in Linguistic Domains, since it deals, in a satisfactory way, with *natural langage Conditionals* (*Cf.* [Pacd92(b), 94], [PdjH95]).

4 Conclusion

We have presented a Logico-symbolic System dealing with Uncertainty encoded into a Qualitative way. We keep working in a Finite-valued Predicate Logic to represent the Uncertain Knowledge. We use Qualitative terms to express partial Certainty. Its management can be made within a Semantic Model using two Detachment Rules, i.e. the Logical and the Conditional Inferences. So, we can use Generalizations of either classical Deductions Rules, or classical Conditional Probabilities. We have also pointed out that our approach leads to the basis of a Symbolic Theory of Probability.

References

[ADGP92] H. Akdag, M. De Glas & D. Pacholczyk – *A Qualitative Theory of Uncertainty.* Fundamenta Informaticæ. Vol. 17. N°. 4. p. 333-362. 1992.

[Alel88] R. Aleliunas – *A new normative theory of probabilistic logic.* in Proc. of the Canadian A.I. Conf. San Mateo, California. p. 67-74. 1988.

[Alel90] R. Aleliunas – *A summary of New Normative Theory of Probabilistic Logic.* in Uncertainty in A.I. 4 . Elsevier Science Pubs. North Holland. p. 199- 206. 1990.

[Bell90] J. Bell – *Nonmonotonic reasoning, nonmonotonic logics and reasoning about change.* in A. I. Review 4. p. 79-108. 1990.

[Bobr84] D. G. Bobrow – *Qualitative Reasoning About Physical Systems.* Amsterdam. Elsevier Science Pubs. 1984.

[Bout94)] C. Boutilier – *Modal Logics for Qualitative Possibility Theory.* in Int. Journal of Approximate Reasoning, 10. p 173 - 201. 1994.

[CGSc91] G. Coletti, A. Gilio & R. Scozzafava – *Assessment of qualitative judgements for conditional events.* in Expert Systems. Lecture note in Computer Sc. Nu. 548. 1991.

[CoGr83] P. R. Cohen & M.R. Grinsberg – *A framework for Heuristics Reasoning about Uncertainty.* in Prooc. AAAI. p 355 - 357. 1983.

[Cohe85] P. R. Cohen – *Heuristic Reasoning about Uncertainty : An A. I. approach.* Pitman Pubs. Inc. 1985.

[DaGi92] A. Darwiche & M. Ginsberg – *A symbolic generalization of probability theory.* in proc. of the Am. Ass. for A. I. San Jose. p. 622-627. 1992.

[Darw92] A. Darwiche – *A symbolic generalization of probability theory.* Ph.D. D. Computer Science Dpt., Stanford University. Palo Alto, California. 1992.

[Davi90] E. Davis – *Representation of Commonsense Knowledge.* Morgan Kaufmann. 1990.

[DrHe93] M.J. Druzdzel & M. Henrion – *Efficient Reasoning in Qualitative Probabilistic Networks* Proc. of AAAI. p 548 - 553. 1993.

[FPKE93] J. Fox, S. Parsons, P Krause & M. Elvang-Goransson - *A General Framework for Uncertainty Reasoning.* in Proc. of IMACS Inter. Worshop. Barcelona. p 461 - 470. 1993.

[Gold92] M. Goldszmidt – *Qualitative probabilities, a normative framework for commonsense reasoning.* Ph.D. D. University of Los Angeles. 1992.

[GoPe92] M. Goldszmidt & J. Pearl – *Reasoning with qualitative probabilities can be tractable.* in proc. of the 8th Conference on A. I. Stanford. p. 112-120. 1992.

[HaFa92] J. Y. Halpern & R. Fagin – *Two views of belief : belief as generalized probability and belief as evidence.* in A.I. 54. p. 275-317. 1992.

[Haec92] W. van der Haeck - *On the Semantics of Graded Modalities.* Journal of Applied Non-classical Logics, 2 (1). p 81 - 123. 1992.

[HeDr91] M. Henrion & M. J. Druzdzel – *Qualitative propagation and scenario- based schemes for explaining probabilistic reasoning.* in Uncertainty in A. I. 6. p. 17-32. 1991.

[Pacd92(a)] D. Pacholczyk – *Contribution au Traitement Logico-symbolique de la Connaissance.* Thèse d'Etat. Université P. et M. Curie. PARIS VI. 1992.

[Pacd92(b)] D. Pacholczyk – *A New Approach to Vagueness and Uncertainty.* in C.C.-A.I. Vol. 9. Nu. 4. p. 395-435. 1992.

[Pacd93] D. Pacholczyk – *Symbolic Reasoning under Vagueness and Uncertainty.* LAFORIA, Rapport interne n° 93/19.

[Pacd94] D. Pacholczyk – *A Symbolic Probability Theory for the Management of Uncertainty.* in CC-AI, Vol 11, Nu 4, p 3 - 70. 1994.

[PdjH95] D. Pacholczyk, J-M. Pacholczyk & G. Hunault - *Explicit Management of the Natural Language Uncertainty via a Logico-symbolic Probability Theory.* To appear in Proc. WOCFAI'95. Paris. July 1995.

[PaDo93] S. Parsons & M. Dohnal – *A semiqualitative approach to reasoning in probabilistic networks.* in Applied A. I. Vol. 7, Nu. 3. p. 223-236. 1993.

[PaMa93] S. Parsons & E.H. Mandani – *Qualitative Dempster-Shafer Theory.* in Proc. of IMACS Worshop. Barcelona. p 471 480. 1993.

[Pars93] S. Parsons – *On Reasoning in networks with qualitative Uncertainty.* in Proc. 9th Conf. on Uncertainty in A. I. Washington. DC. 1993.

[Pear88(a)] J. Pearl – *Evidential Reasoning Under Uncertainty.* in Exploring A. I. (H. E. Shorbe Ed.). M. Kaufman, San Mateo. p. 381 - 418. 1988.

[Pear88(b)] J. Pearl – *Probabilistic reasoning in intelligent systems.* Morgan Kaufmann Pubs. San Mateo, California. 1988.

[Pool91] D. Poole – *Representing diagnostic knowledge for probabilistic Horn abduction.* in Proc.s of IJCAI'91. p. 1129 - 1135. 1991.

[Pool93] D. Poole – *Average-case analysis of a search algorithm for estimating prior and posterior probabilities in Bayesian networks with extreme probcbilities.* in Proc. of IJCAI'93. p 606 - 612. 1993.

[Stru88] P. Struss – *Mathematical aspects of qualitative reasoning.* A.I. Eng. 3. p 156-169. 1988.

[Well90] M. Wellman – *Formulation of tradeoffs in Planning under Uncertainty.* Pittman. London. 1990.

[Will86] B. C. Williams – *Doing Time : Putting qualitative reasoning on former ground.* in IAAAI-86, Philadelphie. p. 105 - 112. 1986.

[XBPo90] Y. Xiang, M.P. Beddoes & D. Poole – *Can Uncertainty Management be realized in a finite totally ordered Probability Algebra.* in Uncertainty in A. I 5. Elsevier Science Pubs. p. 41 - 57. 1990.

Systematic Construction Of Qualitative Physics-Based Rules For Process Diagnostics

Jaques Reifman
Argonne National Laboratory
Reactor Analysis Division
Argonne, Illinois 60439
U.S.A.
e-mail: jreifman@anl.gov

Thomas Y. C. Wei
Argonne National Laboratory
Reactor Engineering Division
Argonne, Illinois 60439
U.S.A.

Abstract

A novel first-principles-based expert system is proposed for on-line detection and identification of faulty component candidates during incipient off-normal process operations. The system performs function-oriented diagnostics and can be reused for diagnosing single-component failures in different processes and different plants through the provision of the appropriate process schematics information. The function-oriented and process-independent diagnostic features of the proposed expert system are achieved by constructing a knowledge base containing three distinct types of information, qualitative balance equation rules, functional classification of process components, and the process piping and instrumentation diagram. The various types of qualitative balance equation rules for processes utilizing single-phase liquids are derived and their usage is illustrated through simulation results of a realistic process in a nuclear power plant.

1.0 Introduction

For over a decade researchers and engineers have been developing expert systems (ESs) for process fault diagnostics. In the early systems, the knowledge base (KB) was constructed through pre-analysis of the failure of each process component based on an event-oriented approach. Once the symptoms or process signal trends associated with each component fault were identified, diagnostic rules were constructed that directly mapped symptoms into specific component faults.[1] In the later systems, the KB was constructed by modeling the process through graph structures[2,3] where a function-oriented approach was generally used for diagnostics. Once the functions of each process component were known and the process model developed, diagnostics were accomplished by comparing the process functions that were disrupted with the components responsible for performing the disrupted functions. The advantage of this approach over event-oriented is that there is a limited number of functions that a component is designed to provide, while there are numerous possible combinations of component failures.

In spite of the progress made over the last decade, process diagnostics ESs are still limited in one fundamental aspect. They are designed to diagnose component faults for one specific process. New ESs need to be designed for different processes, unless the processes are identical, even if the processes share common properties such as similar thermal-hydraulic (T-H) geometrical configurations, operating conditions, and fluid material and phase.

Here, we propose a novel function-oriented first-principles-based concept for developing process diagnostic ESs that overcomes this limitation. Except for the self-contained process schematics representation, the KB of the proposed system is process-independent, which allows for usage of the same diagnostic system with different processes and plants. This possibility not only decreases the effort involved in developing a new system, but it also eliminates the time-consuming process of KB verification and validation, which needs to be performed only once in the proposed approach. The process-independent diagnostic capability of the proposed ES is attained through the use of qualitative reasoning where a small number of values are taken to represent the values of continuous real-valued variables.

Figure 1 illustrates the three types of knowledge of the proposed diagnostic ES and their corresponding usage, in a three-step mapping, that relates process symptoms into component faults.[4,5] When a process component fails, it causes the process T-H variables, e.g., pressure P, flow W, temperature T, and level L, to vary or trend from their expected values. The physical rules database (PRD) is used to map the trend in the T-H variables into imbalance trends in the three conservation types of mass, energy, and momentum, e.g., mass increase, momentum decrease. Then, the component classification dictionary (CCD) is applied to map the identified imbalance type and trend into generic faulty component types, e.g., pump, valve, heat exchanger, whose failure could have been responsible for the identified imbalance, i.e., the inadequate performance of one of the three T-H functions, mass transfer, energy transfer, or momentum transfer. Finally, the piping and instrumentation diagram (PID) containing the process schematics information, the only system-dependent portion of the KB, is applied to identify specific faulty components, e.g., pump A, valve CV-121, regenerative heat exchanger C, as the possible faulty component candidates.

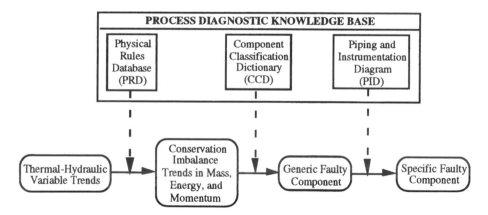

Fig. 1.   Three Distinct Types of Knowledge in the Knowledge Base Perform Three Mappings Required for Process-Independent Function-Oriented Diagnostics

In previous work reporting the proposed concept,[4,5] the first-principles qualitative rules of the PRD used to map trends in the T-H variables into imbalances of mass, energy, and momentum, were solely derived through the equations of state (EOS) and the definition of momentum. Furthermore, each process component was associated with one control volume that required *complete* instrumentation, i.e., each control volume was characterized by lumped values of P, W, T, and L, which are rarely available for each process component in real-world applications. Here, in addition to the EOS and definition of momentum, we apply the basic mathematical description of the macroscopic conservation equations to construct qualitative rules[6] that characterize imbalances in mass, energy, and momentum. The locations of the existing process instruments that measure the T-H variables define the boundaries of the control volume for each rule, which may now involve one or more connected components. That, in addition to the provision of different types of rules with different instrumentation requirements and rules capable of inferring the trend of nonmeasured variables, reduce the need for complete instrumentation. In the following sections, we derive the various types of qualitative rules of the PRD and illustrate their usage through simulation results of a process in a nuclear power plant. In this paper, the derived rules are limited to single-component failures in generic T-H processes consisting of single-phase liquid, i.e., subcooled water. However, the rules in the PRD of the developed ES also account for separated volume components containing noncondensable gas over single-phase liquid.

2.0 Qualitative Physics-Based Rules

The qualitative physics rules that we derive in this section are generic rules in the sense that the same set of rules can be applied to different component types and different T-H processes without any need for customization. This approach differs from the qualitative physics reasoning methods based on De Kleer and Brown's work,[6] where a set of balance equations or confluences that model the process are customized for each device (process) based on the device topology. However, to permit the generalization of the rules, the geometrical configuration of the T-H system is decomposed into T-H loops, which are classified as being of two types, open and closed. A loop is defined as a continuous circuit of fluid flowing monotonically in one direction. A closed loop starts and ends at the same location, while an open loop starts at two different pressure boundaries. This decomposition of the T-H system into decoupled T-H loops allows the physical rules representing the mathematical conservation equations to be applied to any control volume configuration, i.e., one specific component or a group of connected components, within a T-H loop. The rules can not be applied to control volume configurations composed of components belonging to different T-H loops. This is due to our approach which follows a monotonically varying pressure distribution with account taken for the step discontinuity at the pump.

The qualitative physics rules of the PRD are of two classes: Q rules and CV rules. A Q rule indicates the type and trend of the imbalance in a control volume inferred from the trends in the T-H variables. Corresponding to the three balance equations of mass, energy, and momentum, we have three types of Q rules, Q_{mass}, Q_{eng}, and Q_{mom}, respectively, which can have one of three trends or qualitative values, increasing($\uparrow$), decreasing ($\downarrow$), and unchanging (-). Thus, if a control volume is experiencing a loss of mass, a Q rule identifying such imbalance would characterize the Q status of the control volume as $Q_{mass}^{\downarrow}$. A CV rule infers the trend status of nonmeasured T-H variables, pressure P, flow W, temperature T, and level L, in a process component, from the other T-H variables and the Q status of the component. In the following paragraphs, we illustrate the derivations of the Q rules and CV rules.

2.1 Derivation of Q Rules

Different classes of Q rules, with varying degree of diagnostic precision, can be derived as a function of the type, trend, and number of T-H variables. Specific groups of three-signal variables with specific trends are required to form the minimum set for *unique* identification of an increasing or decreasing Q status in a control volume. For instance, the three-signal variables [$P^{\downarrow}$ $W_{in}^{\uparrow}$ $W_{out}^{\downarrow}$], can uniquely identify $Q_{mass}^{\downarrow}$ in the control volume defined by the two flow measurements in both open and closed T-H loop configurations. In the above notation, $P^{\downarrow}$ indicates a pressure decrease measurement anywhere in the T-H loop, $W_{in}^{\uparrow}$ represents an increase in the control volume inlet flow and $W_{out}^{\downarrow}$ represents a decrease in the control volume outlet flow. Unique Q status identification can also be obtained for Q_{mom} and Q_{eng} if the specific variable trends are available for the sets [W P_{in} P_{out}] and [W T_{in} T_{out}], respectively. However, in many practical situations, the instrumentation set is insufficient to provide this minimum set. There are cases where only two- or one-signal variables are available in a loop. In such cases, Q rules can also be constructed to provide some malfunction Q diagnostics. But as can be expected, the precision of the diagnostics decreases with a larger number of possible Q malfunctions being inferred. For instance, if only the two-signal variable set [P W] is available in the loop, then a Q rule would indicate both Q_{mass} and Q_{mom} problems.

In the following paragraphs, we derive Q rules with both three- and two-variable sets. Also, we show that three-variable rules can be systematically constructed through the logical intersection of two two-variable rules, and that two-variable rules can be constructed through the logical union of two three-variable rules.

Three-Variable Rules

We start the derivation of three-variable rules for Q rules that infer imbalances in the conservation of mass inventory. For the control volume shown in Fig. 2, associated with one or a group of connected components, the static mass conservation equation is given by

$$Q_{mass} = W_{out} - W_{in} , \qquad (1)$$

where W_{in} and W_{out} are the control volume inlet and outlet mass flow rates, respectively, and Q_{mass} is the mass source/sink term in the mass balance. Reference 7 discusses how we separate the dynamic effects of a process component malfunction from the analysis of the static conservation equations. Transforming Eq. (1) into qualitative differential expressions using De Kleer and Brown's[6] methodology and notation, gives the following confluence:

$$[dW_{in}] - [dW_{out}] = -[dQ_{mass}], \qquad (2)$$

where the square brackets [·] represent the qualitative value or trend ($\uparrow$, $\downarrow$, -), of the argument basic quantity, i.e., W_{in}, W_{out}, and Q_{mass}. Equation (2) represents the general confluence, from which Q rules characterizing imbalances in Q_{mass} can be derived by applying the different trend combinations of W_{in} and W_{out}, and using the operations of qualitative algebra.[6] For the case where inlet flow into the control volume is increasing and outlet flow is decreasing, the confluence in Eq. (2) infers that Q_{mass} is decreasing ($Q_{mass}^{\downarrow}$), or, equivalently, that the control volume is loosing mass, represented through the rule:

$$\text{rule (A)} \qquad \text{If} \quad W_{in}^{\uparrow} \text{ and } W_{out}^{\downarrow}, \quad \text{Then } Q_{mass}^{\downarrow}. \qquad (3)$$

While Q_{mass} in the actual balance equation is the source/sink term, in the qualitative analysis rule in Eq. (3), it should be thought of as a conservation imbalance indicator, viz. a malfunction status indicator characterizing the fact that one of the components within the control volume is malfunctioning and causing the mass inventory to decrease.

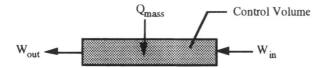

Fig. 2.   Control Volume with Moveable Boundaries Defined by the Location of the Flow Measurements W_{in} and W_{out}

Similarly, we can also derive a rule from the general confluence in Eq. (2) corresponding to rule (A), for the case where Q_{mass} is increasing,

$$\text{rule (B)} \qquad \text{If} \quad W_{in}^{\downarrow} \text{ and } W_{out}^{\uparrow}. \quad \text{Then } Q_{mass}^{\uparrow}. \qquad (4)$$

Trend combinations that cause ambiguous inference in Eq. (2), e.g., both W_{in} and W_{out} increasing, are not represented in the PRD. These two rules, (A) and (B), formed with two variables of the same type, i.e., W, in the condition part of the rule, uniquely identify Q_{mass} imbalances in open loops. However, in closed loops, where the definition of "in" (upstream) and "out" (downstream) has two possible combinations, both rules would be simultaneously activated regardless of the fault location and type of mass problem.

This undesirable situation can be eliminated, by the addition of information, if a P instrument measurement is available. Through perturbation analysis of the single-phase liquid equation of state $P = P(\rho, T)$, where ρ is the liquid density, we obtain

$$dP = \frac{\partial P}{\partial \rho} d\rho + \frac{\partial P}{\partial T} dT. \tag{5}$$

By initiating the fault diagnosis when dT is *small* and using the fact that the bulk modulus $(\rho \partial P / \partial \rho)$, for liquid water is positive, the qualitative differential equation for Eq. (5) becomes

$$[dP] = [dM], \tag{6}$$

where M is the liquid water mass inventory in a control volume V with density ρ. Instantiating the confluence in Eq. (6) with a decreasing pressure trend, translates into the rule

$$\text{rule (C)} \qquad \text{If } P^{\downarrow}, \quad \text{Then } M^{\downarrow}. \tag{7}$$

If a P meter is available in a closed (or open) loop, an indication of $P^{\downarrow}$, and hence $M^{\downarrow}$, would contradict an inference made by rule (B). Thus, the logical combination of rule (C) with rules (A) and (B) eliminates the possibility of applying rule (B) and uniquely identifies the $W^{\uparrow}$ instrument as being upstream of the malfunction and $W^{\downarrow}$ instrument as being downstream of the malfunction. The logic intersection of rules (A) and (C) is therefore

$$\text{rule (D)} \qquad \text{If } P^{\downarrow} \text{ and } W_{in}^{\uparrow} \text{ and } W_{out}^{\downarrow}, \quad \text{Then } Q_{mass}^{\downarrow}. \tag{8}$$

Analogously, there is a corresponding rule for Q_{mom} when three-signal variables, [W P_{in} P_{out}], are available,

$$\text{rule (E)} \qquad \text{If } W^{\uparrow} \text{ and } P_{in}^{\downarrow} \text{ and } P_{out}^{\uparrow}, \quad \text{Then } Q_{mom}^{\uparrow}, \tag{9}$$

where $Q_{mom}^{\uparrow}$ is downstream of P_{in} and upstream of P_{out}, and W is measured anywhere in the loop. Rules (D) and (E) are examples which illustrate that only three-signal variables, [P W_{in} W_{out}] or [W P_{in} P_{out}], are required to form the minimum set for *unique* $Q_{mass}^{\uparrow\downarrow}$ and $Q_{mom}^{\uparrow\downarrow}$ identification for the complete set of loops.

Two-Variable Rules

When only two- or one-signal variables are available in a loop, rules can also be constructed to provide some malfunction Q diagnostics. But as can be expected, the precision of the diagnostics decreases with a larger number of possible Q malfunctions being inferred. We provide an illustration of one such rule, for the case when only two-signal variables [P W], are available and show how the rule is constructed.

For the case where [$P^{\downarrow}$ $W^{\uparrow}$], rule (D) could be activated, if another flow meter downstream of W was present with a decreasing trend, or rule (E) could be activated, if another pressure meter downstream of P was present with an increasing trend. Since either rule could be activated in this [$P^{\downarrow}$ $W^{\uparrow}$] combination, then the logic union of rules (D) and (E), could be applied

$$\text{rule (F)} \qquad \text{If} \quad P^{\downarrow} \text{ and } W^{\uparrow}, \quad \text{Then } Q^{\downarrow}_{mass} \text{ or } Q^{\uparrow}_{mom}, \qquad (10)$$

where $Q^{\downarrow}_{mass}$ is located downstream of the W instrument and $Q^{\uparrow}_{mom}$ is located downstream of the P instrument. Thus, when two-variable rules with different T-H variables are activated, the location of one of the variables (W for Q_{mass} and P for Q_{mom}) is used to define one boundary of the control volume with the other boundary defined by either end of the loop.

The construction of rule (F) shows that there is a systematic procedure using Boolean logic, logic union in the case of two-signal variables, to derive Q rules with two- or one-signal variables from the set of rules which uses the minimum three-variable sets [P W_{in} W_{out}] and [W P_{in} P_{out}]. However, the two-variable rules can also be used to reconstruct the three-variable rules, if the signal variables can be grouped in blocks of two. For instance, if we consider a two-variable rule analogous to rule (F), i.e.,

$$\text{rule (G)} \qquad \text{If} \quad P^{\downarrow} \text{ and } W^{\downarrow}, \quad \text{Then } Q^{\downarrow}_{mass} \text{ or } Q^{\downarrow}_{mom}, \qquad (11)$$

and a signal set [$P^{\downarrow}$ $W^{\uparrow}_{in}$ $W^{\downarrow}_{out}$] is available, it can be grouped as two two-variable sets [$P^{\downarrow}$ $W^{\uparrow}$] and [$P^{\downarrow}$ $W^{\downarrow}$]. This would mean the activation of both rules (F) and (G), where the logical intersection of these rules is $Q^{\downarrow}_{mass}$, which is the identical conclusion of the activation of rule (D). This shows the logical consistency between the derivation of the sets of the different-variable-number rules. We apply logical union when we construct two-variable rules from two three-variable rules and logical intersection when we construct three-variable rules from two two-variable rules.

2.2 Derivation of CV Rules

CV rules infer the trend status of nonmeasured variables of a process component based on the trends of other T-H variables and the Q status of the component. We illustrate the derivation of a CV rule that infers the trend of the flow W_a, through the cold side of a counter current heat exchanger. For the control volume shown in Fig. 3, the static energy conservation equation is given by

$$Q_{eng} = W_a (h_{out} - h_{in}) = W_a c_p (T_{out} - T_{in}), \qquad (12)$$

where h_{in} and h_{out} are the control volume inlet and outlet enthalpy, respectively, c_p is the specific heat and Q_{eng} is the energy source/sink term in the energy balance. Transforming Eq. (12) into a qualitative differential expression and solving for W_a yields the confluence

$$[dQ_{eng}] + [dT_{in}] - [dT_{out}] = [dW_a]. \tag{13}$$

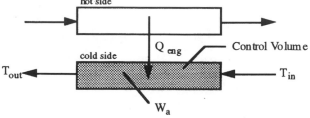

Fig. 3.   Control Volume Representation of the Cold side of a Counter Current Heat Exchanger where the Energy Balance Equation Allows for the Inference of the Trend of the Flow W_a Through the Heat Exchanger

For the case where the energy source into the control volume is not increasing, the inlet temperature is not increasing, and the outlet temperature is increasing, the confluence infers that the flow rate is decreasing, represented through the rule:

rule (H)   If $Q'^{\uparrow}_{eng}$ and $T'^{\uparrow}_{in}$ and $T^{\uparrow}_{out}$,   Then $W^{\downarrow}_a$,   (14)

where the symbol "/" indicates negation. Other CV rules for inference of W_a can be obtained by instantiating the quantities in the left hand side of the confluence in Eq. (13) with different trend combinations. A similar procedure is used to derive CV rules for other types of T-H variables and components.

The synthetic signal trends obtained through the CV rules extract the most information possible from the process and increase the total number of instruments (virtual and real) available for diagnostics. Once inferred, synthetic signals are combined with actual signals and used to determine the Q status of components through the Q rules. In the following section, we illustrate the usage of CV and Q rules in the diagnostics of a component failure in a nuclear power plant process.

3.0 Simulation Results

The concepts discussed in the previous section have been incorporated into the process diagnostic system PRODIAG. The current version of PRODIAG is written in Quintus Prolog[8] and has been designed to identify single-component failures in generic T-H processes consisting of single-phase liquid, i.e., subcooled water, and single-phase liquid plus noncondensable gas. In the following, we show simulation results of one, out of many fault events, in the Chemical and Volume Control System

(CVCS) of a pressurized water nuclear reactor for which PRODIAG has been used to perform diagnostics.[9,10] A blind test with thirty-nine events simulated with a full-scale operator training simulator has been used to validate PRODIAG. Out of the 39 events, 37 were correctly identified within the first 40 seconds with graded degree of accuracy, i.e., uniquely identified, identified as one of two candidates, etc.

Figure 4 illustrates a portion of the letdown line and charging line of a CVCS for a pressurized water reactor. Letdown water leaves the Reactor Coolant System (RCS), indicated in the upper left portion of the figure, and flows through the shell-side or hot-side of the regenerative heat exchanger (RHX) where it gives up its heat to makeup water being returned to the RCS. From there, letdown water proceeds through a series of components (not represented in Fig. 4) until it reaches the Volume Control Tank (VCT). Then, the charging pump (pump A in the figure) takes the coolant from the VCT through the tube-side or cold-side of the RHX and back to the RCS. This simplified piping and instrumentation diagram configuration of the CVCS is decomposed into two open T-H loops, loop 1 representing the letdown line from the RCS to the VCT and loop 2 representing the charging line from the VCT to the RCS. Other flow lines, i.e., T-H loops, are represented in the PID database of PRODIAG but have been removed from the figure for simplification.

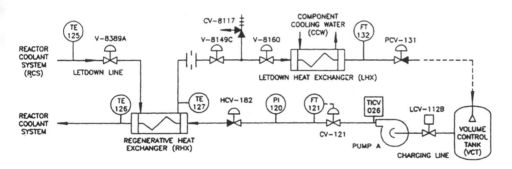

Fig. 4. Simplified Letdown Line and Charging Line of a Chemical and Volume Control System for a Pressurized Water Reactor

Let us consider the fault event where the pipe in the charging line (loop 2) connecting valve HCV-182 and the RHX starts leaking. The charging line leak causes an instantaneous decrease in loop 2 pressure, except for the separated volume VCT, measured by PI-120, increase in mass flow rate from the VCT up to the leak location measured by FT-121, and decrease in mass flow rate from the leak location to the RCS. The absence of a flow meter downstream of the leak precludes the detection of the decrease in makeup water through the tube-side (cold-side) of the RHX. A decrease in the RHX cold-side flow causes an increase in the heat exchanger outlet temperatures measured by TE-126 in loop 2 and TE-127 in loop 1. However, due to the heat exchanger thermal inertia, there is a time delay before the RHX outlet temperatures increase to reflect the pipe leak in loop 2.

When the fault event starts, PI-120 indicates a pressure decrease and FT-121 indicates a flow increase. With only these two $[P^{\downarrow} \ W^{\uparrow}]$ measurements, the two-variable rule in the PRD, rule (F), is activated by PRODIAG to hypothesize that there is either a mass decrease in loop 2 downstream of FT-121 or a momentum increase in loop 2 downstream of PI-120. The lack of an additional flow meter downstream of the leak location, precludes the differentiation between the two hypotheses. However, a few seconds into the transient, the RHX outlet temperature measured by TE-126 starts to increase, allowing PRODIAG to rule out the momentum problem and narrow down the diagnostics to a mass decrease problem.

The ES diagnostic rules of the PRD arrive at the correct diagnosis by sequentially applying CV rule (H), and then Q rule (D). First, CV rule (H) is applied to infer that flow W_a through the cold-side of the RHX is decreasing. With this information, Q rule (D) is applied by *creating* a control volume from valve CV-121 to the RHX, by matching W_{in} with FT-121 and W_{out} with W_a, to infer that mass is decreasing.

PRODIAG applies a few other rules, not described in this paper, before CV rule (H) can be activated. First, the enthalpy (or temperature) transport rules are applied in both loops to transport the constant temperature trend measured by TICV-026 and TE-125 to the inlet of the RHX for the cold- and hot-sides, respectively, of the heat exchanger. This procedure allows for the inference of a constant inlet temperature T_{in} in both sides of the RHX and accounts for the second term $T_{in}^{/\uparrow}$, in the condition part of rule (H). The third term in the expression $T_{out}^{\uparrow}$, is directly accounted through the measured value of TE-126. Finally, the first term $Q_{eng}^{/\uparrow}$, is accounted for by solving an energy balance equation similar to Eq. (13) for dQ_{eng} in loop 1, and reversing the obtained trend to infer Q_{eng}^{-} if TE-127 is unchanging and $Q_{eng}^{\downarrow}$ if TE-127 is increasing. Either case satisfies $Q_{eng}^{/\uparrow}$.

Once the diagnostics of the charging line leak is narrowed down to a mass decrease problem between flow meter FT-121 and the estimated flow W_a inside the RHX, the ES proceeds to hypothesize the faulty component. Faulty components are hypothesized through the last two mappings illustrated in Fig. 1. First, the CCD database is searched to identify generic component types whose failure could have caused the detected mass imbalance. For mass decrease, closed valve or component break are identified. In out abstract classification of generic components, a break is classified as a sink of mass since when a component breaks or leaks it affects the mass balance causing a *loss* of mass. Next, the PID database is searched to determine if there are closed valves or component break between the two flow measurements. Since there are no closed valves, PRODIAG correctly hypothesizes that the faulty component is a break between FT-121 and the RHX.

4.0 Conclusions

In this paper we present a novel function-oriented first-principles-based ES for on-line diagnosis of incipient process component failure. Diagnostics are performed through a three-step mapping process, where trends in T-H variables are mapped into trends in imbalances of mass, energy, and momentum, which are then mapped into generic faulty components and next mapped into specific faulty components. The mapping from T-H variables to imbalances in the conservation equations is performed through qualitative physics-based rules that are systematically derived in the paper. Both three- and two-variable rules are constructed, which can be used to identify imbalances in control volumes with varying diagnostics precision, depending on the type, trend, and number of instruments available. Unlike prior work describing the use of qualitative physics-based rules, here the approach is generic, with no need to customize the rules as a function of the process to be diagnosed. The proposed approach is system-independent and can be applied to different processes and plants, with the provision of the appropriate process-specific piping and instrumentation diagram.

Initial simulation results for the CVCS of a nuclear power plant indicate that the proposed ES can correctly diagnose single component failures in T-H processes consisting of single-phase liquid plus noncondensable gas. Future work will include the testing of the ES to diagnose malfunctions in different T-H systems consisting of similar fluid properties, and extension of the current work to include T-H processes utilizing two-phase flow and multiple-component failures. Future work will also include the implementation of signal processing techniques such as low frequency bandpass filters to account for noisy signals in the determination of signal trends.

Acknowledgments

This research was supported by the U.S. Department of Energy, Energy Research Program, under contract number W-31-109-ENG-38.

References

1. W. R. Nelson, "REACTOR: An Expert System for Diagnosis and Treatment of Nuclear Reactor Accidents," *Proceedings of the National Conference on Artificial Intelligence*, AAAI, pp. 296-301, Pittsburgh, Pennsylvania, August 18-20, 1982.

2. F. E. Finch and M. A. Kramer, "Narrowing Diagnostic Focus Using Functional Decomposition," *AIChE J.*, **34**, 25, 1988.

3. J. E. Larsson, "Hyperfast Algorithms for Model-Based Diagnosis," *Proceedings of the IEEE/IFAC Joint Symposium on Computer-Aided Control System Design*," pp. 533-538, Tucson, Arizona, March 7-9, 1994.

4. J. Reifman, L. L. Briggs, and T. Y. C. Wei, "A First-Principles General Methodology for Representing the Knowledge Base of a Process Diagnosis Expert System," *Proceedings of the 4th International Conference on Industrial*

and Engineering Applications of Artificial Intelligence and Expert Systems, pp. 255-265, Kauai, Hawaii, June 2-5, 1991.

5. J. Reifman, L. L. Briggs, and T. Y. C. Wei, "Nuclear Power Plant Diagnostics Using Qualitative Analysis and Component Functional Classification," *Proceedings of the Frontiers in Innovative Computing for Nuclear Industry*, pp. 227-236, Jackson, Wyoming, September 15-18, 1991.

6. J. De Kleer and J. S. Brown, "A Qualitative Physics Based on Confluences," *AI*, **24**, 7, 1984.

7. J. Reifman and T. Y. C. Wei, "PRODIAG - Dynamic Qualitative Analysis for Process Fault Diagnosis," *Proceedings of the 9th Power Plant Dynamics, Control and Testing Symposium*, pp. 40.01-40.15, Knoxville, Tennessee, May 24-26, 1995.

8. Quintus Corporation, Palo Alto, California, Release 3, 1991.

9. J. Reifman, T. Y. C. Wei, R. G. Abboud, and T. M. Chasensky, "Cooperative Research and Development for Artificial Intelligence Based Reactor Diagnostic System," *Proceedings of the American Power Conference*, pp. 365-370, Chicago, Illinois, April 25-27, 1994.

10. J. Reifman, T. Y. C. Wei, R. G. Abboud, and T. M. Chasensky, "Function-Based Approach to Plant Diagnosis," paper submitted to the American Nuclear Society 1995 Winter Meeting, San Francisco, California, October 29-November 2, 1995.

Integrated Process Supervision : A Structured Approach to Expert Control

C.Quek, P.W.Ng and M.Pasquier

Intelligent Systems Laboratory, School of Applied Science, Nanyang Technological University, Singapore 2264

Abstract. There is much interest in the use of expert systems in on-line process supervision and control. One of the better known Expert Control (EC) [1] architecture is that proposed by Karl J. Astrom. In this architecture, there are several alternative algorithms used for the same function. This is because there is seldom one single algorithm that works for the entire operation. These algorithms are coordinated by an expert system, which decides which algorithm to use and when to use it [1]. It is at this point that the architecture offers little assistance. As a result, most applications of the Expert Control (EC) tend to have ad hoc rules [1]. This is compounded by the need for additional safety logic rules when performing adaptation. The Integrated Process Supervision (IPS) [1] [9] [10] is a refinement of the EC architecture by allowing the integration of different control techniques within a single generic framework. The IPS framework introduces a generic structure for the rules used by the coordinating expert system. The IPS has been validated using both classical [10] and AI control techniques [11] such as neuro-control.

1 Introduction

There is much interest in the use of Artificial Intelligence techniques in Control Engineering, particularly knowledge based systems. This is due to the ease of translating human operators experience to computer readable rules.

The use of knowledge based systems in Control Engineering falls into several categories [7] [8]. The first involves the use of the rulebased system as part of the feedback loop. The second involves the use of expert systems in designing the controller. Closely related to this is the use of knowledge based system in tuning the controller parameters during operation. Such a use of the expert system is normally referred to as process supervision. The third use of expert system is in fault diagnosis.

The focus of this paper is in the use of knowledge based systems in the area of on-line process supervision. Current approaches to on-line process supervision tends to be very application specific. This is due mainly to the following reasons:

1. Specific plants (i.e. different plant transfer functions, different faults to monitor)

---

[1] MIPS: A Toolkit for Multivariable Integrated Process Supervision, Applied Research Grant 7/92, Nanyang Technological University, Singapore.

2. Specific controllers (PID, relay, fuzzy)
3. Specific methods to change controller parameters
4. Safety logic to ensure that controller and tuner operates correctly.

As a result of the uniqueness of each application, there is littile attempt to provide a methodology to specify the rules. Hence, rules for on-line process supervision tend to be ad hoc.

There are many research efforts to develop a framework for the use of knowledge bases in on- line process supervision. Recommendations include the use of temporal reasoning, blackboards, hierarchy, etc. However, they seldom provide details on how to specify the rules. Most literature does not list out the rules which are used in their application. As a result, the engineer has to develop the rules individually.

The Integrated Process Supervision (IPS) provides a generic framework for the proper organization and separation of distinct tasks for on-line process supervision. Through this framework, the rules for supervision becomes well structured and the control problem becomes modular. An added advantage of this generic framework is that it allows the integration of various control techniques.

In the following section, the Expert Control (EC) architecture is examined. Next the Integrated Process Supervision (IPS) architecture is discussed in details to demonstrate its generality. To demonstrate the generality of the IPS, results of two instances of the IPS are presented. In both cases, the same rules were used by the process supervisor.

2 Expert Process Supervision

Astrom's Expert Control (EC) architecture is examined in details in this section since the IPS framework is a refinement of the EC architecture. Figure 1 shows the EC architecture. The various layers (shaded) at each component indicate the use of several algorithms for each task. This is because there is seldom a single algorithm that works for the entire operating regions of the plant. The knowledge base in the EC selects the appropriate algorithm and adjust the parameters used by the algorithm. The knowledge base also includes safety logic that ensures that the tuning of the controller parameters does not cause the system to become unstable.

The EC is generic to the extent in that it allows the use of various algorithms where appropriate. All these algorithms are coordinated by the knowledge base. It is natural to group rules into classes that are associated with different algorithms and different task to be performed. It is also very convenient to have generic rules that apply to classes of objects. However, the EC architecture provides little assistance here. The knowledge base needs to supervise and interact with the various tasks of tuning, identification, supervision, etc. Consequently, the knowledge base becomes complex. This is because there is no former definition of what process supervision entails. As a result, any function can fall within the confines of process supervision.

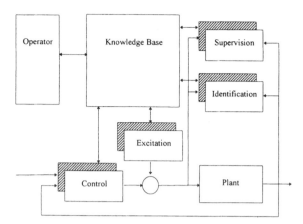

Fig. 1. Expert Control Architecture

A survey of current literature [7] [8] reveals that process supervision has the following functions :

1. Detection of plant parameter deviations and instability
2. Guidance of controller tuning, adaptation and synthesis
3. Identification and Diagnosis of process faults

Each of these functions is non-trivial and significant efforts are employed in these areas. Furthermore, these functions need not necessarily be limited to knowledge base techniques. It is useful to separate these functions and have the knowledge base activate them when necessary and select the appropriate algorithm for the activated function. In theIPS the following definition for process supervision is adopted :

Process supervision is the selection and activation of appropriate techniques so as to drive the system to meet the required system performance objectives.

It is up to the activated technique to perform its intended function. The process supervisor is not involved in that function except to verify that the selected technique is able to perform its intended function. Hence the interaction between the process supervisor and other tasks is minimized. Through this separation of supervisory function from the task specific functions, the Integrated Process Supervision (IPS) achieves generality, in that any technique can be used for the task specific function, and elegance, in that the rules becomes very modular.

This separation is the point where the IPS deviates from the EC. In the EC architecture, the adaptive mechanism is generally in-built within the rulebase. This incorporation gives rise to two disadvantages. Firstly, it complicates the rulebase as the rulebase has other functions (e.g. fault monitoring, etc.) to do. Secondly, the use of a rulebased adaptation is usually limited to the heuristic tuning of classical controllers such as the PID controller [5]. Other adaptation approaches such as Self Tuning Regulation (STR) [3] and Model Reference

Adaptive System (MRAS) [4] are difficult to express using rules. Furthermore, training of neural network controllers, such as backpropagation based controllers [12], by virtue of their complexity can never be trained using rule-base heuristics. In addition, even with the common PID controller, good tuning rules for the entire operating region are extremely difficult to find; even though much research effort has already been put in. With the separation of supervisory and task specific functions, IPS is able to overcome these two difficulties.

3 Integration of Approaches Using IPS

In this section the IPS concept is further explored. There are two principal concepts to IPS, namely the classification of control tasks and the use of performance indices to select the control tasks. It will be shown that the use of performance indices alone is sufficient criteria in the selection of appropriate control tasks.

3.1 Basic Control Regimes

The functions needed to be performed by any control system can be classified into three categories, namely :

1. Primary Control
2. Adaptive Control
3. Fault Diagnosis

The primary control function is to ensure that the controlled variable maintains at some fixed level (regulation) or follow some values (servo). In most cases, the primary controller can only work well when the operating conditions fall within the design assumptions. If the design assumptions are violated, the adaptive control regime is invoked to adjust the parameters of the primary controller. If the adaptive regime is unable to effectively adjust the control parameters, this is an indication that some severe system deviations has occurred. In this case the fault diagnosis regime is invoked. Figure 2 shows the basic control regimes as well as the IPS framework.

Any technique can be used for each regime, although they have to be properly matched. For example, if a fuzzy linguistic controller is used as the primary controller, a STR cannot be used as the adaptive controller. Other than this minor restriction, any technique can be used for each control regime. Consequently, the tuning rules used in the EC rulebase, can be viewed as an adaptive controller. From this perspective, the IPS can be seen as a framework that encapsulates the EC.

The emphasis here is the classification of basic control functions. The criteria for the activation of these basic regimes is specified by a performance index (or a combination of performance indices). This is done by the process supervisor.

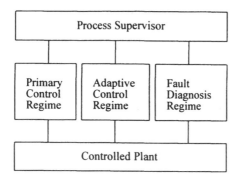

Fig. 2. Control Regimes in IPS

3.2 Performance Index

The aim of any control system is to satisfy some performance requirement. This is usually expressed in terms of a performance index whose value is to be minimized. When the performance index meets the system requirements, the system is considered to exhibit acceptable behaviour. If the system deviates from the design assumption, the performance index increases. The system is now considered to exhibit malfunction behaviour. This can be due to changes in operating conditions or changes in system parameters through degradation (i.e. wear and tear). If the degradation persists further, the performance index will increase even more. The system is then considered to exhibit faulty behaviour. This use of performance index to classify system behaviour is shown in Figure 3. The boundaries for the system behaviours are specified by the values X and Y. These values are design parameters for the IPS. Percentages are used to specify deviation from the reference model.

This classification of system behaviours matches exactly that of the control regimes described earlier. When the behaviour is acceptable, the primary control regime suffices. When the system exhibit malfunction behaviour the adaptive regime has to be invoked. The adaptive regime attempts to adjust the primary controller parameters so as to bring the system performance back into the acceptable region. If stability is not preserved during adaptation, the performance index will increase further and thus provides an indication that the adaptive algorithm used is not suitable. Finally, when the system is faulty, the fault diagnosis regime is activated. Through the matching of the basic control regimes with system behaviours, the IPS provides a generic framework for the integration of various control techniques.

3.3 Fuzzy Scheduling

The boundaries for the different behaviours are not crisp but fuzzy for two reasons. Firstly, the plant model may not represent the actual plant well and hence

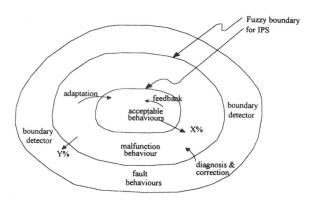

generic tasks: feedbacks, adaptation & diagnosis

Fig. 3. Classification of System Behaviours

introduces some uncertainties. Secondly, the measurement of the performance index is not accurate due to noise. The use of fuzzy sets to account for the fuzzy boundaries is not discussed in this paper so as not to distract the reader from the main focus of this paper. Details on the fuzzy scheduling of control regimes will be reported separately.

4   Simulation Results

In order to study the validity of the IPS architecture, an experimental testbed based on a computer simulation of an industrial process was developed. This testbed has been implemented on a SUN Sparc 10 workstation. Figure 4 shows a simplified block diagram of the process rig. Two distinct mass or energy flow loops can be identified. They are: the fluid and thermal loops and shall, henceforth, be referred to as the flow and the temperature loops respectively. For brevity, only experiments on the flow loop is discussed. The flow loop consists of four major components, namely the heater tank, the sump, the forced air convection radiator and the DC motor pump. Water is pumped from the sump into the tank via the radiator. The radiator consists of a radiating manifold through which the fluid flows. An electric fan forces a steady stream of air between the radiating surfaces and the fluid is cooled as it flows through the manifold. The rate of flow of the fluid through the radiator is monitored by an impeller type flow meter. Fluid in the tank drains under gravity into the sump via a solenoid valve. This circulation of fluid through the components under both the pump action and gravity forms the flow loop.

In the simulation tests, a gradual pipe blockage was introduced into the radiator fins of the flow loop. The blockage progressed gradually from zero percentage blockage of the radiator till it reached 40 %. This parametric drift produced performance degradation and could be detected by the IPS. The IPS automatically

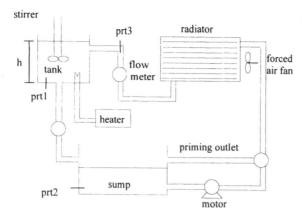

Fig. 4. Simplified Block Diagram of Process Rig

scheduled the appropriate control regime on the basis of the amount of degradation produced by the drift. The process supervisor used the closed loop integral square error (ISE) and the control effort as supervisory inputs.

In order to demonstrate the generality of the IPS framework, two instances of the IPS were implemented to control the process rig. The first instance [9] used a PI controller for the primary regime and an Model Reference Adaptive System (MRAS) for the adaptive regime. The second instance [11] used a Modified Cerebellar Model Articulation Controller (MCMAC) for the primary regime and the MCMAC training algorithm for the adaptive regime. In both cases, the same fault diagnostic algorithm is used, but is left out of this discussion for clarity. Figure 5 and Figure 6 shows the two instances of the IPS framework.

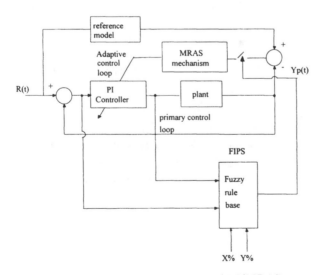

Fig. 5. IPS Implementation using PI/MRAS

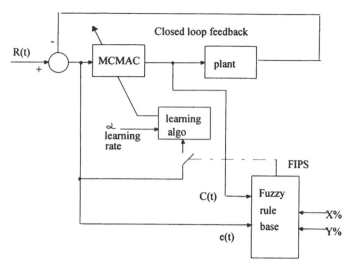

Fig. 6. IPS Implementation using MCMAC/learning algorithm control regime

In both instances the same rules were used in the process supervisor. The rules used are shown below:

If system performance is low and control effort is acceptable
    then behaviour is acceptable
If system performance is medium and control effort is acceptable
    then behaviour is malfunction
If system performance is high and control effort is acceptable
    then behaviour is faulty
If system performance is low and control effort is unacceptable
    then behaviour is faulty
If system performance is medium and control effort is unacceptable
    then behaviour is faulty
If system performance is high and control effort is unacceptable
    then behaviour is faulty

These rules can be represented by a rule map as shown in Figure 7.

There is only a single boundary for control effort instead of two. The blockage at the radiator fins causes an increase in the control effort. The adaptive regime is unable to decrease the control effort as it can only adjust the controller parameters. Consequently, there is no need to schedule in the adaptive regime when the control effort drifts while the performance is still acceptable.

Figure 8 shows the results of the experimentation with PI/MRAS based IPS scheme. The plant ISE index of the closed loop error is normalized to the reference model ISE index. The reference model is a first order model with a time constant of 35 seconds. A probing signal in the form of toggling the reference level about 2% of the reference setting was used to excite the system. The sensitivities of the detection mechanism, X and Y% [9], were defined using fuzzy sets

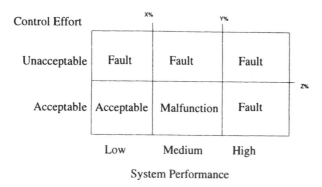

Fig. 7. Rule Map for Process Supervisor

about 120 and 130% of the reference model ISE, Jref. A full paper on the details of the fuzzy scheduling scheme is currently being prepared for publication.

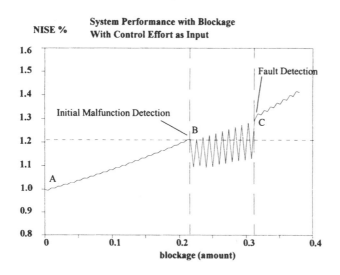

Fig. 8. Control regime scheduling according to performance classification for PI/MRAS IPS scheme.

At instant A, a radiator gradual blockage was introduced, see Figure 8. As the blockage progressed malfunction was detected by the IPS at the instant B. The MRAS was then scheduled to retune the PI controller on-line to bring performance within the acceptable class. Adaptation was stopped by the scheduler at instant C when the performance was deemed faulty due to larger performance degradation. The scheduling between the PI and MRAS regimes alternated during the period between B and C when the system underwent prolonged degradation as a result of further blockage. The MRAS brought the system behaviour within the acceptable class whenever performance exceeded the lower sensitivity detection mechanism (120%). The scheduling between the two continued until the system performance degraded beyond 130% and was considered as a fault by the scheduler. The MRAS was then stopped and the appropriate fault diagnostic technique invoked at instant C. Research work based on synchronous fault tracking [14] [15] using qualitative reasoning techniques [16] are currently being addressed within the MIPS project. Some initial results was reported in [17].

In the second experiment the MCMAC neural network replaced the PI controller as the primary control regime and the corresponding encoding algorithm for the MCMAC replacing the MRAS as the adaptive technique. Figure 9 shows the experimental results of the scheduling of the neural network controller and its learning algorithm as the system's performance degrades with continuous gradual blockage of the radiator. The integral error square of the closed loop error was used as the supervisory input to the fuzzy integrated process supervisor, FIPS This index was normalized to the same ISE, Jref, produced by the reference model used in the first experiment. Owing to the superior closed loop performance of the MCMAC neural network controller the lower behaviour transition boundary (X%) from acceptable to malfunction was set at 40% of the ISE of the reference model, Jref, used in the first experiment. The upper behaviour boundary (Y%) was set at 130%.

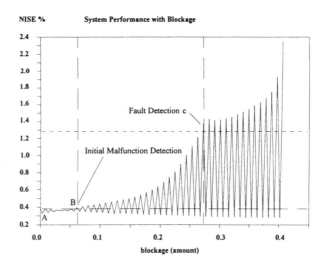

Fig. 9. Control regime scheduling according to performance classification for MC-MAC/learning algorithm IPS scheme

Figure 9 shows the results of the performance by scheduling the MCMAC neural network controller, its encoding algorithm (adaptation) and fault diagnosis regimes as the system performance degrades with the gradual radiator blockage. It shows the changes in the normalized ISE index as the FIPS schedules the different AI control regimes. The two boundary detection settings are shown at 40% and 130% of Jref. Parametric drifts in the form of gradual radiator blockage was initiated during the experiment at the instant A. This is depicted in Figure 9. The performance index increased with increasing blockage until the FIPS detected the behaviour transition at instant B. This was the initial malfunction detection by the FIPS. The encoding algorithm for MCMAC was then initiated by the FIPS to do on-line retuning of the primary controller. Adaptation was then stopped at instant C by the FIPS when the behaviour exceeded the upper behaviour boundary (Y%) fault and the diagnostic regime started. In both experimental setups no actual diagnostic regime was scheduled as this is outside the scope of this paper. The above experiments effectively demonstrated the generality of the architecture to accommodate AI-based control techniques and the scheduling of the primary control and the associated learning algorithm.

5 Conclusion and Future Work

In this paper, the Integrated Process Supervision (IPS) is proposed as a generic framework to provide a structure for Expert Control (EC). By distinguishing between supervisory function and control tasks, the IPS framework offers an elegant way to integrate both traditional and AI-based control techniques. This point has been successfully demonstrated by in the two experiments [9] [11].

The scheduling of the control regimes is achieved through the use of a fuzzy rule based system within the process supervisor. At present further work is being done to enhance the fuzzy integrated process supervisor within the IPS scheme and to extend the IPS to deal with multi-variable and multiple- loop control. Also, the selection of switching boundaries is being studied.

References

1. Astrom K.J., Arzen K.-E., Expert Control in An Introduction to Intelligent and Autonomous Control, Panos J. Antsakis, Kevin M. Passino (Editors), Kluwer Academic Publishers, 1993.
2. Astrom K. J. , "Intelligent Control" in Proceedings of the 1st European Control Conference, Grenoble, France, pp 2328-2339, 1991.
3. Astrom K.J. "Self Tuning Regulators - Design Principles and Applications" in Applications of Adaptive Control, Kumpati S. Narendra, Richard V. Monopoli (Editors), pp 1-68, Academic Press, USA, 1979.
4. Kumpati S. Narendra, Yuan-Hao Lin, "Design of Stable Model Reference Adaptive Controllers" in Applications of Adaptive Control, Kumpati S. Narendra, Richard V. Monopoli (Editors), pp 69-130, Academic Press, USA, 1979.
5. Astrom K.J., Hang C.C., Persson P., Ho. W.K. "Towards Intelligent PID Control" in Automatica Vol 28. No. 1, pp 1-9, Great Britain, 1992.
6. Krijgsman A.J., Verbruggen H.B., Brujin P.M., "Knowledge Based Real-Time Control" in 3rd IFAC Workshop on Artificial Intelligence in Real-Time Control, Clyne Castle, Swansea, UK, pp 13-19, 1988.

334

7. H.B. Verbruggen, A.J. Krijgsman, P.M. Brujin, "Towards Intelligent Control : Integration of AI in Control" in Application of Artificial Intelligence In Process Control, L. Boullart, A. Krijgsman, R.A. Vingerhoeds (Editors), pp 223-249, Pergamon Press, 1992

8. F. Morant, M. Martinez, J. Pico, "Supervised Adaptive Control", in Application of Artificial Intelligence In Process Control, L. Boullart, A. Krijgsman, R.A. Vingerhoeds (Editors), pp 223-249, Pergamon Press, 1992.

9. R. Leitch and C. Quek, "Architecture for integrated process supervision", IEE Proceedings-D, Control Theory and Application, Vol. 139, No. 3, pp 317-327, May 1992.

10. R. Leitch and C. Quek "A behaviour classification for integrated process supervision", IEE Proceedings of the 3rd International Conference on Control, Vol 1, pp 127-133, Edinburgh, Scotland, March 91

11. Quek H.C., Ng P.W., Ng G.S., "Fuzzy Integrated Process Supervision of Neural Network Control Regimes" in Proceeings of the 2nd Singapore International Conference on Intelligent Systems, pp 153-158, Singapore, November 1994.

12. W.H.Schiffman and H.W.Geffers, "Adaptive Control of Dynamic Systems by Backpropagation Networks", Neural Networks, Vol. 6, pp 517-524, S.Grossberg, M.Kawato and J.Taylor (Ed.), Pergamon Press, USA, 1993.

13. C. Quek and R. Leitch, "Direct method for model reference adaptive PI controller using the gradient approach", Proceedings of IEEE Region 10 International Conference, Tencon 93, Vol. 4, pp 447-450, Beijing.

14. Q. Shen, Fuzzy qualitative simulation and Diagnosis of continuous dynamic systems, Ph.D. Thesis, Heriot-Watt University, Edinburgh, September 1991.

15. D.L. Dvorak and B. Kuipers, " Model based monitoring of dynamic systems", Proceedings of the 11th International Joint Conference on Artificial Intelligence, Vol. 2, pp 1338-1343, 1989.

16. D. Weld and J. DeKleer, Readings in qualitative simulation about physical systems, Morgan Kaufman Publisher, San Mateo, CA, 1989.

17. C. Quek, S.Y. Huang and J.C. Tay, "Qualitative synchronous fault tracking for dynamic process diagnosis", Proceedings of the 2nd International Conference for Intelligent Systems, pp 249-255, Singapore, 1994.

Using Stochastic Grammars to Learn Robotic Tasks[*]

Pedro U. Lima[1] and George N. Saridis[2]

[1] Instituto de Sistemas e Robótica/Instituto Superior Técnico
1096 Lisboa Codex, PORTUGAL
[2] ECSE Dept., Rensselaer Polytechnic Institute
Troy, NY 12180-3590, USA

Abstract. The paper introduces a reinforcement learning-based methodology for performance improvement of Intelligent Controllers. The translation interfaces of a 3-level *Hierarchical Goal-Directed Intelligent Machine* (HGDIM) are modeled by a 2-stage *Hierarchical Learning Stochastic Automaton* (HLSA). The decision probabilities at the two stages are recursively updated from the *success* and *failure* signals received by the bottom stage whenever a primitive action of the HGDIM is applied to the environment where the machine operates.

The top translation stage and the use of regular stochastic grammars to accomplish the translation of commands into tasks are described here. Under this framework, subsets of conflicting grammar productions represent different task strategies to accomplish a command. At this stage, an LSA is associated to each subset of conflicting grammar productions. Results of simulations show the application of the methodology to an Intelligent Robotic System.

1 Introduction

Intelligent Control (IC) techniques [1] particularly qualify for applications to Robotics, due to the need to coordinate a diverse and large number of sensors and actuators. They differ from "conventional" control techniques by aiming to attain higher degrees of *autonomy*, thus dealing with higher *uncertainty*. Among IC techniques, we are especially interested on learning-based methodologies, due to the repetitive nature of some robotic tasks or at least of some of the primitive operations which compose them. Reinforcement Learning is particularly interesting as it involves the exchange of small bandwidth information (failure and success signals only) between robotic subsystems. In typical applications, such as unmanned space and underwater missions, the cost of large bandwith for communications between the central command (earth controller or main vessel

---

[*] The first author was supported by the portuguese National Board for Scientific and Technological Research (JNICT), under Grant #BD/1357/91-IA. The second author was supported by the NASA Center for Intelligent Robotic Systems for Space Exploration (CIRSSE) under Grant #NAGW-1333.

controller) is prohibitive and can be reduced by increasing the autonomy of the machine involved in the mission.

This paper summarizes work done towards establishing an analytic design methodology for Intelligent Controllers whose feedback is essentially based on reinforcement learning. An analytic design based on measures of performance recursively improved through feedback assures some degree of certainty about the measurability, repeatability and verifiability of that design. To the best of our knowledge, such a methodology does not currently exist. Here, we focus on learning the optimal tasks of an Intelligent Controller, although this is just a piece of the hierarchical learning methodology we proposed in previous work [2, 3].

Fu [4] was probably the first author to write about Learning Control Systems and to coin as *Intelligent Control Systems* those systems of interdisciplinary nature, in the intersection of Artificial Intelligence and Automatic Control. He also introduced the concepts of *Stochastic Automata* and *Stochastic Grammars*. The former has been developed, although in different directions, by Narendra and his associates [5]. In the last few years, Sutton and his associates explored reinforcement learning solutions which associate these two views of stochastic automata [6].

The paper is organized as follows: in Sect. 2, we summarize basic concepts related to the Theory of Stochastic Grammars. In Sect. 3 we give some insight into the more general problem we are addressing (selection of the optimal tasks and primitive actions from a robotic language hierarchy), focusing later on the particular problem of learning the optimal task selection. Section 4 describes the application of the theory to an intelligent robotic system. Finally, Sect. 5 summarizes the paper and provides suggestions of future research.

2 Stochastic Grammars

Grammars are usually employed to describe the syntax of languages or structural relations defining a pattern. They are useful in the context of Hierarchical Intelligent Controllers to describe the constraints imposed to the ordering of subtasks composing a task. In particular, *Stochastic Grammars* (see a survey by Fu and Booth [7]) allow the assignment of probabilities to conflicting productions or rewrite rules. This turns out to be equivalent to the assignment of probabilities to the different strings of the generated *language*. The probabilities of the productions in each conflicting set can be learned by a *Learning Stochastic Automaton*. Hence, stochastic grammars combined with *Reinforcement Learning* provide the means to learn the ordering of subtasks composing a task.

Let us first define formally a stochastic grammar:

Definition 1. A *stochastic grammar* is defined by the quintuple $G = (V_T, V_N, \mathcal{R}, \mathcal{P}, S)$, where

1. V_T is a finite set of *terminal symbols*;
2. V_N is a finite set of *nonterminal symbols*;

3. $\mathcal{R}$ is a finite set of productions or rewrite rules;

4. $\mathcal{P}$ is a finite set of probabilities that are assigned by a one to one mapping to the elements of $\mathcal{R}$;

5. S is the start symbol.

Only *stochastic regular grammars* will be considered here, that is stochastic grammars whose productions have the general syntax

$$A \to \alpha \ \text{ or } \ A \to \alpha B, \ \alpha \in V_T^*, \ A, B \in V_N$$

where the symbol to the left of the arrow is called *premise* while the term to the right of the arrow is the *consequent*. V_T^* denotes the set of all the possible strings composed by elements of V_T, including the null string.

The set of productions $\mathcal{R}$ can be partitioned into m disjoint subsets $\mathcal{R} = \{\mathcal{R}_1, \ldots, \mathcal{R}_m\}$, where m is the number of nonterminal symbols, $m = |V_N|$. In particular, $\mathcal{R}_i$ is the subset of productions with the same premise A_i, corresponding to the ith nonterminal symbol.

Correspondingly, the set of probabilities $\mathcal{P}$ can be partitioned into m disjoint subsets, where subset $\mathcal{P}_i$ contains the probabilities of the productions of $\mathcal{R}_i$.

A stochastic grammar is *proper* if

$$\sum_{k=1}^{m_i} p_{ik} = 1, \ \ p_{ik} \in \mathcal{P}_i, \ \ |\mathcal{P}_i| = m_i, \ i = 1, \ldots, m$$

i. e. if for each subset of productions $\mathcal{R}_i$ the production probabilities in $\mathcal{P}_i$ add to one.

To each string x of the language $L(G)$ generated by G corresponds a word function $f(x)$. If the grammar is unambiguous, that is, if there is only one leftmost derivation for each x,

$$f(x) = \prod_{k=1}^{K(x)} p(k, x), \ \forall x \in L(G)$$

where $K(x)$ represents the number of steps in the derivation of x, and $p(k, x)$ is the probability of the production used in the kth step of the derivation of x.

A language $L \subset V_T^*$, where V_T^* represents all strings of finite length composed by elements of V_T, including the null string ϵ, is called a *stochastic language* if there is a function $0 \leq f(x) \leq 1$, $\forall x \in L$, called *probabilistic word function*, $f(x): L \to \mathbb{R} <$, such that $\sum_{x \in L} f(x) = 1$. This is the same as to say that the probabilities of each of the strings of L add up to one.

Not all stochastic grammars generate stochastic languages. Some restrictions must be imposed to the stochastic grammar.

A stochastic grammar G is a *consistent grammar* iff the word function defined over $L(G)$ is a probabilistic word function, that is, iff $L(G)$ is a stochastic language.

If the grammar is proper, then it will be consistent.

3 Hierarchical Learning of Optimal Robotic Tasks

3.1 General Concepts of the Model Proposed

A hierarchical architecture for autonomous intelligent control systems which encompasses most of the concepts described in related work was proposed in the 70s by Saridis (see a recent book by Saridis and Valavanis [8]). This architecture is based on a 3-level hierarchy, where more abstract actions are taken at the top **Organization Level** and more precise actions are taken at the bottom **Execution Level**. Given an *external command* (goal), the Organization Level is responsible for sequencing the pre-defined *primitive tasks* into a *task*. The Execution Level executes a detailed translation of the task, generated by the intermediate **Coordination Level**. This level successively decomposes the *subtasks* composing the task into *primitive tasks*, and distributes them by a number of coordinators specialized in specific sub-tasks, such as vision or motion planning for an Intelligent Robotic System. The coordinators invoke the Execution Level *primitive actions* to precisely execute the task.

At the interfaces between IM levels, specific *translations* must be made: the **Organization-to-Coordination Translation Interface** has to choose among different *tasks* capable of attaining a goal. The goal is expressed by a *command* sent to the machine. Any task is composed of *primitive tasks*, usually corresponding to the primitives of a given language. For each primitive task, the **Coordination-to-Execution Translation Interface** has to determine the best *primitive action* from the set of those capable of reaching the elementary subgoal associated to the primitive task.

To compare the different alternatives at each translation interface, we need a *cost function* [3]. In robotic systems, the uncertainty involved in the design of the algorithms implementing *primitive tasks* (move, locate, plan-path) is mostly due to approximate or incomplete modeling and statistical fluctuations around nominal parameters. This uncertainty can be quantified by estimating the reliability of the algorithm, roughly defined as the frequency of successes when attempting to meet its specifications. However, generally the computational cost increases with reliability, in terms of the time it takes to complete, the amount of memory it uses, or the number of resources (e.g. processors) required. Thus, it makes sense to think of a selection technique which includes both reliability and computational cost, but first the two measures must be coherently defined in a context where information is noisy and incomplete [3].

We presented elsewhere [3] equations wich propagate bottom-up the cost function originally defined for *primitive actions*. Hence, the cost function of *primitive actions*, *primitive tasks* and *tasks* is expressed by the balance between cost and complement of reliability of a *task*. *Task* cost and reliability are a direct result of the costs and reliabilities of the *primitive tasks* which compose the task. *Primitive task* cost and reliability are propagated from the same measures for the corresponding *primitive actions*.

The success and failure signals used to estimate the reliability of the algorithms at all levels of the Intelligent Controller are implicitly propagated bottom-up through the hierarchy by the described scheme. The **Execution Level** receives a reinforcement signal as the result of applying a *primitive action*. This occurs each time the *primitive action* is applied by checking if the corresponding specifications were met. The success or failure signal is used to recursively estimate the reliability of the *primitive action*, which is propagated to the reliability of a *task* as explained before.

3.2 Learning Task Selection

When the design is based on the hierarchical model just described, we must define the set of available *primitive tasks* and corresponding *primitive actions* first, and then define the alternative *tasks* for each *command* as strings of a language whose terminal symbols are the *primitive tasks*. If we view the alternative *tasks* for a command as different decompositions of that command into *primitive tasks*, a stochastic grammar is a well suited model of the job performed by the **Organization-to-Coordination Translation Interface**. Each subset of productions of the grammar represents a set of alternatives in the decomposition process.

This use of a stochastic grammar resembles an expert system where the production rules have associated certainty factors. However, the association of a LSA to each subset of productions and the introduction of a performance measure provides a consistent and quantifiable method of learning the best decisions.

We have proposed before a methodology for performance improvement of *Hierarchical Intelligent Controllers* (HICs) based on *Hierarchical Reinforcement Learning*. The two translation interfaces of Saridis' 3-level hierarchy are modeled by a 2-stage *Hierarchical Learning Stochastic Automaton* (HLSA), as sketched in Fig. 1. The HLSA includes a *Hierarchical Reinforcement Learning Scheme* which recursively updates the decision probabilities at the two stages from *success* and *failure* signals received by the bottom level whenever an action of the HIC is applied to the environment. Under this learning scheme, the probability of selecting the best tasks and primitive algorithms converges to 1 with probability one (w.p.1) [2].

The *task* selection process is improved recursively as the cost function estimates improve from the propagation of the cost and reliability learned at the **Coordination-to-Execution Interface**. However, we fill focus here on the top **Organization-to-Coordination Interface**, that is on learning the optimal *task* selection. Nevertheless, it is important to note that this differs from other Hierarchical Reinforcement Learning methods described in the literature (e.g. Lin [9]) aiming to teach some complex task to a robot. Here a primitive action fails or succeeds due to a failure or success to meet its specifications, and the overall task is evaluated from the performance of its composing primitives, while in those works the overall task is directly reinforced from the success or failure of its application, evaluated by an external agent. This evaluation is assumed to be either performed either by a human or by a sensing system which may be itself very unreliable or too complex.

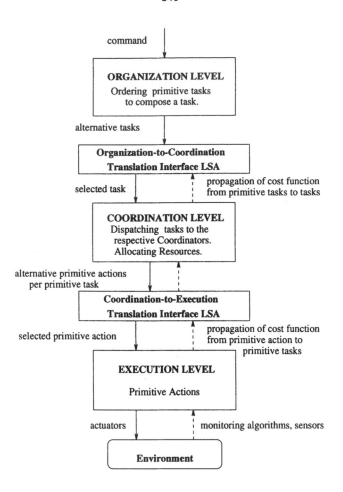

Fig. 1. HLSA and HIC

The solution presented is valid under the general assumptions that the HIC moves inside an environment which can be modeled as a multi-state stochastic process, the HIC can recognize the different states of the model of the environment, and there is a mechanism of error detection and error recovery to detect and recover from situations which could compromise the integrity of the HIC and/or of the environment.

Each *command* interpretable by the HIC is the starting symbol of a regular stochastic grammar. The grammar expresses the constraints imposed by the *command* to the set of *primitive tasks*, the terminal symbols of the grammar. Each string of the language generated by the grammar represents a *task*. Hence, a *task* is generated by the successive application of grammar *productions*.

As we are dealing with regular grammars, the *premise* of each production of the grammar is a non-terminal symbol of the grammar. Each subset of grammar productions with the same premise (refer to Sect. 2) represents one (or more) alternatives on the derivation of the translating *task*. There is a LSA associated to each of these subsets. The productions in each subset are the actions of the LSA, and their probabilities are learned according to the LSA reinforcement scheme explained below. The set of all these LSAs represents the top stage of the hierarchy. The optimal *task* is indirectly learned along time, as a result of learning the optimal production of each production subset. The *task* is optimal in the sense of minimizing the cost function which balances algorithm reliability and cost.

At every step, a (sub)optimal *task* is selected by random decision, based on the current subsets of production probabilities. Each *task* is a string of *primitive tasks*. The *primitive tasks* composing *task t* will also be in the *consequent* of some production involved in the generation of t.

The **cost function**, valid at all levels of a Hierarchical Intelligent Controller, is defined by:

$$J = 1 - R + \rho C \tag{1}$$

where R is the reliability, C the cost and ρ a weighting factor such that $\rho C \in [0, 1]$. In general ρ will be such that the cost does not overwhelm the reliability when directing the search for the optimal action.

Equation (1) applies to the three levels of the HIC, i.e., the performance of a *primitive action*, *primitive task* or *production* can be evaluated by (1), if the cost and reliability are appropriately propagated bottom-up through the hierarchy. The propagation equations can be found in Lima and Saridis [3].

To update the probability density function over the set of *tasks* for a *command*, Fu's stochastic approximation reinforcement learning scheme used in this work is based on the generalized LSA proposed by Nikolič and Fu [10].:

$$p_{ij}(n_i + 1) = p_{ij}(n_i) + \gamma(n_i + 1)(\lambda_{ij}(n_i) - p_{ij}(n_i + 1)) \tag{2}$$

where $n_i = \sum_j n_{ij}$, $0 \leq \lambda_{ij}(n_i) \leq 1$, $\sum_j \lambda_{ij}(n_i) = 1$, $i = 1, \ldots, d$ denotes environment states, $j = 1, \ldots, r$ denotes *tasks*. As the environment is assumed to be multi-state stochastic, we must create a LSA per environment state.

Given the estimates of the performance function for the top stage, $\lambda_{ij}(n_i)$ is given at each step by

$$\lambda_{ij}(n_i) = \begin{cases} 1 \text{ if } \hat{J}_{ij}(n_{ij}) = \min_k \hat{J}_{ik}(n_{ik}) \\ 0 \text{ if } \hat{J}_{ij}(n_{ij}) \neq \min_k \hat{J}_{ik}(n_{ik}) \end{cases} \tag{3}$$

We use $\gamma(n_i + 1) = \frac{1}{n_i+1}$, which satisfies the condition of Theorem 2 in [10]. Given this, it has been proven that the probability density function of the action probabilities for state i converges w.p.1 to zeros for all the actions (*tasks*) except the optimal action m at each stage. The optimal action is the one which minimizes J. If m is the index of the optimal action, $J_{im} = \min_{k=1,\ldots,r}\{J_{ik}\}$, where J_{ij} is the cost function at the decision stage under consideration. Hence, the theorem implies that $\Pr\{\lim_{n_i \to \infty} p_{im}(n_i) = 1\} = 1$, for state i, $i = 1, \ldots, d$ and action j, $j = 1, \ldots, r$.

4   Application to an Intelligent Robotic System

The coordination of vision and motion algorithms is one of the typical problems in Intelligent Robotic Systems. This is the subject of the case study described in this section.

A manipulator PUMA 560 has to grasp a cylindrical strut whose 3D pose (position + orientation) is roughly known. There is a pair of cameras in the ceiling, overviewing the working space of the manipulator and used by a stereo vision system to determine more accurately the 3D pose of the object. The manipulator has position, velocity and force sensors. The scene is well illuminated but from time to time lights go off, deteriorating the accuracy of vision algorithms. The environment has 2 states, one corresponding to lights on (state 0) and the other to lights off (state 1).

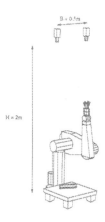

Fig. 2. Workspace setup for case study 2

A realistic simulation of this setup has been performed, including PUMA dynamics, realistic vision system parameters and dimensions, and compliance. Detailed description of the *primitive actions* used for each *primitive task* can be found in [2].

The only *command* available is c=Grab-Strut. The *primitive task* set is composed by 5 *primitive tasks*, $E = \{e_1, e_2, e_3, e_4, e_5\}$, where $e_1 \stackrel{\Delta}{=}$move manipulator, $e_2 \stackrel{\Delta}{=}$grasp object with compliance, $e_3 \stackrel{\Delta}{=}$locate object, $e_4 \stackrel{\Delta}{=}$plan trajectory, and $e_5 \stackrel{\Delta}{=}$grasp object hard.

Primitive task e_1 represents the motion of the manipulator tip along a preplanned trajectory in joint space. Uncertainty is due to unmodeled dynamics and noise.

The goal of *primitive tasks* e_2 and e_5 is to slowly move the tip (tool) of the manipulator to the object and grasp it. The *Position Accommodation Control* method is used by all algorithms translating e_2 to accomplish compliance control of the manipulator. Different parameterizations of the required impedance (similar to a mass, spring and damper system) result in different algorithms with different costs and reliabilities. Motion driven by some desired force moves the tool tip to the object. e_5 is position controlled and has only one translating algorithm. Only passive compliance exists in this case.

Primitive task e_3 determines the pose of an object using stereo vision algorithms. The uncertainty on pose determination by stereo vision is mainly due to matcher errors when determining which image pixels in the two cameras correspond to the same point in the observed scene. This may be due both to spot noise and pixel resolution, and leads to disparity errors which affect the 3D pose estimation.

Changing the state of the environment deeply affects the two algorithms. Switching the lights off increases spot noise which affects the estimation (by any of the algorithms) of the strut end-points in each of the images. This will increase disparity errors and consequently pose estimation errors.

Primitive task e_4 plans a trajectory in joint space whose end-points are the joint-space vectors corresponding to the initial and final pose required for the manipulator tip when moving from a standby position to the grasping position. A *minimum-jerk trajectory generator* is the only algorithm used. It generates the desired joints acceleration, velocity and position at a number of pre-specified points along the trajectory by a method which minimizes the jerk, or third derivative of joint position.

Table 1 shows the costs of the *primitive actions* for the different *primitive tasks*. Cost does not change with the state of the environment. During the simulation, the reliabilities of the *primitive actions* were estimated based on the rewards resulting from the successes of their application over the simulated environment.

Table 1. Primitive tasks, primitive actions and computed costs.

pr. task	e_1		e_2				e_3		e_4	e_5
pr. action	a_1^1	a_2^1	a_1^2	a_2^2	a_3^2	a_4^2	a_1^3	a_2^3	a_1^4	a_1^5
cost	0.55	0.44	0.18	0.14	0.16	0.22	0.35	0.35	0.00	0.3

To grab the strut, the system must first estimate the strut pose. Then, it plans a path from the current pose of the manipulator tip to the neighborhood of the strut pose, and moves along that path. Finally, the manipulator slowly approaches the strut and tries to grasp it. Alternative tasks differ by the inclusion or not of compliance in the final move, and by using or not using stereo vision to refine the *a priori* knowledge of the strut pose. The stochastic regular grammar for the command is:

$$
\begin{aligned}
G &= (V_T, V_N, R, P, S) \\
V_N &= \{ S, A, B \} \\
V_T &= \{ e_1, e_2, e_3, e_4, e_5 \} \\
R &= \{ \\
0.5\ S &\to e_3\ A \\
0.5\ S &\to A \\
1.0\ A &\to e_4\ e_1\ B \\
0.5\ B &\to e_2 \\
0.5\ B &\to e_5\ \}
\end{aligned}
$$

The numbers to the left of the productions are the initial production probabilities. Productions such as $S \to A$, with no terminal symbols in its right-hand side, are assigned zero cost and 0.5 reliability.

The simulation described in the previous section was run for several different situations in order to point out the main concepts and tradeoffs of the proposed execution and design methodologies, and also to suggest future research avenues.

All results shown are the average over 50 sample functions of some stochastic process, such as the evolution of action probabilities or cost function, except when noted. Each sample function consists of 150 *task* runs (iterations in the figures), except when noted. The production and algorithm probabilities are updated after a task is applied. The initial state of the environment is always state 0 (lights on).

The plots of action probabilities and cost functions for "conflicting" productions 0 and 1 are displayed at the top of Fig. 3. Their evolution is slow. The bottom of the same figure shows the result of using a convergence acceleration method which combines a modified version of the algorithm proposed by Nikoliç and Fu [10], with the use of initial estimates for the reliabilities, based on models or past experience of the designer. initial estimates $R(0)$ are weighted by a confidence factor.

Figure 4 shows the results of testing the adaptiveness of the learning scheme to an unacknowledged change in the state of the environment. Only one sample of the stochastic processes is shown. The state of the environment switches from state 0 (lights on) to state 1 (lights off) at iteration 150, but state 0 remains the estimated state for the HLSA, which does not recognize the change. The simulation consisted of 400 task runs. A recursive sample mean algorithm with *forgetting factor* was used to improve the adaptiveness of cost function and probability estimates at the bottom stage. No proof of convergence exists for this algorithm, which resembles the stochastic approximation algorithm described before, but gives more weight to recent samples than to old samples.

After the state switching, production 0 is no longer the best production, since the performance of the stereo algorithms deteriorates under poor lighting conditions, and the initial rough estimate of the strut pose is preferred. In this run, the HLSA learned the change.

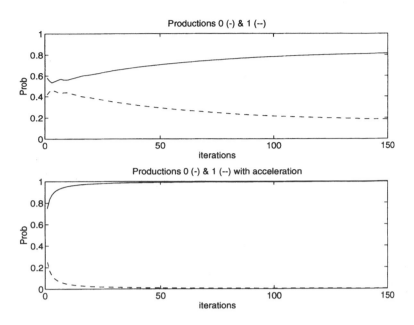

Fig. 3. Learning the best between productions 0 and 1. Top: without acceleration; Bottom: with acceleration

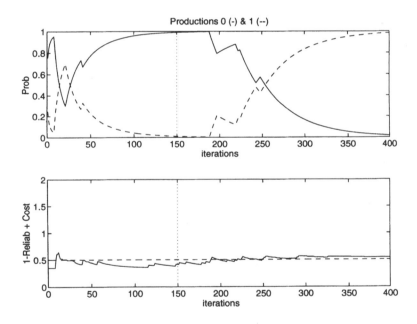

Fig. 4. Adaptiveness of learning scheme when seeking the best between productions 0 and 1

5 Conclusions and Future Research

Measuring its performance and improving that performance using feedback from the environment are desirable features of any Intelligent Controller. We have described part of a model of a Hierarchical Intelligent Controller which uses a Hierarchical Reinforcement Learning Scheme to converge w.p.1 to the actions which minimize a proposed cost function. The cost function balances the complement of reliability and cost at all levels of the Intelligent Controller.

The paper focused on the translation from commands to tasks, performed by a regular stochastic grammar. The probabilities of production subsets of the grammar are learned along time from estimates of the tasks cost function. These are obtained by bottom-up propagation of the cost function of the primitive actions of the Intelligent Controller, estimated from successes and failures of these actions to meet the specifications for the primitive tasks they translate.

Future research should contemplate the extension from regular to more complex grammars (such as context-free) in order to accommodate a broader language for task generation from commands. The behavior of Hierarchical Learning Stochatic Automata (used to model the whole Hierarchical Intelligent Controller) in the presence of non-stationary environments is a subject of current research.

References

1. Technical Committee on Intelligent Control, "Report of task force on Intelligent Control, IEEE Control Systems Society," *IEEE Control Systems Magazine*, vol. 14, June 1994. P. Antsaklis, editor.
2. P. U. Lima and G. N. Saridis, "Hierarchical reinforcement learning and decision making for Intelligent Machines," in *Proceedings of 1994 IEEE Int. Conf. Robotics and Automation*, May 1994.
3. P. U. Lima and G. N. Saridis, "A performance measure for Intelligent Machines based on complexity and reliability," in *Proceedings of SY.RO.CO 94*, September 1994.
4. K. S. Fu, "Learning Control Systems - review and outlook," *IEEE Transactions on Automatic Control*, vol. AC-15, no. 2, 1970.
5. K. S. Narendra and M. A. L. Thathachar, *Learning Automata - an Introduction*. Prentice Hall, 1989.
6. R. S. Sutton, A. G. Barto, and R. J. Williams, "Reinforcement learning in direct adaptive optimal control," *IEEE Control Systems Magazine*, vol. 12, no. 2, pp. 19–22, 1992.
7. K. S. Fu and T. L. Booth, "Grammatical inference: Introduction and survey – part II," *IEEE Transactions on Systems, Man and Cybernetics*, vol. SMC-5, no. 4, 1975.
8. K. P. Valavanis and G. N. Saridis, *Intelligent Robotic Systems*. Kluwier Publishers, 1992.
9. L.-J. Lin, "Scaling up reinforcement learning for robot control," in *Proceedings of the Tenth International Conference on Machine Learning*, 1994.
10. K. S. Fu and Z. J. Nikoliç, "On some reinforcement techniques and their relation to the stochastic approximation," *IEEE Transactions on Automatic Control*, vol. AC-11, no. 2, pp. 756–758, 1966.

Constraint Categorial Grammars

Luís Damas, Nelma Moreira
{luis,nam}@ncc.up.pt

LIACC, Universidade do Porto
Rua do Campo Alegre 823, 4150 Porto, Portugal

Abstract. Although unification can be used to implement a weak form of β-reduction, several linguistic phenomena are better handled by using some form of λ-calculus. In this paper we present a higher order feature description calculus based on a typed λ-calculus. We show how the techniques used in $\mathcal{CLG}$ for resolving complex feature constraints can be efficiently extended. $\mathcal{CCLG}$ is a simple formalism, based on categorial grammars, designed to test the practical feasibility of such a calculus.
Keywords: constraint satisfaction, computational semantics, high-order programming.

1 Introduction

Unification based formalisms show a clear inability to deal in a natural way with phenomena such as the semantics of coordination, quantification scoping ambiguity or bound anaphora. As a matter of fact, although unification can be used to implement a weak form of β-reduction, it seems that this kind of phenomena is better handled by using some form of λ-calculus [DSP91, Per90]. One possibility, which is at the heart of systems like λProlog[NM88], is to extend both the notion of term, to include λ-abstraction and application, and the definition of unification to deal with λ-terms. For this extension to be technically sound it is necessary to require λ-terms to be well typed. On the other hand, it turns out that if instead of using terms we use complex feature descriptions (where conjunction replaces unification), we still can follow the same plan to produce a higher-order calculus of feature descriptions. $\mathcal{CCLG}$ is a simple formalism, based on categorial grammars, designed to test the practical feasibility of such an approach. The main reason for selecting a categorial framework for this experiment was that, due to the simplicity of the categorial framework, it allowed us to concentrate on the constraint calculus itself. Another reason was also the close historical relationship between categorial grammars and semantic formalisms incorporating λ-abstraction. $\mathcal{CCLG}$ extends categorial grammar by associating not only a category but also a higher-order feature description with each well-formed part of speech. The type of these feature descriptions are determined by the associated category. Note also that a derivation leading to an unsatisfiable feature description is legal. When compared with other formalisms (for instance, [ZKC87]) one of the main distinguishing features of $\mathcal{CCLG}$ is the fact that it computes partial descriptions of feature structures and not the feature structures themselves.

It is important to notice that this calculus is easily modified to deal with constraints over finite or rational trees, instead of feature trees. Also, the advantages of this kind of calculus, namely its decidability, over the use of general high-order logic programming systems, for processing semantic representations in NLP systems should be obvious. The rest of the paper proceeds as follows. We start by defining a feature description calculus as an hybrid of λ-calculus and feature logics and we present its denotational semantics. In section 2.1 we describe a complete constraint solver for higher-order feature descriptions. In section 3 we define constraint categorial grammars and briefly present its implementation. Some final remarks are considered in section 4.

2 Feature Description Calculus

The feature description calculus $\Lambda_{\mathcal{FD}}$ at the heart of our formalism is inspired both on the λ-calculus and on feature logics [Smo89, ST92]. For technical reasons, namely that we want to ensure the existence of normal forms, it is a typed calculus. Our base types are **bool** for truth values and **fs** for feature structures.

Our types are described by

$$\tau ::= \mathbf{bool} \mid \mathbf{fs} \to \tau \mid \tau \to \tau'$$

Note that we exclude **fs** as the type of any feature description. This reflects our commitment to compute partial descriptions of feature structures rather than feature structures.

Now assume we are given a set of *atoms* a, b, ..., a set of *feature* symbols f, g, ..., a set of *feature structure variables* x, y, ..., and, for each type τ, a set of *variables of type* τ x_τ, y_τ, ... Then the set of *feature descriptions* of type τ is described by

$$
\begin{aligned}
e_\tau \quad &::= \mathbf{true} \mid \mathbf{false} \mid x_\tau \mid e_\tau \wedge e_\tau \mid e_\tau \vee e_\tau \mid \neg e_\tau \mid e_{fs \to \tau} x.p \mid e_{fs \to \tau} a \mid e_{\tau' \to \tau} e_{\tau'} \\
e_{bool} \quad &::= t.p \dot{=} s \mid t = s \\
e_{fs \to \tau} \quad &::= \lambda x.e_\tau \\
e_{\tau' \to \tau} \quad &::= \lambda x_{\tau'}.e_\tau
\end{aligned}
$$

where s and t denote either atoms or feature structure variables, and p is a, possibly empty, sequence of feature symbols denoting a path in a feature structure.

Note that the language thus defined includes both feature logics and a typed λ-calculus.

We import from both theories such notions as substitution, free and bounded occurrences of variables, $\alpha-$ and $\beta-$reductions and $\beta\alpha$-normal form. In particular, a *closed feature description* is a feature description with no free variables. Moreover, feature constraints of feature logics, widely used in unification grammars, correspond to a subset of *feature descriptions* of type **bool**, without abstractions or applications.

To define a semantics for the calculus of feature descriptions we adopt the standard model $\mathcal{RT}$ of rational trees for feature structures (see [DMV94]) and associate with each type τ a semantic domain D_τ as follows

$$
\begin{aligned}
D_{\mathbf{bool}} &= \{0,1\} \\
D_{\mathbf{fs}\to\tau} &= \mathcal{RT} \to D_\tau \\
D_{\tau'\to\tau} &= D_{\tau'} \to D_\tau
\end{aligned}
$$

From this point on a semantics for feature descriptions is defined in the same way as for feature logics and the typed λ-calculus by noting that the standard boolean operations can be extended to all the semantic domains involved in a component wise fashion, e.g.

$$
(\lambda x.e) \vee (\lambda x.e') =_{def} (\lambda x.e \vee e').
$$

More precisely, let an *assignment* ρ be a mapping defined on variables, such that $\rho(x) \in \mathcal{RT}$ and $\rho(x_\tau) \in D_\tau$, for each type τ. As usual, $\rho[d/\sigma]$ denotes the assignment obtained from ρ by mapping σ to d. Let $f^{\mathcal{RT}}$, $p^{\mathcal{RT}}$ and $a^{\mathcal{RT}}$ denote the interpretation of features, paths and atoms in $\mathcal{RT}$, respectively. Furthermore, let $t^{\mathcal{RT}}\rho$ be $\rho(t)$ if t is a variable and $t^{\mathcal{RT}}$ otherwise. Then, the semantics of feature descriptions $\Lambda_{\mathcal{FD}}$ given an assignment ρ is defined inductively, as follows:

$$
\begin{array}{ll}
[\![x_\tau]\!]\rho = \rho(x_\tau) & [\![\lambda x.e_\tau]\!]\rho = \lambda\!\!\lambda v.[\![e_\tau]\!]\rho[v/x] \quad (v \in \mathcal{RT}) \\
[\![t.p \doteq s]\!]\rho = \begin{cases} 1 & if\ p^{\mathcal{RT}}(t^{\mathcal{RT}}\rho) = s^{\mathcal{RT}}\rho \\ 0 & otherwise \end{cases} & [\![\lambda x_\tau.e'_\tau]\!]\rho = \lambda\!\!\lambda v.[\![e'_\tau]\!]\rho[v/x_\tau] \quad (v \in D_\tau) \\
 & [\![e_{fs\to\tau}x.p]\!]\rho = ([\![e_{fs\to\tau}]\!]\rho)[\![x.p]\!]\rho \\
[\![t = s]\!]\rho = \begin{cases} 1 & if\ t^{\mathcal{RT}}\rho = s^{\mathcal{RT}}\rho \\ 0 & otherwise \end{cases} & [\![e_{fs\to\tau}a]\!]\rho = ([\![e_{fs\to\tau}]\!]\rho)a^{\mathcal{RT}} \\
 & [\![e_{\tau\to\tau'}e'_\tau]\!]\rho = ([\![e_{\tau\to\tau'}]\!]\rho)[\![e'_\tau]\!]\rho
\end{array}
$$

where $\lambda\!\!\lambda$ denotes function "abstraction" in set theory and $(x \in D)$ means that D is the domain of x. For the conjunction operation, we define:

$$
\begin{array}{ll}
[\![e_{bool} \wedge e'_{bool}]\!]\rho = \begin{cases} 1 & \text{if } [\![e_{bool}]\!]\rho = 1 \text{ and } [\![e'_{bool}]\!]\rho = 1 \\ 0 & \text{otherwise} \end{cases} \\
[\![e_{fs\to\tau} \wedge e'_{fs\to\tau}]\!]\rho = \lambda\!\!\lambda v.d \wedge d' \text{ where } [\![e_{fs\to\tau}]\!]\rho = \lambda\!\!\lambda v.d \ (v \in \mathcal{RT}) \\
\qquad\qquad\qquad\qquad\qquad\qquad\qquad\qquad [\![e'_{fs\to\tau}]\!]\rho = \lambda\!\!\lambda v.d' \ (v \in \mathcal{RT}) \\
[\![e_{\tau'\to\tau} \wedge e'_{\tau'\to\tau}]\!]\rho = \lambda\!\!\lambda v.d \wedge d' \text{ where } [\![e_{\tau'\to\tau}]\!]\rho = \lambda\!\!\lambda v.d \ (v \in D_{\tau'}) \\
\qquad\qquad\qquad\qquad\qquad\qquad\qquad\qquad [\![e'_{\tau'\to\tau}]\!]\rho = \lambda\!\!\lambda v.d' \ (v \in D_{\tau'})
\end{array}
$$

and analogously for the other boolean operations. If $1_{bool} \equiv 1$, $1_{fs\to\tau} \equiv \lambda v.1_\tau$, and $1_{\tau'\to\tau} \equiv \lambda v.1_\tau$ then the semantics of **true**, for each type τ is defined by:

$$
\begin{aligned}
&[\![\mathbf{true}_{bool}]\!]\rho = 1_{bool}, \\
&[\![\mathbf{true}_{fs\to\tau}]\!]\rho = \lambda v.1_\tau \ (v \in \mathcal{RT}) \\
&[\![\mathbf{true}_{\tau'\to\tau}]\!]\rho = \lambda v.1_\tau \ (v \in D_\tau)
\end{aligned}
$$

and analogously for **false**.

An important property of the feature description calculus is the existence of normal form under β-reduction which is a simple consequence of well-typedness. Another important property is that for any closed feature description of type

τ we can decide if it is equivalent to **false**. This last property is essentially an extension of the satisfiability problem for a complete axiomatization of feature logics. For this reason we will say that a feature description of type τ is satisfiable iff its semantics is not that of **false**.

2.1 Constraint Solver

Our implementation of the feature description calculus is based on the reduction to normal form followed by the techniques used in $\mathcal{CLG}$ [DV92, DMV94] for resolving complex feature constraints. In order to face the NP-hardness of the satisfiability problem, our approach was based in factoring out, in polynomial time, deterministic information contained in a complex constraint and simplifying the remaining formula using that information. The deterministic information corresponds to a conjunction of (positive) atomic constraints in *solved form*[1], which we denote by $\mathcal{M}$. We say that $\mathcal{M}$ is a *partial model* of $\mathcal{C}$ if and only if every model of $\mathcal{C}$ is a model of $\mathcal{M}$. When every model of $\mathcal{M}$ is a model of $\mathcal{C}$, but no proper subset of $\mathcal{M}$ satisfies this condition, we will say that $\mathcal{M}$ is a *minimal* model of $\mathcal{C}$. By using disjunctive forms it can be proved that any set of feature constraints $\mathcal{C}$ admits at most a finite number of minimal models[2]. In [DV92, DMV94, Mor95] a rewrite system was presented that from a complex feature constraint $\mathcal{C}_0$ produces a pair $\langle \mathcal{M}, \mathcal{C} \rangle$, where $\mathcal{M}$ is *solved form*, $\mathcal{C}$ is smaller than C_0 and such that $\mathcal{RT} \models \mathcal{C}_0 \leftrightarrow \mathcal{M} \wedge \mathcal{C}$ and any minimal model of C_0 can be obtained by conjoining a minimal model of $\mathcal{C}$ with $\mathcal{M}$. Moreover the rewriting system is complete in the sense that $\mathcal{M} \wedge \mathcal{C}$ is satisfiable, unless it produces **false** as the final model.

We now extend that rewrite system to higher-order feature descriptions. First we give some more characterizations of feature descriptions. A *basic normal description* of type τ is described by:

$$
\begin{aligned}
e_\tau \quad &::= \textbf{true} \mid \textbf{false} \mid x_\tau \mid x_\tau \wedge e_\tau \mid x_\tau \vee e_\tau \mid \neg e_\tau \mid x_{fs \to \tau} x.p \mid x_{fs \to \tau} a \mid x_{\tau' \to \tau} e_{\tau'} \\
e_{bool} \quad &::= t.p \doteq s \mid t \doteq s \\
e_{fs \to \tau} \quad &::= \lambda x.e_\tau \\
e_{\tau' \to \tau} \quad &::= \lambda x_{\tau'}.e_\tau
\end{aligned}
$$

Then, every closed feature description in basic normal form will be of the form $\lambda \bar{x}_\sigma . e_{bool}$ where $\bar{x}_\sigma$ denotes a sequence of bound variables of some types and e_{bool} is not an abstraction. Omitting the λ prefix, given a feature description of

---

[1] A conjunction of feature constraints $\mathcal{M}$ is a *solved form* if:

1. every constraint in $\mathcal{M}$ is of the form $x.f \doteq s$ or $x = s$
2. if $x = s$ is in $\mathcal{M}$ then x occurs exactly once in $\mathcal{M}$
3. if $x.f \doteq s$ and $x.f \doteq t$ are in $\mathcal{M}$ then $s = t$

Any conjunction of atomic constraints is satisfiable if and only if it can be reduced to a *solved form* [Smo89, Mah88, DMV94]

[2] Actually it is necessary to extend the notion of models to include negative atomic constraints, but that will not be addressed here.

type **bool**, e_{bool}, the solver will produce a partial model $\mathcal{M}$ and a smaller feature description e'_{bool} or **false**:

$$\langle \mathcal{M}, e_{bool} \wedge \mathbf{false} \rangle \rightarrow \langle \bot, \mathbf{false} \rangle$$
$$\langle \mathcal{M}, e_{bool} \wedge \mathbf{true} \rangle \rightarrow \langle \mathcal{M}, e_{bool} \rangle$$
$$\langle \mathcal{M}, e_{bool} \wedge s = t \rangle \rightarrow \langle \mathcal{M} \wedge s = t, e_{bool} \rangle$$
$$\langle \mathcal{M}, e_{bool} \wedge t.p \doteq s \rangle \rightarrow \langle \mathcal{M} \wedge t.p \doteq s, e_{bool} \rangle$$
$$\langle \mathcal{M}, e_{bool} \rangle \rightarrow \langle \mathcal{M}, e'_{bool} \rangle \text{ if } e_{bool} \longrightarrow^{\star}_{\mathcal{M}} e'_{bool}$$

with the convention that after each application of one of the rewrite rules the new partial model is reduced to solved form (or **false**). The complete rewrite system $\longrightarrow_{\mathcal{M}}$ is:

$$
\begin{array}{llll}
(\lambda x.e_\tau)x.p & \longrightarrow_{\mathcal{M}} e_\tau[x.p/x] & \neg(\lambda x.e) & \longrightarrow_{\mathcal{M}} \lambda x.\neg e \\
(\lambda x.e_\tau)a & \longrightarrow_{\mathcal{M}} e_\tau[a/x] & (\lambda x.e) \wedge (\lambda x.e') & \longrightarrow_{\mathcal{M}} \lambda x.e \wedge e' \\
(\lambda x_{\tau'}.e_\tau)e'_{\tau'} & \longrightarrow_{\mathcal{M}} e_\tau[e'_{\tau'}/x_{\tau'}] & (\lambda x.e) \vee (\lambda x.e') & \longrightarrow_{\mathcal{M}} \lambda x.e \vee e
\end{array}
\tag{1}
$$

$$
\begin{array}{lll}
e_\tau \wedge x_\tau & \longrightarrow_{\mathcal{M}} x_\tau \wedge e_\tau & \text{if } e_\tau \text{ is not a variable} \\
e_\tau \wedge (x_\tau \wedge e'_\tau) & \longrightarrow_{\mathcal{M}} x_\tau \wedge (e_\tau \wedge e'_\tau) & \text{if } e_\tau \text{ is not a variable} \\
(e_\tau \wedge e'_\tau) \wedge e''_\tau & \longrightarrow_{\mathcal{M}} e_\tau \wedge (e'_\tau \wedge e''_\tau) & \\
e_\tau \vee x_\tau & \longrightarrow_{\mathcal{M}} x_\tau \vee e_\tau & \text{if } e_\tau \text{ is not a variable} \\
e_\tau \vee (x_\tau \vee e'_\tau) & \longrightarrow_{\mathcal{M}} x_\tau \vee (e_\tau \vee e'_\tau) & \text{if } e_\tau \text{ is not a variable} \\
(e_\tau \vee e'_\tau) \vee e''_\tau & \longrightarrow_{\mathcal{M}} e_\tau \vee (e'_\tau \vee e''_\tau) & \\
(x_{fs \to \tau} \wedge e_{fs \to \tau})x.p & \longrightarrow_{\mathcal{M}} (x_{fs \to \tau})x.p \wedge (e_{fs \to \tau})x.p & \\
(x_{fs \to \tau} \wedge e_{fs \to \tau})a & \longrightarrow_{\mathcal{M}} (x_{fs \to \tau})a \wedge (e_{fs \to \tau})a & \\
(x_{\tau' \to \tau} \wedge e'_{\tau' \to \tau})e_\tau & \longrightarrow_{\mathcal{M}} (x_{\tau' \to \tau})e_\tau \wedge (e'_{\tau' \to \tau})e_\tau & \\
(x_{fs \to \tau} \vee e_{fs \to \tau})x.p & \longrightarrow_{\mathcal{M}} (x_{fs \to \tau})x.p \vee (e_{fs \to \tau})x.p & \\
(x_{fs \to \tau} \vee e_{fs \to \tau})a & \longrightarrow_{\mathcal{M}} (x_{fs \to \tau})a \vee (e_{fs \to \tau})a & \\
(x_{\tau' \to \tau} \vee e'_{\tau' \to \tau})e_\tau & \longrightarrow_{\mathcal{M}} (x_{\tau' \to \tau})e_\tau \vee (e'_{\tau' \to \tau})e_\tau &
\end{array}
\tag{2}
$$

$$
\begin{array}{lll}
\lambda x.e_\tau & \longrightarrow_{\mathcal{M}} \lambda x.e'_\tau & \text{if } e_\tau \longrightarrow^{\star}_{\mathcal{M}} e'_\tau \\
\lambda x_{\tau'}.e_\tau & \longrightarrow_{\mathcal{M}} \lambda x_{\tau'}.e'_\tau & \text{if } e_\tau \longrightarrow^{\star}_{\mathcal{M}} e'_\tau \\
(x_{\tau' \to \tau}e_\tau) & \longrightarrow_{\mathcal{M}} (x_{\tau' \to \tau}e'_\tau) & \text{if } e_\tau \longrightarrow^{\star}_{\mathcal{M}} e'_\tau
\end{array}
\tag{3}
$$

$$
\begin{array}{llll}
false_{fs \to \tau}x.p & \longrightarrow_{\mathcal{M}} false_\tau & true_\tau \wedge e_\tau & \longrightarrow_{\mathcal{M}} e_\tau \\
false_{fs \to \tau}a & \longrightarrow_{\mathcal{M}} false_\tau & e_\tau \wedge false_\tau & \longrightarrow_{\mathcal{M}} false_\tau \\
false_{\tau' \to \tau}e_{\tau'} & \longrightarrow_{\mathcal{M}} false_\tau & e_\tau \wedge true_\tau & \longrightarrow_{\mathcal{M}} e_\tau \\
true_{fs \to \tau}x.p & \longrightarrow_{\mathcal{M}} true_\tau & false_\tau \vee e_\tau & \longrightarrow_{\mathcal{M}} e_\tau \\
true_{fs \to \tau}a & \longrightarrow_{\mathcal{M}} true_\tau & true_\tau \wedge e_\tau & \longrightarrow_{\mathcal{M}} true_\tau \\
true_{\tau' \to \tau}e_{\tau'} & \longrightarrow_{\mathcal{M}} true_\tau & e_\tau \vee false_\tau & \longrightarrow_{\mathcal{M}} e_\tau \\
false_\tau \wedge e_\tau & \longrightarrow_{\mathcal{M}} false_\tau & e_\tau \wedge true_\tau & \longrightarrow_{\mathcal{M}} true_\tau
\end{array}
\tag{4}
$$

$$
\begin{aligned}
e_\tau & \longrightarrow_\perp & false_\tau & \\
x & \longrightarrow_{\mathcal{M}} & t & \quad \text{if } x = t \in \mathcal{M} \\
a.p \doteq s & \longrightarrow_{\mathcal{M}} & false & \\
x.p \doteq s & \longrightarrow_{\mathcal{M}} & t = s & \quad \text{if } x.p \doteq t \in \mathcal{M} \\
a = b & \longrightarrow_{\mathcal{M}} & false & \\
t = t & \longrightarrow_{\mathcal{M}} & true & \\
x = t \wedge e_{bool} & \longrightarrow_{\mathcal{M}} & x = t \wedge e'_{bool} & \quad \text{if } e_{bool} \longrightarrow^\star_{\mathcal{M} \wedge x = t} e'_{bool} \\
x = t \wedge e_{bool} & \longrightarrow_{\mathcal{M}} & false & \quad \text{if } \mathcal{M} \wedge x = t \to \perp \\
x.p \doteq t \wedge e_{bool} & \longrightarrow_{\mathcal{M}} & x.p \doteq t \wedge e'_{bool} & \quad \text{if } e_{bool} \longrightarrow^\star_{\mathcal{M} \wedge x.p \doteq t} e'_{bool} \\
x.p \doteq t \wedge e_{bool} & \longrightarrow_{\mathcal{M}} & false & \quad \text{if } \mathcal{M} \wedge x.p = t \to \perp
\end{aligned}
\tag{5}
$$

$$
(e_\tau \vee e'_\tau) \wedge e''_\tau \longrightarrow_{\mathcal{M}} (e_\tau \wedge e''_\tau) \vee (e'_\tau \wedge e''_\tau) \text{ if both } e_\tau \text{ and } e'_\tau \text{ are } \mathcal{M}\text{-dependent with } e''_\tau
\tag{6}
$$

We assume that α-reductions will be performed whenever necessary. For simplicity we omitted the rules concerning negation. The rewrite system is divided in six groups, each one dealing with: (1) β-reduction (where $e[d/x]$ denotes the substitution in e of x for d), abstraction and boolean operations for higher order types; this rules are applied before any other rule (2) application and boolean operations (3) rewrite inside abstractions and applications (4) **false** and **true**; (5) feature description of type **bool**, e_{bool}; this rules essentially correspond to the feature constraint rewrite system in [DMV94] (6) distributive law; this rule must apply only when both e_τ and e'_τ have variables in common with e''_τ, eventually through "bindings" in $\mathcal{M}$ [3]. If this last rule is omitted, the rewrite process becomes polynomial although incomplete.

Theorem 2.1 *Given a closed feature description e_τ the rewrite system is correct, terminating and complete in the sense that e_τ is satisfiable unless **false** is produced. Moreover the final feature description is in basic normal form.*

For a proof of the above results see [Mor95].

3 Constraint Categorial Grammar

In this section we show how the expressiveness of categorial grammars can be augmented using feature descriptions.

We will use a basic (rigid) categorial grammar (CG), consisting of a set of categories, a lexicon which assigns categories to words and a calculus which determines the set of admissible category combinations. Given a set of basic categories Cat_0 we define recursively the set of categories Cat by: the elements of

---

[3] The notation of $\mathcal{M}$-dependence coincides with the one for complex feature constraints [DMV94], if $x \in c$ means x occurs free in c. Given two constraints c_1 and c_2 and a model $\mathcal{M}$, c_1 and c_2 are $\mathcal{M}$-*dependent* if and only if $Var_{\mathcal{M}}(c_1) \cap Var_{\mathcal{M}}(c_2) \neq \emptyset$, where $Var_{\mathcal{M}}(c)$ is the smallest set satisfying: if $x \in c$, then $x \in Var_{\mathcal{M}}(c)$; if $x \in Var_{\mathcal{M}}(c)$ and $x.f \doteq z \in \mathcal{M}$, then $z \in Var_{\mathcal{M}}(c)$.

Cat_0 are categories; if A and B are categories then A/B and $A\backslash B$ are categories. Some unary (lexical) rules (lifting, division, etc) will be added to provide a flexible CG which can cope with discontinuity and other linguistic phenomena. Semantically these rules allow functional abstraction over displaced or missing elements.

A Constraint Categorial Grammar is a tuple $< Cat_0, \Upsilon, Lexicon, Rules >$ where

1. Cat_0 is a set of base categories
2. Υ is a map which associates with each category C a type $\Upsilon(C)$ and satisfies

$$\Upsilon(A/B) = \Upsilon(B\backslash A) = \Upsilon(B) \to \Upsilon(A)$$

3. *Lexicon* is a set of triples $< w, A, c >$, where w is a word, A a category and c is a feature description of type $\Upsilon(A)$
4. *Rules* is the set of inference rules to combine pairs $A - c$ of syntactic categories and feature descriptions (semantic representation).

The inference rules used in the current grammars are:

$$(app/) \; \frac{A/B - c_f \quad B - c_b}{A - (c_f c_b)} \; \text{if } c_f c_b \text{ is satisfiable}$$

$$(app\backslash) \; \frac{B - c_b \quad B\backslash A - c_f}{A - (c_f c_b)} \; \text{if } c_f c_b \text{ is satisfiable}$$

plus a set of unary rules.

3.1 A sample grammar

In figure 1. is given a fragment of an English grammar written in $\mathcal{CCLG}$. We use '\' for 'λ', '&' for '$\wedge$' and '|' for '$\vee$'. All variables are bound and can be any string of letters. The **let** constructor allows the use of macros in the writing of the lexicon. The **transformation** constructor implements unary rules for type raising. Type raising rules are just allowed for some categories and their application is controlled during execution. The **lex** constructor is used for each lexical entry. In this experiment we do not impose any type discipline (HPSG style) in the feature structures themselves[4]. If we assign to each part of speech a feature structure, then an associated feature description will be of type $fs \to \ldots \to$ **bool**. For instance, if we assign the type $fs \to$ **bool** to "John", with semantics $\lambda s.s = john$, and assign the type $fs \to fs \to$ **bool** to "runs", with semantics $\lambda x.\lambda s.s.reln = run \wedge s.arg1 = x$, the sentence "John runs" would have the type $fs \to$ **bool** and semantics $\lambda s.s.reln = run \wedge s.arg1 = john$. Once more we note that the use of partial descriptions allows us to express directly, the relations between the several constituents. The semantic used is inspired in the ones in [PS87].

---

[4] Neither the distinction between "syntactic" and "semantic" features is made.

Base_Categories   % Define the set of base categories
      s = fs— >bool,   % and their types
      iv = fs— >fs— >bool,
      np = s/iv,
      tv = iv/np,
      dv = tv/np,
      n = fs— >fs— >bool,
      det = np/n,
      pp= fs— > bool;
transformation   % define a type raising rule
      np = (s/np)/(iv/np) : \S \Vt \C. S (Vt C);
%%%%%%% some useful abbreviations
% agreement specifications
let 3RD_SG = \X. X.pers=p3 & X.nb=sg;
let NOT_3RD_SG = \X. X.pers\=p3 | X.nb\=sg;
let ANY = \X. X=X;
% proper nouns (generalized quantifier type)
let PN(W) = \P.\s. s.quant=exists_one & s.arg.reln=naming
    & s.arg.arg1=W & 3RD_SG(s.arg) & P s.arg s.pred ;
% common nouns (AGR is an agreement)
let CN(W,AGR) = \s. s.reln=W & s.arg1=x & AGR s;
%determiners
let DET(Q,AGR) = \N. \P. \s. s.quant=Q & AGR s.var &
    N s.var s.range & P s.var s.scope;
% intransitive verbs
let IV(W,AGR) = \s.\p. p.reln=W & p.arg1=s & AGR s;
% transitive verbs (Obj is the semantics of the object)
let TV(W,AGR) = \Obj. \su.\p. Obj (\o \q. q.reln=W & q.arg1=su & q.arg2=o) p;
let V_PP(W,AGR) = \SS. \su \ s. SS s.arg2 & s.reln=W & s.arg1=su & AGR su;
%ditransitive verbs
let DV(W,AGR) = \Ci. \Cs. \subj. \si. Cs (\ind. \s. Ci (\obj \p. p.reln=W &
    p.arg1=subj& p.arg2=obj & p.arg3=ind s) si & AGR subj;
%%%%%%%%%%%%% lexicon
lex a, det, DET(exists_one,3RD_SG); lex every, det, DET(all,ANY);
lex book, n, CN(book,3RD_SG); lex man, n, CN(book,3RD_SG);
lex john, np, PN(john); lex mary, np, PN(mary);
lex died, iv, IV(die,3RD_SG); lex loves, tv, TV(love,3RD_SG);
lex read, tv, TV(read,ANY); lex said, iv/pp, V_PP(say,ANY);
lex gave, dv, DV(give,ANY);
lex that, pp/s, \s.s;
% coordination lex and, s\(s/s), \S1\S2\s. s.type=coord & S1 s.arg1 & S2 s.arg2;
lex and, np\((tv\iv)/np), \NP1\NP2\VT. \subj\s. s.type=coord &
    VT NP1 subj s.arg1 & VT NP2 subj s.arg2;
lex and, iv\(iv/iv), \V1\V2. \subj.\s.
    s.type=coord & V1 subj s.arg1 & V2 subj s.arg2;
lex and, np\(np/np), \NP1\NP2\VT\s. s.type=coord &
    NP1 VT s.arg1 & NP2 VT s.arg2;

Fig. 1. Sample grammar

Processing $\mathcal{CCLG}$ is implemented in Prolog augmented with the constraint solver for feature descriptions[5]. In this section we briefly describe this implementation. Although the feature descriptions used in the grammar are untyped, a type inference algorithm is used to infer types for each expression. Moreover, for each lexical entry the type of the feature description is checked with that of the category and whenever possible the *normal form* of the feature description is computed. The inference rules are build-in in the grammar processor. Currently, we use a bottom-up chart parser that builds a context-free backbone. Each edge is a (Prolog) term $arc(Begin, End, Cat, Sref)$ where Cat is the category spanning from $Begin$ to End and $Sref$ is the information to be used to extract the semantic representation, and that reflects how this edge was formed: if it was a lexical entry $Sref$ is a reference to it; if it results from a left (right) application rule, it is a pair of references for its daughters; if it results from a unary rule, it is a pair of references to the initial category and to that rule. When the parse trees are successful built, the semantic representation is extracted and the constraint solver applied. These two components can be interleaved in order to prune, as soon as possible, inconsistent edges. As is apparent from the sample grammar (figure 1.) the semantic representations can become very cumbersome to write and visualize. So a graphical "workbench", based on a Tcl/Tk interface to Yap Prolog, was provided to edit grammars and lexicon, as well as to visualize the parse trees and semantic representations (as matrix boxes).

An Example As an example we analyze the parsing of the sentence "a man said that john read a book and mary died". There are two possible parse trees of this sentence, one with the coordination in the scope of the relative clause and other with a wider scope. The semantic representation of this sentence will be a feature description \x_1.X1|X2 where X1 and X2 are partially represented in figures 2. and 3.. Figures 4. and 5. show the semantics of the sentences "john read a book" and "mary died", respectively. In the feature description X2 (figure 3.) the former semantics is identified with the value of x_1.arg1.scope.arg2 and the latter is identified with the value of x_1.arg2. In the feature description X1 (figure 2.) the value of x_1.scope.arg2 is the feature structure corresponding to the coordination of the these two sentences. As remarked in the previous section, the parsing process first builds a parse forest using only the categories of lexical items and the inference (and unary) rules for syntactic categories. The parse tree of sentence we are considering is too large to be considered here, so figure 6. shows only the parse forest of "john read a book". In the first row we have the syntactic categories of each lexical item (given in the lexicon or derived by a unary rule). In the following rows each entry corresponds to the possible ways of deriving a category spanning a portion of the input sentence. For instance, the category iv can be derived in the third row from iv/(s/iv) and s/iv, spanning "read a book". Then for each parse tree that spans the whole sentence with root category s, the semantic representation of the constituents

---

[5] So it can be seen as an instance of $\mathcal{CLP}(\Lambda_{FD})$.

are combined and if the constraint solver does not produce **false**, a semantic representation is derived.

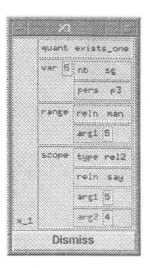

Fig. 2. Coordination inside relative

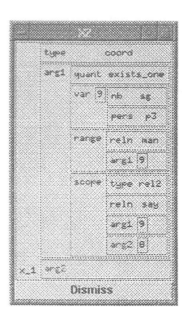

Fig. 3. Coordination wider scope

4 Final Remarks

The current implementation of $\mathcal{CCLG}$ shows the practical feasibility of using higher order feature structure descriptions as semantic representations. This reflects the fact that the complexity of the satisfiability problem for higher order feature descriptions is essentially the same as for feature logics. We should also point out that the good performance of the system results in part from its hybrid nature where a categorial grammar with atomic base categories is used to guide parsing. Some more toy English grammars where written that can handle some kinds of discontinuity, modifiers and quantifier scope. However, the introduction of a type discipline and more general treatment of recursive lexical rules ([BvN94]) must be considered, in future work. On the other hand, most recent developments of categorial grammars are based on the Lambek calculus [Lam58, Moo88, Mor94] (an intuitionist fragment of Linear Logic). Some implementations for the propositional fragment are based on chart parsers [Kon94, Hep92] and we conjecture that $\Lambda_{\mathcal{FD}}$calculus can be successfully used in such a systems, for process semantic representations. From an implementational perspective it would be helpful to study how current techniques employed in

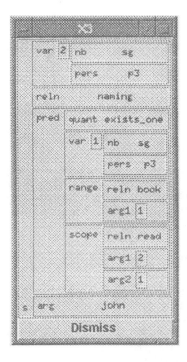

Fig. 4. Semantics of "john read a book".   **Fig. 5.** Semantics of "mary died".

john	read	a	book
s/iv (s/(s/iv))/(iv/(s/iv))	iv/(s/iv)	(s/iv)/n	n
s/(s/iv)		s/iv (s/(s/iv))/(iv/(s/iv))	
	iv		
s			

Parse Forest (john read a book)

Dismiss

Fig. 6. A parse forest

functional programming implementations, namely the use of combinators, can be imported for improve the computation of β-reductions.

Acknowledgments The authors would like to thank Sabine Broda and the anonymous reviewers for their valuable comments on an earlier draft of this paper.

References

[BvN94] Gosse Bouma and Gertjan van Noord. Constraint-based categorial grammars. In *Proceedings of the 15th International Conference on Computational Linguistics and the 22nd Annual Meeting of the Association for Computational Linguistics (COLING)*, 1994.

[DMV94] Luís Damas, Nelma Moreira, and Giovanni B. Varile. The formal and computational theory of complex constraint solution. In C. Rupp, M. A. Rosner, and R. L. Johnson, editors, *Constraints, Language, and Computation*, Computation In Cognitive Science, pages 149–166. Academic Press, London, 1994.

[DSP91] Mary Dalrymple, Stuart M. Shieber, and Fernando C. N. Pereira. Ellipsis and higher-order unification. *Linguistics and Philosophy*, 14:399–452, 1991.

[DV92] Luís Damas and Giovanni B. Varile. On the satisfiability of complex constraints. In *Proceedings of the 14th International Conference on Computational Linguistics (COLING)*, Nantes, France, 1992.

[Hep92] Mark Hepple. Chart parsing lambek grammars. In *Proceedings of the 14th International Conference on Computational Linguistics (COLING)*, pages 134–140, Nantes,France, 1992.

[Kon94] Esther Konig. A hypothetical reasoning algorithm for linguistic analysis. *Journal of Logic and Computation*, 1994. to appear.

[Lam58] Joachim Lambek. The mathematics of sentence structure. *American Mathematical Monthly*, 65, 1958. Reprinted in: Buszkowski, W., W. Marciszewski, and J. van Benthem (eds): Categorial Grammar. Amsterdam, 1988.

[Mah88] Michael J. Maher. Complete axiomatizations of the algebras of finite, rational and infinite trees. Technical report, IBM Thomas J. Watson Research Center, P.O. Box 704, Yorktown Heights, NY 10598, U.S.A., 1988.

[Moo88] Michael Moortgat. *Categorial Investigations: Logical and Linguistic Aspects of Lambek Calculus*. Foris, Dordrecht, 1988.

[Mor94] Glyn Morrill. *Type Logical Grammar:Categorial Logic of Signs*. Kluwer Academic Publishers, Dordrecht, 1994.

[Mor95] Nelma Moreira. *Formalismos e técnicas de implementação de gramáticas lógicas com restrições*. PhD thesis, Faculdade de Ciências da Universidade do Porto, 1995. to appear.

[NM88] Gopalan Nadathur and Dale Miller. An overview of λprolog. In Robert A. Kowalski and Kenneth A. Bowen, editors, *Logic Programming: Proceedings of the Fifth International Conference and Symposium*, volume 1, pages 810–827, Seattle, WA, 1988. MIT Press.

[Per90] Fernando C.N. Pereira. Categorial semantics and scoping. *Computational Linguistics*, 16(1), 1990.

[PS87] Fernando C.N. Pereira and Stuart M. Shieber. *Prolog and Natural Language Analysis*. Center for the Study of Language and Information Stanford, 1987.

[Smo89] Gert Smolka. Feature constraint logics for unification grammars. Technical report, IBM Wissenschafliches Zentrum, Institut für Wissensbasierte Systeme, 1989. IWBS Report 93.

[ST92] Gert Smolka and Ralf Treinen. Records for logic programming. In Krzysztof Apt, editor, *ICLP92*. MIT, 1992.

[ZKC87] Henk Zeevat, Ewan Klein, and Jo Calder. Unification categorial grammar. In Nicholas Haddock, Ewan Klein, and Glyn Morrill, editors, *Categorial Grammar, Unification Grammar and Parsing*. Centre for Cognitive Science, University of Edinburgh, 1987. Volume 1 of Working Papers in Cognitive Science.

A New Translation Algorithm from Lambda Calculus into Combinatory Logic

Sabine Broda and Luís Damas

LIACC, Universidade do Porto
R. do Campo Alegre 823, 4150 Porto, Portugal
e-mail: {sbb,luis}@ncc.up.pt

Abstract. Systems of lambda calculus are of importance for most knowledge representation theories and in particular for several systems for Natural Language Processing. During the implementation of lambda systems several problems arise that are directly related to the presence of bound variables. These problems can be avoided using translations from lambda calculus into combinatory systems, which give origin to extremely simple reduction machines. In this article we present and prove the correctness of a translation algorithm, that, when compared with other systems, has quite good properties in terms of memory space as well as in terms of length of evaluations.

Keywords

Combinatory Logic, Lambda Calculus, Knowledge Representation

1 Introduction

Systems of lambda calculus are of importance for most knowledge representation theories, which are based on higher order logic, e.g. [3]. In particular several systems for Natural Language Processing, see [6], [12], [11] and [5], use lambda terms as semantic values for syntactic expressions. Then the meaning of more complex parts of speech is obtained by evaluation of compound terms aiming for efficient implementations of systems of lambda calculus. The main problems that arise here, during compilation and even evaluation of expressions, are due to the presence of bound variables that give origin to complicated instantiation mechanisms. One way to avoid these α-conversion problems is based on combinatory logic and exploits an ideia of Schönfinkel [14], that dates back to 1924. Schönfinkel's work originated the appearance of an algorithm for transforming lambda expressions into combinatory expressions that, besides combinators and constants, use only free variables. This correspondence between lambda calculus and combinatory logic has been well studied by Curry and Feys [4], though more from a mathematical rather than a practical point of view. In practice, the implementation of the combinatory representation gives rise to an extremely simple reduction machine, but runs into some other main problems. In fact, the translation of lambda terms into combinatory logic is very expensive and creates extremely large terms that need a lot of memory space. On the other hand, the reduction of the combinatory expressions consists of a huge number of simple reduction steps, which constantly create intermediate expressions, that will be destroyed right afterwards and that naturally consume a lot of transient storage space. Several attempts have been made to improve the original translation algorithm in order to produce more compact combinatory terms. One kind of approaches, used for example by Abdali [1], Kennedy & Sleep [9] and Statman [15], is based on the definition of multiple abstraction operators that abstract on any number of variables simultaneously. However, these algorithms only produce compact output when the number of simultaneous abstractions performed is large. But as remarked by Turner [16], in practice the need to abstract on different variables arises at successive stages what makes it more convenient to have a definition of simple abstraction which is well behaved under self-composition. Another method that fits into the former category is the use of supercombinators which were proposed by Hugues[7] (see also [13]). This approach is frequently used in implementations of functional programming languages and uses an extended notion of combinator. In fact, supercombinators are defined by combinations which among their arguments may contain also other supercombinators, in contrast to regular combinators which are defined by combinations of their arguments only. Turner (see [16], [17]) proposed a method based on a single abstraction operator. This approach was used to implement the high-level functional programming language SASL and is probably one of the most adequate techniques for practical applications (compare with remarks in [10], [13] and [2]). Turner added three new combinators to Schönfinkel's combinatory system and obtained a satisfactory improvement on the size of the produced combinatory terms. Schönfinkel's algorithm translates lambda expressions of size $\mathcal{O}(n)$ in worst case into combinatory terms of size $\mathcal{O}(n^3)$, whereas Turner's method produces output, which is worst case of size $\mathcal{O}(n^2)$. The same relation stands between the number of reduction steps needed to evaluate expressions in the three systems.

In what follows we present another translation algorithm with a single abstraction operator and which is based on Schönfinkel's method. We propose to translate each lambda term into a combinatory expression together with a set of combinator definitions. The translation is quadratic, thus comparable to Turner's technique, in terms of the memory space needed to store the combinatory counterpart of a lambda term and it is linear in the sense that it produces output, which needs at most as many reduction steps for evaluation as the original lambda expression. The implementational advantages are obvious, in terms of storage space as well as of the efficiency of evaluation.

The idea is very simple. Schönfinkel's algorithm produces, when abstracting a variable from a combinatory term, an expression that contains a sequence of successively introduced combinators. We propose to substitute this sequence by one single combinator, whose reduction rule is implicitly defined by the sequence. By this, each abstraction in the original lambda term is expressed by at most one combinator together with its definition. Apart from generating much more compact compilation code, the evaluation of terms can be done with much fewer reduction steps than in other, on combinatory logic based implementations. On the other hand, this method needs a very simple reduction machine avoiding the usual problems caused by α-conversion.

2 Schönfinkel's algorithm

We start by establishing some notational conventions and recalling the main definitions and results that will be needed later on. We denote lambda and combinatory terms respectively by capital letters $M, N, \ldots$ and $X, Y, \ldots$. The letters $x, y, \ldots$ and $c, c_1, \ldots$ mean respectively variables and constants, whereas cv can be both.

Definition 2.1 *The set of lambda terms is defined by the following rules*

- *any constant or variable is a lambda term;*
- *(MN) is a lambda term, if M and N are;*
- *$\lambda x.M$ is a lambda term, if x and M are respectively a variable and a lambda term.*

The abbreviations $M_1 M_2 \ldots M_n$ and $\lambda x_1 \ldots x_n.M$ will respectively stand for $(\ldots (M_1 M_2) M_3 \ldots) M_n$ and $\lambda x_1.(\ldots (\lambda x_n.M) \ldots)$, whereas $\to_\beta$ is the reflexive and transitive closure of $\to_{1\beta}$, defined by the well-known relation

$$(\lambda x.M)N \to_{1\beta} M[N/x].$$

Now, we define the notion of combinatory term, as well as Schönfinkel's combinators together with their reduction rules.

Definition 2.2 *Let $\mathcal{K}$ be a set of combinators. Then the set of combinatory terms is given by the following rules*

- *every constant or variable is a combinatory term;*
- *every combinator $\tau \in \mathcal{K}$ is a combinatory term;*
- *(XY) is a combinatory term, if X and Y are.*

Schönfinkel used the combinators I, K, C, B and S, that are respectively of arity 1, 2, 3, 3 and 3. A term of the form $\tau X_1 \ldots X_n$, where τ is a combinator of arity n, is called a weak redex. The contractum $\kappa(R)$ of a weak redex R in the $\{I, K, C, B, S\}$-system is defined by

$$\begin{aligned}
\kappa(IX) &= X \\
\kappa(KXY) &= X \\
\kappa(CXYZ) &= XZY \\
\kappa(BXYZ) &= X(YZ) \\
\kappa(SXYZ) &= XZ(YZ).
\end{aligned}$$

A combinatory term X reduces to Y in one reduction step, denoted by $X \triangleright_{1w} Y$, if Y is obtained from X by substitution of a subterm R, which is a redex, by its contractum $\kappa(R)$. The relation $\triangleright_w$ is the reflexive and transitive closure of $\triangleright_{1w}$ and $=_w$ is the symmetric closure of $\triangleright_w$.

Schönfinkel established a correspondence between combinatory logic and lambda calculus, presenting an algorithm, described in Figure 1, that transforms any lambda term M into a combinatory term M_H.

$$(MN)_H = M_H N_H$$
$$(\lambda x.M)_H = \mathbf{abstr}(x, M_H)$$
$$(cv)_H = cv$$

Translation

$$\mathbf{abstr}(x, x) = I$$
$$\mathbf{abstr}(x, cv) = Kcv$$
$$\mathbf{abstr}(x, XY) = \mathbf{opt}(S\ \mathbf{abstr}(x, X)\ \mathbf{abstr}(x, Y))$$

Abstraction

$$\mathbf{opt}(S(KX)(KY)) = K(XY)$$
$$\mathbf{opt}(S(KX)I) = X$$
$$\mathbf{opt}(S(KX)Y) = BXY$$
$$\mathbf{opt}(SX(KY)) = CXY$$
$$\mathbf{opt}(SXY) = SXY$$

Optimization

Figure 1: The translation algorithm.

On the other hand he defined the inverse transformation $(\ )_\lambda$ that computes for every combinatory term X a lambda term X_λ:

$$(XY)_\lambda = X_\lambda Y_\lambda$$
$$cv_\lambda = cv$$
$$I_\lambda = \lambda x.x$$
$$K_\lambda = \lambda xy.x$$
$$C_\lambda = \lambda xyz.xzy$$
$$B_\lambda = \lambda xyz.x(yz)$$
$$S_\lambda = \lambda xyz.xz(yz)$$

These translations are faithful in the sense expressed by the two following propositions, which are proved in [8].

Proposition 2.3

1. $\quad X \vartriangleright_w Y \quad \Rightarrow \quad X_\lambda \to_\beta Y_\lambda;$
2. $\quad X =_w Y \quad \Rightarrow \quad X_\lambda =_\beta Y_\lambda.$

Proposition 2.4 $\quad (M_H)_\lambda =_{\beta\eta} M$

The two previous results are the main reason why combinatory logic can be used as an intermediate language for evaluating lambda terms. This aspect is important since the former system provides us with an extremely simple reduction machine. On the other hand it is an inefficient method, because the algorithm produces combinatory terms of huge size. Though complex reductions are substituted by simple ones, the relation between the number of reduction steps for evaluating lambda terms and their combinatory counterpart is so bad, typically $\mathcal{O}(n)$ to $\mathcal{O}(n^3)$, that the translation algorithm is merely of theoretical interest.

In 1979, Turner proposed an optimization of Schönfinkel's algorithm, see [16]. By the introduction of three extra combinators he improved the size of the translation by the factor n, i.e. lambda terms of size $\mathcal{O}(n)$ are transformed into combinatory terms of size $\mathcal{O}(n^2)$ with the same relation between the length of their reductions. This system is actually used to implement the high-level functional programming language SASL, see [17].

In the next section we present a combinatory system, where lambda terms can be represented and especially evaluated in a rather compact way.

3   The combinatory system $\mathcal{Cl}(\mathcal{K})$

We give now the formal description of the combinatory system $\mathcal{Cl}(K)$, which is based on a set of recursively defined combinators.

Definition 3.1 *The set of combinator indexes $\mathcal{A}$ is given by the following rules:*

- $\epsilon \in \mathcal{A}$
- $\alpha \in \mathcal{A} \Rightarrow c{\cdot}\alpha \in \mathcal{A};$
- $\alpha \in \mathcal{A} \Rightarrow b{\cdot}\alpha \in \mathcal{A};$
- $\alpha_1, \alpha_2 \in \mathcal{A} \Rightarrow (\alpha_1, \alpha_2) \in \mathcal{A}.$

Here ϵ denotes the empty word and $\cdot$ the concatenation operation.

The set of combinators K is defined by

- $K \in \mathcal{K};$
- $\alpha \in \mathcal{A} \Rightarrow \Phi_\alpha \in \mathcal{K}.$

The combinator K has still arity 1 and the arity of a combinator Φ_α is defined by $\sharp\alpha + 1$, where $\sharp\alpha$ is the number of c's and b's that appear in α. The contraction of redexes in $\mathcal{C}\!\ell(\mathcal{K})$ is defined inductively:

$$\kappa(KXY) = X$$
$$\kappa(\Phi_\epsilon X) = X$$
$$\kappa(\Phi_{c\cdot\alpha}XX_1\ldots X_{\sharp\alpha+1}) = (\kappa(\Phi_\alpha X_1\ldots X_{\sharp\alpha+1}))X$$
$$\kappa(\Phi_{b\cdot\alpha}XX_1\ldots X_{\sharp\alpha+1}) = X(\kappa(\Phi_\alpha X_1\ldots X_{\sharp\alpha+1}))$$
$$\kappa(\Phi_{(\alpha_1,\alpha_2)}X_1\ldots X_{\sharp\alpha_1}Y_1\ldots Y_{\sharp\alpha_2}Z) = (\kappa(\Phi_{\alpha_1}X_1\ldots X_{\sharp\alpha_1}Z))\,(\kappa(\Phi_{\alpha_2}Y_1\ldots Y_{\sharp\alpha_2}Z))$$

4 The extended algorithm

In this section we present an extension of Schönfinkel's algorithm, which translates lambda expressions into $\mathcal{C}\!\ell(\mathcal{K})$-combinatory terms. The translation produces terms that have at most as many combinators as there are abstractions in the original lambda term. Consequently each lambda term is represented by a combinatory term of smaller or equal length. We propose to give new names, $\$X, \$Y, \ldots$, to the combinators in order of appearance and store them together with their reduction rules. Thus every lambda term yields a set of combinator definitions plus a combinatory expression to be evaluated. The memory space, stemming both from term size and combinator allocation, which is necessary to store the combinatory representation of a lambda term of size $\mathcal{O}(n)$ is, as in Turner's system, in worst case of size $\mathcal{O}(n^2)$. But the evaluation of combinatory terms in $\mathcal{C}\!\ell(\mathcal{K})$ consists of at most as many reduction steps as the β-reduction of the original lambda term, which represents an important improvement in terms of execution time and transient storage. In order to extend Schönfinkel's algorithm, we substitute the definition of ( )$_H$ on abstractions by the following line.

$$(\lambda x.M)_H = \mathbf{comp}(\mathbf{abstr}(x, M_H))$$

The function **comp**, described in Figure 2, only applies to those terms X, where the abstraction algorithm introduced a sequence of I's, C's, B's and S's. This sequence is substituted by a new combinator, denoted by $\$X$ and the rest of the term is written in a new order by the function **term**. At the same time the rule

$$\$Xx_1\ldots x_{\sharp(\alpha)+1} = \kappa(\Phi_\alpha x_1\ldots x_{\sharp(\alpha)+1}),$$

with $\alpha = \mathbf{ind}(X)$, is added to the set of combinator definitions. The algorithm can be very easily implemented. A prototype implementation in Prolog for the translation and reduction of lambda terms is given in the Appendix.

$$
\begin{aligned}
\mathbf{comp}(I) &= \mathbf{term}(\$X, I) \\
\mathbf{comp}(CXY) &= \mathbf{term}(\$X, CXY) \\
\mathbf{comp}(BXY) &= \mathbf{term}(\$X, BXY) \\
\mathbf{comp}(SXY) &= \mathbf{term}(\$X, SXY) \\
\mathbf{comp}(X) &= X
\end{aligned}
$$

Compactation

$$
\begin{aligned}
\mathbf{term}(A, I) &= A \\
\mathbf{term}(A, CX_1X_2) &= \mathbf{term}(AX_2, X_1) \\
\mathbf{term}(A, BX_1X_2) &= \mathbf{term}(AX_1, X_2) \\
\mathbf{term}(A, SX_1X_2) &= \mathbf{term}(\mathbf{term}(A, X_1), X_2) \\
\mathbf{term}(A, X) &= AX
\end{aligned}
$$

Combinatory expression

$$
\begin{aligned}
\mathbf{ind}(I) &= \epsilon \\
\mathbf{ind}(CX_1X_2) &= c \cdot \mathbf{ind}(X_1) \\
\mathbf{ind}(BX_1X_2) &= b \cdot \mathbf{ind}(X_2) \\
\mathbf{ind}(SX_1X_2) &= (\mathbf{ind}(X_1), \mathbf{ind}(X_2)) \\
\mathbf{ind}(X) &= b
\end{aligned}
$$

Combinator definition

Figure 2: The extended algorithm.

5 Correctness

In this section we prove the correctness of our method, showing that it preserves the correspondence between lambda terms and their combinatory representations established by Schönfinkel's translation. By $FV(X)$ we denote the set of variables occuring in the combinatory term X.

Let the λ-transformation be given by

$$
\begin{aligned}
cv_\lambda &= cv \\
(XY)_\lambda &= X_\lambda Y_\lambda \\
K_\lambda &= \lambda xy.x \\
(\$X)_\lambda &= \lambda x_1 \ldots x_n.M,
\end{aligned}
$$
where $\$X x_1 \ldots x_n = M$ is the definition of $\$X$.

Then the following Lemmas can be proved by induction on n.

Lemma 5.1 *For every combinator τ of arity n there is $(\tau)_\lambda = \lambda x_1 \ldots x_n.M$, for some lambda term M that contains no abstraction.*

Lemma 5.2 *Let τ be a combinator of arity n such that $(\tau)_\lambda = \lambda x_1 \ldots x_n.M$. If $\kappa(\tau X_1 \ldots X_n) = B$, then $(B)_\lambda = M[(X_1)_\lambda/x_1, \ldots, (X_n)_\lambda/x_n]$.*

Proposition 5.3 *Let X, Y be $\mathcal{Cl}(\mathcal{K})$-combinatory terms, then:*

1. $X \triangleright_w Y \Rightarrow X_\lambda \rightarrow_\beta Y_\lambda$;
2. $X =_w Y \Rightarrow X_\lambda =_\beta Y_\lambda$.

Proof

1. It is sufficient to show that for every combinator τ of arity n and combinatory terms $X_1, \ldots, X_n$, if $\tau X_1 \ldots X_n \triangleright_{1w} Y$, then $(\tau X_1 \ldots X_n)_\lambda \rightarrow_\beta Y_\lambda$. In fact
$$
\begin{aligned}
(\tau X_1 \ldots X_n)_\lambda &= (\tau)_\lambda (X_1)_\lambda \ldots (X_n)_\lambda && \text{def. of ( )}_\lambda \\
&= (\lambda x_1 \ldots x_n.M)(X_1)_\lambda \ldots (X_n)_\lambda && \text{Lemma 5.1} \\
&\rightarrow_\beta M[(X_1)_\lambda/x_1, \ldots, (X_n)_\lambda/x_n] \\
&= (Y)_\lambda && \text{Lemma 5.2}
\end{aligned}
$$
2. $X =_w Y$ if and only if there is some combinatory term Z such that $X \triangleright_w Z$ and $Y \triangleright_w Z$. From (1.) we conclude that $X_\lambda \rightarrow_\beta Z_\lambda$ and $Y_\lambda \rightarrow_\beta Z_\lambda$. Thus, $X_\lambda =_\beta Y_\lambda$. •

Lemma 5.4 *Let x be a variable and $X \in \mathcal{Cl}(\mathcal{K})$. Then,*

1. $x \notin FV(\mathbf{abstr}(x, X))$;
2. $(\mathbf{comp}(\mathbf{abstr}(x, X)))x \triangleright_w X$.

Proof

1. Trivial.
2. By observation of the abstraction and optimization routines, **abstr** and **opt**, it is easy to show that
   - the function **abstr** creates a new combinator K when abstracting x on a term X if and only if $x \notin FV(X)$ and in this case there is $\mathbf{abstr}(x, X) = KX$;
   - $\mathbf{abstr}(x, Ux) = U$ iff $x \notin FV(U)$;
   - $\mathbf{abstr}(x, X) = I$ iff $X = x$;
   - $\mathbf{abstr}(x, X) = BUV$ iff $X = UZ$, $x \notin FV(U)$, $x \in FV(Z)$, $Z \neq x$ and $V = \mathbf{abstr}(x, Z)$;

   Now suppose that $x \notin FV(X)$. Then $\mathbf{comp}(\mathbf{abstr}(x, X))x = \mathbf{comp}(KX)x = KXx \triangleright_w X$.

   From now on let $x \in FV(X)$.

   If $X = Ux$, with $x \notin FV(U)$, then $\mathbf{comp}(\mathbf{abstr}(x, X))x = \mathbf{comp}(U)x = Ux = X$.

   For the remaining case it is sufficient to show that for any $\mathcal{Cl}(\mathcal{K})$-term X, with $x \in FV(X)$, and for $\alpha = \mathbf{ind}(\mathbf{abstr}(x, X))$ and $\$XX_1 \ldots X_{\sharp\alpha} =$

term$(\mathbf{abstr}(x, X))$ one has $\kappa(\Phi_\alpha X_1 \ldots X_{\sharp\alpha} x) = X$. We will prove this result by induction on $\sharp\alpha$.

Let $\sharp\alpha = 0$. Then $\alpha = \epsilon$ and $\mathbf{abstr}(x, X) = I$. Thus $X = x$ and obviously $k(\Phi_\epsilon x) = x$.

Otherwise $\alpha = c \cdot \alpha'$, $\alpha = b \cdot \alpha'$ or $\alpha = (\alpha_1, \alpha_2)$. We show the result for $\alpha = b \cdot \alpha'$, which is the most complex of the three cases.

First there might be $\alpha = b$, $\sharp\alpha = 1$, $X_1 = U$, $x \notin FV(U)$ and $X = Ux$. Indeed $\kappa(\Phi_b X_1 x) = X_1 = X$.

Otherwise, $\mathbf{abstr}(x, X) = BUV$, with $X = UY$, $V = \mathbf{abstr}(x, Y)$, $X_1 = U$, $\alpha' = \mathbf{ind}(V)$ and $\Phi_{\alpha'} X_2 \ldots X_{\sharp\alpha} = \mathbf{comp}(\Phi_{\alpha'} V)$. By the induction hypothesis there is $\kappa(\Phi_{\alpha'} X_2 \ldots X_{\sharp\alpha} x) = Y$. Thus
$\kappa(\Phi_{b \cdot \alpha'} X_1 \ldots X_{\sharp\alpha} x) = X_1(\kappa(\Phi_{\alpha'} X_2 \ldots X_{\sharp\alpha} x)) = UY = X$. $\quad\bullet$

Proposition 5.5 *For every lambda term M there is $(M_H)_\lambda =_{\beta\eta} M$.*

Proof By induction on M. The cases for $M = x$ and $M = M_1 M_2$ are trivial. Let $M = \lambda x.P$. Then

$$
\begin{aligned}
((\lambda x.P)_H)_\lambda &= (\mathbf{abstr}(x, P_H))_\lambda & \text{Definition of ( )}_H \\
&=_\eta \lambda x.(\mathbf{abstr}(x, P_H))_\lambda x \\
&= \lambda x.((\mathbf{abstr}(x, P_H))x)_\lambda & \text{Definition of ( )}_\lambda \\
&=_\beta \lambda x.(P_H)_\lambda & \text{Prop. 5.3 and Lemma 5.4} \\
&=_{\beta\eta} \lambda x.P & \text{induction hypothesis.} \quad\bullet
\end{aligned}
$$

6 An example

The following example belongs to the field of natural language representations. In the framework of Montague's universal grammars (for an introduction to the subject see [6]) lambda terms are used as semantic values for syntactic expressions. For example, one can give the following semantic values to the expressions "every", "man" and "walk" (note that man' and walk' on the right hand side are lambda constants).

$$
\begin{aligned}
[\![\text{every}]\!] &= \lambda xy.\forall_c(\Rightarrow (x(c))(y(c))) \\
[\![\text{man}]\!] &= \text{man'} \\
[\![\text{walk}]\!] &= \text{walk'}
\end{aligned}
$$

Then it is necessary to evaluate the expression

$$
M = \lambda xy.\forall_c(\Rightarrow (x(c))(y(c))) \text{ man' walk'}
$$

in order to obtain the meaning of the sentence "Every man walks". In an implementation for lambda terms based on Turner's combinatory system, M is represented by

$$
\boxed{B'B\forall_c(C'(B' \Rightarrow)(CIc)(CIc)) \text{ man' walk'}}
$$

and the evaluation of M consists of the following reduction sequence.

$$B'B\forall_c(C'(B' \Rightarrow)(CIc)(CIc)) \text{ man' walk'} \rightarrow B\forall_c(C'(B' \Rightarrow)(CIc)(CIc) \text{ man'}) \text{ walk'}$$
$$\rightarrow \forall_c(C'(B' \Rightarrow)(CIc)(CIc) \text{ man' walk'})$$
$$\rightarrow \forall_c(B' \Rightarrow (CIc \text{ man'})(CIc) \text{ walk'})$$
$$\rightarrow \forall_c(\Rightarrow (CIc \text{ man'})(CIc \text{ walk'}))$$
$$\rightarrow \forall_c(\Rightarrow (I \text{ man' } (c))(CIc \text{ walk'}))$$
$$\rightarrow \forall_c(\Rightarrow (I \text{ man' } (c))(I \text{ walk' } (c)))$$
$$\rightarrow \forall_c(\Rightarrow (\text{ man' } (c))(I \text{ walk' } (c)))$$
$$\rightarrow \forall_c(\Rightarrow (\text{ man' } (c))(\text{ walk' } (c)))$$

Using our algorithm one obtains a representation for M, containing two combinators, together with their definition.

$$\$Xxyzt = x(y(tz))$$
$$\$Yxyztu = y(z(ut))x$$

$$\$Y \ c \ (\$X\forall_c) \Rightarrow c \text{ man' walk'}$$

Now the reduction of M can be done in only two steps.

$$\$Y \ c \ (\$X\forall_c) \Rightarrow c \text{ man' walk'} \rightarrow \$X\forall_c(\Rightarrow (\text{man'}(c))) \ c \text{ walk'}$$
$$\rightarrow \forall_c(\Rightarrow (\text{man'}(c))(\text{walk'}(c)))$$

7 Conclusion

In this article we proposed a new translation algorithm from lambda calculus into combinatory logic and proved the correctness of the translation. The algorithm yields a system in which reductions are executed in a particularly efficient way. This is obviously crucial for implementations of lambda systems, with special interest for several theories of knowledge representation as well as for functional programming languages.

Acknowledgments The authors would like to thank the referees for their helpful comments on the preliminary version of this paper.

References

1. S. Abdali. An abstraction algorithm for combinatory logic. *Journal of Symbolic Logic*, 41:222–224, 1976.
2. H. Barendregt. Functional programming and lambda calculus. *Handbook of Theoretical Computer Science*, pages 322–63, 1990.

3. L. Cardelli. Semantics of multiple inheritance. In Kahn, MacQueen, and Plotkin, editors, *Semantics of Data Types*, volume 173 of *LNCS*. Springer Verlag, 1984.

4. H. Curry and R. Feys. *Combinatory Logic Vol. 1*. North-Holland, Amsterdam, 1958.

5. M. Dalrymple, S. M. Shieber, and F. C. N. Pereira. Ellipsis and higher-order unification. *Linguistics and Philosophy*, 14:399–452, 1991.

6. D. Dowty, R. Wall, and S. Peters. *Introduction to Montague Semantics*. D. Reidel Publishing Company, Dordrecht, 1985.

7. J. Hugues. Supercombinators, a new implementation method for applicative languages. *Proc. ACM Symp. on Lisp and Functional Programming*, pages 1–10, 1988.

8. J. P. S. J. Roger Hindley. *Introduction to Combinators and λ-Calculus*. Cambridge University Press, 1986.

9. J. R. Kennaway and M. R. Sleep. Counting director strings. University of East Anglia, Norwich, 1984.

10. J. Mulder. Complexity of combinatory code. Preprint 389, University Utrecht, Department of Mathematics, August 1985.

11. F. Pereira. Categorial semantics and scoping. *Computational Linguistics*, 16(1), 1990.

12. F. Pereira and S. Shieber. Prolog and natural-language analysis. *CSLI Lecture Notes*, 10, 1987.

13. S. Peyton Jones. *The implementation of functional programming languages*. Prentice-Hall, 1987.

14. M. Schönfinkel. Über die Bausteine der mathematischen Logik. *Mathematische Annalen*, 92:305–316, 1924.

15. R. Statman. On translating lambda terms into combinators; the basis problem. pages 378–382. IEEE, 1986. Proceedings of the LICS'86.

16. D. Turner. Another algorithm for bracket abstraction. *Journal of Symbolic Logic*, 44:267–270, 1979.

17. D. Turner. A new implementation technique for applicative languages. *Software-Practice and Experience*, 9:31–49, 1979.

A Appendix

```
:- op(400,yfx,'@').
execute(M,Result):- reset,
        translate(M,X),
        reduce(X,Result,0,N).
reset:- abolish(red/2),
        (recorded(comb,_,R),erase(R),fail;
        recorda(comb,0,_)).
reduce(A,C,N,N1):-
        l_reduce(A,B,N,N2),
        (A=B -> r_reduce(B,C,N2,N1);
        reduce(B,C,N2,N1)).
l_reduce(k@X@Y,X,N,N1):- !, N1 is N+1.
l_reduce(A@B,C,N,N1):- !,
        (red(A@B,C),N1 is N+1 ;
```

```
            l_reduce(A,A1,N,N1),
            C=A1@B).
l_reduce(A,A,N,N).
r_reduce(A@B,A1@B1,N,N1):- !,
        r_reduce(A,A1,N,N2),
        reduce(B,B1,N2,N1).
r_reduce(A,A,N,N).
translate(M@N,M1@N1):- !,translate(M,M1),translate(N,N1).
translate(lambda(X,M),Exp):- !,
        translate(M,M1),abstr(X,M1,M2),comp(M2,Exp).
translate(CV,CV).
abstr(X,X,i):-!.
abstr(X,Y@Z,T):- !,abstr(X,Y,Y1),abstr(X,Z,Z1),opt(s@Y1@Z1,T).
abstr(X,CV,k@CV).
opt(s@(k@X)@(k@Y),k@(X@Y)):-!.
opt(s@(k@X)@i,X):-!.
opt(s@(k@X)@Y,b@X@Y):-!.
opt(s@X@(k@Y),c@X@Y):-!.
opt(s@X@Y,s@X@Y).
comp(A,Exp):- (A=i;A=c@Y@Z;A=b@Y@Z;A=s@Y@Z),!,
        new_comb(C),term(C,A,Exp),ind(A,List,Res),
        make_term([C|List],[],Cterm),asserta(red(Cterm,Res)).
comp(A,A).
new_comb(C):- recorded(comb,C,Ref),erase(Ref),
        D is C+1,recorda(comb,D,_).
make_term([X|R],R,X):-!.
make_term(List,R,A@X):- !,make_term(List,[X|R],A).
term(A,i,A):-!.
term(A,c@X1@X2,Exp):- !,term(A@X2,X1,Exp).
term(A,b@X1@X2,Exp):- !,term(A@X1,X2,Exp).
term(A,s@X1@X2,Exp):- !,term(A,X1,E1),term(E1,X2,Exp).
term(A,X,A@X).
ind(i,[A],A):-!.
ind(b@_@Y,[A|R],A@E):- !,ind(Y,R,E).
ind(c@X@_,[A|R],E@A):- !,ind(X,R,E).
ind(s@X@Y,R,E1@E2):- !,ind(X,R1,E1),ind(Y,R2,E2),last(R1,A),
        last(R2,A),join(A,R1,R2,R).
ind(_,[A,B],A@B).
last([X],X):-!.
last([X|R],Y):- last(R,Y).
join(A,[A],L,L):-!.
join(A,[X|R],L,[X|T]):- join(A,R,L,T).
```

Interlocking Multi-Agent and Blackboard Architectures

Bernhard Kipper

Dept. of Computer Science, Univ. of Saarbrücken, 66041 Saarbrücken, Germany
E-Mail: kipper@cs.uni-sb.de

1 Introduction

In order to handle the challenges that arise in the construction of artificial intelligence (AI) systems, advanced system architectures are needed. Two kinds of architectures that are often used for complex, modularly designed AI systems are multi-agent and blackboard architectures. These two architectures have many similiarities, but they differ in two main respects: in the way processing is controlled and in the way in which the modules communicate with each other.

The differences between multi-agent and blackboard architectures imply that for different application domains, different architectures seem to be more appropriate. This paper addresses the following question: What happens if one aims at realising an application for a domain of which one part better fits one architecture and another part better fits the other architecture?

The proposal is made to integrate multi-agent and blackboard architectures by interlocking them in order to exploit the advantages of both architecture types within one application system.

2 Comparing multi-agent and blackboard architectures

2.1 The main principles underlying the two architectures

The concept of multi-agent architectures relies on the idea that a collection of autonomous modules, called *agents*, can achieve intelligent problem-solving behavior by coordinating their knowledge, goals, skills, and plans. Communication between the agents is attained via a message passing mechanism. The agents in a multi-agent system may be working toward a single global goal, or toward separate individual goals that interact. They must also reason about the processes of coordination among the agents. The task of coordination can be quite difficult in multi-agent systems, because there may be situations where there is no possibility for global control or globally consistent knowledge.

A blackboard architecture consists of a global database, called the *blackboard*, several separate modules, called *knowledge sources* (KSs), and a control unit. Blackboard architectures model the following type of problem-solving behavior: The KSs are gathered around the blackboard that is commonly used to write and read results and intermediate hypotheses. Depending on the current state of the blackboard, the control unit determines which KS can contribute to the problem-solving process (by checking activation conditions given for each KS), mediates between competing KSs, and gives control to the choosen KS. After the KS gives back control to the control unit, a new cycle begins.

2.2 The main characteristics of the architectures

In the following, some basic properties of multi-agent and blackboard architectures are compared:

Modularity: Both multi-agent and blackboard architectures are strictly modular because of the subdivision in terms of agents and KSs, respectively. This subdivision can be used to incorporate different processing and reasoning methods within one system. It is also advantageous that this modularity allows for relatively easy replacement and addition of modules.

Flexibility: Both multi-agent and blackboard architectures are very flexible architectures, not only with respect to the specific modules used (i.e. from the architectural point of view, there are no special requirements concerning the modules), but also with respect to the process of activity selection:

- Both types of architectures allow for sophisticated handling of the flow of control.
- Both multi-agent and blackboard architectures can benefit from a concurrent or distributed implementation.

Communication between modules: In multi-agent architectures, communication between agents is achieved via a message passing mechanism: If some agent needs information from other agents or wants to inform other agents about its own results, it sends it a message, which usually includes specifications of sender, recipient(s), message type, and message content.

In blackboard architectures, communication between the KSs is possible only via the blackboard. This shared global database allows indirect communication between modules: A KS does not need to know addresses or possible recipients of messages, because the information written on the blackboard is visible to all KSs.

Control mechanisms: While control in most multi-agent architectures is distributed, blackboard architectures usually have a central control unit that enforces the following control cycle: In each cycle, the control unit first determines which KSs can make further contributions to the actual solution state and chooses one of the competing KSs, which is then executed.

Availability of implementation tools: Experiences with existing systems led to the development of generic shells, i.e. tools for the development of multi-agent and blackboard applications that facilitate the implementation of a concrete system.

2.3 Which architecture for which domain?

Blackboard architectures have been applied in many systems covering a wide range of application domains such as interpretation, planning, and control tasks.

On the basis of an examination of various blackboard systems, [Nii 86] summarized the applicability conditions of blackboard architectures as follows:

> Generally, the occurence of some combination of the following characteristics in a problem makes it an appropriate candidate for the blackboard approach:

[1] • A large solution space
[2] • Noisy and unreliable data
[3] • A variety of input data and a need to integrate diverse information
[4] • The need for many independent or semi-independent pieces of knowledge to cooperate in forming a solution
[5] • The need to use multiple reasoning methods (for example, backward and forward reasoning)
[6] • The need for multiple lines of reasoning
[7] • The need for an evolutionary solution   (p. 102–103, numbers added)

As follows from the discussion in the previous subsection, multi-agent architectures are also appropriate for domains with the characteristics mentioned in the items 3–6 because of their modularity and flexibility, whereas the characteristics mentioned in the items 1,2, and 7 go better with blackboard architectures, because in these cases, the blackboard data structure is used extensively.

For domains having one or several of the characteristics mentioned in the items 3–6, the question therefore arises whether there are other criteria stating if either a multi-agent or a blackboard architecture is preferable to the other, because of their differences with respect to communication between modules and control mechanisms. The answer proposed here is that the predictability of the way to a successful solution is such an additional criteria: If it is relatively clear which module communicates with which other or in which ordering the modules work, than the application can very well take advantage of the characteristics of multi-agent architectures. On the other hand, if it is not clear which modules cooperate or in which order they work, a blackboard approach is better, because for each module of a blackboard architecture, it can be checked via the activation conditions when it can contribute to the solution.

This claim is corroborated by [Cawsey et al. 92] where the use of multi-agent and blackboard architectures is empirically compared. They defined certain problem types in terms of the number of the modules involved, the spread of areas of expertise, and the accuracy of knowledge of areas of expertise. For each architecture and for each problem type, they created 50 random scenarios. They summarize their results as follows:

> If knowledge is well distributed, with each agent having distinct types of knowledge they can reason about, and having accurate models of the areas of expertise of other agents, an actor model is appropriate, especially where large numbers of agents are involved. ...
> If there is more overlap in the areas of expertise, or if the agents have only limited knowledge of each others expertise areas, then the blackboard

model may be more appropriate. We expect this to be a general result. (p. 251)

An attempt to summarize the criteria for choosing between multi-agent and blackboard architectures for a given application domain is given in Table 1.

Aspect of domain	Multi-agent architectures	Blackboard architectures
Need to integrate diverse information and/or different processing and reasoning methods	high	high
Possibility to divide the problem solving knowledge into independent pieces	given	given
Size of solution space	small or medium	large
Noisiness or unreliability of data	low	medium or large
Need for an evolutionary solution	not given	given
Working order of and cooperation between modules	largely predictable	largely unpredictable
Knowledge of a module about other modules	accurate	limited
Number of modules	large	small or medium

Table 1. Conditions under which multi-agent and blackboard architectures are especially suitable for a given domain.

3 Interlocking multi-agent and blackboard architectures

The discussion above illustrates that there are some criteria which can be applied when choosing an appropriate architecture for an application. But what is to be done if one aims to implement an application for a domain with the property that in one part, a multi-agent architecture seems most appropriate and in another part, a blackboard archtitecture seems most appropriate? This is, e.g., the case when realising a natural language (NL) dialog system: The merits of multi-agent architectures can on the one hand be exploited in NL systems (see, e.g., the approach of [Fum et al. 88]), but on the other hand, as [Kipper 94] shows, it can be advantageous to realise a NL analysis module as a blackboard architecture.

The approach proposed here is to integrate multi-agent and blackboard architectures by interlocking them. This is possible, because in these architectures, the internal structure of agents and KSs, respectively, is not restricted: An agent of a multi-agent architecture could itself internally be structured as blackboard architecture and - vice versa - a KS of a blackboard architecture could internally have a multi-agent architecture.

In this way, it is possible to handle the above mentioned problem of finding an appropriate architecture for a heterogenous application domain as follows:

1. Determine for which part of the domain which architecture is to apply.
2. Choose the architecture that is appropriate for the main part of the application domain as the "top-level" architecture. (If the domain is bipartite – i.e. the parts which call for a multi-agent or a blackboard architecture, respectively, are of approximately equal importance –, make a choice that depends on implementational criteria.)
3. Interlock the architecture chosen for the remaining parts in the top-level architecture by structuring one of the agents or KSs respectively of the top-level architecture as blackboard or multi-agent architecture respectively.

This proposal was realised in the NL dialog system PRACMA. With the domain of NL processing, it was demonstrated how the two architectures can be combined when an application domain has partly both characteristics: According to the criteria given in Table 1, the overall architecture of the NL dialog system PRACMA is a multi-agent architecture (see [Jameson et al. 94]) whereas for the subtask of NL analysis, a blackboard architecture is used (see [Kipper 94]). The peculiarity of this blackboard architecture consists in acting as a whole as a single agent within PRACMA's multi-agent architecture. Communication between the KSs of the blackboard agent and the other agents is achieved while maintaining the priniciple that in blackboard architectures, all information is written on the blackboard data structure.

The experiences with the PRACMA system succesfully show how the merits of different types of architectures can be exploited within a single AI system.

References

[Cawsey et al. 92] A. **Cawsey**, J. **Galliers**, S. **Reece**, and K. **Jones**. *A Comparison of Architectures for Autonomous Multi-Agent Communication*. In: Proceedings of the 10th European Conference on Artificial Intelligence (ECAI 92), Vienna, Austria. John Wiley & Sons, New York, 1992, pp. 249–251.

[Fum et al. 88] D. **Fum**, G. **Guida**, and C. **Tasso**. *A Distributed Multi-Agent Architecture for Natural Language Processing*. In: Proceedings of the 12th International Conference on Computational Linguistics (COLING 88), Budapest, Hungary, 1988, pp. 812–814.

[Jameson et al. 94] A. **Jameson**, B. **Kipper**, A. **Ndiaye**, R. **Schäfer**, J. **Simons**, T. **Weis**, and D. **Zimmermann**. *Cooperating to Be Noncooperative: The Dialog System PRACMA*. In: KI-94: Advances in Artificial Intelligence (Proceedings of the 18th German Annual Conference on Artificial Intelligence (KI-94), Saarbrücken, Germany). Springer, Berlin, 1994, pp. 106–117.

[Kipper 94] B. **Kipper**. *A Blackboard Architecture for Natural Language Analysis*. In: Proceedings of the 7th Florida Artificial Intelligence Research Symposium (FLAIRS 94), Pensacola Beach, USA, 1994, pp. 231–235.

[Nii 86] P. **Nii**. *Blackboard Systems: Blackboard Application Systems, Blackboard Systems from a Knowledge Engineering Perspective*. AI Magazine Vol. 7, No. 3 (August 1986), pp. 82–106.

A Model Theory for Paraconsistent Logic Programming

Carlos Viegas Damásio and Luís Moniz Pereira*

CRIA, Uninova and DCS, U. Nova de Lisboa
2825 Monte da Caparica
Portugal
{cd|lmp}@fct.unl.pt

Abstract. We provide a nine-valued logic to characterize the models of logic programs under a paraconsistent well-founded semantics with explicit negation $WFSX_p$. We define a truth-functional logic, $\mathcal{NINE}$, based on the bilattice construction of Ginsberg and Fitting. The models identified by $WFSX_p$ are models of logic $\mathcal{NINE}$. We conclude with a discussion on the conditions to obtain an isomorphism between the two definitions, and thereby characterizing $WFSX_p$ model-theoretically.

1 Introduction

One of the main issues in logic programming is the definition of semantics for negation(s). Quite recently, a second form of negation besides the older default negation, was proposed by several authors [12, 8, 11, 21, 13]) providing a mechanism for explicitly declaring the falsity of literals, which was not available before. The importance of extending LP with a second kind of negation $\neg$, has been stressed for use in deductive databases, knowledge representation, and non-monotonic reasoning. Different semantics for extended LPs with $\neg$-negation have appeared (e.g. [8, 18, 13, 22]). The specific generalization for extended programs of well-founded semantics [7], $WFSX$, defined in [13, 2] using "explicit negation", is taken as the base semantics in this paper.

The introduction of explicit negation requires being able to reason with, or at least detect, contradictory knowledge. Indeed, information is not only normally incomplete but contradictory as well. As remarked by [22] there are three main ways of dealing with inconsistent information:

Explosive approach: If the program is contradictory then every formula is derived from it. This corresponds to the usual approach in mathematical logic, and of several semantics for extended logic programs [18, 8, 13, 2].

Belief revision approach: The program is revised in order to regain consistency. This is the view adopted by some authors in the LP community [17, 14, 10, 1, 2]. It does not necessarily require an explicit paraconsistent semantics: the procedural revision operators suffice.

---

* We thank Esprit BR project Compulog 2 (no. 6810), and JNICT for their support.

Paraconsistent approach: Accept contradictory information and perform reasoning tasks that take it into account. This is the approach of [4, 19, 22], and the one we will follow in this paper.

The first approach is rather naïve and only makes sense when dealing with mathematical objects. For instance, if we have a large knowledge base being mantained or updated by different agents, it is natural to encounter inconsistencies in the database. Most of the time, this inconsistency is local to some part of the knowledge base and it shouldn't affect other, independent, information. If we adopt the explosive approach, and a single contradiction is found then we must discard the entire knowledge base. This is uneconomical.

Sometimes the contradictory information can be due to a specification error, and we'd like to fix it through debugging. In other situations the information provided is in itself contradictory. In the former, we can use belief revision techniques. In the latter, a paraconsistent deductive mechanism is necessary. Notice however that to perform belief revision we need in any case to detect the inconsistencies and the reasons supporting them. Thus, paraconsistent reasoning is an, at least implicit, intermediate step to attain belief revision.

Since we want to assign meaning to every program we will make use of the paraconsistent version of $WFSX$, $WFSX_p$ which can be found in [1, 2]. The semantics complies with two basic principles: coherence and also a form of introspection. The "coherence principle" of [13, 2] relates the two forms of negation, default and explicit: it stipulates that the latter entails the former, i.e if L ($\neg L$) is entailed then so is $not \neg L$ ($not\, L$). In other words, coherence requires that if I'm convinced of the truth of a proposition then I must believe (i.e. be weakly convinced about) the truth of the proposition.

The introspection mechanism too provides the derivation of new weak convictions. To express it we need the notion of "doubt": I doubt the truth of L iff I have weak conviction for the falsity of L; I have conviction in the truth of L iff I doubt the weak conviction in the falsity of L. Now we can state the principle of introspective doubt: if I doubt all the bodies of rules for L then I'm weakly convinced of the falsity of L. The joint application of these principles is brought out in example 1.

Example 1. Let P be the extended logic program containing the five rules $\{a; \neg a;$ $b \leftarrow a; c \leftarrow not\, b; d \leftarrow not\, d\}$. It is clear that the model of this program must entail a, $\neg a$ and b; therefore I'm convinced of the truth of a and b (a and b are true) and convinced of the falsity of a ($\neg a$ is true). By applying coherence we should also have $not\, a$, $not\, \neg a$ and $not\, \neg b$, i.e. I'm weakly convinced of the falsity of a ($not\, a$ is true) and weakly convinced of the truth of a and b ($not\, \neg a$ and $not\, \neg b$ are true). By doubt introspection, I believe in the falsity of b ($not\, b$ is true) if I have doubts about the truth of a; and indeed I'm reserved about the truth of a because I believe in the falsity of a, i.e. $not\, a$ is true. Therefore $not\, b$, and thus c, should belong to the model. By the same introspective doubt, I'm weakly convinced of the falsity of c ($not\, c$ is true) if I doubt my belief in the falsity of b, i.e. if I'm convinced of the truth of b; this is so (b is true), therefore $not\, c$

should belong to the model of the program. Regarding literal d, I'm convinced of the truth of d iff I doubt the truth of d, therefore I remain agnostic about my conviction, i.e. d and $not\, d$ are not entailed. On the other hand, I'm weakly convinced of the truth d since I have no rule for $\neg d$.

Therefore we equate conviction in the truth (resp. falsity) of a proposition with L (resp. $\neg L$), and belief with "$not\, \neg$", i.e. belief in the truth (resp. falsity) of a proposition with $not\, \neg L$ (resp. $not\, \neg\neg L = not\, L$).

We assume the reader acquainted with the terminology of extended logic programs, in particular that atoms or explicitly negated atoms are called objective literals, and that default literals are the default negated objective literals. For details see [8, 13, 2]. All definitions and results in this paper are valid only for the ground instances of programs.

We refer the reader to [1] for the alternating fixpoint definition of $WFSX_p$. Different, but equivalent, definitions of $WFSX_p$ also appeared in [16, 15, 2]. In these works the paraconsistent version of $WFSX$ is used only to detect contradictions to be removed. This is not the stance taken here. We wish to analyse the intrinsic properties of the semantics to shed new light on the subject, and also to turn the connectives into truth-functional ones. We provide a nine-valued logic to characterize the models of logic programs explicit negation under $WFSX_p$, based on the bilattice construction of Ginsberg and Fitting. The models identified by $WFSX_p$ are models of logic $\mathcal{NINE}$. We conclude with a discussion on the conditions to obtain an isomorphism between both definitions, thereby characterizing $WFSX_p$ model-theoretically.

2 Model theory for $WFSX_p$

One of the main criticsms to the original definition of well-founded semantics with explicit negation regards its model theory. In [13, 2] the definition of the logical implication operation is not truth functional and literals a and $\neg a$ are viewed almost as separate entities: though $\neg a$ entails a false nothing else follows for other truth values. Furthermore, in some cases the head of a rule is assigned the truth value $\mathbf{f}$ the body $\mathbf{u}$, but the rule is satisfied ($\mathbf{f} \leftarrow \mathbf{u}$). This is due, in such cases, to the coherence principle, and it might be considered awkard in a three-valued logic. In other situations, with the same assignment of values to head and body a rule, and where coherence does not intervene, the rule is unsatisfiable, showing again the non-truth functional character of the model definition used. These problems are illustrated with example 2.

Example 2. Let P be the logic program containing the following rules: $\{a \leftarrow b;$ $b \leftarrow not\, b; \neg a\}$. The $WFM(P)$ is $\{\neg a, not\, a, not\, \neg b\}$. According to the notions of interpretation and model of [13, 2], literal b is assigned truth value undefined, a is assigned false, and $\neg a$ true. The first rule of the program is satisfied by this interpretation, even with false head and undefined body. The intuition being that $\neg a$ overrides the undefinedness of a obtained on the basis of the first rule.

The basic mechanisms we want to capture and formalize are illustrated in examples 1 and 2. Literals are entailed with three different degrees of epistemic entrenchment: conviction, weak conviction and undecidedness. Convictions are represented by objective literals and the rule implication sign in extended logic programming propagates them. Weak convictions are drawn by default or result from the mandatory application of the coherence principle.

A by now standard way of generating new logics for reasoning with missing or conflicting information is via Ginsberg's bilattices [9], who generalizes the ideas behind Belnap's four valued logic [3]. We follow Fitting's proposals [6] on how to construct a bilattice.

Definition 1. [6] Given two complete lattices $C = \langle \mathbf{C}, \leq_1 \rangle$ and $D = \langle \mathbf{D}, \leq_2 \rangle$ the structure $\mathcal{B}(C, D) = \langle \mathbf{C} \times \mathbf{D}, \leq_k, \leq_t \rangle$ is a bilattice, with $\langle c_1, d_1 \rangle \leq_k \langle c_2, d_2 \rangle$ iff $c_1 \leq_1 c_2 \wedge d_1 \leq_2 d_2$, and $\langle c_1, d_1 \rangle \leq_t \langle c_2, d_2 \rangle$ iff $c_1 \leq_1 c_2 \wedge d_2 \leq_2 d_1$. To each ordering are associated join and meet operations as usual. Conjunction and disjunction are, respectively, meet and join in the truth-ordering.

The intuition here is that C (D) provides the arguments for (against) believing in the truth of a statement. If $\langle c_1, d_1 \rangle \leq_k \langle c_2, d_2 \rangle$, then situation 2 has more information than 1, i.e. knowledge is increased. If $\langle c_1, d_1 \rangle \leq_t \langle c_2, d_2 \rangle$ then we have more reasons to believe in situation 2 than in 1, because the reasons for believing the statement either increased or the reasons against it are weaker, i.e. $\langle c_2, d_2 \rangle$ is truer than $\langle c_1, d_1 \rangle$.

Next we define our truth-space using the bilattice construction. We have identified the reasons for believing, disbelieving, or abstaining in the truth of a proposition: conviction, weak conviction and undecidedness. Using these degrees we can form two complete lattices, one with the reasons for the truth of a proposition and other with the reasons against it (or for its falsity): *For* $= (\{\} < \{not\ \neg L\} < \{L, not\ \neg L\})$ and *Against* $= (\{\} < \{not\ L\} < \{\neg L, not\ L\})$. The set $\{L\}$ $(\{\neg L\})$ is not an element of lattice *For* (*Against*) because of the coherence principle: If I am convinced of the truth of L $(\neg L)$ then I must believe in L $(\neg L)$, i.e. $not\ \neg L$ $(not\ L)$ should hold. In fact, we can abstract from the lattices *For* and *Against* by defining their isomorphic lattice of opinion. The bilattice $\mathcal{NINE}$ is then constructed from the opinion lattice.

Definition 2. The opinion lattice is the complete lattice $O = < \{none, weak, strong\}, (none < weak < strong) >$. Bilattice $\mathcal{NINE}$ is defined as $\mathcal{B}(O, O)$. To each one of the nine pairs $\langle o_1, o_2 \rangle$ of $\mathcal{NINE}$ we assign it a value as follows:

Pair	Value	Pair	Value	Pair	Value
$\langle none, none \rangle$	$\perp$	$\langle none, strong \rangle$	**f**	$\langle strong, weak \rangle$	**II**
$\langle none, weak \rangle$	**df**	$\langle strong, none \rangle$	**t**	$\langle weak, strong \rangle$	**III**
$\langle weak, none \rangle$	**dt**	$\langle strong, strong \rangle$	**I**	$\langle weak, weak \rangle$	**IV**

By $\perp$ we mean no opinion (or undecidedness or undefinedness), and corresponds to the bottom element of the lattice according to the knowledge ordering. The two extra logical values correspond to default falsity (**df**) and default truth

(dt). We have also the classical **t** and **f** values and four degrees of contradictory information. Figure 1 is the Hasse diagram of bilattice $\mathcal{NINE}$. In order to ob-

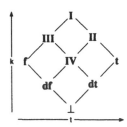

Fig. 1. Logic $\mathcal{NINE}$

tain a correspondence with the paraconsistent semantics for extended logic programs we need to define two forms of negation and the interpretation of the rule implication sign. According to Fitting [6] a negation operator in a (interlaced) bilattice should satisfy the following three properties: (1) $a \leq_k b \Rightarrow \neg a \leq_k \neg b$; (2) $a \leq_t b \Rightarrow \neg b \leq_t \neg a$; (3) $a = \neg\neg a$. If the double negation condition (3) is not verified then the negation operator is said to be weak. The intuition is that negations should reverse truth but preserve knowledge. In what follows we will also use $\mathcal{NINE}$, when no confusion arises, to represent the set of logical values induced by bilattice $\mathcal{NINE}$.

Definition 3. Let $\neg : \mathcal{NINE} \mapsto \mathcal{NINE}$ and *not* $: \mathcal{NINE} \mapsto \mathcal{NINE}$ be the unary operators defined by the following truth-tables.

a	$\perp$	df	dt	f	t	I	II	III	IV
$\neg a$	$\perp$	dt	df	t	f	I	III	II	IV
not a	$\perp$	t	f	t	f	I	I	I	I

Proposition 4. *Operators* $\neg : \mathcal{NINE} \mapsto \mathcal{NINE}$ *and not* $: \mathcal{NINE} \mapsto \mathcal{NINE}$ *are, respectively, a negation and a weak negation.*

The rationale is that $\neg$ finds the degree of conviction for the negation of a proposition, exchanging the roles of what counts for and what counts against. The *not* operator determines if the negation of a proposition is at least believed. We have four cases to consider: there is no conviction in the truth nor falsity of a proposition; there is at least weak conviction in the falsity of a proposition and no conviction in its truth; there is no conviction in the falsity of a proposition and at least weak conviction in its truth; there is at least weak conviction for both the falsity and the truth of a proposition. In the first case we remain undecided. In the second case *not* returns true, and in the third case false. In the fourth and last case we have contradictory information and *not* returns contradiction.

The definition of the rule implication sign is rather simple: it enacts the principle that if we have conviction in the antecedent we must have conviction in the consequent.

Definition 5. Let $\leftarrow: \mathcal{NINE} \times \mathcal{NINE} \mapsto \mathcal{NINE}$ be the binary operator defined by the following rules: Rule implication $a \leftarrow b$ is **f** iff b is **I**, **II** or **t** but a is none of these truth values; otherwise, $a \leftarrow b$ is **t**.

Our goal is to define a notion of model which complies with the alternating fixpoint definition of $WFSX_\mathrm{p}$. Namely, we would like the paraconsistent well-founded model to be a $\mathcal{NINE}$ model of the program. To attain this we first define as usual the syntax, and the notions of interpretation, valuation function, and model.

Definition 6. Let $\mathcal{L}$ be a set of atomic propositions. The language $\mathcal{L}_9$ is defined inductively as follows: constants **t** and **f** belong to $\mathcal{L}_9$; if $a \in \mathcal{L}$ then $a \in \mathcal{L}_9$; if $A \in \mathcal{L}_9$ then $\neg A$ and *not* A are in $\mathcal{L}_9$ too; if A and B belong to $\mathcal{L}_9$ then their boolean combinations $A \wedge B$, $A \vee B$ and $A \leftarrow B$ also belong to $\mathcal{L}_9$; nothing else belongs to $\mathcal{L}_9$.

We define a nine valued interpretation as a function assigning to each atomic proposition one of the truth values of $\mathcal{NINE}$. The definition of truth valuation $\hat{I}_9$ wrt to an interpretation I_9 is a function mapping formulae into logical values of $\mathcal{NINE}$, with the logical connectives "$\wedge$", "$\vee$", "$\neg$", "*not*" and "$\leftarrow$" as per definitions 1, 3, and 5. An interpretation is a model of a set of formulae iff there is conviction in each formula of the set.

Definition 7. Let I be a $\mathcal{NINE}$ interpretation. Interpretation I is a $\mathcal{NINE}$ model of a set of formulae S, represented by $I \models_9 S$, iff $\forall_{s \in S} \hat{I}(s) = \mathbf{I} \vee \hat{I}(s) = \mathbf{II} \vee \hat{I}(s) = \mathbf{t}$

For simplicity, we write $I \models_9 s$, standing for $I \models_9 \{s\}$, where s is an arbitrary formula of $\mathcal{L}_9$. By definition of valuation of implicational formulae, we have for any formula s of $\mathcal{L}_9$ the equivalence $\hat{I}(s \leftarrow \mathbf{t}) = \mathbf{t}$ iff $I \models_9 s$.

The commutative, associative, idempotency and absorption laws of '$\wedge$' and '$\vee$' are inherited from the complete lattice structure of $\mathcal{NINE}$. Remark that property *not not* $A = $ *not* $\neg A = \neg$*not* A holds in $\mathcal{NINE}$, and therefore all possible combinations of the negation operators can reduce to one of the four following cases, where a is an atomic proposition: a, *not* a, $\neg a$ or *not* $\neg a$.

The mapping between single literal based interpretations and $\mathcal{NINE}$ truth-values is immediate. The formal mapping aspects can be found in definition 8.

Definition 8. Let I be a set of literals, default or objective, and $\mathcal{L}_I$ the set of atoms of the language of I. The $\mathcal{NINE}$ interpretation $\tau(I)$, with underlying language $\mathcal{L}_I$, is the interpretation where to an atomic proposition a of $\mathcal{L}_I$ is assigned one logical value, as follows:

$\perp$ iff $a \notin I \wedge \neg a \notin I \wedge not\, a \notin I \wedge not\, \neg a \notin I$ **I** iff $a \in I \wedge \neg a \in I \wedge not\, a \in I \wedge not\, \neg a \in I$

df iff $a \notin I \wedge \neg a \notin I \wedge not\, a \in I \wedge not\, \neg a \notin I$ **II** iff $a \in I \wedge \neg a \notin I \wedge not\, a \in I \wedge not\, \neg a \in I$

dt iff $a \notin I \wedge \neg a \notin I \wedge not\, a \notin I \wedge not\, \neg a \in I$ **III** iff $a \notin I \wedge \neg a \in I \wedge not\, a \in I \wedge not\, \neg a \in I$

f iff $a \notin I \wedge \neg a \in I \wedge not\, a \in I \wedge not\, \neg a \notin I$ **IV** iff $a \notin I \wedge \neg a \notin I \wedge not\, a \in I \wedge not\, \neg a \in I$

Notice that the τ mapping is a bijection among the set of interpretations and the set of $\mathcal{NINE}$ interpretations based on the same set of atomic propositional symbols.

Our first result is the desirable statement relating the paraconsistent partial stable models of a logic program with $\mathcal{NINE}$ models, i.e. the fixpoints of $\Gamma\Gamma_s$. For the definition of Γ and Γ_s operators see [1, 2]. According to theorem 9 we have succeeded in finding in $\mathcal{NINE}$ a model theory for the paraconsistent well-founded semantics with explicit negation.

Theorem 9. *Let P be an extended logic program. If T is a fixpoint of $\Gamma_P\Gamma_{P_s}$ then $I = \tau\left(T \cup not\, \mathcal{H}_P - \Gamma_{P_s}\right)$ is a $\mathcal{NINE}$ model of P, i.e. $I \models_9 P_9$. The theory P_9 is obtained from P by replacing all rules $L_0 \leftarrow L_1, \ldots, L_m, not\, L_{m+1}, \ldots, not\, L_n$ by the $\mathcal{L}_9$ formula $L_0 \leftarrow L_1 \wedge \ldots \wedge L_m \wedge not\, L_{m+1} \wedge \ldots \wedge not\, L_n$*

Example 3. Consider again program P of example 2. Its WFM_p is $\{\neg a, not\, a, not\, \neg b\}$. We obtain its $\mathcal{NINE}$ model by using the τ transformation. To a is assigned the value **f** and to b the value **dt**. As the reader can check, this is a $\mathcal{NINE}$ model of the corresponding P_9 program.

3 Supported Models

The program of example 2 has other $\mathcal{NINE}$ models which do not correspond to any fixpoint of $WFSX_p$. One such model is obtained by assigning **f** to a, and to b the undefined truth value $\perp$. But this model is smaller under the knowledge order than the corresponding model generated by the WFM_p. This raises the question why we infered **dt** for b instead of $\perp$. In general terms, we have an additional mechanism for infering weak conviction, i.e. negation by default. Because we have no conviction in the falsity of b we may weakly believe in its truth. This form of reasoning provides new insights into the stronger conditions that the $\mathcal{NINE}$ models generated by $WFSX_p$ obey.

Definition 10. Let I be a $\mathcal{NINE}$ model. We define relation $I \rightsquigarrow F$ as follows, where L is an objective literal and A and B $\mathcal{L}_9$ formulae without occurrences of the rule implication symbol:

$I \rightsquigarrow L$ iff $I \models_9 not\, L$ $I \rightsquigarrow (A \wedge B)$ iff $(I \rightsquigarrow A)$ or $(I \rightsquigarrow B)$

$I \rightsquigarrow not\, L$ iff $I \models_9 L$ $I \rightsquigarrow (A \vee B)$ iff $(I \rightsquigarrow A)$ and $(I \rightsquigarrow B)$

When $I \rightsquigarrow F$ we have reasons to doubt of F. The cases on the left express formally the intuitions given in the introduction of the paper. Now we can give a better characterization of the properties obeyed by $WFSX_p$ fixpoints.

Definition 11. Let P_9 be a $\mathcal{NINE}$ theory generated by a logic program P. We say that I is a supported model of P_9 iff the following holds: $I \models_9 L$ iff there is an implication in P_9 with consequent L and antecedent *Body* such that $I \models_9 Body$; $I \models_9 not\, L$ iff $I \models_9 \neg L$ or for every implication with conclusion L and premise *Body* we have $I \leadsto Body$.

According to the above definition, we have conviction in the truth of a literal if we have at least one rule for that literal for which we are convinced of the truth of the body. We believe in the falsity of a literal iff we are convinced of its falsity (coherence principle), or we doubt each body of the rules with that literal in the head (principle of introspective doubt).

Theorem 12. *Let P be an extended logic program and P_9 its corresponding $\mathcal{NINE}$ theory. If T is a fixpoint of $\Gamma_P\Gamma_{P_s}$ then $I = \tau\,(T \cup not\,\mathcal{H}_P - \Gamma_{P_s})$ is a supported model of P_9.*

The converse of the above theorem is not valid, i.e. there are supported models which are not fixpoints of $\Gamma\Gamma_s$. Therefore supported models do not fully characterize the fixpoints of $\Gamma\Gamma_s$, as illustrated in the following example.

Example 4. Consider the following two-rule program $\{a \leftarrow b; b \leftarrow a\}$. The corresponding $\mathcal{NINE}$ theory has four supported models, namely $\{a = \mathbf{dt}, b = \mathbf{dt}\}$, $\{a = \mathbf{t}, b = \mathbf{t}\}$, $\{a = \mathbf{II}, b = \mathbf{II}\}$ and $\{a = \mathbf{IV}, b = \mathbf{IV}\}$. The least model under the knowledge ordering is the first one listed. Mark that the unique fixpoint of the original program corresponds to the latter model.

The problem with example 4 is the "positive loop" between a and b. In general, when programs have no infinite positive dependencies among literals, the supported models are isomorphic to the fixpoints of $WFSX_\mathrm{p}$. We first define the positive dependency graph:

Definition 13. Let P be an extended logic program. The vertices of the positive dependency directed graph $Dep^+(P)$ of P are the literals of $\mathcal{H}_P$. For each rule $L \leftarrow L_1, \ldots, L_m, not\, L_{m+1}, \ldots, not\, L_n$ of P there is an edge from node L_i, $1 \le i \le m$, to node L. If there are no infinite descending chains in $Dep^+(P)$ we say that the program has no infinite positive recursion.

Theorem 14. *Let P be an extended logic program without infinite positive recursion, if $I = \tau(T \cup not\, F)$ is a supported model of the corresponding P_9 theory then $T \cup not\, F$ is a fixpoint of $\Gamma\Gamma_s$.*

The importance of this result is due to the circumstance that an extended logic program P can be transformed into an equivalent program with no objective literals in the bodies of rules. This means that it is possible to find an equivalent program where the characterization of $WFSX_\mathrm{p}$ fixpoints by the supported models holds, i.e. a model-theoretic definition for $WFSX_\mathrm{p}$. This program is obtained by iterated application of an appropriate partial evaluation transformation: let $no^+(P)$ be the set of rules in P which do not have positive literals in their bodies. Let $L \leftarrow Body$ be a rule in $no^+(P)$. Substitute every positive occurrences of L in a body of P by the conjunction $Body, not \neg L$. Add these new rules to P. Iterate this step till all rules of $no^+(P)$ were substituted, obtaining program P'. Repeat the whole process with program P' till no new rules are added, resulting program P_f. Program $no^+(P_f)$ is equivalent to the original program P. This bottom-up construction is similar to Brass and Dix's residual program computation [5].

Example 5. Consider the program of example 4. By applying the above process we obtain as a result the empty program, which has the unique supported model $\{a = \text{IV}, b = \text{IV}\}$, corresponding to its paraconsistent well-founded model.

4 Conclusions

We have provided a new truth-functional nine-valued logic which furnishes an elegant model-theory for *WFSX* and *WFSX*$_p$. In this logic, a bilattice, it is possible to define, by a truth table, the meaning of the "*not*" and "$\neg$" negation operators, besides the usual boolean connectives "$\vee$", "$\wedge$" and "$\leftarrow$". We were able to prove that every paraconsistent partial stable model is a model of the theory readily obtained from the program, under our $\mathcal{NINE}$ logic. Then we introduced the notion of supported model in order to establish a one-to-one correspondence between supported models and paraconsistent partial stable models. We have shown that this is not possible in general, but we have identified a class of the programs (the ones which do not have infinite positive dependencies) where the "equivalence" holds. Fortunately, every extended logic program has an equivalent one in this stricter class of programs, and therefore we can characterize model-theoretically the semantics of any extended logic program. It remains to be settled if such one-to-one characterization is possible without using this other equivalent, but distinct, program. It would also be very interesting if the main ideas underlying our *WFSX*$_p$ semantics could be generalized for arbitrary interlaced bilattices. A similar nine-valued logic was independently proposed in [20] to formalize a semantics for disjunctive extended logic programs, but with different interpretations of the negation operators, and based on an Answer-Set like semantics. There are results showing the natural embedding of the semantics [4, 18, 19, 22] in *WFSX*$_p$, which will be the subject of a forthcoming paper.

References

1. J. J. Alferes, C. V. Damásio, and L. M. Pereira. A logic programming system for non-monotonic reasoning. *Journal of Automated Reasoning*, Special Issue on Implementation of NonMonotonic Reasoning(14):93–147, 1995.
2. J. J. Alferes and L. M. Pereira. *Reasoning with Logic Programming*. Springer–Verlag, 1995. In print.
3. N. D. Belnap. A useful four-valued logic. In G. Epstein and J. M. Dunn, editors, *Modern Uses of Many-valued Logic*, pages 8–37. Reidel, 1977.

4. H. A. Blair and V. S. Subrahmanian. Paraconsistent logic programming. *Theoretical Computer Science*, 68:135–154, 1989.

5. S. Brass and J. Dix. A disjunctive semantics based on unfolding and bottom-up evaluation. In *Proc. IFIP '94-Congress, Workshop FG2: Disjunctive Logic Programming and Disjunctive Databases*, pages 83–91. Springer, 1994.

6. M. Fitting. Bilattices and the semantics of logic programming. *Journal of Logic Programming*, 11:91–116, 1991.

7. A. V. Gelder, K. A. Ross, and J. S. Schlipf. The well-founded semantics for general logic programs. *Journal of the ACM*, 38(3):620–650, 1991.

8. M. Gelfond and V. Lifschitz. Logic programs with classical negation. In Warren and Szeredi, editors, *7th ICLP*, pages 579–597. MIT Press, 1990.

9. M. L. Ginsberg. Multivalued logics: a uniform approach to reasoning in artificial intelligence. *Computational Intelligence*, 4:265–316, 1988.

10. C. M. Jonker and C. Witteveen. Revision by expansion. In G. Lakemeyer and B. Nebel, editors, *Proceedings ECAI'92 Workshop on Theoretical Foundations of Knowledge Representation*, pages 40–44. ECAI'92 Press, 1992.

11. R. Kowalski and F. Sadri. Logic programs with exceptions. In Warren and Szeredi, editors, *7th ICLP*. MIT Press, 1990.

12. D. Pearce and G. Wagner. Reasoning with negative information I: Strong negation in logic programs. In *Language, Knowledge and Intentionality*, pages 430–453. Acta Philosophica Fennica 49, 1990.

13. L. M. Pereira and J. J. Alferes. Well founded semantics for logic programs with explicit negation. In B. Neumann, editor, *Proc. ECAI*, pages 102–106. John Wiley & Sons, 1992.

14. L. M. Pereira, J. J. Alferes, and J. N. Aparício. Contradiction Removal within Well Founded Semantics. In A. Nerode, W. Marek, and V. S. Subrahmanian, editors, *LPNMR'91*, pages 105–119. MIT Press, 1991.

15. L. M. Pereira, J. J. Alferes, and J. N. Aparício. Contradiction removal semantics with explicit negation. In M. Masuch and L. Pólos, editors, *Knowledge Representation and Reasoning Under Uncertainty*, volume 808 of *LNAI*, pages 91–106. Springer-Verlag, 1994.

16. L. M. Pereira, J. N. Aparício, and J. J. Alferes. Non-monotonic reasoning with logic programming. *Journal of Logic Programming. Special issue on Nonmonotonic reasoning*, 17(2, 3 & 4):227–263, 1993.

17. S. G. Pimentel and W. L. Rodi. Belief revision and paraconsistency in a logic programming framework. In A. Nerode, W. Marek, and V. S. Subrahmanian, editors, *LPNMR'91*, pages 228–242. MIT Press, 1991.

18. T. Przymusinski. Extended stable semantics for normal and disjunctive programs. In Warren and Szeredi, editors, *7th ICLP*, pages 459–477. MIT Press, 1990.

19. C. Sakama. Extended well-founded semantics for paraconsistent logic programs. In *Fifth Generation Computer Systems*, pages 592–599. ICOT, 1992.

20. C. Sakama and K. Inoue. Paraconsistent stable semantics for extended disjunctive programs. *Journal of Logic and Computation*, 5(3), 1995.

21. G. Wagner. A database needs two kinds of negation. In B. Thalheim, J. Demetrovics, and H.-D. Gerhardt, editors, *Mathematical Foundations of Database Systems*, pages 357–371. LNCS 495, Springer-Verlag, 1991.

22. G. Wagner. Vivid logic: Knowledge-based reasoning with two kinds of negation. *LNAI*, 764, 1994.

Promoting Software Reuse Through Explicit Knowledge Representations *

Carmen Fernández-Chamizo, Pedro Antonio González-Calero
and Mercedes Gómez-Albarrán

Dep. Informática y Automática. Universidad Complutense de Madrid
28040 Madrid, Spain
email: cfernan@eucmvx.sim.ucm.es

Abstract. Selection and adaptation of software components are fundamental issues to attain effective reuse in object-oriented programming.
Component understanding is essential to both processes. In this paper
we propose a knowledge-based approach to the component understanding problem which includes the explicit representation of design commitments, design decisions and customizing alternatives. This proposal
is being implemented in the ORA (Object Reuse Assistant) system, a
tool to support the retrieval, understanding, and adaptation of software
components in general purpose object-oriented libraries.

1 Introduction

Software reuse can improve software quality and productivity [1]. But, as stated
in [4] there remain several problems that still limit software reuse, ranging from
the scarce availability of reusable objects to the difficulty of retrieving, understanding and adapting the required software objects. Class reuse in object-
oriented languages constitutes an important contribution on the way to reusability [16]. However, object-oriented programming (OOP), while improving the
whole software development process, adds its own drawbacks to the software
retrieval problem [18]. The use of polymorphism and inheritance introduces a
large number of dependencies between components. Dynamic binding increases
the number of implementations to be examined, and the dispersion of functionality into different components makes global understanding difficult. General
purpose object-oriented libraries (GPOOLs), as the libraries included in generally available environments for object-oriented languages, have a high reuse
potential due to their generality. Software development using GPOOLs usually
involves the extension of existing classes to meet the particular requirements.
In this paper we address the problem of component understanding as the central issue to attain effective reuse of software components in class libraries. We
present a knowledge-based approach which includes the explicit representation
of design commitments, design decisions and customizing alternatives extracted

---

* This work is supported by the Spanish Committee of Science & Technology (CICYT,
TIC92-0058 & TIC94-0187)

from the class library implementation and documentation. This proposal is being implemented in the ORA (Object Reuse Assistant) system, a tool to support the retrieval, understanding, and adaptation of software components in general purpose object oriented libraries. Section 2 describes the problems associated with component reuse, in particular, retrieval, understanding and adaptation of software components. In Section 3, a discussion about the specific characteristics of reusing classes in general purpose class libraries can be found. Section 4 describes the ORA system, presenting the knowledge representation as the central part of the system, along with some specific examples of its use. In the last section, we conclude making a comparison of related systems and stating the current state of the system and its foreseen evolution.

2 Component Reuse

Software development with reuse [17] involves mechanisms for (1) specifying reuse needs, (2) retrieving a set of reuse candidates from a component base which match certain key characteristics of the reuse needs, (3) evaluating the potential of each retrieved reuse candidate for satisfying the key characteristics at an acceptable cost and selecting the best-suited candidate, if any, (4) modifying the selected component in order to satisfy the given reuse specification, if necessary, and (5) integrating the modified component into the ongoing development project. In this paper we are concerned with the retrieving and adapting processes. But usually, to assess the adequacy of a selected component, or to adapt it to a new context, it is necessary to know the behavior, structure and interrelationships of the component. So, the problem of component understanding underlies both processes.

2.1 The Retrieval of Software Components

Traditional approaches to software retrieval can basically follow two approaches which are described below.

The goal of the automatic indexing approach is to characterize each component by a set of indices that are automatically extracted from its natural language documentation. [11, 14] describe systems based on this approach. Some recent proposals [9] include a partial natural language analysis of the component descriptions in order to improve the retrieval effectiveness. With these techniques, retrieval is in general efficient, but help with selection and correct usage must be found outside the retrieval system.

On the other hand, the key feature of the knowledge-based approach is that it draws semantic information about software components from a human expert. Knowledge-based systems are often very sophisticated. Unfortunately, as a tradeoff, they require domain analysis and a great deal of pre-encoded, manually provided semantic information. The systems proposed in [7, 19] use knowledge bases to represent knowledge about software components. The LaSSIE system [5] embodies a frame-based knowledge representation. Software components are described in terms of the operations they perform. This knowledge is classified into a conceptual hierarchy by a knowledge representation system.

All these knowledge-based systems represent the knowledge in frame-like structures with similar sets of slot-fillers. They all organize the knowledge around the functions performed by the components, although some of them also include frame representations of the objects involved. In every single case, the characterization of the components with slot-fillers is done manually, following a pre-established model of the domain.

2.2 Understanding and Adaptation

Understanding the behavior, structure, and interrelationships between various entities of a software component is essential to its selection, and even more to its adaptation in order to integrate it into a new context, or to solve a somehow different problem. Adaptation is needed when the component does not fulfill all the requirements of the new context or the new problem. It involves locating the inappropriate choices and replacing them; this may in turn affect other choices, and therefore cause additional adaptations. Most of the knowledge-based systems address, to a certain extent, the understanding problem. In the LaSSIE system [5], Devanbu undertook the task of building an information system to aid in the discovery problem, that is, the process of learning about an existing system to use or modify it. More specifically, the GTE environment [10] uses domain knowledge to support understanding and adaptation of the components. Domain knowledge is expressed through explicitly represented patterns within the reusable components, helping to understand the component semantics. The IPSEN environment [2] uses typed links between software components to describe the complex relationships existing in a software system. The links serve to understand a component context when retrieving it and integrating it into a new context. All these systems rely on domain knowledge and, if the application domain is well defined, they provide an acceptable support. In this paper we are concerned with the problem of supporting reuse in general purpose software libraries. The lack of a pre-specified application domain adds new difficulties to the problem of knowledge representation.

3 Reusing General Purpose Object-Oriented Libraries (GPOOLs)

There are two important properties that cause class libraries to be reusable: generality and extensibility. Generality refers to the ability of one system, without modification, to serve in a large range of circumstances, while extensibility refers to the ability of a system to be easily modified to better meet a particular need [13]. To understand extensible software we have to represent explicitly not only the client interface, but also the interfaces and organization among the internal modules of the system. GPOOLs are a clear example of extensible software, because subclassing and inheritance allow multiple variants to coexist, cooperate, and be easily constructed. The problem with extensible systems is that they can not be arbitrarily extended, since some restrictions and dependencies must be met in order to preserve the consistency of the system. The description of these commitments needs to be as little restrictive as possible, since there must be room for alternative components. We must specify the responsibility each module has to, and its effects on, the system as a whole. Specification at this level would describe the architecture of the systems that can be developed, rather than their particular behavior. When designing a general purpose class, the designers have in mind the potential extensions of this class that will be consistent with their design. Accordingly to these potential extensions, many design decisions are taken and many design commitments are established. All this information has a high parallelism with the notion of software architecture. Our proposal consists of (1) identifying this design knowledge, and (2) representing it explicitly, along with all the knowledge about behavior and structure of the class that may be required to reuse it. We are investigating the utility of this proposal to support the extensibility of GPOOLs. In this way, we have partially implemented the ORA system, which is described below.

4   The Object Reuse Assistant (ORA)

Since understanding and adaptation are so central to reuse, we believe that there is a need for tools that support them directly. Our work has concentrated on general purpose software libraries for object oriented languages, due to their higher reuse potential. The generally available object-oriented environments include some basic libraries with general purpose components for graphical interfacing, data structure manipulation, communication with the host system and some utilities considered of general interest. When building applications for a particular domain, these components are a crucial part of any implementation. We have used a knowledge-based approach, by constructing an explicit representation of each component in the library. Because of the reuse potential of the selected libraries and their expected use life, we believe that a complete hand-coded representation of those components is well justified, and that it will demonstrate a high enough benefit to be regarded as a profitable effort. We are developing the Object Reuse Assistant (ORA), a system to support the retrieval, understanding and adaptation of software components in general purpose object oriented libraries. ORA consists of a knowledge base, representing the functionality, structure and relationships of the components, and a user interface, allowing different ways of access to the knowledge base. A previous version of the ORA system [8] included another module implementing an automatic indexing approach. That module is still available but its description, and the description of the user interface, are out of the scope of this paper since they have little influence on the component understanding problem. The following subsections describe the representation mechanisms exemplified with components from a Smalltalk class library, and the retrieval and adaptation processes implemented in ORA.

4.1 The Representation of the Class Library

The underlying representation we have used is Loom, a language and environment for knowledge representation and reasoning [15], descendant of the KL-ONE system. Loom has the ability of automatically classifying a structured concept with respect to a taxonomy of other concepts. The knowledge base is implemented as a frame network, where every node represents a concept. Concepts are restricted by a number of slots that relate them to other nodes in the network. Along with this taxonomic-based reasoning, Loom features an object-oriented assertional language which is dynamically truth maintained. The natural way of using Loom involves defining a terminological knowledge base that serves as the lexicon for assertions about objects in the world being represented. The terminological component is defined off-line, while the assertional component is designed to provide efficient reasoning suitable for a smooth interaction with the final user. Loom has certain characteristics that make it appropiate for building an information system for software component reuse: consistency checking, conceptual retrieval, deductive capabilities and support for incremental descriptions and simple rules.

We identify two different knowledge sources: terminological knowledge about programming and knowledge about implementation specifics of the class library. Although several realizations [3, 12] of programming knowledge ontologies can be found in the research literature, there is no consensus about what such a representation should include. Therefore, although being aware of its limitations, we have built our own classification of programming concepts.

In the ORA system, the root concepts of the programming knowledge representation are ACTION and OBJECT. Operations and objets manipulated by those operations are represented as specilizations of the ACTION and OBJECT concepts, respectively. Direct specializations of the OBJECT concept are DATA and DEVICE which are in turn further specialized. A complete description of the terminological component falls outside the scope of this paper.

The second component of the knowledge base is the one where implementation specifics are represented. This knowledge component can be further subdivided using the following criteria: knowledge automatically extracted from the class library and hand-coded knowledge. For every class and every method in the library a Loom concept is defined. These concepts are automatically classified by the Loom classifier into the hierarchy of component descriptions. Figure 1 shows the common slots for the classes, on the top, and the methods, on the bottom, whose fillers are automatically extracted from the source code. Notice that the information extracted directly from the code, allows ORA to provide the functionality for code browsing included in conventional object-oriented programming environments. Implementors of a given message can be displayed, as well as senders of a given message, or the user can ask for a list of the messages sent in a method and get information about those messages.

What is more interesting is the use that can be made of the hand-coded knowledge included in the descriptions. This knowledge, represented as additional slots in the descriptions, serves several purposes:

```
(:about class
    { fixed-class | variable-class | bytes-class }
    (has-superclass superclass)
    [ (has-class-variable class-variable) ]+
    [ (has-instance-variable instance-variable) ]+
    [ (has-pool-dictionary-variable pool-dictionary-variable) ]+
    [ (has-class-method class-method) ]+
    [ (has-instance-method instance-method) ]+)

(:about method
    [ primitive-method ]
    (has-selector selector)
    (has-code code-string)
    (has-comment comment-string)
    { (send-message-with-selector selector) }+)
```

Fig. 1. Information extracted automatically from the source code

- Relating the classes and methods to the programming concepts previously defined. In this manner, the classes and methods are viewed as specific implementations of programming concepts. Notice that this correspondence does not need to be established on a one-to-one basis. Programming concepts can correspond with groups of collaborating classes or methods.
- Stating design decisions and commitments. For example, class libraries are designed in such a way that certain groups of methods must remain consistent, i.e. these methods have to be overridden together or not at all. In ORA these constraints are represented explicitly.
- Stating feasible customizations. Abstract classes are used in reusable libraries to gather together the common functionality of a number of classes. Typically, in abstract classes some methods are implemented in terms of other non implemented methods, which are the responsibility of the subclass. When designing abstract classes a number of possible specialization parameters are in the mind of the designer, but this information does not appear explicitly in the implementation. We elicit that knowledge and represent it in ORA.
- Stating dependencies among implementations. One of the design guidelines in object-oriented programming is "do not duplicate functionality". This commitment leads to a cleaner architecture where every class has a well defined functionality, and where many components rely, through a client relationship, on the functionality provided by classes located in different places of the class hierarchy. In ORA these dependencies are explicitly represented for two purposes: to help in understanding the implementation; and to assist in the adaptation of methods by accessing to functionally related components which are close in the ORA semantic representation.

4.2 Component Retrieval

The first goal of ORA is to help in the retrieving and understanding of components from the class library. This goal can be illustrated with the following questions:

– Is there a component *c* that implements the programming concept *p*?.
– Where is component *c*?
– How should component *c* be used?

Component retrieval in the ORA system is conducted by the classifying mechanism of the knowledge base. Basically the user has two access modes: to build a frame description, or to browse the concept hierarchy. For users unfamiliar with the terminology employed in the representation, the natural approach is to browse the knowledge base from the root. Since the concept taxonomy is organized in an intuitive way, the user is likely to find the programming concepts where s/he thinks they should be. However, the access is faster if a frame description is provided, since the system will then return the most specific concepts matching that frame. When using the frame-based mode, the user has to select, either a verb describing the action the component performs, or a noun representing an object manipulated by the component. From the user input, the system displays a skeleton frame corresponding to the action or the object. For each frame slot the system prompts the user for the corresponding filler. The user can ask for help regarding appropriate responses, but it is not necessary for every slot to be filled. If the answer to an initial query is unsatisfactory, the user can reformulate the query or browse in the neighborhood of the selected concept. Traditional information retrieval systems assume that users know exactly what they are searching for. At the other end, browsing systems make the users explore the information space, taking the risk of getting lost. Our system can close the gap between exact queries and browsing by allowing retrieval by reformulation and conceptual browsing. Retrieval by reformulation [5] considers retrieval as an incremental process of retrieval cue construction. With this technique, the user and the computer system cooperate, the former being able to incrementally improve his or her query according to the results of the previous queries. In addition to finding software components that match the query, we can explore the conceptual hierarchy to obtain near matches. This provides a means to browse amongst functionally related components instead of browsing components related by the inherited code, as browsers usually supplied with class libraries do. From a given concept, the user may ask for more abstract or more specific concepts than the one selected, or follow any link from that frame to any of its fillers, since these are also concepts in the knowledge base. These requests will result in the system displaying the corresponding frame(s). Once the user has found the desired concept, s/he will ask the system to follow the implementation link, which must point to the actual component implementing that concept in the class library. The selected component may be a single method, a class, or a framework of collaborating classes and methods.

4.3 An Example of Component Adaptation

In this section we present a brief example of how the explicit knowledge representation in the ORA system can help in component adaptation. Let us assume that a user is in the process of implementing a method for "extracting words from a

```
(:and select                                    (defconcept select-adjacent-sequence
   (the obj                                         is (and select
      (and sequence                                    (the obj sequence)
         (the item-type alphanumeric-char)))          (the source sequence)
   (the source string)                                (relates has-adjacent-subsequent
   (relates has-adjacent-subsequent                       source obj)
      source obj))
```

(a)

(b)

```
(defconcept extract-words-from-string           (defconcept string-without-spaces
   is (and select-adjacent-sequence                 is (and string
      (the obj string-without-spaces                   (not-filled-by item-type
      (the source string))                                i-space-char)))
   constraints
      (the has-implementation
         met-cl-string-asArrayOfSubStrings))
```

(c)

(d)

Fig. 2. Component descriptions

string". Figure 2(a) presents the query of the user, where s/he has specified a
component which selects adjacent sequences of alphanumeric characters from a
string. Figure 2(c) shows the closest match for this query, i.e., the selection from
a string of adjacent sequences of characters different from the space character.
The description in 2(c) is a direct subsumer of the user query, and for that reason, it is retrieved by the Loom classifier as the closest match. The definition of
this concept relies on the concepts *select-adjacent-sequence* and *string-without-
spaces*, shown in Figure 2(b) and 2(d), respectively. *extract-words-from-string* is
an implemented component, and, therefore, it includes a slot pointing to the
description of its implementation, the method asArrayOfSubstrings.

This method divides a string into substrings at the occurrences of one or
more space characters. At first glance, this may look like a good solution to the
problem at hand, but notice that the "words" extracted by this method will be
any sequence of characters different from the space character, including punctu-
ation characters. If the "words" that the user meant to extract were sequences of
alphanumeric characters, then it would be necessary to find a different method
or to adapt this one. There is no method that implements this operation exactly, and so, adaptation is the only choice. As for any other method, ORA has
information about the functionality that asArrayOfSubstrings borrows from
other classes and methods. Figure 3 shows the information that ORA would
show about dependencies, by paraphrasing the underlying representation. The
origin of the undesired functionality (the isWhiteSpace method) can be inferred
from these dependencies. Now, the user can follow a link to the representation
of isWhiteSpace and browse amongst functionally related components. In that
area of the knowledge base are located the methods that test some kind of condition on characters, including the isSeparator method, which should replace
isWhiteSpace in asArrayOfSubstrings to implement the desired function.

asArrayOfSubtrings relies on:
 OrderedCollection which provides an extensible ordered collection
 isWhiteSpace method from Character class to identify space char occurrences
 Stream which provides sequential access to collections
 copyFrom:to: method from IndexedCollection class to extract a subcollection
  from an indexed collection

Fig. 3. Functional dependencies for the asArrayOfSubstrings method

5 Conclusions and Future Work

We have presented the Object Reuse Assistant, a system to support the retrieval, understanding and adaptation of software components in general purpose object oriented libraries. This system uses a knowledge-based approach to represent the general programming knowledge and the implementation-specific knowledge which are embedded into the class library (in the code, in the class hierarchy, in the class dependencies, etc.). The main advantages of our approach are:

- The explicit representation of design commitments, design decisions and customizing alternatives, which has proved to be useful to attain a more effective reuse of general purpose class libraries.
- The connection of the description of component implementations to the related programming concepts, facilitating the location and understanding of the required component.

The ORA knowledge base and the user interface have been implemented in Loom, and Lisp as the underlying programming language, for a SUN SPARC-Station platform. Our work has concentrated on building the descriptions of a subset of the Smalltalk/V [6] class library, along with the general purpose programming concepts needed to articulate this representation. The system needs to be completed with the descriptions of the rest of the class library, and the related programming concepts. Future work focuses on refining the representation of programming knowledge and applying it to different class libraries, in order to test the generality of the resulting knowledge base.

References

1. Biggerstaff, T. J. and Richter, C., 1987. "Reusability Framework, Assessment, and Directions". *IEEE Software*, vol. 4, 2.
2. Börstler, J., 1994. "IPSEN: An integrated environment to support development for and with reuse", in *Software Reusability* (Schäfer, W., Prieto-Díaz, R. and Matsumoto, M., eds.), Ellis Horwood.
3. Booch, G., 1987. *Software Components with Ada: Structures, Tools, and Subsystems.* Benjamin Cummings.
4. Caldiera, G. and Basili, V.R. 1994. "The qualification of reusable software components", in *Software Reusability* (Schäfer, W., Prieto-Díaz, R. and Matsumoto, M., eds.), Ellis Horwood.

5. Devanbu, P., Ballard, B.W., Brachman, R.J. and Selfridge, P.G., 1991. "LaSSIE: A Knowledge-Based Software Information System", in *Automating Software Design* (Lowry, M.R. and McCartney, R.D., eds.), AAAI Press/ The MIT Press.

6. Digitalk, 1986. Smalltalk/V. *Tutorial and Programming Handbook*.

7. Embley, D.W. and Woodfield, S. N., 1987. "A Knowledge Structure for Reusing Abstract Data Types", *Procs. of the Ninth International Conference on Software Engineering*, ACM, 360-368.

8. Fernández-Chamizo, C., Hernández-Yáñez, L., González-Calero, P. A. and Urech-Baqué, A., 1993. "A Case-Based approach to Software Component Retrieval". *Symposium on Case-Based Reasoning and Information Retrieval*, Standford University, AAAI Spring Symposium Series, March 1993.

9. Girardi, M. R. and Ibrahim, B., 1993. "A Software Reuse System Based on Natural Language Specifications". *Procs. of International Conference on Computing and Information (ICCI '93)*, Sudbury, Ontario, Canada, May 27-29, 1993, pp. 507-511.

10. Gish, J.W., Huff, K.E. and Thomson, R., 1994. "The GTE environment-Supporting Understanding and Adaptation in Software Reuse", in *Software Reusability* (Schäfer, W., Prieto-Díaz, R. and Matsumoto, M., eds.), Ellis Horwood.

11. Helm, R. and Maarek, Y. S., 1991. "Integrating Information Retrieval and Domain Specific Approaches for Browsing and Retrieval in Object-Oriented Class Libraries". *OOPSLA-91*.

12. Jonckers, V., 1991. "Inheritance Hierarchies in an Environment for Knowledge-based Programming Research", in *Inheritance Hierarchies in Knowledge Representation and Programming Languages* (Lenzerini, M., Nardi, D., and Simi, M., eds.), John Wiley & Sons.

13. Kiczales, G. and Lamping, J., 1992. "Issues in the Design and Specification of Class Libraries". *OOPSLA '92*.

14. Maarek, Y.S, Berry, D. M. and Kaiser, G. E., 1991. "An Information Retrieval Approach for Automatically Constructing Software Libraries". *IEEE Trans. on Software Eng.*, vol. 17, 8.

15. MacGregor, R., 1991. "The evolving technology of classification-based knowledge representation systems". In *Principles of Semantic Networks: Explorations in the Representation of Knowledge* (Sowa, J. ed.), Morgan Kaufmann.

16. Meyer, B., 1987. "Reusability: The Case for Object-Oriented Design". *IEEE Software*, vol.4, 2.

17. Rombach, H.D. and Schäfer, W., 1994. "Tools and environments", in *Software Reusability* (Schäfer, W., Prieto-Díaz, R. and Matsumoto, M., eds.), Ellis Horwood.

18. Wilde, N. and Huitt, R., 1992. "Maintenance Support for Object-Oriented Programs". *IEEE Trans. on Software Eng.*, vol. 18, 12.

19. Wood, M. and Sommerville, I., 1988. "An Information Retrieval System for Software Components". *ACM SIGIR*, vol. 22, 3,4.

Efficient Learning in Multi-Layered Perceptron Using the Grow-And-Learn Algorithm

Gildas Cherruel[1][2], Bassel Solaiman[3] and Yvon Autret[1]

[1] Université de Bretagne Occidentale, Laboratoire LIMI,
BP 809, 29285 BREST Cedex France
[2] TNI, ZI du Vernis – 29608 BREST France
[3] ENSTB, Département Image et Traitement de l'Information,
BP 832 – 29285 BREST Cedex FRANCE

Abstract. The well-known Multi-Layered Perceptron[4] has gained power thanks to the Back Propagation Algorithm. The difficulty which still subsists is its time-wasting. In fact, the learning process can be improved by using the Grow-And-Learn (GAL) algorithm. In this paper, we present such a hybrid system: the cooperation between GAL and MLP networks. The obtained system is more rapid and more efficient than the classic Back Propagation which computes on the MLP.

Keywords – *character recognition, co-operation, neural networks.*

1 Introduction

The Back Propagation algorithm has emerged as one of the most efficient learning procedures for the Multi-Layered Perceptron (MLP). This algorithm has been widely used in several fields such as pattern recognition, signal and speech recognition. A common complaint, however, is its slow learning: back propagation needs to use the training data numerous times before yielding an acceptable performance. However, several studies have been conducted [1] to reduce the learning time for the MLP with the back propagation algorithm.

During the learning procedure of the MLP, random samples are chosen from the training set in order to be presented to the network. The performance rate depends on the training set: a well trained network with an effective training set has a clear advantage over one that is poorly trained or has a training set that doesn't properly exemplify future operations. This kind of training produces various MLPs which can have poor or good performances on generalization.

In every learning base, there are samples that can be easily learned: they belong to their class in a clear way, and they are known as *typical*. Other samples are very often misclassified: they are known as *confusing*. A good learning method is to present in turns typical and confusing samples to the MLP, as mentioned by Ohnishi [2]. According to Ohnishi, the recognition rate is better and quicker obtained. Nowadays, the classification of samples in confusing and typical has to be already known before the beginning of training phase. Effectively, Ohnishi has studied this method on a theoritical problem: a separation in a two-dimensional space, with a pre-computed set of confusing samples. This experiment suffers from lack of power: in real problems, manipulated spaces are rarely in two dimensions. In these conditions, it is very hazardous to extract confusing and typical elements from the learning base.

---

[4] *MLP*

Our main subject is to provide a new method for the learning phase. This learning method is based upon Ohnishi works, and an incremental neural network algorithm called *GAL* (Grow-And-Learn – [3] –). The learning system is able to compute automatically the confusing and typical examples of a learning base.

2 Presentation of the GAL Network

The GAL algorithm [3] has been developped to deal with incremental problems. The main problem of traditional networks (after the slow learning phase) is their incapabilities to learn a domain that is fundamentally unknown entirely at the network's birth. Indeed, when the initial learning base is probably able to grow in time, the MLP can't learn it with a good recognition rate: the learning base contains a given set of classes and then fixes the amount of neurons in the output layer of an MLP. If there are more classes later, the output layer has to grow. This cannot be done dynamically. After growth, the weights are disturbed so all the learning has to be rerun.

GAL gives its own solution to the incrementality problem. It is able to grow and manage its internal structure. If a new sample of a new class occurs, it will append a new neuron in the output layer and the connections set to able to recognize this new class. Furthermore, it has the capacity to learn only the samples that are necessary to perform a good recognition in the future. Effectively, if GAL can respond the correct class to a presented sample, it is unnecessary to learn it.

2.1 The GAL Network Structure.

The GAL network has the structure shown in figure 1 . It is structured in three layers: (1) the Input Layer P contains the sample which is presented to GAL; (2) the Examplar Layer A and E contains the necessary samples for performing a good recognition (the memorized samples count will grow); (3) the Class Layer C is composed of all the classes already known.

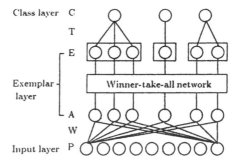

Fig. 1. The *GAL* network

The weights between the layer P and the layer A are noted: W_{ie} (from input i to unit e). And the weights between the layer E and the layer C are noted: T_{ec} (from unit e to class c). The weights T_{ec} are binary: if unit e is connected (element of) to class c then $T_{ec} = 1$ else $T_{ec} = 0$.

2.2 Propagation Process

When a sample is presented to GAL the following steps are computed:

First, the activations of all neurons of layer A are calculated:

$$A_e := \sum_i P_i \times W_{ie} \tag{1}$$

Then a "Winner-Take-All" is computed on the layer A, so that only the units for which A_e is maximum are activated:

$$E_e := \text{ if } A_e == max_i(A_i) \text{ then } 1 \text{ else } 0 \tag{2}$$

The examplar unit E_e for which weights are the closest to input is the only active unit. The GAL response is computed by the formula:

$$C_c := \sum_e E_e \times T_{ec} \tag{3}$$

After this calculation, only one class neuron is active (because the weights T are binary values). This neuron is the response of the GAL network.

2.3 Learning Process

The learning process consists of the two following phases (they are repeated until GAL doesn't miss any of the samples of the learning database):

1. The first, *the awake phase*, deals with selecting the samples that have to be integrated from the learning base. With a given sample from a given class, GAL responds right or wrong. If it is right, nothing has to be done. Otherwise, the sample has to be memorized. Two cases can occur:
   - The misclassified sample belongs to a known class c. In this case, GAL appends only one examplar unit connected to the good class c. The sample is learned "by heart" (i.e. the sample is copied into the W_{ie}).
   - The misclassified sample belongs to an unknown class c'. GAL has to append a new class c' with one examplar unit connected to. The sample is also learned "by heart".
2. The second, *the sleep phase*, handles garbaging the learned samples whereas they were redundant. All of them are sequentially presented to GAL. For each, the weights are inhibited so that GAL's response cannot use its data for the classification. If the response is right then the sample was redundant and is forgotten. Otherwise, it is kept.

3 The Proposed System

The main problem that we encounter using a large learning database with neural networks is the correctness regarding several criterions. One of them is the representativity of each class in the database. The right number of the representative items cannot be easily known. These items are known as the confusing patterns. Using GAL we can find them. To illustrate this, Alpaydin applied in [3] his GAL to a theoritical problem: given a circle inside a square, the problem was to say if a given point was in the circle or out of the circle and in the square. In fact, we can easily see that only the frontier between the circle and the square has a real signification. But a usual neural network cannot deduce it by learning.

The main problems of this test is that it was academic. Effectively, the frontier is very smoothed compared to a real database with, for example, hand-written characters. Furthermore, the circled frontier can be easily deduced by a human; but the second kind of learning database cannot be.

For doing so, a real application is considered in this paper. It concerns the problems of hand-written characters recognition. The main ideas of our approach can be summarized as follows: (1) Using GAL to obtain the confusing patterns, (2) Training the MLP network over the chosen patterns, (3) Testing the MLP over the generalization database.

The most important advantage is that the size of the learning database is drastically reduced. Another non-negligible advantage is that the obtained learning database can be easily enlarged: when a new class has to be added to the main database, it is not necessary to rebuild the confusing database from nil. This can be done by learning the new confusing patterns with the GAL network. Then, the MLP structure has to be modified accordingly to the new number of classes. Finally, the training phase can be redone over the confusing database. Similarly, if the database is enlarged with new patterns we can know if they belong to the confusing patterns only by running GAL over them. If some of they belong to, the confusing database is enlarged and the MLP learning time is much more reduced than in the normal case. If they don't belong to, the MLP don't need to be modified. The final structure is shown in figure 2 : B represents the initial learning database and B' stands for the confusing database obtained after the GAL learning process. The samples of B' are presented one from each class in a cyclic manner.

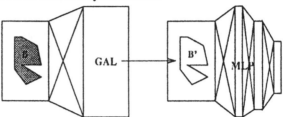

Fig. 2. The *GAL* and *MLP* cooperation system

4 Experiments

In order to test the validity of this idea, we have used a database of 10000 handwritten digits. Those digits were written by 100 different "writers". Each of them has written ten digits into grids of ordered forms. These digits are composed of a matrix of 16×16 pixels of 16 gray levels. The initial learning database (B) contains the first 5000 digits, and the generalization database contains the last 5000 ones.

GAL memorized 439 digits of B (known as B'). And MLP is composed of three layers: the input layer (256 neurons), the hidden layer (70 neurons) and the output layer (10 neurons).

To evaluate the results, an identical MLP network has learned the initial database B. Both MLP networks have been tested on the generalization database. The results, given in figure 3 , show the obtained error for the generalization. For the cooperation, one iteration is composed of the whole B'; for the MLP alone, one iteration is composed of the whole B.

5 Discussions

The first interest of the co-operation is, thanks to the extraction of confusing patterns by GAL, the decrease of the error level rate after the same iterations count. MLP has to memorize only the confusing patterns, so that it can perform a better generalization. Effectively, among the typical digits, there are digits which can confuse the accuracy of MLP, especially the irrelevant ones.

The second interest is a better quality of both learning phases. Without the GAL phase, MLP performs a learning process in fits and starts. In other words, it sometime breaks down its experience trying to obtain a better recognition rate. This technique hard-wired

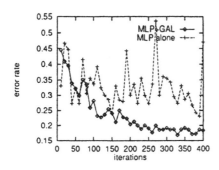

Fig. 3. Compared results of the *GAL* and *MLP* cooperation

in the backpropagation process allows the error to jump out of the local minima of the error surface. This has to be done because this surface is very chaotic for such problems (the frontiers between classes are not well defined). This is shown in figure 3 by the peaks observed and a chaotic trend of learning. With the GAL pre-phase, the trend is much more regular and smoothed. The peaks occur less often and less pronounced. The convergence is also more rapidly obtained. This is because the error surface is smoothed by GAL. All the irrelevant patterns have been eliminated. Most of the local minima have been reduced because the frontiers between the classes are better identified.

The final interests of the cooperation is the shorter learning-process time and the guarantee that MLP will not 'change completely its mind' several iterations before the learning phase is stopped, giving us a worse error than before the change. The count of samples to be learned is cut down by a factor of ten (in our test). The process time of one sample being the same in both learning methods (due to the same MLP skeleton), cuts down the global learning time by a factor of ten as well.

6   Conclusions

The GAL-MLP co-operation is a typical example of a co-operation which raises the performances of a well-known network such as MLP. One of the great powers of this cooperation is the addition of restricted incrementality capabiblities to MLP. Effectively, the extra cost of the relearning phase of GAL and MLP when a new class is integrated into the system (GAL has to integrated the new class in order to increment the confusing database, and MLP has to be modified accordingly and relearned) is diminished thanks to the co-operation.

References

1. Y. L. Cun, "Generalization and network design strategies," *technical report crg-tr-89-4*, University of Toronto, 1989.
2. N. Ohnishi, A. Okamoto, and N. Sugie, "Selective presentation of learning samples for efficient learning in multi-layered perceptron," *Proceedings of the International Joint Conference on Neural Networks*, vol. 1, pp. 278–289, Jan. 1990.
3. E. Alpaydin, "Grow-And-Learn: an incremental method for category learning," *Proceedings of the International Conference on Neural Networks*, pp. 761–764, July 1990.

A Non-Diffident Combinatorial Optimization Algorithm

Gilles Trombettoni, Bertrand Neveu, Pierre Berlandier, Maria-Cristina Riff
and Mouhssine Bouzoubaa

INRIA-CERMICS, B.P.93 06902 Sophia-Antipolis Cedex, France

Abstract. Branch and bound is a well known, all-purpose optimization strategy. It relies on the availability of a search space evaluation function and maintains an upper bound cost as a reference for the pruning. This upper bound is updated each time a better solution is encountered. In this paper, we propose a non-diffident optimization strategy that imposes this value. The computation of the bound is based on some heuristics that use probabilistic knowledge of the problem. Setting an arbitrary low bound enables a faster convergence towards the best solution. The counterpart is that the search space might be traversed more than once. However, we show in an experimental evaluation that our approach remains beneficial.

1 Introduction

Constraint satisfaction problems (CSP) have proved useful in the encoding of various instances of combinatorial problems such as planning or scheduling and industrial constraint solvers such as CHIP [Chip 91] or ILOG SOLVER [IlogSolver 94] have been developed. However, in many cases, one looks for the *optimal* solution with respect to the minimization of some given criterion. An optimization strategy as the *branch and bound* (B&B) should then be adopted.

Basically, B&B uses a heuristic function that, given a position in the search space, returns an underestimation of the cost of every solution that could be reached from this position. Each position in the search space is weighted by the heuristic function. If the returned underestimation is greater than the current upper bound, the B&B strategy simply abandons the exploration from this position.

Applications of B&B generally exhibit a heuristic function that is finely tuned to the considered problem [Malik 93, Lee 91]. Unfortunately, for some problems and criteria, the approximation provided by the heuristic function is not sufficient to prune the search space efficiently.

We propose an optimization strategy that uses an upper bound that can be smaller than the cost of the current solution so that the search might converge more quickly. However, we guarantee that the algorithm does not miss the best solution since we allow ourselves to traverse the search space several times. The computation of the upper bound is based on a heuristics that uses some probabilistic knowledge about the problem and the criterion (e.g. the expected number of solutions).

2 Overview of the algorithm

The algorithm we are presenting is based on a depth first traversal of the search space (DFS). The memory space used by DFS is linear in the number of variables of the problem.

We suppose that we initially know the interval $[c_l, c_u]$ in which the possible costs are ranging. Each step of our non-diffident optimization algorithm (NDO), presented on figure 1, is a search for a better solution than the current one : it will either increase c_l or lower c_u until c_u goes below c_l. The upper bound b of the search process can be chosen in the currently remaining cost interval. We can then distinguish two cases for a NDO step:

1. *A solution with cost c is found.* We can concentrate on the new cost interval $[c_l, c[$ (line 5). It is the standard action taken by the B&B strategy.
2. *No solution is found.* We will not be able to progress in the search tree, but we then know that there is no solution with a cost between c_l and b. The new possible cost interval is thus $]b, c_u]$ (line 6).

Note that the ϵ parameter (line 1) allows the algorithm to stop when the cost interval is sufficiently reduced.

```
function NDO(cl, cu);
1 while cu ≥ cl + ε do
2     b ← choose-upper-bound(cl, cu);
3     (solution, c) ← find-solution(cl, b);
4     if solution ≠ ⊥ then
5         cu ← c − 1;
6     else cl ← b + 1.
7 return (solution, c).
```

Fig. 1. the NDO algorithm

3 The Upper Bound Choice Heuristics

The *choose-upper-bound* function yields the upper bound that is computed and used at each step of the NDO algorithm.

A simple heuristics implements a dichotomy of the cost interval: it always returns the middle point c_m of the segment $[c_l, c_u]$. Its advantage is to eliminate at each step half of the potential cost interval. However, the average influence of this easy heuristics did not make NDO a definite winner over B&B.

A second and more complex one is based on two quantities that yield some knowledge about the problem to optimize and also on the given optimization criterion: for a given cost interval, $\#sol$ yields an estimate of the number of solutions and $\#arcs$ an estimate of the number of arcs traversed during the search. The design of a good heuristics is then guided by the following desiderata. We want to avoid a search tree traversal without finding any solution, and to ensure that, in that unfortunate case, a sufficient part of the cost interval will be pruned. The bound also should not be set below c_u if the number of arcs then traversed is not significantly smaller than with c_u

The best heuristics we came out with (figure 2) did not need any estimate of the $\#arcs$ quantity. $\#sol\text{-}min$ tries to ensure a not too severe upper bound that should maintain at least $\#sol\text{-}min$ solutions in the tree to explore. The parameter $segment\text{-}rate$ maintains a minimum rate of cost interval to explore in a step. The best results have been obtained by choosing a severe upper bound ($\#sol\text{-}min$ is small) until we find a first solution. After this first stage, no more risk is taken and c_u is always chosen as upper bound.

```
function choose-upper-bound(c_l, c_u);
1 if a first solution has been found then
2     return c_u
3     else return max(b_1, b_2)
4          with #sol(c_l, b_1) = #sol-min and
5               b_2 - c_l = segment-rate × (c_u - c_l).
```

Fig. 2. finding a non-diffident upper bound

4 Experimental Evaluation

We have been primarily interested in applying NDO to the resolution of constraint satisfaction problems. A constraint satisfaction system usually includes a solution search component based on domain enumeration. To simulate the search trees developed by CSP solvers, we have developed a weighted tree generator, parametrized by a depth d, a width s, a couple of bounds (w_l, w_u) for the weights associated to each arc and a pruning factor p. A solution is represented by a leaf at depth d, its cost comes from the aggregation of the weights along the path to the solution.

4.1 First results on random trees

Additive criterion The aggregation of the weights is done by addition. Comparisons were done about the number of arcs traversed by a conventional B&B approach and NDO. Results with different sizes of trees and a null initial minimum cost c_l appear in the left table on figure 3 (average on 100 instances with

#sol-min set to 100 and *segment-rate* set to 0.01). The results are positive (the number of arcs visited is reduced by 50% using NDO).

Maximum weight criterion The best solution is the one for which the heaviest weight among the arcs is minimum. The NDO results are here better than for the additive criterion. For this criterion, both algorithms are very efficient: the number of visited arcs is very small allowing us to make tests on greater trees. In the results in the right table on figure 3) (average on 100 instances), the depth of the tree varies between 50 and 80, the width is 5.

d	15	16	17	18
B&B	4565	6954	10521	14606
NDO	2432	3648	5714	8091
NDO/B&B	.53	.52	.54	.55

d	50	60	70	80
B&B	1797	2627	3687	4528
NDO	237	320	414	754
NDO/B&B	.13	.12	.11	.17

Fig. 3. Comparison NDO/BB for the additive and maximum criteria

4.2 Comparisons with Value Ordering Heuristics

A common way to improve the results with B&B is to use value ordering (VO) heuristics in order to find good solutions faster. For both criteria we have studied, this consists in traversing the tree by ordering the branches with respect to the increasing order of the weights.

Although both algorithms should get a benefit from this heuristics, the tests show that this is especially interesting for the B&B. Indeed, this heuristics is useful for the entire B&B search tree, but for our algorithm, it is only useful in the steps where a solution is found. The tests on the same random trees as in previous section, are shown on figure 4.

For the additive criterion, the VO heuristics is as efficient as our algorithm and the combined use of this heuristics and our algorithm does not improve efficiency. For the maximal criterion, the use of our algorithm is still interesting when using the VO heuristics.

depth	15	16	17	18
B&B	2279	3483	5061	7434
NDO	2279	3843	5574	8726
NDO/B&B	1.	1.1	1.1	1.17

depth	50	60	70	80
B&B	696	986	1300	1637
NDO	235	306	342	669
NDO/B&B	.34	.31	.26	.41

Fig. 4. Comparison NDO/BB with value ordering

4.3 Results on Random CSP

The algorithm has also been implemented in the CSP framework. First tests on random binary CSP [Sabin 94] show an improvement of the B&B for the maximum criterion (minimization of the maximum of a variable value in a solution). These tests were done with a forward checking scheme, a dynamic variable ordering heuristics (smaller domain first) and a value ordering heuristics (smaller value first). The constraint density was fixed to 0.2, the domain size to 40. We have made vary the size of the problem (number of variables) and the tightness of the constraints. The expected number of solutions is estimated as in [Prosser 94]. For a given size, the improvement we obtained with NDO is greater on CSP with many solutions, where the B&B is for this maximum criterion already very efficient.

size (nb variables)	30	30	30	35	35	35	40	40
tightness	.2	.3	.4	.2	.3	.4	.2	.3
B&B	360	578	1990	616	1566	10284	904	4504
NDO	160	293	1574	277	924	8747	660	3358
NDO/B&B	.31	.46	.75	.38	.58	.78	.47	.73

5 Conclusion and future works

We have presented a new combinatorial optimization algorithm which manages a non safe upper bound. We have also designed a heuristics that allows a non-blind choice of this upper bound using an estimate of the number of solutions. Although the algorithm may traverse the search space several times, a comparison with B&B on random search trees and CSP has shown its interest. However, its effect is lowered when used conjointly with a value ordering heuristics. Tests over real life problems should show how does the algorithm behave when the quantities $\#sol$ and $\#arcs$ are less easy to estimate.

References

[Chip 91] Cosytec. CHIP *Users' Reference Manual*, 1991.

[IlogSolver 94] ILOG, 2 Av. Galliéni, F-94253 Gentilly. ILOG SOLVER *Users' Reference Manual*, 1994.

[Lee 91] K. Lee, H. Leong. An improved lower bound for channel routing problems. In *IEEE International Symposium on Circuits and Systems*, 1991.

[Malik 93] K. Malik, G. Yu. A branch and bound algorithm for the capaciated minimum spanning tree problem. *Networks*, 23(6):525–532, 1993.

[Prosser 94] P. Prosser. Binary constraint satisfaction problems : Some are harder than others. In *Proc. ECAI*, pages 95–99, Amsterdam, the Netherlands, 1994.

[Sabin 94] D. Sabin, E. Freuder. Contradicting conventional wisdom in constraint satisfaction. In *Proc. ECAI*, Amsterdam, Netherlands, 1994.

Modelling Diagnosis Systems with the Logic Programming

Iara de Almeida Móra* and José Júlio Alferes**

CRIA, Uninova and DM, U. Évora
2825 Monte da Caparica, Portugal
{idm | jja}@fct.unl.pt

Abstract. The evolution of logic programming semantics has included the introduction of an explicit form of negation, beside the older implicit (or default) negation typical of logic programming. For the richer language, called extended logic programming, much theoretical work has been done. Mainly resulting from the theoretical work, the language has been shown adequate for a spate of knowledge representation and reasoning forms. However, the theoretical work has not been accompanied by the usage of the language for building real-life implementations. In this paper we report on the experience of using extended logic programming to model the diagnosis system. By using extended logic programming, we can rely on a well established language, with a clear declarative semantics, and for which implementations exist. Moreover, some issue of the diagnosis process are automatically dealt by the contradiction removal methods developed for extended logic programming. Due to the greater expressive power of extended logic programming, the process of implementing diagnosis of distributed systems has been quite simplified. The form of the resulting program is rather simple and has a very clear and declarative reading. Thus, we deem that extended logic programming can be used in practice to solve some "real-life" problems.

1 Introduction

Reliability is the property that allows one to fairly trust on the service provided by a computational system. When the desired reliability of a system is greater than the actual reliability of its individual components, it is necessary to make use of additional procedures and/or methods, at least to protect the systems against faulty hardware, as the physical components tend to degrade. The purpose of fault tolerance is to provide, through redundancy, a service that meets its specifications in spite of fault occurence.

Distributed systems components present a series of potential advantages over nondistributed ones, for the implementation of fault tolerance, such as: indepen-

---

* Thanks to the CNPq - Brazil for their support, and to the "Fault Tolerance Group" of UFRGS.

** Partially supported by JNICT-Portugal and ESPRIT project Compulog 2 (no. 6810). Thanks to Luís Moniz Pereira for his valuable comments.

dence from hardware faults, greater facilities to isolate errors, and greater flexibility to reconfigure the system after fault occurrence. In a distributed system the system units are autonomous, and so when a fault is detected the faulty unit can be isolated from the system without affecting the other units. Moreover, because of the inherent redundancy in fault tolerant systems, the other units will be able to supply the services of the faulty one.

For the reconfiguration to be possible it is necessary to identify the faulty components. This identification procedure is called fault diagnosis. The application of diagnosis at system level may occur on systems where units are sufficiently complex to perform tests on other units. The diagnosis process, which must be periodically started when an error is detected or before a critical process is delivered to a specific unit, consists of discovering the differences between the ideal unit model and the real unit behavior. These differences are not the result of direct observations. On the contrary they should be derived, through tests, from the behavior of the units components. To execute the diagnosis it is necessary to model the system behavior, i.e.: (a) the expected behavior (logic description of the correct working of the system components); (b) the system components themselves; and (c) the observed behavior(the results of the tests performed in the systems).

Besides this system model, it is also necessary to define the units that will perform the diagnosis and what units will be diagnosed. In this respect, it is possible to distinguish between two approaches: (1) a centralised one, where one system unit is responsible for the diagnoses of the the whole system; or (2) a decentralised one, where a group of units starts by performing individual systems diagnoses and, afterwords, reach a consensus about what is the correct system diagnosis.

The centralised diagnosis approach requires the unit that performs the diagnosis to be fault-tolerant, i.e., it must have redundant components and use special algorithms. This makes the system more expensive. In the decentralised approach, there can be different possible units organizations that perform the system diagnosis. We follow the organization proposed in [5], consisting of: one group of units, the *diag_group*, which is responsible for diagnosing only another group of system units, the *test_group*. Compared with the (extreme decentralized) case where all system unit diagnose all systems units, this grouping strategy has the advantage of avoiding the overloading of communication means, because each unit exchanges messages only with a subset of the system units.

Based on this organization, the required steps for the whole diagnosis process of a distributed computer system are:

- Step I - *Testing Requests* : one of the diag_group units is responsible for requesting the tests defined for each unit in its test_group[3].
- Step II - *Testing* : each unit of a test_group performs the requested tests.

---

[3] Since the responsible unit might itself be faulty, one must define methods (beyond the scope of this paper) to guarantee that one of the units indeed sends the messages.

- Step III - *Tests Results Gathering* : each test group unit sends its test results to the whole diag group. At this stage, it is possible that the testing results are not delivered, meaning that: (a) a component of an unit is faulty, if that component has not sent back any of its results; or (b) the whole unit is considered faulty - fail-stop - if none of the unit components have answered to any request.
- Step IV - *Diagnosis* : given the tests results and the expected behavior of units, each diag group unit generates a diagnosis for each test group unit.
- Step V - *Consensus* : diag group units, based on the resulting diagnoses, reach a consensus on the final diagnosis of every test group unit.
- Step VI - *Diagnosis Propagation* : one of the diag group units sends the consensus result to the other groups, so that the whole system has its real state registered everywhere.

Next we report on an implementation of distributed systems diagnosis, that uses extended logic programming (ELP). By using ELP, we can rely on a well established language, with a clear declarative semantics, and for which implementations exist. Moreover, some issue of the diagnosis process are automatically dealt by the contradiction removal methods developed for ELP. Due to the greater expressive power of ELP, the process of implementing diagnosis of distributed systems has been quite simplified. The form of the resulting program is rather simple and has a very clear and declarative reading.

In this paper, we concentrate on the appropriateness of ELP without any message passing mechanism, to deal with the parts of the process above that do not involve exchanging messages. So, after a brief introduction to the logic programming basis (section 2), this paper focus on the implementation of step IV (section 3). Finally, in section 4, we draw some conclusions and breifly mention subsequent work, including the implementation of the whole process in a distributed logic programming language.

2   Logic programming basis

The evolution of Logic Programming semantics has included the introduction of an explicit form of negation, beside the older default negation typical of Logic Programming, cf. [7, 8, 12]. The richer language, called Extended Logic Programming (ELP), has been shown adequate for a spate of knowledge representation and reasoning forms (see e.g. [2]). For these new semantics of logic programming implementations exist (e.g. [1, 3]).

An extended program is a (possibly infinite) set of ground rules[4] of the form

$$L_0 \leftarrow L_1, \ldots, L_m, not\ L_{m+1}, \ldots, not\ L_n\ (0 \le m \le n)$$

---

[4] For simplicity, in examples we use non-ground rules. These non-ground rules simply stand for its grounded version, i.e. for the ground rules obtained from it by substituting in all possible ways each of the variables by elements of the Herbrand universe.

where each L_i $(0 \le i \le n)$is an objective literal, i.e. an atom A or its explicit negation $\neg A$, plus a set of integrity contraints. An integrity constraint is simply a rule whose head (L_0) is the reserved atom $\perp$.

In our implementation, we've used a LP system based on the *WFSX* semantics for ELP (for details of the semantics see [8], and of the corresponding derivation procedures see [1]). *WFSX* follows from WFS for normal programs [6] plus the coherence requirement relating the two forms of negation: *"For any objective literal L, if ¬L is entailed by the semantics then not L must also be entailed"*. This requirement states that whenever some literal is explicitly false then it must be assumed false by default.

By adding the possibility of expressing, in the language of logic programs, both truth and falsity of propositions, a new issue is raised in logic programming – how to remove contradictions. Several approaches to contradiction removal in ELP appeared [4, 9, 10]. The possibility of expressing inconsistencies, and removing them, within the language of ELP, opened logic programming for the application to several new domains. This is the case of declarative debugging of programs, where there is a contradiction between the result given by the program and the results expected by the user, and also of model-based diagnosis [10], where there is a contradiction between the observations made in the artifact and its expect behavior.

Now we briefly recap contradiction removal of extended logic programs as defined in [10]. Here we simply present a declarative definition of what is expected to be a revision. For a description of the method for achieving these revision, and a discussion on the revision semantics obtained, see [1, 10][5].

Without loss of generality (cf. [1]), contradiction removal is obtained by changing the truth value of objective literal with no rules in the original program. Moreover, not every such literal is allowed to change its truth value – only those in a pre-defined set of *revisable* literals. This set is provided by the user along with the program (see [10] for how the use of revisable allows for control over revisions).

Definition 1 Removal Set. A set of objective literals S is a removal set of a program P iff all elements of S are revisables and $P \cup S$ is non-contradictory.

Definition 2 Revision of a Program. A set of objective literals R is a revision of a program P iff R is a minimal removal set of P.

3 Diagnosing system units

In this section we concentrate on the process of diagnosing system units (step IV above) and, as a case study, we will present a computer network as the target of diagnosis system. As already mentioned, each unit in some diagnosis group must provide a diagnosis for all units in its respective test group. For performing

---

[5] The implementation of both the contradiction removal method, and the top-down procedures for *WFSX* are available on request.

the diagnosis, each diagnosis group unit will execute a contradiction removal process on a given extended logic program. The contradictions to be removed are those resulting from differences between the expected and the observed system behaviors. Thus, the revisions of the program are the diagnoses of test group units.

The extended program of each diagnosis group unit must contain a description of: *the system's expected behavior* (a logic description of the correct behavior of the system members); and *the system's observed behavior* (the results of the tests performed). The system expected behavior does not depend on the previous steps of the diagnosis process. The system's observed behavior is the result of the previous steps in the whole diagnosis process. Here we assume that the result of each test (generated by step III) is asserted in the logic program of each diagnosis group unit as a fact of the form exc(u,c,t,r) where u (resp. c, t) is the name of the test group unit (resp. component, test) and r is the result.

Before starting performing the diagnosis, a diagnosis group unit must know what are the units of the system in its test group, and which are each test group units components. Moreover, it is also necessary to model the tests for each system component. This is done simply by inserting facts to describe units, components and component tests, of the form:

```
unit(unit_name,diag_id,test_id).
group(id,[unit_names],size_group).
component(unit_name,component_name).
tests(component_name,[test_names]).
```

Note that unit components and component tests are independantly defined. This is so because, in fact, the tests do not depend on a given component of a unit but rather on a component type. This allows for flexibility on modifying the composition of the system: adding (resp. excluding) units and components simply involves adding (resp. excluding) the facts for the desired unit and its components, and adding (resp. excluding) the unit name in the facts of the diagnosis and test groups.

In the following examples we consider that the test group, named t1, in consideration includes:

```
group(t1,[sirius,spica],2).
unit(sirius,d1,t1).              unit(spica,d1,t1).
component(sirius,cpu).           component(spica,cpu).
component(sirius,memory).        component(spica,memory).
component(sirius,disc).          component(spica,disc).
tests(cpu,[program]).
tests(memory,[mparity,mecc,mread,mwrite,madressing]).
tests(disc,[dparity,decc,dread,dwrite]).
```

3.1 Diagnosis Process – a first approach

The diagnosis process is performed using contradiction removal. Contraditions appear when an expected behavior and an observed behavior are compared and differ. The modelling of such contradictions in logic programs can be done by introducing[6]:

```
false <- unit(U,_,_), problems(U).
problems(U) <- component(U,C), problems(U,C).
problems(U,C) <- test(C,T), test_result(U,C,T,R),
                 expected_result(U,C,T,CR), R \= CR.
```

The predicate `test/2` just picks up (from the facts for `tests/2`) one test name for the component C. In this simplified version, `test_result(U,C,T,R)` simply looks for a fact `exc(U,C,T,R)` in the program.

Now, it is necessary to model what is the expected result for each component test: the expected result is the correct result for the test, on the assumption that "the component is working properly". This statement is easily modelled in logic programming, by using default negation[7]:

```
expected_result(U,comp,test,CR) <- correct_result(comp, test, CR),
                                   not abnormal(U,comp).
```

By default, `not abnormal(U,comp)` is assumed to be true, and so the expected result is the correct one. If this provokes a contradiction, then we must revise our assumption of normality of the component. To achieve this, in the framework we are using, it is enough to declare `abnormal/2` as a revisable literal.

Example 1. Suppose that, in the system described in page 5, the `dparity` test on sirius's disc, and the `program` test on sirius's cpu, return incorrect results, and all other tests return correct ones, i.e. the facts for `exc/4` in the program have incorrect results for those two tests, and the correct one for all other tests. The revision of the resulting program is `[[abnormal(sirius,cpu),abnormal(sirius,disc)]]`.

3.2 Components dependences

In the example above the diagnosis process did not consider the dependence between components, i.e., it did not consider if one of the faulty components could cause others to present a incorrect behavior. In fact, the result of the incorrect test on the disc could be the result of a failure on the cpu and not on the disc. In this case, we would like the system to present as faulty just the component capable of affecting the others (the cpu); a verification of the possibly affected components should be performed in subsequent diagnosis process.

It has been rather easy to model these dependences in logic programming. Intuitively, we want to say that the result of the `dparity` test on the disc depends not only on the disc itself, but also on the cpu of the unit. Translating this statement directly to ELP we obtain:

---

[6] In the implementation of contradiction removal, instead of ⊥, the reserved word `false` is used.

[7] Of course, this modelling requires the addition to the program of a fact for defining the correct result of each test.

```
expected_result(U,disc,dparity,correct_res) <-
                           correct_result(comp, test, CR),
                           not abnormal(U,disc), not abnormal(U,cpu).
```

In general, to the body of the `expected_result` rule for a given test we must add a literal `not abnormal(U,compD)` for each `compD` component on which the test depends.

Example 2. By replacing in the program of example 1 the rule for the expected result of the `dparity` test by the one above, the single revision of the program is now `[abnormal(sirius,cpu)]`, as desired.

3.3 Strong dependence

Unfortunately, this dependance modeling creates another problem: suppose all sirius's cpu tests return a correct result and the sirius's disc `dparity` test does not. The revisions of the resulting program are $\{abnormal(sirius, cpu)\}$ and $\{abnormal(sirius, disc)\}$. The rational for these diagnosis are, respectively, that `dparity` returned the incorrect value because the cpu is influencing the disc behavior, or simply because the disc is really faulty. However, since all of sirius's cpu tests return the correct value, and in our implementation we are considering quite a large set of tests for a realistic case, one would prefer to assume that the cpu is in fact working properly, and that the fault comes from the disc.

To obtain this result we simply declare that it can never happen that all tests of a given component return the correct value and, simultaneously, the component be assumed abnormal. In logic programming[8]:

```
false <- abnormal(U,C), -problems(U,C).
-problems(U,C) <- tests(C,LT), all_ok(U,C,LT).
all_ok(_,_,[]).
all_ok(U,C,[T|L]) <- correct_result(C,T,R), exec(U,C,T,R), all_ok(U,C,L).
```

Note that, in the case descriped above, $\{abnormal(sirius, cpu)\}$ is no longer a revision since it creates a contradiction between having and not having problems with the cpu. So, as expected, the only diagnosis is $\{abnormal(sirius, disc)\}$.

3.4 Non-responding units

With the above described model of the system behavior, whenever some component test does not return any result (i.e. there is no fact for `exec` regarding that test) no contradiction is generated. In fact, the absence of such fact simply causes the corresponding `test_result` to fail. So, when a component test does not provide a result, the diagnoses are the same as if it had returned the correct result. This is clearly not the intended behavior. On the contrary, we wish the component to be assumed faulty. It is easy to check that to obtain this desired behavior, it is enough to add the rule:

---

[8] In the implentation we are using explicit negation ¬ is denoted by -.

```
test_result(U,C,T,not_responding) <- not exc(U,C,T,_).
```

When, for a given unit, none of the test's results are returned then, instead of having diagnoses stating that each component is faulty, we'd like to have a single diagnosis stating that the unit is in a *fail_stop* situation. In practice, this situation occurs when the diagnostic group cannot "see" the unit, either because there is some problem in communications, or because the unit is not "alive". To model this exceptional situation, we must add to the program the integrity constraint:

```
false <- unit(U,_,_), not abnormal(U,fail_stop), not exec(U,_,_,_).
```

Moreover, when a *fail_stop* abnormality is encountered, all other possible faults must be ignored. In other words, all other faults depend on the *fail_stop* abnormality. So, keeping to the way dependence was modeled above, one must add the literal not `abnormal(U,fail_stop)` to each of the `expected_result` rules[9].

3.5 Fault modes

Until now, regarding tests results, we've only distinguish between the correct and the incorrect ones. In fact, the *expected result* is always the correct one, and all incorrect results are unexpected. However, for certain tests, some incorrect results are well known. By taking into account the knowledge of these incorrect results, more informative diagnoses can be provided. Moreover, this distinction helps on building the diagnoses, by eliminating sooner some possibilities for diagnosis of the system[10].

If a given incorrect result is well know then, when the test returns that result, it is not completely unexpected. We can say that the given incorrect result is expected, on the assumption that the component has abnormal behavior, and the abnormality is of a certain known type. In logic programming:

```
expected_result(U,comp,test,IR) <- -correct_result(comp,test,IR),
                    abnormal(U,comp), known_fault(U,test,IR).
```

A fact of the form - `correct_result(comp,test,IR)` must be added for each known incorrect result. Moreover, to relate the incorrect result with the name of the fault type, we also add a rule of the form:

```
known_fault(U,test,faulty_result) <- fault_mode(U,comp,fault_type).
```

This rule can be read as: "the `faulty_result` is known on the assumption that the component is in a given fault mode of type `fault_type`. `fault_mode` is an assumption that can be revised in order to remove contradictions, i.e. in order to find a diagnosis one can assume that the system is in a given fault mode. Thus the predicate `fault_mode/3` must be declared as revisable.

---

[9] The solution can be improved for the cases where some components do respond, and others don't. Lack of space preclude the presentation of the solution.

[10] Lack of space preclude the discussion here on how fault modes can make diagnosis more efficient.

Now, whenever a test result equal one known incorrect result, the latter most be expected. This is to say that if it is not expected, a contradiction should appear. As before, for modularity in modeling units and components, we represent contradictions in a component via the predicate problems/2. So, we must also add the following rule for this predicate:

```
problems(U,C) <- test_result(U,C,T,R), -correct_result(C,T,R),
                 not expected_result(U,C,T,R).
```

Example 3. Suppose the *cpu* component has a known fault, fault_1, when the *program* test returns the incorrect result res_1. We must add:

```
-correct_result(cpu,program,res_1).
known_fault(U,program,res_1) <- fault_mode(U,cpu,fault_1).
```

If the sirius's cpu program test returns res_1 and all other tests return the correct result, the only diagnosis is [abnormal(sirius,cpu),fault_mode(sirius,cpu, fault_1)].

4   Conclusions and Future Work

Before opting for the ELP language, we've implemented diagnosis of distributed system using a representation formalism based on *frame models*, where the hierarchy top level are the unit definitions with components as its slots. Usual frame features, such as default and if-needed deamons were used in the model.

Over the previous implementation, the one described in this paper presented several advantages. First, the representation formalism of the previous implementation was not suitable for usage with the Reiter's algorithm [11] for diagnosis. This modification that had to be done took a great implementation effort. On the contrary, by using ELP, we could rely on its contradiction removal methods to automatically deal with some issues of the diagnosis process. Moreover, the ELP implementation, contrary to what happened with the previous one, resulted quite clear, and with an intuitive declarative reading. It is also worth mentioning that some feature of diagnosis present here, such as the usage of fault modes and treating fail-stop situations, were not treated in the previous implementation due to the great complexity involved in doing so. With the ELP implementation these issues were rather simple to implement.

We are now extending the use of logic programming to all other steps of the process. For doing so we rely on an execution enviroment of logic programming languages in heterogeneous multiple processor architectures, which is presently being developed in our institute in the EERP project PADIPRO, supported by DEC. We foresee that, except for step II (testing), the usage of logic programming can bring several advantages: (1) By using logic programming in the testing request step the program can make use of the set of facts, already necessary for the diagnosis step, defining what are the test group units and what are the tests needed for each unit. This allows for an easy and modular way of gathering the knowledge on what tests are needed, and avoids the duplication of information for different steps. (2) The tests results gathering and the diagnosis step can be interleaved. By implementing both these two step in logic programming, finding the diagnoses of test group units can start before all results were returned. The contradiction removal process needed in step IV, being based on a top-down procedure, can start even without any of the results, and wait for the result of a given test only when that result is indispensable. This will, we expect, cater for an increase on the efficiency of the whole process. (3) The implementation of the consensus step also gains from being described in a declarative language.

The testing step, relying on hardware tests, is best suited for implementation on a low-level language. Thus we intend to keep with the low-level implementation of tests. This implementation can easily be called from, and return its results to the logic programming environment.

References

1. J. J. Alferes, C. V. Damásio, and L. M. Pereira. A logic programming system for non-monotonic reasoning. *Journal of Automated Reasoning*, Special Issue on Implementation of NonMonotonic Reasoning(14):93–147, 1995.
2. C. Baral and M. Gelfond. Logic programming and knowledge representation. *J. Logic Programming*, 19/20:73–148, 1994.
3. W. Chen and D. S. Warren. Query evaluation under the well founded semantics. In *PODS'93*, 1993.
4. C. V. Damásio, W. Nejdl, and L. M. Pereira. REVISE: An extended logic programming system for revising knowledge bases. In *KR'94*. Morgan Kaufmann, 1994.
5. I. de Almeida Móra. Diagnóstico de Falhas em Sistemas Distribuídos. Master's thesis, Universidade Federal do Rio Grande do Sul, Porto Alegre, Brasil, March 1994. (In portuguese).
6. A. V. Gelder, K. A. Ross, and J. S. Schlipf. The well-founded semantics for general logic programs. *Journal of the ACM*, 38(3):620–650, 1991.
7. M. Gelfond and V. Lifschitz. Logic programs with classical negation. In Warren and Szeredi, editors, *7th Int. Conf. on LP*, pages 579–597. MIT Press, 1990.
8. L. M. Pereira and J. J. Alferes. Well founded semantics for logic programs with explicit negation. In B. Neumann, editor, *European Conf. on AI*, pages 102–106. John Wiley & Sons, 1992.
9. L. M. Pereira, J. J. Alferes, and J. N. Aparício. Contradiction Removal within Well Founded Semantics. In A. Nerode, W. Marek, and V. S. Subrahmanian, editors, *LP & NMR*, pages 105–119. MIT Press, 1991.
10. L. M. Pereira, C. Damásio, and J. J. Alferes. Diagnosis and debugging as contradiction removal. In L. M. Pereira and A. Nerode, editors, *2nd Int. Ws. on LP & NMR*, pages 316–330. MIT Press, 1993.
11. R. Reiter. A theory of diagnosis from first principles. *Artificial Intelligence*, 32:57–96, 1987.
12. G. Wagner. Logic programming with strong negation and innexact predicates. *J. of Logic and Computation*, 1(6):835–861, 1991.

Agreement: A Logical Approach to Approximate Reasoning

Luis M. M. Custódio and Carlos A. Pinto-Ferreira

Instituto de Sistemas e Robótica - Instituto Superior Técnico
Av. Rovisco Pais, 1096 Lisboa Codex, Portugal.
Ph. 351-1-8418272 Fax 351-1-8418291

Abstract. In this paper, some aspects of the human reasoning process, such as commonsense knowledge, uncertainty and approximate reasoning are discussed. A new way to approach these concepts — the point of view of agreement — and the relationships among them are addressed. It is shown that the concept of agreement provides a framework for the development of a formal and sound explanation for concepts (*e.g.* fuzzy sets) which lack formal semantics. Based on the notion of agreement, a multi-valued logic — logic of agreement — that has been proved to be sound, is then presented.

1 Introduction

Most of the knowledge used by human beings in their day-to-day activities is based on concepts that result from a kind of tacit agreement among people. In this paper a research exploring the idea of agreement and its use to model human knowledge and reasoning in what concerns commonsense is presented. The fact that agreement among individuals is not always perfect suggests a kind of uncertainty exhibiting some similarities with the concept of fuzziness introduced by Lofti Zadeh [11]. However, the fuzzy approach can be criticized due to its subjectivity: this is the reason why logicists argue against "fuzzy logics" (see a reply from Sheridan to [3]). The controversy that has emerged between the fuzzy, and AI and other communities suggests that, in some extent, the fuzzy approach is not satisfactory [4][7]. The basic reason for this controversy is the lack of a formal definition of fuzzy sets, *i.e.*, so far, a fuzzy set is a concept based on intuitive grounds.

In the present paper, the concept of agreement is used to state a formal definition of fuzzy sets, allowing to raise, reframe, and solve some of the deficiencies of the Fuzzy Set Theory while providing a framework for the development of a formal system to commonsense representation and reasoning — the Logic of Agreement, an extension of Classical Logic.

2 Commonsense and Agreement

Commonsense reasoning and representation is one of the most relevant issues in Artificial Intelligence [8]. The present approach is based upon the idea that commonsense derives from the knowledge that is held, used, and shared by a group of individuals. Recall that the etymology of the word "common-sense" is just the "sharing of feelings" (among people about themselves and the world).

What we call reality is nothing but agreement. As a consequence, a commonsensical concept like "tall", for instance, should be framed with respect to a certain group of individuals, when characterizing a certain person. Of course, being tall differs strongly if commonsense emerges from a group of bushmen or swedish individuals.

The key issue in what regards reasoning under agreement is to determine whether the mechanisms of derivation used by people are sound with respect to a given semantics. In other words, for instance, if a group of individuals agrees, in some extent, with propositions A, $A \rightarrow B$, and B, (given a degree of agreement for each proposition), then, there should be an inference system capable of deriving, say B (and the corresponding degree of agreement) given A, and $A \rightarrow B$. If such an inference system would not exist, then it would be impossible to reason under agreement (at least with some degree of accuracy). This should be a very puzzling conclusion as people usually derive conclusions from premises stated under agreement. For instance, most of the people agrees that Spielberg movies are good. When a new Spielberg movie comes up, people should agree, at least *a priori*, that it should be good. Of course, the degree of agreement of the former proposition should positively influence the degree of the latter.

It is important to notice that, in those cases where agreement is perfect (that three is greater than one, that Tweety is a bird, for instance), Logic of Agreement should provide the same results as Classical First Order Logic.

3 Fuzziness and Agreement

At first sight, a good candidate for dealing with ambiguity and vagueness (which derive from incomplete agreement) is the fuzzy approach. However, "fuzzy logic" is not a logic in the sense that, (i) it does not have a formal model theory — a semantic system, (ii) it does not rely on a unique inference system — there are several inference mechanisms to be applied according to the situation, and (iii) fundamental concepts, as membership function, for instance, are ill-defined and intrinsecally vague. As recognized by Zimmermann [12]: "Fuzziness has so far not been defined uniquely semantically...". So, "fuzzy logic" is *arbitrary, unsound* and *vague*. Arbitrary, because one should choose rules of inference adequate for the problem in hand; unsound, as any set of inference rules does not provide suitable explanations, even with respect to an informal semantics; and vague, as there is the lack of a formal and unique definition of basic concepts. As a consequence, when applied to certain problems (see the pencil of Sheridan-Fine example in Sect. 5) it delivers puzzling answers and weird results.

Nevertheless, the main problems are not in the "logic" itself but in its very foundations: the Fuzzy Set Theory. In fact, Fuzzy Set Theory is supposed to be an extension of Classical Set Theory. However, as fuzzy sets are defined by the way of membership functions, and nobody knows for sure where do they come from, the whole building of fuzzy lies on poor foundations. Furthermore, basic operations such as union and intersection of fuzzy sets can be performed using different mechanisms as the min, max, drastic product and sum, to name but a few. You can even define your own operators and "prove" their advantages and fitness in a bunch of examples.

The point of departure of this research is that vague concepts vary from individual to individual (hereafter referred as agent) according to her/his knowledge, environment, social and cultural aspects, to name a few. Moreover, agents can have two differing roles: as *individual* agents and as *commonsensical* agents. When asked if a women with, say, 1.70 height is tall, a particular individual does not have difficulties in answering yes or no. It is clearly a matter of true/false decision on the logic value of a proposition [5] [6]. However, when raising the same question to a group of individuals it is conceivable to finding a degree of acceptance of that particular proposition ranging from zero (complete rejection) to one (complete acceptance). When an individual associates degrees of acceptance to a proposition she/he is behaving as a commonsensical agent, who interprets the feelings of a group with a sufficiently high number of individuals.

Therefore, to define a class, several individual agents are questioned concerning the membership of an element on a particular class or category. The proportion of the number of positive answers versus the total number of answers is called degree of agreement. If this degree is interpreted as the membership grade of the element in the class, it is possible to define a membership function representing the sethood of the class. For instance, if the number of agents that agree with the fact that a 1.7m height individual is tall, is 80 out of 100, then the degree of agreement is 0.8. So the membership grade of a 1.7m height element in the set of tall individuals is 0.8.

As it is assumed that an individual agent uses the classic set theory in order to answer to questions relatively to membership of an element in a set, the following expressions summarize the traditional definitions of set complement, union and intersection.

Let A be a subset of X and x an element of X, the universe of discourse.
To represent the agent's opinion, a ternary function is used as follows:

$$cc(i, x, A) = \begin{cases} 1 \text{ if agent } i \text{ accepts that } x \text{ is a member of } A \\ 0 \text{ } otherwise \end{cases} \quad (1)$$

Using this function, the traditional set operations are defined as follows:
Let $\bar{A}$ be the complement of a set A

$$cc(i, x, \bar{A}) = 1 - cc(i, x, A) \quad (2)$$

$$cc(i, x, A \cap B) = cc(i, x, A)cc(i, x, B) \quad (3)$$

$$cc(i, x, A \cup B) = cc(i, x, A) + cc(i, x, B) - cc(i, x, A)cc(i, x, B) \quad (4)$$

Based on these expressions, it is possible to define the degree of agreement for operations on sets. Suppose that N agents are questioned concerning the membership of x in a set A.

Definition 1. Degree of agreement

The degree of agreement $ac(x \in A)$ among N agents relatively to the membership of x in a set A is defined by the proportion of the number of agents agreeing that x belongs to A, i.e.,

$$ac(x \in A) = \frac{\sum_{i=1}^{N} cc(i, x, A)}{N} \tag{5}$$

Using this definition, the extension of the concept of agreement to operations for sets can be easily performed.

Definition 2. Degree of agreement for the complement of a set

According to equation 2, the degree of agreement $ac(x \in \bar{A})$ among N agents w.r.t. the membership of x in a set $\bar{A}$ is defined as

$$ac(x \in \bar{A}) = \frac{\sum_{i=1}^{N} cc(i, x, \bar{A})}{N} = \frac{\sum_{i=1}^{N} 1 - cc(i, x, A)}{N} = 1 - ac(x \in A) \tag{6}$$

Definition 3. Degree of agreement for the intersection of two sets

According to equation 3, the degree of agreement $ac(x \in A \cap B)$ among N agents w.r.t. the membership of x in a set $A \cap B$ is defined as

$$ac(x \in A \cap B) = \frac{\sum_{i=1}^{N} cc(i, x, A)cc(i, x, B)}{N} \tag{7}$$

Definition 4. Degree of agreement for the union of two sets

According to equation 4, the degree of agreement $ac(x \in A \cup B)$ among N agents relatively to the membership of x in a set $A \cup B$ is defined as

$$ac(x \in A \cup B) = \frac{\sum_{i=1}^{N} cc(i, x, A) + cc(i, x, B) - cc(i, x, A)cc(i, x, B)}{N} \tag{8}$$

The following definition establishes a function that provides the covariance between two collection of answers obtained concerning the membership of an element x in a set A and in a set B. It reflects the quantity of agents that give the same answer for both questions and the quantity of agents giving different answers.

Definition 5. Covariance

A covariance function in terms of agreement is defined as

$$cov(x \in A, x \in B) = \frac{\sum_{i=1}^{N} [cc(i, x, A) - ac(x \in A)][cc(i, x, B) - ac(x \in B)]}{N} \tag{9}$$

Now it is ease to prove the following propositions

Proposition 6.

$$ac(x \in A \cap B) = ac(x \in A)ac(x \in B) + cov(x \in A, x \in B) \tag{10}$$

Proposition 7.

$$ac(x \in A \cap B) \leq ac(x \in A) \ (or \ ac(x \in B)) \leq ac(x \in A \cup B) \qquad (11)$$

Proposition 8.

$$ac(x \in A \cup B) = ac(x \in A) + ac(x \in B) - ac(x \in A \cap B) \qquad (12)$$

Interpreting the grade of membership $\mu_A(x)$ of an element x in a fuzzy set A as the degree of agreement among N agents w.r.t. the membership of x in A, demonstrates that the operators usually used in fuzzy set theory should be re-evaluated.

The most popular choice of operators for intersection and union is min and max, respectively [2][12][10]. Based on the new interpretation of grade of membership it is clear that both operators are not adequate considering equations 10 and 12. Also the pair product/probabilistic sum has been frequently used as operators for those operations. However, based on the agreement definitions, this pair is also inadequate to represent the intersection and union of fuzzy sets. Moreover, in fuzzy literature the choice of a particular pair of operators either is not justified or is justified in practical terms (application dependent) or it is justified based only on algebraic arguments. The agreement concept is therefore a possibility to fulfil this gap and to give a real semantic interpretation of the membership grade notion.

With this interpretation of the meaning of vague concepts, it is possible to define a rigorous but clear semantics of a logic involving classic and non-classic propositions. A classic one is represented by a degree of agreement that it is 1 (or 0), *i.e.*, all the agents agree (or disagree) on the membership of an element in a class.

Since it is supposed that each agent is a rational individual using first order logic to reason about the world [9], one of primary priorities of this new logic was that it would be a extension of the classical logic. When propositions involved are classic ones, the logic provides the same results as the classical logic, giving only two logical values: true and false.

Moreover, each proposition is logically evaluated by a set of N agents generating a degree of agreement in the interval $[0, 1]$. Based on a proof theory, presented in [1], this logic is capable of infering new propositions and, more important, to determine its degree of agreement.

4 Logic of Agreement: the Semantic System

In order to create the semantics of a logic, it is necessary to establish a conceptualization of reality, defining the relevant objects of the world for a specific problem, as well as the relations among the objects. The set of objects of the conceptualization is called universe of discourse.

Since the existence of several agents is assumed, the semantic system considers that each agent defines her/his own conceptualization of reality. However, when agents are asked about a property of an object, each one conceptualizes the property differently, but the object involved should be the same so the aggregation of answers would make sense. For instance, if agents are asked if John is tall, all the agents must be considering the same John. The same hypothesis is assumed for functions. For instance, when the question involves the son of Peter (for example, John), all agents should consider the same John. Finally for the relations of the conceptualizations of reality, it is assumed that the agents have total freedom of conceptualizing each relevant property. Therefore, supposing that there are N agents, the semantic system considers N conceptualizations of reality, with the same objects and functions, but different relations.

Prior to the full definition of the semantic system, it is essential to have a formal language allowing the representation of propositions about the world conceptualized. Those propositions are represented by formulas of the language, according to a specific alphabet and certain rules of formation (see [1]).

The evaluation of a formula depends on the interpretation given to each element in the formula, $i.e.$, it depends on the relation between the elements of the language and the elements of the conceptualization — objects, functions and relations. As usual, the concept of interpretation I is defined as the mapping from the elements of the language to the elements of the conceptualization.

Since there are different conceptualizations, it is also assumed different interpretations I_i, one for each conceptualization (agent). As the objects and functions are the same in all conceptualizations, all the interpretations map an object or function constant of the language into the same objects or functions of the conceptualization.

According to the definition of agreement, an agent agrees or not with the fact that an object possesses a certain property. So each agent should conceptualize a property by a classical relation through the definition of a crisp set of objects that satisfy the property.

4.1 Formal Definition of the Semantic System

Definition 9. Interpretation

An interpretation I_i (used by the agent A_i) is a mapping from the elements of the language to the elements of the conceptualization satisfying the following properties:

i) if c is a constant symbol of object, then $I_i(c) \in D$ and $\forall_j,\ I_i(c) = I_j(c)$, where D represents the universe of discourse common to all conceptualizations.

ii) if f is a constant symbol of function, with rank n, then $I_i(f) : D^n \to D$ and $\forall_j,\ I_i(f) = I_j(f)$.

iii) if p is a constant symbol of relation, with rank n, then $I_i(p) \subseteq D^n$.

Now it is possible to define the concept of *concordance*, denoted by $\models_I \phi$, representing the fact that the agent using the interpretation I accepts the proposition represented by the formula ϕ.

Definition 10. Concordance

i) an agent A_i concords with the proposition represented by the atomic formula $p(c_1, \ldots, c_n)$, according to her/his interpretation I_i, if and only if the tuple $< I_i(c_1), \ldots, I_i(c_n) >$ belongs to the relation $I_i(p)$, i.e.,

$$\models_{I_i} p(c_1, \ldots, c_n) \quad \text{iff} \quad < I_i(c_1), \ldots, I_i(c_n) > \in I_i(p)$$

ii) an agent A_i concords with the proposition represented by the formulas $\neg\phi$, $\phi \wedge \psi$, $\phi \vee \psi$, $\phi \rightarrow \psi$ and $\phi \leftrightarrow \psi$ according to her/his interpretation I_i, if and only if

$$\models_{I_i} \neg\phi \quad \text{iff} \quad \not\models_{I_i} \phi$$
$$\models_{I_i} \phi \wedge \psi \quad \text{iff} \quad \models_{I_i} \phi \text{ and } \models_{I_i} \psi$$
$$\models_{I_i} \phi \vee \psi \quad \text{iff} \quad \models_{I_i} \phi \text{ or } \models_{I_i} \psi$$
$$\models_{I_i} \phi \rightarrow \psi \quad \text{iff} \quad \not\models_{I_i} \phi \text{ or } \models_{I_i} \psi$$
$$\models_{I_i} \phi \leftrightarrow \psi \quad \text{iff} \quad \models_{I_i} \phi \wedge \psi \text{ or } \models_{I_i} \neg\phi \wedge \neg\psi$$

The concordance concept can be defined by a mathematical function $conc : I \times \mathcal{L} \rightarrow \{0, 1\}$, where I is the set of interpretations and $\mathcal{L}$ is the set of formulas. The former definitions can be stated as:

Definition 11. Function $conc$

i)

$$conc(I_i, p(c_1, \ldots, c_n)) = \begin{cases} 1 \text{ if } < I_i(c_1), \ldots, I_i(c_n) > \in I_i(p) \\ 0 \text{ otherwise} \end{cases}$$

ii)

$$conc(I_i, \neg\phi) = 1 - conc(I_i, \phi)$$
$$conc(I_i, \phi \wedge \psi) = conc(I_i, \phi) \, conc(I_i, \psi)$$
$$conc(I_i, \phi \vee \psi) = conc(I_i, \phi) + conc(I_i, \psi) - conc(I_i, \phi) \, conc(I_i, \psi)$$
$$conc(I_i, \phi \rightarrow \psi) = conc(I_i, \neg\phi \vee \psi)$$
$$conc(I_i, \phi \leftrightarrow \psi) = conc(I_i, \phi \wedge \psi) + conc(I_i, \neg\phi \wedge \neg\psi)$$

Since an agent creates her/his own conceptualization of reality, it can be said that the agent defines a possible world. Assuming N agents, N possible worlds are created, each one associated with a particular interpretation. Let $W = \{w_1, \ldots, w_N\}$ be the set of possible worlds created by N agents.

Definition 12. Let w be the possible world defined by an agent A. A function $In : W \rightarrow I$ is defined, associating to the possible world w the interpretation $In(w)$ used by the agent A. Then, $In(W) = \{I_1, \ldots, I_N\} = I$ is the set of all interpretations.

In order to aggregate the information given by N agents, it is defined the concept of (agreed) satisfaction in the logic of agreement (LA).

Definition 13. Satisfaction of a formula

Let A be a formula of the language and α a real number in the interval $[0, 1]$, if the formula A is satisfied (agreed) by a degree α, in the set W of possible worlds, it is denoted by $W \models_\alpha^{LA} A$.

Definition 14. Satisfaction

The set W of possible worlds satisfies by a degree α a formula in the following cases:

i) $W \models_\alpha^{LA} A$ iff exist in W, αN worlds w_i such that $\models_{In(w_i)} A$, where A is an atomic formula.

ii) $W \models_\alpha^{LA} \neg A$ iff exist in W, αN worlds w_i such that $\models_{In(w_i)} \neg A$.

iii) $W \models_\alpha^{LA} A \wedge B$ iff exist in W, αN worlds w_i such that $\models_{In(w_i)} A \wedge B$.

iv) $W \models_\alpha^{LA} A \vee B$ iff exist in W, αN worlds w_i such that $\models_{In(w_i)} A \vee B$.

v) $W \models_\alpha^{LA} A \rightarrow B$ iff exist in W, αN worlds w_i such that $\models_{In(w_i)} A \rightarrow B$.

vi) $W \models_\alpha^{LA} A \leftrightarrow B$ iff exist in W, αN worlds w_i such that $\models_{In(w_i)} A \leftrightarrow B$.

Definition 15. Logical value

If a formula A is satisfied by a value α, by the set of possible worlds W, then it is said that α is the logical value of the formula A.

Definition 16. Collective or simultaneous satisfaction

A set of formulas $\{P_1, \ldots, P_m\}$ is satisfied by the set of possible worlds W, according to the set of logical values $\bar{\alpha} = \{\alpha_i, \ldots, \alpha_m\}$, denoted by $W \models_{\bar{\alpha}}^{LA} \{P_1, \ldots, P_m\}$, iff

$$W \models_{\alpha_i}^{LA} P_i$$

i.e., the set of possible worlds satisfies the formula P_i with a logical value α_i.

Definition 17. Logical consequence

Let $\Gamma = \{P_1, \ldots, P_m\}$ be a set of formulas and $\bar{\alpha} = \{\alpha_i, \ldots, \alpha_m\}$ a set of logical values, where α_i is the logical value of the formula P_i. Let also be a formula A and the correspondent logical value α. It is said that A is a logical consequence of Γ, according to $\bar{\alpha}$ and α, denoted by $\Gamma \models_{\bar{\alpha}, \alpha}^{LA} A$, if for the set of possible worlds W, Γ has a collective satisfaction $\bar{\alpha}$, then A is satisfied in the value α.

Theorem 18. *The logic of agreement is sound.*

Proof. The proof is provided in [1].

5   The Pencil of Sheridan-Fine: a Simple Example

The following example was mentioned by Sheridan in a reply to Dubois and Prade [3] and it will be used here to illustrate the differences between agreement based operators and "popular" fuzzy ones.

Suppose that there is a pencil that is fairly red and fairly orange. Sheridan claims that it is at least *conceivable* that the pencil is very red or orange. Intuitively, this means that the grade of membership of the disjunction should be greater than the grade of membership of each disjuncts.

Assuming that N agents were questioned concerning the acceptance of the following propositions: i) orange(pencil), and ii) red(pencil), suppose that both propositions have a degree of agreement of 0.7, which are denoted by

$$< orange(\text{pencil}), 0.7 >$$
$$< red(\text{pencil}), 0.7 >$$

representing that the Sheridan-Fine pencil is fairly orange and fairly red.

Consider that based on expression 12, an inference rule is defined which has the following form when applied to the pencil example:

$$< orange(\text{pencil}), a >$$
$$< red(\text{pencil}), b >$$
$$\frac{< orange(\text{pencil}) \wedge red(\text{pencil}), c >}{< orange(\text{pencil}) \vee red(\text{pencil}), a + b - c >}$$

According to expression 12 the union and intersection operators (and consequently the disjunction and conjunction operators) are not independent. Therefore, it is necessary to consider another proposition: $orange(\text{pencil}) \wedge red(\text{pencil})$. Suppose also that the grade of agreement for this proposition is 0.5. This could be interpreted as: for half of the N agents, the pencil is red and orange, and for the other half, the pencil is not simultaneously red and orange, i.e., there is a maximum disagreement concerning the proposition $orange(\text{pencil}) \wedge red(\text{pencil})$.

Applying now the inference rule stated above, it can be derived:

$$< orange(\text{pencil}) \vee red(\text{pencil}), 0.9 >$$

which denotes that the grade of agreement among the N agents, for the proposition $orange(\text{pencil}) \vee red(\text{pencil})$, is 0.9. This could be interpreted as the pencil being very red or orange. As it was refered by Sheridan, using the "most popular choice of fuzzy operators" (min and max) it is impossible to obtain such conclusion. In fact, the utilization of the max operator for union (disjunction) "leads" to a pencil fairly red or orange.

As the union (disjunction) operation depends on the intersection (conjunction) one, it is possible to obtain different grades of agreement for the proposition $orange(\text{pencil}) \vee red(\text{pencil})$. For instance, if the conjunction's degree of agreement is 0.4, the disjunction degree would be 1.0, meaning that the pencil is completely red or orange. On the other hand, if the conjunction degree is 0.7, the disjunction one is 0.7. Only in this case the result given by the fuzzy operator max is equal to the one obtained based on agreement. Therefore, as the degree of agreement for the disjunction "orange(pencil) or red(pencil)" varies according to the value of the conjunction, it confirms the idea of Sheridan that it is conceivable that the grade of agreement (membership) of the disjunction could be greater than the grade of agreement (membership) of each disjuncts.

6   Conclusions

In this paper, a novel way to formalizing approximate reasoning, based on the concept of agreement, was introduced. The relation between agreement and fuzzy membership was used to emphasize some aspects of the fuzzy theory that have been criticize by other research communities. For instance, the notion of agreement was utilized to allow a formal semantical definition for the concept of degree of membership. Moreover, some fuzzy set operators were re-evaluated in terms of the new way to define fuzzy membership.

Based on the agreement concept, a multi-valued propositional logic — logic of agreement — was presented in terms of its semantic system.

References

1. Custódio, L., Pinto-Ferreira, C.: Logic of Agreement. Technical Report ISR/IST **10-95** (1995)
2. Dubois, D., Prade, H.: Fuzzy Sets and Systems: Theory and Applications. Academy Press (1980)
3. Dubois, D., Prade, H.: An Introduction to Possibilistic and Fuzzy Logics. in: Smets et.al. (eds), Non-Standard Logics for Automated Reasoning. Academic Press (1988)
4. Elkan, C.: The Paradoxical Success of Fuzzy Logic. Proceedings of the National Conference on Artificial Intelligence, The MIT and AAAI Press (1993) 698-703
5. Gardenfors, P.: Knowledge in Flux: Modeling the Dynamics of Epistemic States. The MIT Press (1988)
6. Hayes, P.: Some Problems and Non-Problems in Representation Theory. In: Brachman, R., Levesque, H. (eds), Readings in Knowledge Representation. Morgan Kaufmann (1985) 3-22
7. Laviolette, M., Seaman, J.: The Efficacy of Fuzzy Representations of Uncertainty. IEEE Trans. on Fuzzy Systems, **2-1** (1994) 4-15
8. McCarthy, J.: Programs with Common Sense. Proceedings of the Teddington Conference on the Mechanization of Thought Processes (1959)
9. Omar, R.: Artificial Intelligence through Logic. AICOM, **7-3/4** (1994)
10. Yager, R.: Expert Systems Using Fuzzy Logic. in: Yager et.al. (eds), An Introduction to Fuzzy Logic Applications in Intelligent Systems. Kluwer Academic Publishers (1992)
11. Zadeh, L.: Fuzzy Sets. Information and Control, **8** (1965) 338-353
12. Zimmermann, H.: Fuzzy Set Theory and its Applications. Kluwer-Nijhoff Publishing (1985)

Constructing Extensions by Resolving a System of Linear Equations

MESSAOUDI Nadia*

LIM, URA CNRS 1787, Université Aix-Marseille II, Faculté des Sciences de Luminy

163 Avenue de Luminy, case 901, 13288 MARSEILLE Cédex 9 FRANCE

Tél (33) 42 25 45 54, e-mail : messao@lim.univ-mrs.fr

1   Introduction

The fixed-point approach is essentially represented by the default logic (construction of extension E) and the autoepistemic logic. In this paper, we present the way to transform the construction of extensions for logic default into a resolution of a system of linear equations in order to reduce the complexity of the problem : $BC(BF) = E \iff M_{BC} \times X_E = B_{BF}$. Then the calculus become similar to a classical problem of numerical calculus from which we can borrow the methods. We will see then how it could be interesting to adapt iterative algorithms of the numerical calculus to improve our method.

2   An introduction to default logic

We assume the reader familiar with basic notions on default logics (see e.g. [6] and [4]). A theory with only normal defaults (normal theory) has at least one extension. But we can't assure the same property for the seminormal default theories Though there is a large class of consistent seminormal default theories which have at least one extension (this is to say, there is no cycle of inference). The following definitions present a syntaxical method to determine if there is a cycle in seminormal default theory [1].

Definition 1 *[1]($\prec$ et $\preceq$) Let $\Delta = (D, W)$ be a closed, seminormal default theory. The partial relations, $\prec$ and $\preceq$ on Literals $\times$ Literals, are defined as follows :*
1. If $\alpha \in W$, then $\alpha = (\alpha_1 \vee \ldots \vee \alpha_n)$ for some $n \geq 1$. For all α_i, $\alpha_j \in \{\alpha_a, \ldots, \alpha_n\}$, if $\alpha_i \neq \alpha_j$, let $\neg\alpha_i \preceq \alpha_j$.
2. If $\delta \in D$, then $\delta = \frac{\alpha \ : \ \beta \wedge \gamma}{\beta}$. Let $\alpha_1, \ldots, \alpha_r$, $\beta_1, \ldots, \beta_s$, and $\gamma_1, \ldots, \gamma_t$ be the

*This research is supported by a CEA-EDF project for the developpement of an expert system helping for nuclear fuel casing defaults diagnostic in nuclear reactors.

literals of the clausal forms of α, β *and* γ, *respectively. Then :*
(a) If $\alpha_i \in \{\alpha_1, \ldots, \alpha_r\}$ *and* $\beta_j \in \{\beta_1, \ldots, \beta_s\}$, *let* $\alpha_i \preceq \beta_j$.
(b) If $\gamma_i \in \{\gamma_1, \ldots, \gamma_t\}$, $\beta_j \in \{\beta_1, \ldots, \beta_s\}$ *and* $\gamma_j \notin \{\beta_1, \ldots, \beta_s\}$ *let* $\neg\gamma_i \prec \beta_j$.
(c) Also $\beta = \beta_1 \wedge \ldots \wedge \beta_m$, *for some* $m \geq 1$. *For each* $i \leq m$, $\beta_i = (\beta_{i,1} \vee \ldots \vee \beta_{i,m_i})$, *where* $m_i \geq 1$. *Thus if* $\beta_{i,j}$, $\beta_{i,k} \in \{\beta_{1,1}, \ldots, \beta_{m,m_m}\}$ *and* $\beta_{i,j} \neq \beta_{i,k}$, *let* $\neg\beta_{i,j} \preceq \beta_{i,k}$.
3. The expected transitivity relationships hold for $\prec$ *and* $\preceq$:
(a) If $\alpha \preceq \beta$ *and* $\beta \preceq \gamma$, *then* $\alpha \preceq \gamma$. *(b) If* $\alpha \prec \beta$ *and* $\beta \prec \gamma$, *then* $\alpha \prec \gamma$. *(c)If* $\alpha \prec \beta$ *and* $\beta \preceq \gamma$ *or* $\alpha \preceq \beta$ *and* $\beta \prec \gamma$, *then* $\alpha \prec \gamma$.
A seminormal default theory is said to be ordered *if and only if there is no literal,* α, *such that* $\alpha \prec \alpha$.

Theorem 1 *[1] If a seminormal default theory is ordered, then it has at least one extension.*

3 Rewriting the problem of constructing extensions

The propositional calculus formulae can be interpreted, this is to say, can receive a value of the domain of the semantic interpretation, for example $\{T, F\}$ for the classical bi-valued logic. We add to this set the new value $\emptyset$ to characterize ignorence about a proposition or "lack of coefficient" (we'll see below what it means). We are begining to present a set of operators which will be used to formalise the spread of information in the knowledge base.

Definition 2 *We introduce the operators* $\odot$ *and* $\oplus$ *such as :*
$\oplus, \ominus : \{T, F, \emptyset\} \times \{T, F, \emptyset\} \longrightarrow \{T, F, \emptyset\}, \odot : \{T, F, \emptyset\} \times \{T, F, \emptyset\} \longrightarrow \{T, F, \emptyset\}$

$\oplus$	$\emptyset$	T	F
$\emptyset$	$\emptyset$	T	F
T	T	T	T
F	F	T	F

$\odot$	$\emptyset$	T	F
$\emptyset$	$\emptyset$	$\emptyset$	$\emptyset$
T	$\emptyset$	T	F
F	$\emptyset$	F	T

$\emptyset$ *is the neutral element for* $\oplus$ *and* T *is the neutral element for* $\odot$. *The operators* $\odot$ *and* $\oplus$ *are commutative and associative.*

Definition 3 *Let* M_A *be the set of matrices* $(n \times m)$ *for* n *and* m *integers, with their coefficients in* $\{T, F, \emptyset\}$. *The operators* $\odot$ *and* $\oplus$ *are generalised to the elements of* M_A.

We introduce two new values ε, $-\varepsilon$ to the domain $\{T, F, \emptyset\}$, characterizing what is placed on justifications in the default. For example : $\frac{A:B}{C}$ will be noted
$$(Value_P(A) \odot f_A) \odot (Value_J(B) \odot f_B) = Value_C(C) \odot f'_C \qquad (1),$$
with $\forall x \in Literals$, $Value_I(x) = T, F, \emptyset$ (I for Prerequised or Consequent) if respectively x, $\neg x$, or neither x or $\neg x$ is in I, $Value_J(x) = \varepsilon, -\varepsilon, \emptyset$ (J for Justifications) if respectively x, $\neg x$, or neither x or $\neg x$ is in J, $f_x = T$ if $x \in W$, $f_x = F$ if $\neg x \in W$, $f_x = \emptyset$ if neither x or $\neg x \in W$, f'_y is the unknown variable

which is in the final extension we are going to compute. If at the end of the computation, $f'_y = T$ then $y \in E$, if $f'_y = F$ then $\neg y \in E$, else neither y or $\neg y \in E$. Then, (1) $\iff (T \odot f_A) \otimes (\varepsilon \odot f_B) = T \odot f'_C$. The following arrays present the definition of the operators $\otimes, \oslash : \{T, F, \emptyset\} \times \{T, F, \emptyset\} \longrightarrow \{T, F, \emptyset\}$ and how the values ε an $-\varepsilon$ are used :

$\otimes$	$\emptyset$	T	F
$\emptyset$	$\emptyset$	T	F
T	T	T	$\emptyset$
F	$\emptyset$	T	$\emptyset$

$\oslash$	$\emptyset$	T	F
$\emptyset$	$\emptyset$	T	F
T	T	T	F
F	F	F	F

$\odot$	$\emptyset$	T	F	ε	$-\varepsilon$
$\emptyset$	$\emptyset$	$\emptyset$	$\emptyset$	$\emptyset$	$\emptyset$
T	$\emptyset$	T	F	T	F
F	$\emptyset$	F	T	F	T
ε	$\emptyset$	T	F	-	-
ε	$\emptyset$	F	T	-	-

This traduces that a default $\frac{A \wedge B : C}{D}$ is rewritten into the equation
$(Value_P(A) \odot f_A \oslash Value_P(B) \odot f_B) \otimes (Value_J(C) \odot f_C) = Value_C(D) \odot f'_D$, (3)
if the data base gives $f_A = F$, $f_B = T$ et $f_C = F$, (3) is rewritten in
$(T \odot F \oslash T \odot T) \otimes (\varepsilon \odot F) = T \odot f'_D \iff F \otimes F = T \odot f'_D$.
If $F \otimes F = T = T \odot f'_D$, the resolution of the equation gives $f'_D = T$, this is to say, D is inferred, although we have $\neg A$ and $\neg C$. To avoid this sort of inconsistence, we must have $F \otimes F = \emptyset$ not to be able to conclude anything about D.
These operators are generalised to the matrices with their coefficients in $\{T, F, \emptyset\}$ and more precisely for $\otimes$, by a "multiplication" of coefficients with coefficients of the same indices.
For each knowledge base consisting in a set of defaults D and a data base W, each rules is rewritten in the formalism presented above. Also we obtain a system of linear equations to solve in $\{T, F, \emptyset\}$.

4 Constructing extensions and resolution of linear equations

To solve the system of equations we have established, it's interesting to have a look at Numerical Calculs algorithms. Also, as for systems in $\mathbb{R}$, we concluded that direct resolution should need prohibitif computational time for big systems. To limit this problem, we interested ourselves in iterative methods, more effectives and more precisely, we use an adaptation of Gauss-Seidel method [2]. Let the system to solve : $M_G \odot X = B$. (1)
M_G is decomposed as follows : $M_G = D \ominus E \ominus F$
with D diagonal matrix, E strictly upper triangular matrix and F strictly lower triangular matrix.
We deduce from (1) the following iterative system :
$$\begin{cases} X^0 = F : \text{data base vector} \\ D \odot X^{k+1} = E \odot X^{k+1} \oplus F \odot X^k \oplus B \end{cases} \quad (2)$$
But to take into account in the computation that X^k and X^{k+1} computed before have to be consistent with justifications of the applied defaults of the knowledge base, (2) is rewritten in :

$$\begin{cases} X^0 = F \; : \; \text{data base vector} \\[2mm] D \odot X^{k+1} = \left(E \oslash X^{k+1} \oplus F \oslash X^k \ominus D \odot X^k \right) \otimes \left(M_\epsilon \oslash \begin{pmatrix} \left(X_i^{k+1} \right)_{1,\ldots,k} \\ \left(X_i^k \right)_{k+1,\ldots,n} \end{pmatrix} \right) \oplus B^{k+1} \\[4mm] B^{k+1} = \left(M_G \oslash \begin{pmatrix} \left(X_i^{k+1} \right)_{1,\ldots,k} \\ \left(X_i^k \right)_{k+1,\ldots,n} \end{pmatrix} \right) \otimes \left(M_\epsilon \oslash \begin{pmatrix} \left(X_i^{k+1} \right)_{1,\ldots,k} \\ \left(X_i^k \right)_{k+1,\ldots,n} \end{pmatrix} \right) \end{cases}$$

To be able to use this procedure, as in Numerical calculus, we have to condition the matrix M_D to obtain the most as possible values on the diagonal different from $\emptyset$. This operation consists in permuting rows and columns of the triplet $(M_D, \; M_G, \; M_\epsilon)$ in order to obtain on the diagonal of M_D a maximum of values not equal to $\emptyset$.

If the matrix M_D has opposed values on a same column i, then it means that the formalised defauls theory may have more than one extension. Thus, the system is replaced by two new systems, one with only the positive values of the column i, the other with only the negative values of the column i. We subdivise like that, in order to never have in each system a column with opposed values. This operation have to be applied only for the formalisation of the defaults, not for classical rules. So for a theory $\Delta = (W, \; D)$, only D is concerned, for any W.

Example : For the following default theory $W = \{A, \; (A \to B), \; (A \to C)\}$
$D = \left\{ \frac{A : \neg D}{\neg D}, \; \frac{A : \neg F}{\neg F}, \; \frac{B : D}{D}, \; \frac{C : F}{F}, \; \frac{B : E}{E}, \; \frac{E : \neg H}{\neg H}, \; \frac{E : G \wedge \neg D}{G}, \; \frac{G : H}{H}, \; \frac{E : I \wedge \neg F}{I}, \; \frac{I : \neg J \wedge \neg H}{\neg J} \right\}$
We have to subdivise the first formalised system into six new systems and after conditionning and computation, we obtain six extensions :
$E_0 = \{A, \; B, \; C, \; D, \; E, \; F, \; \neg H\}$
$E_1 = Th(W \cup \{A, \; B, \; C, \; \neg D, \; E, \; F, \; G, \; \neg H\})$
$E_2 = Th(W \cup \{A, \; B, \; C, \; D, \; E, \; \neg F, \; \neg H, \; I, \; \neg J\})$
$E_3 = Th(W \cup \{A, \; B, \; C, \; \neg D, \; E, \; \neg F, \; G, \; \neg H, \; I, \; \neg J\})$
$E_4 = Th(W \cup \{A, \; B, \; C, \; \neg D, \; E, \; F, \; G, \; H\})$
$E_5 = Th(W \cup \{A, \; B, \; C, \; \neg D, \; E, \; \neg F, \; G, \; H, \; I\})$

Definition 4 Let $BC = \mathcal{R} \cup \mathcal{F}$ with $\mathcal{R}$, the set of rules and $\mathcal{F}$, the set of facts.
$Tr(BC) = Tr(\mathcal{R}) \cup Tr(\mathcal{F}) \cup \{f_x = f'_x; \; \forall x \in Literals(BC)\}$
with $Tr(BC)$, the set of equations with their coefficients in $\{T, \; F, \; \emptyset\}$ obtained after rewriting BC following the procedure exposed above.

Theorem 2 For finite, ordered, default theory, the procedure given above always converges on an extension.

Proof : Suppose that W is consistent. To show that $Th(Tr^{-1}(X^{i+1})) \, (Tr^{-1}(X)$ is the traduction of the vector X into a set of literals corresponding to its coefficients different from $\emptyset$, for example if $X_a = T$ then $a \in Tr^{-1}(X)$, if $X_a = F$ then $\neg a \in Tr^{-1}(X))$ is an extension for Δ, we use the theorem defining an extension in [4] and we show that $Th(Tr^{-1}(X^{i+1})) = \bigcup_{i=0}^{\infty} E_i$,
1. we are going to show first that $\bigcup_{i=0}^{\infty} E_i \subseteq Th(Tr^{-1}(X^{i+1}))$. By definition : $E_0 = W = Tr^{-1}(X^0) \subseteq Th(Tr^{-1}(X^{i+1}))$.
Suppose that $E_i \subseteq Th(Tr^{-1}(X^{i+1}))$ and considere $\omega \in E_{i+1}$
(a) if $\omega \in Th(E_i)$, then $\omega \in Th(Tr^{-1}(X^{i+1}))$ by hypothesis and closure.
(b) otherwise $\omega \in \left\{ \omega / \frac{\alpha : \omega \wedge \beta}{\omega} \in D, \; \alpha \in E_i, \; \forall x \in F_i \cup \{\beta, \; \omega\}, \; Tr^{-1}(X^i) \cup \{\alpha\} \not\vdash \neg x \right\}$.

Therefore $Tr^{-1}(X^{i+1}) \not\vdash \neg\omega \vee \neg\beta$. Here $Tr^{-1}(X^i) \not\vdash \omega \vee \beta$ since $Tr^{-1}(X^0) = W \subseteq Tr^{-1}(X^{i+1})$. Also, $\alpha \in Th(Tr^{-1}(X^{i+1}))$, by hypothesis. It follows that $Tr^{-1}(X^{i+1}) \vdash \omega$. Hence $E_{i+1} \subseteq Th(Tr^{-1}(X^{i+1}))$.

2. Finally, we show that $Th(Tr^{-1}(X^{i+1}) \subseteq \bigcup_{r=0}^{\infty} E_r$. Since $\bigcup_{r=0}^{\infty} E_r$ is logically closed, it suffices to show that $Tr^{-1}(X^{i+1}) \subseteq \bigcup_{r=0}^{\infty} E_r$. By definition, $Tr^{-1}(X^0) = W = E_0 \subseteq \bigcup_{r=0}^{\infty} E_r$. Assume that $Tr^{-1}(X^i) \subseteq \bigcup_{r=0}^{\infty} E_r$ and considere X^{i+1}, $X^{i+1} = f(X^i) = X^i + \left(\emptyset \ \ldots \ X_\omega \ \emptyset \ \ldots \right) + R^{i+1}$ for some $\omega \in CONSEQUENTS(D)$, where R^{i+1} is all the other solutions generate by the resolution. Since $X^{i+1} \subseteq \bigcup_{r=0}^{\infty} E_r$ by hypothesis, we have only to show that $\omega \in \bigcup_{r=0}^{\infty} E_r$. Since $\omega \in CONSEQUENTS(D)$ there is a $\delta = \frac{\alpha : \omega}{\omega \wedge \beta} \in D$ such that $\alpha \in Tr^{-1}(X^{i+1})$, $Tr^{-1}(X^i) \not\vdash \neg\omega \vee \neg\beta$ and $Tr^{-1}(X^{i+1} \not\vdash \neg\omega \vee \beta$. By hypothesis, since $\alpha \in Tr^{-1}(X^{i+1})$, $\alpha \in E_j$ for some j. Since $\omega \in Tr^{-1}(X^i)$, it follows that $Tr^{-1}(X^i) \not\vdash \neg\omega \vee \beta$. But then by definition of E_{j+1}, $\omega \in E_{j+1} \subset \bigcup_{r=0}^{\infty} E_r$. With (1) and (2) we obtain the desired result.

5 Conclusions-Perspectives

We have shown that for a large class of default theories for which coherent reasoning is always possible, we can use an inference algorithm based on a resolution of a system of linear equations in order to reduce the complexity of the computation. This could be very interesting when we know that defaults are extremely common in AI and there is a wide variety of common situations to which they can be applied, including several AI knowlege representation schemes.

Now we implement our method in the developpement of an expert system for a french entreprise. Then we will think of extending this to other nonmonotonic logics as the Paradoxical logic[3].

References

[1] D.W. Etherington, *Formalizing Nonmonotonic Reasonning Systems*, Artificial Intelligence 1987.

[2] Gene H.Golub, Gérard A.Meurant, *Résolution numérique des grands systèmes linéaires*, 1983 Eyrolles.

[3] A. Kohler, N. Messaoudi, *Modélisation de l'Incertain*, 1994 Congrès RFIA Paris.

[4] Lukaszewicz W., *Considerations on Default Logic-An Alternative Approach.* Computational Intelligence 4.

[5] N. Messaoudi, *Constructing Extensions with Matricial Resolution*, 1994 AIMSA Sofia.

[6] Reiter R., *A Logic for Default Reasoning.* Artificial Intelligence, 13.

Presenting Significant Information in Expert System Explanation*

Michael Wolverton

Computing and Information Systems Department, Daresbury Rutherford Appleton Laboratory,Chilton, DIDCOT, UK, OX11 0QX; mjw@inf.rl.ac.uk

Abstract. This paper presents a method for eliminating *insignificant* portions of an explanation of a conclusion – those portions that include terminology and inferences that the user does not have the expertise to understand, and those portions that add little to the user's belief in the conclusion. The method exploits a user model to select for presentation only those portions of an expert system's reasoning that add significantly to the user's belief that the conclusion is the right one. Examples demonstrate how the method generates concise explanations with only significant information, and how it tailors the explanation to the user.

1 Satisficing Explanations

Today's knowledge-based systems can use quite complex chains of reasoning to produce conclusions, and producing good machine-generated explanations for those conclusions can be difficult. Some explanations will involve complex domain concepts and detailed reasoning steps that the user has no hope of understanding. These kinds of problematic explanations are especially likely to occur with non-expert users. Other explanations will be unnecessarily long and contain great deals of information that, while technically correct and understandable to the user, does not add to the user's belief in the system's conclusion. This explanation problem is especially likely to occur with expert users. These two specific problems can be viewed as instances of the same general problem: in both cases, the explanation is made unnecessarily long by including information that adds little or nothing to the user's belief in the conclusion. We want to produce explanations that still reflect the expert system's reasoning, but that eliminate as much of this "insignificant" information as possible.

The goal of the project reported in this paper, then, is to produce explanations of long reasoning processes that attempt to balance *completeness* with *conciseness*, and to strike this balance paying specific attention to the user's understanding of the domain. The paper concerns itself only with explaining *conclusions* of reasoning. I.e., it does not address other types of explanation studied in the literature – answering user questions about how requested inputs might

---

* This research was supported by an ERCIM Post-Doctoral Fellowship 94-05. Thanks to Cindy Wolverton for the signal processing example of Sec. 3, and to Myles Chippendale and Gerhard Wickler for helpful comments on an earlier draft of this paper.

be used, defining system terminology and concepts, or tutoring. Furthermore, it is specifically concerned with generating explanations that satisfy one particular user information need about a conclusion: we want to convince the user that the conclusion is the correct one (as opposed, for example, to convincing the user that the system's reasoning is generally robust).

With these goals in mind, we propose a type of explanation called *satisficing conclusion-substantiating explanation* (SCS explanation), defined informally as:

Definition 1 (Satisficing Conclusion-Substantiating Explanation). Given a system S, some conclusion produced by that system C_S, and a user U, an SCS explanation of C_S to U with belief threshold p is either: (1) the shortest sequence of facts that convince U that there is a high probability ($> p$) of the conclusion C_S being true; (2) or, if no sequence of facts can give the user confidence greater than the threshold p, the set of facts that gives the user the maximum possible confidence in C_S.

This definition is designed to have SCS explanations be free of the two sources of insignificant information mentioned earlier. First, any portion of an explanation that the user cannot understand presumably will not add to his belief in the conclusion, and will thus not be included in the SCS explanation because of the minimality requirement. Second, portions of an explanation that add very little to the user's belief in the conclusion will not be included, provided they are not required to push the user's belief in C_S over p. The next section gives a method for producing a particular subclass of SCS explanations.

2 Method for Producing SCS Explanations

The method described here produces a class of explanations that specialize the class defined by Def. 1 in two ways. First, the user's domain theory τ_U is assumed to be a subset of the system's knowledge. I.e., we use the *overlay* approach to user modeling [2] . Second, the final explanation produced by this method will correspond to the basic sequence of reasoning steps used by the expert system to produce the conclusion. I.e., the explanation's content will be a subset of the trace of the expert system's inferences.

The method for producing SCS explanations is shown in Fig. 1. First, following the guidelines of Def. 1, the algorithm finds the smallest subset of the expert system's reasoning steps that either (1) produces a confidence in the conclusion of greater than p, or (2) maximizes confidence in the conclusion. Then the algorithm outputs the subset in textual form, filling in missing steps of the expert system's reasoning with heuristically chosen general text. One aspect of the algorithm that require some elaboration is the method of finding the sequence E (step 1), which is not specified in Fig. 1. A number of combinatorial optimization methods could be used; one of the simplest would be a heuristic search (e.g., branch-and-bound) of the subsets of R. An important requirement of finding the optimal subset is that there be a method of combining arbitrary sets of evidence from the expert system's reasoning. In many cases, the explanation module will be able to use the expert system's method for combining evidence.

Given
- R, a sequence of inferences the system used to produce the conclusion C_S.
- $\tau_U \subseteq \tau_S$, a user model represented as a subset of the system's knowledge.
- a belief threshold p

Produce an explanation of C_S as follows:
1. Find the sequence of reasoning steps E such that (a) the members of E are both a subset of R and a subset of τ_U, and (b) E meets either criterion (1) or, failing that, criterion (2) of Def. 1 above.
2. Output in sequence textual translations of the members of E. Whenever there are reasoning steps in R that are not included in E, produce text with a *textual linking heuristic* in lieu of the missing reasoning step.

Fig. 1. Method for producing SCS explanations

3 Example

This section contains an example illustrating the effect of the SCS explanation method of Sec. 2 and of different user models on the explanations produced. The explanation module's goal in this example is to produce an explanation substantiating the diagnosis of a hypothetical expert system designed to diagnose problems in a digital signal processing system. The system diagnoses problems using a fault hierarchy by performing tests that successively refine its hypothesis.

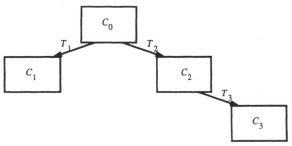

C_0 = Signal output of system is faulty
T_1 = Verify values stored in hardware registers
C_1 = No problem in initialization software
T_2 = Oscilloscope signal level check of gain boards
C_2 = Analogue gain board faulty
T_3 = Observe time response of T&C signals
C_3 = Timing component should be replaced

$Prob(C_3 | T_1 \wedge T_2 \wedge T_3) = .95$
$Prob(C_3 | T_2 \wedge T_3) = .92$
$Prob(C_3 | T_3) = .75$
$Prob(C_3 | T_1 \wedge T2) = .7$
$Prob(C_3 | T_2) = .5$

Fig. 2. Example reasoning of digital signal processing expert system

Fig. 2 shows the reasoning sequence of small portion of the system for a single diagnosis of a problem with the system. In this example, the system is attempting to diagnose the problem (C_0) that the observed output signal of the system is too weak. The system firsts tests the hypothesis that the problem is caused by a fault in the initialization software by verifying the values stored in the hardware registers (T_1). This test indicates that the software is initializing the registers correctly (C_1), so the system can give up on this branch of the hierarchy. Next, the system tests the hypothesis that there is a hardware fault by performing an oscilloscope signal level check of the two (analog and digital) gain boards (T_2). This test reveals that the analog gain board is faulty, while the digital gain board is fine (C_2). Finally, the system attempts to refine its current diagnosis by observing the time response of the analog gain board's timing and control signals (T_3). This test reveals that the board's timing component is faulty (C_3), and this is returned as the expert system's diagnosis.

Outputting the system's entire line of reasoning as an explanation for the conclusion C_3 – i.e., not using Sec. 2's method for eliminating insignificant information – might produce an explanation such as this:

> I verified the values stored in the hardware registers. The result was that all hardware register values were correct. This test indicated that the hardware initialization software is working correctly.
>
> Next, I did an oscilloscope signal level check of the gain components of the hardware. The result was that the signal level on the analog gain stage was too weak, and the signal level on the digital gain stage was fine. This test indicated that the analog gain board is faulty, and the digital gain board is fine.
>
> Next, I observed the time response of on-board timing and control signals of the analog gain board. The result was that the rising edge of the START timing signal occurs after the raw signal event of interest. This test indicated that the hardware timing component of the analog gain board is faulty and should be replaced.

This explanation might represent an accurate account of all the tests performed and conclusions reached in the process of producing the final diagnosis, but it also is probably unnecessarily long and detailed for most users. And this is only a simple example of a small portion of a fault hierarchy; explanations of realistic complex diagnoses can quickly grow to be completely unmanageable.

Now let us examine two different SCS explanations of the same diagnosis. The first explanation will be generated for an expert user – he is assumed to know about all the concepts and all the tests that the system knows about, and therefore his user model is identical to the system's knowledge base. Assume that the belief threshold for an explanation is set to 0.9. For this user and this belief threshold, the results of test T_1 constitute insignificant information. Knowing the results of tests T_2 and T_3 already support a .92 level of belief in conclusion C_3, and additionally knowing the result of test T_1 raises that value only a very small amount to .95. So the method of Sec. 2 will produce an explanation without the first paragraph of the previous explanation:

> I did an oscilloscope signal level check ... the analog gain board is faulty, and the digital gain board is fine.
>
> Next, I observed the time response ... the hardware timing component of the analog gain board is faulty and should be replaced.

Now consider a user with less expertise. This user has an understanding of the higher-level components of the system, but doesn't understand the detailed workings of those components. In particular, he does not know about the timing and control components of the gain boards. Thus, his user model includes tests T_1 and T_2, but does not include T_3. Therefore, the SCS explanation method will not present the detailed description and results of test T_3. It will present the results of both T_1 and T_2, rather than T_2 alone, because (1) both tests taken together give more confidence in the conclusion than T_2 by itself, and (2) since the confidence level for T_1 and T_2 (.75) is less than the belief threshold (.9), the method wants to find the explanation that maximizes confidence. So the explanation produced is the same as the first one presented in this section, except with "bridge" text to the final conclusion generated by the linking heuristic replacing the detailed description of test T_3:

> I verified the values ... the hardware initialization software is working correctly.
> Next, I did an oscilloscope signal level check ... the analog gain board is faulty, and the digital gain board is fine.
> A more detailed test of the analog gain board indicated that the hardware timing component of the analog gain board is faulty and should be replaced.

4 Related Work and Other Discussion

Other projects have addressed the elimination of portions that detract from the usefulness of the whole explanation [3, 1, 5]. The method reported in this paper is unique in that it uses the expert system's own mechanism for reasoning under uncertainty to decide on a set of inferences that imply a high level of confidence in the conclusion, given a particular user model. Our explanation method can also be viewed as a particular type of *reconstructive explanation* [4]; within that view, however, this work extends Wick and Thompson's work by automatically generating the explanation type based on the user model and belief threshold.

There are a number of interesting issues related to this project that are areas for future research: (1) adapting this approach to other information needs, e.g., tutoring or convincing the user of generally robust reasoning by the expert system, (2) abstracting a sequence of reasoning steps for presentation in the explanation and reasoning about that abstraction's effect on the user's beliefs, and (3) extending the approach to allow for "user-driven", hypertext explanations.

References

1. P. Gautier and T. Gruber. Generating explanations of device behavior using compositional modeling and causal ordering. In *AAAI-93*, pages 264–270, 1993.
2. I. Goldstein. The genetic graph: A representation for the evolution of procedural knowledge. *Int. J. Man-Machine Studies*, 11:51–77, 1979.
3. J. Wallis and E. Shortliffe. Customized explanations using causal knowledge. In Buchanan and Shortliffe, editors, *Rule-Based Expert Systems*. Addison-Wesley, 1984.
4. M. Wick and W. Thompson. Reconstructive expert system explanation. *Artificial Intelligence*, 54:33–70, 1992.
5. I. Zukerman and R. McConachy. Generating discourse across several user models: Maximizing belief while avoiding boredom and overload. In *IJCAI-95*, 1995.

A Cognitive Model of Problem Solving with Incomplete Information

Nathalie CHAIGNAUD

LIPN - CNRS URA 1507 - Institut Galilée
avenue J.B. Clément - 93430 Villetaneuse - France
e-mail: nat@lipn.univ-paris13.fr

Abstract. This paper presents a human behavior model of problem solving where information is deliberately incomplete and is to be obtained by the execution of some actions. This model is based on an experimentation set up with psychologists and simulates the observed behavior as faithfully as possible. We show how it allows a modular implementation with opportunistic aspects.

1 Introduction

Our purpose is to develop a cognitive model of planning activities when information is deliberately incomplete and is to be obtained by executing some actions. Clearly, the subject does not wait until he/she has an exact and complete representation of the problem to begin to work: on the contrary, the first attempts of solution are used to refine the problem representation. Plans thus constructed can be questioned when new information is incompatible with what has been taken into account up to there.

This interdisciplinary work is made in collaboration with psychologists. Our results show that the subject reasons in a less organized way than we assumed. The subject attempts to optimize his/her actions as long as no problem arises and reacts more instinctively in case of difficulty. His/her activity is related to planning by its anticipative character (see (Newell and Simon, 1963), (Hayes-Roth and Hayes-Roth, 1979) and (Tate et al., 1990)).

2 Experimentation

In the problem, the subject has to build a Hi-fi system. A complete system is made of five different elements: an amplifier, a tuner, a tape recorder, a record player and a compact disc reader. Several constraints are enforced: the budget is limited, elements must be compatible with the amplifier and their availability has to be checked with a restricted numbers of "phone calls". The availability of the elements is initially unknown. The subject can perform four different actions: select an element, throw an element chosen, test the configuration and phone. One phone call is necessary for each element chosen.

The subject is given a text describing the problem and is asked to think aloud while performing the task on a computer program. We have collected one hundred fifty individual protocols: one hundred of them have been analyzed to build the model and the remainder has been put aside for validation.

3 Protocol analysis and modeling

3.1 General behavior

Roughly speaking, the subject optimizes his/her actions as long as he/she is not in trouble and takes emergency measures when necessary. More precisely, when he/she does not meet obstacles, he/she organizes his/her activity. He/she chooses the elements of his/her Hi-fi system and manages his/her phone calls. That forces him to anticipate his/her resolution. However when an obstacle appears, the subject adopts a short-sighted reasoning and attempts to resolve the problem step by step. We distinguish several *phases* where the subject behaves differently according to his/her estimation of the situation.

Moreover the subject does not respect simultaneously all constraints of the problem. He/she can misunderstand or forget one of them or push it deliberately into the background of his/her activity.

Finally, the subject simplifies the problem insofar as he/she works on an abstraction of constraints called *criteria*.

3.2 The elements of the model

Phases. There are four different phases in the resolution differentiated by the subject estimation of the situation. These are "configuration building", "correction", "deadlock solving" and "test".

The configuration building phase is generally the longest in terms of actions. During it, the subject builds his/her Hi-fi system as long as he/she encounters no difficulty. When this happens, he/she can have two types of reaction:

On the one hand, the subject can be consider that there is simply constraint violation. He/she enters then a short correction phase in order to rectify his/her selection. On the other hand, if the subject thinks that the situation is a deadlock, he/she enters an deadlock solving phase. This consists in a restart of the resolution. This phase is short because it is only a starting point for a new configuration. The test phase is even shorter insofar as it boils down to perform a single "test" action. This ends the problem in case of success and leads to a correction or deadlock solving phase otherwise.

Criteria. The four phases constitute a first level of the protocol analysis. The criteria taken into account during the resolution form a second one. Four criteria have been highlighted in the protocols and the wording of the problem.

- *compatibility*: the subject focuses on the compatibility between the different elements he/she chooses,
- *price*: the subject takes care of the price of the elements,

– *availability*: the subject wants to check as soon as possible the availability of elements,
– *phone calls*: the subject controls the number of phone calls.

As already specified, the subject does not take in account all the criteria but only a subset that varies as new information comes along. This subset is called *state of mind*. It follows the evolution of the situation and its changes trigger modifications in the subject's behavior. In the deadlock solving or correction phases, the subject focuses entirely on the obstacle met. His/her state of mind is often restricted to criteria directly linked to its cause. However, when he/she enters a configuration building phase, he/she takes more criteria in account, which makes him anticipate on his/her resolution. His/her behavior is stable and his/her state of mind does not evolve very much.

Strategies. A first level of the criterion interpretation in the current phase is the strategy which describes the kind of action to undertake in priority (select or phone), and the kind of element to put forward (amplifier or component). The strategies are divided into two categories: those concerning elements and those concerning actions. We have identified seven different strategies:

– Strategies on elements
    1. configuration built on the amplifier,
    2. *multicompatible* configuration: components are picked to delay as much as possible the choice of the amplifier,
    3. no strategy.
– Strategies on actions
    4. select then phone,
    5. phone then select,
    6. phone and select simultaneously,
    7. no strategy.

The subject chooses a strategy in each category according to the current phase and to his/her state of mind. Strategies 3 and 7 apply when the subject's behavior appears disorganized or when the use of a particular strategy makes no sense.

Tactics. A second level of interpretation is the tactics which instanciate the elements on which the actions are performed. While strategies concern the type of element or action put forward by the subject, tactics provide the different ways to choose elements. We have recognized nineteen tactics, that are not listed here for the sake of brevity. Some of them allow to choose the amplifier (e.g. "amplifier compatible with the most components"), the components (e.g. "available components"), etc. Tactics depend on the strategies, the phase and the state of mind of the subject.

Observations. At a given time of the resolution, the state of the system is determined by a phase, a state of mind and the use of strategies instanciated by tactics. Any change to this state initiates a new *stage* depending on the observations made by the subject on data. These observations may concern the current configuration as a whole or a particular element.

In order to model the diversity of the behavior encountered, we must parameter the "personality" of the simulated subject. Thus, we have defined five features (thrifty, scatterbrained, opportunistic, systematic, good appraiser) taking values "not at all", "poor", "fair" and "a lot". Observations and choices are made partly according to these parameters.

4 Computer implementation

The system IGGY, currently being written in Common Lisp, implements the model using a *blackboard* architecture (Engelmore and Morgan, 1988) with a hierachical control (Terry, 1983). It includes a blackboard, domain specialists grouped in six families and control specialists (see figure 1).

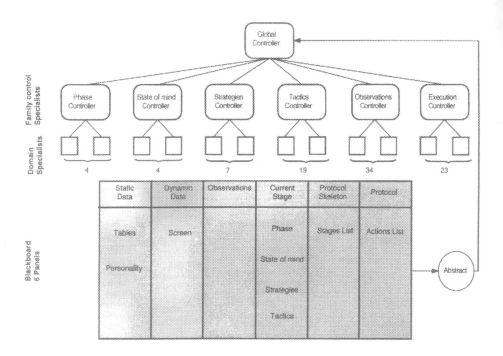

Fig. 1. Architecture used

The blackboard. It includes six thematic panels: the static parameters of the problem, the dynamic data of the problem, the current observations list, the current stage, the historic of the different stages of the resolution and the list of undertaken actions. An *abstract* updated at each change on the blackboard informs the system on the nature of the last event.

Domain specialists. They are grouped in six families. Each one represents a possible choice in his/her family and is represented as "condition/action" rules.

Control specialists. In each family, domain specialists are supervised by a control specialist, called family controller and also specified by condition/action rules.

A global controller supervises the system. At the beginning of the resolution, the global controller triggers the "observations" family that generates the writing of observations on the blackboard. Each stage of the resolution is achieved in the same way: "phase", "state of mind", "strategies" and "tactics" families are successively triggered depending on observations. Then comes the turn of the "execution" family to execute the current stage and to generate the protocol. For each action undertaken, the global controller triggers the "observations" family to check if everything is all right. In this case, the execution is carried on, else a new stage begins from the involved family.

5 Conclusion

We have shown that, in our problem, the subject plans under uncertainty. Our model based on the set phase, state of mind, strategies, tactics and observations is general enough to be applied to other applications. Indeed, the two kinds of situation ("normal" and "abnormal") appear in most problems with incomplete information.

It appears that artificial systems able to detect two degrees of abnormality (correction and deadlock) and to react without complex reasoning might, in some cases, be as efficient as more sophisticated systems.

References

Engelmore and Morgan, *Blackboard Systems*, Addison-Wesley Publishing Company, 1988.

Hayes-Roth and Hayes-Roth, "A cognitive model of planning", *Cognitive Science*, vol 3, 1979, pp. 275-310.

Newell and Simon, "GPS, a program that simulates human thought", in Feigenbaum, E. A. and Feldman, J. eds *Computers and Thought*, 1963, pp. 279-293.

Tate, Hendler and Drummond, "A review of AI planning techniques", in *Readings in planning*, Allen, Hendler et Tate, Morgan Kaufman Publishers, Inc, San Mateo, 1990, pp. 26-49.

Terry, "The CRYSALIS Project: Hierarchical Control of Production Systems", Technical Report HPP-83-19, Heuristic Programming Project, Computer Science Department, Stanford University, 1983.

Filtering Software Specifications Written in Natural Language

Núria Castell and Àngels Hernández

Universitat Politècnica de Catalunya, Departament de Llenguatges i Sistemes
Informàtics, Pau Gargallo, 5. Barcelona 08028. Spain

Abstract. The specification phase is one of the most important and
least supported part of the software development process. We have conceived SAREL (Assistance System for Writing Software Specification in
Natural Language) as a tool to improve the specification phase. SAREL
is a continuation of a program of research and development called LESD
(Linguistic Engineering for Software Design). The purpose of SAREL[1]
is to assist engineers in the creation of software specifications written in
natural language. It is divided into three modules: the first one controls
the requirement according to the writing norms, the second one obtains
a conceptual representation using the Knowledge Base, and the third one
carries out a series of optional analyses taking into account the following software quality properties: consistency, completeness, traceability,
verifiability and modifiability. Once a requirement has been labeled as
correct, its conceptual representation is added to the Requirements Base.

1 Introduction

The software development process starts generally with the specification phase.
At this stage it is very important to control the quality of specifications in order
to detect possible mistakes as early as possible. The correction of errors in the
development and implementation phases implies spending more time and effort
than in the specification phase. This is the reason why developers increasingly
try to identify possible mistakes in the early phases of software development.

During the initial phase, software specifications for complex systems result in
bulky documents since they are often written in natural language. Documentation writing is guided by norms which define the linguistic restrictions required
to satisfy the specifications. These norms are of two types: those relating to the
use of natural language in general (for example, [2] and [3]); and those that are
based on terminological restrictions related to a particular domain (for example,
the ESA - European Space Agency - norms). Both of them restrict the use of natural language through a set of rules which limit various irregularities (polysemy,
paraphrase, ambiguity, vagueness..). Even though the norms define linguistically
precise restrictions, the frequent failure to observe them makes it difficult for the
consequences of such breaches to be detected afterwards. In addition to linguistic restrictions, the norms also include Software Engineering constraints related

---

[1] This work is supported by CICYT (TIC93-420). email: castell,ahernandez@lsi.upc.es

to the quality factors of the specifications, such as consistency, completeness, traceability, modifiability and verifiability.

The purpose of the system we are developing (SAREL) is to assist engineers in writing specifications in natural language taking into account the writing norms and the software quality properties.

Other systems which tackle the problems associated with the specification phase are RA [13] [14], FRORL development system [17] and OICSI [11] [15]. The Requirements Apprentice (RA) assists a human analyst in the creation and modification of software requirements. The FRORL development system facilitates the specification, analysis and development of a software system. The OICSI is a system prototype that supports the analyst in the process of problem-statements acquisition, elicitation modelling and validation. Although the goals of the above systems vary slightly from SAREL system's goal, they form a reliable set of references for our research work. A comparative study can be found in [10].

In section 2, we describe our system (SAREL) in a general way. Sections 3, 4 and 5 describe each module of SAREL. The paper concludes with a discussion of the future goals of our research.

2 SAREL: an Assistance System for Writing Software Specifications in Natural Language

The SAREL system is a continuation of a program of research and development called LESD (Linguistic Engineering for Software Design). This project was instigated by the ARAMIIHS center in Toulouse (France) and was carried out by French and Spanish researchers. LESD aimed [4], [5], [16] to develop computational tools which would (1) allow conceptual interpretation of functional or preliminary software aerospace specifications written in English; (2) permit evaluation of quality factors by means of reasoning algorithms applied to the conceptual representation; and (3) help the engineers handle documentation.

In this context, the main goal of SAREL is to assist an engineer in the creation of software specifications written in natural language. To be exact, the specifications are written in English because this is the most common language in the aerospace domain (the LESD domain). The examples we present in this paper are taken from aerospace system documents. A preliminary version of our system was described in [10]. The assistance process, broken down into several steps, validates every requirement introduced by the engineer taking into account the writing norms (for instance [2], [3]) and the quality properties [9]. This process incrementally constructs a conceptual representation of the specification. The controls, shown in figure 1, can be grouped into three modules: the Style Refinement Module, the Conceptual Refinement Module and the Software Quality Control Module. Once a requirement has been checked and is correct, its conceptual representation is added to the Requirements Base.

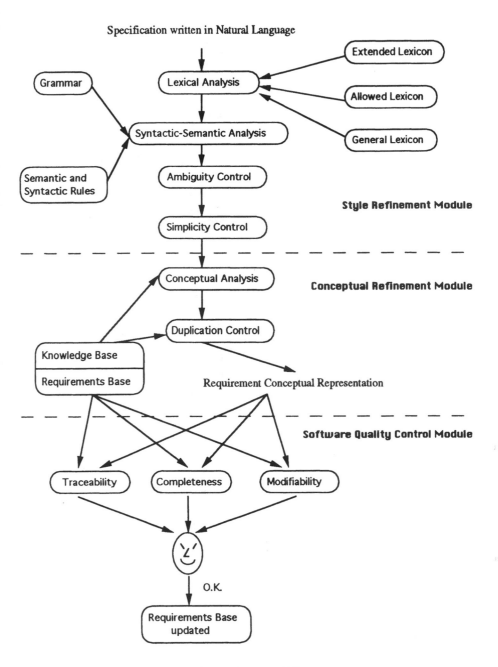

Fig. 1. The Modules of SAREL

3 Style Refinement Module

This module controls the requirement according to the writing norms and is broken down into four steps: lexical analysis, syntactic-semantic analysis, ambiguity control and simplicity control. This module first controls the lexicon used in a requirement, then analyses its coherence and finally validates its surface form.

3.1 Lexical Analysis

This analysis carries out the control of lexicon used in the specification. Given a requirement, the lexical analysis verifies that the words belong to the application domain lexicon. To do so, SAREL uses three different lexicons:

- The extended lexicon includes all words related to the application domain.
- The allowed lexicon is an extraction of the previous one. Every word in the allowed lexicon represents a set of synonyms on the extended one.
- The general lexicon contains general English words.

Firstly the analyzer will ensure that all words contained in the requirements belong to one of the three lexicons. After that, all words belonging to the extended lexicon will be substituted by synonyms from the allowed lexicon. The lexicon division offers the engineer some kind of writing flexibility, because he can use an extended lexicon instead of the allowed lexicon which is more restrictive.

At present we are adapting an On-line Lexical Database (WordNet) [12] to the aerospace domain in order to build the above lexicons. But the lexical validation process is independent of the application domain.

3.2 Syntactic-semantic Analysis

In this step, the Alvey parser [6] is used. This parser is based on Montague's logic and its output is a tree-like semantic representation. This environment has been modified and adapted to the aerospace domain and it provides satisfactory results.

Although semantic rules are associated with syntactic ones, the GDE (Grammar Development Environment) is not able to capture the whole meaning of a requirement and a conceptual analysis must subsequently be performed.

3.3 Ambiguity Control

It is possible to obtain more than one semantic representation from a requirement. This situation appears when the requirement contains some kind of ambiguity. The goal here is to identify the representation which corresponds to the engineer's idea. For example the requirement "*The AEROS will monitor the computer on-board and the status of the space-vehicle*" can give rise to two possible interpretations:

a) "*The AEROS will monitor the computer on-board the space-vehicle and the AEROS will monitor the status of the space vehicle*"

b) *"The AEROS will monitor the computer on-board and the AEROS will monitor the status of the space vehicle"*

The ambiguity controller applies a series of rules to the set of semantic representations in order to qualify them. An example of a possible rule is the one which asserts that the preposition *of* is always related only with the last nominal group. This controller cooperates with the engineer to select the correct semantic representation.

3.4 Simplicity Control

One of the properties expressed by the writing norms is simplicity. From the semantic representation of the requirement the controller detects whether the structure of the sentence is simple or compound. The following requirement does not have this property.

Req.: *"The AEROS will control the computer on-board the space-vehicle and the AEROS will control the automatic systems of the flight configuration"*

If the requirement is composed of two simple requirements, the validation process can continue with these two in a sequential way.

4 Conceptual Refinement Module

This module validates the requirement in relation to the Requirements Base (RB). At first it obtains a conceptual representation using the Knowledge Base (KB). Both RB and KB use a frame-based formalism [16]. From the conceptual representation this module detects duplicated information. At present we have already defined the Knowledge Base, and the Requirements Base is manually incremented when requirements have been analysed. The automatic process to integrate requirements is still at a development phase.

4.1 Conceptual Analysis

This analysis identifies in the Knowledge Base those entities involved in the semantic representation and constructs the requirement conceptual representation. Figure 2, from [16], shows the conceptual representation of two requirements:

Req-1: *"The AEROS will monitor the systems of the space-vehicle"*
Req-2: *"The AEROS will control the automatic systems of the space-vehicle"*

4.2 Duplication Control

The function of the duplication controller is to verify that the requirement introduced by the engineer contains new information. To do so, it matches the requirement conceptual representation to the Requirements Base in order to discover possible duplications. The following example shows a set of equivalent requirements since the system obtains the same conceptual representation for them.

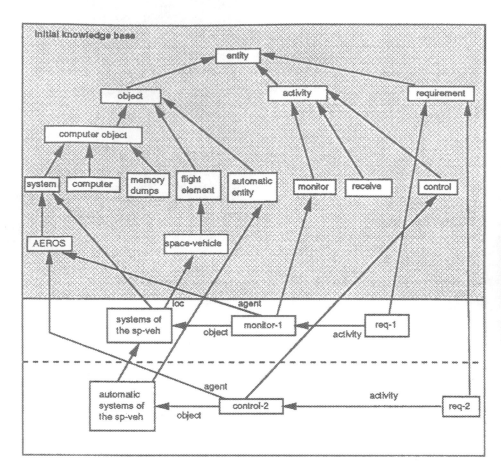

Fig. 2. Conceptual Representation

Req-1: "*The AEROS will monitor the computer on-board the space-vehicle*"
Req-2: "*The computer on-board the space-vehicle will be monitored by the AEROS*"
Req-3: "*In the space-vehicle, the computer on-board will be monitored by the AEROS*"
Req-4: "*The computer on-board the space-vehicle will be monitored*"

At first the duplication controller searches on the Requirements Base all requirements containing the activity which appears on the new requirement. All of them will be tested in order to discover if both the agent and object are the same. When the controller detects duplication, it will offer the engineer the possibility of refining it.

5 Software Quality Control Module

This module carries out a series of optional analyses which validate the global Requirements Base incremented with the new requirement. The goal is to offer information about the software quality properties which have been considered most relevant in LESD (*completeness, traceability, consistency, verifiability* and *modifiability*).

Once a requirement has been validated and the information about software quality has been presented to the engineer, he decides if the conceptual representation of requirements must be added to the Requirements Base. This process incrementally constructs the conceptual representation of the specification written in natural language.

Taking into account that these analyses are optional, the engineer could decide not to use them (it is a normal decision when adding the first requirements). In any case these modules can be used in the future to control the global quality software specification at that point. The analyses related to the quality properties already studied are described in the following paragraphs.

5.1 Analysis of Traceability

The goal here is to provide the engineer with information about the traceability links of the requirement. To do so, SAREL activates a set of existing algorithms [16] which control the traceability in order to show the relationships between the introduced requirement and a subset of requirements of the RB (either more specific or more general). From this information the engineer can see the relationships between requirements introduced up to this point. From the next requirement :

Req-1: *"The AEROS will receive the data of the space vehicle"*
the system displays, among others, the following more general requirement:

Req-2: *"The system will monitor the data of the space vehicle"*

The second requirement is more general than the first because AEROS is the main instance of "system" and "receive" is part-of "monitor".

The lack of links shows that the requirement is isolated in relation to the rest of requirements.

5.2 Analysis of Completeness

At this stage SAREL activates reasoning mechanisms which are being developed [1] taking into account several aspects of completeness. In order to control completeness, it is necessary to have available a general hierarchy of actions-subactions that can be associated to any set of specifications related with an aerospace system. An example of this hierarchy is present in the activity *monitor*, which comprises three subactivities: *receive, analyse* and *display*. Given the next requirement:

Req.: *"During the launch phase, the AEROS will analyse and display the status of the space vehicle"* taking into account the hierarchy described above, the system analyses the relationships among requirements in the Requirements Base. If there is no requirement containing the *monitor* activity, it will inform the engineer. In the same way, if the system notices that there is a requirement that contains the *monitor* activity but there is no requirement containing the subactivities in the hierarchy, it will inform the engineer that the current specification could be incomplete.

5.3   Analysis of Modifiability

The complexity and consistency of future modifications of software specifications depends on the level of propagation of a given modification in all requirements affected by that modification. The concept of modifiability in LESD has been formalized [7] [8] according to the levels of interconnection between the specifications requirements. The range of possible values is [0..1], but the range of acceptable values is a subinterval of this. In case the obtained measure does not fall within this second range, the engineer must study a possible problem of excessive or insufficient interconnection.

6   Conclusion and Future Research

Our research deals with the control of quality in specifications written in natural language. Since the specification phase is performed by a human analyst, we have designed an assistance system for writing software specifications in natural language. The quality of the specification is studied from two points of view: writing norms and software quality properties.

The assistance process is divided into three modules: the Style Refinement Module, the Conceptual Refinement Module and the Software Quality Control Module. Once a requirement has been validated by these modules, it is added to the Requirements Base. During this process we incrementally obtain a conceptual representation of the specification.

In order to exhaustively develop our system, future research work will be focused on a) designing an automatic mechanism which provides Conceptual Representations from Semantic Representations, b) developing semiautomatic mechanisms which build domain Knowledge Bases from technical documents, and c) defining the validation process of the obtained Knowledge Base. Moreover, the study of selected quality factors will continue.

References

1. Alvarez J., Castell N. "An Approach to the Control of Completeness Based on MetaKnowledge", Technical report, LSI-94-50-R Dept. of LSI, Universitat Politècnica de Catalunya, 1994.
2. ANSI/IEEE Std 729-1983. *IEEE Guide to Software Requirements Specifications* 1983.

3. Association Européene des Constructeurs de Matériel Aéronautique. *AECMA Simplified English, A Guide for the preparation of aircraft maintenance documentation in the international aerospace maintenance language*, December 1989.

4. Borillo M., Borillo A., Castell N., Latour D., Toussaint Y., Verdejo M.F. "Applying Linguistic Engineering to Software Engineering: The traceability problem". In *Proceedings of the European Conference on Artificial Intelligence (ECAI92)*, pages 593-595, Viena, Austria, August 1992.

5. Borillo M., Toussaint Y., and Borillo A. "A. Motivations du project LESD". In *Conference on Linguistic Engineering'91*, Versailles, France, January 1991.

6. Briscoe T., Grover C., Boguraev B., Carroll J. "The ALVEY Natural Language Tools Project Grammar: A Large Computational Grammar". Technical report, ALVEY Documents, Cambridge Univ., Computer Laboratory, UK, 1987.

7. Castell N., Slavkova O. "The Modifiability Factor in the LESD Project: Definition and Practical Results", Technical report, LSI-95-7-R Dept. of LSI, Universitat Politècnica de Catalunya, 1993.

8. Castell N., Slavkova O. "Metrics for Quality Factors in the LESD Project". In 5th European Software Engineering Conference (ESEC'95), Sitges, Spain, 1995.

9. Castell N., Slavkova O., Toussaint Y. and Tuells A. "Quality Control of Software Specifications written in Natural Language". In *Proceedings of the Seventh International Conference on Industrial and Engineering Applications of Artificial Intelligence and Expert Systems (IEA/AIE'94)*, Austin, Texas, USA, 1994.

10. Hernández, A. "SAREL: An assistance system for writing software specifications in natural language". In *Proceedings of the IBERAMIA'94*, ISBN 980-6168-16-X Caracas, Venezuela, 1994.

11. Jarke M., Bubenko J., Rolland C., Sutcliffe A. and Vassiliou J. "Theory Underlying Requirement Engineering: An Overview of NATURE at Genesis". In *Proceedings of the IEEE International Symposium on Requirements Engineering (RE'93)*, San Diego, California, USA, 1993.

12. Miller, G.A. "Wordnet: A Dictionary Browser" in *Information in Data, Proceedings of the First Conference of the UW Centre for the New Oxford Dictionary*, Waterloo, Canada: University of Waterloo. 1985.

13. Reubenstein H.B. and Waters R.C. "The Requirements Apprentice: Automated Assistance for Requirements Acquisition". *IEEE Transactions on Software Engineering*, 17:226-240, 1991.

14. Rich C. and Waters R.C. *The Programmer's Apprentice*. Reading, MA: Addison-Wesley, and Baltimore, MD. ACM Press, 1990.

15. Rolland C., Proix C. *A Natural Language Approach for Requirements Engineering"*. Conceptual Modeling, Databases and CASE: An Integrated View of Information Systems Development, P. Loucopoulos, R. Zicari (eds.) WILEY, 1992.

16. Toussaint Y. *Méthodes Informatiques et Linguistiques pour l'Aide a la Spécification de Logiciel*. PhD thesis, Universidad Paul Sabatier, Toulouse, 1992.

17. Tsai J.P., Weigert T. and Jang H.C. "A Hybrid Knowledge Representation as a Basis of Requirement Specification and Specification Analysis". *IEEE Transactions on Software Engineering*, 18:1076-1100, 1992.

Parsimonious Diagnosis in SNePS

Pedro A. de Matos and João P. Martins

Secção de Sistemas/DEM,
Instituto Superior Técnico,
Technical University of Lisbon,
1096 Lisboa Codex, Portugal

Abstract. Kernel Diagnosis has been developed to overcome some problems found in Diagnosis from First Principles. Although the results obtained when using the Kernel Diagnosis method are not incorrect, this method is not parsimonious in the sense that every diagnosis must be computed in order to find the Kernel Diagnoses. The method we have developed re-introduces the parsimony criteria in the computation of the Kernel Diagnosis. According to our method the computation of every possible diagnosis is no longer needed and, therefore, the computation of the diagnoses may become greatly simplified. After presenting our method, we briefly introduce the SNePS Semantic Network and we present an implementation of the method based in SNePS.
Keywords: Automatic diagnosis and common sense reasoning.

1 Introduction

The purpose of this paper is to present a diagnosis method called Parsimonious Diagnosis that was developed in [5]. This method is the result of adding the parsimony criteria to Kernel Diagnosis [4]. The parsimony criteria formalizes the common sense rule *"a diagnosis that explains a failure by assuming the fault of a set of components is better than a diagnosis that assumes the fault of a superset of those components"*. The main result achieved by adding the parsimony criteria to Kernel Diagnosis is that we no longer need to find *all* the possible diagnoses to characterize the interesting ones.

Before we present our approach, we discuss its ancestor methods, Reiter's Diagnosis from First Principles (Sect. 2), where only knowledge about correct behavior is used, and Kernel Diagnosis (Sect. 3), where knowledge about failure behavior is also used. Parsimonious Diagnosis is then presented in Sect. 4. In Sect. 5 we discuss an implementation of Parsimonious Diagnosis in SNePS and in Sect. 6 we present an example using SNePS [1].

2 Diagnosis from First Principles

In this section we briefly present Diagnosis from First Principles (henceforth, DFFP) [6]. We show the need for Kernel Diagnosis by presenting an example where DFFP fails.

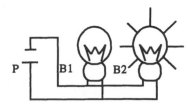

Fig. 1. Two light bulbs and one light power supply

To perform a diagnosis using DFFP we must have a model of the system describing its topology, the correct behavior of its components, and the set of measurements made. From this model, assuming that the components are ok, we compute the system's expected outputs. If we observe a difference between the expected values and the measured values, we conclude that some of the components have failed. We can use a TMS [2] to identify these components.

Unfortunately, this simple approach sometimes fails. Consider, for example (adapted from [7]), a system that has a power supply, P, connected in parallel to two light bulbs, B_1 and B_2 (see Fig. 1). It is known that "If a light bulb is working properly then it is on if and only if there is voltage". One of the light bulbs is on and the other is not. From this description, we would expect both light bulbs to be on, if they were working properly. From the observation that B_1 is not on but B_2 is on we conclude that B_1 is not working properly.

DFFP produces rather strange results for this example. The method proposes two diagnoses, $\{Ok(P), \neg Ok(B_1), Ok(B_2)\}$ and $\{\neg Ok(P), Ok(B_1), \neg Ok(B_2)\}$. Obviously, the last diagnosis is incorrect. The reasoning follows like this: If both P and B_1 are working properly then B_1 should be on. Since it isn't, we can conclude that at least one of P or $B1$ is not ok. If we assume that P is working properly then B_1 is not (otherwise B_1 would be on). On the other hand, if B_1 is working properly then the reason why it is not on is that there is no voltage, the power supply has failed. Since the power supply has failed, B_2 should not be lighted, but it is. Therefore, it must be the case that B_2 is also faulty!

The reason for this behavior is that DFFP has not used all the knowledge we have used about what happens when a bulb and a power supply fail.

3 Kernel Diagnosis

Kernel Diagnosis [4] solves the problems described by adding to the system's model knowledge of what happens when components fail.

The fundamental difference between the Kernel Diagnosis and DFFP is that we use the description of how components fail. For example, if we add the propositions "An improperly working light bulb will never be on" and "An improperly working power supply doesn't produce voltage" it will be possible to deduce that both P and B_2 are working correctly. The incorrect diagnosis is, then, discarded.

To compute Kernel Diagnosis we need the concept of a world. A *world* is defined to be a set of assumptions about the working status of the components of a system, containing one assumption for each component. An assumption, in this context, is the statement that the component is either faulty or ok. In the previous example, $\{Ok(P), Ok(B_1), Ok(B_2)\}$ is a world. A *possible world* is a world that is consistent with the measurements made. Given a world and the inputs of a system, we can predict the output of every component. If we measure the outputs of some components and if they contradict the expected value, then this is not a possible world. If we use a TMS, we can find which are the components responsible for these outputs. We know, then, that the assumptions raised about how these components work cannot be correct, that is, we know that a certain subset of the world's assumptions is inconsistent. Any world that is a superset of an inconsistent set of assumptions is not a possible world. If we can identify all inconsistent sets of assumptions, we know which worlds are possible worlds and which worlds are not.

Let us now suppose that there is a component C that is not responsible for any of the measured values. Clearly, whether C is working or not is irrelevant. Therefore, there is a diagnosis where it is assumed that the component C is working, and there is another diagnosis, exactly like it except for C that is supposed to be faulty. If we remove the assumption regarding the component C, the set thus obtained will be called a partial diagnosis. We generalize this idea in the following definition: For any component C, if there is a diagnosis (or a partial diagnosis) PD_1 such that $PD_1 = \Delta \cup \{Ok(C)\}$, where Δ is a set of assumptions that doesn't contain any assumption about the working status of C, and there is another $PD_2 = \Delta \cup \{\neg Ok(C)\}$ we may represent both diagnoses (or partial diagnoses) by the partial diagnosis Δ.

Some partial diagnoses are of special interest and are called Kernel Diagnoses. A *Kernel Diagnosis* is a minimal partial diagnosis in the sense that none of its strict subsets is also a partial diagnosis.

4 Parsimonious Diagnosis

In this section we present another diagnosis method, the Parsimonious Diagnosis method. Parsimonious Diagnoses are the possible worlds that satisfy the parsimony criteria, a criteria that rejects every possible world whose faulty assumptions contain a superset of the faulty assumptions of another possible world. We don't need to know the set of possible worlds in order to find the Parsimonious Diagnoses, and, therefore, we no longer have to find all the conflicting sets of assumptions, the hard part of finding Kernel Diagnoses.

Let C_1 and C_2 be two components of a system. Suppose that some measurements have been made and that the failure of C_1 explains the measurements. Suppose furthermore that there is another diagnosis that explains the same measurements by assuming that C_1 and C_2 are not working properly. The second diagnosis is proposed because we haven't yet made all the possible measurements; otherwise, we would know which components were working properly and which were not, and there would only be one diagnosis. Since there are additional measurements that could have been made, there must exist possible worlds that represent every possible outcome. Common sense tells us that it is not usual that many components fail at the same time and if we can explain the measurements by assuming the malfunction of a subset of those components we should prefer this explanation. This is why the first diagnosis is preferred to the second diagnosis. This is the idea that is captured by the parsimony criteria.

To compute Kernel Diagnoses we must know the set of possible worlds (Kernel Diagnoses are representations of all possible worlds). We can find out which worlds are possible worlds if we know all the conflicting sets of assumptions. All the worlds that are supersets of any conflicting set of assumptions are known to be inconsistent with the measurements and cannot represent possible worlds. Once we know the possible worlds, we can select the Parsimonious Diagnoses.

There is, however, an alternative way to compute the Parsimonious Diagnoses that avoids, in some cases, the need to know all the conflicting sets of assumptions. This is not surprising if we remember that we are not interested in computing all the possible worlds but only some of them, namely the parsimonious possible worlds. The method is similar to the method proposed in [3]. We proved [5] that, given a set of inconsistent sets of assumptions, if the parsimonious worlds that are not supersets of any of the inconsistent sets of assumptions are possible worlds (that is, if they are consistent with all the observations) then they are the Parsimonious Diagnoses. Notice that if a parsimonious world that is not a superset of any of the inconsistent sets of assumptions discovered so far is found to be inconsistent with the observations then a new set of inconsistent assumptions has been found. The process must be repeated, updating the set of inconsistent sets of assumptions, until all parsimonious worlds that are not supersets of any of the inconsistent sets of assumptions known so far are consistent with the observations. In the worst case, all conflicting sets of assumptions will be found. There are cases, however, in which there are some conflicting sets of assumptions that don't need to be computed because the worlds that are their supersets are not parsimonious.

5 An implementation in SNePS

In order to perform diagnosis we must use a TMS. We decided to use SNePS as a basis for building our diagnosis system because it has an ATMS incorporated. We will briefly introduce SNePS and describe some changes that were made to SNePS to use the Parsimonious Diagnosis method. These changes concern both a new kind of node, the assumption node, and the definition of new commands.

SNePS is a semantic network with reasoning capabilities. Nodes represent intensional concepts and labeled arcs represent relations between concepts. These arcs are introduced by the user when building the network or built by the system when inference is drawn. A node introduced by the user is called a hypothesis. Each node has associated a set of supports that represent reasons for the node to be believed. Each support has two kinds of information: the origin set, which is a set of hypotheses that underly the derivation of the node, and the origin tag, which tells whether the proposition was derived by the system or introduced by the user. Given the set of hypotheses and, for each node, the set of supports, we may determine whether a node is believed or not. The set of believed nodes is called a belief space. The SNePS belief revision system, SNeBR, uses this information to detect contradictions. A node that belongs to the current belief space is represented by the node label followed by an exclamation mark "!".

To produce diagnoses we must be able to deal with assumptions. We've added the possibility of representing assumptions in SNePS. An assumption is weaker than a hypothesis in the sense that if a contradiction is found and an assumption is involved, we drop the assumption, after recording the inconsistency. Without assumptions, a contradiction requires the user to change the current context. An assumption is represented by two nodes, the assumption node and the assumed node. The assumption node is introduced as a hypothesis and the assumed node is believed as a consequence. An assumption is raised by the command (assume <node>). In our example, we use the case frame MEMBER/CLASS to represent membership of a class. The representation of the input and output value of a component is done by the case frames COMP/IN and COMP/OUT, in which the arc COMP points to the component and the arc IN (or OUT) points to the value of its input (or output). Since the input (or output) of a component is a function of that component, a node representing that the input of a component is zero is inconsistent with a node representing that the input of the same component is one. The command (function-application <function> <arg>) tells SNePS that a contradiction should be found whenever there are two nodes (Mx! (<function> $value_1$>) (<arg> <argument>)) and (My! (<function> $value_2$>) (<arg> <argument>)), with $value_1 \neq value_2$.

There are two types of inference in SNePS: node-based or path-based inference. In the first type, there are nodes that represent deduction rules and other nodes that represent facts and derived nodes are built by applying the inference rules of the underlying logic. In the second, the idea is to substitute a path of labeled arcs that connects two nodes by another labeled arc. Orthogonally, SNePS may perform either forward or backward inference. The command new-measurement receives, as arguments, the descriptions of the nodes representing the measured values. Forward inference is then performed with those nodes. The command pars-diagnosis executes the cycle previously described to find the Parsimonious Diagnoses.

6 An example

We now present an example of Parsimonious Diagnosis. There are three inverters connected in serial, I1, I2 and I3 (see Fig. 2). The output of I1 is connected to the input of I2, and the output of I2 is connected to the input of I3. Three measurements have been made: I1's input and output are both ONE and I3's output is also ONE. The kernel diagnoses are $\{\neg Ok(\text{I1}), Ok(\text{I2}), Ok(\text{I3})\}$ and $\{\neg Ok(\text{I1}), \neg Ok(\text{I2}), \neg Ok(\text{I3})\}$. What we claim is that the last diagnosis

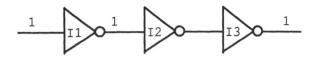

Fig. 2. Three inverters

is not based in common sense. The reason for this claim is that abnormalities are unusual. We should not consider abnormalities unless we are "forced to" in face of evidence. In this example, we are not "forced to" consider that the three components are faulty because assuming that component I1 is would explain the measurements. Using the parsimony criteria the proposed diagnosis is $\{\neg Ok(\text{I1}), Ok(\text{I2}), Ok(\text{I3})\}$. The other non-parsimonious diagnosis is discarded.

We start by telling SNePS[1] what representations are function applications, the components that exist in our circuit, and its topology. And we assume that all the inverters are ok. This is done by the following commands:

```
(function-application in comp)
(function-application out comp)
(function-application what suposedtobe)
(assert member i1 class inverter)
(assert member i2 class inverter)
(assert member i3 class inverter)
(assert comp i2 conn i1)
(assert comp i3 conn i2)
(assume suposedtobe i1 what ok)
(assume suposedtobe i2 what ok)
(assume suposedtobe i3 what ok)
```

Next, we use the command **new-measurement** to describe the measurements we have made.

```
(new-measurement (comp i1 in one) (comp i1 out one) (comp i3 out one)))
```

As result of this command, SNePS shows the inferences drawn which include (M14! (COMP I1) (OUT ONE)) and (M15! (COMP I1) (OUT ZERO)). These two nodes generate a contradiction. Since M15 was based on the assumption that I1 is ok, the set containing this assumption is added to the set of inconsistent sets of assumptions. The next command triggers the computation of the parsimonious diagnosis. From the inconsistent sets of assumptions found so far, $\{\{Ok(\text{I1})\}\}$, it is easily seen that $\{\neg Ok(\text{I1}), Ok(\text{I2}), Ok(\text{I3})\}$ is the only parsimonious world. Since the parsimonious world doesn't contain any of the inconsistent sets of assumptions found so far and it is consistent with the measurements, the parsimonious world is the parsimonious diagnosis.

---

[1] Due to lack of space, path descriptions, which describe the behavior of the inverters, and some other aspects were not described.

```
(pars-diagnosis)
Parsimonious diagnoses
(((M10! (ASSUME (M9! (SUPOSEDTOBE I2) (WHAT OK))))
  (M12! (ASSUME (M11! (SUPOSEDTOBE I3) (WHAT OK))))
  (M25! (ASSUME (M24! (SUPOSEDTOBE I1) (WHAT NOT-OK)))))))
```

7 Conclusions

We have developed and implemented a method for performing diagnosis, named
Parsimonious Diagnosis, that re-introduces the parsimony criteria used in Reiter's DFFP. We claim that Kernel Diagnosis is not common sense reasoning
because the diagnoses obtained by this method are unnatural, as they assume
more abnormalities than necessary. We have presented an example of such a
case. This problem was solved with the re-introduction of the parsimony criteria, which lead to the development of the Parsimonious Diagnosis. Using this
method, it may no longer be necessary to identify the whole set of inconsistent
sets of assumptions, the hard part of finding the Kernel Diagnoses, but only the
inconsistent sets necessary to find the Parsimony Diagnoses.

8 Acknowledgements

We would like to thank all the members of the Artificial Intelligence Group of
IST for their comments and support, in particular M.R. Cravo for suggesting
the use of common sense to perform diagnosis and João Cachopo for providing
LaTeX support. We would also like to thank Stu Shapiro for his helpful comments
on an earlier version of this paper. This work has been partially supported by
JNICT under Grant PMCT/C/TIT/176/90 and by IDMEC.

References

1. Martins, J. P., Shapiro, S. C., "A Model for Belief Revision", *Artificial Intelligence*
   35, pp. 25–79, 1988.
2. Martins, J. P., "Belief Revision", *Encyclopedia of Artificial Intelligence*, vol. 1, S.
   C. Shapiro (ed.), John Willey & Sons, pp. 58–62, 1987.
3. de Kleer, J., Williams, B. C., "Diagnosing Multiple Faults", *Artificial Intelligence*
   32, pp. 97–130, 1987.
4. de Kleer, J., Macworth, A. K., Reiter, R., "Characterizing Diagnoses", *Proc. AAAI-
   90*, pp. 324–330, 1990.
5. Matos, P. A., *Diagnóstico Parcimonioso: Um Método de Detecção de Falhas.* Master's Thesis. Lisbon, Portugal: Instituto Superior Técnico, Technical University of
   Lisbon, 1992.
6. Reiter, R., "Theory of Diagnosis from the First Principles", *Artificial Intelligence*
   32, pp. 57–95, 1987.
7. Struss, P., Dressler, O., "Physical Negation - Integrating Fault Models into the
   General Diagnostic Engine", *Proc. IJCAI-89*, pp. 1318–1323, 1989.

Syntactic and Semantic Filtering in a Chart Parser

Sayan Bhattacharyya[1] and Steven L. Lytinen[2]

[1] University of Michigan, Dept. of Electrical Engineering & Computer Science,
Ann Arbor, MI 48109, USA
[2] DePaul University, Dept. of Computer Science, 243 S. Wabash,
Chicago, IL 60604, USA

Abstract. This paper describes a method to enhance the performance of a unification-style bottom-up chart parser by means of top-down filtering techniques. The filter developed consists of a syntactic module which prevents the construction of redundant edges in the chart by ensuring that a proposed edge in the chart can really be syntactically combined with neighboring edges later, and a semantic module which ensures that the semantic information in a proposed edge in the chart is compatible with semantic information in other edges.

1 Introduction

Chart parsers used in natural language processing parse an input sentence by building up a data structure called the chart. A chart is a network of vertices representing points in the sentence which are linked by edges which represent constituents of the sentence. In a unification-style chart parser [5] the chart is augmented step by step by adding pieces of description according to the grammar. Each partial description added remains in the chart and serves to constrain the possibilities for further augmentation. In LINK, a bottom-up unification-style chart parser described by Lytinen [3], a directed acyclic graph (DAG) is built to represent the analysis of a sentence. Edges built by LINK are labeled by DAGs incorporating syntactic as well as semantic information. New edges are added to the chart by applying unification rules. This guarantees that the new constituent added to the parse has the necessary syntactic and semantic features. We present a way of integrating bottom-up parsing with top-down parsing, both in terms of syntax and semantics. Our approach can be described as bottom-up parsing with top-down filtering. We modified LINK using this approach. Similar approaches have been variously called in the literature a "filter" [1] and an "oracle" [4].

2 Necessity For Top-down Filtering Methods

In a top-down parser, parsing is rule-driven while in a bottom-up parser, parsing is data-driven. Thus in a top-down chart parser an active edge in the chart is sought to be expanded with all rules in the grammar which have the current symbol as the left-hand side, causing the parser to be over-productive in edge construction. In a bottom-up parser on the other hand only complete edges are combined, by the application of rules whose right hand sides correspond to the completed edges. A bottom-up parser is also over-productive because it will build some useless edges that cannot be combined with edges lying to the left or to the right. So top-down filtering is effective in a bottom-up parser by reducing the production of useless edges by checking whether the edge that is sought to be built has any chance of combining with an adjacent edge to form part of a larger edge. Making use of top-down information about the semantic context as well can help to reduce redundancy by anticipating and blocking out unlikely choices.

3 Implementing the Filter

Ordinarily, LINK traverses the input sentence from left to right, building up possible edges as it does so. At the outset, during the initialisation of the chart, link-building is a strictly left-to-right process. After chart initialisation (after all word-level, i.e. primitive, edges have been built), phrase-level edges will be attempted to be built, guided by the heuristic that edges will be first sought to be constructed out of previously unused edges. (Thus phrase-level edge construction may not always occur strictly from left to right.)

3.1 Syntactic Component of the Filter

Chart Initialisation. The objective of initialising the chart is to build edges around each word in the input sentence. For each word of the input sentence, LINK was made to look up its corresponding lexical entry in the LINK lexicon to check for possible syntactic ambiguity, ambiguity being defined here as the existence of multiple definitions belonging to different syntactic categories. If no syntactic ambiguity is detected for the candidate word, LINK is allowed to proceed to build edge(s) around the word in the ordinary way. On the other hand, if syntactic ambiguity is detected, then for each candidate syntactic category a check is made on the chart constructed so far to determine whether a valid left-adjacent predecessor exists. The edge is constructed only if such a left-predecessor exists.

Constructing the Complete Chart. The objective is to build progressively larger edges, combining words into phrases and phrases into increasingly larger phrases until an edge is ultimately constructed which spans across the entire sentence and corresponds to a complete parse. Link construction is an iterative process that continues until the parse is complete or until there are no further edges in the chart that can be constructed. At each step of the iterative process, the chart is examined from left to right to check if there is a constituent sequence of edges that unify with the right-hand-side of a grammar rule. For the first sequence so obtained, it is checked whether there exists any left-adjacent phrase contiguous to the candidate phrase for which the edge is being sought to be built that corresponds to a syntactic category which is a valid predecessor of the syntactic category of the proposed candidate edge. The attempt to build the edge is abandoned if such a left-adjacent phrase does not exist. If such a left-adjacent phrase does exist, a similar check is carried out for right-adjacency. However, as in general it is not guaranteed that a complete non-primitive right-adjacent edge will exist (because of the left-to-right nature of the parsing process) the right-adjacency check is limited to checking the existence of only valid right-adjacent *words* (i.e. primitive edges) and not valid right-adjacent *phrases* (i.e. non-primitive edges). A edge will be finally built if and only if both the left-adjacency and right-adjacency checks are successful.

3.2 Semantic Component of the Filter

The task of the semantic filter is to perform word-sense disambiguation early on in the parse in order to prevent construction of edges in the chart which correspond to word-senses which are apparently irrelevant in the given context. This is expected to lead to considerable savings as word-sense ambiguity is a big source of parsing inefficiency in most large applications; for example, Waltz [6] estimates that in English, on the average, each word has as many as 3.7 different senses.

LINK maintains a semantic hierarchy consisting of IS-A relationships between semantic categories. In order for the fillers of the slot of a certain semantic category to find something to unify with, either an entity belonging to the same semantic category of the slot filler, or an entity belonging to a descendant semantic category of the slot filler in the semantic hierarchy (not necessarily immediate descendant) must be present. Our strategy is to generate a table listing the valid semantic associates of every semantic category. The semantic associates of a semantic category would include all the slot-filler semantic categories for that semantic category and all the descendants of each slot-filler semantic category in the semantic hierarchy. Then, while parsing, as soon as an edge is sought to be built which would assign to an edge a particular semantic category, the table of valid semantic associates is looked up to determine if any valid semantic associate for that semantic category exists within the input sentence. If yes, the proposed edge is passed for construction (provided it is also passed by the syntactic component of the filter) and if not, the proposed edge is rejected. Thus a proposed edge must pass through both the syntactic and semantic filters before it is cleared for construction.

For example, for the semantic hierarchy shown in Figure 1 and the following semantic category definition:

PTRANS:

(actor) = ANIMATE

the table of semantic associates generated will be:

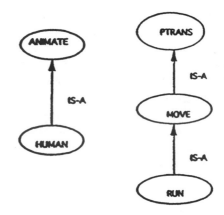

Fig. 1. An example semantic hierarchy

semantic category	semantic associates
PTRANS	ANIMATE MAN
MOVE	ANIMATE MAN
RUN	ANIMATE MAN
ANIMATE	PTRANS MOVE RUN
MAN	PTRANS MOVE RUN

As another example, consider the two sentences **John shot some bucks** and **John spent some bucks**. The word **bucks** is a source of ambiguity here. Syntactically, the two sentences are exactly alike, so that the syntactic component of the filter cannot help resolve the ambiguity. In the grammar that we used for this sentence, the word **shot** had the semantic category PROPEL and the word **spent** had the semantic category ATRANS. The word **bucks** had the choice of two semantic categories, ANIMAL and MONEY, among which it was necessary to disambiguate.

The semantic definitions of ATRANS, PROPEL, ANIMAL and MONEY were as follows:

ATRANS:

```
is-a (ACTION)
(actor)  = HUMAN
(object) = PHYS-OBJ
(from)   = HUMAN
```

PROPEL:

```
is-a (ACTION)
(object) = ANIMAL
```

MONEY:

```
is-a (PHYS-OBJ)
```

ANIMAL:

```
is-a (ANIMATE)
```

For our example grammar, the table of semantic associates had the following as entries for the semantic categories **ANIMAL** and **MONEY** after stepwise construction according to the aforementioned algorithm:

semantic category	semantic associates
ANIMAL	PROPEL PHYS-STATE
MONEY	POSSESSION ATRANS DIVIDE

Note that **ATRANS** was not a valid semantic associate of **ANIMAL** and **PROPEL** was not a valid semantic associate of **MONEY**. Thus, the edge corresponding to **MONEY** will not be built in the first sentence as no valid semantic associate of **MONEY** is present in the first sentence. Similarly the edge corresponding to **ANIMAL** will not be built in the second sentence.

Our method of semantic filtering is similar in some ways to some semantic disambiguation techniques described in the literature, such as the preference semantics used by Wilks [7] and the polaroid words technique described by Hirst [2].

4 Performance Issues

We measured the performance of our system (LINK with the filter described) *vis-a-vis* that of LINK without filter by parsing a set of forty-eight sentences, with a grammar that had been expressly written for the domain. Figure 2 shows the comparative performance improvement obtained by using the syntactic component of the filter. In this figure the ratio of rules applied during the parse for the two methods and the ratio of time needed to parse a sentence by the two methods have been plotted against the number of words per sentence. It can be seen that performance improvement appears to increase the longer is the input sentence. Figure 3 and Figure 4 show how the semantic component of the filter leads to a further improvement in performance for those sentences which can be parsed after the addition of the semantic filter. These two figures show the results of parsing a subset of 24 sentences from our domain.

Figure 3 compares the performance of the combined syntactic and semantic filter to that of the syntactic filter taken singly while Figure 4 separately compares the performance of the combined syntactic and semantic filter and the syntactic filter to the performance in the absence of any filter.

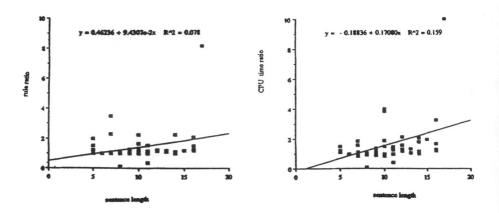

Fig. 2. (a) Plot of ratio of number of rules used by parser without filter to number of rules used with syntactic filter. (b) Plot of ratio of CPU time needed by parser without filter to CPU time needed with syntactic filter

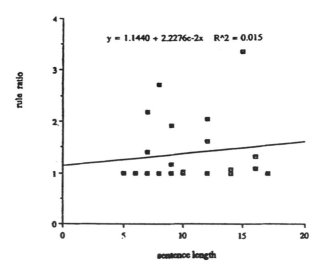

Fig. 3. Plot of ratio of number of rules used by parser with only syntactic filter to number of rules used with both syntactic and semantic filter.

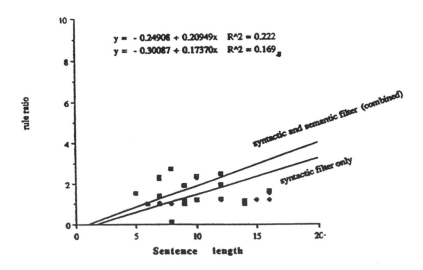

Fig. 4. Plot of ratio of number of rules used by parser with no filter to number of rules used by parser with both syntactic and semantic filters.(The plot of rule ratio improvement using syntactic filter only has also been shown for the sake of comparison)

References

1. Grishman, R.: Computational Linguistics. Cambridge University Press, Cambridge (1986)
2. Hirst, G.: Semantic Interpretation and the Resolution of Ambiguity. Cambridge University Press, Cambridge (1987)
3. Lytinen, S.L.: A unification-based integrated natural language processing system. Computers Math. Applic. Vol. **23**, no 6-9 (1992)
4. Pratt, V.: Lingol, a progress report. Advance Papers 4th Intl. Joint Conf. Artificial Intelligence **422-8** (1973).
5. Shieber, S.: An Introduction to Unification-Based Approaches to Grammar. Lawrence Erlbaum Associates, Hillsdale, NJ (1986).
6. Waltz, D.: Semantic Structures. Lawrence Erlbaum Associates, Hilldale, N.J. (1989)
7. Wilks, Y.: Preference Semantics. in E. Keenan, ed, Formal Semantics of Natural Language. Cambridge University Press, Cambridge (1975)

Any solution should, therefore, satisfy the following set of constraints:

$$\sum_{k=1}^{m} N^k = n$$ there are m routes, each supplying its subset of points N^k

$$\sum_{l=1}^{N^k} p^l \leq p_{\max}$$ the capacity of a single vehicle should not be exceeded

$$\min \sum_{i,j \in N^k} d_{ij} \leq d_{\max}$$ the maximum reach of a single vehicle should not be exceeded and each subtour N^k represents the Travelling Salesperson Problem

$$\min \sum_{k=1}^{m} (\min \sum_{i,j \in N^k} d_{ij})$$ the objective function

The previous algorithm, described in [2], used a decomposition approach. It decomposed the overall problem into m subproblems, namely TSPs, and then solved each TSP by very simple, but popular method described in [3]. Many m subsets, representing a complete solution, were investigated. The subsets were chosen in clockwise or counter-clockwise direction and some heuristic interchanges between two out of m subsets were made. The algorithm proved to be extremely time consuming and the quality of the final solution was merely sufficient. The global optimum could not be reached due to decompositon to relatively independent subsets that were separately investigated. Thus, the need for faster and more appropriate algorithm arose.

2 Genetic Algorithms

The genetic algorithms are a family of computational procedures that use randomly created initial population of solutions, commonly called the first generation, and direct it, over numerous generations, to an optimum through the use of evolution-like operators. The operators commonly used are selection, recombination and mutation. The selection ensures that better solutions get higher probability of being selected in the next generation. The recombination and mutation provide means of creating new individuals through exchanging the *genetic material* between the members of the current generation and by randomly introduced changes in a single individual. The experiences in solving the TSP are used in the Multiple Vehicle Routing Problem.

GA Approach to Solving Multiple Vehicle Routing Problem

Slavko Krajcar, Davor Skrlec, Branko Pribicevic, Snjezana Blagajac

University of Zagreb
Faculty of Electrical Engineering and Computing
Unska 3, 41000 Zagreb, Croatia
email: caddin@zvne.fer.hr

Abstract

Paper deals with the application of a genetic algorithm in the Multiple Vehicle Routing Problem. A short overview of a previously on-site developed algorithm is given. The genetic algorithm is developed on basis of experiences in solving the Travelling Salesperson Problem. A few heuristic improvements are added in order to prevent converging to local optima and to reduce the search domain. The performance of the algorithm is investigated on two configurations, and so is the influence of each genetic parameter on the algorithm's effectiveness. The final assessment is given in conclusion.

1 Introduction

The Multiple Vehicle Routing Problem is very common to technical as well as to non-technical fields, such as economical dispatch. It can be stated as follows:

There is a single supply point and n consumer points. If there are m vehicles, each of finite capacity and maximum reach, how to supply all consumer points at a minimum cost? The number of vehicles is not a constraint and each vehicle comes to and leaves the consumer point only once.

2.1 TSP genetic operators

Even though the Travelling Salesperson Problem is quite famous, its definition, for the sake of completiveness, is repeated here:

A salesperson has to visit N cities, starting at any city, visiting each city only once, and finally returning to the starting one. This route should be done at a minimum cost (time, length or any other measure of quality).

In developing different genetic operators suitable for use in TSP one can observe the tendency of increased preservation of critical paths; that in turn emphasizes the ability of the genetic operator to preserve most of parents' segments. In authors point of view an average inheritance rate less than 80% is unsufficient for a proper converging. Since the natural representation of the TSP is the decimal coding, although there have been atempts of using genetically classical binary representation, a short overview of decimal recombination operators is given.

Firstly, there are operators which use special kinds of reorderings in two randomly chosen parents. Most common are PMX (partially mapped crossing), OX (order crossing) and CX (cycle crossing) and their derivatives. In PMX, sections chosen in a certain manner (called the *mapping sections)* are exchanged between two individuals. Similarly, other two operators tend to acomplish simple and fast reordering along with the maximal rate of inheritance. There have been atempts to apply simple inversion in a randomly chosen segment. This approach proved to be suitable only if the positions of two neighbouring cities were substituted. The inversion of larger segments lead to the loss of critical paths. The *elitist* operator, works as follows [5]: the first city is chosen randomly, but the next city is chosen from the parent with the shortest path to previously chosen city. The procedure continues until the full path is completed. In case of a shortest path introducing already used path, any longer but legal path would do. There have been atempts [4] of introducing matrix representation of TSP in order to give subtler qualitative evaluation of solution, but they seem to be quite computationally burdensome. Finally, we have decided to use *edge recombination* operator for its adequacy in treating Multiple Vehicle Routing.

2.2 Edge Recombination Operator

The operator, considering edges between cities, was introduced in [7]. Let two parents be [A B C D E F] and [B D C A E F] (where capital letters represent cities). An *edge table* is formed in the following way:

A has edge to : B F C E   B has edge to : A C D F   C has edge to : B -D A

D has edge to : -C E B   E has edge to : D -F A   F has edge to : A -E B where negative are edges common to both parents. Note that edges **F-A** and **F-B** at the end of the tours are taken also into consideration. The new tour starts with a city **A** or **B**, which are both starting points in parent tours. Let **B** be randomly chosen. Now **B** must be wiped out from each city's table. The next point is chosen from the edge-table of city **B**. The problem encountered here was appearing of isolated cities which had not a single connecting city left in table. To avoid this shortcoming the city chosen must have a minimum of unused edges, and, along with that, the greatest probability of remaining isolated. Since only city **A** has 4 edges and **C D** and **F** have 3 edges each, one out of the last three cities must be chosen. Let **C** be the next one and wiped out from tables. There are two cities left **A** and **D**. Since **C-D** is a shared edge among two parents, city **D** has to be chosen no matter of unused edges left. Following aforementioned rules one possible solution is [**B C D E F A**]. In case of the edge-table being empty, a random point is chosen. It was reported that the inheritance rate was 95-99% which proved to be an excellent result.

3 Genetic algorithm used

Before any genetic action can take place, a certain preprocessing has to be done in order to reduce the search space. For each consumer point a set of the closest neighbouring consumer points is determined. The upper limit of the number of these points is determined as $2^{num\_closest} < n < 2^{num\_closest+1}$ (*n* being the number of configuration points). For the supply point the same set is determined, but with *num_closest*+2 or *num_closest*+1 members, because the starting point is the same for each route. Now one can start forming the initial population. A consumer point is randomly selected from the aforementioned set of the supply point. The next consumer point is chosen from the previous point's set of the closest points and the same procedure continues with this and any following route. The forming of the single route continues until a constraint on the maximum capacity or the maximum length of the route is violated. In case of previous point's set being empty, i.e. all points in the set have already been used, a random point out of remaining ones must be chosen.

Once the entire population is created and each member evaluated (i.e. overall cost depending on distances between points), a simple ranking is applied. The fitness function applied here is embedded in a ranking position of an individual. The member that represents the best solution becomes the first, and the worst solution comes to the last position. Since the aim of the selection process is to give priorities to better solutions, a function that randomly selects *upper* members with greater probability is required. The formula [6] of the function used is:

index_of_member = population_size*(bias - sqrt (bias*bias - 4.0*(bias - 1)* fracrand ())) / 2.0 / (bias - 1)
fracrand ( ) = ((double) random ( ) / 2 147 483 647)

where *random( )* is a 32-bit random number generator, while *bias* is a special parameter of the function. If *bias* is between 1.0 and 2.0 the selection function is linear, i.e. linearly distributed over the entire population in a manner that the best (the first one in the population) individual, with a value of 1.x for *bias*, gets x*100% higher probability of being selected than the worst one. For values of *bias* over 2.0 function gets nonlinear, i.e. good solutions are too frequently selected. It should be noted that values above 1.2 are not of practical use for the Multiple Vehicle Routing Problem. Low values for *bias* prevent the population to converge to local optima, by artificially prolonging the convergence process, since less good solutions are not cut off during early generations.

Once the two members are selected the edge operator is applied in order to form just one offspring (this procedure is known in literature as "one-at-the-time" recombination). If the previous point's edge-table is empty, a point out of the table of closest points should be used; otherwise completely random point is chosen. When a constraint on a maximum capacity of a vehicle is violated, the route is finished. If the *child* produced is better than the worst member of the current population, the child replaces it and ranking is applied again (unlike the typical procedure - replacing parents). The procedure continues until convergence. The population is said to converge when 90% of the population members represent the same solution or the arbitrarily prefixed number of generations is reached. Convergence is checked in steps of 100 generations.

4 Comparison and results

The tendency of incorporating lengthy edges was observed, but was effectively suppressed by using penalty function. The penalty function is supposed to be simple, so lengthy links received additional ponders. Therefore, the cost of such individuals was not real anymore, but adapted to the selection process. The algorithm was investigated in two configurations representing electrical power distribution networks. The supply point is now a transformer station x/20(10) kV and consumer points are transformer stations 20(10)/0.4 kV. The routes are now feeders constrained by maximum capacity (12 or 6 MVA) and maximum length (due to the maximum voltage drop allowed and the minimum availability).

A real configuration of 54 points was the first one investigated. The typical initial individual, representing a complete solution, is shown in Fig. 4.1. The structure of the configuration is obviously unacceptable and rather meshy, but it does not impose any problem on the performance of the genetic algorithm.

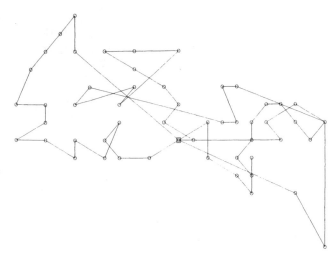

Fig. 4.1 Initial 54-point configuration

The program was run many times under different genetic parameters. Some of the results are shown in Tab. 4.1.

Population	bias	num_closest	penalty	exec. time (s)	cost (million)
100	1.2	2 (3)	1	13	3.75
300	1.1	5 (7)	1	158	3.78
500	**1.05**	**5 (7)**	**1**	**338**	**3.74**

Tab. 4.1 Results of 54-point configuration

The penalty function is suppressed in order to examine algorithm's performance with huge populations. In this example the penalty ponder proved not to have any significant impact on the performance. One can observe the algorithm's sensibility to its parameters. If the quick solution is needed, not an exhaustive search, a small population should be used, but parameters have to be adjusted too. The *bias* should have relatively higher value, which introduces the spreading of a couple of good solutions on the entire population. But *num_closest* should be less than previously suggested to ensure that good solutions are really few and hard to find. The best solution represents an exhaustive search with very low *bias* rate that enabled the prolonged convergence.

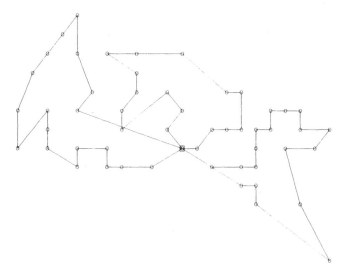

Fig. 4.2 Final 54-point configuration

The best configuration found is given in Fig. 4.2. The results shown are the best of many investigated, and the process of finding good solutions should be preferrably guided by an experienced user.

The second configuration investigated consists of 105 points. The results with the same population sizes are given in Tab. 4.2.

Population	bias	num_closest	penalty	exec. time (s)	cost (million)
100	1.05	6 (8)	1	183	16.14
300	1.2	2 (3)	1	346	15.65
500	**1.2**	**2 (3)**	**1**	**877**	**15.17**

Tab. 4.2 Results of 105-point configuration

Comparing the examples with the same population sizes it could be stated that the execution times were now between two or three times longer than previous ones. Therefore, the search time seems to grow approximately linear with the number of the configuration points. The 300-population size example from the Tab 4.2 is shown in Fig 4.3.

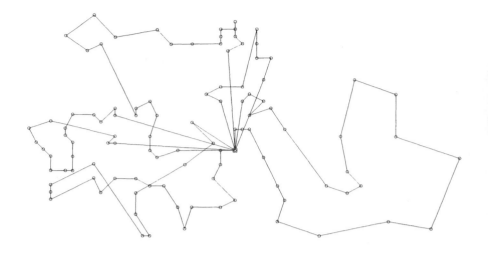

Fig. 4.3 Final 105-point configuration

Although one can be suspicious, overlappings of a single route and between different routes do not necessarily lead to costly solution. The points are unpleasantly distributed, in sense that there are some scarce and some dense areas, and the formation of routes is burdened with previously mentioned constraints. Although different, genetic parameters were now chosen with the intent to shorten the execution time. In general, the greater the population size, the better is final solution, but the time increase is linear. Higher values for *bias* should be used along with the lower values for number of closest points to ensure that the best individuals in the current generation are really good enough. The algorithm was run on SUN-Sparc station 20 with the coding written in C language.

5 Conclusion

The method of solving the *multiple dispatch problem* by genetic algorithm, along with the application in distribution networks was described in this paper. Two real configurations were presented. The results are promising, but there should be a room for various improvements. Although the TSP is one of the problems frequently investigated by different genetic algorithms, this paper deals with an upper-step problem consisted of multiple simultaneous TSPs which, in authors knowledge, has not yet been successfully solved by genetic algorithms. In searching for further improvements the work on parallel genetic algorithms and on possibilities of integrating genetic algorithm and a *simulated annealing*-like mutation operator continues.

Literature

[1] D.E.Goldberg: *Genetic Algorithms in Search, Optimization and Machine Learning.* Addison-Wesley, MA, 1989.

[2] S.Krajcar: *Algorithms for interactive optimal planning of distribution networks.* Doctoral thesis, ETF Zagreb, 1988.

[3] S.Lin and B.W.Keringhan: *An effective Heuristic Algorithm for Traveling Salesman Problem.* Oper. Research 21, 498-516, 1973.

[4] Z.Michalewitz: *Genetic Algorithms + Data Structures = Evolution Programs.* Springer-Verlag, Berlin, 1992.

[5] J.Y.Suh and D.Van Gucht: *Incorporating Heuristic Information into Genetic Search.* Proceedings of the 2nd International Conference on Genetic Search, 100-107. Lawrence Erlbaum Associates, 1987.

[6] D.Whitley: *The Genitor Algorithm and Selection Pressure: Why Rank-Based Allocation of Reproduction Trials is Best.* Proceedings of the 3rd International Conference on Genetic Search, 116-121. Morgan Kaufmann, 1989.

[7] D.Whitley, T. Starkweather and D'A. Fuquay: *Scheduling Problems and Travelling Salesman: The Genetic Edge Recombination Operator.* Proceedings of the 3rd International Conference on Genetic Search, 133-140. Morgan Kaufmann, 1989.

Multilevel Refinement Planning in an Interval-Based Temporal Logic*

Werner Stephan and Susanne Biundo

German Research Center for Artificial Intelligence
Stuhlsatzenhausweg 3, D-66123 Saarbrücken, Germany
email: {stephan,biundo}@dfki.uni-sb.de

Abstract. We present a strategy for deductive plan formation where prefabricated general solutions are adapted to special problems. The strategy is an instance of refinement planning with a particular technique for representing abstract solution patterns. It is developed within an interval-based temporal logic where plans are treated as an executable form of specification. Following the paradigm to view plans as programs basic actions as well as composite plans are built using a programming language with *add* and *delete* as elementary operations.

1 Introduction

In this paper we propose an approach which in some sense compares to operator abstraction in hierarchical planning. In our case, prefabricated general solutions are in a deductive process adapted to special problems using several levels of abstraction. The generality of these solution schemes, which are often recursive, demands for abstraction: not all details of the scenario are considered at this level. The basic formal framework of our approach is based on elementary *add-* and *delete* operations as they underly STRIPS-like systems (e.g., [7]). We use a kind of programming language in order to define basic actions as well as composite plans in a way similar to that proposed in [10], but now add- and delete operations as well as the programming language notation are used coherently for all levels of abstraction. To do so, we introduce an interval-based modal temporal logic in the style of [9] and [1]. The reason for prefering this modal logic to formalisms like Situational Calculus [5], Fluent Theory [4], or Dynamic Logic [8] is that this logic allows for a flexible treatment of more or less abstract specifications and plans on the same linguistic level.

First, the basic logical formalism is introduced. We then give the general idea underlying refinement planning in our variant of temporal logic and sketch the main technical prerequisites for our particular strategy. For a full version of the paper and a detailed discussion of related work we refer the reader to [11].

---

* This work was partly supported by the German Ministry for Science and Technology (BMBF) under contract ITW 9404 0.

2 Logical Framework

Planning scenarios are as usual modelled by *objects* having certain properties and by *relations* holding between (some of) them. In our example (cf. figure 1), it consists of four rooms, doors, and a couple of blocks.

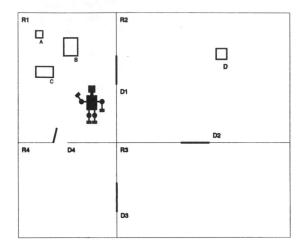

Fig. 1. A Planning Scenario

The *syntax* of a particular planning scenario is based on a finite set of *sort symbols*. As usual, a set of *variables* and a set of *constants* is provided for each sort. The set of *relation symbols* is divided into a *flexible* and a *rigid* part. Rigid symbols remain static in each situation while the meanings of flexible symbols may change from one situation to the next as an action occurs. In our example, the *in* relation, among others, is assumed to be flexible.

A model $\mathcal{M}$ consists of a nonempty *domain* $\mathcal{D}$ for each sort and a global *interpretation* $\mathcal{I}$ that assigns relations to the rigid symbols. A *valuation* w.r.t. $\mathcal{M}$ assigns domain elements to variables of the respective sort.

The dynamic aspect in our planning scenarios is mirrored by the semantic concept of *state*: States are interpretations assigning relations over the domains to the flexible symbols.

In order to describe state changes we provide a *programming language* to build up basic actions and plans. For each flexible symbol r there are elementary operations **delete-**$r(\ldots)$ and **add-**$r(\ldots)$ of the same arity as r. *Programs* are then given by the following rules:

$$\pi ::= \mathbf{skip} \mid \mathbf{delete\text{-}} r(\bar{\tau}) \mid \mathbf{add\text{-}} r(\bar{\tau}) \mid (\pi_1; \pi_2) \mid$$
$$(\pi_1 \ \mathbf{or} \ \pi_2) \mid \mathbf{if} \ \phi \ \mathbf{then} \ \pi_1 \ \mathbf{else} \ \pi_2 \ \mathbf{fi} \mid \mathbf{while} \ \phi \ \mathbf{do} \ \pi \ \mathbf{od} \mid$$
$$\mathbf{choose} \ \bar{x} : \phi(\bar{x}) \ \mathbf{begin} \ \pi \ \mathbf{end} \mid a(\bar{\tau}) \mid a(\bar{x}). \ \pi \ (\bar{\tau})$$

where in addition we have used a system of names for (procedural) *abstractions*. ϕ is a first-order formula and the occurrences of $\bar{x}$ following **choose** are binding occurrences.

Using this programming language a basic action in our scenario moving a block from one room to another reads:

move(b, r_1, r_2) **.** **if** $\neg in(b, r_1)$ **then skip else** delete-$in(b, r_1)$ **;** add-$in(b, r_2)$ **fi.**

Reasoning about basic actions and plans is done using an interval-based modal temporal logic the syntax being basically the same as the one used in other temporal formalisms (cf. [3]). It provides modal operators o (*next*), $\Diamond$ (*sometimes*), and $\square$ (*always*). In addition we use the binary modal operator **;** (*chop*) expressing the sequential composition of formulae, operators corresponding to the elementary **delete**-$r(\bar{\tau})$ and **add**-$r(\bar{\tau})$ operations, and a recursion operator[2].

As is the case with *choppy* logics in general (cf., e.g., [9]) the semantics is based on *intervals* which are nonempty sequences of states. The modal operator o is interpreted using the immediate subinterval relationship while for $\square$ and $\Diamond$ we use its reflexive and transitive closure. **;** is interpreted as the composition on intervals.

3 Refinement Planning

In refinement planning an initial plan specification is refined via intermediate steps to an executable plan. A possible format for initial specifications φ_0 is

$$\text{FIN} \land \text{EF} \land \text{SAFE} \land \text{INV} .$$

These four conjuncts describe the properties an interval has to meet in order to be accepted as a possible solution. Thus φ_0 specifies a set of intervals (computations) $\hat{\varphi}_0 := \{\sigma \mid \mathcal{M} \models_\sigma \varphi_0\}$. We have

FIN $:\leftrightarrow \Diamond$o **false** ,   EF $:\leftrightarrow \phi_{pre} \rightarrow \square$ (o **false** $\rightarrow \phi_{post}$) ,

SAFE $:\leftrightarrow \phi_{pre} \rightarrow \square (\phi_{safe_1} \land \ldots \land \phi_{safe_n})$, and

INV $:\leftrightarrow \square$ (**inv** $- r_1(\bar{x}_1) : \phi_1(\bar{x}_1) \land \ldots \land$ **inv** $- r_m(\bar{x}_m) : \phi_m(\bar{x}_m))$.

The formula FIN states that the interval is *finite*. The *effect* of a computation (EF) is described by pre- and postconditions which are first-order formulae. In addition to the desired effect the initial specification contains *safety conditions* which have to hold in all intermediate states. Again, these conditions are first-order. Finally, one might wish to specify that certain parts of the state space are not affected by the computation. This is done by *invariance*-clauses, **inv** $-$ $r(\bar{x}) : \phi(\bar{x})$, which stand for formulae

$$\forall \bar{x}.((\phi(\bar{x}) \land r(\bar{x})) \rightarrow \text{o } r(\bar{x})) \land \forall \bar{x}.((\phi(\bar{x}) \land \neg r(\bar{x})) \rightarrow \text{o } \neg r(\bar{x}))$$

The restriction formula ϕ is again first-order.

---

[2] The formal treatment of recursion in this context is described in [11].

Starting from the initial specification φ_0 in the refinement process we try to construct an executable plan π whose set of computations $\hat{\pi}$ is a subset of $\hat{\varphi}_0$. This is done by transforming φ_0 gradually by a sequence of intermediate specifications

$$\varphi_0 \succ \varphi_1 \succ \ldots \succ \varphi_n = \pi \, .$$

to a *plan formula* π. In each step we restrict the set of computations, that is we have $\mathcal{M} \models \varphi_{i+1} \rightarrow \varphi_i$, for all $0 \leq i < n$.

Plans as given by plan formulas π are *well-defined* in the sense that for each state $s \in S$ there exists a computation $\sigma = \langle s, \ldots \rangle \in \hat{\pi}$. Note that as opposed to plan formulae specifications might be *inconsistent*.

For a particular *refinement strategy* we are given an admissible set of (intermediate) specifications and a collection of (refinement) rules operating on these specifications. For each such rule we have to provide a *validating tactic* that generates a proof of the implication resulting from the application of the rule. Given all these proofs by a simple transformation we end up with a proof of the assertion $\pi \rightarrow \varphi_0$ which expresses the correctness of π with respect to φ_0. Since $\hat{\pi} \neq \{ \}$, in the end we know that our initial specification was consistent. In a sense we have constructed a model (defined by π) for that specification.

4 Stuttering

Now we are going to describe a strategy where abstract recursive patterns are refined to plans made up of basic actions from a lower, more concrete, level. In our example the abstract level consists of a scenario where we only have blocks and rooms which may be related by *in*. The problem of moving an arbitrary set of blocks from one room to another is solved by the following recursive plan:

move*$(s,r_1,r_2) \Leftarrow$ **if** $\forall b.(b \in s \rightarrow in(b_1,r_1)) \wedge s \neq \emptyset$ **then**
 choose b $: b \in s$ **begin** move(b,r_1,r_2) ; move*$(s - \{b\},r_1,r_2)$ **end**

It moves one block after the other from r_1 to r_2 by means of the abstract operation move defined in section 2.

The idea is to refine this plan on a lower level where in addition there are doors and a robot but where the move* and move operations are no longer available. In a sense these abstract operations have to be *implemented* by sequences of operations from the lower level. Unfortunately, in the current setting this cannot be done since the above plan *exactly* defines a computation. The first computation in figure 2 is a computation of move(A,R1,R4).

A solution to this problem is known as *stuttering* (cf. [6],[2]). We allow additional (stuttering) steps which however do not affect the relations we are interested in on the abstract level. Stuttering versions of abstract operations still exhibit essentially the same behaviour while they leave room for later refinements.

Stuttering can be introduced in this setting by redefining the basic add- and delete-operations. In our example on the abstract level we are only interested in the *in* relation between blocks and rooms. We would then like to allow stuttering

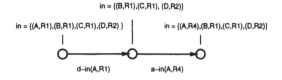

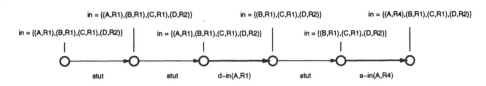

Fig. 2. Two Computations

steps that change only relations other than in. The appropriate stuttering version of **add**-$in(b,r)$ is **add**-$in_{\{in\}}(b,r)$ defined by

$$\mathrm{STUT}_{\{in\}} \; ; \; \mathbf{add}\text{-}in(b,r) \; ; \; \mathrm{STUT}_{\{in\}} \;, \text{ where } \mathrm{STUT}_{\{in\}} \text{ is the formula}$$
$$\Diamond_\circ \; \mathbf{false} \; \wedge \; \Box \; \mathbf{inv} - in(b,r) \; : \; \mathbf{true} \;.$$

The second computation in figure 2 is a computation of the stuttering version of move(A,R1,R4). As a main result we obtain that a plan π satisfies a plan specification φ iff a plan $\bar{\pi}$ does which allows stuttering w.r.t. the flexible symbols in φ provided that $\hat{\pi} \subseteq \hat{\bar{\pi}}$ holds (cf. [11]).

References

1. S. Biundo, D. Dengler, and J. Köhler. Deductive Planning and Plan Reuse in a Command Language Environment. In *Proc. ECAI-92*, pages 628–632, 1992.
2. L. Lamport. The Temporal Logic of Actions. Tech. Rep., DEC, Palo Alto, 1991.
3. Z. Manna and A. Pnueli. *The Temporal Logic of Reactive and Concurrent Systems*. Springer, 1991.
4. Z. Manna and R. Waldinger. How to Clear a Block: Plan Formation in Situational Logic. *Journal of Automated Reasoning*, 3:343–377, 1987.
5. J. McCarthy and P. Hayes. Some Philosophical Problems from the Standpoint of Artificial Intelligence. In *Machine Intelligence 4*, pages 463–502. 1969.
6. A. Mokkedem and D. Méry. A Stuttering Closed Temporal Logic for Modular Reasoning about Concurrent Programs. In *Proc. ICTL-94*, pages 382–397, 1994.
7. E. Pednault. ADL: Exploring the Middle Ground Between STRIPS and the Situation Calculus. In *Proc. KR-89*, pages 324–332, 1989.
8. S. J. Rosenschein. Plan Synthesis: A Logic Perspective. In *Proc. IJCAI-81*, 1981.
9. R. Rosner and A. Pnueli. A Choppy Logic. In *Symposium on Logic in Computer Science*, pages 306–313. IEEE Computer Society Press, 1986.
10. W. Stephan and S. Biundo. A New Logical Framework for Deductive Planning. In *Proc. IJCAI-93*, pages 32–38, 1993.
11. W. Stephan and S. Biundo. Multilevel Refinement Planning in an Interval-Based Temporal Logic. Research Report, German Research Center for AI, 1995.

Lecture Notes in Artificial Intelligence (LNAI)

Lecture Notes in Computer Science